MW01036567

ANGELS OF THE
UNDERGROUND

ANGELS OF THE UNDERGROUND

THE AMERICAN WOMEN WHO RESISTED THE JAPANESE IN THE PHILIPPINES IN WORLD WAR II

THERESA KAMINSKI

OXFORD
UNIVERSITY PRESS

OXFORD
UNIVERSITY PRESS

Oxford University Press is a department of the University of
Oxford. It furthers the University's objective of excellence in research,
scholarship, and education by publishing worldwide.

Oxford   New York
Auckland   Cape Town   Dar es Salaam   Hong Kong   Karachi
Kuala Lumpur   Madrid   Melbourne   Mexico City   Nairobi
New Delhi   Shanghai   Taipei   Toronto

With offices in
Argentina   Austria   Brazil   Chile   Czech Republic   France   Greece
Guatemala   Hungary   Italy   Japan   Poland   Portugal   Singapore
South Korea   Switzerland   Thailand   Turkey   Ukraine   Vietnam

Oxford is a registered trademark of Oxford University Press
in the UK and certain other countries.

Published in the United States of America by
Oxford University Press
198 Madison Avenue, New York, NY 10016

Library of Congress Cataloging-in-Publication Data
Kaminski, Theresa, 1958–
Angels of the underground : the American women who resisted the Japanese in the Philippines in World
War II / Theresa Kaminski.
pages cm
Includes bibliographical references and index.
ISBN 978–0–19–992824–8
1. World War, 1939–1945—Underground movements—Philippines.
2. World War, 1939-1945—Participation, Female.   3. Philippines—History—Japanese
occupation, 1942-1945.   4. Women guerrillas—Philippines—History—20th century.
5. Americans—Philippines—History—20th century.   I. Title.
D802.P5K36 2015
940.53'599082—dc23
2015015185

1 3 5 7 9 8 6 4 2
Printed in the United States of America
on acid-free paper

For Charles

CONTENTS

ACKNOWLEDGMENTS

The final phase of this book project coincided with the twenty-fifth anniversary of my marriage to Charles Clark, the best husband I could have ever hoped for. Researching and writing a book is never easy, but his support made it bearable. And his keen eye on the copyedited version of the manuscript was invaluable.

Without my agent, Jacqueline Flynn, this book would not exist. Over the last twenty years, I researched, wrote, and published two academic books about American women, war, and imperialism in the Philippines. I was fascinated with this topic and couldn't imagine why everyone else wasn't as well. Still, it was with some surprise that I received a query from Jacquie, asking if I'd ever thought about writing a book about Margaret Utinsky. Jacquie had seen the movie *The Great Raid*, was intrigued by the portrayal of Peggy, and thought there was a great story there. I agreed. She found the book a home at Oxford, where Tim Bent and Keely Boeving helped turn a rough manuscript into something better. Alyssa O'Connell was a whiz with images and permissions.

Many people generously helped me along the research path. Sascha Jansen promptly answered numerous questions about the Manila people. Carol Guarzzo, Pat Bloodworth, Kathy Bower, Teresa Booth, and David Grant Stewart shared stories about Margaret Utinsky. Sig Unander, Edna Binkowski, and Deb Hagermann did the same for Claire Phillips. James Zobel provided invaluable research assistance, and Stacy Cordery, Kurt Piehler, Chris Schaefer, and Jason Ridler contributed their historical expertise. My apologies to anyone I've overlooked.

I was fortunate to be working on this project when my place of employment still supported research leave for faculty. Thanks to a semester at the Institute for Research in the Humanities at the University of Wisconsin–Madison, I managed to complete a wobbly first draft.

For more than twenty years, the most supportive trio of friends/colleagues has seen me through the frustrations and joys of research and writing: Susan Brewer, Leslie Midkiff DeBauche, and Valentina Peguero. What brilliant scholars you are.

This is the first book I've written while my son, Sam Clark, lived away from home. He graduated from college in four years and is now out there in the great wide world. My parenting duties are over, but I'm still a mother.

PHILIPPINE ISLANDS

LUZON

PHILIPPINE SEA

Lingayen Gulf

Baguio

Clark Field

Manila

Cavite

SOUTH CHINA SEA

MINDORO

PANAY

Bacolod CEBU LEYTE

NEGROS

Dumaguete

PALAWAN

SULU SEA

MINDANAO

Davao City

BRITISH NORTH BORNEO

NORTH

SCALE: 1 Inch = 125 Miles (Approx.)

Courtesy of Michael C.J. Kaminski.

INTRODUCTION

O N THE LATE AFTERNOON OF APRIL 2, 1945, the SS *JOHN LYKES* maneuvered out of the Port of Manila on the island of Luzon in the Philippines, skirting the remains of dozens of vessels the Japanese had sunk during the Battle of Manila, which had ended only weeks earlier. Here in the Pacific theater, World War II was still in its protracted final stage, with the United States military fighting enemy forces island to island on the way to an invasion of Japan. The battle for the Philippine Islands, a vast archipelago in the western Pacific Ocean that the Japanese occupied back in 1942, had been underway since October 1944.

It took over three months for the Americans to reach the capital city of Manila, the big prize of this fight. From early February to early March 1945, US forces and their Filipino allies squared off against the Japanese—who were determined to either hold the city or destroy it. By the beginning of April, when the *Lykes* left port, Manila was securely in American and Filipino hands, but the Japanese had left the city a smoldering ruin as they moved north to continue the fight.

Designed as a cargo ship, the *Lykes* had been converted to an American troop transport at the beginning of the war, its modest 418-foot length capable of carrying as many as 1,300 military personnel. But on this day, the first of a month-long voyage to Los Angeles, the *Lykes* bore a split manifest: some five hundred American soldiers and sailors and about an equal number of civilians returning to their stateside homes.[1]

Most of the civilians were American men, women, and children recently liberated from the internment camp at the University of Santo Tomas in Manila, where Japanese occupation forces had confined them in early 1942. After three years of captivity, these Americans welcomed their berths on the *Lykes*, anxious and relieved to depart the war-ravaged Philippines. Not everyone took advantage of it. For example, Gladys Savary, a tall, white-haired woman in her early fifties who had owned a popular Manila restaurant before the war, declined passage home. Gladys had also not been interned in Santo Tomas with the other Americans, and now that the war was winding down, some tension and hard feelings developed among a once close-knit and amiable community. Questions surfaced about exactly how Gladys had managed to remain free, how she had managed to negotiate the occupation.

Despite—or perhaps because of—what she had been through during the war, Gladys decided to stay in Manila and open another restaurant. She intended it to serve as a kind of way station for any American military prisoners of war who might have survived the labor camps in Japan and would soon be passing through Manila on their way home from the Pacific theater. Gladys had known some of these young men at the beginning of the war when they were stationed in and around Manila. She made sure to set aside extra food and booze for the soldiers trying to defend the capital. After the surrender to the Japanese in 1942 and the occupation that followed, she devised ways to help them while they were incarcerated on the island of Luzon before they were shipped off to Japan.

To Gladys, that clandestine assistance, along with similar aid she provided to some of the very same Santo Tomas internees who now seemed to resent her, represented resistance to the Japanese occupation. She had defied the enemy's rules against helping POWs and civilian detainees, and believed that this proved she had not had an easy war—that she had sacrificed and had taken risks. Above all, it proved she had not collaborated with occupation officials.

As the SS *John Lykes* picked its way out of the Manila harbor that day in April, it carried three other American women who, like Gladys Savary, had also managed to avoid internment in Santo Tomas. And like Gladys, all three used their freedom during the occupation to engage in resistance work in and around Manila. One was Claire Phillips, a striking, gregarious brunette in her late thirties, traveling with her young daughter, Dian. Once she found herself on the ship and surrounded by her own countrymen, Claire could not stop talking about her wartime activities. The more she gabbed, however, the more the other Americans on board avoided her. They found her bragging distasteful and her stories outlandish.

Desperate for a sympathetic ear and hoping to find someone who could lend credence to her tales, Claire tried to befriend one passenger in particular, an American woman a few years her junior—slender, dark-haired, of Filipino heritage—traveling with her three children. Yay (rhymes with "why") Panlilio, Claire assumed, would understand better than anyone else what she had been through. After all, both of them had been involved with the guerrillas on Luzon and both knew how the underground worked.

A journalist in Manila before the war, Yay developed a web of political and military contacts throughout Luzon. During the Japanese occupation, Yay chafed at the regulations that prevented her from aiding what remained of the American and Filipino forces. So she deposited her children with trusted friends and fled to the hills east of the capital city where she joined a band of Filipino guerrillas. She became indispensable to the organization and training of the unit. Yay talked with Claire Phillips a few times on board the *Lykes*, even sympathized with her at least a little, but shied away from further involvement in this particular drama. Yay had had plenty of her own during the war and did not feel strong enough to deal with someone else's.

Unable to win Yay's support, Claire told a couple more stories in an attempt to bolster her reputation. She spread the word that she had been engaged in undercover work for the Federal Bureau of Investigation. This backfired as actual FBI agents were on the ship, and denied Claire had any connection to their organization. Claire also spun a grand romantic tale about her relationship with an American soldier named John V. (Phil) Phillips. Asserting that she had been widowed by the war, she hinted she would file a claim for Phil's army insurance policy and for reimbursement from the US government for her prisoner relief efforts. Claire assured anyone who still listened to her that she had documents to prove all of this.[2]

Four days before the *Lykes* made its port-of-call in Honolulu, Claire claimed someone had rifled through her belongings. Her personal papers, along with promissory notes worth about 100,000 pesos ($50,000 in 1945, equal to about $660,000 in 2015) had vanished—stolen, she was certain, by people who wanted to discredit her. The ship's transport commander, Major Gilbert, did not believe a theft had occurred and refused to investigate. Claire's near hysteria over the missing items attracted the further attention of an FBI agent on board, who interviewed her at length and turned up disturbing discrepancies in her stories.

Despite the alleged robbery, Claire still had in her possession over $1,000 in US currency and 565 pesos in Philippine National Bank notes, rarities for anyone who lived through Japanese-occupied Manila. The FBI agent rejected Claire's explanation that before departing on the *Lykes*, friends helped her exchange the Philippine money she managed to hide earlier in the war. Why would anyone steal IOUs and personal papers yet leave hard cash untouched? Did she fabricate the robbery because the documents she claimed would prove her involvement with the guerrillas and the POWs did not, in fact, exist?[3]

The G-man also grew curious about the mangled condition of Claire's passport—which lacked a photograph—and when she could not provide a clear explanation he became suspicious about her actual nationality. First Claire told him she had buried the passport along with other important documents near the beginning of the occupation, and three years in damp soil had caused significant deterioration. Then, to account for the missing photograph, Claire blamed her daughter, Dian, claiming the little girl ripped it off—either while playing or during a temper tantrum—after they boarded the ship. These stories, combined with the revelation that

Claire held two life insurance policies made out in different names, prompted the agent to take her fingerprints to verify her identity.[4]

Conversations with other passengers led the agent to Margaret (Peggy) Utinsky, a petite redheaded American nurse in her mid-forties. Curiously—and what further heightened the agent's suspicions—was that Claire had not directed the FBI to Peggy to verify her stories, though the two women knew each other. Peggy had run a Manila-based underground organization that coordinated the smuggling of food and other necessities into POW camps on Luzon, and her relief efforts therefore would have often overlapped with Claire's.

Peggy did indeed know Claire, quite well, but refused to vouch for her character. She did, however, confirm to the FBI agent that Claire intended to collect John Phillips's insurance. Moreover, as far as the documents that Claire claimed had been stolen from her bunk, during the war Peggy had—for safekeeping—buried Claire's papers along with her own. Peggy dug them up after the Battle of Manila and examined the documents before returning them to Claire. She maintained there were no promissory notes from any guerrillas or POWs. As far as Peggy was concerned, Claire may have destroyed them simply to create some drama and gain sympathy.

Later, some of the ship's passengers overheard Peggy and Claire arguing about money and IOUs. When the *Lykes* finally docked in Los Angeles in May 1945, the two women were no longer speaking to each other. They went their separate ways.[5]

AS THE WAR CORRESPONDENT MARTHA GELLHORN observed, "War happens to people, one by one." This is the story of a restaurateur, an entertainer, a reporter, and a nurse—four American women who found themselves trapped in a city occupied by an enemy army and thousands of miles from home. Though caught up in the same extraordinary and perilous situation, and responding to it in remarkably similar and courageous ways, these women barely knew each other. They did not forge a sisterhood of anti-Japanese resistance and, as evidenced by their interaction above, even denigrated one another. Yet each contributed in her own way to networks of people committed to thwarting the occupiers.

One by one, as the enemy occupation unfolded, Gladys, Claire, Yay, and Peggy each determined how the war would happen to them, and to them alone.[6]

Their independence from—even suspicion of—each other reveals how the experience shaped them. Survival meant keeping to oneself, even within the networks in which they worked. Otherwise everyone would be compromised. The four women spent three grueling years engaged in a desperate, and often lonely, solitary fight for survival that stemmed from their resistance to the occupation. Each in her own way felt a duty to resist the Japanese by helping the American military prisoners of war survive and assisting the guerrilla forces operating on Luzon. Both these actions carried stiff penalties; the penalty for the latter would have been summary execution.

Though they could not, or would not, corroborate each other's stories, those stories can still be told. "Angel of the underground" reads the caption on the back of a photo taken of Peggy Utinsky in 1945. It briefly describes how she spent her own money and raised additional funds so she could smuggle food, vitamins, medicine, and cash to American POWs. This book reveals the full extent of Peggy's wartime activities, as well as those of Claire, Gladys, and Yay. Their experiences illustrate how their lives were stretched to, and beyond, the breaking point. They were forced to dissemble to the degree that they had not only to deny who others were, but who they were themselves. To merit the designation of angel, they had to be anything but.

CHAPTER 1

THE COLONIAL PHILIPPINES

THE WAR THAT HAPPENED TO Gladys Savary, Claire Phillips, Yay Panlilio, and Peggy Utinsky had its roots in a conflict that took place at the end of the nineteenth century over the fate of two Spanish colonies, Cuba and the Philippine Islands. That war, the Spanish–American War of 1898, secured independence for Cuba. But it resulted in a new colonial master for the Philippines and launched an imperialist struggle between the United States and Japan for supremacy in the Pacific.

Confrontation over territory was not unfamiliar to Americans. From its own colonial beginnings, the United States has been an expansionist country, assimilating land on the North American continent by conquering and relocating indigenous people, and negotiating with or going to war against rival imperialist European powers. Land meant security, power, and wealth, but Americans justified their actions with the softer language of manifest destiny—the divinely sanctioned spread of democracy. By the end of the nineteenth century, the United States had secured vast national borders, from the Atlantic Ocean to the Pacific.[1]

With those continental successes, Americans began looking toward the Pacific for new opportunities, attracted to the economic possibilities presented by the vast China market. The United States acquired the Midway Islands in 1867, challenged Germany in Samoa in 1885, and established settlements in Hawaii during the 1880s. Then, when the indigenous populations of Cuba and the Philippine Islands began agitating against their Spanish colonizers, the United States, seeing its role as a savior, inserted itself into that imperialist drama.[2]

The Philippine Islands, located about 7,000 miles from the west coast of the United States, is a vast southeast Asian archipelago of about 7,100 islands stretching over 115,000 square miles in the western Pacific Ocean. By the late 1800s, its indigenous population, made up of a variety of Southeast Asian and Oceania ancestry, numbered around seven million. These inhabitants had already set up trade networks with China, Malaysia, and other neighboring countries before Spanish explorers arrived in 1521. The first Spanish settlement was established about forty years later, launching some three hundred years of colonial rule there. One of the most visible signs of Spanish power in the Philippines was Fort Santiago, built on the island of Luzon at the mouth of the Pasig River to protect the newly-established city of Manila, now designated the capital of the Philippines.[3]

During the early nineteenth century, Spain began to lose its grip on the islands, challenged from the outside by rival European powers and from the inside by both religious and civil agitation that grew into an independence movement. By the mid-1890s, revolutionary change was in the wind, and the United States proved willing to use it to push the Spanish out.[4]

A similar situation developed in Cuba, located just ninety miles off the coast of Florida, which the Spanish explored in the 1490s and followed with permanent settlements in the early 1500s. About the size of the state of Pennsylvania, by the early 1800s the island contained a population of more than 631,000, both free and enslaved, European, African, and indigenous. Resistance to Spanish rule developed into a fledgling independence movement in the late 1860s and surged during the 1890s.

The political stability of Cuba concerned Americans who had millions of dollars worth of business investments there, especially in sugar. The idea of a colony intent on overthrowing its oppressor struck a chord with Americans because of their own history. The chance to bestow the benefits of the American way of life on a "lesser" but deserving group of people was impossible to resist.

As President William McKinley tried to convince Spain to give up its colony, he gambled that a show of force would underscore his determination. So he sent the USS *Maine* to Havana to demonstrate American intentions to protect US citizens there. In February 1898, the ship blew up in the harbor, killing more than 260 American sailors. A hasty investigation revealed that a mine caused the explosion, and the United States held Spain responsible. In April, at McKinley's request, Congress declared war. American troops were dispatched to Cuba, while Admiral George Dewey, then commanding the Asiatic Squadron in the Pacific, was ordered to Manila to confront the Spanish there. By mid-August, the American flag flew over Fort Santiago. The war on both fronts ended with an American victory before the year was out.

Cuban independence—along with the sinking of the *Maine*—had been the justification for the war, and the United States Congress passed the Teller Amendment in 1898 to guarantee it. But the US government viewed the Philippine Islands as too valuable to give up, not only for their proximity to China and its lucrative trade, but because of the Philippines' natural resources and thriving hemp, sugar, and tobacco plantations. The contentious issue of race complicated relations between the United States and the Philippines; Americans debated the ability of Filipinos to rule themselves. Some believed that if the United States retained control of the islands it could properly guide Filipinos in establishing a functioning democracy, but those who went on to form the American Anti-Imperialist League saw these actions as condescending and contrary to their country's own revolutionary heritage.[5]

While the United States negotiated the Treaty of Paris with Spain during the fall of 1898, President McKinley sent thousands of American troops to the Philippines in case the impending US occupation required enforcement. Proponents on both sides of the annexation question pushed their respective agendas so strongly that the final Senate vote in February 1899 was close, swinging narrowly in favor of the treaty. The United States agreed to pay Spain $20 million (worth around a half billion dollars in 2015) for the Philippines.

The treaty confirmed the worst fears of the Filipinos: Americans were not liberators, but occupiers. When it became clear the United States had no intention of recognizing Filipino nationalist Emilio Aguinaldo's new republic, he launched a revolt against the American forces in the islands that lasted until 1902.[6]

Of the 126,468 American troops sent to the Philippines to quell the "insurrection," over 4,200 died. No one knows the exact number of Filipino casualties, but estimates suggest 220,000 civilians and soldiers perished. The fighting was vicious on both sides, intensified by racial hostility. Because Filipinos engaged in guerrilla warfare, a tactic the US military dismissed as "uncivilized," American soldiers used it as justification to torture and/or kill any Filipino they considered a threat. Civilians were rounded up into "recon-centration" camps to prevent them from joining the insurgency, and some were subjected to the "water cure," a form of modern day water-boarding, to extract information about the rebellion. Thus did the Americans begin their mission of establishing democracy in the Philippine Islands.[7]

The velvet glove that surrounded this military iron fist came in the form of the first Philippine Commission, designed to win over the Filipino elites (known as *ilustrados*) by drawing them into a political and economic collaboration of mutual benefit. The five-man commission, including Admiral Dewey and General Elwell Otis, the newly-designated US military governor of the islands, arrived in Manila in March 1899, soon after the outbreak of hostilities. The commission was charged with studying the current situation in the Philippines and recommending a course of action for American rule. President McKinley expected the *ilustrados* and all Filipinos would quickly understand the benefits of the American policy of "benevolent assimilation."[8]

In 1900 the commission issued the unsurprising recommendation that the United States needed to remain in the Philippines to put the country on the path to full independence. That year the second Philippine Commission arrived, tasked with setting up a functioning civilian government. Its head, William Howard Taft, a federal circuit judge from Cincinnati, Ohio, had initially opposed the acquisition of the Philippines. But soon Taft—the man who referred to Filipinos as "little brown brothers"—saw this appointment as a way of making his mark and of bringing democracy to the Filipinos.[9]

In addition to the creation of an American-controlled civilian government, the United States retained its military grip on the islands. In 1901 Elihu Root, US Secretary of War, appropriated some land six miles southeast of Manila, just south of the Pasig River, to house the American forces tasked with pacifying the remnants of the Filipino "insurrection." Named Fort William McKinley, it gave birth to the 31st Infantry in 1916, a rarity of US Army units for its primary location on foreign soil. Still, during the early 1900s, the Philippines constituted the biggest overseas posting for the army.[10]

Official transfer of military power to civilian rule occurred on July 4, 1901, when Taft was sworn in as the islands' first American civilian governor-general. Three months earlier, Emilio Aguinaldo had been captured, dealing a huge blow to the nationalist movement, especially when he subsequently swore allegiance to the United States. In the meantime, Taft had been working with the *ilustrados* as they established the Federal Party in December 1900 to encourage all Filipinos to accept American sovereignty and guidance toward self-rule. Taft believed self-rule would not be possible until Filipinos attained a quality education rooted in the English language. He coordinated the establishment of local and provincial governments, the writing of municipal codes, and the implementation of primary, intermediate, and secondary schools throughout the Philippines.[11]

Such large-scale collaboration required subterfuge and force, which was provided by intelligence-gathering, a loyal Filipino police force and military, and the continued presence of US soldiers. In late 1900, prior to the establishment of civilian rule in the Philippines, General Arthur MacArthur implemented martial law and created the Military

Information Division (MID) within the adjutant general's office. MID's commander, Ralph Van Deman, created a network capable of vast data collection, which he employed to root out anti-American elements in the Philippines, arresting anyone who defied American rule, court-martialing civilians, and curbing the press. When the active phase of the guerrilla war ended in 1902, MID continued to not only neutralize Filipino nationalism but to identify and keep track of Japanese spies and sympathizers.[12]

Order—American-style, supported by the Filipino elite—slowly returned to the islands, though it was not buttressed by the large-scale presence of American citizens. An influx of immigrants from the United States might have reinforced its authority over the islands and muted further calls for Philippine independence. In 1903, the first year of peace following the "insurrection," only about 8,000 Americans lived in the Philippines, a number that would remain fairly constant over the next decades. Some were colonial officials, others were entrepreneurs, and still others were former American soldiers who had been stationed in the islands and did not want to leave.[13]

By 1907, Filipino voters had been prepared to participate in the election for the first Philippine Assembly, which would share legislative power with the American commission. Cebu native Sergio Osmeña, a member of the Nacionalista (Nationalist) Party and a strong advocate for self-rule, was elected Speaker of the Philippine Assembly. During the first decade of the twentieth century, American rule allowed Filipinos to establish their own national assembly but made sure that the road to full independence would be a long one. Many Filipino politicians did not disapprove. They willingly collaborated with the Americans as long as the Philippines somehow profited, and as long as independence was still on the table.[14]

Philippine independence appeared within reach when Woodrow Wilson won the presidential election in 1912, and Democrats, many of whom were anti-imperialist, took control of Congress. A progressive Democratic congressman from New York, Francis Burton Harrison, was named governor-general of the Philippines. Upon his arrival in the Philippines on October 6, 1913, the tall and mustachioed Harrison told a crowd of thousands at Luneta Park, "We regard ourselves as trustees acting not for the advantage of the United States but for the benefit of the people of the Philippines Islands. Every step we take will be taken with a view to the ultimate independence of the islands. . . ."[15]

During Harrison's eight-year tenure, he became one of the Filipinos' favorite Americans, mostly because of his plan for "Filipinization" of the country. Harrison also appointed as many Filipinos as possible to government administrative posts, unseating Americans who had held them for years. This action prompted the resignations of those who refused to work as subordinates to Filipinos. While these changes clearly illustrated a commitment to independence, many Americans involved with the Philippines still predicted disaster, arguing that Filipinos were not ready for home rule.

Harrison's Filipinization plan was supported by William Atkinson Jones, an anti-imperialist congressman from Virginia who served on the Insular Affairs Committee that directed Philippine matters. During the summer of 1914, Jones introduced a bill to Congress that called for replacing the commission portion of the Philippine government with an elected Senate and renaming the Assembly the House of Representatives. The Jones bill passed the House of Representatives in October 1914, mostly along partisan lines, but failed in the Senate and died in March 1915.

The bill was introduced again in December, and President Wilson signed it into law in the summer of 1916. The position of American governor-general was retained, appointed by the president and still wielding veto power. Free trade would continue between the United States and the Philippines. However, the preamble of the Jones Act prevaricated over independence, stating that "it is, as it has always been, the purpose of the people of the United States to withdraw their sovereignty over the Philippine Islands and to recognize their independence as soon as a stable government can be established therein." The preamble further clarified the need for "the speedy accomplishment of such purpose" but without "impairing the exercise of the rights of sovereignty by the people of the United States. . . ." The Jones Act paved the way for the creation of the Philippine Commonwealth, the final step to independence.[16]

As important as the act was to US–Philippines relations, many Americans did not pay much attention to it. During the debates over the legislation, Manuel Quezon observed that "the people at large are not interested enough in this subject to write to their congressmen." The attention of most Americans was focused on the war that had broken out in Europe in the summer of 1914.[17]

The United States stayed out of that conflict until 1917. Japan, however, used it to increase its power in the Pacific by seizing Germany's colonial possessions in the region. Although Japan joined the Allies in the war, the Germans tried to convince Japan that an alliance with the Central Powers would allow the Japanese to fight against the three countries (England, Russia, and the United States) that were hampering their Asian expansion, especially in the Philippines. Despite its determination to dominate in the Pacific, Japan declined Germany's overture.[18]

Fed up with unrestricted submarine warfare and worried about the stability of its Mexican border region, the United States declared war on Germany in April 1917, making Japan and the United States allies. The War Department's interest in military intelligence revived, and over the next year and a half, the government created an extensive intelligence setup, including what would become the US Counter Intelligence Corps, plus the staffing designation "2" for all intelligence and security units in the military. In the summer of 1918, just months before the Allied victory, the US Army made military intelligence a discrete division of the general staff. This would all prove instrumental in fighting the next world war.[19]

Though the United States retreated into isolationism after the Great War, this did not spur it to grant independence to the Philippines. During the 1920s and 1930s, Americans continued to travel there, but by the end of the 1930s the American-born population in the Philippines still fluctuated between 8,000 and 9,000. These numbers paled in comparison to those of Japanese and Chinese immigrants (about 16,000 and 100,000, respectively), though the Americans and the Spanish wielded considerably more economic and social power.[20]

Before leaving office in 1921, Woodrow Wilson declared that "the moment had come to move on to independence" for the Philippines, but he did not mean immediately. Warren Harding, Wilson's Republican successor, did not consider repealing the Jones Act, though he also had no intention of granting Philippine independence anytime soon. The reciprocal trade relationship was too lucrative, and Harding and other Republicans worried that an independent Philippines would not be strong enough to withstand expansionist threats from nearby Japan. Harding dispatched an investigative commission to the islands in 1921, headed by Cameron Forbes and General Leonard Wood. Its conclusions reinforced Harding's view that the Philippines were not ready for independence.[21]

Harding then appointed Wood as the new governor-general of the islands. At the time Wood was in his sixties and already had a distinguished career as a soldier, participating in the capture of Geronimo, commanding the First Volunteer Cavalry regiment (known as the Rough Riders) in Cuba, and orchestrating attacks against the Moros in the Philippines. After heading the US military in those islands from 1906 to 1910, Wood returned to the United States to serve as Army Chief of Staff. Described as a "good man [who] found himself in the wrong job," Wood often behaved in an imperious manner as governor-general, doing little to give the Filipinos the impression that he believed they were capable of self-rule, frequently clashing with native politicians.[22]

Wood's successor, Henry Stimson, offered up a new approach. Both Manuel Quezon and Sergio Osmeña, political rivals who set aside their differences in a common opposition to Wood, supported Stimson's appointment in 1928. They took it as a step toward independence when Stimson reinstituted the council of state to get Filipino politicians' input on matters of government and economics. Stimson's governorship did much to smooth over the hostilities left by Wood, but it was a short tenure. He returned to the United States in early 1929 to serve as President Herbert Hoover's secretary of state.[23]

Another governor-general, Dwight Davis, arrived as Filipinos continued to push for independence. Two thousand delegates converged on Manila in February 1930 to discuss and pass a resolution supporting independence. The Philippine legislature sent a new delegation, led by Osmeña and the Speaker of the Philippine House Manuel Roxas, to Washington, D.C., where they spent two years lobbying Congress. The authority of the delegation was diminished by the continuing political feud between Osmeña and Quezon. Quezon, already suffering from tuberculosis, followed the original delegation to the States, attempting to undercut Osmeña's growing power. Quezon ultimately won out.[24]

More important than this political infighting, however, was the question of when, not if, Philippine independence would occur. Congress responded to lobbying efforts by passing the Hare-Hawes-Cutting Act in December 1932. The act provided for a ten-year commonwealth period, during which the United States would continue to militarily protect the islands, ending with complete independence. Hare-Hawes-Cutting did not reflect a sudden revelation that Filipinos were capable of self-rule; rather it was based on the growing economic hardships of the Depression. An independent Philippines would not likely receive special consideration with trade or with immigration, and with current conditions, most Americans willingly promoted protectionism and nativism.

Finally, the Commonwealth lay just ahead. It would be formed under a new American presidential administration, that of Democrat Franklin Roosevelt, who took the oath of office in March 1933. That same year, Adolf Hitler assumed power in Germany and the Japanese renewed their attacks in northern China. Stung by the economic reverses of the Great Depression, the Japanese had embarked on a plan to dominate Asia to seize the raw materials and the laborers it needed to revive prosperity. In 1931, Japanese troops occupied Manchuria, setting up the puppet regime of Manchukuo. The following year they staged an unsuccessful attack on the rich, bustling port city of Shanghai. When the League of Nations criticized these actions in 1933, the Japanese withdrew from the international body rather than end their attacks on China. The Japanese intended to take as much of Asia as possible.

Despite the dominance of isolationist sentiment in the United States and Japanese intentions to expand and conquer, during the 1920s and 1930s, most Americans viewed the Philippine Islands as a safe place—it was, after all, under American protection. That was what drew Gladys Savary, Claire Phillips, Yay Panlilio, and Peggy Utinsky.

CHAPTER 2

FOUR WOMEN

P EGGY, GLADYS, YAY, AND CLAIRE—each woman was an adventurer, willing to travel halfway around the world to Manila, the capital city of the Philippine Islands, in search of a better life. Manila exuded glamour and romance. Its country clubs hosted dances and sporting events, nightclubs offered the coolest drinks and the hottest music, American films played at local movie theaters, and shoppers indulged in the current fashions, courtesy of modern American-style department stores. As expatriates in this colonial location, Americans enjoyed a privileged position. Even those who worked for a living typically earned enough to live in nice villas or in smart apartments in good neighborhoods, perhaps hire a servant or two. For them, this Pearl of the Orient, as Manila was called, was a paradise.

Peggy Utinsky was the first of the four to head to Manila, arriving in 1926 or 1927 for an extended vacation. Born Margaret Doolin in 1900 in St. Louis, Missouri, probably to Irish immigrant parents who may have left her an orphan, Peggy grew up on a Canadian wheat farm. Around the age of sixteen she married a man named John Rowley, and they had one child together, Charles. John may have fallen victim to one of the rounds of Spanish influenza so lethal at the time, because by 1919 Peggy was a widow.[1]

Scarcely twenty years old, alone, and with a small child to care for, Peggy's situation was not unique among American women in the World War I era. Thousands had been left on their own in the late 1910s, either because of the Spanish influenza or the Great War, both of which succeeded in carrying off large numbers of young men. So Peggy needed steady, respectable, well-paid employment, and for a white middle-class woman that typically meant teaching, secretarial work, social work, or nursing. Peggy decided on the last. After completing her training as a registered nurse in 1924, she could have chosen a hospital position, something in a doctor's office, or even contracted with private patients, any of which would have been enough to provide food, shelter, and clothing for her son Charley and herself.[2]

Yet Peggy probably had not abandoned the hope that her years as a working woman would be temporary. She was young and attractive—with arresting blue eyes and head-turning red hair—smart, funny, loyal, always in the mood for a glass of beer and a good game of poker. She could fall in love again, get married again, have the life most young women dreamed about. But a couple of years passed and the still-widowed Peggy was wearing herself out with work. She longed for a change, an extended vacation in a faraway place tinged with the exotic, so she booked passage to go as far west as possible.[3]

As the ship made its way into the harbor, Peggy and Charley would have caught their first view of Manila, a discordant jumble of the Philippines' colonial past and present: Intramuros, the old Walled City of the Spanish occupation; Luneta Park, the site of the execution of Dr. José Rizal, hero of the Philippine Revolution; stylish marble and concrete buildings along the very modern American Dewey Boulevard; bamboo and nipa palm shacks in the native, or Tondo, section of the city. The ship would have docked, as did all on international voyages, at Pier 7, a massive double-decker concrete structure built in the 1920s at the cost of millions of pesos.

The planned six-month visit stretched into a year, then two, until there seemed no point in returning stateside, because, as Peggy later wrote, "I loved the Islands." She probably worked in Manila, too, picking up nursing jobs and scrambling a little to earn money. Still, life in the Philippines was likely more pleasant than it had been in the States. Manila had warm weather, beautiful scenery, a low cost of living with affordable domestic help, and a close-knit, sociable American community.[4]

Then, finally, came romance. John (Jack) Paul Utinsky cut an imposing figure: six feet tall with curly dark brown hair, inviting emerald eyes, and an Errol Flynn pencil moustache. Jack had been born in 1897 in West Virginia and raised in Springfield, Illinois, the eldest of four children of Russian-Lithuanian immigrant parents. At seventeen, he joined the US Army and was stationed in the Philippines. By the end of November 1917, the year the Americans joined the Great War, he had been promoted to first lieutenant in the army infantry, and he may have been with US troops in Siberia. After separating from the service, he took a job as a civil engineer for the American government in the Philippines, settling on the small island of Corregidor, just off the southern tip of the Bataan peninsula.[5]

Corregidor, the island referred to as "the Rock"—as in Gibraltar—a nod to its defensive capabilities, was all about fortification. Located at the entrance of Manila Bay, the island was four miles long and just over a mile across at its widest. Everyone's livelihood there, including Jack Utinsky's, stemmed from its strategic location. It would protect Manila in the event of an enemy attack. In 1907, Corregidor was designated a US Military Reserve, and Fort Mills, an army post, was constructed there. During 1909, the Corps of Engineers began to strengthen the seaward approach area of the island with a variety of weapons batteries.

Engineers started blasting into Malinta Hill during the 1920s and 1930s to construct the Malinta Tunnel, a massive military complex over eight hundred feet long. In addition to this main east–west passage, thirteen laterals were built on the north and another eleven on the south. Between the batteries and the tunnel, the US military believed it could protect Corregidor as well as Manila. By the mid-1930s, the island contained an underground city, complete with military headquarters, radio and decoding rooms, repair and storage facilities, and a hospital large enough to accommodate a thousand patients. An efficient tram system zipped workers to and from their jobs.[6]

Peggy met Jack sometime during the early 1930s, either when he had gone to Manila to indulge in some big-city nightlife, or she had come to Corregidor to visit friends—Americans in the Philippines routinely indulged in that kind of socializing. However they met, an immediate attraction pulled them together. Jack captivated Peggy with his stories, witty tales about his experiences all over the Philippines. A born raconteur, fluent in Spanish and several Philippine dialects, he seemed to know everything about the islands. When Jack proposed, presenting Peggy with a stunning three-carat diamond ring, she did not have to think twice. They married in 1934.[7]

Corregidor became Peggy Utinsky's new home. Although the island was small, its amenities were vast. During the latter half of the 1930s, luncheons and bridge games filled Peggy's long afternoons and cocktail parties enlivened the evenings. "Easy warmth and gay companionship," she observed of those years. It was simple enough to ignore the fact that Corregidor had been developed for its defensive capabilities. Nothing in Peggy's immediate vicinity seemed remotely threatening—signs of American power were visible everywhere on the island that the United States had been militarizing over the previous decades. Jack earned a comfortable living from his work as an engineer, they had dozens of friends, Charley seemed happy, and they all had a lot of time to enjoy the privileges of the American colonial lifestyle.[8]

THE YEAR AFTER THE UTINSKYS MARRIED, the Philippines took another step closer to independence. The United States established a Commonwealth government in the Philippines designed to last for ten years, at the end of which the islands would receive independence. The Hare-Hawes-Cutting Act, which outlined this arrangement, had passed the US Congress in late 1932, but to become effective, the act also had to pass the Philippine legislature. The two most powerful political leaders of the time, Sergio Osmeña and Manuel Quezon, both members of

the Nacionalista Party yet already at odds with each other, sharply disagreed about the act, with Osmeña for it and Quezon against. Quezon
and his faction, who opposed the act out of concern for the harm it would
do to Philippine trade and immigration, ultimately won out. A new governor-general arrived in Manila during the Osmeña-Quezon debate:
Frank Murphy, the former mayor of Detroit, a bachelor, and a Catholic.
Murphy's contribution to the controversy was to remain neutral and let
the Filipino politicians hash it out.[9]

The Philippine legislature ultimately rejected Hare-Hawes-Cutting,
and Manuel Quezon went back to Washington in 1934 to renegotiate
terms of independence. The resulting Tydings-McDuffie Act was, as
Sergio Osmeña complained, "merely Hare warmed over." It was, however,
Quezon's creation and proved popular in both the United States and the
Philippines. The legislation provided for a Commonwealth government
largely concerned with domestic issues, independence in ten years, and
Philippine imports subjected to American tariffs—with no promises that
the United States could maintain army bases in the islands. The Philippines
now had a firm commitment to independence, with the Commonwealth
period as the final transition phase. In early 1935 a constitutional convention created the structure of the new Philippine government. Quezon and
Osmeña devised a coalition ticket to foster political unity, with Quezon
elected president and Osmeña vice president.[10]

The passage of Tydings-McDuffie in the United States was entangled in
economic fears, xenophobia, racism, and isolationism. President Franklin
Roosevelt, like many of his predecessors, had no clear idea on the question
of Philippine independence. In 1934, during the debates over the legislation, Roosevelt remarked in private, "Let's get rid of the Philippines—that's
the most important thing. Let's be frank about it." Severing the colonial
relationship would benefit the United States by eliminating free trade and
by removing the costly military obligation to protect the islands.[11]

The Commonwealth setup proved popular with most Filipinos, though
not all. Frank Murphy had to guard against actual uprisings as well as threats
of them. In May 1935, just before the plebiscite for the new Constitution,
Sakdalistas—rebels who wanted immediate independence—attacked

fourteen municipalities near Manila, seizing government buildings and constabulary garrisons, then hoisting their own flag. The constabulary quelled the uprising but in the process killed fifty-nine Sakdals. After the election of Commonwealth officials, hundreds of people met almost every night in the Cavite backyard of aging insurrectionist and losing candidate Emilio Aguinaldo to listen to speakers denounce Manuel Quezon as an enemy of independence. Some called for his assassination. Rumors abounded that Aguinaldo planned a massive protest parade on inauguration day, but neither the assassination nor the protest occurred.[12]

In addition to concerns over these kinds of threats, plans for the inauguration ceremony became complicated by a protocol dispute that revealed continuing tensions over Philippine autonomy. Manuel Quezon believed that his inauguration as president of the Commonwealth should be marked with a twenty-one gun salute and Frank Murphy's inauguration as American High Commissioner with a nineteen-gun salute. A twenty-one gun salute was normally reserved for the head of a sovereign state, which the Philippines would not become until after the Commonwealth period. The US Secretary of War, George Dern, told Murphy, "There can be no question as to the status of the High Commissioner to the Philippine Islands as the representative of the President of the United States as long as the sovereignty of the United States continues." A subsequent telegram from the War Department made President Roosevelt's position clear: "It is proper that the High Commissioner be regarded as the senior official and, therefore, that as between the two he take precedence over the President of the Commonwealth." In the end it was decided that Quezon and Murphy would each receive a nineteen-gun salute, with the High Commissioner's going off first.[13]

When he was inaugurated in 1935 as the first president of the Commonwealth of the Philippines, Manuel Quezon implemented the National Defense Act to create a strong national army. Quezon planned to spend a quarter of his budget to raise and train 10,000 regular troops by 1945, with an additional 400,000 in reserve. To boost the strength of the fledgling force, he merged the Constabulary, created in 1901 as the civil government's police force, into the army as its First Regular Division.

He chose the most experienced officer he knew to head his armed forces: Douglas MacArthur.[14]

MacArthur was born with connections to the Philippine Islands and to the American military: his father, Arthur MacArthur, had been a military governor there in the early twentieth century. After graduating from West Point, Douglas took a posting for a short time in the islands until malaria prompted reassignment. He then served with distinction during the First World War, and in 1922 took command of a US infantry brigade in the Philippines. Over the next dozen years, a series of promotions bounced him back and forth between the islands and the States. In 1930 he became the US Army's Chief of Staff in Washington.

Manuel Quezon had known since at least 1934 that he wanted MacArthur at the head of a new Philippine military. While in Washington that year trying to both negotiate independence and lay the groundwork for a new government, Quezon asked him, "Can the Philippines be defended?" The general replied, "I *know* that the islands can be protected, provided of course you have the money which will be required." MacArthur proposed that 11,000 Filipino soldiers be readied to train 400,000 reservists. Their job would be to harass the Japanese if they attacked and to hold the islands until American reinforcements arrived. Quezon offered MacArthur the position of military adviser.[15]

Tired of his position in Washington, MacArthur accepted and negotiated a sweet deal: the rank of field marshal (the first American to wear five stars), an $18,000 annual salary with a $15,000 personal allowance, and accommodations in the top-floor suite of the Manila Hotel (which enjoyed the ultimate luxury of air-conditioning). Despite the perks, the military adviser position was a kind of consolation prize for MacArthur, who coveted the post of American High Commissioner for the Philippines, which he was never given. President Roosevelt endorsed MacArthur's retirement from the US Army and subsequent acceptance of the field marshal position in the Philippines.[16]

Although the United States maintained a steady military presence in the Philippines during the Commonwealth period, absolute defense of the islands was not a top American priority. In fact, military experts agreed after World War I that in the event of an attack by Japan, there was no scenario in which the United States *could* hold its colony. War Plan Orange (WPO), developed in the early 1900s by the US Army and Navy, changed many times over the years, but throughout remained focused on the fortification of Manila Bay and Corregidor Island to protect Manila. By the end of the 1930s, the basic military strategy called for stopping a Japanese invasion at Manila Bay. If for some reason that proved impossible—and it certainly would—American and Filipino forces would resort to a holding action against the Japanese and withdraw to the Bataan Peninsula, a thirty-mile-long extension of the Zambales Mountains on the island of Luzon that divided Manila Bay from the South China Sea. There, troops would await reinforcements.[17]

The strength of these combined forces hovered at a very low point because the isolationism of the interwar period led to troop reductions and disarmament. By 1939, when war began in Europe, seventeen countries had armies stronger than the United States. Japan had nearly two-and-a-half million troops with another three million in reserve. American military experts estimated the Japanese could send 50,000 to 60,000 men to the Philippines on a week's notice. In the entirety of East Asia, the United States—along with Great Britain and Holland—had about 350,000 troops. During World War I, Japan came in on the side of the Allies. This time it was clear that the country's sympathies lay with the Axis powers of Germany and Italy.[18]

GLADYS SLAUGHTER SAVARY HAD, by her own admission, a "simple, normal childhood in a small town in the Middle West." As she put it, "I went to school, had dozens of dogs and cats and pet chickens, played hooky, got spanked with regular frequency for my many misdemeanors." She ended up in Manila by way of Paris and South America. Born in 1893 in Genoa, Nebraska, a town so small it was only on the map because of its Indian Industrial School, she was the last of six children in a prosperous farming family.[19]

At seventeen Gladys headed west to college, possibly to California, but did not stay long enough to graduate. She was interested in too many things, few of them academic. Chicago beckoned next, and Gladys settled there around 1919. Working at a dull clerical job, she grew restless and unfocused. With at least two broken engagements behind her, she headed off in 1921 to visit friends in Shanghai, which she found to be the "gayest, maddest city in the Orient."[20]

Gladys cut a striking figure there—a willowy 5'7" tall, with dark blonde hair, blue eyes, straight nose, and a firmly rounded chin accented with a mole on its right side—and she was very popular in the European immigrant community. She loved Shanghai: "Parties, clubs, races, dances, sight-seeing, houseboating—it was a life such as none of us will ever know again." Footloose, attractive, and flirtatious, Gladys fell in love with a young American naval officer and followed him to Chefoo, a port city in northeastern Shandong Province under Japanese control. From there she traveled to Peking, changing boyfriends along with cities, never finding the right man to settle down with. In January 1922 she returned to Chicago, no less restless than when she had left.[21]

This time an opportune job offer quenched her wanderlust. In China Gladys had learned mah-jonhgg, a game of strategy and chance played with dozens of picturesque tiles, which became a craze in the United States during the first half of the 1920s. An American game company headquartered in Chicago hired Gladys to promote its version of mah-jonhgg in Europe. This dream come true—getting paid for traveling—did not last long. While Gladys was in Budapest, the company went out of business and she found herself unemployed. Undaunted, she headed for Paris because "Who doesn't want to go to Paris?"[22]

Gladys enrolled in language and history classes, took up residence in a student hostel, and hired tutors to make sure she aced her coursework. Her French language tutor introduced her to André Savary, a young electrical engineering student from Bapaume, a small town in northern France. "He was interesting, well-read and was a walking history of France," Gladys later recalled. "As we became closer to each other, I realized I had to decide." So in late 1924 Gladys returned to the States to think about André's marriage proposal and to talk it over with family. "Disapproval was the unanimous response." Still, she was over thirty and the family's blessing was only a courtesy. Gladys headed back to Paris where she and André married on April 14, 1925.[23]

The newlyweds took a house outside the city, on the banks of the Marne River, where Gladys enthusiastically settled into her idyllic French life. It turned out to be short-lived, however, because André, as Gladys put it, "had a roving foot, and when he had an opportunity to go to Venezuela on an engineering project, there was nothing else to do but go!" The Savarys settled in Maracay, capital of the state of Aragua, with a population of about 10,000, in the north-central part of the country near the Caribbean coast. Gladys was the only American woman in the city, but Venezuelans assumed that she was, like her husband, French.[24]

Gladys considered Maracay "comic opera living," mostly because of the aging Venezuelan dictator General Juan Vicente Gómez, who ran the country from his home in the small city. While Gladys later acknowledged that Gómez "ruled the lives of his people with a truly iron rod," she did not take him seriously. In 1929, using her maiden name Slaughter, she wrote a letter to *Time* magazine ridiculing the general by pointing out the eighty-four illegitimate children he sired by a string of mistresses.[25]

When Venezuelan officials figured out who wrote the letter, they suggested Gladys leave their country. She departed Maracay in January 1930; her husband followed two months later. The couple ended up in Brooklyn, where André found work as an electrical engineer and Gladys as a secretary at a publishing company. The money was enough to live well, but Brooklyn was hardly the kind of exotic locale they craved. So when Savary received an offer to work on the construction of an electrical plant on the Philippine island of Culion, the couple did not hesitate to pack their bags.

Culion is an island divided in halves. At the time, about 7,000 lepers lived in a colony on one side, while on the other were all of the people who supported and treated them. André's job at the electrical plant involved supervising some of the leper patients who also worked as laborers. Life was comfortable for the Savarys on their side of the island. They lived in a small, well-appointed cottage perched on a picturesque hillside, and they socialized with missionaries, doctors, and scientists. The men hunted wild pig in their spare time; Gladys collected orchids.[26]

When the electrical plant was finished, so was Savary's job on the island, and the couple needed to look for a new opportunity. They moved to Manila in 1931 to consider their options. Gladys favored returning to France, but her husband concluded his best employment opportunities were either right there in Manila or in Mexico. They ended up staying in Manila, doing something neither of them had ever anticipated they would do.

"We got into the restaurant business!" Gladys later explained. "The whole venture was whipped up over a couple of Dubonnets. We met some French people who deplored the dearth of good eating places in Manila [and thought] how nice it would be to have a French restaurant." Gladys had some savings and André had been raised in a family with sophisticated culinary tastes, so it all made sense. The Savarys rented a Spanish mansion at 233 Isaac Peral, on the corner of Dewey Boulevard, in Manila's elegant Ermita district. To ensure authentic cuisine, they hired a chef from France.[27]

Renovations on the property fulfilled Gladys's vision of a cozy, intimate place that projected an atmosphere of good friends sharing a meal. The cocktail lounge was decorated in red, with the dining area made into a "tropical copy" of a Paris restaurant the Savarys particularly admired. Menus from different French restaurants, along with old French prints, adorned the walls, banquettes provided comfortable seating, and a large Provençal-style sideboard displayed an eclectic collection of carvings and porcelains. The terrace, with its spectacular view of Manila Bay and Dewey Boulevard, offered open-air dining. The Restaurant de Paris, advertising itself as "Manila's Smartest Restaurant," opened in 1932. Few of its considerable clientele called it by that name; they simply referred to it as "Gladys's."[28]

And to her amazement, the restaurant turned a profit. "André was a fanatic on the subject of good food and wine, I liked to eat and drink well myself and the chef was splendid. . . . In the words of one of our friends, we ran the place like a blankety-blank house-party. But it was a huge success," she later wrote. Everyone showed up at Gladys's in the 1930s, including Peggy and Jack Utinsky, and probably the noted journalist Yay Panlilio.[29]

YAY PANLILIO MOVED TO MANILA without a second thought—she viewed it as her real home. Her mother, Valentina, was a Filipina who allegedly had stowed away on a ship bound for San Francisco. After making her way to Denver, Valentina met an Irish-American man and bore him a daughter named Valeria (but called "Yay") on May 22, 1913. Yay's biological father apparently did not figure into her early life, and she wrote sparingly about those years with her mother, Filipino stepfather Ildefonso Corpus, and younger half-brother Raymond: "In my childhood we had lived in tenements, boxcars, ranch shacks; and through one severe Colorado winter somehow we had survived in a canvas tent." By 1930 the Corpus family had moved to Auburn, California. Yay left home as soon as she could, at sixteen marrying Edward (or Eduardo) Panlilio, a Filipino national nine years her senior. For a brief time the newlyweds lived in Roseville, about sixteen miles away from Yay's parents.[30]

The exact circumstances and date of Yay's arrival in the Philippines are uncertain, though it is clear that her husband accompanied her. Their first child was born in Manila in 1933, and they had two more before separating. Then Yay fulfilled her dream of becoming a journalist. *The Philippines Herald* hired her on as a reporter and photographer, and she later also broadcasted the news on radio station KZRH. Yay's newspaper work turned her into, according to *Fortune* magazine staff writer Florence Horn, "Probably the best-known woman in the Islands." Some of that had to do with Yay's sartorial splendor. When she worked in Manila, she typically wore a white sharkskin suit, the bulbs for her camera awkwardly stuffed in her blouse pockets. Other times she donned pants in vivid colors and tied a scarf over her head. Everyone in the city knew Yay Panlilio on sight.[31]

The other part of Yay's notoriety had to do with her fearlessness in getting a story. She did not hesitate to cover controversial topics involving the tangle of colonial-era politics, and in the Philippines the media and politicians were intertwined. Yay's boss at *The Philippines Herald*, Carlos Romulo, studied in both the Philippines and the United States before becoming a professor of English at the University of the Philippines in 1923. While holding that position Romulo also served as secretary to Philippine Senate president Manuel Quezon, who had founded the *Herald* in 1920 to promote Philippine independence. During the early 1930s, Romulo became publisher and editor of the newspaper.[32]

He gave Yay a loose rein in deciding which stories to cover and how to cover them, and she did not confine her stories to Manila. The Philippines is a big country, full of all kinds of interesting people and events, and she wanted to bring as many of them as she could to the *Herald* readers. Because of her American and Filipino heritage, Yay easily moved among all communities in the islands, and she held a steadfast allegiance to both countries.

CLAIRE PHILLIPS CAME TO MANILA because she wanted to be famous. "Call it restlessness, fate, wanderlust or the whirligig of chance, Bill Shakespeare said that 'all the world's a stage' and maybe I was not fond of sitting in the wings," she later explained. Her original name, in fact, was tailor-made for a stage career: Claire Mabel De La Taste. Her father, George, was born in England in 1878 and immigrated to the United States in 1887. He met and married Mabel Melvina Cole, from Howard City, Michigan, and their union produced three daughters. Claire, born in 1907, was the middle child. George died when the girls were still young, but Mabel did not remain a widow long. She married a marine engineer named Jesse Snyder, and in 1914 the family settled in Portland, Oregon.[33]

As a teenager, Claire considered Portland a dead end for a show business career, so she did not even stick around to graduate from high school. She left home in search of work as a chorus girl and a vaudeville actor, moving around—Kansas City, Denver, and Seattle—trying out different stage names. Fame eluded Claire as she struggled to keep body and soul together, especially once the Depression set in. Local authorities in Seattle picked her up for vagrancy at least once, in May 1933, while she was using the name Dorothy Smith.[34]

When Claire hit her late twenties, she decided she had to do something drastic if she was going to make it big. Her knockabout companion Louise De Martini, originally from the coal mining town of Black Diamond, Washington, seemed to have encouraged this bold move. The pair pinned their hopes on Honolulu and traveled to Hawaii in 1938, but even this shot at fame fizzled. So they continued moving across the Pacific, booking passage to the Philippines, America's westernmost colonial outpost. They scraped together enough money to travel on the SS *President Pierce*, part of the popular American Presidents Line. The 535-foot-long ship offered its 550 passengers a variety of amenities—from dancing to sports to beauty parlors—that guaranteed a pleasant voyage between ports of call in China and Japan.[35]

By the time she reached Manila Claire Phillips was in her early thirties, still vibrant, attractive, and ambitious. By playing up her previous stage experience, she snagged a job at the 1,600-seat Metropolitan Theatre. Located on the corner of Padre Burgos Street and Quezon Boulevard, the art deco Metropolitan represented the modern glitz of colonial Manila. It had opened in 1931, boasting a roofline that resembled a gracefully arched eyebrow, the exterior punctuated with statues created by an Italian sculptor, and the interior lobby walls decorated with stylized reliefs of Philippine flora.[36]

For twenty-five pesos (about $2 then) a week, Claire danced in the chorus line. This did not provide the star billing for which she yearned, but she viewed it as a good first step to fame. Within a couple of months, though, romance trumped her budding stage career. Claire jettisoned her show business plans for Manuel Fuentes, a forty-year-old Filipino mestizo from Capiz, a city about 250 miles southeast of Manila, in the western Visayas region of the Philippines.

Manuel had been a civilian employee of the American military for nearly twenty years. In 1938 he worked as a steward on the SS *Corregidor*, a job that took him all over the vast archipelago. When his ship docked in Manila, he probably attended the shows at the Metropolitan Theatre, likely had an eye for the pretty dancers. In fact, at first glance Manuel may have taken the new girl at the Metropolitan, with her light caramel skin, black hair, and brown eyes, for a mestiza.

Very soon after their first meeting—perhaps within weeks—Manuel proposed and Claire accepted. In Manuel, Claire found the head-over-heels romance she dreamed of, swept away by this slightly older yet still-handsome man with a well-paying, steady, and rather glamorous job. The whirlwind courtship blurred the reality that Claire shared the

Metropolitan stage with dancers a full decade younger than she. Marriage to a well-traveled, attractive man would provide enough excitement and glamour. Or so Claire hoped.

She assumed Manuel could not bear to be separated from her, and that she would join him on most of his inter-island trips. But the romance did not last and the adventure never panned out. After their wedding in the Manila suburb of Caloocan in August 1938, the couple settled into a comfortable middle-class life. Claire found herself bored. Manuel proved an inattentive husband. Moreover, he did not want his wife to work, especially not on stage, so returning to the Metropolitan was not an option for Claire. As for his exciting travels, when Manuel headed off on business, he left Claire at home. Head-over-heels romance landed with a dull thud.[37]

Resentful of her husband's lengthy and repeated absences, and by now bored to distraction, Claire decided she wanted a baby. When Manuel returned after a seven-month trip in 1939, Claire presented him with a daughter named Dian who, she said, had been born in February. Given the timing of their original meeting and the quick marriage, it is possible that a suspected pregnancy was the main reason for the nuptials. What Claire failed to tell her husband, and what he insisted he did not know for years, was that Dian was the daughter of one of their servants. Claire had either never been pregnant or she suffered a miscarriage shortly after the wedding; still, she found a way to get what she wanted.[38]

The baby did not save the faltering marriage. One day later in 1939, with Manuel again away on business, and probably without his knowledge, Claire took Dian and sailed for the United States. By the time she returned to Manila in September 1941, rumors of war were in the air.

★ ★ ★

CHAPTER 3

THE TWILIGHT OF OLD MANILA

Y AY PANLILIO'S CAREER AS A JOURNALIST MEANT SHE KEPT current on all matters pertaining to the Commonwealth of the Philippines, including impending independence and the potential Japanese threat to it. Once war broke out in Europe in 1939, her work drove her at such breakneck speed that not even a brush with death deterred her. While Yay was out chasing down a story, the brakes on her car failed, sending her head-on into a garbage truck. The doctors treating her injuries did not expect her to survive, yet she defied the prognosis, retaining a noticeable limp—sometimes accompanied by enormous pain—that intensified with overexertion.[1]

One of Yay's 1939 stories was about the growing number of Japanese immigrants in the islands, which she worried would undermine the country's security. She traveled over six hundred miles to Mindanao, the southernmost island of the Philippines, to research an article on the thriving plantations near its largest city, Davao, where Japanese had rapidly taken over local businesses.

Victor Takizawa, a Japanese businessman, showed Yay around Davao, pointing out with pride the many laborers and businessmen who lived in *Dabao-kuo*, or Little Japan, a self-segregated community with its own schools and shrines. When Yay caught sight of a Japanese flag flying out in public, she snapped a picture and sent it to the *Herald*'s city editor, who turned it over to local authorities. A fracas over the flag ensued between the office of the American High Commissioner and the Japanese Consulate, highlighting the rivalry between the two countries.[2]

By the late 1930s it was clear Japan had designs on the Philippines and had been sending its people there to establish a foothold, to lay the foundation for a fifth column. Eighty plantations in the Davao area were owned by Japanese who grew rubber, a native banana called the abaca, coconuts, and trees prized for their lumber. Overall, the Japanese made up 6 percent of the 68,000 people in this section of Mindanao. Although a 1939 census revealed just over 29,000 Japanese living in the Philippines out of a total population of over sixteen million, the Japanese now seemed particularly noticeable. In response, the following year the Commonwealth government restricted Japanese immigration to the Philippines, drawing sharp protests from Tokyo.[3]

Yay's journalism career expanded when she began augmenting her *Herald* work with broadcasting news stories on KZRH, also known as Radio Manila. The radio station had been launched in July 1939 by Samuel Gaches, owner of Heacock's Department Store. The station's most popular broadcaster was Clarence Beliel, known on air as Don Bell. Beliel was an old Asia hand who started off with the US Marines in China in the 1920s before joining the *Shanghai Evening Post & Mercury* as a reporter. When the Japanese attacked Shanghai in 1937, Beliel decided to leave China—much of his reporting had been critical of the Japanese—and ended up in Manila.[4]

Though Yay said little about her work in the two years leading up to the outbreak of the Pacific war, she spent a lot of time reporting on what she could of the military, making numerous contacts along the way. And the military realized she could be a tremendous asset to them. At some point, Colonel J. K. Evans, the liaison between the American War Department and the Philippine Commonwealth government, ordered Captain Ralph Keeler, Assistant Chief of Intelligence at Fort Santiago, to recruit Yay as an S-2 agent. In the Army, S-2 was responsible for intelligence, including gathering information on enemy movements, providing security clearances, and handling radio codes and maps. Keeler instructed Yay to pass along anything interesting she picked up during her routine reporting. Her work as a journalist provided a natural cover, and the fact that she was half Filipina might get her into places where Caucasians could not go.[5]

Because of her newspaper work, Yay probably knew another Filipina journalist who worked as the society editor for the Manila *Herald*. Pilar Campos, daughter of Pedro Campos, President of the Bank of the Philippines, was twenty-four years old in 1941. Petite and slender, with black hair, brown eyes, and light tan skin, Pilar was a graduate of Marygrove College in Detroit, Michigan, and considered herself Americanized. She frequented many events that brought Filipinos and Americans together.

During a party at the Army-Navy Club that August, Pilar met Ralph Hibbs, a doctor in the US Army Medical Corps. Born in Iowa in 1913, Hibbs graduated from the University of Iowa's medical school in 1936, enlisted in the army in February 1941, and landed in Manila in June. Whether they were enlisted men or officers, American servicemen tended to lead a cushy life in the Philippines, that is, until December 8, 1941. Enlisted men were on duty from 6:00 a.m. until 1:00 p.m., known as "tropical hours." This earned them about $21 (or 42 pesos) a month, enough to pay $1.50 each month for a servant to keep their uniforms and bunks in impeccable shape. Extensive leisure time meant abundant opportunities to watch American movies in air-conditioned theaters, and free hours to fill with bowling, swimming, tennis, baseball, or basketball. A night on the town was very affordable as well. Most bars charged five cents for a bottle of beer; a turn with a prostitute could cost as little as fifty cents.[6]

As a surgeon assigned to the second battalion of the 31st Infantry, Ralph Hibbs looked after about seven hundred patients at a clinic in Fort Santiago, now occupied by the US military, but he still kept an officer's version of tropical hours. "Days in garrison in Manila opened with sick call at 0630 hours. I was free by 1100 daily for golf at Fort McKinley or Manila's lovely Wack Wack course," he later recalled. After golf came lunch with Manila's social elite at one of the city's clubs, followed by late afternoon gambling at the Army-Navy Club, then dinner at a fine restaurant. "Neither of us sought help in finding the moral path," Hibbs later admitted of his relationship with Pilar Campos. "We dated, drank and danced as stateside Americans would." Their romance blossomed into a sexual affair.[7]

Even with tropical hours, there was a lot to be done, especially in terms of medical care, to prepare for what everyone seemed to know was coming. While Hibbs spent most of his time treating patients, other medical personnel departed to the Bataan peninsula to work out the logistics of emergency medical care for combat troops and more long-term hospital care in the rear. Officers and enlisted men alike received crash courses in field medicine and/or first aid. Sternberg General Hospital, located on the corner of Calle Arroceros and Calle Concepcion near the Pasig River, was designated as the primary hospital to treat battle injuries. Additional hospital annexes were assigned throughout Manila to care for projected casualties. If—when—those thousands of casualties became reality, tropical hours would become a dim memory for Ralph Hibbs.[8]

PEGGY UTINSKY ENJOYED LIFE on Corregidor with Jack, but as the 1930s drew to a close she started thinking about a stateside visit. This was not unusual. Many Americans living in the Philippines went home every few years, and for Peggy the 1939 World's Fair provided the ideal justification. She had always wanted to attend a world's fair, and its theme, "Building the World of Tomorrow," sounded intriguing. Plus it was taking place in New York City, where Peggy had never been. The trip was likely a high school graduation gift for her son, Charley. Now a young man, he was eager to get on with his life on his own terms, perhaps away from the Philippines.[9]

By the time Peggy made travel arrangements, though, the World's Fair had been open for about a year, and its title had taken on a bitter irony. Germany's invasion of Poland in 1939 encouraged Japan to step up its efforts to subdue China. In early 1940, Japanese troops tried to take Longzhou, a circular valley area in southwest China that contained an important railroad line linking it to the bordering northern French Indochina city of Hanoi. The railroad provided a supply line of fuel and other provisions the Chinese needed to continue their struggle against Japan, and for several months they put up a fight to keep that line open.

Because of these hostilities and the uncertainties they presented, the US Army needed all of its military and civilian personnel to maintain a strong presence in the Philippines and to keep its fortifications in good repair. So it was out of the question that Jack, still working as an engineer on Corregidor, would accompany his wife and stepson on their stateside trip. In fact, when Peggy boarded an army transport ship headed for San Francisco, her husband may have hoped she would not return. Peggy would be safe there. But Jack had been married to this woman for six years; he should have known she would not turn from a fight.

Peggy arrived in San Francisco on June 22, 1940, the day Adolf Hitler signed an armistice with France, the culmination of Germany's springtime blitzkrieg across Western Europe. As news spread, she traveled on to San Antonio, to visit relatives. Then she stopped in Illinois, eager to see the sights of Chicago, and detoured to Springfield to meet Jack's father and stepmother before heading on to New York. There Peggy spent time with one of Jack's sisters, regaling her niece and nephew with tales of the Philippines and of her smart white parrot. Aunt Peggy was a big hit, and photos were snapped to commemorate the visit. Dressed fashionably in a short-sleeved shirtwaist dress, peep-toe heels, and a brimmed hat, she looked to be in the prime of her life.

The United States, meanwhile, inched closer to war. In September 1940, President Roosevelt signed the Selective Training and Service Act, the first ever peacetime draft in the United States. Japan, Germany, and Italy created a military alliance known as the Tripartite Pact on September 27th. By October, Japan forced an agreement from the new Vichy government acknowledging Japanese rights to station its troops in Indochina and freely move supplies and personnel through the country. This last move particularly alarmed US officials, who worried about Japan's next potential conquest. In an attempt to slow down the Japanese military, Roosevelt signed an export embargo on American steel, scrap metal, and oil to Japan.

President Quezon's response was to try not to antagonize Japan, which he worried could invade the Philippines at any time. His country held many attractions for the Japanese, especially the natural resources that Japan's military could make good use of: iron, nickel, copper, lumber, acres of arable farmland, and numerous harbors, including Manila Bay. And if they controlled the Philippines, the Japanese could also humble the United States and wring important concessions from it.

So Quezon undercut General MacArthur's authority over the military and stopped the draft. In September 1940, he requested and received from the Philippine National Assembly special emergency powers, and the following April he created the Civilian Emergency Administration to safeguard the integrity of the islands and ensure their tranquility. These measures strained Quezon's relationship with the American High Commissioner in Manila, Francis Sayre, who worried that such actions would interfere with America's ability to defend the Philippines. His qualms were compounded by concerns over how Filipinos would respond to a Japanese attack. Would they turn against the Americans and greet the Japanese as liberators? Or would they continue their loyalty to the United States and fight against the Japanese?[10]

Peggy Utinsky realized that these events would probably change her life. As she later recalled, "One morning I was listening to the radio and heard an announcement that the Government would soon order all Navy women to leave the Philippines. That meant the next order would apply to Army women and I had no intention of being shelved somewhere away from Jack, if there was going to be trouble."[11]

She hated being told what to do, even by her own government, and had no intention of being separated from her husband. The order aimed at army dependents would not be issued until the spring of 1941, but Peggy refused to wait and see. She left for the West Coast to hop on the first ship leaving for Manila, likely assuming that if she showed up and was persistent enough, she could talk her way on board a westbound vessel. But an army transportation official proved immune to Peggy's tenacity. Despite the lack of an official statement, the army did not want civilian women traveling to the Philippines.[12]

Peggy went as high over the official's head as she could. She tracked down Major General Walter K. Wilson, commander of III Army Corps at the Presidio of Monterey in California, and convinced him to intercede on her behalf. The general had recently returned stateside from the Philippines after a two-year stint as head of Manila's harbor defenses. There, he had gotten to know the Utinskys. Wilson wrote a letter to the Quartermaster General in Washington, D.C., explaining that Jack Utinsky worked on Corregidor and that his wife had lived in the Philippines for years. Since Corregidor was Peggy's home, the general pointed out, she must be allowed to return.[13]

Wilson's rank carried the necessary weight with the Quartermaster General's office, so Peggy got her way after all. Wilson's involvement is particularly intriguing because from 1925 to 1929 he had been the officer in charge of war plans and training for the Military Intelligence Division (MID). The beginning of another world war in 1939 necessitated a vast expansion of military intelligence. Because of Japanese aggression in Asia, information about Filipinos who expressed anti-American sentiments as well as information about Japanese nationals living in the Philippines would be invaluable to the US military. Someone as perceptive and as intrepid as Peggy Utinsky could be quite an asset, and General Wilson would have known that.[14]

In the late fall of 1940, Peggy secured passage on the *Etelon*, a converted Alaskan fishing vessel bound for Manila, carrying about five hundred American soldiers. After her years on Corregidor, Peggy likely felt very much at home surrounded by these young men in uniform. She had a fine time on board, playing—and almost always winning—poker.

The Corregidor to which Peggy returned resembled a bustling fortress, armed with rifle, mortar, anti-aircraft, and searchlight batteries, including twenty-three such batteries at the head of the tadpole-shaped island alone. It was manned by four coast artillery regiments made up of both American (59th and 60th) and Filipino (91st and 92nd) forces. Theoretically, the Rock could withstand any naval attack and keep Manila Bay and the entire island of Luzon safe from any enemy.

The theory seemed sound enough to Peggy; besides, that was where her home with Jack was. So in the spring of 1941, when the US Army ordered the remainder of its dependents in the islands stateside, she refused to comply. Jack, however, saw things differently. Rules are rules, he insisted, and his work with the army meant Peggy had to leave. He bought a ticket for the SS *Washington*, scheduled to leave Manila's Pier 7 on May 14th, and made sure his wife's trunks were packed and ready for loading. Jack escorted Peggy up the gangplank, all the while assuring her that they would not be separated for long. "We'll make short work of the Japs if they do come. You'll be back before you know it," he told her.[15]

Peggy tried to be dutiful and obedient, but she had just moved heaven and earth—or at least the US Army—to get back to the Philippines, and she did not intend to leave again. She warned Jack, "I won't be one of those thousands of women back in the States who have to sit and wonder every minute what is happening here in the Islands." Dubious that his wife would do as she was told but reluctant to be seen breaking the rules, Jack bid her good-bye and left the pier.[16]

"The *Washington*, last ship to leave the Philippines carrying Army wives, had sailed from Manila, and I was supposed to be on it," Peggy later recalled. But when the ship sounded the final going-ashore bell, Peggy ordered her trunks removed, walked down the gangplank, and melted into a group of people waving good-bye from the pier. She stood next to General Jonathan Wainwright, commander of the Philippine Division at Fort McKinley, who had put his wife Adele on board. They watched the *Washington* steam off into the horizon.[17]

Jack did not raise an eyebrow when his wife strolled into the Manila hotel where he had booked a room. He had known her too long to be surprised. Though resigned to Peggy remaining in the Philippines, Jack was adamant about one thing: she must stay in the hotel rather than return to their home on Corregidor. He had to return to work—the army needed him for some work on the Bataan peninsula—and Peggy could not go with him. The hotel, he assured her, would be safe in case something happened.

Peggy accepted that she would have to stay in Manila. Still, she did not like the idea of living at a hotel, so she looked around for a place of her own. She found it at 21 A. Mabini Street in the Ermita district of Manila. It was a modest second-floor apartment carved out from what had been a single-family home, and it was the perfect size for one person: one bedroom, a bathroom, a tiny kitchen, and a living room with a nice picture window. The street was named for Apolinario Mabini, one of the great leaders of the Philippine independence movement.

As Peggy adjusted to her new surroundings in Manila during the summer of 1941, Japanese troops occupied Saigon and announced a protectorate over Indochina. President Roosevelt responded by directly intervening in military matters. He ordered the 120,000-man Philippine military to merge with the 31,000 US Army troops already in the islands. And he named MacArthur as Commanding General of the new United States Army Forces Far East (USAFFE). Throughout that summer, MacArthur insisted it was possible to defend the Philippines with strategically placed motor torpedo boats and additional B-17 bombers. Dedicated Filipino soldiers would hold the beaches, preventing an enemy attack from becoming an occupation. As long as all of this was in place by April 1942, MacArthur asserted, USAFFE could repel any Japanese attack.[18]

Peggy decided to stay busy by doing something useful. In October 1941 she brushed up on her nursing skills by taking a job with the Red Cross in Manila. And with so many American soldiers and sailors arriving every day in the city, she wanted to offer them a comforting reminder of home so she began working in a soldiers' canteen. It was impossible to ignore the signs of impending war.[19]

BY THE TIME THE WAR had started in Europe, Claire Phillips considered her marriage to Manuel Fuentes finished. As she later wrote, "Next to death, marriage is probably one of the greatest of life's adventures. Mine culminated in a misadventure and as the aftermath, I took my infant daughter, Dian, and returned home." But Manuel, not convinced the marriage was over, followed his wife and daughter to Portland, Oregon, where they were living with Claire's mother. Despite his entreaties, Claire looked into filing for divorce in Reno, Nevada, and talked Manuel into taking care of it, though she never followed up to see if he had done so.[20]

After Manuel returned to the Philippines, Claire struggled to adjust to life in Portland. She had left it years before because she could not launch a show business career from there, and her return served as a painful reminder of her failures. Dian may have been an added complication—a Filipino child living with her white mother on the West Coast of the United States, an area particularly hostile to Asians. Once again Claire concluded she would be better off in the Philippines.

By the time Claire prepared to leave Portland, the Japanese had concluded their push into Indochina. Nonetheless, the State Department did not prevent Claire from going to the Philippines, because forbidding travel of American citizens to the islands could look like the government was abandoning them to the Japanese, an impression it wanted to avoid to prevent panic among Philippine residents.

In late August 1941, as Claire remembered, "Despite the dire warnings and vehement protests of my well meaning family, I packed my bags, took Dian in my arms, and walked up the gang-plank." She had booked passage for two on the SS *Annie Johnson*, a small Swedish ship that took twenty-six days to reach its destination. The vessel had such a stellar reputation for its cuisine, tropical drinks, and leisure activities that celebrities like Bertolt Brecht and Greta Garbo regularly chose it for their overseas travels, but Claire found the trip boring and taxing. Her entertainment was limited to the endless food buffets, which held little attraction because of her seasickness. And Dian, an energetic toddler, required constant attention, of which Claire was in short supply.[21]

The *Annie Johnson* docked at Pier 7 on Saturday, September 20th, as clouds hung over Manila, bursting into occasional storms, the warm air thick with humidity. After passing their health, immigration, and customs inspections, Claire and Dian disembarked and were greeted by Louise De Martini, Claire's original travel companion and close friend. Louise pronounced Claire a fool for returning to the Philippines with a young child. "Didn't it occur to you that the navy escorted your tub into the Bay because it is mined?" Louise asked. "Take a look at the army and navy activity on the water front."[22]

Indeed, the *Annie Johnson* required a Navy escort to negotiate the two-mile wide North Channel of Manila Bay. Otherwise it would have tripped one of the mines floating just below the surface of the water. The South Channel, normally an option for ships heading into the Bay, was now impassable. Mines had been so thickly planted there, according to some, that they provided a solid enough surface for people to walk across. Americans and Filipinos alike took comfort in this heightened protection, convinced that it would prevent the Japanese from attacking Luzon.[23]

Claire looked at all of the military personnel and equipment around the dock area and drew the same conclusion. The Japanese, she told Louise, "threaten and bluff, but I don't think they will ever fight us. They are not crazy." Besides, Claire pointed out, if it was so dangerous, why was Louise still in Manila? They were both fools, Louise conceded, so they should stick together. She invited Claire and Dian to move into her apartment and split expenses, an offer Claire gratefully accepted, though she intended to stay only as long as it took her to find a job.[24]

Whenever the two women spent an evening at home, all sorts of people popped by, usually bringing bottles of liquor. Among the frequent drop-ins was Charley De Maio, a good-looking Italian-American chief petty officer in the US Navy, and his charming twenty-year-old fiancée. Claire called the redheaded young woman "Mona" because of her Mona Lisa smile. While Claire found Mona quick-tempered, self-centered, and unfaithful, she liked Charley, who only saw the good in his fiancée. Claire did not want to be the one to open his eyes to Mona's true character.

Besides, Claire was not around for many of those impromptu parties. Gigs were more easily had and better than they had been in 1938. Competition for nightclub engagements had all but vanished because so many American women had already left the Philippines. Claire also found herself in demand because she had brought back from the States the latest popular songs and the most current fashions, which were a big draw to the Americans remaining in Manila, particularly those in military uniform. Using her original stage name, Claire De La Taste, she appeared regularly at both the staid Manila Hotel ballroom and the modern-chic Alcazar Club. Located at the corner of Echague and Avenida Rizal in downtown

Manila, the Alcazar was officially a nightclub, though most patrons made a beeline for its private illegal casino, run by Ted Lewin.

The Pearl of the Orient had a decidedly seamy side. Lewin, who had experience in running gambling cruises along the California coast for American mobsters, shifted his operations to the Philippines when US law enforcement officials started looking at him too closely. He opened the Alcazar in 1938. Manila's underground metropolis pulsated with vice—gambling, prostitution, drugs—as American and Filipino officials looked away while pocketing their bribes. The police had some success in closing down liquor establishments and curbing opium use. Prostitution and gambling, both run from cabarets, continued with the cooperation of the police and other city officials. Men like Lewin made small fortunes while entertainers like Claire earned an adequate living.[25]

Politics were woven into these illegal vices, especially gambling. Throughout the 1920s and 1930s, politicians in the Philippines embraced gambling as a way of financing their careers; consequently, they had to deal with the organized criminal syndicates that ran the gambling houses. The Commonwealth government willingly turned a blind eye to these illegal establishments, and upward of forty clubs opened by the late 1930s, run by men like Ted Lewin. Because of his well-connected Filipino business partners and his equally well-connected customers, Lewin's casinos remained untouched by the police.[26]

President Manuel Quezon concluded that regulation and licensing would accomplish more than periodic ineffective busts. In the late 1930s, the Games and Amusement Board granted a twenty-five-year license to the Jai Alai Corporation, populated with several of Quezon's friends. The license legalized betting on jai alai, a Basque form of racquetball that used a long basket-type catcher instead of a flat racket. Building began in 1939 of a grand four-story art deco Jai Alai Club on Taft Avenue in Manila, which contained a playing court, a betting room, four restaurants, and four bars. The club's crowning glory was the elegant (and air-conditioned) Sky Room, where its patrons flocked for dinner and cocktails.[27]

The Jai Alai Club, popular as it became, was only one attraction of many in Manila, and places like the Alcazar continued to draw a steady clientele.

Claire Phillips did not lack for work and quickly saved up enough money to move out of Louise De Martini's place. Claire and Dian settled into a unit in the Dakota Apartments, a new building in the Ermita district of Manila, just blocks away from Peggy Utinsky.

In keeping with the practices of other middle-class Americans living in this colonial city, Claire hired two domestic workers: a young Filipina nurse named Lolita to work as an amah to care for Dian, and the elderly Maria to prepare meals and clean the apartment. Lolita lived in because her husband had joined the Philippine Constabulary, and in these uncertain times he was more often than not away on maneuvers. This arrangement allowed Claire the freedom to pursue both career and social life since Lolita stayed in at night to take care of Dian.

During the fall of 1941, Claire's life was a jumble of work, endless rounds of parties at Louise De Martini's apartment, and war preparedness. In mid-October, she participated in a black-out drill at the Alcazar, the first of many. The sirens blasted at nine o'clock as club employees hurried to close the window curtains, and airplanes and army trucks roared so loudly the orchestra stopped playing. As soon as the outside noise faded, though, the music resumed, and when the all-clear sounded at ten o'clock, the evening returned to its normal rhythms. "At this time, this make-believe was a novel experience," Claire later mused.[28]

A perhaps less-novel experience for Claire was that a new man walked in to her life. Private John V. Phillips, known as Phil, showed up at the Alcazar Club with a group of friends on a warm and rainy Wednesday evening in October. He and his fellow soldiers were in the mood for a special celebration. General Jonathan Wainwright, out viewing military maneuvers that day and checking the progress of war preparations, pronounced that the Filipino and American troops had passed with honors. Phil's group may have decided to spend time at the Alcazar in particular because the club had been advertising its new orchestra, along with a headline singer nicknamed "Sweetness."[29]

The young private cut an impressive figure: over six feet tall, well-proportioned and muscular from his years laboring on ranches, wavy brown hair, warm eyes. Phil grew up in his parents' home state of Missouri, spent his teenage years in the flatlands of Oklahoma where his father worked as an engineer, and was inducted into the army in California after his family made its final move west. Phil ended up in Manila as a radio man with Headquarters Company of the 31st Infantry at Fort McKinley. Of all the military men who frequented Manila's bars and clubs, it was most typical to find members of the 31st in such places. The only strictly American infantry regiment in the islands, its reputation for hard drinking was reflected in its nickname, the "Thirsty-First."[30]

When Claire finished singing her encore that evening, Phil asked her to dance and did not let her out of his arms for the rest of the night. He escorted her home and gave her a good-night kiss—just one, she would later insist. They had lunch the next day and the next, and soon Phil was talking marriage. He was serious enough about it that he wrote home about the wonderful woman he was going to marry, Claire Fuentes.[31]

Although Phil was ready to jump in, Claire, not relishing a repeat of what happened with Manuel Fuentes, saw no need to rush. Moreover, she had a few years on Phil, and had her daughter's welfare to consider. "I had made one mistake [already]; it seemed like good sense to wait until Phil received his discharge," Claire wrote after the war. "Then if we still felt the same, it was back to the States, a big family wedding, the dreamed-of ranch, and 'live happily ever after.'" From experience Claire knew that feelings change and that after the war she and Phil would be better able to decide whether they wanted to spend their lives together. She did not yet fully realize how short life can be.[32]

Claire attempted to use her romance with Phil to block out what was happening around them, but this proved futile, as signs of an impending war were now everywhere. During the first couple of weeks of their relationship, she noticed the increasing frequency of spontaneous blackout drills. The Manila newspapers ran several stories about the advisability of building air-raid shelters, complete with detailed instructions of how to build them. And Phil mentioned many times to Claire his concerns about the green army recruits arriving from the States. [33]

During the second half of 1941, more and more young men were arriving in the Philippines. This was the result of wrangling between the US War

Department and General MacArthur over appropriate troop levels in the islands, as well as the kinds of weapons and supplies needed. MacArthur rarely lost this kind of debate and in November 1941, the War Department authorized him to implement his plan, known as Rainbow 5. In addition to the torpedo boats and B-17s that would soon arrive, MacArthur called for a doubling of American troop strength in the Philippines by the end of the year, and he expected more pursuit plans and heavy guns. The force that MacArthur envisioned in Rainbow 5 would take months to become a reality. But he did not have months.[34]

William (Bill) A. Berry, the grandson of two Civil War veterans, was one of the last arrivals of American military personnel to the Philippines as part of Rainbow 5. That summer of 1941, the twenty-five-year-old Berry had a comfortable, draft-exempt job as the prosecuting attorney for Payne County, Oklahoma. As he later explained, he found that "the air was filled with patriotism. I could breathe it. I could feel it. I had it in my bones. When I listened on the radio to the fireside chats of President Roosevelt, I, like millions of other Americans was inspired."[35]

Berry gave up his draft exemption and applied for a Navy commission, receiving it and his orders on September 3rd. Now an ensign and a reserve intelligence officer, he was told to report to "Cavite, P.I.," having no idea what or where that was. "It wasn't until I looked it up in an atlas that I determined that 'P.I.' referred to the Philippine Islands, and that Cavite was a US Navy base located on Manila Bay," he later admitted. Berry was a typical raw recruit"—no military background or training, no knowledge of navy regulations or of ships.[36]

After a thirty-day layover in Honolulu, the *President Harrison*, on its last voyage before it was captured by the Japanese, deposited Bill Berry in Manila on November 17th. Berry and his cabin mate, Jack Woodside, quickly got into the swing of tropical military duty. With their monthly ensign's pay of $125, Berry and Woodside rented a fourth-floor apartment in the Admiral Apartments on Dewey Boulevard, about a mile from the port. They hired a Filipino servant to take care of all the domestic chores, and spent their evenings, like Ralph Hibbs and others, at the Army-Navy Club, drinking and socializing. And if Berry had not known anything about Cavite or about the US Navy, he was equally clueless about the District Intelligence Office where he was told to report. He learned that it was located in the Marsman Building on the Manila waterfront, along with the headquarters of the Sixteenth Naval District and the commander in chief of the Asiatic Fleet, Admiral Thomas C. Hart.[37]

When Berry arrived that first day, someone handed him a sheaf of papers, saying, "Here, deliver these." That was how he learned his main job was to courier documents between the Naval Intelligence Headquarters and the Army Intelligence Office, and that was how he met Colonel Charles Willoughby, head of the Army's G-2 unit, mastermind of wartime intelligence. Gathering, interpreting, and utilizing intelligence is crucial in any war. Berry, however, was a novice at it, little more than a paper pusher—or runner—who lacked any useful knowledge about the Philippines. It would be generous to say that everyone had to start somewhere; the clock was ticking in Manila, though. Time was short, and what military intelligence needed now were people with real knowledge of the islands.[38]

Despite Claire's hesitation about marriage, Phil continued an ardent pursuit: "Claire, darling. You'll have to marry me soon. Please say that you will." She finally agreed to a Christmas wedding. Planning for the nuptials took a backseat to a more imminent celebration: Claire's 34th birthday on December 2. It was a day of mixed excitement. On the one hand, Manila newspapers ran stories about Secretary of State Cordell Hull resuming talks with Japanese envoys and about President Quezon reaffirming his loyalty to the United States.[39]

On the other—and what probably caught most of Claire's attention—was the used blue coupe Phil gave her, an extravagant gift that would come in very handy over the next few weeks. The couple combined Claire's birthday celebration with an engagement party at the Jai Alai Club. "A sight for the gods," Claire remembered of that evening in the club, "men in uniforms and women in dinner gowns drank at a swank bar or danced slowly to the music of a softly playing orchestra." Their gala mood continued over the next few days, the couple blissfully unaware that their dual celebration at the Jai Alai would, in hindsight, look more like a *Götterdämmerung*—the twilight of old Manila.[40]

During the late 1930s, the public side of Gladys Savary's life in Manila hummed along. The Restaurant de Paris continued to make money, which the Savarys augmented with rental income. The upper floors of the old Spanish mansion that housed the restaurant contained about a dozen rooms leased to paying guests. The "inmates," as Gladys fondly referred to them, were mostly young single men seeking their fortunes in Manila. The private side faltered as the Savarys' marriage collapsed. It may have been a point of pride or a reflection of decorum in a heavily Catholic country, but Gladys never publicly acknowledged her divorce from André. She left Manila twice in the late 1930s, returning each time, perhaps in hopes of reviving the marriage, perhaps because she missed Manila more than she imagined she would.[41]

Years later, Gladys explained, with a certain amount of vagueness, "Like everyone else in the Philippines, about that time, I had played the gold stock market a bit, and with my small winnings, I felt I had earned a vacation on my own merits. Naturally, I went to Paris, the long way round, via Suez." It was the summer of 1937, and Gladys sailed alone. She found the city as lovely as she remembered, but noticed "people were uneasy, unhappy, and fearful. War was in the air, in the minds of everyone."[42]

Though it would be two more years before war broke out in Europe, Gladys picked up on Parisians' unease over Germany's recent actions. During 1936, Germany had violated the Versailles Treaty and occupied the Rhineland, demilitarized territory adjacent to Belgium. It also signed the Anti-Comintern Pact with Japan, binding the two countries together with their resistance to communism. In that fall of 1937, Adolf Hitler promised to recognize the integrity of Belgium's borders, but he also sent German supplies to aid fascist forces in the civil war that had been going on in Spain since the year before.

Gladys traveled on to the United States to visit family before returning to Manila, where she probably tried one last time to work things out with André. She did not stay long and left again at the beginning of 1938, this time going directly to the States, where she remained for more than a year. A telegram from André brought Gladys back to Manila in 1939. With the war in Europe underway, he had been called up for active duty in French

Indochina. He informed Gladys that if she expected the restaurant to remain open, she would have to come back to Manila as soon as possible. By the time she reached the city in November, though, André had already gone, and their divorce had likely been finalized by this time.[43]

Despite the failed marriage and the increasingly tense world situation, Gladys had no qualms about going back to the Philippines. After all, she still had the restaurant, which was her livelihood. Besides, Gladys remembered, "Manila is at its best, the fall of the year. Cool, no rains worth mentioning, the social season at its height, gay parties, polo games, swimming, golf, the town full of Army and Navy." She acknowledged that war would probably come to the Philippines, but certainly not while the United States still controlled them: "I even became a convert to the popular theory that Japan wouldn't do any attacking of the Philippines because she could just walk into them in 1946 when Philippine independence would become effective."[44]

Even with her husband gone and her marriage over, and with more American civilians leaving the Philippines and more military personnel arriving, Gladys labeled 1940 and 1941 as "pleasant years" in Manila. She thrived as a restaurateur and landlord, and was especially pleased when in 1940 her nephew Edgar Gable and his wife Marian took up residence in an apartment in the old Spanish mansion. Edgar had been hired as the purchasing agent for Nielson & Company, a Philippine business conglomerate that dealt in everything from stocks and securities to mining and aviation. For a year or so, until the summer of 1941, he, Gladys, and Marian formed a tight, happy trio.[45]

Like most other Americans in Manila, Gladys contemplated the likelihood of war with Japan and concluded it would not happen soon, though "soon," of course, is a relative term. Still, the signs of preparedness were everywhere; she saw them every day while working in her restaurant. Her nephew and tenant Edgar, adhering to the better safe than sorry maxim, put his wife Marian on a ship for home in the summer of 1941.

Gladys continued watching the military traffic near the Restaurant de Paris. "All that fall of 1941, before the terrace dining room on the boulevard passed swarms of ambulating armament, men were arriving in ever-increasing numbers, planes were being shipped in in crates or flown in." The creation of USAFFE, envisioned as a force powerful enough to defeat the Japanese, did not, in fact, result in a particularly large or well-trained organization. By December there were only eight 7,000-man Philippine Army divisions on Luzon, and they had not all been fully mobilized.[46]

Filipino soldiers—with the exception of the elite Philippine Scouts who had access to the best weapons—received minimal training, usually drilling with wooden models of guns. They wore ill-fitting made-in-the-USA canvas shoes and shiny helmets that during the day made them human targets. USAFFE rifles were old Springfields and Enfields, some dating from 1917, and they tended to jam or misfire. There were not quite enough of them to supply each man who was mobilized. Two newly-arrived National Guard tank battalions brought 118 new M-3 Stuart light tanks to the islands along with forty-six half-tracks. Thirty-five B-17s and seventy-two pursuit planes were also in place to defend the Philippines, adding up to less than half the number planned.[47]

While Gladys watched all the military traffic pass by her restaurant, she hoped hostilities, should they break out, would hold off until USAFFE was better prepared. In November, Japanese special envoy Kurusu Saburo stopped in Manila on his way to the United States in a last-ditch attempt to maintain peace. Many Manilans were cautiously optimistic that the fifty-five-year-old Kurusu, married to an American, could prevent war. During the 1910s he had served as Japan's first consul general in the Philippines and received accolades for improving relations between the two countries. Kurusu disapproved of Japanese aggression in China, a major sticking point between his country and the United States. More recently Kurusu had served as Japan's ambassador to Germany, where, despite his opposition to it, he signed the Tripartite Pact. Out of step with his government's wishes, he requested to be recalled and returned home to retirement in early 1941.[48]

Like Ambassador Normura Kichisaburo—whom he would assist in Washington—Kurusu advocated peace with the Americans, so he willingly abandoned retirement for this assignment. Yet both men operated under strict instructions from Tokyo and an inflexible deadline of November 30th. Japan's troops in China and its signature on the Tripartite Pact ultimately proved to be nonnegotiable points. At the end of the month, the War Department sent a message to General MacArthur warning an attack by Japan could come at any time.[49]

In fact, the decision to go to war had already been made. When President Roosevelt froze Japanese assets in the United States in July 1941, he pushed Japan into a corner. Japanese military leaders debated what would come next. The army wanted to start conquering in Malaya, to secure needed natural resources, before moving on to the Philippines. It preferred to shore up its supplies prior to provoking the United States, which would certainly happen with an attack on the Philippines. The Japanese Navy, however, favored starting with America's colony before it became too heavily fortified. Finally, during the late summer of 1941, the Japanese made plans to hit both Malaya and the Philippines and to do it before new supplies could reach MacArthur.[50]

Weighing more heavily on Gladys's mind than the military scenes on her street in early December 1941 was a telegram she received from André, letting her know he was under new orders. Because of wartime censorship, the details had been scissored out of the message so she did not know—and in fact would never know—where he ended up. He had been in London since the fall of France in 1940, working at the headquarters of the Free French, France's government-in-exile. He had already received the Légion d'Honneur and Croix de Guerre for his military service in Indochina. Gladys understood at least the broad outlines of his army duties, and may also have been aware of the details of his private life, though she did not share them with anyone. In London, while working for the Free French, André had married a twenty-one-year-old Englishwoman named Jennifer Pickard.[51]

AS DECEMBER 1941 GOT UNDERWAY, Peggy busied herself with work at the Red Cross and the soldiers' canteen. Yay pursued the best news stories she could find, passing tidbits of information along to the higher-ups in S-2. Claire celebrated her birthday and her engagement to

Phil, and Gladys worried about André. These four women were exactly where they wanted to be, but they could not have anticipated what would happen next.

During the first week of December, everybody in the Philippines prepared for the annual Feast of the Immaculate Conception. Due to the holiday and the uncertainty of the situation with the Japanese, the Philippine government urged nonessential civilians to evacuate Manila that weekend. Various athletic competitions, ubiquitous during the holiday, were canceled. Airplane spotters working for the Civilian Emergency Administration (CEA) now were on duty twenty-four hours a day and USAFFE officials assured the public that the military was taking all precautions. President Quezon, up in the mountain city of Baguio for the holiday, called for his cabinet and for key personnel of the CEA to meet him there.

Taking advantage of the typically warm and dry weather, many Filipinos left Manila for the countryside to participate in the festivities honoring the Holy Mother. Americans, Catholic or not, entered into the spirit and headed off to the beach or to country clubs or at least to the movies. And over that holiday weekend, Manila's Metropolitan Theatre paired the new Disney release, *The Reluctant Dragon*, with an older historical film entitled *The Last Days of Pompeii*.[52]

THE SOUTHWEST PACIFIC AREA (1941)

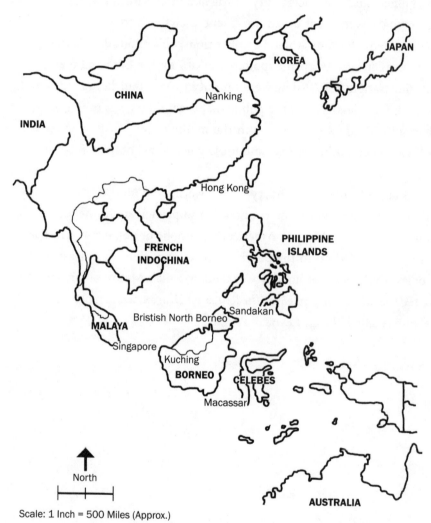

KOREA

JAPAN

CHINA Nanking

INDIA

Hong Kong

FRENCH
INDOCHINA

PHILIPPINE
ISLANDS

Bristish North Borneo Sandakan

MALAYA

Singapore

Kuching

BORNEO CELEBES

Macassar

AUSTRALIA

North

Scale: 1 Inch = 500 Miles (Approx.)

Courtesy of Michael C.J. Kaminski.

CHAPTER 4

THE JAPANESE ATTACK

B OMBS BEGAN FALLING ON THE NINETY-SIX VESSELS OF THE US Pacific Fleet anchored at the American naval base at Pearl Harbor, Hawaii, just before eight o'clock on a brilliantly sunlit Sunday morning, December 7, 1941. A task force of the Imperial Japanese Navy, consisting of six aircraft carriers, launched more than 180 dive bombers, fighters, and torpedo aircraft against US military installations. Divided into four attack groups, Japanese planes also targeted the Marine Corps station at Ewa, the Army Air Corps' Hickam Field, and the Navy seaplane base at Kaneohe Bay. At Pearl Harbor, enemy aircraft sank three American battleships, capsized the *Oklahoma*, and nearly destroyed four others. Three light cruisers, three destroyers, and several smaller ships were also badly damaged. At those nearby airfields, ninety-six army aircraft were obliterated and nearly the same number from the navy, with 128 damaged. Between that first attack and a second, which started around 9:00 a.m., over 2,200 men were killed, another 1,100 wounded. The Japanese did not get away unscathed, but their losses were far fewer: twenty-nine planes and five midget submarines.[1]

Admiral Thomas C. Hart, fleet commander in Manila, received the chilling message, due to the International Date Line, at 3:00 a.m. on Monday, December 8th: "Air Raid at Pearl Harbor—This is No Drill." Hart declined to inform General MacArthur, quietly ensconced with his wife and young son in his penthouse in the Manila Hotel during the long holiday weekend of the Feast of the Immaculate Conception. USAFFE's commander did not learn about the Japanese attack until he received a phone call from his chief of staff, Major General Richard K. Sutherland, who received the news via a California radio station. MacArthur later remembered receiving a call from Washington at 3:40 a.m., but since "no details were given" he assumed "the Japanese might well have suffered a serious setback." Confirmation and additional details arrived about twenty minutes later; in the interval MacArthur had taken no steps to safeguard the Philippines.[2]

General Lewis Brereton, MacArthur's air commander, showed up at headquarters at 5:00 a.m. seeking permission to strike at Japanese bases on Formosa. He needed MacArthur's authorization to order the nineteen B-17s at Clark Field aloft. When Brereton attempted to speak to MacArthur, Sutherland blocked him, explaining that their boss was busy. Brereton continued to prepare the planes for a strike, though he could not execute it. The Japanese had about two hundred Zeros and Mitsubishi bombers on Formosa, initially delayed by early morning fog, ready to take off later in the morning. They had been expecting to encounter stiff resistance from USAFFE and intended to obliterate it.[3]

Brereton still could not get in to see MacArthur, reportedly busy with intelligence and reconnaissance reports, though he tried twice more that morning. MacArthur later denied that he knew of any meeting between Sutherland and Brereton, and that Brereton had ever suggested to him an attack on Formosa. Besides, MacArthur viewed an attack on Formosa impractical because it was too far away and would strain the range of the American planes to the point where it would be a suicide mission. While the generals discussed and planned, no action was taken to protect the Philippines.[4]

Military leaders were not the only ones groping their way through the morning's events. Francis Sayre, the American High Commissioner, learned about Pearl Harbor at 4:00 a.m. and immediately understood the implications for the Philippines: "Our entire military strategy had been based on holding Corregidor and some territory on the Bataan peninsula against capture, and waiting for the American main fleet to fight its way to our rescue. We now learned that there was no American fleet which would come." Sayre's last point was perhaps the fatal reality many military planners had not wanted to recognize. If US strategy relied on troops falling back and holding out until reinforcements arrived, what would happen if those reinforcements *could not* arrive?[5]

President Manuel Quezon was in Luzon's northern resort city of Baguio that morning, recuperating at the Mansion House from an illness. His private secretary, Jorge Vargas, telephoned him from Manila with the news, and Quezon's response echoed MacArthur's initial disbelief: "You are joking; Pearl Harbor is the best defended naval station in the world. Where did you get that nonsense?"[6]

CLAIRE PHILLIPS, LIKE OTHER MANILANS, woke to the news of the Pearl Harbor attack on Monday morning. "I was sleeping late on the morning of December eighth when Lolita knocked quietly at my door. I heard her but pretended that I did not," Claire remembered. Undaunted, the amah entered the bedroom, touched Claire's shoulder, and asked, "Senora, excuse me, please, but there is a war. What shall I do?"[7]

Claire thought Lolita had merely concocted a novel way to get her out of bed. She tried to go back to sleep. Lolita insisted she was not making it up; still, Claire ignored her until she heard the newspaper boys outside shouting about the bombing of Pearl Harbor. When she bolted out of bed to see what was happening, a glimpse out her bedroom window revealed a few people standing around on a street corner and military vehicles speeding past. If there was a war, it was not here, she thought. To Claire, this looked like all the Monday mornings she had seen over the past several months. Nevertheless, as a precaution, Claire called Dian inside from where the little girl had been playing on the patio.

While mother and daughter ate breakfast, John Phillips showed up at the apartment, and one look told Claire he was not there for an early date: "My soldier stood there in full battle dress—pack, gas mask, tin hat on his back, canteen, mess kit and a .45 automatic hooked to his belt." Phil instructed her to hail a cab, take Dian and Lolita, withdraw the money in her bank account and change it into US currency. Then she should buy enough medical supplies and canned goods to fill a large suitcase, and have the blue coupe fully serviced. When Claire returned from these errands, she should pack a bag of suitable outdoor clothing for herself and Dian in case they had to evacuate the city. Before he left for his barracks, Phil told her she needed to stay in Manila until she heard from him.[8]

Many Manilans had the same idea that morning. Claire pushed through lines at the bank to get her money. The drugstore, though crowded, had all of the medical supplies she wanted. The grocery stores had imposed purchasing limits on canned goods, so Claire dragged Lolita and Dian through five markets before she stockpiled enough food.

She did not hear from Phil again until he telephoned late in the afternoon, asking her to meet him at Fort McKinley to talk through their plans. Reluctant to travel alone, Claire took Lolita and Dian along. Phil met the trio at the gate of Intramuros—the Old Walled City—and escorted them to a lunchroom where he and Claire discussed a variety of contingency plans over cups of cold coffee. Despite his position as a radio man with the 31st Infantry's Headquarters Company, Phil did not have much concrete information to pass along to Claire. The only thing they could think for her to do was to go back to her apartment and wait.

By this time on Monday, the Japanese had attacked Hawaii, Guam, and Wake Island, and were now bringing the war to the Philippines. Ensign Bill Berry's job with naval intelligence exploded in a frenzy of activity the morning of the attacks. His roommate, Jack Woodside, woke him up at five o'clock with the news about Pearl Harbor, and a driver from the District Intelligence Office picked up both men. "Immediately I was put to work delivering correspondence between Navy Intelligence and the Army G-2 office and running various other errands. It seemed to me that everyone had something that needed to be done," Berry recalled. He and the others were issued .45 automatic pistols, and although he learned how to pop in its cartridge, he did not know how to shoot it.[9]

While General MacArthur waited for the reconnaissance reports that morning, the Air Corps prepared for battle. At Clark Field, forty miles northwest of Manila, adjacent to Fort Stotsenburg, B-17s were loaded with bombs and Curtiss P-40 fighter escorts were refueled, awaiting MacArthur's orders. Sometime before 11:00 a.m. Brereton received permission to attack Formosa. Even then it took time to get the planes ready. They were sitting on the ground, recently returned from various scramble and reconnaissance missions, when the first Japanese fighters arrived at 12:20. One of the Japanese pilots recalled, "Instead of encountering a swarm of American fighters diving at us in attack, we looked down and saw some sixty enemy bombers and fighters neatly parked along the airfield runways." The planes at Clark were sitting ducks—all nicely lined up. In all, fifty-three bombers and forty-five Zeros participated in the attack, hitting Clark Field to destroy aircraft and nearby Iba Airfield to take out the only functioning radar equipment on the islands. The incomprehensible delays of that morning cost USAFFE eighty American lives and about half of its most effective bombers and fighters. Enemy bombers returned that evening, hitting several more locations, including Nichols Field, just south of Manila. The Japanese had not encountered any resistance.[10]

Air raid sirens sounded in Manila throughout the rest of the day and into the night. Claire created a safe place in the apartment for Dian under her bed, doubling up mattresses for extra protection, keeping one corner propped up to ensure a good air supply. Claire heard the Japanese planes, the bombs dropping off in the distance, the response—mostly futile—of the big American anti-aircraft guns. All night, Claire later remembered, "I sat trembling on the edge of the bed, alternately thinking and praying until daylight."[11]

Claire and Lolita got an early start the next morning packing up the supplies they had bought the day before. Around noon, Claire's frustrating friend Mona telephoned. The young redhead blithely assumed the Japanese would soon occupy Manila—only for a month or two until the

Americans rallied to toss them out. In the meantime, Mona predicted with romantic optimism, it would be easy enough to wait out the occupation in whatever internment camp the Japanese set up for civilians. Then she would be happy to be rescued by a handsome American soldier. "We will all be heroines soon," she assured Claire.[12]

Nothing about this scenario appealed to Claire, and she asked Mona, "Do you really want to be here in Manila when, as, and if the Japs take over?" Mona remained adamant that nothing very bad would happen. She preferred internment—three months, tops—to the plan their mutual friend Louise De Martini had made to hide out at the Catholic shrine in Antipolo, about twenty-five miles east of Manila in Rizal province. Dozens, perhaps hundreds, of Manilans had already begun the trek along the well-known route for pilgrims paying homage to, ironically, Our Lady of Peace and Good Voyage.[13]

The thought of an internment camp horrified Claire. She worried that Dian would never thrive in such a place, and that their very survival would be at stake. Exasperated with the conversation, Claire hung up on Mona. She went outside to watch an aerial battle raging over the Cavite naval base, about twenty-three miles south of Manila. Claire counted twenty Japanese planes against five American. "I was both elated and surprised to see any of our planes in the air," she remembered, but they did little good. Enemy bombs destroyed the oil storage tanks at Cavite, and the remaining American planes turned tail. Claire went back into to her apartment and resumed packing.[14]

A second night of bombing lasted until the morning light, and Claire spent another sleepless night in bed, horrible "what-if" scenarios running through her head. At six-thirty she gave up trying to get any rest and got out of bed for breakfast. With some food in her stomach, she fell back into an exhausted sleep, at least until Lolita woke her in the early afternoon with the latest news. The most recent dogfights and bombings had been right over Fort McKinley, where Phil was headquartered.[15]

Claire had to see for herself that Phil was all right. She, Dian, and Lolita piled into the little blue coupe, and headed southeast out of Manila toward McKinley. In normal times it would have been a quick and pleasant six-mile trip across the Pasig River and away from the city, but now the roads were rough from exploded bombs and clogged with military traffic and checkpoints. A Filipino sentry stopped them at the city limits, and Claire told him, "Official business. Very official." She continued bluffing sentries along the way, claiming to be on unspecified official business, and said to the final guard at the gate to Fort McKinley, "My husband is an army officer stationed here. He expects me."[16]

Once Claire maneuvered the blue coupe onto the grounds of the fort, she looked around the vast area and realized she had no idea how to find Headquarters Company. She drove aimlessly, hoping to see a sign or a likely looking building. The car stalled, and the soldier who came to her aid informed her that Headquarters Company had already moved out, just the night before. Claire refused to believe him. She made one more loop around the post, and again the car stalled. A tank driver came to the rescue this time, and told her, "Sister, if I was you, I'd go gettahell away from here and beat it home. It's liable to get plenty rough here most any time. Your old man will look for you when he has time."[17]

The soldier had a point, Claire realized with a sinking feeling. If Phil had gone to Manila, he would find her apartment empty and worry. She headed straight back to the city and was relieved not to find Phil waiting at the apartment. Still, Claire did not know where he was, and nightfall brought a sense of dread: "The streets were empty. We seemed to be living in a vacuum; a steadily menacing and tightening vacuum." She lay down on her bed and cried.[18]

The sound of a truck pulling up to the curb outside ended her tears. Claire listened to the familiar footsteps and the familiar knock, and opened the door to Phil. He bore the signs of the rapidly deteriorating military situation: his torn uniform caked with mud, his eyes red-rimmed, his face unshaven. "Hello, sweetheart. I did come back for you," he said. Phil told Claire that Headquarters Company had left Fort McKinley for the Bataan peninsula, and he had gone AWOL to retrieve her. Phil wanted Claire and Dian out of Manila, now, and with him on Bataan under USAFFE's protection.[19]

Within days of the first Japanese attack, Manila had turned into a different city. The Pearl of the Orient was in danger of being crushed: blackouts and bombings at night, random weapons discharged by nervous soldiers, people crowding the streets, snarling traffic as they searched for ever-dwindling food and gasoline supplies. Within a week, Manilans had to rely on shortwave radios to pick up local broadcasts, many city businesses refused to accept credit, and passenger ships could not sail from Manila Bay. President Quezon authorized the military to seize all of the food and fuel it needed even as he continued assurances that Filipinos would fight against the Japanese, side by side with Americans.[20]

John Phillips shaved, took a bath, and put on a clean uniform while Claire cooked for him, so happy to see her fiancé that she sang while she worked. Phil knew he could get in trouble for this unauthorized trip into Manila, so he needed to move fast and get Claire and Dian to Bataan. If he could do this quickly enough, maybe his superiors would not notice his absence, and he could spare Claire the terror of living in an enemy-occupied city. Phil said, "I wouldn't leave you there unless you had a gun with two bullets in it, one for you . . . the other for Dian."[21]

Claire knew what he meant. They both remembered the Japanese attack on and subsequent occupation of Nanking, China, in 1937, which has come to be known as the Rape of Nanking. For six weeks invading Japanese troops terrorized the civilians there, raping thousands of Chinese women. Phil would not leave Claire and Dian to that fate, and he assumed they would rather die than endure sexual assault by the enemy.

After Phil downed his meal, he and Claire stuffed the blue coupe with all of the items she accumulated over the previous days. They invited Lolita to come along, and the small group traveled through the night, north out of Manila and around the bay toward the Bataan peninsula, the car's headlights dimmed for the blackout with Claire's coral satin housecoat.

Over the next eighty miles, Claire and Phil may have discussed the newest developments of the enemy attack. The Japanese 2nd Taiwan detachment had made a successful landing on Luzon's west coast at Vigan on December 10th, their thrust to the south only temporarily delayed by the bridges destroyed by USAFFE. They also landed in the north, at Aparri, with two companies. The Philippine Army withdrew rather than attempt to stop them.

The Japanese continued aerial strikes around Manila, too. Nichols Field was hit on December 9th, and again the following day along with nearby Del Carmen and Nielson fields. Across Manila Bay from Corregidor, enemy planes pounded the Cavite naval base for two hours. Lacking sufficient air power for protection, Admiral Thomas Hart moved the American fleet from Manila Bay to safer locations in the southern Philippine islands. The Japanese had succeeded in destroying most of USAFFE's planes, and in dispersing its ships, paved the way for a large-scale invasion.[22]

As the military situation deteriorated, the Philippine government reaffirmed its allegiance to the Allies. President Roosevelt had asked the US Congress for a declaration of war against Japan on December 8th, which easily passed. On December 11th, the day after the Japanese landed at Vigan and the day after they sank the British ships *Prince of Wales* and *Repulse* off of the coast of Malaya, President Quezon asked for and received two things from the Philippine Congress: emergency legislation to deal with the war and an official statement of loyalty and assistance to the United States. Resolution 115 offered "the full support and cooperation of the Filipino people to the government of the United States." As a colony, the Philippines could not issue a separate declaration of war against Japan, but this resolution served the same purpose.[23]

While pledging support to the United States, Quezon took additional steps to protect his people by directing civilian defense and war relief efforts. On December 12th he met with General MacArthur who told him a retreat to Corregidor was likely. At first, Quezon resisted the notion he would have to evacuate Manila along with other high-ranking American and Filipino officials. Quezon believed his place was with the Filipino people. MacArthur replied that it was his duty to make sure that the Japanese did not capture the president of the Philippines. Quezon's freedom would signal, at some level, the continuing freedom of the Philippines no matter what the Japanese had in mind for the islands. Still, Quezon felt torn. If he left, his people might consider him a coward. If he remained, he would have to collaborate with the Japanese.[24]

Claire and Phil had more easily made the decision to evacuate Manila. Their final destination was the small town of Pilar, about midway down the eastern edge of the Bataan peninsula, some three miles away from Phil's unit, which had bivouacked further up in the hills. At two o'clock in the morning, Phil had no qualms about approaching a large house in the barrio—he was US Army, after all, and presumed he would be welcomed. He instructed Lolita, who spoke the local dialect and had good dickering skills, to ask the owners about providing room and board. The family agreed to let the newcomers stay for one peso a day.

Claire left Lolita with the sleeping Dian and drove on with Phil to his camp. He stopped short of their destination and said to Claire, "I would feel much better and fight much harder if you and Dian were really mine. I want to talk with Chaplain Taylor about it." Phil admired the thirty-two-year-old officer a great deal and respected his opinion. Lieutenant Robert Preston Taylor, Texas native and graduate of Baylor University, had been a pastor at the South Fort Worth Baptist Church prior to joining the army in September 1940. Assigned as regimental chaplain to the 31st Infantry, the tall, fair-skinned redhead had arrived in Manila in May 1941.[25]

Claire agreed, only if Phil promised not to go AWOL again. Once, she thought, his commanding officer, Captain Earl Packer, might be sympathetic. Twice would land Phil in a whole lot of trouble. He agreed to no more unapproved leaves, and the couple parted, Phil walking off to his camp and Claire driving back to the house in Pilar. The next morning she woke to the sounds of the local women washing clothes at the town pump. From the window she saw Lolita bathing a happy, laughing Dian in the center of the pump's platform. Claire turned a sharp eye on her surroundings. In addition to the water pump, which drew people from miles around to the heart of town, Pilar had a central plaza, complete with a city hall that contained the mayor's office, police station, and post office.[26]

Most of the day passed with routine chores, as if nothing out of the ordinary was happening on Luzon. Two events of the day, though, illuminated the reality of war. First, Claire had to retrieve Lolita from the local constabulary headquarters. The police, mistaking the young woman for Japanese, arrested her as she walked to the post office to mail a letter, and Claire had to vouch for her. Second, when Claire and Lolita returned to Pilar, they spotted two American soldiers standing in the plaza, filling large water cans at the pump. One was Phil. He reassured Claire he had not gone AWOL. "This, honey, in case you don't recognize it, is punishment. As I expected, the Old Man gave me a week's K.P. for going AWOL. I have to come down here, twice daily for a week. Isn't that awful?" Captain Packer, it seemed, had a soft spot for couples in love.[27]

Claire and Phil established a routine: when he showed up for water detail, she served him a meal while Lolita laundered his dirty uniform. "He was beyond a shadow of a doubt the best dressed and best fed soldier on Bataan," Claire remembered. She figured the other soldiers could also use a home-cooked meal and clean clothing, and suggested Phil bring along some of the other men in his unit. Every morning, Claire and Lolita washed the soldiers' clothes at the town pump, every afternoon they cooked. Soon Claire turned her two rented rooms into a canteen. Some of the soldiers insisted on paying her for their food and laundry, pressing IOUs into her hands. Claire knew they were living on field rations, that they had not been paid since they left Manila, and did not know when they would be paid. She took the IOUs, then tore them up.[28]

The townspeople pitched in to support the canteen, and to show her appreciation, Claire taught English and math to a large group of children and adults. The days flew by in an optimistic lull. The canteen and the makeshift school diverted Claire's attention from the realities of the war, which now seemed further away. She found Pilar calm compared to Manila, despite the long-distance sounds of bombs and the movement of troops and tanks through the area. As long as Phil and the 31st Infantry remained nearby, Claire felt safe.

Once the laundry, cooking, and teaching were done for the day, the nights were spent with Phil. He got away from Headquarters Company for a few hours, always bringing hungry friends and some liquor. They chowed down on fried chicken and cold salads—much better than the field rations the soldiers ate the rest of the time—and drank sarsaparilla laced with gin or beer. These evenings helped Claire handle the grim broadcasts her landlord's radio picked up from San Francisco. Every night as December wore on, she heard the same thing: "Hang on to Bataan! Help is on its way from the United States!" She wanted to believe the Americans could land supply ships off the tip of the peninsula, wanted to believe that fresh troops and fresh food would soon arrive, but she saw no signs of any of it.[29]

Just before the artificial calm broke—in an unspoken recognition that it would—Claire and Phil started their Christmas celebration early. About a week before the actual holiday, her blue coupe went missing, and she assumed it had either been stolen or subjected to an impromptu military requisition. Local police, alerted to the theft, could find no sign of it. On the evening of December 20th, Phil showed up in an army truck, bearing gifts. He admitted to Claire that he appropriated her car so he could drive to Manila to buy gifts.

To take the sting out of the other part of his story—the coupe broke down about four miles outside of Pilar and Claire would have to figure out a way to retrieve it—Phil insisted they open their presents right away. His purchases were thoughtful, but more extravagant than useful. Claire received a blue kid evening bag stocked with lipstick and a compact, there was a doll for Dian, and a good pair of shoes for Lolita. It never occurred to Claire to ask how he could afford such things.

The next day, December 21st, while Claire located and retrieved her car, a Japanese fleet materialized in the Lingayen Gulf, about 135 miles northwest of Manila along the South China Sea. At dawn the following morning, the Japanese launched their invasion, landing 43,110 soldiers from Lieutenant General Homma Masahura's 14th Army and Lieutenant General Tsuchibashi Yuichi's 48th Division. Homma had been tasked with capturing Manila, and he intended to conquer the entire island of Luzon in fifty days. Japanese military officials calculated it would take a mere seven weeks to force the surrender of the Philippine Islands.

General MacArthur rushed everything he could to Lingayen—tanks, planes, submarines—then notified USAFFE beach defenses that the enemy's main attack was upon them. Homma's men faced four USAFFE divisions and a cavalry regiment led by Major General Jonathan Wainwright. Although Wainwright had about twice as many men as Homma, the

American and Filipino troops were poorly trained and equipped, and could do little to slow down the Japanese. By noon, USAFFE was in retreat. Homma, intent on taking Manila, failed to notice where the Fil-American forces were headed. [30]

The Lingayen invasion, though over a hundred miles away, increased military activity in the Bataan peninsula as more and more USAFFE troops dropped back from their more northern locations. Claire happened to take a holiday from teaching the day Japanese troops landed at Lingayen, expecting to spend some extra time with her fiancé. Instead, she received a message that Phil had pulled patrol duty, and would meet her that night. She should bring food. Phil did not show; instead, he sent another soldier to let Claire know he could not come until the following evening. That night, December 23rd, an additional 7,000 Japanese troops landed at Lamon Bay in southeastern Luzon, increasing the threat to the entire island.[31]

Because of the swift Japanese successes, especially over these two days, General MacArthur ordered implementation of War Plan Orange (WPO). The best-case scenario of holding off the Japanese at the beaches—the tactic MacArthur long believed would work—had not been possible. To salvage anything from this debacle, to prevent a wholesale slaughter of his men, MacArthur needed to get them to a safe place. With WPO, the goal became to get to the Bataan peninsula, hold it and Corregidor island, until reinforcements arrived from the United States. Because of the damage inflicted by the Japanese at Pearl Harbor and other locations in the Pacific and because the Japanese controlled the air and sea, it was unlikely those reinforcements would be arriving any time soon.

War Plan Orange required a huge undertaking, moving some 78,000 troops (66,000 Filipinos and 12,000 Americans) plus all of the supplies required to sustain them—more than 18,000 tons of ammunition, fuel, weapons, food, and medical supplies—would have to be funneled to the peninsula, and fast. It was fast, it just was not enough. WPO, which envisioned troops holding off the Japanese for up to six months, had not been based on such large numbers of soldiers. A fighting man required a daily intake of 4,000 calories, and the tons of supplies that ended up on Bataan amounted to enough field rations for one month, not six, and there was only enough rice, a diet staple for Filipinos, for twenty days.[32]

MacArthur moved the men quickly. USAFFE was tasked with delaying enemy forces in northern Luzon long enough for Major General Albert Jones's 51st Philippine Division to get around Manila and onto Bataan by the first week of January 1942. In the meantime, Major General George Parker would shore up defenses on Bataan. Blowing two key bridges across the Pampanga River, which ran across central Luzon from Sierra Madre to Manila Bay, would significantly slow the Japanese advance on to the peninsula, allowing time for General Wainwright's forces to get to Bataan as well.[33]

Claire Phillips concentrated on Christmas. On the morning of December 24th, she took Lolita and Dian with her to the market in nearby Balanga to buy the ingredients for a Christmas Day chicken dinner with all of the trimmings. The war did not take a holiday, though. Through the rest of the day Claire watched military vehicles rumble through Pilar, heading south to Mariveles, at the tip of the Bataan peninsula across from the island of Corregidor.

Christmas Eve was also pivotal for the Philippine government. Two weeks had passed since General MacArthur informed President Quezon that an evacuation to Corregidor might be necessary. Now it was. MacArthur told Quezon to gather a small support staff and prepare to move. Among Quezon's chosen few were his vice president, Sergio Osmeña, Chief Justice José Abad Santos, and General Basilio Valdes. In the final meeting with his full cabinet that day, Quezon asked Secretary of Justice José Laurel to remain and help Jorge Vargas, Quezon's private secretary, who would stay to serve as mayor of Manila. Quezon encouraged the men to "Keep your faith in America, whatever happens."[34]

Laurel and Vargas were left behind to deal—or collaborate—with the Japanese, negotiating the enemy's demands with the needs of the Philippines and with the Philippines' allegiance to the United States. Both men recognized the danger this put them in and asked their president for advice on how to interact with the Japanese when they arrived. Quezon referred their concerns to MacArthur who allegedly told Vargas,

"There is nothing you can do; you have to follow what the Japanese Army of occupation orders you to do. Under international law you must obey the orders of the military occupant. There is only one thing you should not do: take the oath of allegiance to Japan because, if you do, we will shoot you when we come back."[35]

After the disappointment of canceled plans because of all the military developments, Claire planned to spend Christmas Eve night with Phil. "I found myself thrilled and excited as a schoolgirl at the prospect of my midnight rendezvous." She made a special effort getting ready for the evening: a bath, full makeup, fresh nail polish, after which she put on a new blue dress. Claire tucked Dian into bed and sang her daughter's favorite lullaby, "Melancholy Baby."[36]

Taking the sandwiches Lolita had prepared for this romantic encounter, Claire started her journey to the designated meeting place. When she pulled into the clearing, her high spirits deflated at the sight of the several soldiers waiting with Phil. She expected him to be alone. Phil greeted her with a hug and a matter-of-fact explanation: "Bless you for keeping our date for a Christmas wedding." Phil said that Chaplain Taylor could not officiate because of his duties at the field hospital. Father Gonzales, a priest from one of the nearby villages, agreed to preside over the ceremony. Before beginning, Gonzales asked Claire about her background, and she admitted she was not Catholic and that she had been married before. The priest assured her, "This is war, and my only concern is whether you truly desire at this time to enter into a true and lifelong union?" Claire said yes.[37]

Claire and John Phillips took their vows in front of a makeshift altar made of a moss-covered fallen log festooned with tiny white flowers. Claire clutched a bridal bouquet of freshly picked white hibiscus, and dozens of fireflies provided the only light for the ceremony. The newlyweds ate a celebratory meal with their guests and were toasted with citrus punch made from calamansi juice, water, and rum. Then they hurried away for the few remaining hours of their wedding night. It was much too short, but it was all they had.

Though Claire often told this story after the war, whatever took place on Christmas Eve was not a legal marriage. She had no proof of a divorce from Manuel Fuentes, and it is unlikely either a Baptist chaplain or a Catholic priest would be willing to overlook this fact, even in wartime. What is more probable is that during a Christmas Eve party, Claire and Phil exchanged some kind of verbal pledge to each other, signaling a common law marriage. They were never legally man and wife. Yet Claire started using the name Phillips during December 1941 and Phil did not object. Certainly they both realized the protection that name and fabricated marital status conveyed during these uncertain times.

Phil returned to his unit and Claire to her rented rooms. She had more than enough to keep her busy, readying a holiday dinner for Phil and a few of his friends. "Christmas Day passed swiftly as there were five chickens to be roasted, and a washtub of vegetable salad to be made. We prepared baked camotes (native potatoes) and our special treat was to be real bread and butter." By five o'clock, with the work finished, Claire took a bath and dressed for the evening. She expected her guests by eight, so at seven-thirty she positioned herself at the front window waiting to catch the first glimpse of Phil. Instead, she witnessed USAFFE's fallback in full swing: "Trucks, tanks, marching men . . . an endless procession . . . all heading south. . . . The dismal column showed all the visible signs of defeat and retreat."[38]

An hour passed with no sign of Phil, then two. Dian and Lolita ate their share of the Christmas dinner and went to bed. Claire served the remainder of the food to a group of passing soldiers who did not take the time to sit down. They told her everything was snafu—situation normal, all fucked up. Even with a general retreat all the way down to Mariveles, in the southernmost part of Bataan, even if they made the short hop across the North Channel to Corregidor, they might not be safe from the Japanese.

Claire stayed up until midnight before crawling into bed and crying herself to sleep. She woke to even worse news. The remnants of General Wainwright's hard-fighting North Luzon Force could not hold the Japanese back any longer at the Agno River, just south of the Lingayen Gulf. The enemy got around the 26th Cavalry there, quickly reached Highway 3, and pushed back the 11th Division of the Philippine Army, relentlessly driving toward Manila. In south Luzon as well, invading forces rapidly moved from Lamon Bay toward the capital. Manila's days as a free city were numbered, and the war was on its way to Bataan.[39]

Japanese planes bombed the area around the barrio of Pilar on the morning of December 26th. Even before first light, Claire saw the dogged military procession still moving through town on the way to Mariveles. She walked into the backyard to find her landlord digging an air raid shelter, and as they talked about its construction, a bomb exploded nearby. Claire dashed into the house to retrieve Dian and Lolita, and the three of them spent a couple of hours huddled in the backyard refuge until the raid ended. No one exhibited any particular bravery. "With the added shock of each succeeding tremor, my nervous reaction became one of increasing numbness until I felt more like a frightened animal than a reasoning human," Claire recalled.[40]

The attack injured so many people in Pilar that Claire's landlord offered the use of his house to take care of the wounded. Claire turned her makeshift soldiers' canteen into a first aid station and patched up civilians well enough to be moved back to their own homes. At six o'clock in the evening, when the electricity in town was shut off for an enforced blackout, Claire realized she'd had no contact with Phil all day. The next morning a soldier arrived, driving Claire's blue coupe, bearing a note: "Pack all your things and drive to Hermosa. Be there at noon sharp. The first house as you enter town has a windmill. Wait there for me."[41]

It took Claire nearly an hour to get herself, Dian, and Lolita ready for the twelve-mile journey north to the entrance of the Bataan peninsula. En route, Claire noted evidence of the ongoing battle littering the terrain, "We drove past fields strewn with the charred skeletons of airplanes, and scarred by deep holes dug by bombs, or aircraft in their death plunges. Many of the burned planes seemed to be Japanese, but I sadly noted a few American aircraft which apparently had been destroyed on the ground." They had made it about halfway to Hermosa when Japanese bombers appeared overhead, forcing Claire to stop the car and dive for shelter in a roadside ditch with Dian and Lolita. A piece of hot shrapnel cut through Claire's shoe and pierced her toe; otherwise they all emerged unscathed.[42]

The trio arrived at their destination about thirty minutes late. Phil was waiting, jittery and nervous about Claire's delay. He introduced the owner of the house, Judge Fernando Rivera, along with his wife, Rosita, and two young daughters. Rivera refused Claire's offer of payment for room and board, saying, "Señora, it is so little to do for you Americans when you have done so much for us." At the Rivera house, Claire was just a few hundred yards from where the 31st Infantry bivouacked, so Phil could drop by for a home cooked meal, a hot bath, and a comfortable bed when he was not working his midnight shift.[43]

Claire spent her days and most of her nights working alongside two army doctors in a school building next door to the Rivera house that had been converted into an aid station. With the increasing number of casualties, her lack of formal medical training became an impediment. The first time she saw an open stomach wound, she downed the glass of whiskey that was meant for the patient's anesthetic. But, Claire claimed, "I soon became accustomed to the sight of blood and the piteous moans of pain-wracked men."[44]

On December 30th, when Japanese bombs nearly destroyed the nearby barrio of Orani, the townspeople of Hermosa decided to evacuate. The aid station closed, and as the Rivera family prepared to flee to the safety of the hills, Claire agreed to leave only when Phil told her Headquarters Company was pulling out. He found a safe place farther north for Claire, Dian, and Lolita at a hacienda near Dinalupihan, about three miles from his outfit's new location.

———

GLADYS SAVARY HAD NOT EVEN been to bed when Pearl Harbor was bombed. That Sunday night, she invited some friends to the restaurant for dinner, a celebration of the promotion of a British naval officer she knew. After their meal, they headed over to the Jai Alai Club to watch a match—a "great weakness" of Gladys's. Then they stopped at a nightclub before moving on to the Manila Hotel for drinks on the pavilion. Gladys and her friends concluded their evening at an all-night gambling den where they played roulette until dawn. When they finally dropped her at the old Spanish mansion, the newly-promoted British admiral said, "Kids, that's the last fun we'll have together for a long, long time."[45]

It was too late—or too early—for Gladys to go to sleep. As it was, she would have just enough time to shower, change, and eat a bit of breakfast before venturing out to the market to purchase the day's food for the restaurant. When her servant Nick brought her morning coffee and the newspaper, he said, "Honolulu's bombed. What'll we do now?" Gladys's first response was as a businesswoman. The restaurant would be busy, she predicted, because people were always hungry. She told Nick they would do their shopping as usual. "War or no war, we have to eat," Gladys wrote in her diary. "I bought everything in large quantities. Nobody can know what'll happen."[46]

In a matter of hours, Manila had become a dangerous place. Civilians received constant instructions about how to behave during an air raid and how to be vigilant about spotting other enemy activity. Some 25,000 Japanese residents in the islands were rounded up and detained. Manila city officials continued to work on plans for the city's evacuation. And already, people were helping each other. Josefa Escoda, president of the National Federation of Women's Clubs and a social worker employed by the Red Cross, organized Bundles for Emergency. Her volunteers throughout the city collected old clothing and remade them into items needed by those who had been displaced by the bombings. Her relief work expanded over the next several months.[47]

During the ensuing days, as bombs fell on Manila and the utilities stuttered on and off, Gladys worried about how long she would be able to keep the Restaurant de Paris going. It also did not take her long to realize that other people needed help, and the restaurant came in handy for meeting some of those needs. Gladys fed the soldiers who patrolled her neighborhood. "I haven't time to do canteen work or roll bandages," she jotted in her diary on December 16th, "so I have a private canteen for the lads. When they go on duty they get coffee and pastry here, and when they finish duty I hand them out something a bit stronger. Both seem to be appreciated, bless them."[48]

Up until that point, Gladys held to the belief that the US military would quickly defeat the Japanese. Then she talked to a close friend of hers, recently returned to Manila from the United States, who invited her to accompany him on a shopping trip downtown to order new clothes. Gladys was astonished because he had brought back trunks stuffed with new American clothing, and she could not understand why he wanted more. Her friend explained, with a hint of condescension, that the clothes from the States were the wrong kind. Within a month, he told Gladys, the Japanese would control Luzon and would put all of the Allied civilians in concentration camps. He wanted khaki pants and shirts—sturdy items—to wear for the duration. Gladys fumed to herself about his defeatist attitude, yet she started to wonder.

This early in the war, not many Manilans expressed defeatist thoughts, despite the constant enemy bombing. For days, maybe even weeks, most believed that USAFFE and some well-timed reinforcements from the States would turn things around. Rumors and misinformation, rather than fact, fueled much of this optimism. On December 12th, for instance, the *Daily Tribune* ran an unfounded headline claiming USAFFE had halted a Japanese landing at the Lingayen Gulf and was busily mopping up the enemy. It was another ten days before the Japanese invaded there, and USAFFE, with no fresh troops in sight, was unable to stop them.[49]

Many of Gladys's positive thoughts about the progress of the war coexisted with niggling, negative ones. She blamed both the US and Philippine governments for not keeping the public well enough informed about the Japanese threat. Gladys knew that a committee of Americans had convened to work out contingency plans in the event of an enemy occupation. She complained that few of their deliberations "got to the ordinary people, who were completely in the dark. About all I could do was to keep on going—feeding and amusing the frightened patrons who swarmed" into her restaurant.[50]

The American Coordinating Committee (ACC) had organized nearly a year earlier, in January 1941, to work with the military, the American High Commissioner's office, the Philippine government, and the civilian population to plan for civil defense. At the ACC's first meeting that month at the Manila Elks Club, three hundred members selected businessman Frederic H. Stevens as its president. The ACC estimated 8,000 American civilians were living in the Philippines, and the committee wanted all of their names and addresses "in order that the civilian community may render the military and Commissioner Sayre the fullest cooperation should emergencies of war affect the country." Above all, panic had to be avoided. "It is best to know beforehand what to do," the ACC reasoned, "what must be done, and by whom."[51]

As Christmas approached, panic could not be avoided. The enemy landing at the Lingayen Gulf put everyone on edge. How soon, they worried, before the Japanese would make it to Manila? A couple of days before the holiday, two US Navy lieutenants startled Gladys when they "rushed into the restaurant, brushing me aside brusquely. I wanted to know what they were after, but they leapt up the stairs to the third floor." They burst into the apartment of her nephew, Edgar Gable, who, along with his friend John Keevan and another man, was hunched over a shortwave radio in the blacked-out room, listening to the latest news.[52]

The officers accused Edgar and his friends of signaling outside with a flashlight, insinuating they were communicating with the Japanese. Gladys, who entered the apartment on the heels on the Navy men, knew nothing of the kind was going on. She pointed out to the interlopers that Edgar did not even have a flashlight. The only possible source of illumination from within the room was the lit cigar John Keevan had clamped in his mouth. "Everybody laughed," Gladys remembered, "except the Navy lads."[53]

Manila was caught up in a frenzy of movement on Christmas Eve. Not only had the Philippine Army divisions failed to halt the enemy landing at Lingayen, but the 26th Cavalry could not make a dent, either. General Wainwright, commander of the North Luzon Force, ordered in the Philippine Scouts, but they could do little without adequate artillery and tanks. The Japanese kept coming, but the Scouts at least delayed them, making them fight for every step they took. The North Luzon Force crossed the Agno River in the Cordillera mountain region of central Luzon ahead of the enemy. From there Wainwright anticipated his divisions mounting an effective defense to delay or even prevent the Japanese from reaching Manila from the north. Now, examining what happened at

Lingayen, General MacArthur realized the impossibility of it. He knew the Japanese would occupy Manila, and soon.

Gladys, always interested in a good time and a tasty cocktail, celebrated Christmas morning the same way she had for years: attending an eggnog party at a friend's house. This time, however, the event was "rudely interrupted by the bombing." Though everyone headed for the bomb shelter, it was too small and too crowded for Gladys's comfort. She sat on the terrace with her drink and watched the planes in the sky. The party moved over to the Restaurant de Paris for Christmas dinner, complete with tree and gifts, where the conversation revolved around the decamping of the "Royal Family"—President Quezon, High Commissioner Sayre, etc.— to Corregidor. "The criticism at the party that day was pretty severe," Gladys recalled. "Everyone felt very badly let down." They probably also discussed rumors that MacArthur would declare Manila an open city.[54]

He did so the next day, ordering the withdrawal of USAFFE forces, leaving Manila undefended so the Japanese would not feel compelled to destroy it. Gladys bid farewell to Edgar, her beloved nephew, a thirty-six-year-old bespectacled businessman who had joined up with the US Army. Commissioned as a first lieutenant in the Quartermaster Corps, Edgar received assignment to the Philippine Motor Transport Unit on Bataan. Gladys helped him pack—along with the other renters who also volunteered—and, with a sinking heart, helped them write "their last-minute instructions" to loved ones. Then she poured them all a farewell drink. No levity, no hint of a celebration because Gladys knew it was unlikely she would ever see them again.[55]

The open city declaration did not stop the Japanese from bombing Manila. As Gladys noted in her diary, "The open city idea isn't working. We sat yesterday under three hours and twenty minutes of constant bombing. . . . It's enraging, maddening, to see and hear them circle the city to get in the choicest position to bomb, and we sit like clay-pigeon targets below, completely helpless." Just past noon that day, Japanese bombs fell along the port area, sinking a variety of vessels and crippling several piers. Two hours later, shipping concerns at the Pasig River were targeted. The bombs landed either in the water or on the banks; still, the two bombing waves destroyed a college and the building that housed *The Philippines Herald*, and damaged Fort Santiago in Intramuros. Forty people died.[56]

Gladys could have taken refuge across the street at the Bay View Hotel, which had an exceptional air raid shelter. The owner, Dr. Harry Kneedler, served during the Spanish-American War as a surgeon with the 3rd Missouri Infantry and like some other veterans of that conflict decided to continue his career in the Philippines. He married an American woman, Ethel Mason, had two sons, established himself as a physician, and then branched out into other businesses. Kneedler's son Edgar, a graduate of the University of California at Berkeley, ran the hotel, and Edgar's wife, the former Dorothy Douglas of San Francisco, was one of Gladys's closest friends.

Yet this friendship failed to motivate Gladys to cross the street to seek shelter when the air raid sirens went off. She suffered from a touch of claustrophobia and knew she could not tolerate spending time crowded into a small shelter space. Gladys trusted that the sandbags ringed around the inside of her restaurant's dining room would provide adequate protection. She stretched out on the floor "with an old whodunit story, a powder puff between my teeth for concussions, and a bottle of San Miguel beer beside me." From there it was easy to get up and go to bed, "weary but unbowed," once the all-clear sounded.[57]

Through it all, Gladys maintained an attitude she described as "incurably light-minded." She was adamant that she was not weak-minded, but light-minded: coping with the growing horrors of war by embracing levity and rejecting seriousness. Her diary entries contained "yowling about problems of transportation, blackouts, air raids at mealtime, officers who cannot hold their liquor." Had she not been light-minded, she would have written more "about the seriousness of war, the advances of the enemy, and . . . the actual departure of the Army."[58]

A streak of practicality mixed in with Gladys's light-mindedness because she had to tend to business. The Restaurant de Paris was her source of income and independence; she had to keep it going, even during an enemy occupation. She purchased large quantities of food, especially rice, from whoever was selling. She knew that much of what she bought from street vendors had been taken from the quartermaster stores that had thrown open their doors in advance of the occupation. The US military preferred that Manilans have first crack at the supplies that could not be moved before the Japanese arrived. Gladys thought about survival: "Whatever came, we had to eat—everyone had to eat."[59]

She probably did not venture far from the restaurant in the days between Christmas and New Year's because as USAFFE withdrew—all personnel were supposed to be out of the city by December 31st—Manilans panicked. Merchants anxious to evacuate the city began selling their goods at dirt cheap prices. Eager buyers pressed into the stores, leading to arguments and fistfights as people competed for the remaining goods. Looters crashed into stores that had already been closed and carried off what they could. The local police force lifted a feeble finger to restore order. They had given up their weapons so the Japanese would not think they intended to do anything to oppose the occupation. Without weapons, the police could not control the looters.

While the Japanese advanced on Manila, Gladys Savary drank. She opened up the last of her foie gras and champagne and served it to her customers on New Year's Eve. They came to the Restaurant de Paris, as Gladys remembered, "to be cheered up a bit." In an uncharacteristic rejection of light-mindedness, she described the evening as "tragic . . . the Japs were at the gates." After dinner, the party moved across the street to the Bay View Hotel, where Gladys wept into her champagne.[60]

YAY PANLILIO NEVER HAD TIME for tears. As soon as she heard the news about Pearl Harbor, she was on the move. She and Jorge Teodoro, a reporter for the *Daily Tribune*, headed straight for President Quezon's vacation residence in the northern Luzon city of Baguio to score an interview. She may have already been in Baguio, a five-hour drive from Manila, when she learned of the Japanese attack on Hawaii. Quezon had been in the resort city for the Immaculate Conception holiday and to recover from an illness. Yay might have followed him there, searching for the next big story. First thing Monday morning, December 8th, she intended to get it.

While Yay and Teodoro waited for Quezon to receive them, James (Jim) Halsema, a local Baguio reporter and son of the former city mayor, joined them. When the three newspeople were admitted to Quezon's bedroom, Halsema found the president "obviously shaken by events" as he told the trio little beyond the fact that he recalled his chief of staff, Jorge Vargas, from Manila. Yay and Halsema decided to drive down Kennon Road to the Loakan Airport, south of Baguio, to await Vargas's arrival. They wanted to hear what Vargas had to say about what was happening in Manila. Along the way the two reporters saw planes flying toward the John Hay Air Station, commonly referred to as Camp John Hay, and one circling Loakan. They waited for a while at the field but Vargas never arrived.[61]

By the time Yay and Halsema returned to Baguio, the Japanese had already bombed parts of the city, including Camp John Hay. The camp, built during the first decade of the US occupation of the Philippines, was primarily used as a rest and recreation facility. The Japanese targeted John Hay with the intention of killing all the officers from Clark Field they believed would still be there from the weekend's R & R. Beginning at about 8:19 a.m. on December 8th, in what was considered the first Japanese attack on the Philippines, enemy planes dropped more than seventy bombs on the camp. Eleven soldiers died, along with several civilians.

After that morning's event, Yay returned to Manila to file her story, check on her children, and pass along what she had seen in Baguio to the higher-ups in S-2. "Through the Baguio bombing, the Cavite bombing, and the dog-fighting over Manila, I kept my eyes open," she wrote of those first days of the war. "I shuttled from the Fort Santiago Intelligence headquarters at one end of the Walled City [Intramuros] to Victoria No. 1 at the other end. There MacArthur was busy ordering his already battle-worn forces up from the far south, through the defenseless city, and down into Bataan."[62]

After years working at a profession she loved, Yay knew she would give it up in a minute for the chance to help USAFFE. She understood the importance of moving personnel and supplies onto the Bataan peninsula, and she wanted to contribute. "I could drive a truck. I could pound a typewriter. In a pinch, I knew which end of a rifle was the shooting end," she later insisted. She appealed to General MacArthur's press relations aide,

Major LeGrande Diller, to smooth her way. A native New Yorker and 1924 graduate of Syracuse University, Diller had been with the US Army in the Philippines since 1939. Originally part of the infantry, he met MacArthur in July 1941 and was appointed as one of his aides the following month.[63]

As a journalist, Yay probably had had extensive dealings with Diller prior to Pearl Harbor, because at the outbreak of war it was clear she already did not like him. Many members of the civilian press referred to the major as "Killer" for the way he ruthlessly protected MacArthur's image, but Yay called him the "Each-Hair-in-Its Place" major. Diller's response to Yay's request for permission to travel to Bataan was an insulting, "No! No, no-no-no! What do you think this is, a picnic?"[64]

Another S-2 civilian recruit, a man Yay identified only as Glass, had more experience with intelligence work and took her under his wing. Glass, she later recounted, "had been kind to me and taught me a little of sleuthing." Because he was a man, he transitioned into active military service after the Japanese attack. When he pulled out for Bataan, he told Yay, "Save the country if you can, kid." This strengthened Yay's resolve to get to Bataan. She could not save her country—both countries—if she could not get to the fighting. If she could not go with USAFFE, she would figure out another way to get the Japanese.[65]

JACK UTINSKY HAD ALREADY TOLD Peggy that she could not come to Bataan with him. She had taken an apartment on A. Mabini Street in Manila and started working for the Red Cross and a canteen even before Pearl Harbor was bombed. Starting sometime on December 8th or 9th, she put in even more time at one of the Manila hospitals or a Red Cross center, treating the mounting casualties. Colonel Percy J. Carroll, commanding officer at Sternberg General Hospital, designated eight annexes in the city to care for the war wounded, including the Jai Alai Club and the Philippine Women's University. Additionally, about thirty emergency aid stations popped up throughout the city. Trained medical personnel as well as first aid and surgical supplies were at a premium. Doctors, nurses, orderlies all worked long hours during those first days of the war, and then they worked some more. Regular shifts no longer existed.[66]

Peggy stayed on her feet until she could not keep her eyes open, then she picked her way back to A. Mabini Street, careful to avoid the most bomb-ravaged sidewalks. Within a couple of days, repeated bombing raids made Peggy's presence at the hospital all the more imperative. The blackouts made getting there difficult and dangerous. As she recalled, "One night there was a series of heavy, dull reverberations and the windows rattled. I did not know what had happened, but the nurse downstairs had lived in Russia and China. She knew a bomb when she heard it and we ran at top speed for the hospital, in case we were needed." She and the other nurse got lost on the way to the hospital and ended up in a cemetery. They ran through it once, then twice, until Peggy recognized the same white fence they kept passing.[67]

Dashing in circles through a graveyard in the dead of night during a bombing raid convinced Peggy to find a nursing job closer to her apartment. The Red Cross, badly in need of trained medical personnel anywhere, obliged with a reassignment to a new hospital just blocks from her apartment, in the Malate district, just east of Ermita. During the 1930s, both Malate and Ermita developed into residential districts for the upper-middle class—Spanish, French, and some Americans, mostly senior army officers and Protestant missionaries. The neighborhoods contained lovely homes, bungalows or two-story wood houses, each with a small garden, dotting the tree-lined streets.[68]

The Malate Church took up an entire block, bordered on one side by A. Mabini, the street where Peggy lived. The church was home to a group of Irish priests of the Society of St. Columban, founded in 1918 as an overseas missionary organization. It originally sent priests to China, then beginning in 1929, to the Philippine Islands as well. Forty-one-year-old Father Patrick Kelly ran the Malate Church and served as the first Superior of Columbans in the Philippines, with the parish's convent functioning as a "Centre House." The church had its own school, located on the other side of A. Mabini Street, run by Father John Lalor, who had arrived in the Philippines in 1934, the year Peggy and Jack married.[69]

When Japanese bombs started falling on Manila, the Irish priests donated the school building to the Red Cross, which converted it into

Emergency Hospital No. 5, naming Dr. Romeo Atienza as its head. This new Remedios Hospital needed medical personnel, and Father Lalor, having given up his school, donned doctor's whites to tend to the sick and wounded. Peggy joined him there, in what turned out to be a fortuitous placement.

On December 22nd, as enemy troops landed at the Lingayen Gulf, the first wave of medical officers and army nurses left Manila's Sternberg General Hospital for Bataan. They headed for Limay, about two-thirds of the way down into the peninsula, along the eastern shore, where they set up Hospital No. 1. The 1,000-bed hospital, wood framed and open sided with a thatched roof, was situated on an anticipated front line, close to Abucay Hacienda, which would soon see some of the worst fighting of the war. In charge of Hospital No. 1 was Colonel James "Ducky" Duckworth. The former Hoosier was in his early fifties, a career army medical officer who until recently had commanded the hospital at Fort McKinley and the 12th Medical Regiment.[70]

Those days passed in a blur for Peggy, then, around Christmas, Jack returned to Manila. ". . . he came back to see whether I was all right. We had two days together, punctuated by bomb blasts." As happy as she was to see him, her sense of duty would not allow her to shirk her other responsibilities. "I was working at top speed at the hospital, and running the canteen, and helping to pick up the pieces from the bombing."[71]

December 28th was the last day the Utinskys spent together. After General MacArthur issued the open city declaration, all military personnel were supposed to decamp to Bataan. Peggy wanted as much time as possible with Jack that day, but the increased enemy bombing interfered with her intentions. "Mockery," she called it, the way "the Japanese poured on the city the worst bombing it had suffered." On her way to or from the hospital, she had to spend four hours in an iron chicken coop underneath Quezon Bridge until the all-clear sounded. "The longest four hours in the history of man," she described the time she lost with her husband. At their good-bye, Jack said to Peggy, "I came back here thinking I'd have to pull you out of a ditch. Instead of that, I found you scurrying around, pulling other people out. I'd like you to know, darling, that I'm very proud of you."[72]

Peggy had so much to do after Jack's departure that there was no time for self-pity or for mooning, romantic thoughts. Like Gladys Savary, she stocked up on the giveaways from the military quartermasters over the New Year's holiday. Peggy reasoned USAFFE's evacuation would only be temporary. When the soldiers returned to Manila she intended to start up the canteen, and she thought it only fitting the military's own goods should supply the establishment.

Peggy hired eight taxis and a group of able-bodied Filipinos who hauled, packed, and unpacked those cabs seven times. An African-American woman, Margaret Silverton, who lived a block away on A. Mabini Street and ran a laundry, loaned Peggy her truck. "By the time I got through," Peggy boasted later, "my apartment was stacked to the ceiling with everything I could get my hands on: cases of Vienna sausage, corned beef, sardines, vegetables, juices; crackers, flour and sugar; and—most important of all—drugs." But those supplies would be put to a different use.[73]

CHAPTER 5

THE JAPANESE OCCUPATION
OF MANILA

GLADYS SAVARY BEGAN NEW YEAR'S DAY 1942 WITH A
morning eggnog. "Might as well carry on," she figured, since
enemy forces were less than twenty miles from the city. By noontime she
switched to champagne and sparkling Burgundy while she watched the
remnants of the harbor patrol blow up the private yachts bobbing off the
small piers at the Yacht Club.[1]

In the afternoon, a member of the American Coordinating Committee
(ACC) showed up at the Restaurant de Paris and instructed Gladys to
destroy her remaining liquor stock. According to him, "I would be jeopardizing the life, liberty and virtue and what have you of all Manila by not
doing so. That the little yellow rascals would drink liquor, murder, rape
and ruin and rob us all—probably in reverse order." Though Gladys partially complied, she could not resist holding out some alcohol for private

use, especially while she watched from her outdoor terrace as parts of the city went up in flames. She knew she would need that liquor later on.[2]

The ACC official's request was not unduly cautious, though the Japanese were not the immediate problem. Abandoned by USAFFE and by top civilian leaders, awaiting the arrival of enemy troops, the chaos in Manila intensified. After enduring two nerve-shattering weeks of bombing, civilians worried the Japanese planned wholesale slaughter once they reached the capital city. Frightened people jammed the roads, hoping to get away in the nick of time, or they banged on the doors of churches, convents, and schools seeking shelter. Many who remained in the city turned to looting—breaking into stores and other businesses—carrying off whatever they could. The local police and constabulary had already surrendered their weapons so as not to pose a threat to the invading forces, thus they could not subdue the looters. Fires burned throughout the city, the result of vandalism and of strategic military destruction by USAFFE. Manilans, fearful and dejected, awaited the inevitable.

On January 2nd, Gladys wrote in her diary, "I went to market this morning and stocked up with all sorts of things. Prices have gone up dreadfully. It is now eight in the morning and we are still unoccupied." The lack of enemy troops was a small comfort; still, she did not like the feel of the city, which had been her home for ten years. "The streets are nearly deserted, people are huddled in frightened groups, fires raging all about the city—and always rumors, rumors."[3]

At eleven o'clock, Manila's remaining city officials sent out cars with loudspeakers through the streets, advising everyone to stay home. Gladys stayed put, spending the afternoon cooking and socializing with her remaining lodgers and a few brave souls who ventured outside despite the warning. At five-thirty some friends showed up and asked Gladys to come with them across the street to the Bay View Hotel where fellow Americans had been whiling away the hours. She declined, claiming she had guests to take care of, then she packed an emergency bag with a bottle of Scotch and some toiletries in case the restaurant caught fire.

The occupation had proceeded in an orderly fashion throughout the day. The Japanese took over key government and military offices, and their troops drove along Rizal and Taft Avenues, the Rising Sun flag fluttering on the vehicles. By late afternoon, enemy soldiers patrolled city streets, fixed bayonets at the ready, under orders to stop any looting. The violence most Manilans expected did not occur, though they continued to worry about what would happen next.[4]

They should not have had to concern themselves. The 1907 Hague Convention, which Japan signed in 1911, addressed the behavior of an occupying enemy in a conquered land. Article 43 stipulates that once an occupation force takes over, it shall use "all the measures in his power to restore and ensure, as far as possible, public order and safety, while respecting, unless absolutely prevented, the laws in force in the country." The lives and private property of the occupied people, as stated in Article 46, "must be respected."[5]

The Japanese created a structure for the management of their occupied territories. Field Marshal Count Terauchi Hisaichi, Supreme Commander of the Expeditionary Forces to the Southern Area, headed all arenas of Japanese occupation. The Philippines were assigned a commander-in-chief, Homma Masahura, who was followed by three others. However, the chief of the military administration, Wachi Takagi, exerted the most influence on day-to-day life. Military occupation officials spread throughout the Philippines, though they were most numerous on Luzon, where officers supervised every aspect of civilian life, from radio owner-ship to curfews to travel passes. There was a Japanese chief civil adviser to the military administration, a strictly subordinate position since the Japanese military took precedence over everything. To ensure Filipinos acquiesced, the Japanese promoted the Greater East Asia Co-Prosperity Sphere, a pan-Asian, anti-American brotherhood, through its military's Propaganda Corps. Primarily, though, enforcement of the occupation fell to the Kempeitai, the military police of the Imperial Japanese Army. It set up headquarters at Fort Santiago, where Colonel Nagahama Akira directed the arrest, imprisonment, torture, and execution of resisters.[6]

Gladys Savary watched more and more people jam into the Bay View Hotel the first day the Japanese marched into Manila. When its restaurant got overwhelmed, those customers either drifted across the street to the

As Gladys predicted, the Japanese swiftly imposed their authority in Manila, making Americans pay for their imperial hubris. General Homma, presiding over the occupation, issued statements summing up Japan's philosophy behind the Greater East Asia Co-Prosperity Sphere. Japan's aim in the Philippines was to drive out the "evil influence and power" of the United States, which had destroyed the natural development and healthy growth of Asian nations. To start this process, the Japanese Military Police ordered all firearms and weapons surrendered.[14]

A couple of days later, newspapers carried stern warnings about behavior, beginning with, "Anyone who inflicts, or attempts to inflict, an injury upon Japanese soldiers or individuals shall be shot to death." If the attacker escaped apprehension, ten "influential" people would be held hostage until he was caught. But overall, occupation authorities insisted, "The Filipinos should understand our real intentions and should work together with us to maintain public peace and order in the Philippines."[15]

To help maintain order and sever the last remaining thread of American power, Japanese officials compelled the registration of all Allied nationals living in Manila. Radio broadcasts and loudspeakers mounted on cars blared the message instructing them to wait at home with a bag packed with a change of clothes, blanket, mosquito net, and three-day food supply. Japanese soldiers would pick them up.[16]

Registration took place in various locations around the city, including Rizal Stadium and Villamor Hall, a music conservatory on Taft Avenue. The Bay View Hotel, right across the street from the Restaurant de Paris, still housed dozens of Allied civilians trapped there since the first day of the occupation. Among them was a friend of Gladys Savary's who assured her in a telephone call—Gladys had been heeding the warnings about going outside—that after registration everyone would be released, except for men of military age. Gladys did not believe it: "I fear that's too good to be true."[17]

At one o'clock in the afternoon on January 5th, outside in the hot, high sun, the Japanese lined up the American and British guests of the Bay View Hotel. It was another hour and a half before the trucks started driving them off to the registration centers. To ward off her sense of helplessness,

Gladys stood behind the iron grills of her dining room window and distributed Coca-Cola, cigarettes, ice water, and odds and ends people had forgotten to pack. It took the Japanese about four hours to move all of these people, and Gladys admired the civilians for their patience and their pride.

In addition to handing out supplies, she spent the afternoon hours making up care packages of food, blankets, and mosquito nets for herself and her guests. She also stuffed extra food, dishware, and other household items into large duffle bags so she could share with her compatriots—or bribe the Japanese if necessary. Around six-thirty in the evening, all packed and with her business affairs in order, Gladys broke out a bottle of champagne for her guests as they waited their turn.

They did not wait long. When she finally heard the knock and opened the door, Gladys faced a few Japanese officers with their interpreter. She handed over a list of her lodgers—all Americans except one Frenchman—along with their papers. The interpreter was a Japanese photographer who had lived in Manila for years and knew the Savarys. He pointed out to Gladys and the officers that under Japanese law, a woman took the nationality of her husband. Therefore, Gladys, as a French national, was not required to submit to the registration process, and she could stay at the restaurant.

Gladys put up a half-hearted protest. If registration only took a few days, it would not hurt for her to be away from the restaurant. Her staff could certainly handle everything for a few days. But the officers agreed with the interpreter. Though Gladys held an American passport, the Japanese decided she was as French as her husband. Gladys did not mention that André Savary was now her ex-husband, and she remained in the old Spanish mansion that housed her restaurant. "How I wish I'd gone, though," she wrote in her diary that night, without her characteristic light-mindedness. "What can I do alone—and so alone. My whole future—what's the use of thinking about a future?"[18]

Within days, registration turned into internment. Americans and other Allied nationals ended up on the campus of Santo Tomas University. The location had been chosen by the American Emergency Committee

(AEC)—the wartime version of the American Coordinating Committee and a part of the American Red Cross—and agreed to by the occupation authorities. In late December 1941, when it became clear the Japanese would occupy Manila, Frederic Stevens, chair of the AEC, approached the university administration to work out an agreement for using the campus as an internment site. Spread out over sixty acres, Santo Tomas contained many large buildings, complete with sanitation facilities, capable of housing large numbers of people. Tall stone walls surrounded the campus on three sides, providing a sense of security.[19]

The first internees—between three and four hundred Americans and Brits—arrived on January 4th, trucked in from Manila's South Malate District. Many still clung to the belief they would only be here for a matter of days. Earl Carroll, the South Malate District's AEC chair, knew better. If the Japanese intended to keep them for a few days, they would not have chosen him to head an internee committee—which would come to be known as the Executive Committee—to handle daily operations in the camp.[20]

Four days later, Gladys's good friend Helge Janson, the Swedish consul, drove her to Santo Tomas University. They stood outside the fence as people on the other side shouted out orders of what they needed: beds, mosquito nets, clothing, and food. Gladys felt overwhelmed and, watching how her friends were suffering, guilty about her freedom. When she announced she was going to surrender herself for internment, her friends protested. They needed her on the outside, they insisted, where she could help take care of them.

After returning to the restaurant, Gladys wrote in her diary about what she had seen: "A screaming, milling mob, and a most humiliating sight. To think those little yellow boys could do that to us!" Yet the Japanese insisted the British and American internees were doing just fine. According to an official proclamation, the concentration camp at Santo Tomas had been established for protection. "Therefore those who are not under the protective custody of the Japanese Expeditionary Forces are urged to appeal personally to any officer of the Japanese Army Authorities." Enemy aliens who failed to seek this protective custody by January 15th would be considered hostile and "severely dealt with."[21]

Concerned about such harsh yet undefined penalties, Helge Janson advised Gladys to shore up her claim to immunity from internment, especially since she had worked for the Free French Committee, an organization that supported the liberation of France from German control. Her divorce would also likely contribute to her "shaky" standing, so she had no intention of informing the Vichy French consul about it. Acquiescing to Helge, Gladys telephoned the consul and told him she possessed an American passport but was married to a Frenchman. The consul checked his records and confirmed that she had registered with the French Consulate in Manila in 1931 as the wife of Frenchman André Savary. He offered to issue her a French passport, which Gladys declined, asking instead for a certified copy of that record entry to use as proof of her nationality.[22]

Classification as a French national allowed Gladys the freedom to move around Manila, giving her the opportunity to help her interned friends. She successfully talked her way into Santo Tomas on January 13th, the first time she managed a close look at the workings of the camp. Instead of dropping off food and other supplies that day, Gladys met with camp officials to arrange the release of a friend, Mary Berry. Fred Berry, a Manila businessman and now a member of the internment camp's Executive Committee, worried that his wife would not survive in the camp because of heart problems complicated by obesity. He turned to Gladys for help, and she spent hours bouncing from one office in Manila to another, accumulating the proper paperwork, before heading off to Santo Tomas. There the Japanese discharged Mary in Gladys's custody.

Gladys found conditions inside the camp appalling and understood at once why Fred wanted his wife out: "The Japs had put the internees in the college classrooms, forty to sixty in a room; cots, mattresses on the floor, luggage, mosquito nets, all jammed in together with a very few inches allotted to each person. It is horrible, really, to think that people like that should be treated so." She blamed the Japanese for not taking better care of the civilians and praised the members of the Executive Committee for working so hard with limited resources to improve conditions, "getting order out of chaos," in her view.[23]

The situation inside Santo Tomas indeed approached chaos, though the Executive Committee performed near miracles to help thousands of people settle in to their new, reduced circumstances. After the initial deposit of internees on January 4, a steady stream arrived over the next several days until about 5,000 bewildered civilians swelled the campus grounds. Although the AEC originally considered the university a good internment site—especially in terms of likely alternatives—it was far from perfect. Despite the many classroom buildings at Santo Tomas, there were few dormitories. The cots and mattresses Gladys saw in the classrooms represented makeshift sleeping quarters, which remained crowded and uncomfortable until the end.

The lack of dormitories also meant a deficiency of sanitation facilities—not enough toilets and sinks for thousands of people to use every day, several times a day. This proved dangerous on the jam-packed campus since dysentery, malaria, and a host of other diseases could and did develop and spread. When that happened, the lack of adequate medical supplies and personnel perpetuated a cycle of illnesses.

Dealing with all of this, to prevent additional suffering and ward off fatal diseases, required organization. Occupation officials provided little. Japanese civilian authorities, headed by a commandant, administered the Santo Tomas camp for most of the war. The first commandant, 1st Lieutenant Hitoshi Tomoyasu, laid down the basic rules—men and women must live separately, no one should try to escape—then relied on his own discretion to decide additional rules, including the issuance of day passes out of the camp and how to apply for them. For the most part, he allowed the civilian Executive Committee to handle the day-to-day running of the camp, especially the purchase and distribution of food. As long as these activities did not run counter to Japanese objectives, the internees were left to their own devices.[24]

Despite the odd governing style, it was certainly better than what many of the civilian internees must have expected—that the Japanese would simply shoot them. There was a further sense of relief as it became clear the enemy did not have any plans to do so. In fact, there was no evidence these enemy nationals in the Philippines were ever targeted for extermination.

Santo Tomas and the other places of civilian internment were established as concentration camps in the classic sense: contained locations to hold a specific group of people. Santo Tomas was not, in other words, what a concentration camp would come to be known as. It was not an Auschwitz or Treblinka.

Japan had signed the 1929 Geneva Convention Relative to the Treatment of Prisoners of War, and in February 1942 announced intentions to abide by it. In practice, camp commandants rarely did, citing their interpretation that the agreement covered military prisoners, not civilian. The unpredictability of the Japanese running Santo Tomas presented much anxiety for the internees, though in a few months they would realize how much better off they were than the military prisoners. The Japanese treated the POWs in their custody so brutally that the interned civilians, despite their restricted circumstances, would find ways to help those men.[25]

In the first months of the occupation, Gladys Savary did what she could to assist the internees at Santo Tomas. She also kept her business running; she had to. It was the only way she could earn a living to support herself and to help the internees. Gladys's original American lodgers were replaced by an odd collection of civilians like herself who, for one reason or another, the Japanese had not chosen to intern. She forged a new customer base for the restaurant with Americans who had been released from Santo Tomas for medical reasons, which the Japanese allowed early in the war. These people, who had permission for limited travel within Manila, gravitated toward the Restaurant de Paris where they socialized with like-minded people. This was not the paradise of the prewar years, but it was not as bad as Gladys had feared.

ON THAT FIRST DAY OF THE OCCUPATION, Peggy Utinsky nursed patients at Remedios Hospital. Bombing victims arrived in a never-ending stream, leaving her little time to think about what was happening outside the hospital walls. Then, at six o'clock in the evening, with no explanation, the hospital staff received orders to go home. Peggy walked back to her apartment, unaware of anything out of the ordinary, until she came to a crowd of people standing in the street. She asked the man standing next to her if he thought the Japanese would arrive soon. "What the hell do you think that is?" he replied, gesturing to the motorcycle parked in front of them. Then she saw the Japanese motorcycle driver, Japanese flags—the bold Rising Sun—the enemy occupation. "Here they are, they have us," Peggy thought. It seemed unreal, incomprehensible; it was what all the experts said would never happen.[26]

A throng of people pushed into the Bay View Hotel, across the street from the Restaurant de Paris, and Peggy joined them. Inside the hotel, Americans downed cocktails and played cards, trying to ignore the events unfolding outside. Peggy may have nodded in acknowledgement to Gladys Savary, who briefly joined the hotel crush. For some of the more curious, the Bay View provided a bird's-eye view of the arrival of the Japanese. *Life* photographer Carl Mydans and his wife Shelley later described the Japanese they saw from their rooms: "They came up the boulevards in the predawn glow from the bay riding on bicycles and on tiny motorcycles. They came without talk and in good order, the ridiculous pop-popping of their one-cylinder cycles sounding loud in the silent city."[27]

Peggy and the other new arrivals took the elevator up to the hotel's seventh floor where cocktail hour—a euphemism that day since it was clear everyone had been drinking for more than an hour—was in full swing. People started talking at once, asking questions, making comments, speculating, exchanging rumors. Peggy remembered, "No one seemed to know what to do—I didn't either, for that matter, except that it would not be what I was told to do." The conversation turned in circles for nearly an hour until Peggy realized she did not want to remain any longer. Too impatient to wait for the elevator, she dashed down seven flights of stairs. A man stopped her in the lobby and asked where she was going. Home, she said, to which he replied, "You can't. I hear the Japs are going to start shooting at eight o'clock." Peggy responded, "Well, I still have fifteen minutes."[28]

She ran to her apartment, slid open a window, and watched from her living room how the enemy moved into the city. Japanese military vehicles cruised down the street, one right after the other, all night and into the next day. Peggy tried to remain optimistic, consoling herself with the belief the enemy would not stay long . Since Manila was an open city, she reasoned, the Japanese would roll right through on their way to Bataan and perhaps be gone by morning. But they were not; the Japanese would remain for more than three years. Peggy had witnessed just the beginning.

From the second floor apartment on A. Mabini Street, she watched the occupation unfold. "The days crept by and I remained in hiding, with Japs all around me. By now, of course, I knew they had come to stay. And how grateful I was for having disobeyed orders and taken that apartment." Months ago, believing in safety in numbers, Jack had told Peggy to remain in the hotel room he had rented. She did not obey. Now she felt safe here, in an apartment that had windows made of shell rather than glass, which allowed light in without being transparent. Still, Peggy took the extra precaution of drawing the blinds. The Russian nurse who temporarily occupied the first floor had evacuated, so Peggy wanted to create the illusion the entire house was empty.[29]

From this secure perch, she observed the comings and goings in the neighborhood, taking note of the people who cozied up to the Japanese. She watched as more and more Japanese soldiers moved into the city, many of them bivouacking on the streets in the Ermita district. Especially ominous were the Japanese officers, assisted by a translator, who set up a card table on her corner of A. Mabini Street and stopped all passersby. Peggy felt a cold dread. She knew what the Japanese were looking for. "Enemy alien!" She bristled at the designation. "That was a queer thing for an American to be in the Philippines." Yet this was exactly what Peggy had become.[30]

She kept the volume on her radio turned low so as not to attract any unwelcome attention and listened as the orders were broadcast over and over. American and British citizens were instructed to stay home until occupation authorities registered them. Then they would have to report for internment, a temporary measure until the Japanese investigated them all and secured the city. "A formality and it would not last long. Just a matter three or four days," the Japanese said.[31]

Peggy did not buy it for a second. As soon as she stepped outside, she knew, the Japanese would pick her up and would not release her—or anyone else for that matter—in three or four days. She had no intention of sitting out the war in an internment camp. On the one hand she thought, "To obey instructions and go tamely into an internment camp seemed like the sensible thing to do." But on the other, she could not stand being told what to do, and "for the life of me I could not see what use I would be to myself or to anyone else cooped up there."[32]

To be useful—that was what Peggy's sense of duty required. As she later explained, "So I decided to remain hidden, barricaded, rather, in my apartment until it was safe to go out and discover for myself what was going on and how I could get to Bataan where my husband was." She stayed inside for days, then weeks. Japanese soldiers banged on the street-level door several times, even kicked at it as if to test the occupants' resolve. Peggy never moved. One day the soldiers gave up and did not return, finally convinced that the house had been abandoned.[33]

It was ten weeks before Peggy felt safe enough to venture from her apartment. Her only visitor during the entire time was Cam Lee, the Chinese servant who had worked many years for the Utinskys. Lee checked in every day despite his fear of walking along streets populated with Japanese soldiers, making his way to a supposedly empty house to see a woman who should have gone to an internment camp. He continued to do so, Peggy believed, because he felt responsible for her—she had no son or husband with her. Every day Lee showed up, he chided Peggy for her "unreasonable behavior" in refusing to submit to internment.[34]

When she was alone, Peggy passed the time reading. She made her way through every book in the apartment, including Jack's engineering manuals, which she never quite understood. Using a gentle surface touch, she taught herself to type, a skill she believed could be useful in the future. Peggy nibbled at the food she took from the military storehouses, carefully parceling it out, not knowing how long it would have to last. She left the lights off after dark and tiptoed across the floors as she moved from room to room. Each evening, she tuned in the radio, keeping the volume low, and strained to catch the latest news, undoubtedly hoping against hope to hear something good.[35]

Most of all, during those weeks Peggy watched the Japanese soldiers camped outside of her building, learning their routines, trying to understand them. She figured that something she saw or heard might come in handy someday. "Those ten weeks that I lived with Japanese all around the house, sleeping on the sidewalk out in front, going and coming, made me something of an authority on their behaviour [sic]," she concluded.[36]

AT THE BEGINNING OF THE occupation, Yay Panlilio offered a piece of advice to the women of Manila: "Let your children look back and remember how their mother faced war." Women were accountable for their actions during wartime, she believed. They had to choose a side; they had to take action. Yay made her decision. Since she could not travel with USAFFE to Bataan, she intended to provide them with useful intelligence from the heart of the occupation.[37]

Before Yay could undertake this work, she had to find a safe place for her children. The occupation would be dangerous, she knew, and if the Japanese found out she was working against them, they would come for her whole family. It was logistically impossible to send the three children to their father, her estranged husband Edward Panlilio, who was somewhere in the mountains of Palawan Island, over a day's journey from Manila. Yay approached an elderly American couple, Herbert and Janet Walker, currently exempted from internment because of their age, who agreed to take the children.

With that settled, Yay looked for an opportunity to help USAFFE. It turned up in the form of a renewed acquaintance with the Japanese businessman from Davao, Victor Takizawa. Taki, as Yay called him, resurfaced in Manila during the first week of the occupation as a member of Japanese military intelligence. She had not seen him since 1939, yet he greeted her cordially when they ran into each other on a city street. "I climbed out of the *calesa* [horse-drawn carriage] to answer Taki's greeting, and I walked swiftly, with dignity, to keep my knees from buckling. We met once again as friends," she remembered.[38]

Cautious friends, though, at least on Yay's end, since she was already thinking about how to utilize this relationship to USAFFE's advantage.

As Yay and Takizawa chatted in generalities about how the Filipinos were faring in these early weeks of the war, she tried to think of something that would intrigue him. Yay brought up the issue of the availability of food. "The people must eat," she said, and suggested starting a gardening program in Manila. He listened attentively—"Taki showed concern over my concern"—and telephoned Yay a couple of days later with a different offer. He had just been put in charge of radio station KZRH and asked if she would help him re-launch it as a Japanese-run enterprise. Yay jumped at the chance.[39]

The station, now using the call letters PIAM with the tagline "Voice of the Philippines," returned to the airwaves in mid-January 1942, lavishly promoting its news and music programs. In reality it was the mouthpiece of occupation propaganda. Yay was presented with broadcast scripts tightly controlled by Japanese censors, still she concocted phrasing Japanese translators would not fully understand but her English-speaking audience probably would. Using "innuendo so obscure sometimes that only mental telepathy could decode it," she cautioned Filipinos about how to deal with occupation forces, gave advice to the Voice of Freedom broadcasting from Corregidor, and passed along military information to USAFFE officers.[40]

Yay hoped that somewhere, somehow, Captain Ralph Keeler and Colonel J. K. Evans heard her broadcasts and recognized her voice. It was not much of a stretch for Yay to believe those obscure innuendos could be decoded by those listening from Bataan and Corregidor. The Voice of Freedom broadcasts had been initiated by her former newspaper boss, Carlos Romulo, now Major Romulo, aide-de-camp to General MacArthur and press relations officer on Corregidor. Yay figured Romulo knew her well enough to understand what she was trying to do. However it was Colonel Charles Willoughby, head of G-2 and a master of intelligence work, who first caught on. "That woman is trying to give us information," he said when he recognized her voice.[41]

When not on the air, Yay socialized with the Japanese who worked at the radio station, aiming for a nonchalance and camaraderie she did not feel. Close proximity to the Japanese made her nervous and scared. She later admitted, "Sometimes with the Japs at my elbow I was plain yellow."

Yet she knew them enough to sense when they had become suspicious of her. One day Takizawa made a point of showing her his military intelligence badge, as if to remind her of who he was and what he could do to her. Yay contemplated running but felt the time was not quite right. Every day she stayed, she was doing just a bit more to help win the war.[42]

Yay knew it would take a collaborative effort to defeat the enemy. She also knew other Manilans had started organizing underground anti-Japanese networks. Antonio Bautista, a lawyer and Dean of the Graduate School of the College of Law at the University of Manila, a fervent Filipino nationalist, headed one of them. In 1937, he and several other lawyers and journalists had founded the Civil Liberties Union (CLU), dedicated to agitating for immediate independence from the United States. But Bautista, even more worried about growing Japanese aggression in East Asia, in 1940 served as chair of the Committee for Democracy and Collective Security, which organized a boycott against Japanese goods. After December 8, 1941, Bautista and the other CLU members immediately organized for resistance work and soon became a clearinghouse for information and supplies for the guerrilla forces.[43]

Tony Bautista probably already knew Yay Panlilio and trusted her, otherwise he would not have approached her about taking advantage of her friendship with Victor Takizawa. Bautista's wife had been a reporter for *The Philippines Herald* and other members of the CLU were journalists, so Yay would have known them and shared many of their political beliefs. Her frequent conversations with Takizawa meant she could feed him misinformation provided by Bautista. This would give the CLU the time and opportunity to move guns and personnel through Manila with minimal interference from Japanese troops.[44]

According to occupation laws, these were capital offenses. In mid-January 1942, Manila newspapers published a list of "Acts Punishable by Death," which identified seventeen actions as capital crimes, including "intentionally falsely guiding Japanese forces." This was exactly what Yay and Bautista conspired to do with their misinformation. Their scheme could also be counted as rebellion against Japanese forces, espionage, and spreading false information and rumors, all printed on that list.[45]

Yay's work became more dangerous, and her time in Manila was running out. She held on until early March 1942. More and more enemy officers, especially ones who spoke English and dealt with intelligence matters, showed up at the radio station during her shift. They closely monitored Yay's broadcasts and paid attention to whom she spoke. They learned more about her past, that her work as a journalist had led to her acquaintance with important people, and occupation authorities wanted to know where those people were.

When the Japanese launched a search for her former boss, Carlos Romulo, Yay realized she had to get out of the city. Since she had worked with Romulo at the *Herald* and she did, in fact, know him well, the Japanese assumed she could locate him. Yay knew the Japanese would not accept an "I don't know" answer. She feigned a willingness to help them, suggesting Romulo was probably on Bataan, making it clear she would go there to look for him. The Japanese received her offer with such stony silence that Yay understood her freedom was at risk. "I knew when and how to go, and why. Not to die, but to fight and survive to fight again." She would not let the Japanese take her into custody.[46]

In her final radio broadcast, Yay dispensed with discretion and coded language. She directly addressed Carlos Romulo: "Wherever you are, put your feet up and listen. We to whom you were a father—we will keep faith." Yay played it cool in the station, acting like nothing out of the ordinary happened. "I snapped off the mike, faded in the music, waited the remaining minutes of my program to turn the booth over to the regular announcer," she remembered, "then tried not to walk too fast out of the station." Fifteen minutes later, the Japanese issued her arrest warrant.[47]

Before curfew Yay sought refuge at the home of her friend, Dedimia (Ding) Moskaira. Yay had known Ding for about a decade, but did not believe anyone would think to look for her there. Still, Yay would not risk staying in one place for too long. Over the next four days, she made her way through Manila, moving from house to house of generous friends, dressed in the most effective disguise she could manage. Instead of her usual pair of pants and a scarf to keep her hair off her face, Yay donned a dress and makeup and made sure she had a man's arm to hold onto whenever she ventured out on the street. In the guise of a proper, feminine Filipina, Yay left the city and headed for the mountains of Rizal province, about twenty-eight miles to the east. When the Japanese realized she slipped away from them, they began looking for her children to hold them hostage to force her surrender. And they offered a generous reward to anyone who would deliver to them her dead body.[48]

The locations of major U.S. military engagements, spring 1942. Library of Congress, Prints & Photographs Division, FSA/OWI Collection, LC-DIG-fsa-8b08336.

★ ★ ★

CHAPTER 6

BATAAN

A T THE END OF DECEMBER 1941, Claire Phillips was on Bataan, sticking as close as possible to Phil and the 31st Infantry. USAFFE's withdrawal from Manila was a delaying tactic—and everyone knew the Japanese would pursue, everyone knew a bloody confrontation loomed on the horizon. Three days before New Year's Eve, the 31st received orders to set up a defensive perimeter at Dinalupihan and Layac Junction, about ten miles in front of USAFFE's main battle position on Bataan.

Phil told Claire to pack up and leave Hermosa. He did not have to say more than that. Claire knew something big was about to happen; it was time for her to take Dian and go. With considerable unease she listened to stories of the relentless Japanese attacks: dive-bombing and strafing that USAFFE was powerless to stop. Yet every American radio broadcast she heard contained the same encouraging message: "Hang on to Bataan. Help is on the way."[1]

But how to hang on? When would help arrive? These crucial questions went unanswered as American and Filipino soldiers poured into the

Bataan peninsula via the Old National Road that runs along its eastern edge. Their vehicles tore up the landscape, spewing exhaust and churning the hard-packed soil. The noise carried for miles and for days as the men hauled the tons of supplies that were supposed to last until reinforcements arrived, whenever that would be. Eighty thousand soldiers, 6,000 Filipino civilian workers attached to the military, and 20,000 refugees all piled into the several hundred square miles of Bataan.

The enervating weather made the situation worse. Already humid and hot—around ninety degrees when the retreat from Manila began in December—the temperature steadily increased over the next few weeks. Malaria ran rampant on Bataan, plaguing its victims with fevers, chills, headaches, and hallucinations. Over the next weeks, the unexpectedly large military population of Bataan finished the quinine used to prevent and treat malaria. The lack of good latrines meant diarrhea and dysentery spread quickly, and the dearth of food brought scurvy and beriberi, diseases unfamiliar to most Americans. From the beginning, then, there were too many people and not enough food and supplies to go around.

USAFFE did its best to prepare for casualties on the Bataan peninsula. When medical personnel withdrew from Manila, they took as many supplies as possible, but they could not anticipate the circumstances they would encounter on Bataan. The two major hospitals set up in the southern part of the peninsula—Hospital No. 1 in the South Mariveles Mountains and Hospital No. 2 in Cabcaben—were equipped to each treat 1,000 patients. Within a couple of months, both locations would struggle to care for an additional 2,000 patients each. Before April 1942, 24,000 men were ill and many of them never had the chance to see a doctor. No supplies arrived—not medicine, not food, not even ammunition, and the surviving soldiers could barely hold their rifles, much less fight. The military situation was not playing out as USAFFE expected.[2]

The Japanese had not anticipated this scenario either. They began with sufficient troops and supplies and could easily bring in more of both, but they planned for a major battle in Manila. The Japanese considered the capital city the military prize, believing that whoever controlled it would rule the entire country. They could not conceive of a strategy in which

Manila was abandoned. They did not foresee USAFFE's retreat into the Bataan peninsula, had not imagined it would take so long to force their enemy into a corner. The Japanese never expected that in a few short months they would end up with so many debilitated prisoners.

Before the battle for Bataan began in earnest, Phil drove Claire, Dian, and Lolita to what he believed was a safe place at the northern edge of the peninsula. They traveled up from Hermosa, against most of the traffic, dodging the crumbling walls of bombed-out buildings and maneuvering around dead bodies in the road. Phil stopped at a hacienda near Dinalupihan, at the entrance to the Bataan peninsula, about three miles east of his company's new location at Roosevelt Park.

He introduced Claire to the owner's son, Juan Dimson, also the hacienda's manager. Fifty laborers and their families already lived on the property, but Dimson welcomed the newcomers. Over the next few days, Claire made herself useful to the community, nursing when needed, and both she and Lolita helped with housekeeping chores. When Phil visited, which was as often as possible, he showed up tired, hungry, and in a hurry. Given the military situation, it could not have been easy for him to slip away from his duties, even using the excuse of visiting his wife.[3]

On January 4, 1942, Phil informed Claire the Japanese had occupied Manila, and she immediately understood what this meant. "Then we will lose the islands," she replied. Later that evening someone telephoned the Dimson hacienda to report Japanese troops were rolling through San Fernando, only three hours away, the town where General Homma would soon establish his field headquarters.[4]

Claire pulled some supplies together for Phil and drove him back to his unit. "I had a woman's intuition that this parting would be the most difficult of all," she later recalled of that brief time they spent together in her blue coupe. Upon arrival at Roosevelt Park, Phil told Claire he had arranged for Juan Dimson to take her, Dian, and Lolita to the hills for safety. The battle would not reach that far, Phil predicted. Claire should stay there until he came for them. "One of the reasons why I love you so much," Phil said, "is because you are not a weakling." Claire could not bear to hear any more, and she pulled him close. When they disentangled, he said, "Take it easy, darling. I'll be seeing you."[5]

From the very beginning of the battle for Bataan, the 31st Infantry struggled. A member of its Anti-Tank Company, Private Leon O. Beck, later remembered how the Japanese artillery "just tore the hell" out of its line at Layac Junction on January 6, 1942. In the chaos of rapid retreat following the enemy artillery barrage at Layac, Beck did not know exactly where he ended up the next day, somewhere to the south near Abucay. Rumors flew about a desertion at a machine gun outpost, that those absconding men of the 31st left a note: "I will return when the American Army returns."[6]

By January 7th, the day of that alleged desertion, 50,000 troops, including John Phillips, were stationed on or along USAFFE's defensive perimeter at the northern edge of Bataan. Jack Utinsky was there somewhere, as was Gladys Savary's nephew, Edgar Gable. General Jonathan Wainwright commanded I Philippine Corps to the west, with Major General George M. Parker's II Philippine Corps to the east. The only edge USAFFE held at this point could be counted in heads—or feet—it had more boots on the ground than the Japanese. But the enemy, with near-equal troop strength, still dominated the air and sea.[7]

Captain Ralph Hibbs, the young doctor with the 31st Infantry, was also on Bataan with the rest of the 31st, exhausted from working on a fox-hole near the battalion aid station, about two hundred meters to the rear. On January 6th, Hibbs woke to the sound of shooting the next morning, 75 mm fire from the 23rd Field Artillery of the 1st Battalion. The Japanese quickly responded with larger guns, their tanks and foot soldiers soon to follow. American and Filipino forces pulled back.

Hibbs later recalled that daybreak on January 7th "found all three battalions of the 31st safely behind the MLR [main line of resistance]," with the 2nd Battalion in position outside the town of Abucay. The troops "languished in a huge bamboo thicket at the edge of a hillside banana grove, licking their wounds and trying to find something to rebuild morale." The 31st eventually lost that battle at Abucay, but the war was not over—far from it. Medical treatment, hurried and basic, was still possible. Hibbs found that his band of largely untrained first aid soldiers were tireless workers, "always innovative, fun-loving, but not always honest, which is not necessarily a detriment during war."[8]

The battle of Bataan was in full swing by January 9th as enemy troops attacked the II Corps along the Abucay line. The 57th Infantry of the Philippine Scouts and the 41st and 51st Divisions of the Philippine Army tried to hold off Japan's 141st Infantry and 9th Infantry, and had some success with the former. The next day the Japanese dropped leaflets signed by General Homma and addressed to USAFFE troops: "Your prestige and honor have been upheld. However, in order to avoid needless bloodshed and to save the remnants of your divisions, you are advised to surrender." Homma had orders to secure the Philippines by January 26th. He would be delighted to do so sooner rather than later.[9]

The Americans and Filipinos, however, did not have surrender in mind. That same day, January 9th, General MacArthur made his only visit to the troops on Bataan. In the midst of a dive bomber attack, Hibbs and Corporal Paul Decker, a tough but agreeable freckle-faced Oklahoman, took refuge in a foxhole as bombs fell nearby. When Hibbs looked up, he saw MacArthur walking along with his staff, seemingly oblivious to the attack. Hibbs clambered out of the foxhole and saluted the general. As Hibbs recalled after the war, "MacArthur waved to stay put, and swinging his riding crop vigorously with great strides, moved across the open meadow as more Zeros came winging in. A couple of his aides were tugging on his shirt tail telling him to get down. He shrugged them off and kept on walking."[10]

MacArthur's soldiers, at least in January 1942, shared that perseverance. Over the next few days, the Japanese struck with everything they had: heavy infantry, snipers, and coordinated amphibious attacks on "the points," slender tips of land protruding from the southwest end of Bataan. USAFFE held on well enough, but both sides were wearing each other out. On January 15th, Hibbs's battalion received orders to move to Abucay Hacienda to serve as a relief unit. For days on end, Hibbs's hands remained blood stained as he and his medical team struggled to treat the endless onslaught of wounded soldiers.[11]

Among those benefitting from the medical expertise of men like Ralph Hibbs was Lieutenant Colonel Irvin Alexander. During December 1941, the forty-six-year-old officer had worked at his quartermaster post at Fort Stotsenburg, about fifty miles north of Manila, until all moveable supplies had been sent to Bataan. Then he requested reassignment to an infantry unit. Alexander accepted the position of "Senior Advisor" to the Philippine Army's 71st Infantry, which he later described as "an under-strength regiment of which only a few of the officers and enlisted men had had more than a year of service." These men had spent most of that limited time attending to garrison administration; few had ever seen combat or were familiar with Bataan's terrain. They did not have enough weapons, and what they possessed was nearly obsolete. In other words, the 71st was a typical Philippine outfit.[12]

On January 17th, while Hibbs was wrist-deep in blood at Abucay, Alexander received orders to prepare a plan for the 71st Infantry. His men had to defend the Aglaloma Bay area, one of "the points" along the coast of the South China Sea, a particularly dangerous locale with water deep enough for an enemy landing and excellent roads leading to the important West Coast Highway. Alexander sustained serious wounds to his hands and chest as he pushed his company forward on January 24th to engage the enemy and try to hold them off. For his actions, he received two Purple Hearts and the Distinguished Service Cross. The injuries put him in Hospital No. 2 in Cabcaben for sixteen days before he returned to duty.[13]

At Hospital No. 2, Alexander may have been treated by Maude Denson (Denny) Williams. A native Texan in her early thirties who began work there on January 10th as an anesthetist, Denny also took care of shrapnel wounds, dysentery, malaria—anything the men came in with. Denny had served in the Army Nurse Corps in the Philippines in the 1930s and resigned in 1939 when she married Bill Williams, an employee of CalTex, a petroleum oil company. When the war started, Bill, a reservist, joined the army as a 1st lieutenant with the 31st Infantry, and Denny began work as a Red Cross nurse at Sternberg Hospital under Maude Campbell Davison, Chief Nurse of the US Army in the Philippines.

The Williams's situation resembled that of Peggy and Jack Utinsky. However, with the war underway Denny decided, like Claire Phillips, that staying in Manila was not a good idea. Denny wanted to remain as close as possible to the army and continue to nurse; that way, she would never be too far from her husband. She realized that her civilian status would make this difficult. She appealed for help to the officer in charge of coordinating medical operations in Manila, Colonel Percy J. Carroll of the Army Medical Corps. Carroll issued a card for Denny to carry that stated: "The bearer, whose signature appears hereon, is a member of the Medical Corps of the US Army and is a non-combatant left for the care of the sick and wounded only: Maude Denson Williams, nurse."[14]

Bill Williams departed with the 31st for Bataan the day after Christmas 1941. Denny wrote in her diary, "This is one day I shall always remember. I feel that I've lost everything." Believing she would do more good on Bataan or Corregidor, Denny prepared to leave Manila. Even with the card from Colonel Carroll, she was not sure how to get out of the city. Her husband solved that problem on December 30, 1941 by sending a soldier to escort her by car to Mariveles. Accompanied by her friend Marion Lapham and the Laphams' two children, every spare inch of the car packed with supplies, Denny headed south out of Manila and down through the Bataan peninsula.[15]

The timing of the trip must have been perfect, because they did not encounter a single Japanese bombing raid along the way. As Denny recorded that day in her diary, it was difficult to believe a war was going on at all. "The drive was a gorgeous one; all nature seemed to smile on the green woods and the turf. Sunlight rained its gold on the earth, which sent up rich, spicy smells, and the light wind flowing out of the east whispered about stirring things." Denny and Marion spent the next week setting up household along the banks of a river, a little out of the way, but close enough that Denny had easy access to Hospital No. 2. The next weeks passed in a blur of work, the casualties endless—including Irvin Alexander—and constant worry about her husband.[16]

Claire Phillips was probably also worrying about her husband as she, Dian, and Lolita traveled by truck with Juan Dimson's family to the hills just north of Dinalupihan. They wanted to get out of the way of the Japanese troops pouring into the Bataan peninsula. The refugees encountered heavy traffic on the highway because of USAFFE's constant movement and the many other civilians also looking for a safe place. After traveling along the main road, Dimson turned the overloaded vehicle onto a narrow road, little more than a dirt path that ended at a creek. From there, the journey continued on foot with carabao sleds hauling the supplies. It took more than four hours for the group to reach its hilltop destination: a small cabin abandoned by a local hunter. All seventeen evacuees crowded onto the floor to sleep for the remainder of the night.

When Claire woke up, Lolita, who was already making coffee, handed her a pair of binoculars and told her to look outside. "A most unpleasant sight greeted my eyes," Claire remembered, "red and white Nipponese [Japanese] flags flying over the little barrio of Dinalupihan, far below." Her first thought was relief that they had left just in time. Her second was for Phil, wondering where he was, if he had fared as well.[17]

She found out later that day. Juan Dimson slipped back into Dinalupihan during the early morning hours to retrieve his mother, who had initially refused to leave her home there. Dimson watched the remnants of the 31st Infantry pull out of town and happened to run into Phil. The soldier borrowed some money from Juan and gave him a note for Claire, addressed "Dearest Wife," in which he informed her that his unit was falling back to Balanga, a small town south of Abucay. He still planned to come for her, and he wanted her to stay put. He also asked her to reimburse Juan for the loan.[18]

To ease their overcrowding, the evacuees from Dinalupihan used scrounged materials to build a second cabin, providing Claire, Dian, and Lolita with their own room. Still, it was not a harmonious arrangement. On January 10th, worry over enemy patrols probing higher and higher into the hills caused the head of the Dimson family—the elderly and sour Rufino Dimson—to insist Claire separate herself from the rest of the group. He believed if the Japanese caught them with an American, they would all be killed, and Rufino was not willing to sacrifice his life for Claire. Dian and Lolita, however, were welcome to remain with the rest of the group.

At first, Claire complied. In a bamboo thicket about a mile away from the camp, she spent her days writing down her wartime experiences, "notes about what had transpired," she called them. She tanned her face and body, hoping to get dark enough to be mistaken for a native, though the chances of that were slim as her facial features did not resemble a Filipina at all. Isolation from the main settlement made Claire nervous. With every little noise, she thought the Japanese had arrived, and with every passing hour, she missed her daughter. After a few days, Claire offered to hire Damian, one of the young men in the group, to take her, Dian, and Lolita down to Mariveles at the southern tip of Bataan. She believed they would all be safer there, under USAFFE protection, out of the reach of the Japanese, and hopefully with Phil again. Damian, also itching to get away, agreed.[19]

Rufino Dimson grudgingly sold Claire a pound of rice and two tins of fish for their journey, and the small group headed south, keeping the "Sleeping Lady"—the long mountain range that marks Mariveles—in their sights as their guide. They took only what they could carry, staying high enough in the hills to avoid random Japanese patrols. Damian navigated by the large natural landmark because he did not know the area well. After two days the group ended up in Dinalupihan, only a mile away from their original encampment.

It was now late January 1942, and Claire had not managed to make her way back to the American lines or locate Phil. But luck was with her again. Though Rufino Dimson resented sheltering an American, others in the area did not share his hostility. The wife of Dinalupihan's mayor, Enrique Reyes, heard about Claire's predicament. She arranged for Claire, Dian, and Lolita to stay at the Sobrevinas family encampment, three miles further up into the hills. This group—Sobrevinas family members and hacienda employees—proved a congenial lot, and Claire recalled that the "little settlement composed of about twenty huts, was conducted on a cooperative basis, and with little discord."[20]

The pleasant company and the easy work—Claire contributed her medical skills as well as domestic ones—did not quite make up for the problems that plagued the camp, especially diseases, and a dwindling food supply. "Malaria, dysentery, and finally typhoid was the inevitable result," Claire remembered of their isolated location. "Our food supply had diminished and was now limited to rice, salt, and a small amount of sugar-cane." Two people died from illness, probably because of the lack of proper medication and sufficient nutrition.[21]

Eventually, sometime between mid-February and early March 1942, ten of the men in the camp set out to buy food from a neighboring settlement. On their way back, they stayed overnight in the barrio of Meite where they learned that Dinalupihan's priest, Father Eduardo Cabanguis, was sheltering three American soldiers. They had become separated from their unit during the chaos of battle, and two of them were ill. Though none exactly matched Phil's description, Claire had to find out for sure. She announced her intention to go along the next time the food expedition headed out. The men tried to talk her out of it, citing all of the dangers involved, but Claire remained adamant. She prepared for the trip the best she could, securing an adequate pair of walking shoes and stepping up her tanning regimen. Claire was determined not to be a burden to the men.[22]

She departed in early March, wearing clothing similar to her six male companions, tucking her hair inside an old rice sack that served as a hood. The group left the Sobrevinas camp at sundown for its fifteen-mile trip. They made a daring dash across an enemy-patrolled highway and hiked the rest of the way up the hill to Meite. Like the Malate priests in Manila who would become an integral part of the resistance community, Father Cabanguis, a small robust man in his mid-thirties, used his position in Meite to help USAFFE soldiers separated from their units. He welcomed the small contingent from the Sobrevinas encampment and arranged for Claire to spend the night in the home of a local woman. In the morning, a guide took Claire to a wild banana grove just outside the barrio, where the priest had told her she could find the soldiers.[23]

The grove was vast and dense with trees. Claire knew if she tried to look for the men, it would take hours. She could not bear to wait that long, especially if Phil was so close. Banking that the Japanese were not within hearing range, she called out, "Does anyone here speak English?" The response was quick and welcome, "Lady, what do you think I'm doing? Whistling 'Dixie?'" An American soldier stepped out from behind a thick tree trunk.

For a moment, Claire could not speak. The emaciated man standing in front of her in a tattered uniform had quick gray eyes in deep sockets and an incongruously well-maintained Van Dyke beard that added twenty years to his true age. He was not John Phillips. After the long, difficult trip, Claire had stumbled across Corporal John Peyton Boone, one of the men from the 31st Infantry that Leon Beck later claimed had deserted.[24]

Though Claire did not say it, part of her shock at seeing John Boone that day may have been because she recognized his name. Boone had made his living as an entertainment booking agent in Southeast Asia, and he regularly came to Manila. He happened to be there when the Japanese began bombing Luzon, and he decided to join the army. Since he had taken some college classes, he entered the 31st as a corporal.[25]

As soon as she introduced herself, Claire asked Boone if he knew her husband, John Phillips, but he did not. Perhaps the two soldiers who were with Boone might have some information about her husband, Claire suggested. Boone gave a low whistle and his two companions, equally gaunt, emerged from the banana grove. The one Boone introduced as Mramor, a slender man of medium height, about thirty years old, snapped at him for waiting so long to signal an all-clear. He was Private Rudolph J. Mramor, also from D Company of the 31st Infantry, a high school dropout and metal worker prior to his February 1941 enlistment. The other, Alabama native Private Marion F. Henderson, from G Company of the 31st, chimed in with a snide insinuation that Boone had not wanted anyone to horn in on his conversation with Claire.

Corporal Boone cut them off. Claire Phillips was an American lady, he told the men, searching for her husband. Did they know anything about him? Only slightly chastened, the privates admitted no, they did not. The three men sat with Claire for a while, smoking the cigarettes she brought, telling her what happened to them. Henderson and Mramor, suffering from malaria, shaking and sweating from the chills and fever, acted like they were headed for a nervous collapse. Claire felt uncomfortable around them. Boone, in much better physical and mental condition, did most of the talking. He told Claire the basics of their situation, how just before the fighting started at Mount Samat, he and Mramor had gone out on food detail, and when they tried to return they found the area overrun by the Japanese.

At 553 feet high, Mount Samat, located in the mountainous terrain running vertically down the midsection of Bataan, was a valuable position to hold. Whoever controlled it could place artillery on it to fire at strategic points along the lowland coast and the East-West Road below, commanding a great advantage. For weeks through January and February the fighting continued, both sides taking heavy casualties, with USAFFE managing to hold on.[26]

Once separated from their unit, Boone and Mramor could not find it again. They heard about Father Cabanguis who was already sheltering Henderson, and made their way to Meite. By the time Boone finished this brief version of his story, it was getting dark, the best time to travel, so Claire had to leave. She promised Boone she would come back in a week. They all agreed they should stick together until they reached the safety of the American lines, but they disagreed on how to find them. Claire was determined to head south, ultimately getting to the safety of the island fortress of Corregidor. Boone insisted that hiding out on Bataan until the Americans launched a new offensive would be the better bet. Claire figured they could come to terms at their next meeting.

Claire presented her plan of heading to Mariveles and Corregidor at that second meeting. Marion Henderson wanted to give it a shot, especially since he knew Corregidor had a military hospital. Malaria continued to torment him and he wanted medical treatment. Claire remembered Rudolph Mramor snapping back at Henderson, "Aw, go on. They wouldn't put you in the hospital. They throw AWOLs in the guard house." In the turmoil that was the battle for Bataan, there was a fine line between being absent without leave and inadvertently getting cut off from your unit. These men knew this, but they claimed they had been separated from their unit through no fault of their own. "I'm not AWOL. I got lost and you know it," Henderson said.[27]

John Boone, also anxious to justify his actions, explained to Claire the difficulties of reaching the American lines. This version differed slightly from the first he told her. As the fighting in the Mount Samat area began and he was separated from his unit, Boone and a few other soldiers hid for a couple of days so they would not get tangled up in the Japanese lines. Then they hired a Filipino who swore he knew how to get them safely back to the 31st. The Filipino turned out to be a Japanese sympathizer who led them straight to the Japanese. The two men with Boone got shot. After Boone met up with Mramor and Henderson, he hired another local guide—this one truly anti-Japanese—to help the trio get back to the 31st. They found themselves blocked at every turn; the Japanese were everywhere on Bataan.[28]

Mramor sidestepped the technicalities of the AWOL issue but also dismissed Claire's plan to head south. "I don't care if I ever get back to the Army. Leave me in the big, wide open spaces with nothing to do all day," he said. He had met a young Filipina and was thinking about marrying her. For Mramor, the war was over. He was not the only one who thought this way. Other soldiers separated from their units during the winter and spring of 1942 searched for places where they could remain hidden and live quietly until peace returned to Luzon.[29]

For Boone, however, the war had changed, not ended. Like Mramor, he did not like the idea of a journey to Mariveles; his recent hide-and-seek with the Japanese convinced him of the dangers of that kind of travel. Boone had his own plan, with its own kind of peril: to form a guerrilla force and continue fighting the Japanese on Bataan.

"I've been all over these hills," he said to Claire. "There are hundreds of Filipino and American soldiers lost and starving, but still with a burning yen to fight Japs. I believe that I could gather them together into an effective guerrilla band." If those guerrillas could keep the Japanese busy on Bataan, Boone reasoned, they would not be able to cause trouble anywhere else on the islands. Success with this kind of irregular warfare depended on someone reliable and loyal in Manila to send the guerrillas food, medicine, and clothing. Recognizing her appearance in the banana grove as a remarkable opportunity, Boone asked Claire if she would serve as his contact.[30]

In theory, Claire found Boone's plan solid, and she believed he was just the man to pull it off. "He reminded me of a greyhound, straining at a leash," she later wrote. She also remembered her promise to Phil to wait in the hills, and returning to Manila would only take her farther away from him. She declined Boone's proposal. Wishing the three soldiers from the 31st good luck, Claire returned to her own camp.[31]

Like Boone, who thought his best chance was hiding in the hills and participating in guerrilla strikes, and Claire, who wanted to move to the southern tip of the peninsula, where she believed she would be out of the enemy's reach, everybody on Bataan was trying to survive. Everyone had a decision to make.

Food continued to plague USAFFE. In January 1942, American and Filipino military personnel on Bataan were reduced to half rations of 2,000 daily calories, which most men did not receive. And the rations would be cut in half two more times before the fighting ended. As Ralph Hibbs later recalled, the quartermaster had stockpiled only enough food for 100,000 people for one month. Hibbs ate his rations twice a day, morning and evening. There was little variety: rice, oatmeal, evaporated milk, fish, and occasionally potatoes or beans, all flavored with pinches of salt or sugar. Through the month of January, his weight dropped from 178 to 140 pounds.[32]

Some companies struggled more than others. Irvin Alexander learned that on Bataan the 71st Infantry, as a Philippine Army division, had no established mess. He and his men had to find their meals where and when they could, and most of the half-ration they scraped together consisted of poor-quality rice. "A few times per week we received a small piece of meat," Alexander recalled, "but we never knew whether it was going to be horse, mule, or carabao. We were interested, because we soon decided that horse was better than carabao, and mule was better than horse."[33]

Soldiers took their food seriously not only because it was scarce, but because so much of it was new to them. Ralph Hibbs and the rest of the medical staff ranked meat according to palatability: *calesa* pony was the best, then mule, followed by horse and carabao, with monkey "a poor last." The hungry men ate just about anything. Some even hunted the beautiful tropical birds in the area—cockatoos, macaws, and parrots—whatever could supply the desperately needed calories and protein. The men figured out other ways to improvise as well. The Corps of Engineers constructed rice mills, a bakery was rigged by the quartermaster, fish traps were set, yet many still went hungry.[34]

The lack of food would be USAFFE's undoing. Without the ability to resupply, these soldiers were doomed and USAFFE leadership knew it. In the meantime they made the Japanese pay a heavy price for the territory they claimed. General Homma, with his orders to take the Philippines by the end of January, expected the campaign to last no more than fifty days. By the end of the first week of February, though, he had lost about half of his 14th Army. Many of his remaining men suffered from malaria, dengue fever, dysentery, and beriberi just like their USAFFE counterparts. Two weakened, exhausted armies, each trying to take the disease-riddled peninsula, were lying low in February trying to recuperate. Only one could realistically count on resupply and reinforcements.[35]

President Quezon, stunned at what the Japanese managed to accomplish and desperate to save his country, requested that President Roosevelt grant the Philippines independence. With national sovereignty, Quezon would declare the Philippines a neutral country, call on both American and Japanese forces to leave the islands, and demobilize the Philippine Army. These actions, Quezon believed, would save tens of thousands of lives and spare the Philippines further damage. American High Commissioner Francis Sayre approved the plan, and when General MacArthur sent it along to Washington he reiterated the dire situation of USAFFE. Roosevelt rejected the proposal, claiming the Japanese would never honor a declaration of neutrality, and he directed MacArthur not to give up.[36]

Willpower and hope could not win the battle of Bataan for USAFFE. The men needed food, medicine, and ammunition. Frank Hewlett, until recently the United Press Bureau Chief in Manila, now a war correspondent on Corregidor, recorded the catchy poem that many men on the peninsula repeated like a mantra:

We're the battling bastards of Bataan,
No momma, no poppa, no Uncle Sam,

No aunts, no uncles, no nephews, no nieces,
No rifles, no guns or artillery pieces,
And nobody gives a damn.[37]

By March 12, 1942, the battling bastards did not even have General MacArthur. President Roosevelt, adamant that MacArthur not give up, nevertheless did not want the general killed or taken prisoner by the Japanese. Roosevelt ordered MacArthur to leave the Philippines, to direct the Pacific war from the relative safety of Australia. The Philippine Navy was then merged into USAFFE, which was re-designated as the US Forces in the Philippines (USFIL).

With MacArthur's departure, General Wainwright took charge of USFIL, and now it was up to Wainwright and Bataan's new commander, Major General Edward P. King, to hold on. During the early morning hours of March 12th, Bill Berry issued the order to shut down the minefields around Corregidor so MacArthur's PT boats could get out. "I found myself uttering a silent prayer for our commanding general, whom I admired so much, and I wondered if I would ever see him again," he remembered. Not everyone shared Berry's admiration, especially those on Bataan. At an intellectual level the fighting men probably understood MacArthur's departure as tactical and rational. On a gut level they resented it. Using the tune of "The Battle Hymn of the Republic" Lieutenant Henry G. Lee, a twenty-seven-year-old college graduate and poet, penned new and aptly sarcastic lyrics:

Dugout Doug MacArthur lies ashaking on the Rock
Safe from all the bombers and from any sudden shock
Dugout Doug is eating of the best food on Bataan
And his troops go starving on.
Dugout Doug's not timid, he's just cautious, not afraid
He's protecting carefully the stars that Franklin made
Four-star generals are rare as good food on Bataan
And his troops go starving on.
We've fought the war the hard way since they said the fight was on

All the way from Lingayen to the hills of old Bataan
And we'll continue fighting after Dugout Doug is gone
And still go starving on.[38]

In late March 1942, the men had their rations cut again, this time from 200 to 1,000 calories. Soldiers stripped bananas and coconuts off the trees as flour, rice, and even carabao meat ran out, and they continued hunting jungle animals—deer, lizard, wild pig—until those populations were as depleted as USFIL's pack animals. The beautiful cavalry horses were long gone, sacrificed to the never-ending hunger. Pilfering ran rampant as soldiers tried to get food to their friends before the general population. Ralph Hibbs observed how men on supply trucks tossed "cartons of canned food and other goodies to their buddies at a prearranged destination. Even military police assigned to ride on the trucks didn't help. They had friends, too." Soldiers lost between ten to thirty pounds; their combat efficiency dropped anywhere from 20 to 45 percent.[39]

Just as threatening to the health of the Bataan defenders was the dearth of quinine and atabrine to treat malaria. Without enough mosquito nets to protect the men, malaria boomed to epidemic proportions. At the same time starvation set in at the end of March, about 1,000 malaria cases were admitted each day to the Bataan hospitals. Doctors and nurses, about 60 percent of whom suffered from the disease as well, sometimes had luck coaxing the symptoms into remission, but relapses were guaranteed without the proper medicine. When quinine tablets disappeared, doctors made do with the flaky powder of quinine sulfate.[40]

During February and March, while the opposing armies on Bataan mostly rested, trying to shore up for what was coming, Claire Phillips and the other civilians at the Sobrevinas camp in the hills of Bataan experienced their own days of hunger. Increased Japanese patrols coupled with the occupation of Dinalupihan hampered their ability to trade with other barrios, limiting their supplies. The men hunted whatever they could in the area immediately surrounding the settlement, bringing back snakes and monkeys for the women to cook until even those became scarce.

Claire contemplated sending Dian to Manila to stay with her friend Louise De Martini, now interned at Santo Tomas. However, Claire considered Dian her source of daily good spirits, and she could not part with the little girl. Instead, she adopted a wait and see attitude about the progress of the war. Waiting soon provided her with an opportunity to strike at the enemy. During the first two weeks of March 1942, a visitor to the Sobrevinas camp brought information that the Japanese had hidden an ammunition dump in Dinalupihan. Claire realized she was in a position to do something about it. She asked one of the young men, Bonifacio (Pacio) Reyes, to take a message to John Boone, who was holed up nearby in his own camp. Claire relayed the details she had and asked Boone if he had any ideas about how to destroy the dump. Boone replied that he would pass the information along to USAFFE headquarters on Corregidor.[41]

Every night for about a week, Claire looked down at Dinalupihan, expecting to see flames and hear the explosions of blown ammunition, but nothing happened. Tired of waiting, Claire, Pacio, and two other Filipinos decided to take matters into their own hands. She recalled:

[We] made a careful plan and went down the mountain at midnight. I stopped and waited about a mile above the town while the boys went on carrying kerosene-soaked torches.

After giving them ample time to reach their destination, I started a brush fire and kept it going to attract the Nips' attention. When they noticed it, and I saw their distant figures running in my direction, I scrambled higher into the bush and hid. Meanwhile, the three boys had circled the town, crept up and tossed their suddenly-lighted torches into the huts where the ammunition was hidden.[42]

The huts containing the enemy's ammunition went up in a hot popping roar. Then the foursome dashed back to the encampment, taking care to lay a false trail in case the Japanese pursued. The next morning, Claire found that they destroyed the ammunition *and* disrupted Japanese activity. Enemy soldiers temporarily moved out of Dinalupihan until the flames died out the following day, St. Patrick's Day.

Such a small victory could not be celebrated for long. Malaria moved swiftly through the civilian population on the heels of malnutrition, and an outbreak hit the Sobrevinas camp in the second half of March 1942. Claire nursed the afflicted as best she could. Within a couple of weeks, three people in her hut contracted malaria just as her supply of medicine bottomed out. Someone had to go to Manila for supplies and Carlos (Carling) Sobrevinas volunteered. His baby had contracted a particularly severe case so he believed it was his duty. "With a boldness born of desperation," Claire remembered, "he reported to the Japanese commandant in Dinalupihan, begged and received a pass to go to Manila on a Jap army truck. This permission was not so difficult to obtain, as it was the Nip policy to induce refugees to return and till their land, so that the Japs could reap the benefit of the crops."[43]

In an example of Japanese inconsistencies, Carling secured this permission. He was of military age and there should have been questions about why he was not in uniform. Despite Claire's explanation, there was no farming work in Manila, so it seemed odd the Japanese would authorize Carling's travel. Maybe the commandant hoped the favor would be paid back by Carling returning to an agricultural job. Still, luck was with the young man, and he got to Manila easily enough. He had difficulties returning with the needed food and medicine. Carling could not obtain a pass to officially leave Manila so he had to do it secretly, walking the last sixty miles back to the camp. In the two weeks it took him to make the trip, his child died and was buried.

Distressed over their baby's death, Carling and his wife decided they could no longer remain in the hills. They wanted to go to Manila for a fresh start. Carling's brother Doming would accompany them, to round up more food and medicine for the camp. The death of the Sobrevinas baby convinced Claire that Dian would be safer in Manila, so she asked Carling and Doming to take the little girl with them. Lolita wanted to go as well, since she was expecting her first child in about a month and was anxious to be closer to her husband's family. Carling agreed, but pointed out Dian and Lolita would need a place to live in Manila. Did Claire know who might take them in?

She offered the name of Judge Mamerto Roxas, referring to him as an old friend. In fact, Roxas was not only an old friend, but likely a relative of her legal husband, Manuel Fuentes. Japanese occupation officials allowed Roxas to retain his position as a municipal judge, so it was obvious to Claire that he had figured out a way to coexist with the enemy. When Carling proposed that Claire accompany them to Manila, she declined: "I appreciated the gallantry contained in his invitation because I realized full well that he knew the presence of a white woman would endanger the party immeasureably [sic]." Claire decided to stay on Bataan, still hoping to find Phil. Though she was convinced her decision was the right one for her daughter, "It was quite a bad moment for me when I kissed Dian goodbye."[44]

Claire was lucky she sent Dian away when she did. By the first week of April 1942, the lull in fighting Bataan had witnessed for the past two months would come to an abrupt end.

THE CHRISTIAN HOLIDAY GOOD FRIDAY fell on April 3rd that year, and it proved good only for General Homma and his freshly-reinforced troops. The pause in the military engagement had done little to help the American and Filipino soldiers—they were still starving, still crippled by disease. Homma encouraged American and Filipino leaders to surrender, to follow the lead of their counterparts in Hong Kong and Shanghai and accept "an honorable defeat." When they refused to even reply, the Japanese 14th and 21st Divisions set about destroying USFIL. Artillery, bombs, and fire came thick and fast, breaking American lines time and time again. After weeks of partial rations and untreated illnesses, USFIL soldiers lacked the strength to put up any kind of a fight. Even last-minute orders on April 7th to resume full rations from supplies shipped over from Corregidor could not help.[45]

More cautious than his superiors had been in December 1941, General Homma predicted victory in Luzon in a month, but this time the caution was unwarranted. He accomplished his objective in a matter of days. By the end of the first day of the Japanese offensive on April 3rd, USFIL had been well pummeled, the center of its defensive line almost gone, enemy soldiers pushing through everywhere. General King ordered the 31st Infantry back into this fray the following day, but four hundred of its remaining troops, already reduced by two-thirds, were initially unable to pick up their weapons and fight. Somehow they rallied, even launching a counterattack on April 6th that ended in a fiasco. Enemy forces overwhelmed the weakened remnants of the 31st, sending them fleeing into the jungle for their lives.[46]

The day after the rout, General King learned from his officers that only fifteen soldiers out of every hundred were in any condition for battle. The rest were not "effective"—they could not easily walk a hundred yards or scope a rifle to shoot at the Japanese. One of these men was Denny Williams's husband Bill, who was admitted to Hospital No. 2 on April 8th with a high temperature after being sick for days. That same night Denny and the other nurses were evacuated from Bataan to Corregidor, an ominous sign of what was about to happen. Even though she was a civilian, Denny had been working for the military and believed she should follow orders. She did not ask for permission to stay with her sick husband; she thought he might find it humiliating.[47]

Denny Williams described the evacuation from Bataan as "a seething bedlam." The road to Mariveles was jammed with trucks, tanks, and soldiers on foot, all advancing a few meters at a time in a complete blackout. Explosions ripped through the night sky. At Mariveles, Denny learned she missed the last boat that had taken the other nurses across the channel to the heavily fortified Corregidor island. She climbed into a rowboat filled with soldiers. After abandoning this vessel for a yacht, they landed on Corregidor at noon, in the middle of an air raid. There, inside the safety of the Malinta Tunnel, where USFIL was headquartered, Denny joined the other 110 people who made it from the two Bataan hospitals. "The trip has left us exhausted and nerve wracked," she wrote in her diary.[48]

Bill Williams had been left behind on Bataan, along with an estimated 22,000 sick or wounded. Hundreds or even thousands of weak and ill soldiers simply walked away from the fight. General King, recognizing the rapidly deteriorating situation, found himself forced to consider whether USFIL could gain any advantage by continuing to oppose the Japanese.

He concluded they could not. Without informing General Wainwright, and despite orders from General MacArthur to never surrender, King decided to do just that on April 9, 1942. It was his only chance, he believed, to save his troops.[49]

General Homma's senior operations officer, Colonel Motoo Nakayama, was irritated with King—who only offered to surrender the troops on Bataan and who wanted to talk terms. The defeated general expected negotiations, but Motoo wanted an unconditional surrender to come from General Wainwright and to apply to all American troops in the Philippines. King reiterated: he only commanded the troops on Bataan, and he agreed to surrender them unconditionally as long as he had assurances his men would be well treated. Motoo responded to King through an interpreter, "We are not barbarians."[50]

CHAPTER 7

AFTER THE SURRENDERS (OR "IS THE WAR OVER?")

WHILE AMERICAN AND FILIPINO FORCES ON BATAAN fought in vain to hold off the Japanese in early April 1942, Claire Phillips battled malaria. The Sobrevinas family tended to Claire for a week as she shivered under four blankets despite the ninety-degree heat outside, her temperature fluctuating between 102 and 105 degrees. They fed her wild fern tea, a folk remedy substitute for the long-gone quinine. The night before Claire's fever broke, she had nightmares about sprinting through burning forests with John Boone and his guerrillas, getting lost and running in circles.

After Claire woke up on April 10th, as her surroundings came into focus, she registered the uncommon quiet: no machine guns, no howitzers, no planes buzzing overhead. "Is the war over?" she asked Mr. Sobrevinas. He explained that the night before, Bataan had fallen, but that Corregidor still held. "If you listen closely you may still hear their big guns." It was something to cling to, and as long as Claire heard the artillery fire from the Rock she believed the Americans had a chance. She also told herself that Phil may have made it to Corregidor to continue the fight from there.[1]

Though the worst of the malaria was behind her, Claire had to be careful about her recuperation. The first time she felt her strength return she got out of bed, puttered around the hut, ate the food Mrs. Sobrevinas prepared for everyone, and promptly relapsed. She went back to bed for another week. Doming Sobrevinas returned from Manila a few days after Claire left her sickbed for the second time, around April 20th, nearly two weeks after Bataan's surrender. In addition to an impressive supply of food and medicine, he brought an encouraging update about Dian: the little girl did very well on the trip to Manila and made an easy transition into the Roxas household.

The judge sent along a letter to Claire, telling her that under no circumstances should she travel to Manila. It was much too dangerous, and there was no compelling reason to do so, especially since Dian was doing just fine. Reassurances about Dian's welfare eased Claire's mind about her maternal responsibilities so she could concentrate on getting better.

ELSEWHERE ON BATAAN, General Edward King's surrendered troops endured a forced hike north out of the peninsula and into a prison camp. An excruciating journey of sixty-six miles that involved nearly 80,000 men, it would become known as the Bataan Death March.

More than a year earlier, in January 1941, Japanese General Tojo Hideki ordered a copy of the Field Service Code, or *Senjinkun*, distributed to all infantry soldiers. The Code had been prepared under Tojo's direction by the Ministry of the Army, and it gave a contemporary, militaristic twist to the old code of the samurai known as Bushido. *Senjinkun* emphasized discipline and obedience, encouraged soldiers on the battlefield to always attack, never retreat, and never surrender. Fight and win or lose and die were the only options for Japanese soldiers. Inculcated with these beliefs, it was no wonder the Japanese had little to no regard for the tens of thousands of American and Filipino troops who surrendered on Bataan in April 1942. East did not meet West in this matter.[2]

The Japanese anticipated taking prisoners of war, but they had not planned for so many so soon. Camp O'Donnell, the former Filipino training post near Capas, about sixty-five miles north of Manila, was not scheduled to be ready until April 20th to receive about 50,000 POWs. General Homma needed to use Bataan as a base for launching the invasion of Corregidor, so the peninsula had to be cleared of all prisoners as quickly as possible. Homma approved the plan to march the captives out of Bataan, north on the Old National Road to the railway hub in San Fernando, approximately sixty-six miles from Mariveles. The sick and wounded would travel by truck, with stations for food and medical aid set up along the way. From San Fernando, the POWs were to take a train to Capas in Tarlac Province, ending up in Camp O'Donnell.[3]

This was the plan. But instead of no more than 50,000 prisoners, Major General Kawane Yoshikata, in charge of the march north to San Fernando, faced nearly 80,000 men so debilitated they could hardly walk. The two hundred trucks he had allotted to move the sick and wounded were woefully inadequate. This already grim situation turned catastrophic because of Japanese attitudes toward prisoners of war. Many officers resented taking any prisoners at all. Colonel Imai Takeo of the 141st Infantry received a telephone call from a division staff officer who ordered him to kill the prisoners, but Imai refused to do so without written confirmation, which never materialized. Nevertheless, Japanese soldiers began killing some prisoners in Mariveles, random, unpredictable attacks that continued as the enfeebled human convoy dragged its way from the southern tip of the Bataan peninsula to San Fernando.[4]

From the day of the surrender, USFIL troops understood the brutality of their conquerors. The chaos of the situation—the fact the surrender only involved the soldiers on Bataan so fighting continued elsewhere in the Philippines—meant both captors and captives were jumpy, the Japanese quick on the trigger. Enemy troops looked down on the Americans and Filipinos. In their view, honorable soldiers did not surrender; dishonorable ones deserved to be mistreated.

Despite the surrender, Ralph Hibbs continued his work at Hospital No. 1 on Bataan. At mid-morning, Japanese dive-bombers dropped their loads right on the hospital compound, ignoring the prominent Red Cross sign. Hibbs flattened himself into a roadside ditch before dashing to help in a ward that had taken a direct hit. "We heard cries for help as we hurried to the unbelievable carnage. At least thirty were killed and fifty men suffering from malaria and dysentery now had fresh shrapnel wounds," he recalled.[5]

On the morning of April 11th, Hibbs watched as most of the prisoners formed a column, prodded by bayonet-wielding Japanese, heading north. So Hibbs, along with Corporal Paul Decker and another corpsman, fell in with the crush. They walked about two miles to an area known as the Zig Zag, a slender winding path leading up a hill to the jungle. It dawned on Hibbs that the Japanese did not expect their prisoners to survive this hike. Taking an enormous risk, he and his two companions slipped into the jungle unnoticed and made their way back to Hospital No. 1 where they resumed treating patients. The Japanese did not seem to find it unusual that medical personnel had remained behind and did not object to their presence.

Lieutenant Colonel Irvin Alexander, who had been present at General King's headquarters when King made the decision to surrender, returned to his camp with the 71st Infantry to await the enemy. An interpreter showed up the next day, April 10th, and told the captives they would be going to Mariveles to join the other POWs there, a sixteen-mile trip they made by car. From there, Alexander and the others began their trek north on April 13th. After the first couple of miles or so, they hit a bit of luck. A Hawaiian-born Japanese soldier at a roadside supply camp invited Alexander and a few others in for tea. When they finished, the soldier arranged transportation for the prisoners on a bus to Orion, sparing them ten miles of marching.[6]

Such kindnesses often meant the difference between life and death. Alexander arrived in Orion in relatively good shape and stayed there for a day and a half before lining up for the most grueling part of the hike. "We were formed on the road in groups of one hundred and in columns of four," he remembered. "Three mean-looking Nip sentries, all privates who spoke no English, were assigned to each group. Each sentry carried a loaded rifle with fixed bayonet."[7]

The worst day of the march was probably April 17th. Up early only to stand in formation for hours, the prisoners did not start walking until late in the morning. It was already hot—no clouds, no wind, no hint of shade along that endless road. The water some lucky prisoners carried in canteens ran out quickly, and guards allowed few opportunities for refills. Those who tried to reach water supplies without permission were beaten, kicked, bayoneted, shot. Men who could not walk fast enough or took too long getting up from the rare rest periods received the same treatment.

Alexander struggled to his feet after the third rest period. He did not think he had the stamina to go on, but his friends would not leave him. One gave him a salt tablet, another a small piece of candy, then they propped Alexander between them so he could hold on to their arms as they set off again. Over the next six miles, Alexander's men took turns keeping him on his feet, knowing that if he fell or lagged behind, he was dead.

A makeshift camp had been set up for the prisoners in Lubao, twelve miles short of San Fernando, the railway town that provided entrée into Bataan. Alexander remained there for a couple of days to shore up his strength to walk the last stretch. When he arrived in San Fernando, he noted the rail station, a few factories, and some two-story buildings that contained apartments. Instead of receiving billets in those buildings, the prisoners were corralled into a cockfighting arena. After two days, Alexander was loaded into a steel boxcar with about eighty other men for the three-hour, thirty-mile trip to Capas. From there they walked the final eight miles to Camp O'Donnell.

Exhausted and close to death, Alexander made it to the camp because of his friends. Estimates suggest that between 5,000 and 11,000 men died on the hike along the Old National Road. Prison camp—the unprepared O'Donnell—loomed ahead, bringing its own set of life-and-death challenges for the survivors of the Death March.[8]

BATAAN HAD SURRENDERED, but not Corregidor. Not yet. The Rock held through April, a sign the United States had not been beaten, and a blunt reminder to the Japanese they lacked control of the valuable Manila Bay. It did not take long, however, before the myth of the impregnable

Rock unraveled. Bill Berry, stationed here since the navy's retreat from Manila in January, understood the surrender of Bataan made the situation on the island critical. "The Japanese began hauling in artillery pieces to the coast, just two miles away across the strait. From there, they could keep up an unhampered and continuous pounding of our tiny island. We were trapped. We knew it, and the Japanese knew it," he recalled.[9]

The USFIL troops were trapped because of a decades-earlier miscalculation. The big guns, once considered so modern and effective, were, as was now painfully obvious, positioned in the wrong direction. Military experts had expected an attack from the sea, so the gun batteries, mounted on immovable concrete pads, were situated to shoot east at Manila Bay and west toward the South China Sea. They could not simply be redirected at Bataan. The Japanese, now in control of the peninsula, only had to haul their big weapons to the coastline, point, and shoot, keeping up the barrage until the Rock shattered.[10]

Ralph Hibbs witnessed the enemy action from Hospital No. 1 on Bataan, where he remained through the siege of Corregidor, until June 24, 1942. "Daily there were terrific artillery duels between 'The Rock' and the Jap batteries on the Bataan Peninsula," he remembered. "The Jap guns were placed near us, but a greater concentration was in the region of Hospital #2." Hibbs kept working, kept his head down, and luckily for him—for the time being at least—the Japanese focused their attention on Corregidor.[11]

Under constant Japanese bombardment, conditions on the small island got tougher. Food rations were halved in an attempt to stretch the existing supply. Nothing more could be brought in. The troops on Corregidor, who had up to this point lived under tolerable conditions, now got a taste of what had happened to their counterparts on Bataan. Bill Berry ate a lot of horse meat, tinned asparagus, and canned peaches and apricots. There was still milk, though only powdered, and sugar was plentiful. Berry lost thirty pounds; still, he felt fit and energized.[12]

To Gladys Savary's nephew Edgar Gable, even these reduced rations probably tasted heavenly. Gable had spent the first months of 1942 escorting convoys around Luzon, especially through Bataan. When that surrender was announced, he managed to get on a boat to Corregidor where he manned an anti-aircraft battery and kept his strength up by eating a variety and quantity of food unheard of on Bataan.

In addition to the stragglers like Gable, more than 6,000 troops from several Coast Artillery Regiments operated the mostly misdirected big guns. Corregidor was also defended by nearly 4,000 men of the US 4th Marines, who since December 1941 had been preparing a beach defense. They strung barbed wire, set tank traps, dug trenches, dropped sea mines, and installed machine gun nests along 4,000 yards of beachfront. The marines were joined by the Provisional 4th Tactical Battalion, created out of the military personnel who escaped from Mariveles and the Regimental Reserve. They all prepared themselves, and the island, the best they could.[13]

After the surrender of Bataan, Corregidor endured heavy pounding from the more than four hundred enemy howitzers over on the peninsula. Within a matter of days, the Rock's North Shore batteries were nearly obliterated. Denny Williams, working in the hospital in USFIL's fortified underground headquarters in the Malinta Tunnel, wrote in her diary, "That was indeed all that the Rock could do now, stand and take its beating, stripped, scarred, pounded mercilessly from every side, as lonely as a punch-drunk boxer." The bombardments took a toll on the Corregidorians. Denny noticed the men who worked outside, especially the battery crews, resented those whose work kept them inside the relative safety of Malinta. Troops who came over from Bataan were too worn out to do much of anything or care much about anything. Denny thought they had given up already. And the women on Corregidor were no angels. Nurses frequently snapped at others out of fear and exhaustion, and civilian women, many of whom were wives and daughters of military personnel, had to be ordered to lend a helping hand.[14]

Corregidor would have been in Japanese hands even sooner if General Homma had not found his 14th Army low on landing barges and his men suffering from another round of malaria. By April 24th an invasion force bound for the small island organized along the east coast of Bataan. Bombing recommenced the next night, accompanied by crippling artillery fire on April 29th. This relentless assault continued into the first days of May. The landing barges Homma had been waiting for finally arrived, and were prepared and launched at midnight on May 5th. Bill Berry realized it was all over for USFIL when he received instructions to help dump millions of dollars' worth of silver pesos into the bay to prevent it from falling into Japanese hands. Though Berry understood he had a slim chance of surviving, he had not given up. Instead, he took up "an attitude of rock-hard defiance."[15]

Marines did what they could at the beaches to repel the Japanese invasion forces. It was not enough to hold off the eight hundred enemy troops who landed on May 5–6, bringing two light tanks and artillery with them. Taking cover in the cliffs above, Americans and Filipinos dropped grenades and fragmentation bombs on the landing parties, and fired at them with rifles and any other weapons at their disposal. The battle continued through the early morning hours. Jack Utinsky was among Corregidor's defenders; Edgar Gable, too, until the Japanese onslaught forced him to retreat to the Malinta Tunnel.[16]

Despite sustaining huge casualties, the Japanese made their way to the tunnel on the morning of May 6th. Adding to the horror of another imminent surrender, the enemy soldiers positioned in front of the tunnel's east entrance carried flamethrowers. Behind them a tank idled. Eight hundred Americans and Filipinos had already died in the fighting, another 1,000 lay wounded. Corregidor was finished.[17]

The ceasefire came at noon, and General Wainwright prepared for a formal surrender at midday. The men inside the Malinta Tunnel stacked their weapons in a pile outside. Colonel Paul D. Bunker, commander of the 59th Coast Artillery, lowered the American flag at the entrance. Wainwright had ordered Bunker to burn the flag, but the sixty-one-year-old career army officer could not bring himself to do so. Bill Berry remembered what happened next: "A large pair of scissors was brought out, and the flag was cut into small pieces and scattered in the wind. Men were crying." Not all the pieces scattered. Bunker kept a square folded away in his pocket where it remained until he died the following year in a POW camp.[18]

Still holed up in her Manila apartment and determined the Japanese would not find her and force her into an internment camp, Peggy Utinsky clung to the hope that Corregidor would hold fast against the Japanese. She believed what she heard from radio broadcasts, the ones she listened to sparingly, quietly, alone in her apartment. Reinforcements would arrive in time, Corregidor would stand, and the Japanese would finally be driven out. All of this proved to be false. Instead, on May 6, 1942, Peggy remembered the Voice of Freedom announcing, "The men of Corregidor have fought a gallant fight. Here they expected to come to a little rest. They found a seared and burning hell. Here they fought on and on, expecting the help which never came. Now they must surrender, leaving their dead."[19]

Peggy wondered if her husband would be part of this surrender, if he escaped from Bataan only to be caught after all. She found the uncertainty almost maddening. Peggy nearly missed the part of the news story describing how General Wainwright would be boarding a small launch outfitted with a white flag to surrender to General Homma back on Bataan. Then the broadcast ended and there was silence from Corregidor. Peggy later wrote, "I looked around the apartment and knew what had to be done. I was going to Bataan to look for Jack."[20]

ON THE DAY OF CORREGIDOR'S FALL, Gladys Savary was preparing for a visit from some American women. They were out on day passes from Santo Tomas, which camp officials allowed on a case-by-case basis, usually for medical reasons. It was one of the last such social occasions Gladys would host at the Restaurant de Paris. About three weeks earlier several Japanese occupation officials showed up, informing Gladys she could no longer own the establishment. She was welcome, however, to stay on as manager with her regular staff. This offer hinged on certain conditions: "I had to run it as they wanted it run—as a night club, and heaven knows what else." The "what else" Gladys assumed meant a brothel.[21]

A Russian woman employed as an interpreter for the Japanese added extra pressure on Gladys to give up the restaurant. She knew Gladys had worked for the Free French Committee in Manila. She warned Gladys if the Japanese found out, they would take her to Fort Santiago, site of the former headquarters of the US Army in the Philippines and now used as the Kempeitai's headquarters. Gladys took this as a threat. She was certain the woman also spied for the Japanese, and was unsure what else the Russian knew about her activities and allegiances. Gladys would not mind internment in Santo Tomas, but the idea of imprisonment in the Fort terrified her.

She knew her days at the restaurant were numbered. "I dickered along with them for some weeks, but eventually had to give in." Gladys agreed to sign the place over to the Japanese, but asked for a month to find new living quarters. For a few weeks she was a guest in her own establishment, under the close eye of the Japanese. Yet she continued her aid work, visiting patients in several Manila hospitals, making sure they had everything they needed. Every day she sent a supply cart to her friends in Santo Tomas, even launching a laundry service.[22]

On May 6th, Gladys's kitchen staff at the Restaurant de Paris prepared lunch for the women out on their day pass from internment. Gladys wanted them to have an enjoyable afternoon—a game of mah-jongg would follow their meal—so she did not reveal the news about Corregidor she had heard on the radio just before their arrival. When the Santo Tomas guards returned to put the women on the bus back to the camp, someone walked into the restaurant and announced that General Wainwright was surrendering. The war was at an end for Americans in the Philippines.

"My life seemed over," Gladys remembered. "*My people, my country,* asking for terms from a nation we have always considered definitely inferior." She also wondered what the surrender would mean for the immediate future. "Would the Filipinos now agree wholeheartedly with the Japanese idea of Asia for the Asiatics . . . and plunge wholeheartedly into cooperating with the Japs?"[23]

Wainwright was taken to the former US Army airfield at Cabcaben on Bataan to surrender to General Homma, who refused to accept anything less than a complete surrender: Corregidor plus the remainder of the American and Filipino troops throughout the Philippines. Wainwright complied; he had no choice if he hoped to save his men. The American general was relocated to Manila and kept there while the Japanese decided what to do with him. Overall, they ended up with between 10,000 and 11,000 prisoners, probably 10,000 more than they planned on. About 7,000 were

US military personnel, the remainder Filipino civilians. The conquerors had no clear plan for dealing with the POWs beyond moving them out of the tunnel complex. It looked like the Bataan Death March all over again.

Because they knew what happened on Bataan, the prisoners were uneasy about how their captors would treat them. Bill Berry and a group of eighty-four other prisoners were ordered into formation at the front of Queen Tunnel, at the southwest corner of Malinta Hill. They marched until they reached a small clearing where the Japanese gave an ominous order: halt and strip. As soon as all the men shed their uniforms, the Japanese instructed them to get dressed again and marched the prisoners right back to where they started.[24]

Lieutenant John M. (Jack) Wright, Jr. of the 91st Coast Artillery Corps was also part of this surrender. A California native and 1940 graduate of West Point, he arrived that same year at Fort Mills on Corregidor to command a four-gun 155 mm battery. His battery fired the last artillery round on the Japanese before Corregidor surrendered. When Wright returned to the Malinta Tunnel, he could hardly believe his eyes. "American generals and privates, Filipino soldiers and civilians, American nurses, Japanese officers and soldiers, and our wounded and theirs," he wrote, "everyone pushed and jammed, shouted orders, called for friends, searched for loot, bolted food, got drunk on hoarded liquor (a select few), hid personal effects in every crack and hole, and wandered around aimlessly to contribute to the confusion."[25]

Despite the disorder, someone had the presence of mind to begin taking care of the dead bodies, burying some, burning others. On the morning of May 8th, the Japanese moved the living. The American and Filipino prisoners marched in columns along a winding road, still littered with dead American bodies, to the 92nd Coast Artillery tractor garage area on the south shore of Corregidor, east of Malinta Hill. Here, close to 11,000 prisoners lingered outside on a section of the beach that measured about 1,500 feet long by five hundred feet wide. Jack Wright and his fellow POWs could not take more than a step or two before bumping into someone else.[26]

Prisoners in the garage area were separated by nationality: Filipinos in one fenced area, Americans in another, where the Japanese set up a registration center for the approximately 7,000 men. Each provided his name and serial number, and in turn a prisoner of war number was painted on the back of his uniform shirt or pants. The Japanese expected military discipline to continue. Once counted, each group of 1,000 enlisted men was put under the command of an American colonel, with every grouping of one hundred assigned an additional lower-ranking officer. Prisoners had to salute or bow to the Japanese.[27]

As usual in the Philippines this time of year, temperatures were searing. There was no shade on that beach, and for at least the first three days, no shelter. The prisoners were not appropriately clothed, food and water were in short supply, and shell holes functioned as toilets. As Wright remembered, "We existed on the crowded beach for sixteen days. During that time there were probably about thirty deaths. We existed in spite of the bad treatment, the filth, the lack of water, and the lack of any consideration on the part of the Japanese for our needs as human beings."[28]

Because of this lack of consideration, Jack Wright volunteered for a variety of work details in and around the Malinta Tunnel. It allowed him time away from the overcrowded tractor garage area while providing the opportunity to scrounge food and building materials. The remains of the canned food stockpiled in the tunnel prevented malnutrition from setting in on the beach. Pieces of wood and scraps of fabric were fashioned into small shelters that deflected the broiling sun. Some of these things Wright used for himself, some he traded or gave away to his fellow prisoners.

As he slogged through the mud and filth to take his turn with water and burial details, Bill Berry lost track of the number of days he spent jammed with the other POWs at the garage area on the beach. Like the other prisoners, Berry participated in a buddy system to safeguard supplies and pool rations. His included two friends, Dick Tirk and Phil Sanborn, originally executive officers of boats in the harbor patrol fleet. In addition to looking out for each other's welfare, the trio also began hatching an escape plan.

Even in these circumstances, communication continued between Americans in Manila and the surrendered troops on Corregidor. "Somehow my friends in Corregidor got in touch with me," Gladys Savary later wrote, offering up only the barest details of a system established after

USAFFE withdrew from Manila in December 1941. "Often runners of the underground appeared with notes for me to deliver to anxious wives whose husbands were caught there in the engineering squads." The notes themselves contained no specifics, for as Gladys pointed out, "It was far too dangerous."[29]

From the Restaurant de Paris, Gladys received these messages and arranged their delivery to the proper recipients, often performing that duty herself. She usually sent the runners back to Corregidor with supplies as well as replies. This way she kept in touch with her nephew Edgar. After the surrender he managed to get at least one message to her. "Awfully sorry about busniess [sic]," Edgar wrote, acknowledging he received her news that occupation authorities in Manila were confiscating her restaurant. He asked Gladys to send medicine, especially sulfa drugs, further confirmation that couriers still transported these items. "Individually the Japanese [sic] treat us O.K. but we're all afraid of sickness." He needed money, too, preferably in small bills. Edgar signed off, "Chins up."[30]

FOR CLAIRE PHILLIPS, HIDING OUT in the Sobrevinas camp at the northern edge of the Bataan peninsula and still weak from her nearly month-long bout of malaria, the fall of Corregidor came as a brutal shock. "I awakened with the same eerie feeling I had experienced when I emerged from my delirium," she wrote of the morning of May 6th. "The world was much too silent." It did not take her long to realize that the newfound quiet was because the big guns on Corregidor had stopped firing, or to figure that the island had surrendered. Claire now faced a bitter reality. Even if John Phillips had somehow managed in April to get from Bataan to Corregidor, now he was most likely a prisoner of war and he would not be coming back for her. Her grief sent her into a crying jag.[31]

Two of the men in the camp brought word that the Japanese had started moving their prisoners on foot from Mariveles, at the southern tip of the Bataan peninsula. The destination was rumored to be a prison either in Manila or at a place further north on Luzon, Cabanatuan. Claire calculated when the marchers would arrive in her vicinity, and stationed herself in the lookout with a pair of binoculars. "I focused them on a dark mass resembling a large herd of cattle, far down the road, which slowly took shape as it drew nearer," she wrote later. "I could now discern tall figures in the straggling middle lines, with small ones running along on both sides of them. Every now and then a little man would strike a tall one with the butt of a rifle, or kick him. Some of the tall men seemed to be holding up their comrades, and I saw a score of men stagger by, carrying their mates in obviously improvised litters."[32]

The sight of the abused prisoners spurred Claire to action. As she later explained, "I could not stand any more, and made my way somehow unassisted back to the hut. I lay there on the floor in the dark, thinking . . . thinking." That day, she thought in the short term. Might some of the wounded prisoners have been left by the side of the road? Would she be able to offer assistance? Could Phil be one of them?[33]

Bowing to practicality—she would be of no use to anyone if the Japanese caught and killed her—Claire waited for the cover of night. Several men from the Sobrevinas camp accompanied her down the hill to look for Phil and to rescue anyone else left behind. The search party came across five Americans, all dead, and buried the bodies. The men had to carry Claire back to her hut because she suffered another relapse. "I crept into bed without awakening anyone, and passed out cold," she remembered.

By the time Claire shook off the malaria in early June 1942, the situation on Bataan had stabilized. As the victorious occupiers, the Japanese wanted to win the loyalty of the Filipinos, to demonstrate a pan-Asian brotherhood through the Greater East Asia Co-Prosperity Sphere, so they encouraged families to return to Dinalupihan. Many did, and those who remained in the hills received frequent deliveries of food and medicine from friends in town with easier access to supplies. Claire felt safer than she had in months, and she had enough to eat. She also knew the Sobrevinases wanted to return to their family farm. The only reason they did not was out of a sense of obligation to her.

A visit from Father Eduardo Cabanguis, the priest from Meite who introduced her to John Boone, set the stage for Claire's return to Manila. Cabanguis arrived one day in June with news—not the best, but better than Claire hoped for. Just a few days before, as the priest passed the

Japanese commandant's office in Dinalupihan, he saw some Japanese soldiers bring in three captured Americans. He noticed one of them matched Claire's description of Phil, so he loitered for a while to listen to what the men had to say.

One gave his name as Phillips and asked Captain Muri for permission to fetch his wife and child from their hiding place in the hills. The captain refused, countering that if Phillips told him their whereabouts, he would send his men to retrieve them. Phil offered to go along with the soldiers, but was told he would have to stay in the town jail. Since Phil could not accompany the soldiers and would not be able to personally see to Claire's safety, he misdirected the Japanese to the hills around Olongapo, near Subic Bay. After the Japanese put Phil in jail, Father Cabanguis had made his way there and informed Phil that Claire was safe. Phil smiled at the news.

Though Father Cabanguis reassured Claire her husband looked well, she insisted on seeing for herself. "The priest smiled sagely and said nothing," she recounted. "I realized the folly of my remarks a moment after I had spoken, for I knew that Phil would not want me to come out of hiding and give myself up to the Japs after all we had done to avoid that eventuality."[34]

"Looking well" meant that Phil was sick but still on his feet. In April, Private Doyle Decker of the 200th Coast Artillery Regiment had met up with a man who was probably John Phillips. After the Bataan surrender, Decker, like many other men who became guerrillas or were at least determined not to become prisoners, took to the mountains. Decker and his friend, a mess sergeant named Red Wolf, stuck together, along with a Filipino named Nino and an officer named Long, who soon died. They lived as quietly as they could so as not to attract any attention, but food was scarce, illness set in, and there was no medicine. During a wave of sickness that claimed the life of a sergeant they had picked up, Decker remembered, "Phillips wanders into our camp. He has been alone for some time. He is glad to see other Americans."[35]

None of them knew what to do. The Japanese trawled through the hills looking for American stragglers, sometimes assisted by Filipinos, so Americans did not know whom to trust. Decker and the others kept moving, hoping to find a safe place as they slogged through rain, down uncertain trails, marching on less-than-full stomachs. "The trails are getting slick. I am wet and tired as I have been carrying my pack also Sgt. Phillips' pack as he is too sick to carry his pack. He does well to keep up," Decker later explained.[36]

Decker's group found shelter in a barrio for the night, changed into dry clothes, and ate supper before turning in. They woke at daylight and took off again, this time with a destination in mind, a place near Dinalupihan called Fassoth camp. Located below a waterfall and alongside a stream in the secluded foothills of the Pampanga and Bataan mountains, the camp had been set up by twin brothers William (Bill) and Martin Fassoth, Americans who had been living in the Philippines for years. The brothers first thought about joining the US forces on Bataan, but realized they might be of more use doing something else. So the camp they originally planned as a refuge for their families became a gathering place for soldiers separated from their units.[37]

The Fassoths gave Doyle Decker such a warm greeting he felt like he had "reached home at last." Life at the camp was better than anything he had recently experienced. He slept in a clean and dry bunk, and ate regular meals heavy on corn and meat cooked in a well-equipped outdoor kitchen. Decker stayed there for a few weeks and was so busy helping procure food he did not notice John Phillips's departure. But Decker *was* there when John Boone walked into the camp, and Doyle included Boone in the group of "wonderful men" he met at the place: "We kid him about being Daniel Boone." Boone invited Decker to join him when he moved on. However "wonderful" Decker found Boone, there was something he did not quite trust about the man. Decker declined the offer.[38]

He did not remain at Fassoths's for long. After John Boone's departure, Decker left as well because some new arrivals made Decker uneasy. Bill and Martin Fassoth insisted their camp focus on rest and recuperation, but some of the men who stopped there expressed interest in turning it into a base for guerrilla operations. Decker had not yet decided how he wanted to spend the remainder of the war; until he did, he preferred to be around fewer people. Decker and three others headed off across the mountains to Olongapo, near Subic Bay, the place Phil would later misdirect the Japanese in their search for Claire.

For more than a week, Father Cabanguis monitored Phil's detention in Dinalupihan. It took all of Claire's willpower not to sneak down to the village in the hopes of catching sight of him. With the romantic notion of one-last-look, she thought, "It seemed at times that if I could just do that, it would not matter what happened to me afterwards." Still, she waited, because she knew Phil would not want her to risk capture. When Cabanguis returned, he brought the news that Phil had been moved to San Fernando, the railway hub that had been the destination of the Death Marchers back in April.[39]

The priest managed to speak with Phil before he left Dinalupihan, though always in the presence of Japanese guards. Phil told Cabanguis that he and the two other men had been combing the hills nearby for nearly a month looking for Claire and Dian before a Japanese patrol caught them, about three miles from the Sobrevinas camp. Phil had heard Claire was suffering from malaria and was relieved to learn she had recovered. The Japanese had not been mistreating him, Phil claimed, though this may have been for the benefit of his captors' ears. They allowed him to pass his days tending to their horses.

Another five days went by before Claire learned of Phil's removal from San Fernando, either to Bilibid Prison in Manila or to Cabanatuan, further north. There was no longer any reason for her to remain in hiding with the Sobrevinases. She had come to a decision: "This was the last straw! Now all my doubts had vanished, and the miserably long days of watching and waiting were over. The time for action had arrived, and I knew what I must do." Claire sent a message to John Boone: "I'm going to Manila as soon as possible. . . . You know that I want to help. Long live the guerrillas!"[40]

BY MAY 1942, JAPANESE AUTHORITIES in Manila took it for granted that all the enemy aliens had been rounded up and interned. With the focus on Corregidor and the surrender of the rest of the Philippines, Peggy Utinsky felt safe enough to emerge from hiding: "The Japanese were no longer making such a business of stopping people on the streets to look at their passes. Now was my chance to get out of my apartment." Peggy not only wanted out of her apartment; she intended to leave Manila and travel to Bataan. After ten weeks holed up inside and with the news of Corregidor's surrender, she could not sit still any longer. She had to find out what happened to Jack. Still, travel for a lone American woman in Japanese-occupied territory was as difficult as it was dangerous. Not impossible, though, Peggy concluded.

Late one May evening, under the cover of darkness, she made her way to the Malate Convent, the site of Remedios Hospital, where she had worked as a nurse before the occupation. As Peggy later recalled, "I knew I was taking a big risk but I figured that if I kept away from the main streets and the lights, and was lucky in avoiding drunker soldiers, I ought to be all right." At least the route was familiar. Peggy headed to the convent to seek advice from her friend there, the Irish priest John Lalor: "If anyone in Manila could help me, I knew he was the man."[41]

The first item on Peggy's agenda was securing official documentation to allow her freedom of movement within Manila and elsewhere on the island of Luzon. She and Father Lalor talked about the possibility of a medical excuse. It was not an ideal solution. Peggy did not trust the Japanese to honor such excuses indefinitely—time proved her right—and she would worry about getting picked up and put in Santo Tomas. Moreover, Americans exempted from internment there were confined to the Manila city limits. Peggy admitted to Father Lalor that Bataan was her destination, where she hoped to find her husband. "Maybe I can dye my hair and stain my skin and go as a Filipina," she said.[42]

The priest pointed out that her facial features, especially her sharp nose, would give her away immediately, no matter what color her skin appeared to be. Then Lalor made the mistake of saying, "No American can get to Bataan"—a red flag to a bull. Peggy's mind was made up. Back in her apartment, she spent the rest of the night planning how to get to Bataan. The key, she realized, was nationality. Right now being an American was a liability, so, Peggy decided, "If I couldn't be an American, I'd be something else."[43]

Jack Utinsky's family had come to the United States from the Baltic. Peggy knew Lithuania had been occupied by the Germans since the beginning of the war and posed no military threat to the Axis powers. She assumed the Japanese would not consider Lithuanians enemy aliens. Besides, Lithuania did not have a consulate in Manila so the occupation authorities would not be able to prove she was not Lithuanian. A bit risky, Peggy knew, but it was the best she could do.

She decided to adopt the first name Rosena because it sounded Lithuanian to her. She would claim Kovno as her place of birth since it was the only Lithuanian city name she could pronounce. The fact she did not know a single Lithuanian word caused her some concern. Though she doubted she would run into anyone who actually knew the language, it could be the hole in her story that got her into trouble. She thought about her own childhood in Canada—brought to a wheat farm there, growing up speaking English—and made that part of Rosena's identity. With that basic storyline set in her mind, Peggy made one final decision: Rosena Utinsky would be a spinster. She spent the next few hours destroying everything in her apartment that identified her as an American, including items linking her to Jack Utinsky. This, more than anything else, almost shattered her nerve.

At the Malate Convent the following night, Peggy informed Father Lalor of her plan and asked how she could prove Lithuanian citizenship. She needed to find a Filipino—someone the Japanese would readily believe—willing to forge a certificate attesting to her fabricated identity, the priest told her. With this, a residence pass could be issued from Manila City Hall. Peggy enlisted the help of Cam Lee, her family's ex-servant who had checked in on her while she remained hidden. Lee tracked down a man who had worked as a chauffeur for the Utinskys who agreed to the scheme for a modest payment of twenty-five pesos ($12.50).

Reassured about her ability to travel around the city of Manila, Peggy had to figure out how to get to Bataan to find Jack. She had to be careful about arranging this if she wanted to minimize the risk of the Japanese looking too closely at her. Through resourcefulness and no small amount of luck, Peggy found an opportunity. On April 24, 1942, the office of the Commander-in-Chief of the Imperial Japanese Forces had authorized the reorganization of the Philippine Chapter of the American Red Cross as the Philippine Red Cross. The Red Cross headquarters remained at 600 Isaac Peral in Manila. It now operated under Japanese supervision, with four Japanese named to its Executive Committee. Just after the fall of Corregidor, the organization announced its plan to send a small contingent of medical personnel to Bataan to establish civilian relief hospitals and clinics. Peggy intended to be part of that group.[44]

Although she worked with the Red Cross prior to the occupation, Peggy did not know anyone involved with its new incarnation. She started looking for someone to recommend her for the Bataan expedition, which she assumed would be simple. The Red Cross needed trained medical personnel willing to make the trip, and she was trained and ready. "But it did not work out that way," she remembered. "I went from one person to another, begging to be introduced to anybody who could get me into that Red Cross unit. But in those days it was a hard matter to get anyone to vouch for his neighbor—or even his friend. It was not selfishness. People were just being careful."[45]

It was difficult to figure out who might be a collaborator, and Peggy's newly created Lithuanian nationality caused many people to shy away from her. The Filipinos she approached for help distrusted her. They did not know which side she—or any Lithuanian—was on. Finally, Peggy turned to Elizabeth Kummer, one of her oldest friends in the Philippines. A bespectacled, fifty-ish woman who wore sensible suits to match her sensible haircut, Elizabeth had been born into a German immigrant family in New York City in 1892. In 1915 she married Max Kummer, a German national from Dortmund, employed as a coffee bean merchant. That same year, Max filed US naturalization papers. By 1926, he had entered into a business partnership in Manila and he and his wife settled in the Philippine capital.

"A man without a country," Peggy observed of Max Kummer, who refused to embrace the Nazi Party, was unwelcome in the German Club in Manila, and was regarded with suspicion by other Germans living in the Philippines. Elizabeth and Max Kummer were, in fact, quietly supportive of the Allied cause. Peggy was so confident about Elizabeth's loyalties that she had no worries about approaching her. Peggy informed her friend about her intended masquerade and about her determination to find Jack. To do that, she needed help.[46]

Elizabeth telephoned someone she knew with the Japanese High Command and secured permission for Peggy to bypass a personal interview with the occupation official in charge of travel passes. Both women were relieved. Any conversation either of them had with a Japanese might result in a slip-up in Peggy's cover story. The consequences for her could range from internment to execution.

Elizabeth's contacts extended to the Red Cross. She personally introduced "Miss Rosena Utinsky" to one of the organization's Filipino doctors, Antonio G. Sison. In addition to his Red Cross duties, Sison headed the six hundred-bed Philippine General Hospital, located on Taft Avenue, which treated many of the civilian internees from Santo Tomas. The Japanese came to suspect that Sison used the hospital and his position to support resistance work, and in 1944 the Kempeitai arrested him. For nearly two weeks Sison was tortured, beaten, and starved before being released.[47]

But now, impressed with Peggy's nursing degree and experience, Sison was willing to take her story at face value—or perhaps he suspected her real identity and welcomed her assistance. He sent her to Dr. Thomas M. Gann, who ran the Institute of Hygiene for the University of the Philippines and was in charge of putting together the relief expedition to Bataan. Peggy was ecstatic. "When I actually held in my hand the papers that meant the High Command had given me permission to go to Bataan, I was ready to believe in miracles," she later wrote.[48]

In the brief morning cool of a typical May day, Peggy and nine Filipino Red Cross doctors and nurses left Manila. Piled into the station wagon loaded with medical supplies, they drove around the bay, toward the Bataan peninsula. Time and again Japanese soldiers stopped the jam-packed vehicle as it lurched along the roads leading out of Manila. They demanded to see the identity papers of the occupants, interrogating them about their purpose and destination. Each time, the members of the medical team struggled to contain their panic as they exited the vehicle for the required search. The doctors stood erect, their hats placed over their hearts, as if trying to prevent the Japanese from hearing their racing heartbeats. The nurses, all Catholics, kept making the sign of the cross, silently praying to God to look out for them. None of them uttered an extra word, none of them made a superfluous move. They tried to look just like what they were: humanitarians on a relief mission.

Finally, Thomas Gann, the Filipino doctor in charge of the expedition, turned the station wagon west from San Fernando, toward the Bataan peninsula and the small town of Dinalupihan, near where Claire Phillips had been hiding. From there the vehicle chugged south on the Old National Road, traversing the eastern coast of the thirty-mile-long outcrop of land, as the team scouted for the most suitable place among the many barrios and larger towns to set up a makeshift hospital.

In normal times they would have passed through a shifting flora landscape: tangles of bamboo, rigid stalks of cane, patches of razor-edged cogon grass, rice paddies. Springtime on Luzon meant white sunshine and brutal heat, but also bursts of lantana, bougainvillea, gardenias, and orchids—a paradise for the senses even if the temperature called to mind quite the opposite place. But now, after the surrenders, any trace of the natural vegetation and breathtaking flowers was gone. Only the earth churned up by all of those military vehicles, now sun-baked into hardness and packed beneath a thin veneer of dust, remained. And, unavoidably, the bodies.

Peggy remembered when they reached the portion of the road where the Death March had taken place: "We came so soon after the surrender that the dead bodies were everywhere. There was no evidence that a battle had taken place, yet thousands had died here. Bodies lay all around, some beside the road, some in the rice paddies, some in the ditches. I was sick with shock. I could not believe my eyes." The Japanese had stripped the bodies of all their valuables, and hungry dogs tore at the cadavers.[49]

About a third of the way down the east side of the peninsula, the Red Cross workers stopped in Abucay, the site of some of the fiercest fighting on Bataan. Its church, though damaged by heavy bombing, had survived with most of the roof intact. Dr. Gann decided to set up a clinic there. As Peggy and the others unpacked the station wagons, the townspeople gathered around the church to swap information with the new arrivals.

Peggy asked about the dead bodies. The locals told the story behind the steady screaming they had heard over five days and five nights in April as the Death Marchers passed through their barrio.

Peggy later identified the sight of the dead bodies and the stories of the Death March as her reasons for taking up resistance work. "After this trip through filth and nightmare, when everything seemed to be festering death, I knew that I could not stop until I had given every ounce of my strength to help the men who still lived," she decided. "After what those men had endured, nothing seemed too hard or too dangerous. Now I could not think of the Japanese except as beasts, and every weapon or trick that could be used against them seemed not only legitimate but also compulsory."[50]

When Peggy heard the story of the forced march, she became more determined to find Jack and help him survive whatever the Japanese were subjecting him to. Though convinced her husband was alive, she examined all of the dead bodies piled up in the area. That she did not find Jack confirmed her belief that he had survived.

Even as Peggy kept an eye out for Jack, she nursed. Working first out of the bombed-out church in Abucay and then moving on to different barrios, Peggy and the other nurses and doctors treated hundreds of Filipinos stricken with dysentery and malaria. They tended rape victims, some girls as young as seven years old. In Camachile, located between Pilar and Orion, Peggy saw the bodies of two men, shot dead by Japanese soldiers as they were fishing in their own pond. Nearby, the wife of one of the murdered men lay unconscious under a tree. Earlier that morning, with no one to assist her, she gave birth to a stillborn baby.[51]

Every day Peggy saw American prisoners driven by, crammed into trucks, suffering with dysentery and malaria. As a nurse, she understood that all of the afflicted, regardless of nationality, had to be treated if there was any hope of stopping the spread of the illnesses. When she tried to give medicine to the American POWs, however, a Japanese officer told her in very clear English, "You are not to give help to these Americans." He further startled Peggy by revealing he was born and raised in the United States, and was in fact a Protestant chaplain with the Japanese military.[52]

There were a number of such chaplains among the Japanese forces. When the Japanese Imperial Army began planning its invasion of the Philippine Islands, it created a Religious Propaganda Corps (later called the Religious Section) to be sent along with the 14th Army. The Japanese recognized how deeply Christianity was entrenched in the Philippines, a country colonized by Spanish Catholics and American Protestants. In fact, some 90 percent of Filipinos were Christians. To woo Filipinos into accepting the Greater East Asia Co-Prosperity Sphere, the Japanese decided it would be counterproductive to try to suppress Christianity. Instead, the Religious Section would work with the Philippine churches to prove that the Japanese government would support freedom of religion as long as it did not interfere with Japan's war effort. Initially, twenty-five members of the Religious Section, all Japanese Christians, landed on Luzon in December 1941.[53]

The Japanese chaplain observed, almost accusingly, how well Peggy spoke English for a Lithuanian. Her masquerade, only days old, was already getting tested. Peggy kept her wits about her and stuck to her cover story. "I grew up in Canada. And they speak pretty good English there too," she said, which satisfied the Japanese officer. But his refusal to allow her to help the American prisoners did not sit well. Her professional training and sense of fair play made her keep trying. Peggy lost her temper and snapped at the officer, "Unless you let us take care of them, they are going to spread dysentery all through the Japanese Army and you are going to have the biggest epidemic you ever heard of. You'll lose more men than you have lost in battle, I promise you that."[54]

Dr. Gann, who had been silently standing by, was alarmed at Peggy's outburst, worried she would anger the Japanese. The chaplain conceded that an epidemic would have serious consequences, and he allowed the medical team to dispense medicine to the American prisoners. Though Peggy got her way, she soon found that this humanitarian effort posed a danger to her. Many of the men in the trucks had been stationed on Corregidor, Peggy and Jack's former home, and some recognized her. She quietly informed one of them she was here as a Lithuanian, to pass that information along to the other men, and to remember it every time they saw her or heard her name. Still, she took the opportunity to ask each man she knew if he had seen Jack Utinsky. The answer was always no.

All too soon, Peggy was forced to put her search on hold because the Red Cross team had completed its mission, and the team members were returning to Manila. Searching through piles of dead bodies and questioning patients did not yield any information about Jack, yet Peggy felt proud of her contribution to the Red Cross project. She assisted with its survey of the medical requirements of civilians on the peninsula and helped set up clinics to take care of the sick and injured. She defied Japanese orders and provided aid to as many American prisoners as she could by giving them medicine to take along with them. Peggy knew these men represented the tip of the iceberg. There were many, many more of them in need of medical attention and supplies.

Riding along in the station wagon on the way back to Manila, Peggy worried about how she would continue helping those military prisoners, and how she would ever receive news on Jack's whereabouts. A little bundle on her lap caused her additional anxiety. On Bataan Peggy had found a small pile of items left behind by the US military, including an American flag and some papers listing names of spies for the Japanese allegedly working in the area. "I hated to leave them behind and yet I had no right to take them with me," Peggy admitted. "If I involved the Red Cross in any difficulty with the Japanese, they would be refused permission to do any more work in Bataan, to say the least of it."[55]

Peggy wrapped the papers and the flag into a neat package, camouflaging them with heavy paper. Before leaving Bataan, inside the sanctuary of a church she visited with Thomas Gann, she confessed to the doctor what she had done. If he thought it was too dangerous, she told him, she would leave the bundle behind. Perhaps with a bit more bravado than she really felt, she said, "They can only cut our heads off once." Gann instructed her to bring the package along.[56]

As the station wagon made its way toward Manila, a group of Japanese soldiers waved it down for a ride. One of the officers sat next to Peggy, staring at her white skin but ignoring the parcel she clutched on her lap. Out of the blue, he insisted they all stop and have a drink together. It was impossible to refuse, so Peggy climbed out of the vehicle, still holding on to the package, and drank with the enemy. No one mentioned the bundle, and they traveled on to Manila without incident. Back in her apartment, she washed and dried the flag, then hid it, along with the papers, in the building's attic because she thought they might come in handy someday.

Peggy's return to Manila on the last Sunday of May coincided with the arrival of the military prisoners from Corregidor. The American and Filipino soldiers—including Bill Berry, who had been crammed into the small beach area after the surrender—were moved to the capital city. On May 23, 1942, the Corregidor POWs marched to the South Dock where they were taken by launch to Japanese transports. The process continued until dark, and as the prisoners had now come to expect, their captors provided no food or sanitation facilities.[57]

The transports sailed across the bay to Manila the next morning, where landing barges ferried the men to shore, stopping short, giving the Japanese yet another opportunity to humiliate the prisoners. As Jack Wright of the 91st Coast Artillery remembered: "The landing barges moved in toward the beach until in water about four feet deep. The ramps were lowered, and we were ordered to go into water from waist deep to shoulder deep." The men slogged ashore, struggling to keep their meager possessions dry by holding them up over their heads, their already tattered clothing now soaked and filthy.[58]

Bill Berry realized the Japanese had planned a "March of Shame" for them through the streets of Manila, and wanted the prisoners to look as sorry as possible. It was a great piece of visual propaganda for the Japanese to show how completely they had bested the Americans. Before their clothing was dry, before they had a chance to wipe off some of the grime from the wade in, Japanese guards divided the prisoners into groups of 1,000, arranged them four abreast, and ordered them to march up Dewey Boulevard. Whatever the Japanese had in mind, the Filipinos watching did not comply. There were flashes of "V" for victory signs, tears, and the strains of "God Bless America" coming from the crowd.[59]

The men halted at the Manila Yacht Club for a brief watering stop before they resumed their march. As the columns of four turned away from Manila Bay, General Wainwright and a few staff members looked on from their quarters in the University Club. The surrendered officers were not the only interested observers. Peggy later wrote, "I stood on the sidelines, watching that pitiful march. I saw men fall and saw them kicked and beaten with bayonets." That day, of course, she looked for her husband. "As each tired, staggering man came up, I wondered whether the next would be Jack. I didn't know whether I hoped or feared to see him. I could not have helped him." She realized the limits of her masquerade, how little she could actually do to help anyone. "That day it was not easy to pretend not to be an American."[60]

GLADYS SAVARY, IN HER FINAL days of residence at the Restaurant de Paris, also watched the Corregidor prisoners march along the Manila streets. A humiliation for all Americans, Gladys thought, though she could not look away. She admired how the prisoners "bore it like heroes." Like Peggy Utinsky, Gladys had a personal reason for closely scrutinizing the columns of marching men. She wanted to see if Edgar Gable was among them. To her amazement, he was. Gladys caught him with her own eyes but could not go to him. All Caucasians had been warned to stay inside while the prisoners were on the streets. One of the Filipino restaurant employees ran outside and reached Gable as his section of the line turned the corner at the University Club. Gable let the employee know that they were all headed for Bilibid Prison.[61]

Bilibid was a vast prison complex built by the Spanish in 1865 on seventeen acres of land in the middle of Manila. Its Tagalog name meant "to wind around, to coil up" or even "to be bound." Before the end of the century Bilibid had fallen into disrepair, and in the early 1900s, under American rule, it was redesigned into a radial prison—eighteen single-story buildings fanned out from a central guard tower. A New Bilibid Prison was built in nearby Muntinlupa, and most prisoners were transferred there by 1939. Conditions in Old Bilibid continued to deteriorate, yet Japanese authorities decided to make use of it. By the end of May 1942, they had crammed 12,000 prisoners into a compound designed for 5,200.[62]

Considering how the Japanese viewed prisoners of war, it was not surprising that the military did not trouble itself with the poor conditions inside Bilibid. The prison's central location in Manila, however, caused some concern. It made the prison—and its prisoners—much too visible to the capital city's population. The Japanese did not want to give Manilans the opportunity to flout the Great East Asia Co-Prosperity Sphere by trying to help the POWs. When women from the Philippine Red Cross attempted to donate two large truck loads of medical supplies, foodstuffs, clothing, and storybooks, a Japanese officer informed them the items were not needed, that the Japanese could take care of their prisoners.[63]

With official channels closed, some Manilans resorted to under-the-table tactics. When Gladys learned that Edgar Gable was in Bilibid, she smuggled some food and money to him that very night. She never revealed how she accomplished this, but was fortunate not to have wasted any time. For the vast majority of the prisoners, Bilibid was a brief stop of a day or so on the way north. Gable, Jack Wright, and Bill Berry all soon left the prison and walked about a mile through the streets of Manila to the railroad station. There, the Japanese pushed 150 men at a time into steel freight cars. It was standing room only. For hours the tired and hungry men sweated and thirsted in these rolling saunas until they stopped at Cabanatuan, which would become another chapter in their wartime hell.[64]

THAT SAME DAY, AS PRISONERS were forced into cars at the railway station, Peggy Utinsky endured her first beating from two Japanese on a Manila street. As she and Cam Lee rode to the post office in a horse-drawn *carromata*—a two-wheeled cart—she saw the two men running after them, shouting. "I guess they want the cart. They can have it," Peggy said to the driver. When she and Lee got out of the conveyance, the Japanese, with no warning, attacked Peggy. Their fists bounced her against the wheel of the *carromata*, and their hobnail boots lashed her legs, scraping off almost all of the skin. The attack lasted for fifteen minutes. No one dared to intervene; Lee stood on the sidewalk, helpless, waiting for the soldiers to finish. Through a haze of pain Peggy noticed a truck filled with American soldiers had been stopped and the prisoners ordered to watch. Finally, the truck was waved on and the beating stopped. Peggy's body was a purple mass of bruises, her legs shredded and caked with blood. Lee helped her back into the *carromata*—which the Japanese had not wanted after all—and despite her injuries, they continued on to the post office.[65]

If this episode was what Peggy suspected—a signal to the American prisoners of their powerlessness—it also taught her a painful lesson about taking extra precautions in an enemy-occupied city. Although she possessed the official paperwork documenting her Lithuanian nationality and authorizing her travel throughout the city, Japanese soldiers did not always bother to ask for papers. Peggy's Caucasian features made her an easy target for their capricious violence. She would have to learn to be more careful about how she presented herself in public.

The beating was not enough to force Peggy back into the confines of her apartment. When she heard the Japanese had authorized another Red Cross mission to Bataan in June 1942, she made sure to go along. As she later wrote, "There was work to be done there, far more work than there were people to do it, and a chance that I could make some contact with the American prisoners." This also meant many opportunities to find Jack.[66]

Dr. Gann organized this trip as well, but did not lead it. That duty fell to Romeo Y. Atienza, a young Filipino doctor, assisted by his wife, Maria Fe, an expert on home economics and nutrition. On the way to Bataan this second time, Peggy sat in a truck next to an old acquaintance, Doris Robinson, a mestiza nurse in her late twenties. When Doris asked after Jack, Peggy replied that her name was Miss Utinsky, that she was unmarried. Doris said she understood and never raised the issue again. The incident served as another reminder to Peggy about the fragility of her cover story. Doris was willing to keep Peggy's secret. What if other former acquaintances were not so willing or tactful?[67]

Dr. Atienza's Red Cross team set up shop in a bombed school building in the small Bataan town of Calaguiman. Doctors and nurses worked almost around the clock treating malaria and dysentery, feeding the hungry, delivering babies, and providing emergency shelter. During that first day, Peggy later admitted, "I drove people like an avenging fury. We carried out the [wounded and sick] people, swept, cleaned, disinfected, built bamboo cots and by dark we had our patients in it, a functioning hospital."[68]

Peggy performed good and necessary work that did not bring her any closer to the American military prisoners still in the vicinity. She concluded the best way to make contact was to serve as a field nurse so she could travel around the peninsula. This would increase her chances of running into the prisoners whom the Japanese periodically allowed to scrounge for food. One of them might know something about Jack. One of them might be Jack.

When Peggy approached Dr. Atienza with her plan and volunteered for field duty, he tried to talk her out of it. "The job is too hard. You won't be able to stand it," he said. "Do you know what the work entails? You'd be stationed one day at Santa Lucia, the next day at Abucay. You'd have up to 200 cases a day at the clinics, and when that work was done, you'd have to go from house to house, checking the needs of the population." The doctor, who had revealed his pro-American sentiments to Peggy, relented when he realized she would not change her mind. She went on her own to open a clinic in Abucay, one of the towns she ministered to during her first trip to Bataan. The work proved every bit as difficult as Dr. Atienza had predicted, still it gave Peggy the opportunity she had been looking for.[69]

One June day, as she walked along the road, heading for the Red Cross tent, she saw a truck approach. Still smarting from the beating she took in Manila and worrying she was in for a repeat, Peggy hopped into a ditch, hoping the driver would not notice her. The driver behind the wheel was not Japanese but American, and they were both surprised to see each other. Eighteen-year-old Private First Class Marvin T. Ivey had earlier dropped two officers at the tent in hopes of picking up medicine and other supplies. Ivey, tall and baby-faced, an Arkansas native, was part of the Army Medical Department, now working as a driver for the two American officers—Lieutenant John Schock and Captain Andrew Rader—still treating patients at Hospital No. 1, further south on the peninsula. Schock, originally from Nebraska, was a dentist who had been living in the Philippines for more than twenty years. Rader, a graduate of the Wake Forest medical school, ended up on Bataan by way of a 1940 posting to Sternberg General Hospital and a 1941 appointment to the 12th Medical Battalion of the Philippine Scouts.[70]

By the time Peggy walked into the tent, the Americans had already been refused assistance by some members of the Red Cross team. They informed the officers that their organization was forbidden to assist military prisoners; they were on Bataan to provide civilian relief. Peggy wanted to know more about the officers' situation so she interrupted the conversation, telling the men she would give them something to eat before they moved on. Schock and Rader wolfed down the soup, sandwiches, and crackers she brought, managing to get in a few words about their troubles. They told Peggy that Colonel James Duckworth, commanding officer of Hospital No. 1, desperately needed medical supplies. He was too sick to go out to scrounge, so he sent other officers. Peggy had no intention of sending the men back empty-handed. She raided the Red Cross drug supplies—sulfa drugs, brewer's yeast tablets—and threw in some food, as well.

As Schock and Rader packed up the truck, Peggy explained that she worked at both Santa Lucia and Abucay. They should look for her wherever they saw the Red Cross flag and she would give them supplies. She asked one thing in return: "See if you can bring me a complete list of the prisoners, will you? Those who have died, those who are ill, all of them." Jack was still foremost in her mind. The men promised to do their best. The next time, though, three different men would come looking for her because the prisoners took turns on these supply runs.[71]

Peggy almost missed the next contingent of officers. Dr. Joaquin Canuto, one of the Filipino Red Cross officials who had refused to help the American officers, went back to Manila the next day and reported Peggy for violating Japanese orders by. Canuto, Director of General Relief, returned with another member of the Red Cross who was tasked with taking Peggy to Manila. She refused to go: "I was never hired by the Red Cross so they cannot fire me. I volunteered. If the Red Cross doesn't want me, the natives do. I have taken care of a lot of them. Not one would refuse to take me in." She added, "I won't leave Bataan until I am damned good and ready and that will be when there's not another American left here." Peggy stayed put.[72]

A few days later, Captains Jack Le Mire, Neil Burr, and Charles Osborne, all chosen by Colonel Duckworth for this scrounging mission, came looking for Peggy. She ran out from the Red Cross tent to greet the new trio, anxious to know if they brought the documents she requested. The men handed them to her right away, lists of the dead and the prisoners. She did not find Jack's name. As she had done for Schock and Rader, she fed these three captains and gave them as many supplies as they could carry. In her eagerness to help, she forgot to be afraid of making herself too visible to the Japanese. Peggy remembered that time with the three officers: "We sat there eating and drinking and laughing as though we hadn't a worry in the world, though if a Jap had come along just then there would have been a mass beheading. We knew it and still we laughed."[73]

The men told Peggy they would not see her again. The remainder of the prisoners on Bataan were being moved north to Camp O'Donnell, located just to the west of the railway town of Capas. Captain Le Mire pointed at one of the nearby mountain ranges. "There are a lot of guerrillas fighting over there," he said to Peggy. She suggested, perhaps in jest, they could go join them, but Le Mire countered in the same spirit, "Well, it would be a shame to leave these groceries." It was not really because of the groceries that the men declined to head into the hills. A "pointless risk," was how Peggy later described guerrilla activity. Of course, the prison camps carried their own risks, and unfortunately, none of the three captains would survive them.[74]

With the three men well-fed, well-supplied, and ready to leave the Red Cross tent, Peggy promised she would see them in Camp O'Donnell. Since that was where the American prisoners would be, she decided to shift the location of her aid work. That night, before she could do anything more, she contracted dysentery. In a steady downpour of rain, Peggy stumbled out to the latrine nineteen times. By the next morning she had to hold on to the railings of the patients' cots to remain upright while she cared for men as sick as she was. The day after that she could not get out of bed. A Filipina woman, grateful Peggy had treated her son's pneumonia, had Peggy brought to her house and took care of her there for four days.

The last of the Bataan prisoners left for Camp O'Donnell while Peggy was still too sick to send them off with proper food and medicine.

With no more American prisoners on Bataan, Peggy wanted to get back to Manila so she could begin planning her operation for O'Donnell. First she had to recuperate, and Dr. Canuto would not lift a finger to help her. The other nurses warned him that Peggy's case was critical, that she could not stay on Bataan any longer without risking her life. Canuto insisted there was no way to get Peggy to Manila. When Peggy pointed out he had a truck at his disposal and he could drive her, he claimed he was too tired. Peggy's weakened physical condition did not curb her temper, which made her incautious about her cover story. "You'll get me to Manila or I'll write to the Governor of Bataan. He's a friend of mine. If I die, he will see that my letter goes to the Red Cross in the United States and people will know what goes on here," she said. Canuto may have wondered why such a complaint letter about a Lithuanian woman would end up with the American Red Cross. He could have challenged Peggy on that point, but he did not. Perhaps he saw this as his chance to finally be rid of her. Grudgingly, Dr. Canuto drove Peggy back to Manila, where she checked into a hospital.[75]

CHAPTER 8

"MISS U" IS BORN

A T THE END OF MAY 1942, several weeks prior to Peggy Utinsky's second Red Cross trip to Bataan, an African American woman named Millie Sanders approached her before curfew, asking for help. Mildred Brown Sanders had been born to an African American father and Cherokee mother in Marshall, Texas in 1892. She married an army man reported to be part Native American and in the 1920s went with him to the Philippines, where she opened a boardinghouse at 12 Nebraska in Manila's Ermita district. The establishment became well known for its southern cooking, and its boarders affectionately referred to Millie as "Ma Sanders." Her husband was taken prisoner after the surrenders. However, the Japanese could not reconcile Millie's skin color and facial features with "American," so she was not interned in Santo Tomas. Millie was very American, though, and she kept an eye out for fellow country-men in need of assistance.[1]

That evening she told Peggy about an American officer hiding near her boardinghouse, just a few blocks from A. Mabini Street. The man had escaped from the Bataan Death March and made his way to Manila; now he was sick and needed medical attention. Peggy wanted to help, but had to exercise some caution. She could not get to the ailing man and back home before curfew without risking arrest or another beating. She waited until early the next morning to meet the man known as "Captain Burson," who had served two tours of duty in the Philippines, stationed at Fort McKinley with the 45th Infantry. When Peggy met him he was suffering from malaria, dysentery, and shell shock. Burson had the presence of mind to get rid of his uniform, yet he held on to his military-issue pistol and his papers.

Captain Burson initially refused to trust Peggy, claiming he was not an American and did not need her help. She dismissed his protests with a brisk, "Oh, shut up!" Taken aback by her tone, he said, "You are little but you sure are tough." Burson, physically and emotionally spent, reluctantly accepted her help. He shuffled the few blocks to Peggy's apartment, all the while asking where they were headed, who she was, and what she was going to do with him. She reassured him the best she could, and when they arrived at her apartment, she put him to bed.[2]

Peggy was so concerned about Burson's condition that she sent for the Red Cross doctor, Thomas Gann. He did not ask any questions, nor did he even seem surprised to find an American officer in Peggy's apartment. Gann treated Burson and told Peggy what kind of medicine to give him over the next few days. The captain improved. Peggy kept him in her apartment until he was well enough to travel, not an impossible task since her new downstairs neighbor, a Spanish woman, was an Allied sympathizer. Cam Lee, who continued his regular visits to Peggy, was horrified at the risk. The Japanese would have their heads, he warned her, if they found the American officer here.

It was a risk Peggy had to take; turning Burson out of her apartment was the equivalent of a death sentence. He was immediately identifiable as an American soldier and would be picked up and thrown into Fort Santiago. However, it turned out that keeping Burson inside was almost as dangerous as letting him out.

One morning some Japanese soldiers came banging on the street-level door of Peggy's apartment house. Lee turned pale and reminded Peggy about the head-chopping, to which she said, "Of course they will, if we stand here like idiots and don't do something. Help me hide the captain."[3]

They pushed Burson out of the kitchen window so he could hang onto a gas pipe, his toes just grazing a small iron roof below. He had to hold on until the Japanese left. If he lost his grip and landed on the roof, he would cause enough noise for the Japanese to find him and arrest everyone in the building. As Peggy headed to the stairs to meet the Japanese—she presumed they were on their way up—she spotted Burson's gun on her living room table. She shoved it at Lee, telling him to hide it in the attic and then cross the roof to the next building and wait there. Lee was torn. He did not want to leave Peggy to face the Japanese alone, yet he worried about what would happen if they found the gun. He followed Peggy's instructions.

Through a window, Peggy saw the soldiers on the street talking to a Filipino. She heard enough of their conversation to understand the Japanese had come to the wrong building. They wanted this same house number but not A. Mabini Street. The Japanese climbed into their truck and drove off. Lee came down from the attic, returned Burson's gun, and with great indignation said to Peggy that he was very frightened and wanted to leave. Peggy pulled Burson back through the kitchen window. When he grabbed onto the windowsill to steady himself, she lost her grip on his shirt and fell against the kitchen table, breaking all her dishes.[4]

Figuring her time with Burson was running out, Peggy started that very evening searching for his new hiding place. Through connections with sympathetic Filipinos she secured a forged residency pass identifying the captain as a mestizo and rented him a room in a Filipino home in Paco, where she believed he would be safe.

After Peggy returned from her second Red Cross trip to Bataan, in late June, she learned that she was wrong. The Japanese picked up Burson and took him to Fort Santiago for questioning about his nationality, trying to beat a confession out of him. They partially paralyzed his right arm, shattered his left kneecap, and burned his nostrils with lit cigarettes. He would not admit he was American, and the Japanese released him.[5]

Peggy checked up on Burson after his release. Then he sent her a message saying it was too risky for her to try and visit him again. She worried about the captain, and arranged to have food and medicine delivered to him while he recuperated from his torture sessions. Within a few months Burson was well enough to take odd jobs around Manila, and he moved frequently to stay one step ahead of the Japanese. He succeeded until 1944, when the Japanese arrested him and took him to Fort Santiago again. This time Burson did not leave.[6]

After her second to trip to Bataan, while confined in St. Luke's Hospital recovering from dysentery, Peggy received the news about Captain Burson's initial arrest and time at Fort Santiago. It served as a blunt reminder of the dangers of working against the Japanese. Good intentions and careful planning could quickly go awry in enemy-occupied Manila.

At St. Luke's, Miss L. J. Weiser, superintendent of the nurses' training school, personally attended to Peggy the first day she was admitted. Dr. Lindsay Z. Fletcher, an American doctor in the Philippines for more than twenty years, was allowed out of the Santo Tomas internment camp each day to make hospital rounds, and he also checked on Peggy's progress. Given Manila's close-knit American community, especially among medical professionals, Weiser and Fletcher surely knew the true identity of their patient.[7]

The other piece of news Peggy learned was the one thing she had been waiting for these last months: information about her husband. First came a rumor that Jack Utinsky was in Bilibid Prison. For a whole day Peggy reveled in the belief that he was alive and close by. She probably spent her waking hours planning how she would establish contact with her husband, how she would send him all the food and medicine he could possibly need. Maybe, just maybe, there was a way she could get him out.

Then came some less hopeful clarifying information, courtesy of US Navy commander, Lea Bennett Sartin. The middle-aged Mississippi-born doctor had been imprisoned in Bilibid since his capture at the Cañacao Naval Hospital, so he knew a lot about the inmates there. He clarified that Jack had been captured in the Malinta Tunnel on Corregidor at the beginning of May, and spent one night at Bilibid before being moved to an unknown destination. Peggy may have wondered if she missed seeing Jack—may not have recognized him—in the crush of Corregidor prisoners who arrived in Manila the same day she returned from her first trip to Bataan.[8]

This was not the best news, but at least Peggy finally knew her husband survived the surrender and had been spared the Death March. She figured he had been taken to Camp O'Donnell, and she intended to confirm this as soon as possible. Peggy pronounced herself well when she could stand on her own two feet—even if they were wobbly—and left St. Luke's Hospital. With no *carromatas* available for transportation, she started walking to her apartment, supporting herself by holding onto the iron fences that lined the street. The next day she started a private nursing job.

Edwin M. Van Voorhees, Vice President of General Motors Overseas Corporation, had been exempted from internment at Santo Tomas for medical reasons. Since he could afford a private nurse, Elizabeth Kummer recommended Peggy. She needed to earn a living, and taking care of a private patient seemed less risky than working at a hospital where occupation authorities would scrutinize employment records. For all her determination to get back on her feet, Peggy was as much of a patient as her charge. She continued to rely on Cam Lee to help her: "Every morning Lee came for me with a carromata. He would push from behind and the cochero [driver] would pull and between them they got me into the cart and out the same way. I could barely stand and how I looked after Mr. Van Vorries [sic] I don't know."[9]

Through sheer willpower, Peggy determined what had to be done and she did it. As she nursed her patient, her own health returned. One day in July she received a letter from Romeo Atienza, the doctor she worked with during her second Red Cross trip to Bataan. He wrote, "Our people need you." Peggy understood at once that Atienza had figured out a way to help the military prisoners in Camp O'Donnell. The next day Peggy quit her job with Mr. Van Voorhees. She boarded a train to Capas, the railway station closest to O'Donnell.[10]

GLADYS SAVARY CONTINUED TO ASSIST her friends inside the Santo Tomas internment camp by regularly sending in foodstuffs and prepared meals. This became more of a challenge, however, once Gladys lost the Restaurant de Paris, which had been a convenient conduit for her relief work. By the late spring of 1942, the restaurant she had signed over to the Japanese but had not yet vacated was failing. As Gladys noted in her diary, "Business does not warrant my keeping open. There are not enough white people free and I do hate the Japanese business—the little that I do get." Her presence in the restaurant also made her more noticeable, resulting in a few nerve-wracking encounters with the enemy.[11]

Not long after the surrender at Corregidor, a plainclothes member of the Kempeitai showed up at the Restaurant de Paris and questioned the staff and guests. "He was rough with all of them and terrorized the servants," Gladys remembered. He focused on a storage room where Gladys had stashed some thirty trunks belonging to friends and acquaintances now either interned or imprisoned, along with fifty cases of beer for the restaurant. The officer probably wanted a case or two of the brew in exchange for looking the other way, but Gladys worried that an attempted bribe would land her in Fort Santiago. He flung accusations at her about harboring military personnel, started breaking open some of the trunks. Then he stopped, sealed the storeroom, and left.[12]

The Japanese officer returned with two Filipina prostitutes, and the trio ordered food and beer while making "dreadful scenes." Gladys instructed her waiter not to charge for anything, hoping that might ease the officer's hostility. The man insisted on paying, though when he got to the tally at the bottom of the bill, he accused Gladys of profiteering, an offense punishable by death. He waved his pistol around, struck Gladys with it a few times, ordered more beer, and even asked her for money.[13]

If he thought he could intimidate Gladys, he was mistaken. Under the pretext of retrieving the money from her office, she telephoned Kempeitai headquarters to report the officer's conduct. As she understood occupation policies, the Japanese were not supposed to drink on duty or harass civilians without cause, and Gladys believed this man had exceeded his authority. She was brave enough to challenge him through appropriate channels. The offender slipped out of the restaurant before he could be detained and questioned, and Gladys received a reprimand from the military police for charging such a high price for beer. "All good clean fun, but hard on the nerves," Gladys concluded of her attempt to rein in Japanese excesses.[14]

Also hard on her nerves were the additional interrogations about her nationality. Though Gladys believed this issue had been settled in January, occupation officials re-examined the roster kept by the new Vichy French consul in Manila. Gladys's registration as André Savary's wife had taken place in the original French consulate in Manila, but she had not re-registered with the Vichy government. She wanted nothing to do with the Vichy—those French collaborators with the Germans—and did not want to fill out any new paperwork that might compel her to lie.

Sometime in March or early April 1942, all French nationals not on the Vichy list had to report to Santo Tomas to answer questions. Gladys outfitted herself well for the interview with the camp commandant—nice dress, white gloves, hat—and was pleasant to him, almost flirtatious. Since the commandant had Gladys's dossier in front of him, she did not attempt to stretch any truth, at least not one pertaining to her identity. She referred to André Savary as her husband and acknowledged, with as much vagueness as possible, that he went off to fight with his regiment in 1939. Still conflicted about her exemption and perhaps worried that someone had found out about her divorce, she said, "I should be in Santo Tomas since I was American-born." The commandant let her status as a French national stand, though, and sent her on her way. "So I went home, neither fish nor flesh but ready to drag a few red herrings across the Nip path."[15]

About a month later, Gladys received a telephone call from Fort Santiago, headquarters of the Kempeitai, instructing her to report as soon as possible to Captain Ito. This frightened her more than the Santo Tomas summons because of the Fort's reputation. Many of the people taken inside never came out. Now Gladys fretted that the Japanese knew about the underground communication system between Corregidor and Manila. In fact, the day the call came, she received another batch of letters from soldiers on the besieged island. For Gladys it was first things first. She delivered the letters, then gave her restaurant staff instructions for carrying on if she did not return from Fort Santiago.

The conversation with Captain Ito, through his interpreter, proceeded much the same as the one with the commandant at Santo Tomas. She answered the questions and restrained herself from elaborating on any-thing. Finally, Ito got around to his main concern, which only indirectly concerned Gladys's nationality. He wanted to know what Gladys knew about one of her lodgers, an elderly Frenchman, now detained at the Fort. With considerable relief, Gladys realized the captain simply wanted to make sure that he could safely release the old man to her custody. She later observed, "The Santiago episode had left me with less fear of the Japanese; they weren't so smart as I thought them. If I could get away with all I had been doing, then there was no reason I couldn't get away with more."[16]

If Gladys wanted to do more, she would have to do so from a new loca-tion. After the fall of Corregidor, she turned over the Restaurant de Paris to the Japanese. She needed income, so she rented a pair of semi-furnished houses, part of a walled compound of seven homes all owned by the same Filipina, in the Pasay district. Gladys moved into one house at 65 Protacio and rented the other to her close friends, Dorothy and Helge Janson. Helge, the Swedish consul, had retrieved his American wife and their young sons from the northern Luzon city of Baguio where they had been trapped by the Japanese invasion in late December 1941. They needed a place to stay in Manila, and were pleased to remain close to their friend. Civilians that the Japanese considered either friendly or neutral—Danish, Polish, German, Italian, Czech, and Swiss—lived in the other homes in the compound. They were a congenial lot.

Despite Japanese orders not to take anything from the restaurant, Gladys removed many items from there, including dishes, silverware, and linens. She left the furniture because it was too heavy and too obvious for the Japanese to overlook. Smaller things were easily pilfered. Besides, she needed them to take care of the paying guests she had taken on. Four permanent lodgers and a steady rotation of temporary ones occupied the extra bedrooms in the house she rented. Gladys also hired two house ser-vants originally employed by a couple of her boarders and she kept on the cook, maid, and servant from the restaurant. "Quite a household," she observed of the setup that would provide much of her income.[17]

Supported by this domestic help, Gladys continued to operate her mobile food service, daily sending a wagon of supplies into Santo Tomas.

Fifty internees contracted with her, either paying cash or, increasingly, relying on credit, for hot meals and laundry and shopping services. It was a full-time job: "The cook and I partially prepared the food the evening before. Reheating of roasts—or if steaks or chops, cooking of them—was done early in the morning. We got up about four-thirty for this, the cook and I. Salads and vegetables were prepared the night before, and desserts." Three times a week, Gladys traveled by *carretela* to the internment camp to deliver personal messages and news through the package line that served as a lifeline. Located just inside the campus gates, the package line consisted of a series of long counters staffed by internees who checked in the bundles and directed them to the intended recipients.[18]

The Japanese camp authorities sanctioned this system because it reduced their responsibility for providing food and other necessities for the internees. The package line, though, established a kind of caste system within Santo Tomas. Those who had family and friends—or at least acquaintances—on the outside and who had money or valuables to trade, arranged for food, medicine, toiletries, and clothing to be brought in. Camp guards monitored the line to make sure none of the packages contained contraband, especially money, uncensored news, and personal notes. Those items were the underground part of an otherwise above-board operation.

Determined not to get anyone in trouble and smart enough to know how to protect her business, Gladys kept the forbidden items separate from the food baskets and laundry containers she brought into Santo Tomas. "I never put notes or contraband articles in the food or laundry containers," she later wrote, as "it would have jeopardized both parties concerned. I did carry typed sheets of news and notes *on my person*, in my glove usually, which I'd slip out to the Americans on the receiving lines, but I was never caught at that, nor even suspected."[19]

The reason she accomplished this so easily, Gladys surmised, had to do with Japanese beliefs about women. "They have so little regard for women that they never understood that women *could* do any harm." Time and again during her first year in Pasay she watched as Japanese soldiers stopped and searched men out on the streets or riding in buses, ignoring the women right beside them, carrying baskets and bags the Japanese assumed only contained food. The Japanese were not as blind to women's potential for resistance work as Gladys supposed. Though she asserted that women served as the best contacts with the military prison camps, she also conceded, "Many of them lost their lives for it, too." Working as an underground courier for one of the POW camps on Luzon required courage, because the Japanese would, in fact, beat and kill women if they were caught.[20]

PEGGY UTINSKY ALREADY EXPERIENCED ONE of those beatings, yet she moved quickly after receiving Dr. Atienza's note about his aid station at Capas, near Camp O'Donnell. Since she was headed there to work as a nurse, she packed up the food and medical supplies from the quartermaster stores she had been hoarding in her apartment and took them along: "Now at last I had found a use for the provisions with which I had stacked my apartment just before the fall of Manila. At least the food from the American commissary was going to feed Americans."[21]

Peggy bullied and bribed a *cochero*—a cart driver—to help her load up his conveyance and drive her to the train station, where she treated a redcap the same. When the train reached Capas, Peggy's Filipino coach mates made sure all of her boxes and bundles were removed from the baggage car. They were impressed with her cover story—that she was a Red Cross nurse heading to Capas to help Filipino POWs being released by the Japanese from Camp O'Donnell. Eager to prove that they were more beneficent colonial masters than the Americans had been, the occupation authorities decided to pardon the Filipino soldiers and send them home. Many would need medical attention before they could be moved any further than Capas.

Once more the parcels were hefted into a *carretela*. They ended up at a small house located about eight miles from Camp O'Donnell, occupied by Romeo and Maria Fe Atienza and a few Filipino nurses. A local schoolteacher loaned the house to the Red Cross, which used it as its headquarters and residence for the medical staff in Capas. In the absence of any furniture, they all slept on the floor. It was easy enough to accommodate one more.[22]

Dr. Atienza came out of the house to greet Peggy. Amazed at the amount of supplies she brought with her, he said, "I knew you would come, but not in such a big way." The supplies would do much for the desperate POWs in Camp O'Donnell.[23]

The final destination of the Bataan Death March, Camp O'Donnell was a 671-acre site just to the northwest of Capas in Tarlac Province. Originally a training post for Filipino troops, it was now ill-equipped to house such a large number of prisoners. Irvin Alexander, so ill by the end of the hike out of Bataan that he had to be propped up by some of his men, was further sickened by what he encountered when he finally reached O'Donnell. Japanese guards searched the thousands of prisoners before they listened to the "welcome" speech from the camp commandant, Captain Tsuneyoshi Yoshio. The middle-aged reservist, a bit over five feet tall in his knee-high riding boots and sporting a short brush mustache and a shaved head, had been recalled to active duty in 1937 and given the position a week before the first prisoners arrived.[24]

After Tsuneyoshi kept the prisoners waiting long enough to understand who was in charge, he got up on a platform and spoke to them through an interpreter. "Blood rushed into his contorted face as he spoke, and his eyes flashed more venom than a cobra. He told us that Japan won the war already and she would never give back an inch of ground she had gained if she had to fight for five hundred years," Alexander recalled. "He told us we were captives, cowardly and dishonorable, and that we were not to be considered as prisoners of war." The harangue continued for about twenty minutes before the POWs were marched into the camp.[25]

Camp O'Donnell, Alexander realized, had not been constructed to house large numbers of soldiers on a permanent basis. The compound was divided into thirds. The Japanese set up their headquarters, barracks, and storehouses in the middle section, which stretched east–west along a highway. An area to the south had been enclosed for the Filipino prisoners, with a zone to the north designated for the Americans. In their section, the American POWs confronted a few kitchens capable of producing little more than steamed rice, and the barracks—no more than sheds—had thatched roofs and hinged walls designed to stay open at all times except during severe downpours. These barracks, measuring about twenty-four feet wide, contained raised platforms that served as combined living–sleeping space for the men. Irvin Alexander recalled that each man laid "with his head to the wall and his feet to the center, having a space [of] eight feet for himself and all his possessions unless the building was crowded, in which case he was lucky if he had enough room to stretch out."[26]

Thousands of starving, sick, and battered men jostled for position in the barracks hoping for some relief. They soon learned Captain Tsuneyoshi had made only the barest provisions for food and medical assistance. Since the prisoners were, in the commandant's eyes, cowardly and dishonorable, they deserved nothing better. Nor was Tsuneyoshi willing to accept help from outsiders. After Dr. Atienza set up the Red Cross clinic in Capas, he packed supplies into twelve trucks clearly marked with the Red Cross symbol and brought them to Camp O'Donnell. Tsuneyoshi met them at the gate and informed Atienza that Japanese Army regulations did not permit this kind of assistance.[27]

Atienza did not give up, though, and sent a truck almost every day, hoping Tsuneyoshi would change his mind. Major Alvin C. Poweleit, a doctor in the medical detachment to the 192nd Tank Battalion, observed this ritual refusal at the gate of Camp O'Donnell with no small measure of frustration. Initially posted at Fort Stotsenburg, Poweleit had withdrawn to the Bataan peninsula after the Japanese invasion, where he worked at a few medical jobs, including a stint at Hospital No. 1.

When Bataan fell, Poweleit survived the Death March, stood through one of Captain Tsuneyoshi's welcome speeches, then set to work with some other American officers to establish the first hospital at O'Donnell: a large rundown building with space enough for eight hundred to nine hundred strategically bedded patients. The pharmacy was originally stocked with whatever medicine the doctors and medics happened to have with them, which was not nearly enough. Since the Japanese did not contribute any medical supplies or accept Red Cross donations, the camp doctors devised a smuggling system to acquire what they needed. Officers from the 192nd and 194th Tank Battalions scraped some money together and negotiated with the truck drivers who went in and out of the camp to purchase as much medicine as they could.

Captain Fred Nasr of the Dental Corps participated in this scheme along with a friend of his from Manila, Mering Bichara. Mering was the twenty-three-year old owner of Salvador's Beauty Shop on A. Mabini Street, part of a well-to-do Lebanese family involved in the textile and movie theater businesses. Prior to the war, the Bicharas socialized with many American Army officers, and after the surrenders they moved quickly to provide assistance to the prisoners in Camp O'Donnell. Beginning in June, Mering collected and delivered money, food, and medicine. Nasr received the donations and parceled them out to the POWs.[28]

As much as was smuggled into the camp, Major Poweleit soon realized, "The medical situation was so disastrous that the amount we obtained was insignificant." Members of work details allowed beyond the camp gates contributed to the operation; the results were abysmal. "The cost of food and drugs outside the camp was excessive, and the men took tremendous chances bringing in the various items," Poweleit recalled. "If caught, they might be shot, severely beaten or, depending on the whim of the Japanese guard, left alone."[29]

By the time Peggy showed up in Capas in July 1942, the situation had eased just a bit. Colonel James Duckworth and the rest of the medical personnel from Bataan Hospital No. 1 arrived at Camp O'Donnell in July and by the end of the month opened a camp commissary. Though the Japanese helped supply it with food and medicine, the prisoners were in such need that the smuggling continued. Captain Tsuneyoshi continued to refuse Red Cross supplies, yet allowed Dr. Atienza into the Filipino section of the camp to treat the prisoners there.

Once Atienza got into O'Donnell he made contact with the Americans, initially with Colonel Duckworth, Major Wilbur C. Berry, and Lieutenant Frank L. Tiffany. Like Duckworth, Major Berry was a doctor, a South Dakota native who joined the army medical corps in 1936. On Bataan he worked at Hospital No. 2, where he was captured by the Japanese. Tiffany, also from South Dakota, was a minister. He studied at Chicago's Presbyterian Theological Seminary in the early 1930s, was inducted into the Corps of Chaplains in December 1940, and a few months later found himself chaplain at Sternberg General Hospital in Manila.[30]

In furtive conversations these three men told Dr. Atienza about the desperate conditions inside Camp O'Donnell. At the top of their list was starvation. The prisoners were hungry—had been hungry, in fact, since the weeks of reduced rations on Bataan—and the Death March turned a critical health situation into a disastrous one. Irvin Alexander wolfed down the watery evening soup, made from the previous day's vegetable ration. It filled his stomach but did little to advance nutrition. Twice during the first month of imprisonment at O'Donnell he detected a hint of meat in the soup. Once he found an actual sliver of beef. Two hundred pounds of meat and bones did not go far in feeding about 10,000 men.[31]

Colonel Ernest B. Miller, commander of the 194th Tank Battalion and originally headquartered at Fort Stotsenburg along with Alexander, experienced a steady diet of rice during his first two weeks at Camp O'Donnell. Two to four ounces of camotes—native sweet potatoes—soon appeared with the rice, as well as small amounts of the small native mongo beans. Each man received a scant ⅛ to ¼ ounce of meat, usually carabao, approximately once a week. Mealtimes devolved into running battles with swarms of flies that wanted the food as much as the prisoners.[32]

This was a true starvation diet. As Miller later wrote, "Ribs could be counted at a quick glance. We were living skeletons, and that is the way we were destined to remain for the duration of the war. Buttocks sagged—loose skin—devoid of flesh or muscle. Men asleep, might have been dead. There was no difference. We found ourselves, on waking, looking at others still sleeping—wondering whether they were alive." The dead piled up. Fifteen to twenty a day, then thirty to forty, topping out at a record high of fifty-eight in one day. Upwards of 1,000 American prisoners died within the first two months at O'Donnell. Malnutrition took an enormous toll on its own. Compounded with compulsory work, this became a devastatingly deadly combination.[33]

The Japanese paid the POWs in return for their labor in the camp work details. Enlisted men received ten centavos a day—about a nickel—and officers twenty pesos a month, the equivalent of ten dollars. Prisoners used this money to support themselves in camp. However, many men who were too sick to work did not receive the pay and could not afford to purchase their own supplies. It was a vicious, fatal circle. With malnutrition and overexertion, plus the overcrowding and inadequate shelter from the elements, came relentless diseases: dysentery, dengue fever, malaria, beriberi, tropical ulcers.[34]

Despite the establishment of a camp hospital, POWs continued to die. For most patients, the hospital was not the place to get well; it was the last stop before death. Within a few weeks, all of the camp buildings repurposed as medical facilities filled with sick and dying men. Irvin Alexander saw groups of eight or more men lying together under big green mosquito nets that protected them from flying insects. It was a minimal effort; nothing else could be done to keep the rooms or the men clean. The dysentery ward did not have bedpans, and supplies of quinine and sulfathiazole brought into the camp by medical officers to treat malaria and dysentery ran out. The Japanese usually denied requests for more medicine and other supplies, occasionally allowing in small quantities. Capriciousness ruled.[35]

The never-ending need in Camp O'Donnell brought out the best in some people, the worst in others, and caught a few in the gray area in between. Ted Lewin, owner of the Alcazar nightclub where Claire and John Phillips met, proved to be one of the most polarizing figures in camp. It was unclear how Lewin ended up in a POW camp. As a civilian, he should have been interned at Santo Tomas. At the beginning of the occupation he did or said something egregious enough for the Japanese toss him into O'Donnell, and none of his connections could get him out.

Nevertheless, Lewin drew on those connections from inside the camp, his procurement skills reaching legendary status. He never participated in any of the camp work details, yet he arranged for regular shipments of food and medicine, which mysteriously appeared in O'Donnell, unhindered by the Japanese guards. He kept what he needed and sold or traded away the rest. Many POWs found Lewin's actions reprehensible and unworthy of an American. Others considered him a kind of roguish hero. After all, he used the Japanese system to his advantage, bringing much-needed—if very expensive—goods into the camp. Lewin was determined to wheel and deal his way to the end of the war.[36]

In such deplorable conditions, it was no wonder, then, that Duckworth, Berry, and Tiffany looked to Dr. Atienza for help. The prisoners would only survive if the smuggling schemes continued, and they could only continue as long as people outside the camp willingly participated. Dr. Atienza formulated a plan.

When the Japanese began releasing Filipino prisoners from Camp O'Donnell, those who were too sick to walk were taken out in Red Cross ambulances, which guards thoroughly searched on the way out, looking for escapees. No one examined the returning empty vehicles so, Dr. Atienza suggested, they could be packed with the supplies Peggy brought from Manila and driven straight into O'Donnell. Peggy, eager to get the supplies to those who needed them most, supported the idea. The morning they prepared the first delivery, Atienza asked Peggy, "Why don't you send in a note with these things, asking for a receipt? In that way, you may be sure that your supplies are actually reaching the American prisoners."[37]

She liked the idea. Written confirmation that the food had reached the POWs would spur other donations from Manilans who could be assured the supplies were getting to their intended destination. Peggy wrote the note, but hesitated about signing it. Notes were dangerous enough; signed notes could be fatal: "If it were found, there would be trouble for everyone, and trouble in a big way for me. So after a moment's thought, I signed the note 'Miss U.' And with that signature, the Miss U organization came to hazy birth."[38]

The creation of Miss U signaled a transition for Peggy. No longer simply aiding the Americans when an opportunity arose, she committed to a permanent organization that required constant attention. She assumed a variation on her new identity of Rosena Utinsky—Miss U—for the sole purpose of resistance work, and dedicated herself to building a relief network under its auspices. Peggy devoted the next few months to shaping and sustaining Miss U by building a network of donors and couriers, all the while trying to keep her activities as quiet as possible. Safeguarding her identity was key. If the Japanese caught her, she would be in trouble not only for her relief work but also for forging a false nationality. In this, Peggy proved largely successful. All kinds of stories and rumors circulated in Manila and the POW camps about Miss U because no one was sure who she was: Chinese, Russian, or something else entirely.

The first trip was a success. The food supplies were unloaded without attracting the attention of the Japanese, and Dr. Atienza secured a receipt. The system looked simple to Peggy—as long as she supplied items, Atienza smuggled them—so the two of them worked as a team. "I arranged with Dr. Atienza to go up to Capas for each release date, when Filipino prisoners were sent back to Manila. I began traveling back and forth to Capas like a commuter, each time loading with all the food I could carry, but all I could carry was terribly little for so many men in desperate need."[39]

Though Peggy began with a large supply of food, she knew it would not last long; besides, the men needed medicine, toiletries, clothing, and money, too. When she returned to Manila after her first trip to Capas, probably sometime in July 1942, she took stock of her apartment where she had stored her lovely belongings: heavy silverware, Spode and Wedgwood china, jewelry. With a resolve born of the success at Capas, Peggy sold everything, including her electric stove, raising close to $1,000 that she put toward supplies for the POWs. The need was a bottomless pit. As careful as Peggy was with her money, it disappeared quickly, either spent on commodities or parceled out to the POWs.

The project required more funds. So, as Peggy later explained, "I became a regular panhandler. I begged everywhere. In shops, in churches, in the houses of friends, in the offices of total strangers." To minimize the risk that one of these strangers might report her to the occupation authorities, Peggy told them the items were for Filipinos. This lie revealed the persistence of the colonial mentality. Filipinos were in need, too, but Peggy believed Americans' needs were more important. Still, the subterfuge protected her and brought in some donations; yet, she worried that the POWs' needs were too great for her to fulfill on her own. She appealed to people she knew well, those supportive of the United States. That yielded little: "They were afraid. Well, I could understand that. Live under enemy occupation long enough and you begin to breathe an air of suspicion. You don't trust your friends or your neighbors or your own relatives. And most of the time you are probably justified."⁴⁰

To build the kind of trust to produce a consistent flow of donations, Peggy decided to involve at least one well-known Manila fixture, Father John Lalor. Peggy visited Lalor at the Malate Convent and explained the work she had been doing and the needs of her new relief organization. As she had hoped, Lalor agreed to help. One of his first contributions was thousands of pairs of used shoes he dunned from sympathetic friends.

With this, Peggy established a crucial organizational link between Manila and the POW camp: Dr. Atienza in Capas and Father Lalor, along with the other Malate priests, in Manila. She needed additional regulars to work on collection and delivery, and she did not have to look very hard or far for them. One afternoon in July 1942, Peggy visited the Charles Beauty Shop for her usual permanent wave. The shop's owner, an Allied national, had been interned in Santo Tomas. The employees kept the place open. One of the beauty operators was a young Igorot woman, Naomi Flores, who had been educated by an American family in the northern city of Baguio. The petite, quick-smiling woman listened as Peggy related her experiences on Bataan with Dr. Atienza and the Philippine Red Cross. Then Peggy began asking the people in the shop if they were willing to donate clothing to the Filipino prisoners being released from Camp O'Donnell.⁴¹

Peggy recalled the aftermath of that beauty shop appointment: "One day Naomi came to see me and said that she had overheard me talking in the shop, begging for clothing for the Filipinos who were being released. She asked whether she could help me with my work, wrapping packages and things like that. She proved to be so helpful, resourceful and trustworthy that she soon became my right-hand man."⁴²

Naomi Flores was, in fact, astonished to hear Dr. Atienza's name when Peggy talked about Bataan. "I was doing the same thing and asked her if she had any contact with the O'Donnell Camp in Capas, Tarlac," Naomi remembered after the war. Filipinos from all walks of life—like hairdresser Naomi Flores and lawyer Antonio Bautista who founded the Civil Liberties Union—had not been waiting around for others to take the lead in aid and resistance work. Because of the secrecy necessary to protect the underground workers, many conducted their activities alone, never quite sure who else was a comrade.[43]

Another woman involved early on was Maria Martinez, who would be known by the code names Papaya and Sunflower. The first Filipina stock-broker in the islands, Maria also had business interests in real estate and construction material supply. In the fall of 1941 she contracted with the quartermaster construction service to provide stone, sand, and gravel to USAFFE, working closely with Captain Lee Baldwin of the Corps of Engineers. After the Japanese occupied Manila in January 1942, Maria stopped her regular business activities and vowed revenge against the enemy. From her home on Taft Avenue, she had already heard the screams of people tortured by the Japanese in their converted garrison in the American School Building. Then her nephew, Private Robert Bruce Jones, escaped from the Death March and made his way to Manila, where he told Maria about those horrors.[44]

"I immediately volunteered to send food, clothing, medical supplies and 'news' to our American and Filipino war prisoners," Maria later explained. "I tried several ways and means to contact and locate friends, of whom there were many, in the prison camps. In the beginning there was much confusion, much misinformation, but I would not give up and in the end I succeeded in making contacts." One such contact was her old business associate, Captain Baldwin, who managed to get in touch with Maria about a month after the surrender of Corregidor. He let her know he was one of about four hundred hungry and sick prisoners still on the tiny island. Maria collected and sent supplies over to Corregidor at least once a week. Despite the surrender this kind of activity was still possible, as Gladys Savary also knew. In a few short months Maria made another contact that would allow her to expand her activities.[45]

Peggy, then, was a bit of a latecomer to prisoner relief, driven by her own personal connection. She knew Jack was imprisoned somewhere. When she explained to Naomi Flores more about her work with Dr. Atienza to establish a method of getting supplies into the camp, the young Filipina offered to help. Peggy ticked off a verbal list of things the prisoners needed, and told Naomi that if she knew people who had these things, the two of them could go together to collect them.

They made an effective team, and Peggy invited Naomi to come live with her. The Charles Beauty Shop was losing business despite the best efforts of its employees. Under the occupation, too few women had extra money to spend on hairstyling and permanent waves. Naomi brought the tools of her trade with her to establish Peggy's apartment as the site of an in-home business, and Naomi hoped she would pick up a little money now and then providing beauty services. The relocated salon primarily provided a reasonable cover story for the people seen coming and going from Peggy's apartment. As the fledgling Miss U organization grew during the summer of 1942, Naomi took the code name Looter because she was so good at procuring items.[46]

In addition to her "right-hand man," as she came to think of Naomi, Peggy worked closely with Evangeline Neibert, code name Sassy Susie, the daughter of an American father and a mestiza mother. Evangeline's father, Henry Edward Neibert, born in Maryland in 1871, arrived in the Philippines in 1901 as a Thomasite, an American teacher sent to the islands to "civilize and uplift" the local population. Henry met and married teacher Julia Story, and he went on to become a land surveyor and property owner. The couple made sure their daughter Evangeline was well educated, including some nurse's training. "Sweet and infectiously gay, Sassie [sic] Susie was like a little Irish colleen," Peggy remembered.[47]

The Miss U network had finally taken shape, and Peggy found the receipt system worked well. Both she and the donors had their proof that the aid reached its intended targets, and any loans could be scrupulously documented. During Peggy's second trip to Capas, Dr. Atienza helped her divide up the money she raised from selling her to possessions. Some went to Chaplain Tiffany to spend on the needy in Camp O'Donnell and some to Colonel Duckworth for hospital supplies. Peggy and Atienza also used an empty ambulance to carry in the other supplies she brought from Manila. The men sent out receipts and notes listing the things they needed, and, as Peggy recalled, "The notes turned the trick." Upon returning to Manila she worked through Father Lalor to tap American sympathizers—Chinese, Swiss, Spanish, Filipino—for more donations.[48]

For the most part, Peggy's code name held. Many of the donors only knew Peggy as Miss U, but some knew her, recognized her, and became regular members of her organization. Even those people referred to her in conversations as Miss U, just in case someone was listening. Sometimes they called her Aunty, an acknowledgement of the fact that she was not a young woman. Sometimes they called her Shorty, which was either a reference to her height or to her lack of patience, as in short-tempered.

The donations for the POWs were stored at the Malate Convent while Peggy prepared for each trip to Capas. From the beginning, the process of collecting and transporting these supplies was fraught with danger. Not only did Peggy have to be careful about whom she approached, she also had to be careful to limit her time out on the streets. Her first beating taught her the painful lesson that riding in a covered *carromata* was not enough to camouflage her white skin during the day; another incident in the summer of 1942 showed her that nighttime afforded little additional protection.

Through Father Lalor, Peggy was introduced to a group of Maryknoll nuns, Catholic nursing sisters deeply concerned about the plight of the military prisoners. The nuns had spirited away thousands of pairs of pajamas left behind when the Japanese closed down a hospital. They worked with Peggy to refashion them into pants and shirts for the POWs. It was a massive undertaking, and the pajamas were parceled out to others willing to work on the project, including Ethel and Ernest Heise. This elderly American couple had been exempted from internment at Santo Tomas because of their age and because Ernest Heise had been born in Germany. He immigrated with his family to New York, became a naturalized US citizen in 1888, and sometime during the 1910s became involved with a business venture in Manila.[49]

As loyal Americans, the Heises were drawn into prisoner aid work, including the nuns' pajama project. One night, Peggy arrived at their home to pick up a bundle of pajamas. "It was late when I left but I managed to get a *carromata* and climbed in with my big bundle of pajamas. The driver ignored my instructions, which called for following dark streets, and turned into a wide, lighted one. The headlights of an automobile fell on my white face, lighting it up, and some Japanese in a *carromata* between the automobile and me caught the sight of me."[50]

Not only was Peggy spotted, but the soldiers were drunk, a potentially lethal combination for a white woman out alone at night. The cart driver, despite Peggy's order to take off, could not induce the horse to break out of its plod. The Japanese gained on them. When the driver stopped at Peggy's building, she tossed him his fare, leapt out of the *carromata*, and smoothly unlocked the front door on the first try. The unlit street and the big palm tree in Peggy's front yard bought her additional time. The Japanese could not see where she went. Their *carromata*, traveling too fast to safely stop, trotted right past Peggy's apartment.[51]

Worried the soldiers would not give up—that their drunken frustration would turn to anger—Peggy raced into her apartment, locking everything that could be locked. She peered out of the window from her darkened room to see the soldiers on her street on foot, running, yelling, and searching. Peggy watched, frozen in horror, at what happened next: "Two Russian women turned the corner and came down the street. The drunken Japanese grabbed them and dragged them away." There was nothing Peggy could do to help them.[52]

Despite the potential danger of showing her white face, Peggy continued her trips between Manila and Capas that summer and fall. Once, upon entering the small Red Cross headquarters in Capas, she encountered a Japanese who took one look at her and started shouting, "American! American!" Dr. Atienza heard the ruckus and raced over, assuring the man that Peggy was not American but Lithuanian, "That is like German, friends to you." The man remained skeptical so Dr. Atienza touched Peggy's uniform and said she was a Lithuanian *kangofu*, a Lithuanian nurse. Finally the Japanese understood—and believed. The next time he saw Peggy he helpfully repeated this information to anyone else who questioned her identity.[53]

Peggy felt a bit safer, at least while she was in the Red Cross building in Capas. She realized, though, she was operating on borrowed time: "Someone was bound to discover my American nationality in a way that I could not disprove. It was fantastic luck that, after having lived in the Philippines so long, someone had not already recognized me and given me away to the enemy." Peggy tried to keep risks to a minimum, to calculate the relationship between risk and result so she did not get caught or somehow compromise the Miss U organization.[54]

One risk she took offered the possibility of learning something more about her husband. Captain Hix Meir of the 86th Field Artillery, and Vernon Booth, a civilian employee of the Adjutant General Corps, both originally from Indiana, were assigned by the Japanese to work at the light plant in Capas. They sneaked into the Red Cross house at night to pass along information to Dr. Atienza about conditions inside Camp O'Donnell. Peggy heard this, too. She made sure to be around every time the men showed up, and though she always asked, they never had any news about Jack Utinsky.[55]

One day Peggy encountered Meir and Booth while they were out from O'Donnell working on some electrical issues. She could not pass up the opportunity for information, even though it was broad daylight. Soon Dr. Atienza came running. "There's a Jap slapping women around and he is headed this way. Go into the station right away. I'll go the front way and get your ticket," he said. As much as she would have liked to hear more from Meir and Booth, she took off for the train station, the Japanese soldier hot on her trail.[56]

Peggy managed to jump up on the last train car, grabbing at the ticket Dr. Atienza held out for her as the train rolled along the track. The near-escape made her so weak that she could hardly sit up in her seat. Atienza lodged a complaint about the Japanese soldier's behavior with Colonel Ito, a Japanese officer at O'Donnell. Atienza pointed out that nurses were at a premium just now and Peggy was especially valuable because she worked without pay. The colonel took the complaint seriously. The next time Peggy saw that particular soldier, "he was a pretty battered looking specimen." She could not waste any sympathy on him; if she had not run so fast, she would have been the battered one.[57]

Everything Peggy did was risky, but she kept at it because the alternative of doing nothing was against her nature. Besides, there was no other way of finding Jack. "Night after night, when I had gone to bed, I allowed myself to wonder whether any of the food was reaching Jack. I had not heard a word, yet somehow I knew he was a prisoner somewhere. Risks did not seem too dangerous when I thought of him inside those fences." As the summer of 1942 turned into fall, there was still no news. No one seemed to know anything about her husband.[58]

Others worked just as hard as Peggy. In fact, from the very beginning much of the success of the Miss U network relied on Naomi Flores and Evangeline Neibert—Looter and Sassy Susie. Peggy felt more and more conspicuous because of her white skin, and she knew she could not keep up the trips to Camp O'Donnell. However, Naomi and Evangeline, dressed like street vendors with kerchiefs tied around their heads, loaded down with bundles of wares for sale, moved between Manila and Capas without attracting attention.[59]

At least, they did not attract attention for these commercial activities. But during that summer, Naomi Flores found herself in the enemy's crosshairs because of two American soldiers, escapees from the Death March, hiding out in Manila. Naomi worried the Japanese would find them, so she and Peggy hid the men in the deserted Charles Beauty Shop. Once the men were settled in, Peggy made her usual trip to Capas.

Upon returning to Manila a few nights later, instead of heading directly to her apartment, Peggy dropped off the prisoners' receipts with a Filipino friend who told her Cam Lee had been looking for her at the station; she must have missed him. Peggy lost her temper. She had told Lee they should never be seen together because if the Japanese arrested her, they would come for him as well. She did not want that on her conscience.

When Peggy returned to her apartment to confront Lee, she first encountered her downstairs neighbor, Mrs. Carnesa. The woman was beside herself. Mrs. Carnesa told Peggy the Japanese had been to the apartment building three times. Shaken, Peggy crawled into her bed to calm down. Soon Lee showed up to explain his presence at the train station. He needed to warn her. A Spanish woman living next door to the beauty parlor had seen the two American soldiers they had hidden there and reported them to the Japanese. Now the Japanese were trying to track down Naomi, the person who last worked there.

Peggy had to think fast, and the first thing she wanted was to find Naomi before the Japanese. Fortunately, she did. She convinced Naomi their only hope was a pre-emptive strike. Naomi should go to the Japanese at Fort Santiago, ask why they were looking for her, and tell them the young men who had been seen at the beauty shop were mestizos she hired as guards. It was a huge risk, but Naomi agreed. If she was frightened, she did not admit it.

That next day was a long one for both women. As the hours ticked by while Naomi was at the Fort, Peggy kept second-guessing the plan. In the early evening, Naomi returned to Peggy's apartment, shaken but unharmed. The Japanese interrogated her for hours, slapping her once. They seemed to believe her story about the young men. She also told them that she had taken some of the equipment from the beauty parlor to Peggy's apartment, shoring up their cover story for the women who came and went from the building.

The next day—a Sunday—the two Japanese officers who questioned Naomi at Fort Santiago turned up at Peggy's apartment. Naomi knew her story had been convincing, and understood their visit was a social call. She acted as friendly and helpful as she did the day before at the Fort, introducing the two men to Peggy as friends. Naomi made them all some tea, and they chatted through the afternoon hours. Peggy remained vigilant, though, as she saw how closely the Japanese scrutinized her apartment, how carefully they listened to everything she said. The social call was not strictly social. That day, though, the two women were safe.

Despite this scare, Peggy and her network settled into a routine: "We collected money and supplies in Manila. We packed them, hiding the money and notes and drugs. We stored supplies at the Malate Convent. From the contact people in Capas to the contact people in the prison camp, messages and supplies must be taken and lists brought back out. Day in, day out, the game went on. We would try anything."[60]

Some of the prisoner requests were more difficult to fill than others, yet Peggy prided herself on figuring out how to get what was needed.

A lieutenant had his glasses broken when a Japanese guard slapped his face, and asked the Miss U network if the glasses could be repaired. Peggy found an optometrist, Major Willard H. Waterous, willing to do the work. After the Bataan surrender, Waterous ended up back in Manila as a POW, but with sufficient freedom to work on these restoration projects. In addition to such necessities, the Miss U network tried to meet the cultural and leisure needs of the prisoners. Captain (later major) Sidney E. Seid, Army Air Corps, 93rd Bombardment Squadron, requested oil paints. He mentioned in his note to Miss U how dull prison camp life was and he needed something to pass the time. Peggy found the paints.[61]

Sometime during August 1942—a month plagued with typhoons—Peggy, Naomi Flores, and Evangeline Neibert returned to Manila from yet another supply run to Camp O'Donnell. The storm made their trip more difficult than usual as the howling winds and sheets of rain almost knocked the train from its tracks. Tucked into the blouse of her Red Cross nurse's uniform Peggy carried notes and receipts from the prisoners, including General Luther Stevens, Colonel Duckworth, and Chaplain Tiffany. As per their standard practice, the three women did not sit together on the train nor did they walk through the station together.

Peggy alone attracted enough attention. A squad of Japanese soldiers stood at the station gate, their bayonets drawn as they surrounded her. "The Japanese could hardly have picked me up at a time when I had more damning evidence on me, and the worst of it was that it implicated so many of the prisoners as well. My armed escort wheeled and turned into a room at the left of the station," she recalled. There Peggy saw what she first took for German soldiers. When one of them spoke, she realized they were American. Still, this offered little comfort. All she could see were the Japanese soldiers with their weapons, all she could think about were the documents stuffed in her blouse. Peggy was so frightened, her hearing temporarily shut down. Naomi and Evangeline, who followed at a careful distance, saw she had turned sheet-white.[62]

The American officer speaking was Major Clarence C. Heinrich of the 21st Division, Philippine Army. It was understandable that Peggy mistook him for a German because his mother had been born in Germany.

With Heinrich, among others, were Captain Allen F. Crosby of the 121st Infantry, Philippine Army, and Lieutenant Colonel John P. Horan. Horan, a career army officer from Punxsutawney, Pennsylvania, was in command of Camp John Hay when the Japanese attacked. The bombing of the camp on December 8, 1941, coupled with a major landing of enemy troops at Lingayen Gulf just days before Christmas, sent Horan's command into disarray.

When the Japanese occupied Baguio two days after Christmas, Colonel Horan and the rest of USAFFE fought on. After Bataan's surrender in April 1942, Horan assumed command of what had been designated the 121st Infantry Regiment, a group of Filipino and American guerrillas. With Corregidor's fall the following month, General Wainwright ordered all of his men to surrender, and Horan complied. After extensive interrogation, the Japanese moved Horan all around Luzon so he could convince the remaining USAFFE stragglers to surrender.[63]

Peggy happened to run into Colonel Horan and the other men at the train station as they were on their way to Cabanatuan, where the Japanese had set up another POW camp. The American officers had been stuck at the train station for two hours trying to find someone to help them communicate with their Japanese captors. Major Heinrich wanted to get word to his wife and children, interned in Santo Tomas, that he was alive. Peggy used her Red Cross badge to convince the guards to let her make a telephone call. She reached Albert E. Holland, a former sugar company officer, now a member of the Santo Tomas's Executive Committee. He told Peggy that Heinrich's wife and children were staying at the Holy Cross Convent, and he would arrange to send a message to them.

While she waited for Holland to work whatever magic he could, Peggy sent out for food and coffee for Horan, Heinrich, Crosby, and the other men. Because these men needed help and she intended to provide it, she squelched her fear and regained her composure. After an acceptable interval, Peggy telephoned Holland again, and he delivered better than expected news. Heinrich's wife and children were on their way to the train station and should arrive in time for a short visit before he left for

Cabanatuan. Peggy also got word to Captain Crosby's family about his whereabouts, "So, all in all it was a good hour's work," she conceded.[64]

Throughout the summer and fall, the Miss U network continued its efforts and attracted additional helpers. By October, Maria Martinez joined the organization. Rebecca Habibi, a Turkish-born clairvoyant and card reader, introduced Maria to Peggy, and Peggy immediately recognized the Filipina as a valuable asset. Maria later remembered how hard Miss U worked "supplying food, home made Vitamin C, juice, clothes, medicines and money to war prisoners" in Camp O'Donnell.[65]

Colonel Duckworth served as Miss U's inside contact at Camp O'Donnell. He not only collected lists of what was needed and what was dispersed, he also kept track of who was in the camp, who was still alive, who was dead. This was the information Peggy read closely, looking for her husband's name. It was the same kind of information Claire Phillips sought when she arrived in Manila.

CHAPTER 9

THE CREATION OF DOROTHY FUENTES

A T THE END OF JUNE 1942, when the Miss U network was already underway, Claire Phillips talked to Carling Sobrevinas about returning to Manila. He reminded her that he had just been in the city, and was not able to get a pass that would allow her out on the streets. Without it, the Japanese would pick her up in no time and take her to internment at Santo Tomas with the other Allied nationals. Claire insisted on going, reminding him that both Phil and Dian were in Manila. She should be there with them.

Sobrevinas relented. He had done his duty by pointing out she would probably be unsuccessful, and he did not believe he had the right to prevent her from trying. "Through a clever ruse, I smuggled her to Manila right under the very noses of the Japanese," he later recounted. In early July 1942, Carling arranged for some Negritos, indigenous people with the most knowledge of the terrain, to guide them around Japanese lines and into Manila. Without official travel passes from the Japanese, it was the only way they could go. Because she was American, Claire could not bring along any identifying documents. She left her passport and Phil's army papers with the Sobrevinas family for safekeeping.[1]

Claire found the sight of the small, dark Negritos unsettling and was "not reassured by the sight of their glistening white teeth, which had been filed to points. Four of them were partly clad in civilized garb, but the remainder wore G-Strings and little else, save quivers of arrows and hunting bows on their backs." They made their way south to Orani, clambering over hills, pushing through dense brush, sleeping overnight in a small cave, before boarding a *banca* to sail across Manila Bay. When it looked like the white sail might attract too much attention in the dim evening light, it was lowered. The boat drifted for a while, with Claire hidden under the sail and piles of bananas and coconuts. Carling believed he was hiding Claire from hostile Hukbalahaps (Huks) whom he described as "radical Filipino partisans who were assisting the Japs to patrol the Bay."[2]

Sobrevinas may not have known the exact identity of these "radical Filipino partisans." The Huks organized to oppose the Japanese occupation, so they would not have been assisting the enemy with anything. They were fierce nationalists who did not always get along with all ethnic groups native to Luzon. This specific band may have been hostile toward Negritos, and by extension, anyone with them. In any case, Sobrevinas believed these men posed a danger to Claire and he was unwilling to take any chances with her safety.

After arriving on the Manila side of the bay, Sobrevinas and Claire still had to get into the city. They stowed away in a produce truck owned by a Filipino with the proper passes and licenses to travel in and out of Manila. This time Claire hid under sacks filled with charcoal as the truck wended its way through the barrios, stopping at each one for an inspection: "Jap sentries walking around the truck, prodding the bags with their bayonets. I knew full well that a sneeze or cough at such peril-filled moments would have been disastrous, and my lungs ached from the charcoal dust and frequent periods of holding my breath."[3]

While in the countryside Claire had worried that her skin color made her more noticeable. Once she reached Manila she gambled that she could better blend in with the city environment. She had taken care to develop and maintain a dark tan, and when she ventured out in public she wore sunglasses and a hood. Visually she might pass for a mestiza, though she did not have the documentation to support that identity. It was risky to be out on the streets.

Claire willingly took that risk on her first full day in Manila. After she parted from Carling Sobrevinas, she headed downtown to Batangas Street and the home of Mamerto Roxas. Dian, happily ensconced with her extended family members, did not recognize her mother and refused to have anything to do with her. Judge Roxas, concerned with Claire's frail appearance, called in the family doctor who started her on a series of quinine shots for malaria and diagnosed a mild case of scurvy. Overall, as long as she took the medicine and ate fresh fruits and vegetables, the months in the hills would not do Claire any lasting physical damage.[4]

Mamerto Roxas encouraged Claire and Dian to remain in his home. In exchange for shelter and support, Claire had to agree not leave its confines. The Roxas family did not want any trouble with the Japanese, and they would get plenty if they were found harboring an American. While Claire understood the value of the judge's offer, she could not imagine remaining cooped up in one place for an indefinite period of time. It would defeat the purpose of coming to Manila if she could not look for Phil.

The only thing to do was create a new identity that would allow the freedom of movement she needed. Claire's deep tan, her dark hair and eyes all suggested a Spanish or Italian heritage. Either of those nationalities would keep her out of internment. The name she chose to use, that of her first husband Manuel Fuentes, was Spanish, and claiming Spanish citizenship might prove the ideal cover. Spain had colonized in the Philippines long before the United States, and it was not unusual to still find people of Spanish descent who had been born in the islands. Even better, Spain, after its own grueling civil war in the 1930s, had declared neutrality in World War II. Add to that the fact that Manuel Fuentes was a native Filipino, and Claire would have created a very convincing national-ity to keep her out of internment.

Yet she opted to claim Italian heritage and change her first name. Italy was part of the Axis, therefore an ally of Japan rather than a neutral power. Few Italians lived in Manila so there was little chance one of them would uncover Claire's deception. Claire did not speak Italian; neither did most Japanese. Besides, her cover story would account for her lack of Italian. As Dorothy Fuentes, she had been born in the Philippines to Italian par-ents who died when she was young. If circumstances warranted, she could allude to an absent Filipino husband to strengthen her case.

With the plan settled, Claire contacted an acquaintance of hers who had once worked at the Italian Consulate in Manila. Within a week she secured the false papers. Claire then felt confident enough to begin mov-ing around Manila. One of the first things she did was visit Louise De Martini, now interned at Santo Tomas, to bring her friend some food and cigarettes. It was a bold move, turning up at a place filled with people who could recognize her and report her to the occupation authorities. Also a potentially fatal one, as Mamerto Roxas told her when she returned. The Japanese announced that anyone caught sheltering an American or British national would be shot. Roxas knew he could not keep Claire out of sight nor could he turn her in. Instead, he sent a letter to Lieutenant Colonel Ohta Seiichi of the Kempeitai, informing him that "Dorothy Fuentes" was staying with his family. Roxas was willing to vouch for her since she did not have her original papers.

It took a week for Ohta to reply. He ordered Roxas to bring Dorothy Fuentes to his office at Fort Santiago and personally sign as her guaran-tor. On their way to the meeting, Roxas told Claire to leave the explana-tions to him. She should sit quietly and say as little as possible. It was a wise suggestion. During his brief tenure in Manila, Ohta had acquired the nickname "the butcher of Fort Santiago" because of the way he treated prisoners. Thankfully, during Claire's first visit to the Fort, which only lasted thirty minutes, she was not required to say much at all. Through the lieutenant colonel's interpreter, Roxas told Ohta that Dorothy Fuentes had gone to Bataan to visit friends and had contracted a severe case of malaria. Bombs destroyed her identity papers, so when she returned to Manila she had to have new ones drawn up. Ohta bought the story.

Claire had been nervous, but she found Colonel Ohta suave and pleasant, at least until he said that female Philippine nationals were expected to cooperate with the Japanese in one important way. Now Claire held her breath, worried about what would come next. Ohta simply asked her to promise not to aid the enemy. She did, though she kept her fingers crossed. She and Roxas signed the necessary papers and walked out of Fort Santiago.

Though all of Claire's paperwork as "Dorothy Fuentes" was in place, Judge Roxas still urged caution. On the surface, her story sounded good, yet he knew the least little thing would make the Japanese suspicious. If they started following Claire, it would not be long before they figured out she was an American. Claire understood, and since she wanted to find Phil and to help John Boone with whatever he might need, she initially kept a low profile. For four weeks—through the rest of July 1942 and into August—she stuck to the Roxas home, regaining her health through a smart diet and mild exercise. She reconnected with Dian, who eventually stopped seeing her mother as a stranger. Claire traveled to Santo Tomas once a week to bring in supplies to her friends Louise De Martini and Mona. So many Manilans bundled food, clothing, and medicine into packages and brought them to the internment camp that she blended into the crowd.

After a month, Claire expanded her forays into the city, becoming bolder, even incautious. She visited Lolita, recently delivered of a baby boy and still resting in the hospital. Instead of returning directly to the Roxas home, Claire stopped at her old apartment in the Dakota building. She chatted with her former neighbor, Mrs. Lopez, a Spaniard exempted from internment. Mrs. Lopez asked after Phil and Dian, and then told Claire she had her trunk—the one packed with her real documents—moved to the building's storeroom. It was the only thing that had survived the looting that preceded the occupation, and Mrs. Lopez worried that Miss Del Rosario, the building manager, intended to appropriate the trunk.[5]

Claire had no fond memories of her former building manager. Del Rosario quit her job at the Dakota Apartments not long after the Japanese occupation to work as an interpreter at Fort Santiago. She had gone to school in Japan, had even once been presented to the Empress, and could speak the language like a native. Del Rosario was likely one of many "fifth columnists" in the Philippines, a designation for people from within who laid the foundation for and then participated in an occupation. Claire went cold at the thought that Del Rosario might have been in Fort Santiago the day she swore to her false identity.

Even with this realization of how easily her deception could be exposed, Claire continued to take chances being seen in public by people who knew her true identity. Not long after this outing, Mamerto Roxas's sister and sister-in-law told Claire the school at the Malate Convent had been converted into a hospital. The Irish priests who ran it, including Father Lalor, were taking in the Filipino soldiers as they were released from Camp O'Donnell. Remedios Hospital needed all of the nurses it could get, so Claire got busy sewing uniforms. After a refresher course in basic nursing duties and first aid care, she went to work in a ward.

At Remedios Claire met the hospital's chief fundraiser, a young fair-skinned Spaniard with reddish hair and gray eyes named Ramon Amusategui. Born in Spain in 1909, he had settled in the Philippines in the early 1930s, taking a job with a building and loan company in Manila and working his way up to the vice manager position. He married Lorenza Vazquez, the youngest daughter of Spanish parents who had been living on the island of Mindoro. When the war started, the Amusateguis were part of the Manila elite, and though they were Spanish citizens, they had many American and Filipino friends. As Lorenza Amusategui later explained, "When the Japanese blow fell on the Philippines there were more than Ramon and I who had not a single drop of American blood who wanted to do their parts for America." In the fall of 1942, this meant helping the POWs.[6]

Claire found Ramon Amusategui's zeal for the hospital's work and his sincere interest in its patients reassuring enough to risk asking him for help in locating Phil. Ramon knew so much about the military prisoners and the POW camp that Claire assumed he had contacts providing him with information. She was right. Ramon knew a Filipina nurse who worked with an American doctor in Bilibid Prison, Major Willard Waterous—the same doctor who helped the Miss U network. The nurse could ask Waterous to find out about Phil, Amusategui said. Claire would have to be patient because it might take a week or more to relay the information.

Buoyed by the possibility of finally locating Phil and enthusiastic about the good being done at Remedios, Claire decided to emulate Ramon Amusategui. She set out in Manila to collect money and supplies for the hospital, moving through the better residential areas, asking for beds, sheets, towels, dishes, money—anything that would help the men. She talked about them, too, incautiously mentioning John Boone and his guerrillas, how much good they could do for everyone. Claire was astonished when people slammed doors in her face or told her she was out of her mind. No one would give her a thing. Claire's naïveté put her at risk and had the potential to damage others who were much more circumspect at this work.

Though unsuccessful at soliciting supplies, Claire continued with her nursing duties at Remedios. This put her in the path of others connected with the Miss U network. Claire met Dr. Romeo Atienza and learned about his work on Bataan, at Camp O'Donnell, and with the Red Cross. She trusted the doctor as much as she trusted Ramon Amusategui, and asked Atienza to use his contacts at O'Donnell to find Phil. By the end of August 1942, Claire learned from both of her contacts that he was probably in Cabanatuan. Trying to find out for certain would take more time.

Working at Remedios Hospital allowed Claire to make a contribution to the Allied war effort by nursing Filipino soldiers, and it provided her with contacts who could find out about her husband. It did not, however, generate an income. Though Judge Roxas pledged to the occupation authorities that he would provide for Dorothy Fuentes as a guest under his roof, Claire became increasingly uncomfortable with the arrangement. She was a woman accustomed to making her own way and to having her own way. Her financial obligation to the judge undercut that. Moreover, her connection to the Roxas family was a tenuous, indirect one, through her first marriage. As the occupation wore on, the difficulties of remaining in the Roxas home only intensified.

If she left, Claire increased her chances of exposure. Still, she looked around for the same kind of work she always wanted—entertaining—and landed a singing job at Ana Fey's Night Club on Isaac Peral in the Ermita district. Ana Fey, a German Jew who had made her way to Manila via Spain, was a petite blue-eyed platinum blonde who owned a dancing school before deciding a nightclub would be more lucrative. Ana's establishment was patronized almost exclusively by wealthy Japanese, and she had her own protector, a strapping Japanese journalist named Horiuchi, the Manila correspondent for one of Japan's leading newspapers, the *Asahi Shimbun*.[7]

Now that she had a steady income, Claire moved back to her old place in the Dakota Apartments, another risky choice for someone trying to mask her real nationality. Claire hired two servants, just as she had before the war started. She replaced Dian's first amah, Lolita, with Ah Ho, a sixty-year-old Chinese woman, "short, fat, with snapping black eyes and scanty hair skewered into a determined knot atop her head," and hired a Filipina named Pressa as cook. Now, two more people knew about Claire's dual identity.[8]

Claire's performances at the popular nightclub as Dorothy Fuentes attracted scores of Japanese patrons, which intensified the danger that she would be exposed. As she later admitted, "There is only one adequate adjective to describe the state of my mind the first night on my new job . . . jittery." She fielded song requests from the audience, hobnobbed with the guests, and soon Ana Fey encouraged her to "butter up" the important customers. While her boss expected this to encourage the club's patrons to spend more money, Claire had something else in mind. One night, Ana directed Claire to a table of Japanese customers. Sitting there was a young officer named Masamoto, who identified himself as the acting commandant of the Santo Tomas internment camp. With a few drinks under his belt and Dorothy Fuentes's compliments swelling his head, he boasted he could arrange for her to visit Santo Tomas any time she wished. Claire immediately thought of Louise De Martini and wondered if there was more she could do for her friend besides bring supplies. Masamoto might be her key.[9]

Also at the nightclub, Claire met more pro-American Filipino employees who would soon become important to her underground work. She was especially drawn to a young well-educated Filipina, Fely Corcuera, a talented singer and dancer. Fely confided to Claire that she had many relatives fighting in the Philippine Army, and she hated the Japanese. If Fely was the most talented entertainer in the club, the young woman known only as Fahny ran a close second. Claire later described her as "our clever negro mestiza dancer, very dark, but beautiful in an exotic way, witty, spunky, big-hearted, and like Fely, thoroughly patriotic." Fahny's father, an American doctor, was interned at Santo Tomas, and she had not heard from him since January. Fely encouraged Claire to arrange a visit to Santo Tomas with Masamoto. Seeing Louise De Martini would give her the opportunity to pass along a note to Fahny's father.[10]

Masamoto did as promised and arranged a fifteen-minute chat between Claire and both Louise and Mona. On a Sunday afternoon, Claire sat in his office in Santo Tomas with her friends and a Japanese guard who allegedly did not understand English. The women took care not to say anything that could be considered critical of the occupation. Mona, though, risked a few whispered comments to Claire. She had to get out of Santo Tomas, and she wanted Claire to arrange for her to see Masamoto alone. She knew she could convince him to let her out.

The next time Masamoto came to the nightclub, he told Claire how much he enjoyed meeting her two friends, especially the small redhead, Mona. Claire saw the chance to lay the groundwork for Mona's release. She told Masamoto that Mona was only half American, her father was an influential Spaniard, and she actually had very little to do with her mother. Masamoto saw right through Claire's story and said he knew Mona wanted out of the internment camp. He informed Claire that Mona could leave Santo Tomas only if she filed the proper paperwork and renounced her American heritage.

It took Claire a few days to get the documents in order, especially to find two prominent Spaniards or Filipinos willing to act as Mona's guarantors.

After Ana Fey promised Mona a job at her nightclub, Claire presented herself at Masamoto's office at Santo Tomas with the paperwork. He sent for Mona, who renounced her ties to the United States. Claire felt queasy to hear how easily those words flowed from the woman's mouth. Once she finished, Mona declined to spend any time alone with the Japanese officer. She walked out of the room, leaving Claire with Masamoto. He closed the door.

He expected payment for his favor. Claire had put him off once before at the nightclub, mentioning her Filipino husband away attending business on another island. Now, Masamoto insinuated, Claire must be lonely with her husband so far away for so long. He was willing to take her husband's place. Claire tried to deflect by explaining that despite an absent husband, she had her daughter to keep her company at home. She invited Masamoto to visit both her and Mona at the nightclub, which he accepted as a temporary compromise.

Mona was waiting for Claire outside the gates of Santo Tomas, and she told Claire she was very grateful for everything. Claire took this to mean that her impulsive young friend could not bear, under any circumstances, to sleep with the enemy. She soon realized her mistake. Once freed from Santo Tomas, Mona was perfectly willing to exchange sexual favors with the Japanese patrons at Ana Fey's Night Club. There, Mona met a well-off Japanese miner named George, who had been born in California and had citizenship papers from both the United States and Japan. It did not matter to him who won the war. George convinced Mona to find him a nice apartment in Manila, furnish and staff it. When that was all done, she resigned from the nightclub and moved in with him.

This was too much for Claire. Mona, she believed, has crossed a line no woman in an occupied country should cross. But Claire saw that Mona did not care what other people thought of her. Mona wanted a nice place to live and plenty of food on the table, and George could supply that. Claire pushed the point. "Food! Is it really that important? After the war you know what they will say." Mona shrugged it off. She was only half American, she reminded Claire, and she renounced that half. She did not believe anyone would say much of anything. It was the end of their friendship.[11]

Claire's work at Ana Fey's Night Club provided an education in surviving the occupation. Some Japanese could be cajoled and flattered; the key was figuring out which ones. Some would not push for their rewards, and it could be a gamble trying to figure that out, too. At this point in the occupation, the early fall of 1942, Claire tried to draw her own line about acceptable behavior. Flirting, maybe even sex, could be appropriate for securing certain things, like an internment exemption. Openly living with the enemy was beyond the pale.

The Mona drama had curtailed Claire's work at Remedios; once resolved, Claire resumed her regular hospital schedule. She was especially anxious to find out if Dr. Atienza had been able to secure a travel pass to Cabanatuan so she could go there to find Phil. The Japanese had only allowed Atienza and the Red Cross access to Camp O'Donnell as long as Filipino prisoners were there, adamantly insisting the Philippine Red Cross could only aid Filipinos. Since only American POWs were incarcerated at Cabanatuan, Atienza could not think of a valid reason to go there. With that avenue closed to Claire, she was grateful when one of the other hospital volunteers, a young woman named Betty Wright, overheard the conversation and offered to help: "I can promise you anything you write will get in. Don't ask me how I accomplish it, but I have a means of slipping notes in there."[12]

Betty Wright, born in Manila in 1922, claimed Philippine citizenship to avoid internment. With her lifelong connections in the city, she began smuggling supplies to the Cabanatuan prisoners during the summer of 1942. Along with other Manila socialites, including Pilar Campos, Betty organized the Volunteer Social Aid Committee (VSAC), which had ties to similar efforts underway in the city. Newspaperman Tony Escoda and his sociologist wife Josefa (Pepa) worked with the VSAC, and they assisted the Chaplain's Aid Association, which also collected donations in Manila for aid distribution in Cabanatuan. This underground activity grew faster than a spider spinning a web.

Like many of those involved in the VSAC and other groups, Betty Wright had a personal connection to the prisoners. Hers was Lieutenant William James Tooley, Headquarters Company, 31st Infantry, her fiancé. Betty felt a particular connection with Claire because John Phillips was from the same outfit. Claire sat down right away with the tiny piece of paper Betty had given her and poured her heart out to Phil. Betty took the note from her, and then Claire waited. It took a month for the disheartening news to arrive: Bill Tooley had been unable to find out anything about John V. Phillips.

This private sorrow inspired Claire to perform her best at Ana Fey's: "In retrospect, it seems that to escape the ever-present concealed pain and apprehension, I prodded myself into a show of vivacity that stood me in good stead. It gave me a thrill to be so easily accepted in my new role as I made the rounds of the tables between my singing numbers." Claire also perceived the edge of danger in her job. She was among the enemy so always had to be on guard. Soon enough, Claire learned a painful lesson about letting it slip.[13]

On a September night in 1942, when Claire had been working at the nightclub for little more than a week, Ana Fey informed her that she was doing well enough with her requests that she could take a couple of encores after her next number. Impressed with her singing, a group of four Japanese customers invited Claire to join them at their table. As she sat down, one of them asked for ice. Claire moved to call for the waiter. One of the men swatted her on the bottom and ordered her to get the ice herself. Startled and humiliated, Claire turned on him, and seeing the hostility in her face, he burned her leg with his cigarette and said, "In Japan women wait on men." She slapped his face.[14]

The four Japanese took Claire into the club's back room. Though she cast a pleading glance at Ana Fey as she was led away, the club owner did nothing to intervene. Ana instead instructed the orchestra to play loudly to cover any noise, and she stood guard at the door to make sure no one interrupted Claire's "lesson." In that back room, the men lectured Claire on proper female behavior, then directed her to bow and apologize. Just when she thought this would be the end of the matter, they told her to stand with her hands behind her. Claire closed her eyes while the men beat her into semi-consciousness. She hit the floor, and they delivered a few kicks before departing.

After this, the first beating Claire would endure from the Japanese, Ana Fey told her to get back to work. Claire staunched the bleeding from her lip, repaired her makeup, and did just that. The next morning, feeling the effects of the beating—her limbs were stiff, black and blue with bruises—Claire concluded she could no longer work at the nightclub. Ana Fey could not be trusted; she would do nothing to protect Claire. She decided she should have a place of her own. It would be safer, and she could use it as a base of operations: "I had an over-powering desire to obtain money for the American cause. I had not failed to observe how freely the Japanese sometimes talked, particularly when alcohol stimulated their tongues. In my own club, I thought, it would be possible to gather valuable bits of information from the enemy to send to Boone."[15]

Fely Corcuera came to the same conclusion and made the suggestion before Claire raised the subject with her. If Claire opened her own place, Fely promised, both she and Fahny would come work there. Claire knew if she had Fely and Fahny, Ana Fey's customers would switch allegiances to see the best entertainers in the city. Claire faced some big hurdles, though, starting with finances. The kind of nightclub she envisioned—big and swanky—would not come cheap, and she did not have enough money of her own. All of the people she approached about backing the venture turned her down.

A few days after the beating, Claire and Fely lunched together at Chan's Restaurant, located near Manila Bay. Claire knew the restaurant and its owner well because she and Phil ate there many times before the war. Chan seated the two women but did not linger to chat as long as several Japanese occupied a table nearby. Fely went home after she finished her lunch, while Claire lingered, drinking tea until the Japanese left and she could talk to Chan.

When they were alone, Claire told Chan everything that had happened since the war started. She explained that she wanted to open a business so she could help John Boone's guerrillas and the POWs. Chan, intuiting what Claire was after, suggested she rent the building formerly known as La Fonda, located on the next corner of San Luis, at 8 A. Mabini Street: "The well-situated two story building was easily visible from the waterfront. A wide stairway led past the lower floor, which was occupied by small shops, to the second floor which consisted of a big studio room with other small rooms adjoining it."[16]

Claire handed over to Chan all of her remaining valuables—two diamond rings, a watch, and $200 American—as security on a loan of occupation money. The occupation money, now legal tender in the Philippines, enabled Claire to sign a lease on the building. Fely Corcuera and her sister Flora, along with Fahny, started advertising the new place to their favorite customers at Ana Fey's, whispering to them about a new, exclusive club slated to open soon. One patron, a particular fan of Claire's, suggested she name her establishment the Club Tsubaki. Tsubaki, he explained, was "camellia" in Japanese, a favorite flower in his country, and it also denoted something hard to get. The word "club" signaled exclusivity, he added. Putting the two words together virtually guaranteed that Claire's clientele would consist of the upper crust of the occupation society.[17]

After talking up the club and choosing a name, Claire decorated the place like a well-appointed lounge rather than a cocktail bar. She had the walls painted a creamy white, and hung pale orchid satin drapes over the windows and the doorway that led to the stage. Low settees made of rattan lined the walls, with cocktail tables placed conveniently in front of them. Two private booths were available near the entrance for customers willing to pay extra.

Claire chose staff she knew she could trust. In addition to Fely and Flora Corcuera and Fahny, she hired Fahny's two sisters, another employee from Ana Fey's named Judy Geronimo, and a few of the young men she knew from the Sobrevinas camp in the hills. Fely proved instrumental in guiding Claire through the process of securing her business license—the Corcueras' father, Vicente, was well known at City Hall—and facilitated the acquisition of a beer license through one of Ana Fey's customers.[18]

With that, the Club Tsubaki was ready to open.

CHAPTER 10

CABANATUAN

E VEN AS PEGGY UTINSKY SET UP HER RELIEF NETWORK FOR CAMP O'Donnell during the spring of 1942, the Japanese began moving American prisoners further northeast on Luzon to the province of Nueva Ecija. There, a few miles outside of the bustling town of Cabanatuan, was the former training camp for the 91st Philippine Army Division, also referred to as Cabanatuan, which the Japanese turned into a POW camp. Peggy knew enough about Japanese opinions of prisoners and about conditions in O'Donnell to understand the move had nothing to do with providing the men better facilities.

She was right. The Cabanatuan prison complex contained three separate dilapidated camps, each designated a number—Camp 1, Camp 2, Camp 3—and each located a few miles from the others. In late May 1942, as the first American prisoners arrived, only Camp 3 had an efficient working water supply, so the Japanese funneled the men first into Camp 3. Within three days, it was bursting its weak seams. Cabanatuan's newly appointed commandant, Lieutenant Colonel Mori Shigeji, directed the next shipments of POWs to Camp 2, which at least had a water source nearby. When that proved inadequate even by Japanese standards, the prisoners were moved from Camp 2 to Camp 1, the facility closest to the town of Cabanatuan. At its height, Camp 1 would house 9,000 POWs, with an additional 6,000 in Camp 3.[1]

Jack Wright, Bill Berry, and the other prisoners—including, perhaps, Jack Utinsky, John Phillips, and Edgar Gable—began arriving at the town of Cabanatuan in late May 1942, by way of Bilibid Prison in Manila, a trip of about eight hours. The dehydrated and near-starving men fell into columns of four and were marched into the fenced grounds of the local elementary school. The next morning, Jack Wright received a bowl of steamed rice for breakfast, but Bill Berry missed out on his allotment. When the guards lined the prisoners up in columns of two and four to walk them the thirteen miles to their final destination, Wright learned he could not fill his canteen because the water spigot had not been turned on. Berry, however, had the foresight to fill his canteen with runoff rainwater the night before. Deprived of his breakfast, he took restrained swigs to ease his hunger.[2]

The debilitated men traveled a little over two miles an hour, and the Japanese guards allowed them a rest period about every two hours. Some of the POWs were nearly mad with thirst and broke formation during the march when they caught sight of any water supply—carabao wallows or even mud puddles. Some guards laughed at the prisoners' desperation, while others savaged the captives with blows from their rifle butts.[3]

The final destination for Jack Wright was Camp 3, a billet with other officers in the former dispensary, a solidly built wooden structure. The enlisted men crowded into nipa shacks called *bahays*, originally built to house forty Filipino soldiers, each now holding at least one hundred American POWs. Wright remained in Cabanatuan only a few days before he and seventy-five other men were sent back to Corregidor, where the Japanese planned to make use of their knowledge of the coastal artillery. Wright's months at Prison Camp No. 9, most of which were spent working in the mess, afforded him conditions and treatment better than those of his counterparts at Cabanatuan. In June 1943, his luck ran out and he returned to Cabanatuan.[4]

Bill Berry also got out of Cabanatuan within days of his arrival, by his own efforts rather than a decision by the Japanese. On Berry's first night in Camp No. 2, which he regarded as nothing more than a dump, he met up with friends Dick Tirk and Phil Sanborn. They were all of the same mind: they wanted out. Sanborn had picked up a geography textbook from the Cabanatuan Elementary School where the POWs had spent the night on their way into the camp. It contained a map of the Philippines—a golden ticket, the men thought, to their freedom, because it would enable them to stay hidden once they escaped.

Their move the following morning to Camp No. 1 only shored up the men's resolve. This facility was just as bad as the other two at Cabanatuan—overcrowded and lacking modern sanitation—and Berry knew nothing good could come of it. He also knew if he, Tirk, and Sanborn were caught escaping, they would be executed. Only three days before their arrival at Camp No. 1, three enlisted men had walked out of it, and were brought back by Japanese guards who tortured the POWs before killing them. That gave Berry pause, at least until he saw the prisoners from Camp O'Donnell trucked in: "Back on Corregidor we had heard rumors of how badly they were being treated, but we were unprepared for the shock of what we saw. Those guys all had malaria and dysentery and were so skinny that they looked like walking skeletons with skin hanging from their bones. There was absolutely no hope in their eyes."[5]

Berry did not intend to become one of them. That night he stuffed a gunnysack with a blanket, medicine, matches, a few hundred American dollars, and a small framed photograph of his mother. He met Dick Tirk and Phil Sanborn at the latrine and they crawled, one by one, along a ditch and out of the camp. Once clear, they ran east toward the Sierra Madre Mountains, covering nearly eighteen miles by daylight. Along the way they received help from sympathetic Filipinos, including guerrillas, one of whom was Ferdinand Marcos, leader of the Nueva Ecija Province resistance and future president of the Philippines.[6]

That textbook map of the Philippines, their key to freedom, proved no match for the wartime hazards on Luzon. Berry contracted dengue fever, also called breakbone fever, whose accompanying muscle and joint aches made any movement excruciating. Staying in one place for any reason at all was a risky luxury; even sympathetic Filipinos did not want the trio around for long. If the Japanese caught them, they would all be executed.

The escapees stopped at a small fishing village called Magnak on the Pacific coast between Dingalan Bay and Lamon Bay. They decided to stay for several days as Berry struggled with a 105-degree fever, however it was more than a month before the three could push on. Shortly after they did, they were captured near Magnak by pro-Japanese Filipinos and turned over to the enemy. After a brief interrogation during which the Americans managed to convince the Japanese they were stragglers from Corregidor and not escaped prisoners, they were put on a truck to Cabanatuan. Their escape, which neatly encapsulated the problems faced by Americans on the run, had lasted three months.

In the trio's absence, thousands of Americans endured the brutal conditions in Cabanatuan. Lieutenant Colonel Albert Fields, a dentist in his early fifties, managed to record in a journal his observations of life in Cabanatuan. He arrived there, like Jack Wright and Bill Berry, in time to watch the O'Donnell prisoners trucked in at the end of May and the beginning of June 1942. It was two weeks before Fields and the others learned about the possibility of a lifeline. On June 14, 1942, Fields noted in his journal, "We are informed we will be permitted to make outside purchases of food as soon as arrangement can be made—if we have the money. I was lucky I got in here with about P140.00, which is more than most officers have."[7]

Those less fortunate bartered or sold their possessions—shoes, blankets, anything—to obtain food from the commissary, and even its stock depended on the whims of the market as well as the Japanese. When the shelves ran low and when spending money was scarce, the prisoners survived on what they received from the mess. Meals were supposed to be provided three times a day, but water and firewood, which fueled the large iron cauldrons for cooking, were often unavailable. Breakfast was a sticky glop of rice, called by its Tagalog name *lugao*, and lunch and dinner—when it was offered—consisted of a scant handful of rice and a watery soup fortified with shreds of leafy greens. Meat and fat appeared mostly in the men's dreams; when it turned up on a plate it was in the form of dried fish or stringy carabao.[8]

One of the best ways to remain at the top of the food chain was to be part of it through a work assignment. The most lucrative and life-sustaining camp job involved something with the mess. Men with kitchen jobs did not go hungry, nor did those on truck details. The latter were allowed out of the camp to help procure supplies, so they had access to food even before the cooks. Some of these items ended up in the camp kitchens for the general mess, some was destined for the commissary and made available for purchase, and some ended up smuggled in for the camp's black market.

Irvin Alexander spent much of his time thinking and talking about food. Like Albert Fields, he knew money was the key to procuring an adequate supply, but found the process more complicated than the one Fields described. The Japanese could not establish an official purchasing system quickly enough, leaving the POWs to resort to their own devices. "The Filipinos agreed to bring in food under their clothes, purchased with the money that had been left by Americans in convenient places where the Filipinos could pick it up without the knowledge of the Nips," Alexander remembered. "For several days the system worked so well that a surprising amount of canned goods was brought in, but the Nips, becoming suspicious, searched the Filipinos one morning, confiscating all of the food found on them."[9]

Undaunted, Alexander convinced some friends to pool their money, collecting a total of forty pesos, which he believed was enough to purchase a significant amount of food. He drafted a list of things they wanted and passed it along with the pesos to a Filipino working near the camp. "Two days later we were informed that our food purchases had arrived at the house of a Filipino who lived just across the highway from the main gate. It was our big problem to get the food to our side of the fence, for everyone who entered the camp was searched by Nip guards." A sympathetic Japanese medical officer helped them retrieve the package.[10]

By late June 1942, more of this commercial activity was above board as the Japanese allowed the prisoners to use their own money to buy tobacco and food through a commissary officer. The money supply itself, though, was often as big a concern as the food supply. Alexander realized from the beginning of his imprisonment in Cabanatuan that the presence of Filipino laborers in and around the camp made the cash flow possible. The workers acted as go-betweens for the prisoners and their friends in Manila. "As a result of those contacts, large sums of money were smuggled into camp to provide the means by which individuals continued to make commissary purchases," Alexander recalled. "Unquestionably, if it had not been for the opportunity to buy food of heavy protein content, our death rate would have been much higher."[11]

Not all prisoners could count on generous friends in Manila, and for them money remained a problem throughout most of that first summer. The Japanese took their time registering the POWs. By August each man had filled out a card listing his name, rank, and work experience in military and civilian life. That process completed, the Japanese officially pronounced the men prisoners of war. As such they would be paid for their camp work, money that in turn enabled more men to purchase at the commissary.[12]

The POW status accorded the men cold comfort. They already knew how little regard the Japanese had for prisoners, and knew their treatment would not follow the Geneva guidelines. While they welcomed a salary, the physical exertion from the work would likely kill them. Still, the Japanese insisted that only those prisoners who worked would eat. It was not until October 1942 that the Japanese established a basic daily ration for an enlisted man at 570 grams (1 pound 4 ounces), plus 220 grams (7 ounces), if he worked. Compared to the peacetime US Army, when an enlisted man received a daily food ration of 4 pounds 7 ounces (2,013 grams), this was a starvation diet. In Cabanatuan, there was not enough food to provide 570 grams per man, per day.[13]

The commissary officer tried to make up the difference. Under close Japanese supervision, he initially dealt with selected vendors who were allowed to bring their merchandise into the camp. Later, men from the camp commissary were allowed access to Cabanatuan town to make purchases. Demand always exceeded supply, so contraband flowed into the camp as well. Truck drivers sold "extra" items when the Japanese were not looking; members of POW work details purchased goods outside the camp and sold them inside at inflated prices; Americans working in the Japanese messes bought food from the Japanese to resell in camp. Everyone, it seemed, had a hand in something, but as long as all parties—Americans, Filipinos, Japanese—received a cut, everyone was satisfied. As long as they all recognized Japanese authority, the captors saved face.[14]

Without access to this rather convoluted food supply system, the prisoners would have died. With it, they were given a chance to live, though death continued to strike at a high rate. Albert Fields filled his journal with mortality statistics. On June 30, 1942: "One month in War Prison Camp Cabanatuan. . . . Total about 6000 American prisoners. Deaths 498 mostly malaria, dysentery, diphtheria and there is some question but that some of the dysentery is a symptom of malnutrition." For July 4, 1942, thirty-four deaths were recorded, and by mid-month he estimated about thirty deaths per day.[15]

Japanese officials frequently turned up at the camp hospital, where they stood around and shook their heads. They refused to venture into the dysentery ward. Bits of assistance—"fiddling amounts of medicines and supplies" from the Philippine Red Cross, Fields noted, and some access to medical facilities in Cabanatuan town—made no appreciable difference in the lives and deaths of the POWs. Yet over two hundred medical personnel among the POWs continued to treat their comrades as best they could. Not until August would the death rates begin to stabilize and then decline.[16]

As Peggy Utinsky continued her work for Camp O'Donnell during the summer of 1942, she made connections with Philippine Red Cross workers providing civilian relief in the town of Cabanatuan. More and more, as

American POWs were moved from one camp to the other, items collected in Manila and designated for specific prisoners in O'Donnell needed to be sent on to Cabanatuan. Peggy arranged this through Honorata Seraspi, a Red Cross nurse in Cabanatuan town who was willing to help the American prisoners.[17]

Thanks to Seraspi, Peggy already knew relief efforts were underway there. She would not have to start from scratch when Camp O'Donnell was finally emptied and closed down and she shifted the Miss U activities to Cabanatuan. In light of this, it is unclear why Peggy insisted she needed so much time for planning, especially when a quicker move to Cabanatuan would have brought her closer to Jack. By the early summer of 1942 she must have realized her husband was not in Camp O'Donnell. The most likely place he would be was Cabanatuan—if he was still alive. Perhaps after all this time Peggy was afraid to learn the truth.

In early August 1942, Dr. Atienza and Peggy discussed the logistics of extending their relief network to Cabanatuan. Peggy admitted to Atienza she was an American—which may not have been much of a surprise—and had been looking for her husband. The next time he visited Camp O'Donnell, the doctor asked his chaplain contact, Lieutenant Frank Tiffany, what he could find out about Jack Utinsky. Before the end of the month, Peggy had her answer. Jack had been sent to Cabanatuan in June.[18]

Peggy had heard enough of the appalling conditions in Cabanatuan, especially during the first two months, to realize Jack might be dead. He would have found a way to contact her by now if he was still alive. Even if she could not admit it, Peggy had too strong a sense of self-preservation to take off for Cabanatuan to find Jack. She had already been beaten once and had other near-misses with the Japanese. She would have to lie low until she could figure out what to do.

CLAIRE PHILLIPS TOOK THE OPPOSITE tack and flaunted herself by opening the Club Tsubaki on Saturday, October 17, 1942. This was the culmination of her plan to gather information from the unsuspecting Japanese customers and pass it along to the guerrilla John Boone. The night of the opening, Claire debuted a halter-necked white evening gown that clung to her body in all the right places. The hostesses were all outfitted in new dresses as well, with the waiters sporting white coats, pants, and shoes. On each table sat a bowl of peanuts, standard fare to keep the customers thirsty and ordering drinks, while light hors d'oeuvres provided just enough sustenance to balance the effects of the alcohol. By ten o'clock, the club was full; Claire had to turn people away.

The elite who managed to get in included Japanese artists and musicians, five doctors from the Fort Stotsenburg Army Hospital, and Colonel Saito Jiro, a portly forty-seven-year-old intelligence officer who spoke perfect English. An integral part of the Japanese army's occupation administration, first in China and now in the Philippines, Saito had grown up in Honolulu, Hawaii, where his father served as Japan's consul general. Despite his rotund appearance and smooth, soothing voice, the colonel was a dangerous man to cross, but he was exactly the kind of high-ranking official Claire had to attract if she was going to be of any use to Boone's guerrillas.[19]

The customers watched a floor show that began with a Filipino rice planting dance, complete with barefoot young women in native dress. Then Fahny, wearing a gold brassiere and matching panties, over which she layered a long purple taffeta skirt, performed a Siamese Temple dance, accompanied by a male dancer named David. Two more performances—an Igorot wedding dance and David's special torch dance—completed the set. By midnight, Claire realized that opening night was a success: "All the varied parts of my little machine were running smoothly, and compliments showered down on me from the delighted patrons. Our achievement was reflected in my full cash box and the unfeigned gaiety of each member of my staff."[20]

She hoped the opening triumph signaled a turn of luck. Ramon Amusategui, her friend and inspiration from Remedios Hospital, arrived at the Club Tsubaki the next day to congratulate Claire on her achievement. He also offered to introduce her to Father Theodore Buttenbruch, a member of the Society of the Divine Word and the Chaplain's Aid Association. "He is a German priest who has a permanent pass from the Japanese, permitting him to engage in charitable work. He's a real Christian and no Nazi," Ramon told Claire. That Japanese pass allowed

Buttenbruch access to Cabanatuan, where he was a familiar figure among the POWs. Irvin Alexander later recalled that some higher-up in the Catholic Church, perhaps the archbishop of Manila, persuaded the Japanese to allow Buttenbruch's visits. Alexander believed this had more to do with the priest's nationality than with his vocation. The Japanese wanted to show some consideration to their German ally.[21]

Still, Cabanatuan's commandant, Lieutenant Colonel Mori Masao, could not understand why the German wanted to help his enemies. Father Buttenbruch tried to explain that he was above all a man of God and was therefore concerned about all of humanity regardless of nationality. He tried to get Mori to understand that the enemy designation ceased to matter once soldiers became prisoners. Mori could not comprehend either of these points.[22]

The Japanese monitored the priest's Cabanatuan visits. While the clothing he brought was accepted, the Japanese were unsure about what to do with the food. After considerable discussion it was sent on to the mess rather than to individual recipients. Albert Fields also noted Buttenbruch's comings and goings, and somehow got the impression the priest represented the Philippine Red Cross. In addition to food and clothing, Fields observed the priest deliver packages of medicine and supplies—Bibles, song books, sacramental wine—for the chaplains. With the Japanese focusing their attention on Buttenbruch, his driver managed to slip money to some of the prisoners and to whisper the latest war news.[23]

Armed with the address Ramon Amusategui had given her for Christ the King Church, Claire headed off to see Father Buttenbruch. Claire told him straight out she wanted information about her husband, John Phillips, and she wanted to send in supplies to Cabanatuan for him. Buttenbruch advised that he could bring in whatever items Claire collected, but a personal message was a trickier matter. The priest preferred she write something like favorite song lyrics that Phil would recognize as coming from his wife. Anything more specific and personal than that he would not risk. "Get together a few articles that you think your husband will find useful and place them in a small shopping bag. Put the message in the bottom," the priest said. "I will hand the bag over to the American officer in charge, and try to give him your husband's name as I do." He planned his next trip to Cabanatuan in a week.[24]

As directed, Claire stuffed a shopping bag with a pair of shoes and a pair of pants, socks, a shirt, a toothbrush and toothpaste, quinine, aspirin, and several cans of food. Tucked at the bottom was a scrap of paper on which she wrote a line from one of the couple's favorite songs, "I don't want to set the world on fire." When she returned, Claire reminded Buttenbruch one more time of the name—John Phillips—and left his residence with a happy heart.

It was a fine day. Claire decided against hailing a cab or a *carromata*, and walked all the way home. As she entered Luneta Park, she saw a Japanese army truck parked there, with its two inhabitants—a Japanese soldier and an American POW—lounging on the grass. As Claire weighed the odds of speaking to the prisoner, she saw her daughter Dian, accompanied by her Chinese amah Ah Ho, walk into the park. Claire called Dian to her and picked her up. The Japanese soldier took notice, signaled them over, and told Claire in broken English that he liked children. With the soldier diverted by Dian, Claire took the opportunity to ask the POW, Sergeant Joe Rizzo of the 31st Infantry, if he knew her husband.

"Phillips died last July in Cabanatuan," he said. Stunned, Claire refused to believe him, and she cried as she walked the rest of the way to the Club Tsubaki. Fely Corcuera tried to soothe her, saying Claire should not believe Rizzo's story until she received some kind of official confirmation. Claire latched on to this glimmer of hope. After all, she told herself, at least three men by the name of Phillips were enlisted in the 31st Infantry and Rizzo might have gotten his information mixed up. Still, Claire could not shake the feeling of dread. Rizzo had also been with Headquarters Company, and he would have known John V. Phillips.[25]

IN OCTOBER 1942, AS THE Club Tsubaki was opening in Manila, Peggy Utinsky was coordinating relief efforts from her apartment, minimizing her time out in public. She sent Naomi Flores, accompanied by two Filipinos, to Cabanatuan to scope out the situation, and Naomi found the camp population still in flux. Whereas death initially carried the prisoners away—dozens a day in the early weeks—now the Japanese had begun depleting the prison by shipping men off to prison camps elsewhere in Asia. After enduring unspeakable conditions on vessels aptly known as "hellships," the surviving POWs found themselves in slave labor camps in Japan, Formosa, and Korea.[26]

Over the next couple of months, Naomi and her assistants established themselves in Cabanatuan as peanut vendors, local businesspeople trying to make some money from the Japanese and their prisoners. With the constant buying and selling of food in and around the camp, they did not draw undue attention. Still, they found it difficult to get close enough to contact any prisoners. On December 27, 1942, Naomi caught the attention of an American officer working in the camp's vegetable garden, Lieutenant Colonel Edward Mack. A 1925 West Point graduate whose broad face advertised his Eastern European heritage, Mack had been sent in 1940 to Fort William McKinley to join the 57th Infantry of the Philippine Scouts. When the war broke out he was seconded to the 21st Philippine Army and surrendered with the troops at Corregidor.[27]

Ever mindful of Peggy's personal reason for making contact with the American prisoners, Naomi asked Mack if he knew anything about Jack Utinsky. Mack promised to find out, and later the same day passed a note that she took directly to Peggy's Manila apartment. It contained the news Peggy had been dreading: "Your husband died here on August 6, 1942. You will be told that he died of tuberculosis. That is not true. The men say that he actually died of starvation."[28]

Later, Peggy would be unable to remember what she was doing at the time she received the news, or how she made it through the day. She agonized over the fact that Jack might not have died if he had enough food and medicine. She blamed herself for not finding him sooner. Perhaps anticipating this, Mack offered some consolation in his note, "This is terrible news for you, who have, with your unselfish work, been able to save so many others. All of us will always owe you a debt that we can never pay for what you have done." He also added a word of caution: "I do want to say to you that this place is far more dangerous for your work than Camp O'Donnell was. Do not take risks that you took there. If you never do another thing, you have already done more than any living person to help our men."[29]

While Peggy considered this warning, she remembered the last day she spent with Jack in Manila, just over a year ago, as Japanese bombs pounded the city. She had been rushing around between her hospital duties and canteen work, and had little time to spare for him. Jack had said to her, "I came back here thinking I'd have to pull you out of a ditch. Instead of that, I found you scurrying around, pulling other people out. I'd like you to know, darling, that I'm proud of you." The memory helped Peggy make up her mind: she would continue pulling other people out.[30]

Even as she decided this, something about Peggy had changed. Members of the Miss U organization noticed that her personal fire seemed to have gone out. Even more worrisome for the security of the network, they suspected she was drinking—heavily— which led to unpredictable behavior. After the war, when Peggy wrote about this time, there was no reference to alcohol, only vagueness about the chronology and details of learning about Jack's death. She may have been unable to publicly admit how deeply his death affected her.[31]

Yet Peggy carried on with her work. At some point in late 1942 or early 1943, she secured a new travel permit that allowed her to help the "needy" in Cabanatuan, though she used it sparingly. Mostly she operated from her A. Mabini Street apartment, now the headquarters for Cabanatuan relief activities. Edward Mack served as the main contact there for the Miss U organization. Colonel Duckworth, the insider at O'Donnell, remained at that camp a while longer, though Peggy lost touch with him as she shifted her focus to Cabanatuan. Naomi, who had been traveling between Cabanatuan and Manila since October 1942, made the permanent move to the prison camp town by the early spring of 1943. She found two like-minded Filipinas to live with and share the work with, one of whom was married to an African American POW.

Naomi and the others relied on two methods that had been in place since the first weeks Cabanatuan opened. First, they enlisted the help of Filipino merchants already conducting business with the camp, selling items to the prisoners at a reduced rate and adding extra supplies and cash to their purchases. Second, they coordinated efforts with the prisoners who were allowed out of the camp to work on the vegetable garden and then take the produce into town for sale. At Cabanatuan, the importance of the Miss U network was not in any innovations of prisoner relief, but in organization, expansion, and endurance.

All of this commercial activity looked normal, at least on the surface. POWs, as long as they worked, were paid, so they had money to spend. It was not enough to meet their needs. An underground mail system developed in Manila for handling personal checks, written on American banks and cashed by Filipinos. An exchange rate of one peso per dollar on these checks meant a tidy profit if the checks ever made their way back to the States. Prisoners without Manila connections arranged for loans within the camp, to be repaid after the war. It was risky financial business, but the alternative was starvation.[32]

As Peggy later explained the system:

An organization inside the camp co-operated with the smugglers outside to receive pesos, distribute them where they would do the most good, and acknowledge receipt of all moneys received. Some of the officers, who had been stationed in Manila, still had accounts in the banks there, and Manila people cashed checks for them to the amount of hundreds of badly needed pesos, while loans were floated on personal notes payable six months after release.[33]

Actual check blanks were scarce. Prisoners wrote their transactions on any available scrap of paper, and no matter how small or dirty, how negligible the scrawl, the bits of paper were honored in Manila. Despite their original impulse to send in as much as possible, generous Manilans had to rein themselves in a bit with the cash, especially in large denominations. Considering the official pay range for POWs, it looked suspicious for an enlisted man to carry anything much larger than a single peso.

In Cabanatuan, Naomi Flores worked with one Filipino vendor in particular, whom Peggy referred to as Maluto. His name was, in fact, Horacio (Mutt) Manaloto. Naomi realized that Manaloto wanted to help with prisoner relief, but he seemed reluctant to trust her. Peggy put this down to Naomi's appearance: "She wore ragged clothes, with a dirty shawl tied over her head, a typical vendor—which was what she wanted. Probably Maluto [sic], like many people who think of underground workers and spies as glamorous people, expected something mysterious, a woman who looked like a storybook character." To ease his skepticism, Naomi suggested Manaloto visit "Auntie," the head of the network. "Maluto [sic] was afraid and he didn't pretend otherwise," Peggy later recalled. "But he took my address and he came to see 'Auntie.' He listened to my story and he promised to help. Yes, he would let us use his stalls for smuggled goods for the Americans."[34]

This recollection was a misrepresentation of Manaloto, likely crafted by Peggy to emphasize the importance of the Miss U network and to highlight her own leadership abilities. Manaloto's reluctance had little to do with Naomi's appearance or his own fears about getting involved with smuggling. By the time Naomi approached him in Cabanatuan town, Manaloto had already been helping the prisoners and had already connected with anti-Japanese activists in Manila. His reluctance to work with Miss U probably stemmed from concerns about overextending himself.

Horacio Manaloto's market stalls in Cabanatuan town were supplied and supported by Tomas de Guzman, a Manila schoolteacher, and his wife Agustina, a doctor who had been sending her own reserves of medicine into the Cabanatuan camp. The de Guzmans were connected to the Chaplain's Aid Association, which also funded Father Buttenbruch's activities. There were many others participating in the relief efforts as well. The Irish priests at the Malate Convent and members of the Masons in Manila also collected and sent items to Cabanatuan. Newspaperman Tony Escoda and his wife, Josefa, affiliated with the Volunteer Social Aid Committee (VSAC), were likewise already in on the action, as were VSAC members Pilar Campos, Helena Benitez, and Betty Wright, the young woman who tried to help Claire Phillips.[35]

The Miss U network was not the only game in town, but it reinforced the importance of women's participation in the smuggling activities so necessary to the welfare of the American POWs. In addition to Miss U and the VSAC, the Philippine Women's Federation established a canteen about a mile away from the Cabanatuan camp. The canteen's official business was with the Japanese soldiers, but under the table the canteen stored food and medicine destined for the prison camp. Individual women, whether members of a specific group or not, continued to risk their safety to help the POWs. Angelina Castro, a Philippine Red Cross nurse, flirted with a Japanese medical officer at Cabanatuan until he issued permission for her to come and go from the camp as she wished. The equally persuasive Pilar Campos made nice with Japanese officers and guards of Cabanatuan so she could send in parcels for her boyfriend Ralph Hibbs as well as other prisoners.[36]

Hibbs had arrived at Cabanatuan from Bilibid Prison in Manila about two weeks before Christmas 1942, in time to benefit from the Red Cross parcels that were finally brought into camp. "A hot sunny day set the stage appropriately about the 20th of December, 1942 around noon, when a huge unnatural shout went up," Hibbs later wrote. "It was an American war whoop, a celebration like a touchdown cheer." These were serious supplies. Each Red Cross parcel contained evaporated milk, cheese, instant cocoa, sugar, tinned corned beef, coffee, cigarettes, and a few other dreamed-of items.[37]

This manna allowed the prisoners the opportunity to carry on their favorite pastime: *quanning.* The word to define the practice has been traced to Master Sergeant Tabaniag of the 45th Infantry, Philippine Scouts. "Quan"—noun, verb, adjective—was to food as the Marine "gizmo" was to a useful item. Quan referred to anything edible, quanning to any method of preparing it. "Any sort of extra-curricular cooking in prison was called quanning," Major Calvin Chunn later wrote. "We called it quan if it were only a banana added to a kit of rice. And we eagerly sought extra quan at every opportunity." Quan meant survival.[38]

IN ADDITION TO THE RED CROSS parcels, Christmas 1942 was memorable for the gifts the POWs received from civilians in Manila. Gladys Savary, now separated from both the Restaurant de Paris and Edgar Gable, threw herself into holiday preparations. She held a Christmas party for twenty-two children in her Pasay neighborhood—Filipinos, Swedes, Swiss, Brits, and Americans. Gladys draped lights around a pine tree in her garden and found some ornaments, too. "The party was complete with ice cream, cake, presents and all," she remembered. Adults made merry with rum-spiked fruit punch. The laughter from the festivities caught the attention of Japanese soldiers passing by. A few of them climbed the wall surrounding the compound and watched for a while, making no effort to break up the celebration. Gladys later mused, "I marvel now, in the light of the horrible massacres at the end, that they did not murder us all right then!"[39]

Also during this holiday season, Gladys recalled, "Everyone worked like mad, sending turkeys, cakes, and pies into the camps." Though she stuck pretty close to her Pasay neighborhood, she remained in touch with all of her friends in Manila, both inside Santo Tomas and out. Gladys knew about POW relief efforts, and was especially heartened that Tony and Josefa Escoda and Father Buttenbruch persuaded the Japanese to allow parcels into the military prison camps. "We all spent sleepless nights, figuring out how we could get the most into the prescribed packages," she wrote later. Gladys also had a personal connection to the aid work at Cabanatuan. Edgar Gable had been taken there, and she knew he would benefit from these parcels as well as from the Red Cross bundles that had all of Manila talking. Gladys received notes in return for the Christmas packages she sent in to Cabanatuan and was encouraged to find the prisoners "all of fairly good cheer and feeling it was only a matter of time before the end."[40]

The note Gladys valued the most came from her nephew: "The packages from you were perfect. Now I am fixed for several months. Can't thank you enough, but will some day, somehow." Gable let her know he was well—he had an office job which meant he did not have to put in many hours in the physically grueling prison garden—and his eyesight had improved since she sent in vitamins A and D. "I would like to see you and talk to you, have a decent drink and a good dinner, nicely served at a table. This damn war cannot last forever and we'll have fun some day."[41]

FATHER BUTTENBRUCH ARRIVED IN CABANATUAN on Christmas Eve with a truck and a converted bus packed with Christmas presents for the lucky prisoners who had family and friends in Manila. He also probably delivered the gift bags Peggy Utinsky conjured for the men who otherwise would have nothing. Peggy encouraged her friends to cut up their old dresses to make the bags and then fill them with anything they thought was nutritious and useful: nuts, candy, soap, thread. It was not much, but Peggy hoped the bags would cheer the men, and perhaps sustain them just a little longer.

By early 1943, the Miss U organization played an important role in keeping the Cabanatuan prisoners alive. To meet the great, continuing demand of the suffering POWs, Peggy's web of volunteers and suppliers in Manila expanded. By now she understood that people were more will- ing to help specific prisoners, especially if they were personal friends: "So I sent word that the prisoners were to give us the names of anyone whom they might know in Manila. Lt. Colonel Mack talked to them and asked them to send me any names they could." He cautioned the men not to rely on casual acquaintances, only people they were certain could be trusted. "One by one, after that, names would be forwarded to me. I never hesi- tated in approaching these people. They were both rich and poor, and not one ever failed to give me as much as he or she could in money or food," Peggy later wrote. "And never was I betrayed. In all my recruiting of vol- unteer help, indeed, I never met a single fifth-columnist through people whose names were sent me by prisoners in camp."[42]

Yet Peggy's willingness to make these contacts seemed risky to oth- ers in her network, who worried that she was too indiscriminate and might expose the whole scheme. Peggy ignored the concerns. In addi- tion to recruiting more suppliers, she continued to rely on the priests and other personnel working at the Malate Convent. Supplies could be gathered and trucked out from there without attracting too much atten- tion because the priests were known for their charity work. It looked like business as usual.

Juan Elizalde, whom Peggy later identified as a wealthy polo player, donated the use of a truck to move the goods to Cabanatuan. "Several times a week, our truck went back and forth from the convent to Maluto's [sic] stalls at Cabanatuan, and the same system of coded messages employed at O'Donnell was used." With the truck, large quantities of items were trans- ported in a single trip from the Malate Convent. The drivers possessed the necessary travel permissions, and were often accompanied by Red Cross doctors and nurses.[43]

Considering her organizational skills and wide network of contacts, Peggy probably knew that Juan Elizalde was more than a dilettante sportsman. Married to an American, the former Janice Meritt, Elizalde was a wealthy Manila businessman and a reserve captain in the Philippine

Army. A committed patriot, in early 1942 he had organized one of the first underground groups in Manila, an elite team called the "28 Men of Fort Santiago." All well placed in the business community and in politics, Elizalde and the others worked and socialized with the Japanese, collecting information, offering passive resistance, anything to impede the occupation. Elizalde's participation in the Malate Convent relief efforts was just one of his projects. Peggy, however, regarded it as *her* project, and prided herself on his participation in it. The organization, Miss U, was, after all, named for her. She later bragged, "Pretty soon almost everyone in town was either working for me or wanted to work for me."[44]

TWO WEEKS AFTER CLAIRE PHILLIPS spoke with Sergeant Joe Rizzo about her husband, she received a phone call from Father Buttenbruch. He asked if she would come see him at her earliest convenience; he needed to tell her something in person. Claire headed right over to the priest's office at the church. "I can no longer recall his soothing words, but do remember that he showed me the list of deaths in Cabanatuan for the month of July." Buttenbruch may have told Claire about the thirty to forty prisoners who had been dying each day that month. They were not as real as the one name she saw on the list: Sergeant John V. Phillips, died in Cabanatuan Camp No. 1 on Sunday, July 26, 1942. The cause of death was listed as malaria. According to Major Edward R. Wernitznig, a doctor with the 57th Infantry, over 2,300 men were in the hospital that day, and twenty-four died.[45]

Though Claire might have convinced herself that Rizzo could be mistaken about Phil, she knew Father Buttenbruch found out the truth: "Any woman who has lost her loved one under such tragic circumstances will understand my emotions ... emptiness ... anger ... bitterness ... and pity for my poor, gallant husband who had perished so needlessly after heaven knows how much suffering and despair." After leaving Buttenbruch, Claire retired to her room for three days, popping sleeping tablets to blot out time and memories. Fely Corcuera covered for her with the customers at the Club Tsubaki, explaining that Claire suffered from debilitating headaches. Finally, when Dian asked with grave concern if she was well yet, Claire forced herself out of bed. She could not bear for her daughter to worry about her.[46]

Chaplain Frank Tiffany sent Claire a message through Betty Wright, expressing his condolences over Phil's death and clarifying that the young soldier's malaria had been exacerbated by malnutrition. "But I beg of you not to forget the ones that are left. They are dying by the hundreds," Tiffany wrote. Despite her grief, Claire recognized the truth of Tiffany's plea. She resolved to use some of the proceeds from the Club Tsubaki to provide assistance to the prisoners in Cabanatuan.[47]

These intertwined events—learning of Phil's death and deciding to aid the Cabanatuan POWs—are probably what brought Claire Phillips and Peggy Utinsky together for the first time. The details of that first meeting are sketchy. Without identifying her by name, Peggy described how Claire had sought her out sometime in 1943 asking for help in locating a prisoner. "Then one night she brought me fifty pesos to send to a soldier, and later began helping me to collect money."[48]

This may have occurred at the beginning of 1943. Early that year, Claire made contact inside Cabanatuan with Joe Rizzo, who became her main connection to the camp. Betty Wright also told Claire about a woman she knew, Naomi Flores, who might help coordinate deliveries into the camp. Naomi, Betty explained, had first gone to Cabanatuan in the fall of 1942 "for the express purpose of finding a way to communicate with the men buried alive there." Now, after three months, the Japanese guards were so accustomed to seeing Naomi, they did not really notice her, so she went about her real business, smuggling supplies into the camp.[49]

To Claire, Naomi Flores sounded like the perfect operative, which, of course, she was. Naomi already worked for Miss U. Claire asked Betty to set up a meeting. A short time later, Naomi showed up at the Club Tsubaki, posing as a fruit vendor. She confirmed what Betty had already told Claire, that the Japanese guards at Cabanatuan considered her hard-working but simple, and thought nothing of her presence near the camp. Although she hid money or loot in the bottom of bags stuffed with beans—hence, according to Claire, her code name Looter—she wanted to try smuggling in additional items, especially medicine. The prisoners who drove carabao carts in and out of camp to load firewood knew what she was doing and wanted to help. Moreover, Naomi had a reliable supplier in Manila—Evangeline Neibert—who brought the items to Cabanatuan from the city. With such a smoothly running system already in place, courtesy of Peggy Utinsky's organizational skills, Claire decided to work with it rather than duplicate efforts.

Claire invited Evangeline Neibert to the Club Tsubaki for a meeting—a formality, really, since she was sent right out on her first mission. Claire gave Evangeline a hundred pesos and a note for Chaplain Tiffany that asked for the names of ten prisoners who most needed help. Evangeline tucked the money and the note into the false bottom of the shopping bag she always carried, and headed off to meet up with Naomi in Cabanatuan. On her second trip, Evangeline smuggled in the quinine and emetine Claire begged from sympathetic doctors in Manila.

When she returned to the Club Tsubaki that second time, Evangeline carried a letter from Chaplain Tiffany, now using the code name Everlasting. Tiffany provided Claire with the ten names she requested, and emphasized that all of the POWs still required a great deal of assistance. He mentioned that he knew Chaplain Robert Taylor, whom Claire had met on Bataan and who had been a close friend of Phil's. Taylor worked in the prison hospital and knew about the various smuggling operations. He asked a young corporal named Winky, part of a work detail in the rail yards, to get word to Claire in Manila that they desperately needed medicine in Cabanatuan. "With her help," Taylor later recalled, "we not only got some supplies but were also able to smuggle in a short wave radio."[50]

Evangeline made the trip to Cabanatuan for Claire every two weeks, giving Claire the time to scrape together ten pesos for each of the ten men Tiffany identified. She scrounged another twenty pesos for Mack and a few other officers, all to be divided and donated as they saw fit. In addition to the money, which the prisoners used to buy food from the camp commissary, Claire included upbeat notes, hoping to raise their spirits.

Claire's office at the Club Tsubaki served as a clearinghouse for the Cabanatuan donations. Soon it would serve the same function for supplies and information earmarked for John Boone's guerrillas. Couriers scheduled deliveries on her telephone using code phrases; club employees doubled as couriers and contacts. In addition to all of this activity, Claire still found time to drop by Remedios Hospital to find out what Father Lalor needed. The more time she spent with the Irish priests at the Malate Convent, the more involved she became with the Miss U network.

CHAPTER 11

GUERRILLAS IN THE MIDST
OF THE OCCUPATION

D URING THE LATE FALL OF 1942, Claire Phillips kept busy making connections with prisoners in Cabanatuan and running the Club Tsubaki. It was useful work that dulled the grief that had been tugging at her since she received word from Father Buttenbruch about Phil's death. As the Christmas holiday approached, Claire worried she would become preoccupied with memories of the previous Christmas Eve and the midnight ceremony on Bataan.

To keep her mind on all things constructive and positive, she choreographed a new floor show for the club and splurged on engraved invitations to entice customers. Claire also held a Christmas Eve party for the staff, complete with a decorated tree and a round of Christmas carols. She used the occasion to fill the employees in on the motivation for her recent activities: "We must help others who are much worse off than we are." Without telling them straight out who would receive the assistance, Claire believed they understood and supported her, without question.[1]

The new holiday program was a success, and customers jammed the Club Tsubaki every night from Christmas to New Year's. After a huge take on New Year's Eve, Claire paid off the remaining debts she incurred from opening the establishment, which allowed her to redeem the diamond ring and watch she had put up as collateral. Plus she cleared 1,000 pesos. Claire had remained in touch with John Boone through Pacio, one of the men from the Sobrevinas camp, and had been kept informed of some of Boone's activities. Now flush with extra cash, she asked Pacio to deliver some of it, along with a note, to Boone, letting him know the business was profitable. She could send him regular support; she just had to know what he needed. Worried that the Japanese might intercept the message, she signed it "High Pockets," a reference to her habit of hiding valuables in her brassiere.[2]

It was a week before Pacio returned with a reply. Boone, using the code name "Compadre," told Claire that his men needed food, medicine, clothing, soap, and whiskey. Most of all, his unit needed a radio set to connect with other guerrilla groups on Luzon and throughout the islands. Boone wanted to contact a group on the southern island of Mindanao capable of getting messages back and forth to General MacArthur's headquarters in Australia. Boone proposed that Claire employ different couriers at varying times to carry pieces of the radio to his encampment in the hills.

By the time Claire stepped up her involvement with the guerrillas in early 1943, circumstances were rapidly changing for these underground fighters. They were a hodgepodge lot, mostly displaced American soldiers like Boone, either separated from their units during the fighting on Bataan or escaped from the Bataan Death March. As they decided how they wanted to harass the Japanese—if they wanted to harass the Japanese—these men realized they needed supplies and needed to be in touch with each other to pass along useful information. This was where Claire came in.

Couriers were an essential part of the guerrilla communication network, but because of enemy patrols they had limited reach, and therefore limited effectiveness. In late 1942, a lieutenant with the Signal Corps, Robert Ball, was working with guerrilla leader Lieutenant Colonel Wendell Fertig on Mindanao to solve this problem. Fertig, a Colorado native and graduate of one of its mining colleges, had arrived in the Philippines with his family in the 1930s, taking up a job as a civil engineer on the island of Samar. Because of his reserve commission in the US Army Corps of Engineers, Fertig was called to active duty in June 1941, tasked with overseeing military construction projects throughout the islands. In April 1942, General King sent him to Mindanao to build airfields. When General Wainwright surrendered his forces the following month, Fertig refused to turn himself in and instead began gathering guerrilla fighters.

Between their various areas of expertise, Robert Ball and Wendell Fertig rigged a radio and established contact with General MacArthur's headquarters in Australia. Now the guerrillas could receive clear instructions through an established command chain. In February 1943, MacArthur's headquarters sent Major Jesus Villamor to Mindanao via submarine to help coordinate guerrilla activities. On this first trip, Villamor brought along an espionage team to establish a network of intelligence agents throughout the islands.[3]

Lieutenant Commander Charles (Chick) Parsons showed up on Mindanao next to meet with Fertig. Parsons's first encounter with Fertig revealed how much the guerrillas had been left to their own devices. The man who greeted Parsons looked more Asian than Caucasian—Moro hat covering his shaved head, his face highlighted with a trim goatee—and referred to himself as a brigadier general, a self-promotion in the field. Parsons reminded Fertig of the proper chain of command and of his real rank, and that guerrilla activities were no excuse for ignoring military structure and discipline. Parsons then gave Fertig several radio sets to be used for gathering intelligence.

The guerrillas' task was to learn as much as they could about the enemy and his movements and to transmit that information to MacArthur's headquarters. Until American forces returned to the Philippines and launched an effective offensive, the guerrillas were instructed to lie low and avoid antagonizing the Japanese. Any belligerent behavior would only invite reprisals, which might cause the Filipinos to turn against the Americans. Fertig and other guerrilla leaders, including John Boone, did not agree with this strategy. They believed that since they were on the ground in occupied territory, they were the best judges of the situation, and they attacked the enemy when they could.[4]

Those the Japanese caught with an illegal radio might be punished as severely as anyone apprehended engaging in guerrilla activity. In November 1942, *The Tribune* ran a big front-page article under the headline, "21 Are Executed." Their crime: making anti-Japanese broadcasts from an illegal radio station. Twenty-nine others were sentenced to stiff prison terms. The article boasted the arrests as "Revealing that guerrilla and such other anti-Japanese activities are steadily being liquidated . . . [and] the bright dawn of the establishment of the New Philippines is on the point of shining."[5]

Supplying Boone and his men, especially with something as important as a radio, was clearly dangerous business, yet it gave Claire a renewed purpose. This was, after all, why she had returned to Manila. Now, with the Club Tsubaki in full swing and with contacts among the guerrillas and the POWs, she understood the vital nature of smooth-running supply lines. She took an extra precaution against attracting too much attention from the Japanese by changing her living arrangements.

After she had returned to Manila, Claire risked having her real identity revealed when she moved into her old apartment in the Dakota building. Now, because the radio smuggling for Boone's guerrillas required extra caution, the place was an even bigger liability. Plus Manila's midnight curfew had become bothersome. When the Club Tsubaki was busy, which meant most nights, Claire did not have enough time to get home, and she missed seeing her daughter. In early 1943, she decided to move into the club. She hired a carpenter to turn some little-used space at the back of it into a four-room apartment: a bedroom for Dian and her amah Ah Ho, another bedroom for Claire that doubled as her office, a dormitory-style room for any of the female entertainers who could not make it home before curfew, and a kitchen/dining room. "It pleased me very much to have all my precious eggs in one basket," she later recalled of the new addition.[6]

To maintain contact with the guerrillas, Claire utilized Pacio, a trusted acquaintance from the Sobrevinas camp, as her main courier. From his end, John Boone sent a young Filipina named Filomena (Mellie) Guerrero, who joined Boone's band along with her father. Mellie caught Boone's attention when she volunteered to live in Dinalupihan and spy on the Japanese. She made friends with some of the enemy soldiers there, even cooking and sewing for them, before she lit out to the hills with information about troop movements and the locations of ammunition dumps. Then Mellie volunteered to take on the monthly courier runs to the Club Tsubaki. As the weeks—then the months—passed, as his guerrilla unit expanded, Boone needed more and more supplies.[7]

Claire knew that anything she could do through the Club Tsubaki to help Boone and his men was critical. During the late fall of 1942 and into the early winter of 1943, the guerrillas escalated their harassment of Japanese forces on Luzon. The Japanese responded with fury, sometimes destroying entire villages in retribution, killing hundreds of civilians at a time. At the end of October, the Japanese burned the towns of Agoo and Tubao after the guerrillas attacked their garrisons at Ilocos and La Union. The guerrillas needed all the help they could get if they wanted to survive until American forces returned—whenever that might be.[8]

Despite Claire's efforts to keep a low profile, guerrillas on Luzon heard about High Pockets. Doyle Decker, with the guerrilla outfit Squadron 155 near Subic Bay, noted in his journal at the beginning of 1943: "Today is a New Year. I can't help but wonder what this year will bring. Last year was a rough one. So far this year sounds better. A Guerrilla leader in Manila has contacted us. Her code name is Hi [sic] Pockets. She manages to get a newspaper to us. The news sounds good. I hope some day [sic] I can meet Hi Pockets in person."[9]

Although Decker referred to Claire as a guerrilla leader, the only qualification he attested to was her dissemination of news, not the gathering of intelligence. Decker also did not know the real identity of High Pockets. If he heard the name Claire Phillips, he may have associated it with the sergeant he had met and traveled with to the camp of the Fassoth brothers earlier in 1942. After Decker and three other men left Fassoth's that spring, heading for Olongapo, near Subic Bay, a Japanese patrol spotted them and gave chase, but the Americans lost them in the jungle. They hired Negritos, paying them in salt, to guide them the rest of the way, to help pitch camp and find food.

When Decker and the others finally reached the Olongapo area, they found shelter well up in the mountains with a Filipino family. Their arrival attracted the attention of some American army officers also hiding out in the vicinity, and they sent Decker an unfriendly message. They wanted him and his companions to leave, otherwise their presence would call too much attention to the location and put everyone in danger. The Decker quartet moved on, and accepting the premise that congregating was dangerous, they split into two groups of two. They headed for Clark Field where, they had heard, Claude Thorp was organizing a guerrilla force.[10]

Formerly the Provost Marshal at Fort Stotsenburg, Colonel Claude A. Thorp received permission from General MacArthur in early 1942 to organize guerrilla forces on Luzon. Thorp assembled his team: three lieutenants (Robert Lapham, Walter Cushing, Ralph McGuire), Captain David Miller, nine enlisted men, several Filipinos, and two women, including Herminia (Minang) Dizon, Thorp's secretary from Stotsenburg and now allegedly his lover. They took Thompson machine guns, Garand automatic rifles, Springfield rifles, and pistols, and headed off on a forty-day trip to the foothills of Mount Pinatubo, southwest of Fort Stotsenburg.[11]

At Timbo, about halfway between Mount Pinatubo and San Fernando, Thorp set up the headquarters of what would become the Central Luzon Guerrilla Force. After Corregidor's surrender in May 1942, several more Americans, including Edwin Ramsey and Joseph Barker, joined Thorp's group, bringing along a radio set. Unlike Boone's guerrilla unit, which had been harassing the enemy, Thorp's goal was intelligence gathering. On June 15, 1942, Thorp issued a memo identifying John P. Boone, Co. D, 31st Infantry, now of Dinalupihan, as a member of the Central Luzon Guerrilla Force. Boone went on to organize five regiments of guerrillas in the Bataan–Zambales province, mostly locals who continued to live in their own homes, rather than a military encampment. They banded together for training exercises and to conduct raids, but their activities were limited by a lack of equipment and the frequency of Japanese patrols.[12]

By early July 1942, Claude Thorp established the field headquarters of the Luzon Guerrilla Army and issued General Order #1:

> The undersigned hereby assumes the responsibility of Commanding Officer of the U S Guerrilla Forces in the Island of Luzon and that of Personal representative of General Douglas MacArthur for the conduct of all Guerrilla operation and incidental affairs. This is in accordance with verbal instructions from General Douglas MacArthur Jan. 20, 1942.

All guerrilla leaders had to secure written authorization to operate from Thorp's headquarters and all guerrilla units would be responsible to these headquarters. Thorp signed the order, "For General Douglas MacArthur, C. A. Thorp, Lieut. Col. USA, Guerrilla Representative USAFFE."[13]

This was the group Doyle Decker wanted to find. He paired up with Bob Campbell, also a private in the 200th Coast Artillery, for another tough journey. They slogged through relentless rain, coped with illnesses and injuries, and bartered with sometimes suspicious Negritos, all the while wondering if they were headed in the right direction. Finally, they met Qualla, a Filipina guerrilla holstering two .45 pistols and carrying a submachine gun, who led them to Edwin Ramsey's camp. Though it was just the two of them—Decker and Campbell—Ramsey, like the last Americans Decker encountered, was not happy to see them. Nonetheless, he allowed the weary travelers to spend the night. Ramsey sent them on their way in the morning with the explanation that they only had enough supplies for themselves. Decker observed with a bite of his tongue, "Nice people."[14]

Another setback followed. When Decker and Campbell finally reached Thorp's Timbo headquarters in late August 1942, they found it torched and no sign of Thorp. The disappointed duo waited out the rainy season in a nearby barrio until Lieutenant Henry Clay Conner discovered them. An Air Corps signal officer, Conner had managed, along with Lieutenant

Bernard Anderson, to escape from Bataan after the surrender. The two officers had aviation in common. At the time of the Japanese attack, Anderson had been assistant adjutant with the Twentieth Pursuit Group at Nichols Field.[15]

Conner, friendlier than Edwin Ramsey, told Decker and Campbell he was forming a guerrilla organization at a camp about an hour away, and invited them to join. This sounded more sensible than trying to find Claude Thorp, so Decker and Campbell agreed. At Conner's camp, a group of six men drew up plans for a guerrilla unit. Along with Conner, Decker, and Campbell were three other Americans who had escaped the Death March: Frank Gyovai, a tank mechanic from Fort Stotsenburg; Corporal Bob Mailheau, who would become Decker's close friend; and Sergeant Joe Donahey of the 24th Pursuit Group. The men dubbed the unit, which reported to Edwin Ramsey, Squadron 155. Conner, as its head, enlisted the help of the Negritos living in the eastern Zambales Mountains to harass the Japanese.

These guerrilla units proliferated, but because of circumstances and location, it was impossible to keep them organized under the enemy occupation. General MacArthur, who issued the order for Thorp to start pulling together guerrilla forces, was off in Australia and remained out of touch with the day-to-day events in the islands. He blocked the Office of Strategic Services (OSS) from operating in the Southwest Pacific Area Command (SWPA) during most of the war because he did not trust its motives. Instead, he relied on G-2's Military Intelligence Service (MIS), headed by a former member of the Philippine Constabulary, Brigadier General Simeon de Jesus who, along with men like Claude Thorp, began setting up guerrilla units in 1942.[16]

Also away at MacArthur's Australian headquarters were his top intelligence officers. Colonel Charles Willoughby, head of G-2, and Colonel Courtney Whitney, running the Philippine Regional Section of the Allied Intelligence Bureau, used radios and submarines to gather information from the islands and send instructions to the guerrillas and to the spies deployed through a program codenamed SPYRON. At such a distance, transportation was still difficult and dangerous. The guerrillas needed food and information and support—quickly. Claire Phillips was not the only one to step up.[17]

═══════════

AS EARLY AS SEPTEMBER 1942, Peggy Utinsky's apartment on A. Mabini Street in Manila became a meeting place for guerrillas. Some Filipinos from Edwin Ramsey's guerrilla outfit found out through a doctor at Camp O'Donnell that she was helping prisoners there. Word of the Miss U organization spread throughout the various guerrilla groups on Luzon. It did not take them long to contact her. From the beginning, Peggy thought highly of the guerrillas for their bravery and daring: "The guerrillas were hunted men, subsisting on what they could get secretly. They harassed the Japanese at every turn but they had to keep hidden. No man was too young, none was too old to be of their number." She was also impressed to find that not all guerrillas were men. "Whole families were members of the various guerrilla bands, the children acting as lookouts, the women nursing, cooking, running messages."[18]

It was dangerous business. The Japanese and their collaborators were everywhere on Luzon, tracking down and rooting out all guerrillas, but especially the Americans. From the late summer of 1942 and throughout 1943, the underground units suffered a series of losses, beginning with Claude Thorp. The Japanese almost caught him in a raid on his camp at the end of August 1942, but Thorp received advanced warning and made it out in time. Two months later, Thorp's luck ran out when Filipino collaborators betrayed him. He was captured and spent several months in different prisons before the Japanese put him on trial in Bilibid. Joseph Barker, one of his closest aides, was arrested in January 1943 while traveling to Manila disguised as a priest, perhaps in a last-ditch effort to find Thorp and save him. The Japanese nabbed Barker, too, and executed him along with Thorp. Colonel Hugh Straughn, commander of the Fil-American Irregular Troops, had a longer run. The Japanese caught up with him during the summer of 1943 and killed him, as well.[19]

Ralph McGuire, formerly of the 26th Cavalry and now in charge of the western sector of the Central Luzon Guerrilla Force, stepped into Thorp's command. McGuire lived on borrowed time. Some of the Negrito guerrillas allegedly working with him were actually in the enemy's pocket. The Negritos ambushed McGuire sometime around February 1943 and turned him over to the Japanese, who decapitated him.[20]

In October 1943, Edwin Ramsey issued a memo, attempting to clarify this ever-changing situation:

> All senior officers of the Usaffe Luzon Guerrilla Army Forces having been incapacitated, and having issued an order dated 1 June 1943, assuming the responsibility of the command of the Usaffe Luzon Guerrilla Army Forces, the following named officer, Captain Bernard L. Anderson, U.S.A.C. (Inf), is recognized by this Headquarters as the Commanding Officer of the Usaffe Luzon Guerrilla Army Forces.[21]

Both Ramsey and Bernard Anderson wanted Thorp's command, and they quarreled over it. This was not uncommon among the guerrillas—the bickering and the jockeying for leadership. Anderson moved to Bulacan province, then to Tayabas, on the eastern edge of Luzon, along the Pacific coast. Ramsey set up headquarters in Rizal, just to the east of Manila, and tried to unify the guerrilla units in east central Luzon. He eventually claimed 45,000 guerrillas under his command, though it was never entirely clear how much control he had over anything.[22]

Ramsey had strong connections in Manila. Using fake Swiss identity papers, he sometimes traveled into the city, at tremendous risk to himself. More often, though, he dispatched his Filipino officers who easily blended into the population. Sometimes they visited Peggy Utinsky. During the summer of 1943, four guerrillas showed up at her apartment, bearing a message from Ramsey. Peggy already knew one of the men through Miss U: Jeppie (Bert) Richey, a one-legged American civilian who had been using his medical exemption from internment to work with various underground organizations. Another, identified by Peggy as Colonel Santos, could have either been Alejo Santos, associated with Ramsey through the Bulacan Military District, or Abad Santos from Rizal. The message they brought contained written commissions for two young men, former

USAFFE members, who were supposed to meet the guerrillas at Peggy's apartment.[23]

She observed the two "pretty solemn boys" who arrived at her place on A. Mabini Street, giving the correct password to gain admittance. Along with their written commissions, they received enough money to get them into the hills and guns to provide them security along the way. "Those commissions would cost them their lives if the Japanese found them. But the boys wanted to go on fighting." She admired that.[24]

Peggy also felt a special connection to one of the new guerrilla recruits, Robert Bruce (Bobby) Jones, Maria Martinez's nephew. Maria had been one of Miss U's most steadfast workers, though she had not lately spent much time with Peggy. This may have had to do with the change she perceived in Peggy's behavior after Jack's death. Or it could have been because Maria, code name Papaya, had been commissioned a captain in Colonel Hugh Straughn's Fil-American Irregular Troops in July 1943. Maria met Straughn before the war, through mining and construction business interests and activities. He assigned her to the Intelligence Corps of his guerrilla unit, attaching her to the Finance Department. Maria also carried the authority to recruit others, and she brought into the fold Naomi Flores and another young woman, Emma Link Infante.

By this time, however, Naomi was already a busy, experienced guerrilla, and it is unclear how much she actually did for Colonel Straughn's organization. In March, Ramon Amusategui had recruited her, along with Evangeline Neibert, for the Rainbow Unit, without designating her rank. Naomi's job, as she later reported, was to "secure intelligence reports regarding Japanese military activities, installations, movement, strength and war equipment." Two months later she established contact with Bernard Anderson, commanding officer of the Luzon guerillas, and sent him clothing, medicine, and copies of some intelligence reports she thought he would find useful.[25]

Even if Naomi did not have much time to help Hugh Straughn, at least she could help the other guerrillas. However, Maria came to regret bringing in Emma Infante. Though Emma was married to Captain Ramon

Infante, attached to the Alabastro group on Panay under Colonel Macario Peralta, her loyalty to the Allies was questionable. Indeed, by the summer of 1945, Emma was confined to a jail cell, charged by the US military with active collaboration with the Japanese.[26]

After Hugh Straughn's capture by the Japanese in August 1943, Maria began working with Boone and Ramsey. Both men had a hard time finding enough medicine to treat their chronically ill men, and they were always short on funds. Maria facilitated the flow of supplies through Isidro Pongco, code named Eagle. Her nephew, Bobby Jones, assisted in gathering information about Japanese troop movements. Now using a new code name, Sunflower, Maria also helped Boone relay intelligence to other guerrilla units. For this work she collected receipts indicating which supplies had been received and by whom.[27]

In early January 1944, she received one from John Boone, along with a note addressed to "Dear Sunflower." He thanked her for some much-needed office supplies, especially typing paper and carbon, and acknowledged that Pongco managed to deliver vaccines for typhoid, cholera, and dysentery, "which is wonderful." Boone encouraged Maria to raid a Red Cross cache for cotton, adhesive tape, mercurochrome, and Epsom salts, so his men could be better treated for minor gunshot wounds. In closing, he expressed a bit of optimism: "We really are swamped with work now. It is very hard to build a real unit when you are forced to use untrained men as your basis. But the people in this District are 100 per cent loyal and enthusiastic."[28]

It was Bobby Jones and his companion George Arnevic who showed up at Peggy Utinsky's apartment during the summer of 1943 to receive their commissions. After they were sworn in, the meeting broke up, and the guerrillas slipped away. The next morning, Peggy learned of the arrest of one of the men, a Captain Inigo, who had been in her apartment: "This was disquieting news. The fate of everyone at the meeting, of my whole group of workers, and of hundreds in the hills might well be in Inigo's hands. I waited anxiously for some word as to what had happened to him but it was weeks before I learned that he had been set free. He had been tortured but he had not talked."[29]

About a month after that guerrilla meeting, Arnevic turned up on Peggy's doorstep. At six-thirty in the morning, she was already exhausted. To sustain her cover story that she was a Lithuanian nurse, and to earn an income, Peggy took care of private hospital patients every day, most likely at the Philippine General Hospital. Many nights, like the one just past, she also put in long hours at the Malate Convent loading supplies headed for Cabanatuan. Peggy was making a cup of coffee before she had to leave for work. She heard noise from the stairs and assumed a Japanese soldier had followed her from Malate. Peggy opened her front door, prepared to present a good excuse for violating curfew. She saw Arnevic, "unshaven, filthy, sick and stumbling."[30]

When she got him inside the apartment, he explained he sustained a bayonet wound to his arm when the Japanese attacked his guerrilla camp. He came to Manila for medical treatment from the only person he trusted. One look at his wound told Peggy the young man needed a doctor. Worried her pale skin would attract too much attention if she accompanied Arnevic, she telephoned Maria Martinez for help. Maria took him to a Spanish physician Peggy knew from Philippine General Hospital. Arnevic returned to Peggy's apartment to recuperate, and when he was well he tried to leave Manila with a guerrilla compatriot. The Japanese apprehended them both.[31]

As careful as Peggy liked to think she was in dealing with such matters—though she knew the Japanese were keeping tabs on young men like George Arnevic—she could not refuse them the use of her apartment. Not even when it became clear the Japanese were watching her, too. "The fate of those boys drove home the cold certainty that there was danger all around us," Peggy acknowledged. "It came even closer when Father Lalor telephoned late one evening to say that he thought the Japanese were after me and I had better not stay in the apartment that night." She grabbed some overnight essentials and hurried off to stay with Maria Martinez. After three days, when nothing else happened, Peggy returned to A. Mabini Street.[32]

The Japanese were tracking her movements. Everyone in the Miss U network knew it because a friend of Ramon Amusategui tipped him off.

In mid-August, Naomi Flores returned to Manila from Cabanatuan for an early celebration of Peggy's birthday. It was a rare event, this gathering that brought together so many of the people involved in Miss U. The hosts of the party, Joaquin and Angustias Mencarini, were wealthy Spaniards who donated their time and money to Remedios Hospital. As a special surprise for Peggy, Naomi had suggested to some of the Cabanatuan POWs that they design a birthday flag. Naomi intended to personally deliver it to the guest of honor.

As she exited the train station, two Kempeitai officers grabbed her and took her to Fort Santiago. Though this was her third detention, there seemed to be some kind of mix-up. The Japanese were looking for a woman from Pampanga known for her involvement with the guerrillas, and it is possible they mistook Naomi for Herminia Dizon, Claude Thorp's associate. After three hours of questioning, Naomi realized her forged documents had withstood scrutiny. The Japanese had no idea of her true identity.[33]

It was a welcome stroke of luck. Naomi later recounted, "I was utterly relieved when I got out of Fort Santiago because I had with me all the notes and acknowledgement or receipts of the money I had sent to the prisoners in the camp." Had the Japanese searched her, these would have been discovered. Because the Kempeitai concluded they detained the wrong woman, they asked but did not press her about "the activities of Mrs. Utinsky." They accepted what Naomi told them: all she knew of this person was that she was an unmarried Lithuanian nurse. Still, it was an ominous sign that the Kempeitai asked about Peggy—and used her married name.[34]

Confident she fooled the Japanese and certain they were not tailing her, Naomi headed straight to A. Mabini Street. Peggy's maid, Maria, told Naomi the birthday party for Peggy was still going on at the Mencarini home. The guests there were worried about Naomi's absence. Maria added that someone had telephoned several times asking for Naomi Flores. Now Naomi felt uneasy; she realized the Japanese knew where to find her. She had her name listed in the 1942 Manila telephone directory, ostensibly as a supplier of beauty shop services, but really so potential donors to prisoner relief would know where to find her: 128 A. Mabini Street.[35]

As Naomi contemplated what this all meant, the telephone rang and Peggy was on the line, instructing her to sit tight—the party would come back there. Everyone was excited and relieved to find Naomi safe and sound in Peggy's apartment. When they asked what delayed her, Naomi could not tell the truth and add to their concerns: "I refrained from telling anyone about the incident because I knew that Mrs. Utinsky would readily be unnerved." Naomi lied and said the train had broken down. Before this second gathering broke up, all notes and documents connected with the prisoners and guerrillas were gathered up from Peggy's apartment and sent back with Father Lalor for safekeeping at the Malate Convent.[36]

It was a smart move, as the Japanese circled closer to Peggy. A few weeks after Peggy returned from her impromptu visit to Maria Martinez, a man claiming to be a guerrilla showed up at her apartment. Though the timing was right—Peggy had been expecting a courier—something about this man did not sit well with her. "The moment he entered the room I was cold with suspicion. This was a mistake. I knew it." He talked too much, anxious to prove his connections to the Americans. When he offered money, Peggy told him she did not need it.[37]

Evangeline Neibert, in the apartment during the encounter, was certain the man was not a guerrilla and told Peggy so as soon as he left. They noticed he left behind a revolver and some bullets. Plants, Peggy realized, and she knew the Japanese would show up soon to search her apartment. She removed the gun to a safe hiding place and went to bed. Around midnight, her telephone rang. A strange woman's voice said hello and then the connection broke. Frightened but exhausted, Peggy dropped back into sleep for a short while.

Loud noises woke her up, and her maid Maria announced the arrival of the Japanese. Peggy found about fifty soldiers crowded into her apartment, rifling through her belongings: "With typical Japanese dexterity and patience, those soldiers literally took the place apart. They shook out every piece of linen in the drawers, searched every match box, powder box, pillow, picture frame, and book. They even opened two bottles of perfume." The officer in charge fired questions at Peggy: Where are her guns?

What is her name? What does she do for a living? Where is her passport? What is her involvement with Cabanatuan? Why does she own so many books? When Peggy answered one round of questions, the officer began again, going on and on for about eight hours. After instructing Peggy not to leave her apartment, he and his men departed.[38]

It was Friday morning, September 28, 1943. Sleep deprived but far from compliant, Peggy ignored the order. "I had to report to the hospital. There were two emergency cases there whom I was nursing; both of them, as it happened, were members of my group," she later wrote. One was a Russian woman, Zena Jasten, married to Walter Jasten, an American civilian employee of the Adjutant General's Corps, now imprisoned in Cabanatuan. The other was Claire Phillips.[39]

WHILE CLAIRE PHILLIPS AND PEGGY Utinsky scrambled to keep the guerrillas supplied, Yay Panlilio, journalist and S-2 agent, became a guerrilla. Since March 1942, after fleeing Manila one step ahead of an arrest warrant, Yay had been hiding on a secluded farm east of Manila in Rizal province. Though still suffering the chills and fevers of malaria, with a bum knee from a car accident, a weak heart, and an uncorrected case of nearsightedness, she was determined to save her country by joining a guerrilla outfit. She just had to decide which one.

Her choice was made simpler in July when Marking's guerrillas found Yay in her rural hideaway. The organization, founded in April 1942, was named for its leader, Marcos Villa Agustin, known as Marking. In his mid-thirties, Marking had been a cabdriver and an amateur boxer in Manila before the war. After the Japanese attack, he worked as a driver for USAFFE for a time before moving over to Binangonan where he began recruiting a guerrilla force. A triangular-shaped municipality in Rizal province, Binangonan is located between the foothills of the Sierra Madre Mountains and the northeast tip of Laguna de Bay, southeast of Manila. As soon as enemy bombs began falling, residents of Manila and the surrounding suburbs had evacuated to Binangonan, a wharf town on the shore of Laguna Lake, where Marking found a lot of men eager to join him.

Marking established a unit of about 150 men and began patrolling around Binangonan. When the Japanese attacked their camp at Tatala-Binangonan, Marking's guerrillas fled, ahead of their leader. Until he caught up with them, twenty-year-old Leon Z. Cabalhin was in charge. Marking's men did not stop until they reached the farmhouse where Yay had been hiding. Though she was happy to meet these freedom fighters, there were too many of them to go unnoticed by enemy scouting parties. Yay insisted they move on to a safer location, but Cabalhin resisted, "Hostilely respectful," she later acknowledged. The guerrilla pointed out that without orders from Marking, he could not move the men. Yay pressed her point, though, and the owner of the farmhouse concurred. Cabalhin ordered the men to move.[40]

That evening, just as Yay fell asleep, Marking arrived. "Tall, well muscled, but lean, Major Marcos V. Agustin, alias Marking, stood with his fists on his hips, his feet planted wide, and his head high and a little back. In the flickering light his small eyes were challenging, beady," Yay remembered. "I eyed him sleepily, in no mood to be challenged in the middle of the night awakened out of a sound sleep. . . . Now sleepily, grumpily, I eyed the Major." The war had taken away Peggy Utinsky's and Claire Phillips's men; it had brought Yay's to her.[41]

Marking asked what she was doing, and she replied she was helping the guerrillas. "Hotly we looked each other in the eye. I saw a fighting man. He saw a defiant woman. We burst into laughter, having found each other," she later wrote. They started talking. Yay wanted to know everything about Marking's unit and he filled her in with generalities. He had around 150 men, though he would take as many as he could get. They had weapons, and Marking trained his men to the best of his ability, which was not very well. He yelled and hit them to drive home the lessons. This did not encourage the men to learn any better or faster.[42]

Over the next months, Marking revealed the details of his life to Yay. His father was a lawyer involved in local politics, and his mother, a convent-schooled Catholic, had a gambling problem, and fought with her husband and beat her sons. Marking ran away as soon as he could and found a job sweeping up in a movie theater. Over the next years he picked up a variety of skills: driving, car mechanics, boxing, health care, and even a stint as a "secret service man" in Antipolo.[43]

When the Japanese launched their attack in December 1941, Marking first took shifts as an air raid warden then helped convoy troops to Bataan. At the beginning of the new year, he drove an armored car south out of Manila, changed into civilian clothes, and headed for Bataan. Caught by a Japanese patrol, Marking tried to convince them he was a student on his way home. The soldiers saw his tattoos: a star on his right hand and, when they yanked open his shirt, an American eagle and American flag on his chest. They beat him, tied him up, and tossed him in a cattle truck with other prisoners, bound for Manila. As the truck chugged up the ramp to the Calumpit Bridge, Marking jumped into the river. He hiked his way back to the hills where he encountered other men in similar situations.[44]

In June 1942, Marking learned the Japanese were holding 115 American prisoners, mostly pilots and engineers, at the Cine Lumban, an old movie theater, in Laguna. During the day, these men marched out from the cinema at bayonet point to build a wooden bridge across the Lumban River. Marking observed the POWs—"drooping, dying soldiers with desperate, dull, glazing eyes"—and vowed to rescue them. On the night of June 11, 1942, Marking and forty-five of his men crept into Lumban, shot the first Japanese sentry they saw at the theater prison, and proceeded to shoot, bludgeon, and hack the remaining nine. Marking yelled to the prisoners to follow him, but only one, Corporal George Lightman of the 3rd Pursuit Squadron, ran out of the building. The ranking American captain ordered the rest of the prisoners to stay put.[45]

Though the raid ended with one American rescued and dozens of guns confiscated, Marking was unhappy. He had expected to save all the men. Then the chilling news arrived that as punishment for Lightman's escape, the Japanese executed ten POWs, a standard practice for discouraging escapes. Marking had not known that shortly before his raid, an American slipped away from the Cine Lumban, prompting the Japanese to issue their execution warning. The American captain would have had this foremost in his mind when he prevented his men from leaving the theater building. Aware of their poor physical condition, the captain probably believed they could not all make it out and the remaining POWs would be killed in ret-ribution. Marking never made another rescue attempt.[46]

As the two talked that first evening, Yay noticed Marking's men becoming restless. Not tired, but uneasy; they "shifted from foot to foot, squatted wearily, exchanged meaningful glances, hid their disgust behind blank faces. . . . They could see dainty horns coming out of my temples, a forked tail curled about one ankle." The men were suspicious of her and of the attention she received from their leader. If Yay intended to remain with Marking's guerrillas, she had to carve out her own place, establish her own authority. She told Marking he and his men needed time to rest and recuperate. She asked him for a squad of men to set up a camp in the village of Kalinawan, four miles behind the main highway. Punctuated with limestone crags, caves, and underground rivers, it was the perfect guerrilla lair.[47]

With little persuasion, Marking agreed to the hideaway. A bigger chal-lenge was convincing him not to go off half-cocked against the Japanese. When Marking came to see Yay's new camp, he informed her that as a guerrilla, he had to act like one and attack the enemy. Otherwise he was useless. Yay reminded him he could only be effective if he stayed alive, and to do so he needed reliable information about Japanese troop movements and he needed more supplies. She typed up carefully worded letters to her friends in Manila, to be hand-delivered by couriers, asking for help, confi-dent they would come through.[48]

His men were guerrillas, Yay insisted to Marking, not lawless bandits. It was not enough to train them how to handle weapons; they had to under-stand and respect authority. "This is your duty, your responsibility, your cross," she said. "Nobody can carry it but you, for you were marked for it and it was marked for you." If he really cared about his men, he would do everything he could to survive as long as possible. When it came to sur-vival, Yay was fatalistic, telling Marking, "You're not going to live through this. Neither am I. But we can live long enough to do more good than just getting ourselves killed tomorrow."[49]

This impassioned speech did not convince Marking. He wanted to go fight, to kill as many Japanese as possible. Yay persuaded him to wait one more day and had him stay in the new camp long enough to eat some hot soup and have a full night's sleep. That was when they became lovers. Yay hesitated, unsure about the timing. Marking reminded her of the uncertainties of guerrilla life, "Tomorrow might not come. Make up your mind tonight." She agreed. "When a man gives his life for his country, how little a woman's heart!" she later explained. "I turned my head, to meet his lips. War was our marriage, the guerrillas our sons."[50]

The rest and recuperation Yay envisioned for the group never materialized. Within a week, Japanese patrols zeroed in on the new location. For more than eight months, Yay and Marking's guerrillas "played blind man's bluff in a strip four miles long and two miles wide, and little crossroad *sitios* [hamlets] were to be consecrated in suffering and death." Nevertheless, the locals remained largely supportive of the guerrilla unit, and many men joined up to go off with Marking.[51]

Those who remained behind in their hometowns functioned as a home guard, retaliating against the Japanese whenever they could. One member was Trinidad Diaz, a young accountant working at the Rizal Cement Factory in Binangonan, where Marking first organized his unit. Every weekend Diaz transported the company payroll two miles from the factory to the employees at the quarry. She carried a gun because she traveled alone, yet she never had to use it. The people in the area liked her and knew the money belonged to their friends and families.[52]

Diaz worried instead about the increasing presence of the enemy. She saw more and more Japanese patrolling, especially near the waterfront. She decided to take action. One night early that summer, enlisting the help of six men, Diaz attacked and killed five Japanese on the wharf, dumping the dead bodies into a cement mixer. In a final defiant gesture, she confiscated their launch and turned it over to Marking's men. The Japanese rounded up known resisters in the area and executed them in the factory. They eventually arrested Diaz, and she endured interrogation and torture for thirty days. The guerrillas knew the Japanese had her, knew where she was being kept. They could not risk a rescue out of fear the Japanese would extend their retaliation into the community. Diaz did not talk before her execution.[53]

In Rizal province with Marking's guerrillas, Yay spent the summer and early fall of 1942 cementing her leadership role. She refused relegation to the superfluous position of mistress. Yay made sure the guerrillas recognized her authority, and she took every opportunity to assert it, even when it meant standing up to Marking. One day the guerrillas brought in a local suspected of working with the Japanese. Yay recognized him. Pascual helped the Americans in recent weeks, and his wife had provided Yay with food and shelter. Yay could not believe Pascual was involved with the enemy, and she insisted on proof, not rumors, as the basis for any execution order. Marking ignored her, drew his pistol, and announced he would shoot Pascual.

Yay stepped between the two men. "For him, it was a showdown on who was boss. For me, it was a showdown on what was just. For the men, it was a test of courage." Yay won. Marking admitted he could not shoot Pascual because Yay did not want him to. She believed this also earned her the men's respect because she had the courage to stand up to Marking.[54]

Being a courageous guerrilla leader also meant knowing how to issue an execution order once guilt was established. One day when Marking was away from the camp, one of the guerrillas brought in a Sakdal—a pro-Japanese Filipino—accused of spying for the Japanese. The man allegedly revealed to the Japanese that the Filipinos who served as Japanese Volunteer Guards in the area were really the home guard of Marking's forces. Yay ordered the man held under heavy guard until Marking's return, when he could be questioned. Fulgado, the guerrilla who brought the suspect in, reminded Yay that Marking left her in charge, with the right and duty to make that determination herself. Besides, Fulgado asked, "Ma'am, can you not share the blood on our hands?"[55]

Yay knew Fulgado was right. It was her decision and she could not abdicate it to Marking because it was unpleasant. When she heard the captive begging and pleading for his life, even offering up his father as the guilty party, she gave the order to make the man talk. The guerrillas beat him bloody, and then Yay listened to what he had to say. She pronounced him guilty and gave the execution order: "It must be done quickly, mercifully. We cannot waste more bullets. That is an over-all order. You must use the bayonet right through the heart." Though she found killing distasteful, she reminded the guerrillas—or perhaps justified to herself—that it constituted a form of self-defense. Letting the prisoner go free would jeopardize their safety.[56]

Into the fall of 1942, Marking's guerrillas continued to grow, with the core of the outfit the full-timers who lived and fought in the hills. According to Yay, guerrilla activities included other duties: "part-time saboteurs, working for the enemy and undoing all they had done; propagandists writing, printing, passing their down-in-black-and-white defiance; men and women training themselves as intelligence agents, learning to observe and retain and evaluate what they saw and to convey the information accurately and quickly." Anyone who took any action against the enemy was a guerrilla.[57]

Marking spent the majority of his time training his fighters. His big personality and his martial skills, Yay believed, attracted and sustained a large loyal following. A large group required effective organization as well. This was Yay's contribution, handling the administrative details of Marking's guerrillas, keeping troop rosters, assigning duties, and distributing supplies.[58]

Though Marking welcomed this assistance, he tired of Yay's constant reminders about caution. Training was all well and good to a point; he wanted to attack the enemy. Marking and Yay fought about this more than once—huge screaming matches often accompanied by flying fists. During one of these confrontations, Yay threatened to kill herself if Marking refused to heed her advice. He insisted on doing as he pleased. She loaded a .32 snub-nosed Colt revolver and put it to her head. "Filipinos will die for love and Americans will die for principle. I am half-and-half. I die the same way," she said to Marking.[59]

Catching her wrist in his hand, Marking lowered the gun from her head. Yay did not resist. She reminded him again of his responsibilities, telling him the endless work and the endless arguments exhausted her. He took the gun, hugged her, and agreed to stay in the camp until the Japanese scaled back their patrols. This time Marking remained for a week. When he resumed the offensive, he left Yay in charge of fifty ailing, unarmed guerrillas, with the Japanese once again on the verge of discovering their camp.

These were still the early days for guerrilla fighters, and having at least one hundred men with some weapons made Marking a formidable foe of the Japanese. He moved in and out of the camp that fall, sometimes remaining to train new recruits, other times leading the trained ones on missions. Following Yay's lead, Marking harangued his men about proper behavior, reminding them they were fighters, not bandits. He set an example by paying local farmers for the food his men needed. If a farmer refused to sell, Marking honored the refusal—at least while Yay was watching.

The new year of 1943 began with a Japanese raid on Marking's ever-mobile guerrilla camp in Rizal province. As morning broke on January 3rd, the camp received a five-minute warning from the lookout. Yay organized a hasty, successful retreat while Marking and his armed men killed eleven Japanese before they, too, disappeared higher into the mountains.

They built a new camp on Mount Mayton. It provided adequate cover from the Japanese. Water had to be carried in, though, and the area food supply was limited to meager amounts of sweet potatoes and river shrimp, sometimes augmented with the meat from a wild cow. The nutritional imbalance provoked a variety of health problems for everyone. Yay suffered with five abscessed teeth and a fever. The men who now called her Mammy could not bear to see her in such pain. Marking brought in a doctor and a dentist to treat her, and she slowly recovered.[60]

Most of the guerrillas were back to fighting strength in February. Leon Cabalhin, Marking's second-in-command, moved away from the small-scale hit-and-run operations that had been most common. Instead, he led a dozen armed men down the mountain, drawing the Japanese out and away from the guerrilla camp. Cabalhin and his men encountered 150 enemy soldiers and killed ninety-three. Yay later boasted, "It was only one of many such raids, pummeling the enemy everywhere, and it indicated the growing strength of the guerrillas."[61]

Since some of the Japanese escaped the attack, Marking's camp moved again, across the valley from Mount Mayton, which had little natural cover, to Mount Kanumay, blanketed with thick trees. Normally a two-hour trek, it turned into an all-day affair for most of the weakened, weary men. The new camp developed into a vibrant guerrilla headquarters. Volunteers came in for training and were then dispatched where needed, vital information arrived to be passed along, supplies were gathered and parceled out. Still, ill health plagued the camp, and both Yay and Marking wore themselves out providing medical care.[62]

Through March 1943 the guerrillas operated in the area. No matter how well hidden they considered their base, the Japanese found out about it. It was impossible to keep a secret in an area where the guerrillas roamed the countryside, approached farmers for food, chatted with the locals. The Japanese detained one of the farmers and gave him a letter to deliver to Marking, even providing the man with directions to Marking's camp. The letter, written by Captain Ikeda, chief of the Central Luzon Military Police, and addressed to Mr. Marcos Agustin and Mr. [sic] Yay Panlilio, gave a final warning for surrender. If Marking and his men did not give themselves up by April 18, 1943, the Japanese would come for them.

Marking refused. No matter what the Japanese promised or threatened, he would not surrender. Yay pointed out that the guerrillas could not defend their headquarters, that the sick and wounded men in camp would be slaughtered. Marking replied, "You damn woman, you keep your damn mouth shut!" Yay threw her canteen at him, hitting him in the head, and dousing his disassembled gun with water. "Order the sick to go home and lie low. And the next time you throw a canteen, darling, empty it first," he said to her.[63]

The guerrillas stayed put. Hundreds of Japanese swarmed into the hills, as promised, at daybreak on April 18th. "The Japs had a system: the mountain was surrounded, then the patrols cut through, over and over again, like cutting a pie. To go where they had just been was safest—for a while," Yay later explained. One of Marking's patrol leaders, Sidney H. Gorham, originally of the 2d Chemical Survey Company, walked right into a group of enemy soldiers, mistaking them for guerrillas. They quickly pinned Gorham down and took him captive, marching him to Antipolo, where he proudly admitted he was a major with the guerrillas. His actual rank was captain, but he hoped the higher rank would impress his captors enough to treat him well. Before Marking could arrange a rescue, the Japanese moved Gorham to a larger garrison in Laguna, where plans for another rescue could not be carried out before he was moved again. Gorham was executed in Bilibid Prison at the end of September 1943, probably at the same time as Claude Thorp and Joe Barker.[64]

The Japanese had Marking's guerrillas on the run for three weeks following Gorham's capture. Yay, suffering from a slow menstrual hemorrhage and a variety of internal pains, had to be carried along by hammock. They finally found safety in a series of small mountain caves, where, Yay later wrote, "Our defense would be half secrecy and half the Japs' ignorance of which mountain to patrol." As with everything involved in guerrilla life, the safety of the caves proved temporary.[65]

IN THE CITY, CLAIRE PHILLIPS observed the effects of the intensified Japanese campaign. Many prominent Filipinos, Spaniards, Swiss, and Chinese disappeared, arrested in their homes or hustled off the streets by the Kempeitai, landing into Fort Santiago. The "guerrillas minus guns," as Claire referred to the resistance workers in Manila, tried their best to locate these unfortunates. In most cases, success meant the retrieval of a dead body found floating in the Pasig River.[66]

Although Claire no longer volunteered at Remedios Hospital—her work at the Club Tsubaki took all her waking hours—she visited Father Lalor when she could. Occasionally she arranged the delivery of something in particular he needed, other times he had something of interest for her. And one day in 1943 the priest introduced Claire to a young mestizo nurse who was "as daring as you are, my child." It was Bobby Jones, the nephew of Maria Martinez.[67]

Jones and Claire took a walk through the Malate Convent garden, staying out of earshot of the others on the grounds. They talked about the Japanese customers at the Club Tsubaki and Jones admitted he owned a transmitting radio set. It was dangerous to use the equipment because occupation authorities forbade private radio ownership and used detectors scattered around the city to locate violators. When Claire suggested sending the set to the guerrillas, Bobby told her he had been thinking the same. "I told him that I would contact Boone and work out a plan for transferring the set to him, and Jones consented," she later wrote.[68]

While the arrangements for moving the radio were pending, Claire prevailed on Bobby Jones to pass along any news he managed to pick up. Positive stories about Allied progress in the war would go a long way to cheering up the people on Luzon, and Claire decided to publish such news. "Many Filipinos, by this time, were not thinking of abstract right or wrong. They were growing weary of the whole gruesome business of war, and were concerned chiefly with how they and their children could be fed and clothed," she remembered. "They were beginning to fear that it might take years for the Americans to return, and dreaded a future of this miserable, uncertain existence. Our news sheet did much to relieve their mental strain."[69]

Even that work carried risk. In their determination to squelch all opposition, Japanese authorities kept an eye out for and tracked down these kinds of unofficial news reports. Several times they confiscated Claire's sheets and picked up people they suspected of involvement with the publication. Despite the danger, Claire did not want to abandon this enterprise. John Boone told her the news she collected from reliable sources cheered his men, gave them added incentive for their work. Some were itching to strike back at the Japanese, despite orders from Australia to lie low.

The delivery of Bobby Jones's radio took weeks because the set had to be broken down and sent piece by piece with different couriers into the hills. Boone could hardly wait to get it operational, but once reassembled, the small bamboo radio proved disappointing. Its range was too short and failed to improve Boone's communications with MacArthur's headquarters. Not until a new set—smuggled in via submarine to Mindanao then brought piece by piece to Boone's camp on Luzon—was running later in the year could Boone establish consistent communication. "Several months passed without a response," Claire remembered when Boone started using the radio, "then messages started coming in from MacArthur's new G.H.Q. in New Guinea, and some of them were assignments for the 'guerrillas minus guns' or me."[70]

Later, Claire also claimed that with the establishment of this communications network, the Club Tsubaki became the contact center for the
"bona-fide" guerrilla leaders in the area. These men sent messages to each
other and arranged meetings through Claire at the club: "Properly accred-
ited carriers reported the various plans and locations of a given band to
me. I made several copies of this information and relayed it to other guerrilla groups. Thus, in a short time, the activities of half a dozen or more
such bands were coordinated."[71]

Chatting up the club's clientele for information for the guerrillas
remained a core part of Claire's operation. For this, she relied on the assistance of her employees: "After our hostesses had coaxed our high-ranking
official guests into a jovial mood, either Fely or I would join the party and
cajole the alcohol-befuddled Nips into talking. If they were army men, we
led them to tell about troop movements, and the conditions of roads and
bridges. If naval officers, we lured them into talking about their ships. We
pumped many newly arrived business men about the locations and nature
of their establishments."[72]

All this information went to John Boone via courier, but it is difficult
to verify how much of it got sent on and how much was tactically useful.
Yet Claire believed this was important work, and that the information she
gathered played a part in Allied victories. It may have, whether on its own
or combined with additional intelligence from other sources.

During the fall of 1943, for example, Boone asked Claire to keep an
eye out for a Japanese aircraft carrier in Manila Harbor. It had been damaged, and Boone needed to know how long the repairs would take, when
it was scheduled to depart, and where it was headed. The commander of
the carrier, Captain Arita, walked into the Club Tsubaki one evening with
his staff. Claire made sure to give him a warm welcome. "These naval officers, like all newcomers to the club, had to be warmed up through drinks
and flattery, and reassured through more of the same." Arita lapped up the
attention and returned several times. He had fallen for Fely Corcuera and
did not want to miss a night of her singing.[73]

Captain Arita proved to be a quiet man; he did not engage in casual
conversation nor did he drink alcohol. Claire found it a challenge to get

information out of a sober man. With enough visits and enough talk from his officers, she found out the aircraft carrier was headed to Singapore. When she made a fuss about his last evening at the Club Tsubaki, organizing an impromptu farewell party, she picked up additional details. The carrier would shove off at six the next morning, and after a stop in Singapore, it would head to Rabaul. As soon as the captain walked out the door that night, Claire sent a courier to Boone with the information. She knew she would never see Arita again: "I even cried real tears when he left, as I knew I was sending him to his doom . . . but war is war."[74]

This observation about war cut both ways, as Claire soon realized. The staff at the Club Tsubaki were "all grieved and angered" when they read the newspaper account of Hugh Straughn's capture and execution in the fall of 1943. It was the talk of the club that evening, though Claire and her employees could not show any signs of sympathy. Colonel Nagahama Akira, head of the Kempeitai headquarters at Fort Santiago, was drinking at the club the night the news was released. Claire asked him if he had seen Straughn in the prison. Nagahama smiled and bragged that he pulled the trigger at the guerrilla's execution. "I had to pretend to laugh with him," Claire remembered, "but at the first opportunity, I left the room and was violently ill." War was war.[75]

YAY PANLILIO HAD NO TIME or patience for mourning the fate of Hugh Straughn. Marking's guerrillas evolved into a large and powerful organization, and it frequently clashed with other units. Straughn had been an adviser to Marking, but neither had been particularly fond of the other. "I could not weep any tears except crocodile tears," Yay recalled after hearing the news of Straughn's death. "I sincerely would have wished him safe, and I pitied him—but without tears." The spring of 1943 had been difficult as Yay and the guerrillas constantly moved to stay ahead of the pursuing Japanese, especially during June. José Laurel, left behind by President Quezon to work with the Japanese, was shot and wounded early in the month as he played a round of golf at the Wack Wack Club. Marking's guerrillas were alleged to have been behind the assassination attempt of this man they considered a collaborator.

Even with all the moving, Yay's health improved, and the men made time for some fun and celebration. Marking insisted on a grand gesture to celebrate Yay's thirtieth birthday, although "grand" was relative among the guerrillas. "Food was all he could give me, when he would have liked to give the moon, or a guaranteed safety; and I made a point of appreciating all he could offer," she recalled. Marking found a pig to roast, one of Yay's favorite meals, and invited the local parish priest, Father Aramil, to join them.[76]

There was another part of the celebration: Marking arranged for the priest to baptize Yay. Though not a practicing Catholic, Marking had been baptized and believed Yay should be as well. In their situation, he reasoned, Yay needed this sacrament because if they were killed they would not be together in heaven. Yay tried to resist, only giving in when she realized the depth of Marking's determination. After the baptism, the two stood in front of Father Aramil who gave an untypical blessing for that event: "What God hath joined together, let no man put asunder." Yay smiled at the priest and said, "It's nice of you to hope so."[77]

During the summer of 1943, Marking's guerrillas moved to Talim Island, just off the southern tip of Binangonan in Laguna de Bay, which Yay described as "a lovely paradise of forest, farm, and duck yards." The paradise had a couple of other things going for it. There were no Japanese swarming around and the people of Talim seemed genuinely happy to see the guerrillas, even throwing them a party. Marking's men rested, ate well, and stopped running for a time. At least until the Japanese implemented zoning in areas of heavy guerrilla activity. They cordoned off towns, allowing no outsiders to come in. They claimed anyone caught outside was a guerrilla and took them away for interrogation. While they had captive audiences, the Japanese brought in collaborators to identify people involved in anti-Japanese work. The accused were publicly beaten and tortured as a warning to those who opposed the occupation.[78]

In August 1943, the Japanese came to Talim, and destroyed paradise. The locals begged Marking's men to leave as quickly as possible so they would not be caught up in zoning. Yay and the others departed, hoping to draw the enemy away from the generous townspeople who sheltered them. The Japanese were determined to catch Marking this time and mercilessly hounded anyone who assisted him. Yay found out Japanese soldiers "came later to kill six farmers only because we had passed within a mile of the home of one or had drunk from the brook of another or had stopped at the door of a third to buy salt to take with water as we pulled farther and farther away from the people."[79]

The guerrillas took refuge on the mainland with a group of Dumagat people, non-Christian, semi-nomadic descendants of the Negritos. Although temporarily safe from the Japanese, Yay now had other personal issues to deal with. Her relationship with Marking had been tempestuous since the beginning, with shouting matches, threats, slaps, and punches. The physical abuse escalated, with sexual jealousy in particular setting Marking off. He could not stand to see Yay pay any attention to another man.

She was careful, then, when John Schaffer, a former mining engineer who had originally been part of Marking's unit, returned to the group with Bernard Anderson. Schaffer and his fellow engineer Alvin Farretta had become separated from Marking's men during a Japanese raid and found their way to Anderson. Yay's simple greeting to Anderson, "How do you do?" earned her a suspicious look from Marking. By remaining coolly polite to Anderson, Yay hoped to undercut any personal jealousy Marking might feel. Professional jealousy was palpable enough. The guerrillas shared the common goal of getting rid of the Japanese; beyond that, their philosophies, politics, and methods diverged.[80]

Bernard Anderson came to take his measure of Marking, and to determine where he fell in the guerrilla hierarchy. Anderson asked about Marking's rank, the fact that his men called him General. Marking denied any such rank: "I guess if my people want to call me 'General' that's their own business. . . . I sign myself like this: 'MARCOS V. AGUSTIN, Commanding.'" When Anderson offered to help Marking secure official recognition, the Filipino exploded. "Bullshit, recognition! I don't need to be authorized to fight for my own country, I guess! . . . I guess I can run my outfit right! Nobody has to give me permission to fight. I'd like to see anybody stop me!"[81]

Marking calmed down when he agreed with Anderson on the necessity of taking orders from General MacArthur. Marking invited Anderson to stay for a pig roast, then took Yay aside and asked her to talk with Anderson for a while. The visitor instructed Yay on a variety of army procedures, including accounting and other recording keeping. Guerrillas, Anderson insisted, had to toe the army line. Yay liked this man: "He didn't backbite or curry favor by carrying gossip, and thus throw guerrilla outfits against one another. He didn't criticize or complain." She found him sensible and compassionate and devoted to the cause. Yay also probably appreciated that Anderson's professional manner did not provoke one of Marking's jealous rages.[82]

The stresses of guerrilla life were compounding and starting to take a toll on Yay Panlilio. The war was only half over.

CHAPTER 12

THE MANILA UNDERGROUND

CLAIRE PHILLIPS'S DAYS AND NIGHTS REVOLVED AROUND SUP-
porting the guerrillas and the men in Cabanatuan. Her ability
to do so depended on how much money the Club Tsubaki brought in.
Despite brisk business at the club, the voracious needs of the prisoners
and guerrillas stretched Claire to the financial breaking point.

In mid-February 1943, John Boone's most trusted courier—now his
wife—Mellie, arrived at the club with a note. His guerrilla camp had been
raided by the Japanese and all the supplies Claire sent were gone. Claire
knew Boone's men needed new provisions as soon as possible. Because of
her work for Cabanatuan, though, she was low on cash. She made a quick
choice: "I glanced at my diamond ring, and decided it must go the way of
all things."[1]

Claire knew someone at Remedios Hospital who would help pawn the
jewelry. One of the volunteers there was a tall, attractive, forty-year-old
Spanish woman, Angustias Mencarini, who had hosted Peggy Utinsky's
birthday party the previous August. Married to a prosperous Manila

businessman, Angustias divided her time between taking care of her three children and nursing patients at the hospital. Claire heard stories around Remedios that the Mencarinis collected money "for our cause," even selling their own possessions for cash to help the civilian internees at Santo Tomas.[2]

Handing Angustias Mencarini the diamond ring, Claire said she needed quick cash for the guerrillas, a request that did not startle the Spanish woman in the least. Angustias eyed the diamond, estimated it would fetch 3,000 pesos, and completed the transaction in a day. When Claire pocketed the pesos, Angustias said, "Come to my house for lunch day after tomorrow at one o'clock." Trying to beg off, Claire replied that between the Club Tsubaki and her work at the hospital, she did not have time for socializing. "You will have time for this," Angustias assured her. "A few people will be there whom you will enjoy meeting, and you must know."[3]

The Mencarini home was located on Taft Avenue, Manila's most elegant thoroughfare. When Claire arrived, she was surprised to see so many familiar faces among the dozen or so guests: the Amusateguis and the Atienzas, Father Lalor, Naomi Flores, and Evangeline Neibert. When they all sat down at the luncheon table, Angustias said, "Since we are all doing the same kind of work, I thought that it would be nice for us to become acquainted." She introduced each person along with their code name and a description of their activities in aiding the cause. In that room, Claire faced a significant portion of Manila's underground. These were the people the Japanese wanted to neutralize. Yet here they sat, with all the naiveté of amateurs, talking about code names and resistance strategies.[4]

Claire learned the identities of the other guests: German Eroles, young, slender, with blond hair and blue eyes, worked as a cashier in the Marfusa Restaurant, a popular Russian eatery. His code name, Fancypants, was apt as he favored custom-tailored clothing. Sitting next to him was Maria Martinez (Papaya/Sunflower), who lived nearby on Taft Avenue. A large heavyset Filipino, Mr. Torres, known as "The Doctor," sat next to Ramon Amusategui (Sparkplug) and Lorenza Amusategui (Screwball). Angustias used the code name Boots, and her husband Joaquin was known as Rocky.[5]

Peggy Utinsky (right) standing next to Nell Yard (left), Jack Utinsky's sister, with Nell's daughter, Carol, in New York, August 1940. Courtesy of Carol Guazzo.

Jack Utinsky, circa 1917. Courtesy of Carol Guazzo.

Claire Phillips is greeted by Major Kenneth Boggs and a WAC honor guard at La Guardia Airport, April 1951. © Bettmann/CORBIS.

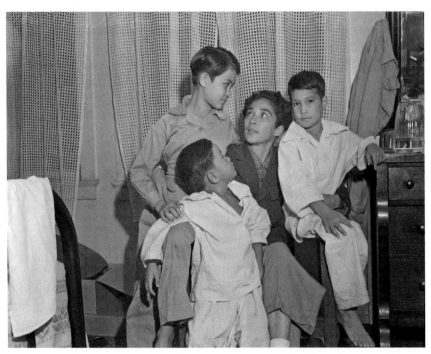
Yay Panlilio and her children in Los Angeles, CA, May 1945. Credit must be given to Los Angeles Times Staff. Copyright © 1945. Reprinted with Permission.

Members of the Japanese "Bicycle Division" head into Manila on January 2, 1942.
Courtesy of the U.S. National Archives and Records Administration.

Santo Tomas University in Manila. Gladys Savary aided the civilian internees incarcerated here. Fred Hill Collection, Pierce Library, Eastern Oregon University. Licensed under Creative Commons Attribution.

The grounds of the Santo Tomas internment camp, where internees were allowed to construct shanties for family use. Courtesy of the U.S. National Archives and Records Administration.

American prisoners at rest along the Bataan Death March, April 1942. Courtesy of the U.S. National Archives and Records Administration.

American and Filipino troops surrender to the Japanese at Corregidor, May 1942. Courtesy of the U.S. National Archives and Records Administration.

Healthiest PWs were selected for group photo. Fort O'Donnell, Death Camp, 15 May 1942, one month after camp was opened.

Prisoners at Camp O'Donnell, May 1942. Courtesy of the U.S. National Archives and Records Administration.

Burial detail at the Cabanatuan prisoner of war camp, May 1942. Courtesy of the U.S. National Archives and Records Administration.

The ruins of Fort Santiago, Manila, 1945. Claire Phillips and Peggy Utinsky were imprisoned and tortured here. Fred Hill Collection, Pierce Library, Eastern Oregon University. Licensed under Creative Commons Attribution.

An unidentified woman posed outside of Claire Phillips's Club Tsubaki, Manila, 1945. Fred Hill Collection, Pierce Library, Eastern Oregon University. Licensed under Creative Commons Attribution.

Claire Phillips with her daughter Dian, Manila, March 1945. Fred Hill Collection, Pierce Library, Eastern Oregon University. Licensed under Creative Commons Attribution.

Peggy Utinsky, still armed, with Dian Phillips in Manila, March 1945. Courtesy of the U.S. National Archives and Records Administration.

Luzon guerrilla leaders in Manila, 1945. John Boone is seated second right. In the center is Manuel Roxas, soon to be the fifth president of the Philippines. Courtesy of the U.S. National Archives and Records Administration.

Luzon guerrilla leaders, April 1945. John Boone is standing forward center, cigarette in hand. Bernard Anderson is on the right. Courtesy of the U.S. National Archives and Records Administration.

Margaret Utinsky, awarded the Medal of Freedom in 1946 for her work in the Philippines. Courtesy of the U.S. National Archives and Records Administration.

In front of all of these committed people, Claire discussed her contributions to Cabanatuan prisoner relief. Since this was not about claiming glory, she acknowledged the involvement of Naomi Flores and Evangeline Neibert. Claire explained how she also devoted a chunk of the proceeds from the Club Tsubaki to John Boone's guerrillas. She concluded with an offer. The club could be used as a headquarters for any coordinating activities this group might need.

Over coffee, the guests debated Claire's proposal and accepted it. Her office at the Club Tsubaki would be the clearinghouse for the collection and dispersal of donations to Cabanatuan, all organized via codes referencing baked goods. Anyone with items ready to send would call Claire's office number and ask, "When are you sending the cookies?" Claire would respond, "Bring your recipes. I'm going to bake today," if a courier was ready to go. When she received written messages from prisoners in Cabanatuan, she would call people to "Come and try my fresh cookies."[6]

No one, it seems, mentioned Peggy Utinsky that afternoon, though almost everyone at the luncheon worked with her, too. Months earlier, the Amusateguis heard about the Miss U network and, intrigued, decided to test its reliability. Lorenza Amusategui, using Peggy's in-home beauty shop as the pretext for a visit, stopped at the A. Mabini Street apartment. Lorenza had with her two hundred pesos she wanted smuggled to Lieutenant Arnold W. Thompson in Cabanatuan. Peggy took the money, said she could have it delivered, and promised a receipt. When that written confirmation arrived, the Amusateguis decided Peggy's organization could be trusted.[7]

Still, Ramon Amusategui moved cautiously. He arranged his first meeting with Peggy through a mutual acquaintance, Jeppie Richey, an American civilian. Richey had worked for US naval intelligence during the First World War and continued as a civilian employee of the navy, ultimately taking a job in the Philippines. While helping to fortify Bataan in December 1941, he was caught in a bombing raid and lost one of his legs. Because of his health, Richey secured a medical exemption from Santo Tomas and established connections with the underground. Since Richey vouched for Peggy, Ramon introduced her to his Spanish and Swiss supporters.[8]

The prisoner relief networks in Manila indeed expanded along with the POWs' needs. Though the name Miss U was easily recognizable, it had perhaps come to refer more and more to general aid rather than a specific person or organization. Still, Peggy's absence from the Mencarini gathering suggests that relations among the underground workers were not always smooth. They shared a common cause, but did not necessarily like each other. Peggy spoke her mind, which could be off-putting. Some found her actions impulsive rather than considered. Persistent rumors of Peggy's drinking may have caused her compatriots to regard her as a security risk.

Claire took great satisfaction from the Mencarini luncheon meeting. Such a large gathering did not make her feel unsafe. Rather, she found comfort in associating names—even code names—with faces. Code names and code phrases, Claire understood, "were designed to aid us in communicating with each other, and also serve as identification, because spurious patriots, either working their own rackets or for the Nips, were in our midst."[9]

She soon received her first lesson about racketeers. A Club Tsubaki employee told Claire about a twenty-two-year-old American soldier, nicknamed Beans, hiding out in Manila. Claire agreed to meet him, and he showed up at the nightclub one evening after closing. He introduced himself as Lieutenant Collins, and while Claire believed this might actually be his real name, she was less convinced about his rank. It was too high, she thought, for someone in his early twenties. He was young, handsome, American, more than a bit charming, and clearly in need. Claire suggested he join John Boone's guerrillas, and Collins concurred.

Before he could set off for the hills, he needed better clothing and some cash. Claire parted with two of Phil's old suits and a bit of money, and provided the young man with a map of where he might find the guerrillas. Collins turned up a few days later, looking spiffy in Phil's clothes, admitting to Claire he gambled the money away. Astonished when he asked for more, she said, "Don't you realize how hard money is to get? You should know that it is needed by the guerrillas with whom you should be fighting."[10]

The scolding fell on deaf ears. Collins walked out of the Club Tsubaki and headed straight for the Malate Convent, where he convinced Father Lalor that Claire told him to stop for some cash on his way to the hills. This time it was the trusting priest who obliged. Claire chalked the whole episode up to an inexpensive but important lesson: "The lad simply disappeared after this, and, at least, did not turn informer, as far as we know. It made me think and think hard, of the very thin ice on which we were all skating, and I resolved to be much more careful in my future dealings with strangers."[11]

GLADYS SAVARY FOUND HERSELF WORKING around the clock in 1943, helping both civilian internees and military prisoners. Like Claire Phillips, she wanted to be generous but not gullible. Gladys was familiar with the "unscrupulous element" in Manila: "knowing the guerrillas had need for aid, they would come asking for money, using names which they knew we would recognize." She always asked for verification: "I had a proved contact to which I sent the little aid I could for the guerrillas, and I am sure my good sense in not believing all and sundry tales saved my life." It was bad enough that some of those begging for pesos were after personal gain; it was life-threatening if they had been put up to it by the Japanese.[12]

One of Gladys's projects involved helping the men in Bilibid Prison. She was not the first to direct her efforts there. Since the summer of 1942, Nancy Belle Norton had been providing aid to the Bilibid POWs. A divorcée, Nancy Belle arrived in Manila along with her adult daughter Mamie, both hired by the Philippine Board of Education to teach school. When Mamie met another American schoolteacher, Roscoe Lautzenhiser, and married him in about 1927, Nancy Belle moved in with the newlyweds. By the time she retired from school teaching, she had become a beloved figure in Manila's American community.[13]

Nancy Belle was nearly seventy years old when the war broke out, barely five feet tall with a slenderness often mistaken for frailty. She wore her gray hair short, and her glasses did little to conceal the brightness of her blue eyes. By all appearances she was a harmless grandmother, an image she cultivated. After the Japanese occupied Manila, they exempted Nancy Belle from internment because of her age. When she learned about the condition of the military prisoners in Bilibid, she hired a horse cart and drove it herself, combing the city for donations of food and clothing. Once Nancy Belle filled the cart, she maneuvered it to the prison gate and talked her way inside. As donations became scarce, she sold popcorn on the streets to raise money to buy the needed supplies.[14]

Although Bilibid's hospital director, Lieutenant Nogi Naraji of the Japanese Army Medical Corps, looked the other way when Nancy Belle came around, he was adamant that she not talk to the prisoners. "So I acted as if those boys, sitting on benches within the gates of the prison, were trees and plants," she later explained. "I never said a word to them—but you can say a lot with your eyes." Though the Japanese gave her wide latitude out of respect for her age, her work was not without risk. One day, in an attempt to break her resolve, some Japanese guards at the prison forced Nancy Belle to sit outside in the scorching sun for four hours with her cartload of goods. She did not give up and leave, so they let her in. The Japanese also kept Nancy Belle under constant surveillance, pulling her in for interrogation many times. Even this failed to deter her. Finally, in 1944 Japanese authorities decided she was doing too much to help the prisoners and interned her in Santo Tomas.[15]

In addition to those outside the prison's walls, some Bilibid inmates did what they could to make connections with sympathetic Filipinos to foster relief efforts. Major Willard H. Waterous, the army reservist and prosperous Manila eye doctor, was allowed to continue his specialized practice. Both the Japanese and their prisoners had glasses in need of repair, and Filipino technicians brought in the damaged eyewear and the necessary supplies to Waterous. In the summer of 1942, Peggy Utinsky had tapped into this system, arranging for repairs for men in Camp O'Donnell. Maxima Villanueva, Waterous's associate, secured her own pass granting routine access to Bilibid prison. Over the next two and a half years, under the guise of performing optometry work, Villanueva smuggled in nearly 180,000 pesos to the prisoners.[16]

Ralph Hibbs also spent some time in Bilibid in mid-1942, working under the direction of Navy commander Lea Sartin, the doctor who sent Peggy Utinsky the first reliable information about Jack. Sartin designated Hibbs as a special project officer at Bilibid, then assistant ward surgeon. One day Hibbs received a visit from Father Theodore Buttenbruch: "Coming into a bare waiting room I was greeted by a stocky Catholic priest. His round cherubic face belied the fierce warrior inside. He was about five feet eight inches tall, wore a broad-brimmed round black crown hat, and moved slowly, with dignity." Buttenbruch carried a note and some money from Hibbs's girlfriend, Pilar Campos. The priest told Hibbs that Pilar had been passing by Bilibid every afternoon at two o'clock just for the chance to get a glimpse of Hibbs. Once she made sure he really was in Bilibid, she planned to send in regular supplies of food, medicine, and money.[17]

Hibbs was grateful for any help Father Buttenbruch and Pilar Campos could provide. The medical staff at Bilibid desperately needed a microscope to facilitate the diagnosis of diseases, and Buttenbruch secured one. In the meantime, Pilar made good on her promise of regular deliveries. Hibbs tied notes to rocks and tossed them over Bilibid's wall as Pilar cycled past each day. She did her best to locate any specific items requested and left them for Hibbs in a drainpipe.[18]

The Campos family's garbage man assisted in delivering the goods Pilar collected, using not only the drainpipe but also areas of the prison wall that had been weakened by loose bricks. The man presented Hibbs with a daring plan of escape to join guerrilla fighters, which the doctor rejected as too risky: "My chances of survival in my estimation improved in prison camp over both front line and guerrilla duty. How much good could I do as a guerrilla? Furthermore, the Japs have threatened reprisals on the other prisoners if anyone escaped. Our first need was contact and not escape."[19]

As a doctor, Hibbs's main concern was healing his fellow soldiers. Seeing how much the prisoners suffered, he could not abandon them. When word filtered into Bilibid in late 1942 that Cabanatuan Camp No. 1 needed additional medical personnel, Hibbs volunteered. It was a testament to his professional commitment that he left a relatively clean and well-supplied prison for an overcrowded death trap. He felt duty-bound to return to his comrades in the 31st Infantry. Hibbs tossed one final rock message to Pilar, telling her of the move and asking her to get out of Manila. As he later explained, "I worried about Pilar and the dreaded 'Kampetei.' [sic] Stories reached us of rape, and the molesting of women and children. Hopefully they would not seize her as they sought out the enemy."[20]

Pilar Campos was as dedicated to the prisoners as Hibbs. She did not heed his advice to leave Manila. Not long after the doctor left Bilibid in December 1942, a Japanese patrol apprehended Pilar as she stood in front of a column of trucks filled with American prisoners, tossing them food. The Kempeitai imprisoned her in Fort Santiago, and eventually released her. She was lucky—but who knew how long that luck would last?

By the time Jack Wright and the other men from the Corregidor Prison Camp No. 9 arrived at Bilibid in early June 1943, little had changed. Wright observed how the war had affected Manila: "Pier seven, which had been the longest covered pier in the world before the Japanese knocked part of the roof off when they were attacking Manila, was back in full opera-tion. There were several hospital ships in the bay. We could only speculate as to their cargo, probably guns and ammunition in addition to patients. Half a dozen freighters were being loaded or unloaded."[21]

Manila was filthy, its damaged streets layered in animal waste and human garbage. The people looked changed, too. Gone was the bewil-derment Wright had detected in Filipinos a year earlier, replaced by "a prayerful hopefulness for the return of the Americans to the Philippines." He believed Filipinos had rejected the Greater East Asia Co-Prosperity Sphere, because when he looked at them, "This time their eyes showed defiance. They encouraged us. And our eyes encouraged them."[22]

Much of Bilibid Prison was used as hospital space for prisoners. POWs were required to do very little work there, and they continued to receive a lot of outside help. Jack Wright noticed a large house across the street from Bilibid, occupied by a family of Filipinos. One of the daughters regularly passed news in and out of the prison. Ralph Hibbs's practice of the rock messages had continued, though it was more risky without Pilar Campos on the other side. As Wright remembered, "News was also received by tying messages to rocks, throwing them over the wall, and hoping that a Filipino, not a Japanese, found the outgoing message and an American found the incoming note."[23]

Gladys Savary, then, was one of many who helped the Bilibid prisoners. This project connected her with the Irish priests at the Malate Convent, who worked with a Japanese interpreter at the prison. The interpreter was a Christian, educated in the United States and sympathetic toward the American POWs. He made occasional visits to Father Kelly at Malate and brought along notes from the prisoners that Kelly sent on to friends and relatives. The interpreter agreed to take back to Bilibid verbal messages for some prisoners. He also brought in items that were either easily concealed or would not attract undue attention from the Japanese authorities: tobacco, books and magazines, games. Father Kelly collected as many of these as he could, supplied by women in Manila like Gladys, who considered Kelly "one of the saints of this war."[24]

Because Gladys knew the good work done by the priests at Malate, she willingly lent a hand. One day a young Irishman named Sullivan, who lived and worked at the convent, came to ask Gladys for advice on cooking. To make the most of available groceries, Sullivan wanted stew recipes or anything similar that could be made in one pot. When Gladys realized the young man had no culinary skills, she accompanied him to the Malate Convent to demonstrate how to make carabao stew with camotes and beans. The prelates, made ecclesiastic jacks-of-all-trade because of the war, joined in. As Gladys remembered, "The sight of Madame Savary busily cooking with the black-robed priests out in an open courtyard was quite a sight."[25]

The tide of the war in the Pacific was already changing in the Americans' favor during the spring of 1943, something Gladys knew because of the radio she kept hidden in her pillowcase. Though the Manila *Tribune* ran stories about Allied defeats and civil unrest in the United States, Gladys had a more accurate view of what was true and what was not. Japan had been turned back at New Guinea, and Admiral Yamamoto was killed when his plane was shot down en route to the Solomon Islands. Gladys shared some of this information with her neighbors, bringing light into their dim situation.

The Japanese responded to this reversal by tightening their grip wherever possible. "We had a heartbreaking time in March," Gladys recalled. "The Japanese went on a cleaning up tour, they insisted too many Americans were wandering around without orders." Gladys's friend Hi initially received a medical exemption from internment because of his ulcers; later the Japanese determined this was not a valid excuse. Hi was picked up and interrogated at Fort Santiago before landing in Santo Tomas. The same thing happened to H. Ford Wilkins, former city desk editor of the *Manila Daily Bulletin* and *New York Times* correspondent. Due to partial paralysis caused by polio, the Japanese had allowed him to live in a refugee community at the Ateneo de Manila with a group of Jesuit priests. Wilkins received a pass for limited movement around the city so he could get to his doctor's appointments. Still, on March 8, 1943, the Kempeitai arrested him and took him to Fort Santiago for questioning.[26]

When the Japanese asked Ford Wilkins if he had any money with him, he lied and said no. Because fourteen pesos were then found in his wallet, he was detained at the Fort for two days. Wilkins then claimed he borrowed the money from a friend, yet he refused to identify the person. Finally, he admitted the money came from the Jesuits. Satisfied with this explanation, the Japanese sent Wilkins to Santo Tomas where he remained until liberation "under special restrictions which allowed him no contact with any persons outside the camp, of any nature, in writing or by word of mouth."[27]

These stepped-up efforts by Japanese occupation authorities to confine and control the alien enemy population reflected growing concerns that Filipinos were rejecting the Greater East Asian Co-Prosperity Sphere. Having too many Americans and other Allied nationals roaming around Manila, making their opinions known about the war, became less tolerable to the Japanese. In addition to rounding up people outside of the Santo Tomas internment camp, they cracked down on the activities of those inside the camp.

On October 7, 1942, the Kempeitai removed Frederic H. Stevens, a Manila businessman and former chair of the American Emergency Committee, from Santo Tomas and imprisoned him at Fort Santiago. He was interrogated and tortured there until Good Friday, 1943. The Japanese believed that Stevens had figured out a way to send money to the military prisoners at Camp O'Donnell and Cabanatuan as well as to various guerrilla leaders on Luzon. Stevens admitted sending money to the POWs, and like many other Americans in Manila he had a personal reason for doing so. His son, Captain Lee R. Stevens, was imprisoned at Cabanatuan, and Frederic Stevens could not resist dispatching pesos and notes to his own child. He denied he had anything to do with the guerrillas. No matter what his interrogators did to him, Stevens refused to admit involvement with any of them.[28]

Nurse Denny Williams, who had been taken prisoner in May 1942 along with the other army nurses on Corregidor, noted Frederic Stevens's return to Santo Tomas on April 23, 1943. He was taken directly to the camp hospital where Denny worked. "He has a protein deficiency; his vision has been impaired and his legs are swollen and numb," she observed. "Mr. Stevens is reticent about discussing his stay in Fort Santiago . . . and we do not care to know just at the present time; however, we know that guests of hotel Fort Santiago come out infected with all sorts of vermin." Denny knew something of the reason for Stevens's imprisonment in the Fort, and she also understood he was guilty as charged. "Well . . . too bad Mr. Stevens was caught at it. He is a gentleman, a thirty-three degree Mason, and I like him," she concluded.[29]

The connections between the internees, military prisoners, and Allied sympathizers on the outside provided a life-sustaining support system that Denny Williams both recognized and profited from. Life in Santo Tomas was easier for her because of the help she received from friends on the outside, particularly the Danish merchant Christian Roesholm and his wife Annie Laurie, who had worked with Denny at the Red Cross prior to the war. Because of her outside contacts and because of the people she knew inside Santo Tomas, she could send messages to her husband Bill, imprisoned in Cabanatuan.[30]

The Japanese did not keep a close watch on Denny's activities—or at least nothing she did aroused their suspicions. Kathleen Twohill McGuire was not as lucky. The Australian wife of an American lumber business-man, she was taken out of Santo Tomas in early 1943 and detained in Fort Santiago. The Japanese wanted to find her husband, Ralph McGuire, who signed on with the 26th Cavalry in December 1941 and later joined Claude Thorp's guerrilla outfit. A letter addressed to Kathleen was inter-cepted outside the camp, raising the Japanese' suspicions that she knew something about her husband's whereabouts. Kathleen was confined for ten days in the Fort. When the Japanese were convinced she knew noth-ing about the guerrillas, she was returned to Santo Tomas.[31]

DESPITE THE CRACKDOWN BY THE Japanese, relief efforts con-tinued. The Miss U network was well staffed for its Cabanatuan project, which Peggy directed from her A. Mabini Street apartment. She remained in regular contact with Ramon and Lorenza Amusategui, Father Lalor, Joaquin and Angustias Mencarini, and German Eroles—all essential partners in this enterprise. Miss U could not operate without their ability to get around the city.

Still worried that she attracted too much attention when she appeared in public, Peggy limited her trips to Cabanatuan. Her white face was a bull's-eye target and she did not want to risk any more beatings. Besides, she had to maintain her paying job as a nurse, otherwise she would have no way to live and the Japanese might look more closely at her identity papers. Evangeline Neibert and Naomi Flores continued to deliver supplies to the prison camp. Naomi settled in the town of Cabanatuan by January 1943, shoring up her cover story as a local vendor, while Evangeline carried on with her courier duties.[32]

Elizabeth Kummer, the woman who facilitated Peggy's spring 1942 trip to Bataan with the Red Cross, helped secure travel passes from the Japanese Military Police for Maria Martinez's trips to Cabanatuan. Maria specialized in smuggling medical supplies to the POW camp and to various guerrilla units on Luzon. Manila attorney Jean L. Arnault provided these items as well as various amounts of money totaling about

15,000 pesos. Maria passed along some of the money to individual prisoners, using the rest to purchase food items to smuggle into the camp. When Arnault could not collect enough, Maria sold her own property— jewelry, silverware, furniture—to fund the relief efforts.[33]

Unlike Peggy, Maria did not ask for receipts from the POWs for her deliveries, though she had been working for Miss U since November 1942. However, she received thank-you notes from some of the grateful prisoners. Sometime around March 1943, Chaplain Frank Tiffany wrote to her: "Your splendid note with its contents came in due time. I do not know how to thank you enough." He told Maria he had passed the money along to some doctors who worked with a commissary officer to buy nourishing food, especially peanuts, for the gravely ill. The extra food boosted the prisoners' morale, too, as Tiffany observed, "It is so encouraging to them to know that others care and are actually showing that care in so evident a way."[34]

A first lieutenant who identified himself only by his first name, Dick, was so grateful that he fell a little in love with Maria Martinez. "I marvel at the things you do," he wrote to her, "It is not only what you do, but also that you do it for us. . . . The words are all mixed up, but perhaps you gather what I am trying to say. . . . I want you to know that I thank you every night before I sleep. . . . I did not actually know there were angels like you. . . . I only hope I have the privilege of meeting you, and I am hoping that I shall someday again soon live instead of exist." He signed off, "Love to you."[35]

Underground workers sometimes delivered distressing news, as Melvin Morgan found out. A civilian employee of the Adjutant General's Corps, Morgan had known Maria since before his imprisonment in Cabanatuan. By mid-July 1943, he estimated she had helped more than ninety POWs there. She kept him abreast of events transpiring outside the camp and informed him that the Japanese had looted his house. Morgan's neighbor, perhaps to curry favor with the occupation authorities or because she was a regular snitch, pointed out his unoccupied home to the Japanese. They stripped the place of everything of value, including Morgan's mining stock certificates. Nearly twenty years of accumulated personal possessions disappeared in a day.[36]

Loss compounded loss for the prisoners, and despite the efforts of the Miss U network, they remained desperate—sick, starving, and overworked. After less than a month in Bilibid, on June 30, 1943, Jack Wright found himself back in Cabanatuan. He had been there briefly, the year before, until the Japanese included him in a work detail sent back to Corregidor, where he may have been a beneficiary of the Miss U network. Maria Martinez had arranged contact with Wright's group after it was sent to Corregidor. Peggy Utinsky questioned a man who identified several Americans being held there, and she recognized the names. Yet she was cautious: "Still, I could not afford to take a chance, so I asked him to bring me a list of men when he returned the next time. When I got hold of the list I felt sure he was telling the truth, as I found on it more names of men I knew. From then on I managed to get food and money to the stranded men."[37]

By the time Jack Wright returned to Cabanatuan, then, he was aware of the prisoner relief efforts. After a thorough baggage inspection, he was billeted in the officers' barracks in Camp No. 1, and was assigned work on the farm detail. Comprised of about three hundred acres, the farm produced a variety of crops, including corn, beans, squash, onions, camotes, and okra. Rain had been falling steadily most of the month, causing some 3,000 prisoners to slog around in a foot of mud. Wright, like the others, went barefoot, wearing only a pair of shorts. Most of the men weeded, some prepared the ground for planting by chopping down anthills and filling in low spots, others used pitchforks to till the soil. Some of the food cultivated on the farm went directly to the camp kitchens. The rest was sold at the market in Cabanatuan town, with the proceeds going back to the camp. Wright did not see the point: "I never could see how we could benefit more than by receiving all the farm produced, but that was the explanation."[38]

On the farm detail, the prisoners were at the mercy of the guards, who supervised the work armed with ax handles and baseball bats they did not hesitate to wield. The head guard was Superior (three-star) Private "Air Raid" Ihara. His nickname came from the POWs who spread a warning—quickly whispering "air raid"—whenever they saw him approaching so no one was caught resting or talking. There was also a guard called "Smiling Boy," known for grinning as he clubbed prisoners. The name "Mickey Mouse" was given to a comparatively benign guard. "Speedo" was so named because he screamed at the men to work faster, and "Donald Duck," because he walked like Charlie Chaplin, and when he talked it sounded as if he was quacking.[39]

In addition to whacks with blunt instruments, the guards meted out a variety of other physical punishments for minor rules infractions. Jack Wright watched as "Two men caught talking were made to stand at attention, facing each other, an arm's length apart. One man slapped the other ten times. Then the second man slapped the first ten times. If the guard was not satisfied with the weight of the blows, he slapped them both." Another man, caught kneeling instead of bending over, was ordered to put his hands in anthills, stretch his arms out, and support his body on his hands and feet. When he did not look miserable enough, the guard ordered him to do pushups.[40]

Farm detail was one of the worst, most physically taxing work assignments. The prisoners did their best to help each other through it or out of it into a different assignment. Sometimes this was determined on the basis of rank or specialized skill. In the spring of 1943, for instance, Ralph Hibbs volunteered as surgeon of the tuberculosis ward, which involved the daily care of about forty men and overall supervision of the ward. "A personal mandate, which I never excused, dictated examining each bare chest twice a day with a stethoscope," he later recalled. It was important work but certainly did not carry the dangers of the farm detail.[41]

Jack Wright's stint out in the fields had a quick negative impact on his health. He weighed 185 pounds upon his arrival in Cabanatuan but lost eleven pounds in eighteen days. He moved fast to prevent a further slide. Before the end of July 1943, he arranged a transfer to serve as an adjutant to Captain Philip H. Lehr. For the next few months, Wright was responsible for organizing work details. Since he did not perform manual labor, he was not issued a worker's ration, which consisted of about one-third more rice than the regular issue. Wright had the time and opportunity to quan—to prepare better meals—and do some washing up. His barracks partner, Captain Gus Cullen, worked on the farm detail and received the worker's ration. Together, they pooled their limited resources to increase their chances of survival.[42]

From time to time, the Japanese cracked down on the smuggling in Cabanatuan. In April 1943, Father Theodore Buttenbruch was banished from the camp, his permit for prisoner relief revoked. The episode occurred when tensions were running particularly high. On the 14th, the Japanese executed Private John B. Trujillo of the 200th Coast Artillery, allegedly for trying to escape. Trujillo was known for the lucrative trades he made with the guards on behalf of other prisoners. The Japanese may have started to believe they were being cheated, or a Japanese guard not in on the schemes may have interrupted a transaction. Trujillo was lured outside the fence on the pretext of negotiating a deal. When the private was caught out of bounds, he was beaten and shot in full view of the other prisoners.

The next day, Father Buttenbruch, accompanied by Tony Escoda, arrived with a truckload of packages for the POWs. The bundles were searched more thoroughly than usual, and something went wrong. Irvin Alexander later remembered the priest's driver getting caught trying to slip a package to a prisoner. Calvin Chunn noted in his diary that Buttenbruch was turned away because a couple of dozen personal notes were found with some of the packages. "Too many individual gifts," the priest was told, and he was permanently banished from Cabanatuan.[43]

This setback meant more work under more difficult circumstances for the Miss U organization. Peggy focused her efforts on supplying Horacio Manaloto's market stalls in Cabanatuan town with goods the men could buy cheaply with the money Miss U provided. The two did not have the best working relationship because Manaloto would not always take Peggy's orders. Manaloto rented a railroad boxcar from the Japanese, which he used to ship items from his Manila warehouses to his vendor stall in Cabanatuan town. Peggy asked him to rent a second car to transport all of the goods Miss U collected. "At first he was reluctant to do so," she later wrote, hinting at a bit of fear on Manaloto's part, "because he had seen too often what happened to his people when the Japanese chose to retaliate on them. But he finally arranged it."[44]

Control, not cowardice, was the point of contention. During the spring of 1943, two of Miss U's major contacts within Cabanatuan, Colonel Harold "Johnny" Johnson and Colonel Edward Mack, became concerned that the scope of the smuggling activities was too big for the organization to handle. Johnson suggested Manaloto take a more active role. In June, Manaloto stopped in to talk to Peggy while he was in Manila. Ramon Amusategui was at Peggy's apartment when Manaloto arrived, and he was forced into the role of peacekeeper as Peggy and Manaloto argued about Miss U's operations. Peggy interpreted Manaloto's proposed expanded role as an insinuation that she was not capable of running the operation. Or she may have had her own concerns about the safety and reliability of altering the Miss U system. Ramon prevented the meeting from spiraling out of control and facilitated an agreement between the two. Afterward, fewer of Peggy's operatives, including Maria Martinez and German Eroles, spent much time in her apartment. They found her difficult to work with, and avoided having to do so.[45]

Still, the smuggling continued, as did Peggy's participation, however reduced. Throughout the spring and summer of 1943, she waited to receive the message, "I am going to visit with my mother." This meant Manaloto was loading a boxcar in Manila. Peggy in turn notified Ramon Amusategui and German Eroles, who headed to the Malate Convent, where Miss U stored its donations. The two men, along with other volunteers, filled carts with the supplies and drove them to the boxcar for shipment to Cabanatuan. They moved quickly because some of the items—green vegetables and fresh fruit, so essential to the prisoners' nutritional needs—were perishable. "The amazing part of the thing," Peggy reminisced, "was that our boxcar traveled up and down on the Japanese railroad right under the noses of Japanese guards in the stations, along the route and at both terminals. Never was there any interference with that enormous flow of food and drugs."[46]

At Cabanatuan, the receiving end of the supply line, carts drawn by carabaos emerged from the prison and headed into town. Once there, the prisoners working for the commissary made a beeline to the market stalls to bargain. Manaloto's four establishments were popular among the buyers. He made sure to rotate his stock, putting out some of his own in a couple of stalls, then Miss U items in the other two. In all, Peggy estimated, "We got from 30,000 to 40,000 pesos into the camp every month, plus all the supplies the men pretended to buy from Maluto [*sic*]. But even so, with 9,000 men on starvation rations, the best we could do was too little."[47]

Despite all their precautions, it would be this scheme at Cabanatuan that finally tore the prisoner relief network apart. Though she limited her time out in public, in the summer of 1943 Peggy noticed someone following her and asking a lot of questions about her nationality.

CLAIRE PHILLIPS DREADED THE HOURS between midnight and 6:00 a.m., curfew time in Manila, when only the desperate or the deranged ventured outside. From her small apartment at the back of the Club Tsubaki she often heard gunshots and rapid footsteps in the streets. If she felt brave, she peeked out of the window to see what happened. She never went out to investigate, much less intervene. Under cover of the curfew, the Japanese used confiscated US military vehicles to transport desirable consumer items—everything from foodstuffs to bathtubs—looted from Manila homes to waiting vessels at the docks. Everything shipped straight to Japan. People also disappeared in those early morning hours. The Kempeitai scooped up unfortunates from the streets or arrested them in their residences or places of business, and deposited them in Fort Santiago. Claire knew the most unlucky were "never heard of again, and it was not an uncommon sight to glimpse bloated, headless cadavers floating in the Pasig River."[48]

Manilans feared more than arrest. Food, clothing, and medical supplies were so scarce that thieves robbed their victims of the clothes off their backs. Filipino men and women were forced into agricultural labor gangs. As food disappeared from store shelves and market stalls, young men followed rice delivery trucks, waiting to scoop up any grains that came loose from the sacks. Gas and electricity were rationed, and those exceeding their allotment had to pay a stiff fine and faced disconnection. Unannounced blackouts rolled through the city. Japanese-backed paper currency, known as "Mickey Mouse" money, plummeted in value.[49]

Claire was so busy she rarely had time to sleep, yet she could not conceive of pulling back on any of her projects, not when she received thank-you notes from grateful recipients of her aid. Charley De Maio, Claire's prewar acquaintance who had been engaged to her friend Mona, turned up on one of the Cabanatuan chaplains' list of needy prisoners so she sent him one hundred pesos and a brief note. Evangeline Neibert delivered a letter from Charley in return, in which he addressed Claire by her code name High Pockets: "When I got your letter I came to life again. Gee, it's good to know someone like you. You've done more for the boys' morale in here than you'll ever know."[50]

"I shed tears of joy as I read his letter over and over. It was wonderful to know that he was alive," Claire remembered. In her excitement she called Mona, the ex-fiancée. Claire assumed the young woman would be relieved to know Charley had survived and would want to help support him. The war had not made Mona a more generous person. "I'm through with all that. What I have, I need for myself," she said. Fortunately for the enormously needy prisoners, few people shared Mona's sentiment.[51]

As the relief work continued, so did the terrible treatment of American prisoners, in Manila and beyond. Though Camp O'Donnell and Cabanatuan were perhaps the most well-known POW camps, the Japanese had set up a few others in the Philippines, smaller concerns associated with a forced labor project.

GLADYS SAVARY WITNESSED THE ATROCIOUS treatment of prisoners at what she referred to as the Park Avenue School. The Pasay Elementary School was located on Park Avenue about three hundred yards east of the spot where F.B. Harrison Street ran past the entrance to the Manila Polo Club Field in Gladys's Pasay neighborhood. Though the prison population fluctuated, several hundred men were held there throughout the war. Each morning they marched to either Nichols or Nielsen Field, stopping work at five o'clock each evening to begin the reverse trip.

The Japanese tried to hide their treatment of these prisoners by clearing the streets twice a day as the men made their shuffling progress to and from the air field. No one was supposed to look at the POWs; still, Gladys found it impossible to ignore the men. She cycled to a cross street of Park Avenue, hid in the bushes, and watched: "It was agonizing to see them, dragging their sore feet, often helping each other walk, and many times one of them would have to be carried by his companions. Too often they carried them back, dead."[52]

Word spread throughout Manila of this pitiable sight, and many— including Gladys, Peggy Utinsky, and Claire Phillips—did what they could to help. First came the brick kickers. Neighborhood residents found an area of loose bricks on the back wall of the school and kicked at them until they fell out. They hid notes, money, and food in the empty space, and covered it back up with the brick. Gladys became particularly adept at this, boasting she was a " 'brick-kicker' par excellence."[53]

When Gladys and her friend Dorothy Janson saw that the guards allowed the prisoners to purchase food at a local *tienda* (shop), they hatched a plan similar to the Miss U scheme in Cabanatuan. The two women convinced the owner to let them make special nutrition-packed *bibinkas* (rice cakes) for the men to buy. Gladys and Dorothy, joined by other women in the neighborhood, worked every day, stuffing meat and eggs into several hundred *bibinkas*, sometimes adding money as well. They resisted the temptation to include personal notes because they wanted to avoid incriminating anyone involved in the operation.[54]

These men needed all the help they could get because they existed in a permanent state of exhaustion and malnutrition. Major Ralph Burdell Scheibley, originally from Toledo, Ohio, weighed a respectable 185 pounds when he arrived at Pasay in June 1943. Every morning he made the long walk—about an hour and a half—to Nichols Field, where he and the rest of the prisoners were divided into work groups, each with its own daily quota. The Japanese needed the airfield, heavily damaged in December 1941, repaired, and the POWs supplied the labor, building runways and airplane barricades.

Scheibley and the others worked from 8:00 a.m. until 5:00 p.m., with thirty to sixty minutes off at noontime. Every thirty days, they received two days off—unless rain disrupted their work—in which case that counted as a day off. As Scheibley later described: "All the work that we did was manual labor, such as pick and shovel, pushing mine carts, which two men would shove maybe two or three miles, unload it, and return." Men who failed to meet their group's quota were punished. Beatings were common, but "Wolf" Ikota and "Cherry Blossom" Matsomura inflicted particularly cruel physical torture for rules infractions. They ordered prisoners tied to a tree by their arms and left them hanging there. They forced them to drink water, then kicked them in the stomach, a form of torture known as the water cure. Only near-fatal injuries that rendered men useless for work received any kind of medical treatment.[55]

Ralph Scheibley never stopped at the *tienda* nor did he benefit from any of the brick kicking. "We tried to buy food on the outside, and a limited amount was allowed through a Japanese merchant at exorbitant prices," he remembered. By the time he was moved from Pasay to Bilibid in July 1944, he weighed just over one hundred pounds.[56]

News about the treatment of the Park Avenue prisoners reached the Miss U network, and Peggy decided to see for herself what was happening to the men: "There was enough horror in Manila without going in search of it, but I felt that I had to know what was going on, that I had to see for myself so there would be someone to make a record for the days when the Yanks would come back." She gained access to a house overlooking the prison, and witnessed the execution, by beheading, of five Filipinos. She also saw two American prisoners stripped and strung up on a mango tree. Another afternoon Peggy watched as two POWs carried in a third man: "I could look down on his face from the window where I crouched. His ribs had been caved in, his whole torso was a mass of bruises and open bleeding wounds."[57]

This man had been beaten, Peggy learned, because he was too weak to do his share of labor. Assigned to a group of four, he was supposed to fill boxcars with gravel and rocks by hand. When he did not perform adequately, Wolf Ikota pushed him up against a wall, shoved a hose into his mouth, and flooded water down his throat. When the prisoner was too weak to put up a struggle, Cherry Blossom Matsomura clubbed him over the head. In this situation, Peggy considered her main roles as that of witness and documentarian. At the end of the war, she intended to turn over the names of these Japanese guards to the US Army.[58]

Claire heard about the Pasay prisoners from Totoy, one of the waiters at the Club Tsubaki. He knew about them from his aunt, Clara (Claring) Yuma, who saw the mistreatment of the POWs by the guards known as Wolf and Cherry Blossom. Claring told her nephew that the conditions at the converted Pasay Elementary School were so appalling the place was referred to as "Devil's Island." Totoy took Claire to meet his aunt, "a sturdy little woman of about thirty, whose righteous anger and unselfishness was reflected in her plain, good face." Claring said, "Those poor men are dying like flies. I've seen the awful food they are given, and a pig would not touch it." She encouraged Claire to come and see for herself.[59]

In the early evening, the two women hired a *carromata* and drove down the road on which the prisoners would be returning from Nichols Field. They stopped at an empty house at the junction of Park Avenue and the National Highway, instructed their driver to pick them up later, and hid inside to wait for the prisoners. Claire later described the same thing Gladys and Peggy had seen: "It was almost impossible that these ragged, bearded specimens of humanity, with shaven heads and red-ringed eyes were once proud American fighting men. It was obvious that many of them were ill or desperately tired, as their comrades supported them to keep them from falling."[60]

Something must be done about this, Claire decided. Claring Yuma knew a local man, Pedro, who worked as a mechanic for the Japanese but who supported the Allies. She was sure he would be willing to assist with whatever scheme they devised to help the Pasay prisoners. Using Claring's name, Claire rented that empty house on the corner to use as a distribution center and began coordinating relief efforts. While Claire solicited donations from sympathetic Manilans, Pedro established contacts among the prisoners, smuggling in an introductory note from Claire: "To the one who gets this: I have been helping Cabanatuan and any one of you who may have been there will know me. Tell me of any way that I can get help to you." She signed it with her signature phrase, "Yours in war, High-Pockets."[61]

A Captain Muir was her first contact. He confirmed the Japanese had set up a commissary for the prisoners to purchase what they needed, and pointed out few men had any money. Claire knew what must be done, and to facilitate donations she asked Muir for a list of the prisoners at Pasay. When she received it the following week, she noticed the name of Sergeant Harold Spooner, one of Phil's friends from the 31st Infantry. She sent Spooner a note and some money, and they struck up a correspondence. He became one of her inside contacts, using the code name Sky Pilot.

Meanwhile, Claring Yuma chatted up one of the Japanese guards who accompanied the prisoners back and forth from Nichols Field. With these good relations established, she hired a carpenter to build a shed on the vacant lot across from their rented house, which would be used as a *tienda* for the prisoners. Claire dressed it up with a prominent display of canned goods—empty cans, but with eye-catching labels. She and Claring stocked the shop daily with about three hundred bananas and other available fruit, conveniently bagged, ready to be taken away. As the long column of prisoners marched past, Claring's friendly guards picked up the bags and passed them on to the men. After a week of this, though, the Japanese started charging the men a peso each for the privilege of receiving one of the bags.[62]

This meant the women had to smuggle more money to the prisoners. Claire and Claring also included peanuts, roasted fresh every day, with the fruit to provide the men with the protein they so desperately needed. To improve the men's vitamin intake, especially to ward off scurvy, they bottled a concentrate made from the juice of a local citrus fruit, calamansi, and sugar. The POWs mixed this with their noontime water ration to create a kind of lemonade. Claire hid clothing and shoes along the side of the road. Using the prearranged instructions they were given, the prisoners picked them up when the guards were not looking.

The Park Avenue School operation worked well for several months. Claire was particularly proud of "Operation Hamburger," launched on July 4, 1943. She celebrated the "Glorious Fourth" in the most American way possible: serving hamburgers to the Pasay prisoners. Fely Corcuera and the other hostesses from the Club Tsubaki helped by slicing some fifty loaves of rice bread, while Claire and the rest of the staff fried the meat patties. They put together a thousand hamburger sandwiches, which they bagged up for distribution at the *tienda* shed. "I was watching from my vantage point," Claire wrote after the war, "and saw the happy-for-a-moment Americans look into their bags . . . heads turned toward my window, and there were smiles on their gaunt faces."[63]

The Japanese guards became greedy for more payoffs and stopped looking the other way. A group of them beat up Claring Yuma one day as she worked at the shop. The women were forced to admit that the food stand had become too risky and decided to close it. They continued to leave other items hidden in the area for the prisoners to find. Pedro proved adept at this because of his daily work interactions with the POWs. He layered on clothing each morning, casting pieces off one by one during the day for the other men to pick up. Though he always wore a pair of shoes to work each morning, he left barefoot at the end of the day.

In addition to the ready-made shirts Pedro shed for the prisoners, others were sewn from drapery and curtain material from the Club Tsubaki. Claire and the other women at the Club Tsubaki pulled down the window coverings, washed them in strong detergent, and laid them out in the sun to soften. After they used up this material, they stripped the sheets from their beds. When someone donated seventy yards of pale pink brocade to the Park Avenue School relief project, a group of Seventh-Day Adventist missionaries turned the material into sixty pairs of men's shorts. The color clashed with the red wool socks other women knitted from other donated material, but Gladys Savary noted that the colorful combination—"Pink brocade shorts and red socks, correct wear for prisoners!"—brought a smile to many faces. The Japanese seemed unconcerned to see so many prisoners sporting new clothing, choosing to believe these items had been donated by the Philippine Red Cross.[64]

Gladys later credited "an odd assortment of women thrown together trying to help those boys" for the widespread prisoner relief efforts at the Park Avenue School. Her "best assistant . . . a whiz at the loose brick business" was an unnamed American mestiza living with a Japanese civilian. Also involved was Camilla Westly, a Norwegian national, who along with her husband Einar raised three sons while living in various places—Hawaii, California, and finally the Philippines—for Einar's work as a sugar technologist. As a citizen of a country the Japanese considered neutral, Camilla received permission to send in some supplies to the Park Avenue School. She joined two other women already working on this project: the retired American schoolteacher Nancy Belle Norton and Lorenza Amusategui, part of the Miss U network.[65]

This high point of prisoner relief activity was about to take a dive.

CHAPTER 13

BETRAYAL

ONE DAY DURING THE SUMMER OF 1943, a Filipino Claire Phillips had never seen before showed up at the Club Tsubaki with a note for her from someone named Captain Bagley. Lately the club had been teeming with activity, both legitimate and illicit. More people—always different people—showed up here, either offering help or requesting it, which made Claire's work all the more dangerous. She read the note: Bagley wanted help for his guerrilla band. Something seemed off, though. Claire had been doing this long enough to sense that nothing rang true about the courier's demeanor or the language of the message. She sent the Filipino on his way, yelling at him that she was Italian, she was not interested in what the Americans were doing or what they needed.

The club's bartender, Mamerto Geronimo, followed the courier outside and watched as he met up with four members of the Kempeitai. It had been a trap. Any underlying concerns Claire had about the safety of her operation now came rushing to the surface: "I was fully aware of the danger that I faced, and this knowledge made me jumpy and at times, irritable." She told Mamerto that she counted on him and Fely Corcuera to take care of little Dian should anything happen to her. If Claire ended up in Fort Santiago, they had to make sure her daughter got up into the hills with John Boone.[1]

Sensing her time could be running out, Claire stepped up efforts to aid the prisoners and transmit information to the guerrillas, trying to get as much done as possible before she was either arrested or killed. To facilitate her work, Claire approached Juan Elizalde, a wealthy Manila businessman who had been at the opening of the Club Tsubaki. The founder of the "28 Men of Fort Santiago," Elizalde worked with the Irish priests at the Malate Convent and with Peggy Utinsky on prisoner relief projects. Claire did not know this until Naomi Flores and Evangeline Neibert brought out a letter from Cabanatuan addressed to Elizalde.

Letter in hand, Claire made a personal delivery to Elizalde to confirm his commitment to the Allied cause. The two got along well, and Elizalde promised to supply the bottles Claire needed for the calamansi juice she made for the prisoners. He also offered to sell her liquor at prewar prices to help boost revenues at the Club Tsubaki: "If I sold the liquor at retail I would only donate the profits to the cause anyhow. Your place can't run without liquor and we can't get along without your place . . . so it's easier for me to make my contribution this way." This new arrangement both helped and hindered Claire's operation, however. Elizalde's material contributions were invaluable, but neither he nor Claire realized that despite all of their precautions, the Kempeitai had Elizalde and his network under surveillance. Now Claire was caught in the crosshairs as well.[2]

September 1943 proved to be a busy month as Claire connected with yet another operative from the Miss U network. Colonel Edward Mack, her contact inside Cabanatuan, suggested she utilize the services of a "Mr. Monoloto." Claire made inquiries about this man, who used the code name Mutt, and learned he had already been vetted by Ramon Amusategui. This was, of course, Horacio Manaloto, who had been working with Miss U since the previous spring. Manaloto, along with the Manila schoolteacher Tomas de Guzman and Guzman's wife Agustina, had been collecting donations throughout Manila. The items were shipped to Manaloto's market stalls in Cabanatuan town where they were either sold to the prisoners at a deep discount or smuggled into the prison camp.[3]

Conditions inside the Cabanatuan POW camp were still abysmal, and for Jack Wright, September 1943 was a particularly tumultuous month. Due to a reorganization of camp facilities, he lost his administrative position and returned to work on the farm. Later, he complained, "I always felt that I was wasting my time on the farm. There was little satisfaction in pulling weeds all day, or in breaking big clods into little ones, or in most of the other jobs that were done by the mass coolie labor system." No one wanted to work on the farm; the labor was backbreaking and it carried increased risks of beatings from the guards. Wright got lucky. After about a week, he received reassignment as the assistant to the barracks leader. Then one day the Japanese came for thirty of the men, all medical corps personnel, and took them to Bataan. Another fifty from elsewhere in the camp were taken as well. The Japanese were making a war movie, and they needed Americans for part of the filming.[4]

The movie, *The Dawn of Freedom*, was a collaborative effort, with a Japanese director, Abe Yutaka, and a Filipino associate director, the noted Gerardo de Léon. Until he became interested in acting and directing, De Léon studied medicine at Santo Tomas University. Between 1939 and 1941, he directed five films, but his career stalled at the onset of the war. The Japanese occupation authorities knew his movies, though, and insisted he work on *The Dawn of Freedom*. A propaganda film, it detailed the invasion and occupation of Manila, portraying the Japanese as heroes and the Americans as murderers and cowards.[5]

A customer came into the Club Tsubaki one night and told Fely Corcuera about a movie company filming some scenes out on Jones Bridge for a picture called *The Dawn of Freedom*. When Claire found out some American prisoners were being used as extras, she and Fely, accompanied by one of their Japanese customers, Mr. Azioka, headed out to the bridge. The two women carried packs of cigarettes and matchboxes Claire had stuffed with pesos. With Azioka leading the way, they secured a good spot near the bridge, next to several truckloads of prisoners, to whom they tossed the small packages.

Claire and Fely were not the only people in Manila to take advantage of this opportunity to demonstrate their support for the Americans. Ted Lockard, one of the POWs, later marveled at the number of Filipinos out on the streets to greet the truckloads of movie extras. "They came out and just bombarded all our trucks with fruit and food. I think it was just a sign of the Filipinos' hope," he remembered, adding, "It exasperated the Japanese." Claire worried the men might be criticized should the movie ever reach the United States: "It would be unjust and unfair to judge those pathetic creatures who sought 'extra chow' and a little break in the bitter monotony of their imprisonment." No American appeared in a speaking role—none would consent—and the film, which Claire considered "ludicrous and foul-smelling" was screened twice, and never in the States.[6]

The pesos Claire tossed to the prisoners during filming came in very handy. Food had become scarcer, and inflation was on the rise as the Japanese kept printing their occupation currency, prompting an upsurge in counterfeiting that further devalued the money and increased consumer prices. One day an egg cost ten centavos, the next, two pesos. To prove they responded to prisoners' needs, the Japanese raised the monthly pay to American officers by five pesos, yet this did not begin to address the intertwined inflation and supply problems. As Arthur L. Shreve, formerly of the Quartermaster Corps and now imprisoned in Cabanatuan, wrote in his journal on September 22, 1943: "I was able to cash a States check on our bank in Ellicotts City for $100.00 for which I received 180.00P. I now can help some of my friends and buy what is available, which is little."[7]

After Shreve penned his entry, Pilar Campos and seven other young women from the Volunteer Social Aid Committee (VSAC) arrived in Cabanatuan on a flatbed truck, wearing crisp blue and white uniforms. When they created VSAC in 1942, it was with the publicly stated purpose of providing assistance to Filipinos adversely affected by the war. They also covertly helped as many American prisoners as possible. To get close to the Americans, to smuggle in food, medicine, and money, the VSAC women put together a song and dance show for the entertainment of the

Japanese stationed at various garrisons. It was not a coincidence they scheduled a performance at Cabanatuan after Pilar's boyfriend, Ralph Hibbs, transferred there from Bilibid Prison.

On September 23rd, Hibbs, alerted earlier about the arrival of the VSAC women, stood outside his barracks watching the progress of the truck. When Pilar caught sight of him, she tossed a package of medicine and vitamins, which he managed to grab before any of the Japanese guards noticed. Also by prior arrangement, Hibbs received a special labor assignment with the camp electrician so he could work on the stage while the women performed. It was a sweet, if brief, moment for the two lovers to be in each other's presence. Though food, medicine, and a variety of other supplies continued to make their way into Cabanatuan, this was the last time Ralph Hibbs saw Pilar Campos.[8]

Aware of the POWs' enormous needs, Claire Phillips kept up a relentless pace of activity during the late summer and early fall of 1943. On top of the constant work, she was confronted with the possibility that her personal cover story might not hold. Italy turned out to be the weakest country of the Axis alliance. Following a successful Allied invasion of Sicily in July 1943, Benito Mussolini was deposed. The subsequent landing of American and British troops on Italy's mainland on September 3rd, forced a quick surrender. This prompted the Japanese occupation authorities in Manila to require Italian nationals to renounce their allegiance to their country. Refusal to do so would result in internment.

Though "Dorothy Fuentes" claimed to have been born in the Philippines to Italian parents, Claire did not want the Japanese looking too closely at her documents to determine if she should take the renunciation oath. Going on the offensive, she took her forged identity papers to the Bureau of Vital Statistics in the National Assembly Building. Judge Mamerto Roxas again greased the wheels, making sure one of his friends handled Claire's paperwork. She believed, or at least she wanted to believe, the Japanese were not paying any particular attention to her. With this nationality wrinkle ironed out, and despite the unease provoked by the appearance of the fake courier, Claire carried on as usual. She did not shy away from any assignment that would help the Allied cause. Smuggling goods and passing along information were by now routine, but occasionally something out of the ordinary turned up.[9]

For instance, at a meeting with Ramon Amusategui at the Malate Convent, probably in the fall of 1943, Claire learned about an American mestizo only known as Rathman who had been caught tampering with Allied communications lines on Bataan back in March 1942. The saboteur disappeared during the ensuing chaos on the peninsula, but Señor Torres, "the Doctor" Claire first met at the luncheon at the Mencarini home, had now located Rathman in Manila. Torres came up with a plan for dealing with the miscreant. Some of Torres's accomplices would get Rathman to the Club Tsubaki in the next night or two. When he arrived, Claire was to telephone Torres, who would follow Rathman from the club and kill him.

Claire never questioned why she and her club had to figure into this assassination plot. "I suppose that it has to be done?" was all she asked Ramon Amusategui. He was emphatic: Rathman was a known informer who also helped interrogate prisoners in Fort Santiago. "That scoundrel has forfeited all his rights either as American or Filipino, and only belongs wherever dead Japs go," Amusategui told Claire. Besides, Torres was convinced Rathman knew something about their organization, so he had to go.[10]

Two nights later, using the prearranged signals, Claire identified one of her customers as Rathman, called Torres, and kept Rathman entertained until "the Doctor" arrived. When Rathman left the club, Claire knew Torres would follow him until they were a safe distance away—no one wanted to compromise the Club Tsubaki—then kill him. When Claire opened for business the following night, there stood Rathman, one of her very first customers, and not a happy one. He showed her his hat, punctuated by a bullet hole in the front. "It looks like someone around here is gunning for me," he said. Claire bought Rathman a drink and sat with him until she convinced him the incident was nothing more than an attempted robbery. She teased him about flashing around his large roll of cash, and Rathman departed the club in a good mood. He never returned. It took about a week, but Torres finally caught up with him and this time, the Doctor did not miss.[11]

These activities left Claire tense and overworked, and caused her to develop an ulcer. In September 1943 she was rushed to the hospital in agony, her temperature spiked to 106. Her doctor, Luis Guerrero, the noted expert on tropical medicine, called in a surgeon to remove Claire's perforated ulcer along with about six inches of intestines. The recuperation did not go smoothly. For the next ten days Claire passed in and out of a heavily medicated sleep. When she finally remained awake long enough to sit up and eat solid food, it was a landmark day. This turning point in her recuperation, however, was not the only reason the day stood out. As Claire later admitted, "something of far greater importance makes it linger in my memory." It was the arrest of Peggy Utinsky.[12]

ON SEPTEMBER 28TH, THE JAPANESE searched Peggy's A. Mabini Street apartment, and departed with a warning. She must not leave her home or the city. Peggy had patients at the hospital who needed her, all incriminating documents had been spirited away to the Malate Convent, and her maid Maria was heading to mass and would soon be in the sanctuary of a church. Determined to carry on as usual, Peggy headed off to work.

The two patients who worked for Miss U concerned Peggy the most: Claire Phillips, still recovering from ulcer surgery, and Zena Jasten, suffering from breast cancer. Peggy had been on duty for perhaps a couple of hours and was at Zena's bedside when she heard the dull noise that signaled to her what was about to happen. There was nothing she could do now to avoid arrest. She listened to the heavy tramp of soldiers' boots along the corridor leading to the ward where she worked. In her last moments of freedom she whispered a request to Zena Jasten. Please let Ernest Johnson know what has happened.

A well-connected American in his early sixties who worked for the Maritime Commission in Manila, Ernest Johnson had been chronically ill since the beginning of the war. Because of this, the Japanese allowed him to remain in a hospital, usually at the Philippine General Hospital, where Peggy sometimes took care of him. From his bed, Johnson received many visitors. Some were the priests from the Malate Convent, and they spent entire afternoons drinking rum and exchanging information that could be passed along to whoever might find it useful. Some were guerrillas who slipped in from the hills, hoping for some of that valuable information. Johnson's room became a meeting place for the underground.

During one of these conversations Johnson learned about Peggy's aid work and asked her to come see him. Their discussion went well, and he offered to solicit donations for Miss U from the many friends who came to visit him. When Johnson, using the code name Brave Heart, had money or important news for Peggy, he sent a messenger to her apartment with a bottle of rum, the signal for her to come to him. Johnson would pass what he had along to Peggy, who in turn issued receipts for Johnson to give to the donors. They never circulated notes between the two of them. "They never knew who I was," Peggy later explained about Johnson's donors. "I did not know their real identity. Only Ernest Johnson knew both ends of the puzzle and kept the funds flying."[13]

When Johnson heard about Peggy's arrest, he notified Ramon Amusategui. Both men were confident the Japanese had no proof Peggy was involved with the guerrillas. They worried instead about how her false nationality would hold up to scrutiny. Ramon bribed a City Hall official to hide the Utinskys' marriage certificate, which identified Peggy as American, and then he paid a call on Mrs. Pearl Yearsley, a Canadian national and one of Miss U's reliable supporters. After the Japanese occupation in January 1942, Pearl received a medical exemption from internment because of blindness, and her husband remained free as well, to look after her. However, their son, Robin, a civilian in his mid-thirties, joined the Army Air Corps, and ended up a prisoner in Cabanatuan. Pearl worked tirelessly with Elizabeth Kummer and Peggy on POW relief efforts.[14]

Ramon Amusategui broke the news to Pearl about Peggy's arrest. Pearl dispatched one of her servants to Cabanatuan with a message for Colonel Mack: "Stop everything." The bluntness of the instruction convinced Mack the situation was critical. With what the colonel already knew about Japanese brutality, once he learned of Peggy's arrest, he worried she would break under torture in Fort Santiago and reveal the details of Miss U. To be on the safe side, Mack and the other officers he worked with in Cabanatuan took extra care to hide all of the items that had made their way into the camp.[15]

288 ≡ ANGELS OF THE UNDERGROUND

Though Mack and Peggy assumed the operation would halt with her arrest, Naomi Flores and the others did not, in fact, stop everything. Since she started her work at Cabanatuan, Naomi routinely changed her tactics from time to time to throw off the Japanese. Whenever there was a hint of something not running as it should, she got word to Ramon, advising him to lie low for a while. Peggy's arrest did not cause a major disruption. Ramon stepped in and, according to Naomi, "the continuous flow of supplies and other materials was going on smoothly."[16]

Maria Martinez carried on as well. "We all continued to work for the cause," she later recalled. "While we were sending supplies to Cabanatuan, we were also taking out from said camp important military information coming from officers in camp." Maria continued to smuggle food and money into Bilibid Prison and the Park Avenue School, and to arrange financial assistance for friends of hers interned in Santo Tomas.[17]

Though the Miss U network was not derailed because of Peggy's arrest, Naomi worried about her, mostly for the same reason as did Colonel Mack. Torture might break her. Naomi suspected Peggy was close to the breaking point even prior to her arrest. The two women quarreled frequently about the notes going in and out of Cabanatuan, though the exact point of contention is not clear. Naomi may have worried that Peggy took too many risks; Peggy may have insisted the risks were worth taking. During one of their fights, something Naomi said led Peggy to threaten "to have the whole lot of us jailed at Fort Santiago."[18]

That Peggy would threaten to turn on her own organization is astonishing, especially when she had poured so much of herself into it. Another of Naomi's revelations about these verbal altercations offers a possible reason for Peggy's outburst. According to Naomi, "There was even a time when she [Peggy] wanted to quit the work because according to her way of reasoning, her husband was already dead." Peggy always said she became involved with prisoner relief in an attempt to locate Jack. When she discovered he died, she kept up the Miss U network as a kind of revenge against the Japanese. As the war dragged on with no end in sight, Peggy's initial sorrow and rage may have devolved into fear and nervousness. Widowed, separated from her only son, almost everything she owned gone—maybe she did not see the point of continuing. Peggy may have been at a very low point to have threatened to stop everything by having her operatives arrested.[19]

Now the Japanese had come for her. That late September morning at the hospital, Peggy steeled herself when the dull thumping sounds stopped. Eight soldiers stood in the doorway, bayonets fixed on their rifles. "You will come," one said to her, and she obeyed. The enemy soldiers fell into formation around her, and they marched out of the hospital.[20]

Two thoughts circled in Peggy's mind. First, she was grateful she was wearing the dark glasses she adopted when she turned herself into a Lithuanian. She reasoned, "If I was going to make a practice of telling lies, I wanted something to hide my eyes, which are always a dead give-away when one is frightened. I had been wearing the things for months and right now they gave me a curious sense of protection." Second, Peggy thought about how lovely the world was. Once the soldiers had her out on the street, she appreciated the strength and brightness of the late morning sun. As they walked—headed for Fort Santiago, she presumed—she wished her journey would take a very long time. With every step, Peggy whispered, "Just a little longer, just a little longer." Then they arrived at the Fort, much too soon.[21]

There was, of course, another witness to Peggy's arrest: Claire Phillips. Awake that morning when Peggy arrived, eating solid food for the first time since her surgery, she remembered, "Aunty, one of our workers, was standing by my bed, watching me eat, and joking about the difficulty I was having in masticating my food." Aunty was one of Peggy's code names, the one that emphasized her age.[22]

Peggy had brought the most recent mail from Cabanatuan, couriered by Evangeline Neibert. Claire was eager to read the prisoners' messages and peruse the receipts. Another nurse interrupted them. "There are four Japanese soldiers in the hall asking for you," she said, pointing at Peggy.

According to Claire, Peggy's response was panic. "For God's sake! What shall I do?" Peggy cried. Despite her weakened state, it was Claire who kept a clear head. She told Peggy to give her all the papers she was carrying. Just as Claire stuffed them under her surgical bandage, the

Kempeitai walked into the room. They searched it, but, fortunately, did not think of frisking Claire. When they found nothing in the room, they took Peggy away. "Aunty, like the brave soul that she was, marched mutely out of the door with the grim-looking quartette who took her to Fort Santiago," Claire recalled. "Sick as I was, I worried, not only for the welfare of the poor woman, but over her ability to undergo the 'examination' certain to be given her, without talking."[23]

The shock of that morning's event may have contributed to Claire's relapse. For two days she was barely conscious, and when she could think straight again she remembered Peggy's arrest. Claire asked a nurse to call Ramon Amusategui, but her speech was so slurred it took several tries to get her request understood. Ramon showed up about an hour later and listened to Claire's story. She assumed he was hearing this news for the first time. Perhaps because of Claire's medical condition, he did not bother to correct her. He promised to let the other Miss U members know, and he collected the notes and receipts she had hidden under her bandage.[24]

Alarmed at Claire's slow recovery, Ramon called for her doctor and also for his father-in-law, Dr. Gerardo Vazquez. The two physicians diagnosed tetanus but had difficulty finding the right medicine to treat it. Few medical supplies of any kind could be found in Manila, so Claire hovered near death for five days until she started to get better, thanks to an improvised serum. Still, she would not return to work at the Club Tsubaki until November.

WHEN PEGGY ARRIVED AT FORT SANTIAGO, she focused on the details around her, attempting to take her mind off what might lie ahead. Years later she remembered the sunshine, not only outside as she walked—marched—to the prison, but inside as well: "The Japanese soldiers took me into a large sunny room on the second floor. Through its open, screened side, I would see the lovely patio, the soft lawn, the flowers." For a few moments, Peggy enjoyed the beauty of the setting.[25]

A Japanese officer and an interpreter sat at a table in that room, a large stack of papers piled in front of them. The interpreter issued orders: sit at the other end of the table and put your arms straight out, palms down on the table. Peggy remembered, "It was a strained, uncomfortable position that made me feel very helpless."[26]

At the beginning, Peggy vowed she would be brave. She felt her heart pounding up in her throat, she swallowed to keep her voice steady. "Whatever happened, I swore to myself, I would never give them any satisfaction by showing fear or by screaming. The first part of the vow I kept; there were a few times, later on, when I broke the second part. You can stand only so much pain."[27]

The pain would come shortly. First, Peggy swore an oath to God to tell the truth, and the interpreter warned her against lying—that it would bring dire consequences. Then the interrogation began. Peggy had anticipated most of the questions. What was her nationality? When and where was she born? Where was her maid? These were followed by others about Peggy's 1940 trip to the United States, which she expected as well. When the Japanese searched her apartment the night before, they found some souvenir menus she had kept from that vacation. Now, the Japanese officer wanted all the details. What exactly had a Lithuanian woman been doing in the United States?

The first blow landed squarely in Peggy's face, knocking her out of the chair, breaking her jaw and several teeth. It came in response to her telling her interrogators she had arrived in San Antonio, Texas, on the fourth of July in 1940. Since she used that particular phrase, they concluded she was an American since the Fourth of July is an American holiday. The officer ordered Peggy up from the floor, then kicked her. She resumed her position at the table, her arms stretched out in front of her.

The questions continued, now with the officer screaming at her, certain he caught her in a lie. He zeroed in on the subject of Peggy's nationality. What documents did she travel on? Why did she return to the Philippines? Peggy answered carefully, knowing she would have to repeat everything and keep all the information consistent. She tried not to stare at that stack of papers on the table. She kept wondering what sort of file the Japanese compiled on her. At the end of the session, the officer said he knew she was American, and would have her interned at Santo Tomas. Peggy replied, "Fine. Then I won't have to earn my living any more."[28]

By the end of the first interrogation session, Peggy lost some of the feeling in her arms, her jaw ached, and her mouth was bloody and swollen. Still, she felt a small ray of hope because the Japanese had spent all this time asking about her nationality. If the only thing they suspected was that Peggy evaded internment for a year and a half, they would likely do what the officer said—send her to Santo Tomas—which would not be so bad. From her Miss U work, she knew she would be able to continue her relief efforts from inside the camp. At least she would still be able to do something, and the other members of her network would remain safe.

The Japanese did not send Peggy to internment in Santo Tomas, nor did they release her. Instead, she was taken to one of Fort Santiago's cells. The cramped space, about eight feet by five feet, lighted by a single bulb above the door, contained a bucket of drinking water and a hole in the floor for sanitary needs. Seven women were in the cell, but only two of them, including the heavily pregnant Mrs. Vicente Domingo, spoke English. Domingo's husband had attacked some Japanese soldiers who tried to rob his office, and then he fled the scene. Enraged, the Japanese took his wife to Fort Santiago as a hostage.

The women asked Peggy for any news about life outside the prison, and they whispered together until a guard came by and heard them. He called Peggy over to the door, punched her in the face, and informed her talking was forbidden in the cell. That was how prisoners learned the rules. Peggy's face turned into a mass of bruises and cuts by the time the women received their *lugao*—boiled rice mush—for dinner. Trying to settle on the stone floor to sleep—there were no chairs, beds, or even blankets—exacerbated the pain throughout her body. Peggy drifted off fitfully, still going over and over in her mind the story she told the Japanese. She knew she would have to repeat it tomorrow. She wanted her lies to be perfect and convincing.

The second day of interrogation began much like the first, with the same officer and interpreter asking question after question, with sharp slaps often following answers that the officer did not like. This pattern continued every day until the fifth. That morning, when Peggy reached the interrogation room, she saw that the Japanese had the application she filled out in

October 1941 for Red Cross volunteer work. On it, she listed her nationality as American. Now the Japanese possessed written proof that she was not Lithuanian. "I was so scared I could hardly move but I sat down, thinking frantically, making up and discarding one story after another." Peggy would not give up easily. "This would have to be good. I had to come through this or I would never leave Fort Santiago." She insisted to the Japanese she had not lied to them—she lied to the Red Cross back in 1941. "I was afraid they wouldn't let me work for them if they knew I was a foreigner," she said. It was the most plausible story she could think of.[29]

The Japanese did not buy it, at least not right away. Over the next hours, they slapped Peggy and forced her to kneel on a split bamboo bench, which cut deep gashes in her legs. Still, she clung to her story. She was in such pain she could not eat the *lugao* that night, though she knew she needed food to keep up her strength.

The next day the Japanese changed interrogation rooms. Gone was the sunshine streaming through the window. Now, in a long and windowless room, Peggy endured another round of torture. "They tied my hands behind my back, attached a rope to the tied wrists and jerked me up several feet above the floor. While I hung there, they screamed questions at me again and again and beat me with their fists." This launched days of alternate tortures. One day Peggy was forced to kneel on the bamboo bench; the next day she was beaten with fists, the flat side of a bayonet, or a leather belt.[30]

Each night when she returned to her cell, her legs and back a runny mess of never-healing sores, Peggy had a single consolation. "One more day and I've stuck to my story. If only I can do it again tomorrow." The Japanese escalated their interrogation, adding psychological torture to the physical. To demoralize her, they forced Peggy to watch the beating of other prisoners. They threatened her with execution, hoping to scare her. Finally, they put her in solitary confinement, a stone cell about four feet square, too small to even lie down in. She ran a fever and gangrene set in on one of her lacerated legs.[31]

On her fourth day in solitary, a guard took Peggy from the cell and escorted her to yet another room where she faced new officers and a new interpreter. They asked Peggy to sign a paper stating she would not work against the Japanese government. She agreed, and the interpreter told her she was free to go. In addition to that promise, the document contained the statement, "Since I have been in Fort Santiago for questioning, I have received courteous treatment from all officers and sentries and been provided with good food." It was an appalling lie. Still, Peggy could not wait to sign. She worried the Japanese would change their minds. They suspected she was not Lithuanian, yet without a confession they did not believe they had a strong case against her. For thirty-two days Peggy refused to confess, and the Japanese allowed her to walk out of Fort Santiago.[32]

Barely among the living when she exited the Fort, Peggy's battered legs gave way once she was outside. She collapsed on a grassy area and stayed there for what seemed like hours. Finally, she flagged down a Filipino riding a bicycle with a sidecar, and ordered him to help her back to her apartment. Peggy's maid, Maria, was relieved to see her again. She helped Peggy bathe, taking special care to clean the worst of her wounds. "But it was a hopeless job," Peggy recalled. "She took me to the hospital. I was a mess. There was a large gangrenous area on my right leg and amputation was clearly indicated. All my organs had fallen from that month of terrific beatings over my back and I needed a major operation to put them back into place again."[33]

Because Peggy insisted she would be useless as a nurse with only one leg, her doctor agreed to try to save it. The operation to repair her injuries proved excruciating. Worried she might start babbling under ether, Peggy would only consent to a spinal anesthetic so she could stay awake. It wore off before the end of the surgery, and for an agonizing forty-five minutes she felt every cut and probe the doctor made. Parts of her body remained paralyzed from the spinal injection for several days, and she ran a dangerously high fever. Still, she did not regret her decision. She kept her leg.

It took Peggy six weeks in the hospital to recover from her "courteous" treatment in Fort Santiago. During this time, two of the Japanese officers responsible for her torture visited her three times a week, sitting silently in her room for an hour each time. She took their presence as a warning against her talking about her treatment in the Fort, so she kept quiet.

Religion provided Peggy a great deal of comfort during those long weeks of recovery. If she could not tell the doctors and nurses about Fort Santiago, she could discuss it with God in her prayers. Although a variety of Protestant religious instruction failed to stick earlier in life, after her release from prison, Peggy became a devout Catholic. She took special solace in a message she received from Colonel Mack. The prisoners in Cabanatuan said daily prayers for her while the Japanese held her in Fort Santiago.

Sometime in November 1943, Peggy was released from the hospital. Her ordeal did not put her off prisoner relief: "Of course, I went straight back to smuggling again, starting with the life-saving supplies moving to Cabanatuan."[34]

LIKE OTHERS IN THE MISS U network, Claire Phillips kept tabs on Peggy's arrest and detention. Some of what Claire heard confirmed Peggy's version of the story: the Japanese could not find any evidence that Peggy was an American, and without a confession, they let her go. Conflicting accounts of Peggy's arrest circulated. Instead of the horrific, painful wounds that Peggy recalled suffering, Claire remarked that Peggy "was tortured a bit," and released two weeks after her arrest. And there were different stories about what prompted Peggy's arrest. According to Claire, "It seemed that a vindictive neighbor had reported her to the military police due to the fact that she had many visitors both day and night."[35]

Claire's description of Peggy's arrest and imprisonment was corroborated by Lorenza Amusategui. Like Naomi Flores, Lorenza had expressed concern about Peggy's erratic behavior. During the spring of 1943, more of the work of the Miss U network was conducted from the Amusategui home or from Ramon Amusategui's office, partially out of concern that the Japanese were watching Peggy's apartment. As far as Lorenza was concerned, the change of venue also stemmed from Peggy's "total lack of tact in dealing with some of these 'customers' [messengers]," which in turn caused resentment among them, "resulting in petty gossip, all harmful to our work." Peggy had become sour and sarcastic, according to Lorenza, so much so that Miss U members preferred to deal with Naomi, Evangeline Neibert, or Ramon.[36]

Peggy's abrasiveness not only had a negative effect on her organization. It may have sealed her fate as well. She antagonized a woman Lorenza identified as Lourdes Campbell, who knew about Miss U. Peggy and the other Miss U members thought Lourdes was too cozy with the Japanese. Peggy confronted her, perhaps about her loyalties, and Lourdes responded by threatening to expose Miss U. This verbal altercation took place in the street, and as Lorenza later wrote, "Let it suffice to say that in those days so many spies for the Japs existed, that to make an enemy was far from worthwhile."[37]

In August 1943, a month before Peggy's arrest, Lorenza learned that five women interned in Santo Tomas had told the Japanese about Jeppie Richey's involvement with the military prisoners. Richey, who had been exempted from internment because of his amputated leg, had been active in the underground. After a while, the Amusateguis convinced Richey his extensive network of acquaintances would make him more useful inside Santo Tomas. From there he could persuade the civilian internees, who Lorenza believed were flush with money, to donate everything they could to the POWs. Richey could also facilitate passing messages between the civilian camp and the military prisons.[38]

Lorenza was at a loss to understand why these women turned on Richey, since most of them had husbands imprisoned at Cabanatuan. Perhaps they blamed him if they received bad news or if they received no news at all. Perhaps at least one of them knew Richey and Peggy Utinsky worked together. Lorenza believed the betrayal had something to do with Peggy: "One of these women . . . once told me she hated Mrs. Utinsky for reasons previously mentioned concerning her character, so her squealing was not too much of a surprise." For Lorenza, it was not a stretch to believe that lingering hatred for Peggy provoked the woman into jeopardizing the whole underground operation.[39]

Despite this betrayal, the circulation of messages did not stop. Instead, the Amusateguis took extra precautions by censoring the messages, reading them closely to make sure they did not contain any incriminating evidence. Lorenza Amusategui discovered that some "thoughtless" people, "in spite of our absolute orders of never mentioning names on their letters to the P.O.W., . . . disobey[ed] the rules of our group and proceed[ed] in their careless manner, writing out names in full when referring to us." The underground had already been compromised, and further breaches were around the corner. Too many people were involved, too many of them well meaning but naïve. All it would take was the wrong people getting hold of even one of these messages, and the whole network would come apart.[40]

The unraveling began when Peggy was arrested. Despite any hard feelings between Peggy and other members, the organization moved swiftly to her aid. Protecting her, they knew, meant protecting Miss U. Ramon Amusategui stepped in to run the organization; he and his brother-in-law Kurt Gantner covered Peggy's household expenses while she was in Fort Santiago. Ramon scraped together 5,000 pesos for a bribe to secure her release. A trusted Miss U donor, "a certain Ernesto Lardizabal who had influential friends dealing with the Jap Kempei" knew whom to slip the money to. Max Kummer, the German husband of Peggy's close friend Elizabeth, also talked to some of his German acquaintances about helping Peggy.[41]

No doubt everyone was anxious to see her released, but perhaps for more self-serving reasons than simply wishing to bring their friend home. Peggy's arrest revealed the hazard of underground workers knowing too much about each other's roles. As Naomi Flores later stated, all of these efforts on Peggy's behalf were necessary because of the possibility that Peggy "might squeal on everybody knowing how she talks." This explanation also casts doubt on Peggy's account of her release from Fort Santiago—it may not have been because of her stoic refusal to talk. The members of Miss U worked behind the scenes to free her.[42]

Lorenza Amusategui, like Claire Phillips, put the length of Peggy's imprisonment at fifteen days, after which Peggy "walked from Fort Santiago to her house, bathed and changed, and went to my father's house to ask him to hospitalize her." Lorenza's father, Dr. Gerardo Vazquez, worked at the Philippine General Hospital, and he was the physician brought in to treat Claire's post-surgery complications. Lorenza was at her father's house the day of Peggy's release, and she noticed two things. First, Peggy had lost weight—fifteen pounds in fifteen days, Lorenza estimated. Second, much to her surprise, neither Peggy's arms nor legs bore any visible signs of torture. Lorenza, her father, her husband, and her sisters all noted Peggy's "flawless white skin, how that skin would have bruised had the Japs mistreated her."[43]

Aside from the weight loss, then, Lorenza saw nothing wrong. Yet Peggy asked Dr. Vazquez to hospitalize her to operate on a small uterine tumor she had had for some time. It was not a medical necessity, nor was it, as Peggy later claimed, a corrective for the collapse of her internal organs brought on by torture. Rather, Lorenza believed, Peggy was petrified the Kempeitai would arrest her again and thought that as long as she was under medical care, the Japanese would leave her alone.

Dr. Vazquez judged Peggy a hysteric and felt relieved when another surgeon decided to handle the operation. Neither Vazquez nor his daughter connected Peggy's mental state with her recent interrogations at Fort Santiago. Vazquez warned Lorenza that Peggy was unstable, which Lorenza saw for herself when she and Ramon visited Peggy in the hospital: "There she lay on her bed waiting to be operated [on], her nerves all shot, trembling like a leaf, crying and pleading with Ramon not to let the Japs arrest her again, and suddenly screaming and threatening, warned she would squeal on all of us were she to be arrested again."[44]

It may have been a threat; it may have been an entreaty. Perhaps Peggy feared she had lost her resolve—if she ended up back in Fort Santiago, this time knowing what the Japanese would do to her, she was not at all certain she could hold up. She did not want to break and ruin the entire Miss U organization. Whatever the true meaning of her words, the Amusateguis kept a close eye on Peggy while she was in the hospital. After Peggy's release, Lorenza stayed away from her, convinced the Kempeitai would come for Peggy again. Her husband continued to visit the A. Mabini Street apartment, however, to help Peggy with the prisoner relief projects, and to keep an eye on her behavior. In the end, Lorenza found Peggy's situation unfortunate. "It really was a pity that Mrs. Utinsky has such an unpredictable character, because she did possess a heart when it came to helping P.O.W."[45]

Claire confirmed that Peggy was shunted aside as the leader of her namesake organization. "Our group avoided her after that, arranging to meet her only when essential, through Father Lolar [sic] at his church or hospital. She resented our aversion, but we had no means of knowing if she was being shadowed, and could not afford to take any chances." They all wanted to come out of the war alive. As evidenced in their memoirs, both Claire and Peggy wanted to remember their wartime selves as strong, dedicated, and admired. The fact they told different stories about Peggy's arrest and imprisonment underscores the solitary nature of underground work.[46]

AS PEGGY RECOVERED FROM HER Fort Santiago ordeal, Claire recuperated from tetanus and returned to work at the Club Tsubaki. Neither woman registered the fact that the Japanese granted independence to the Philippine Islands in October. It was a limited independence, though, as the Japanese never intended to allow the Philippines complete autonomy. Still, the Japanese had moved more quickly than the United States in this matter. After the occupation the Japanese had created the Philippine Executive Commission, a collaborationist government with former Manila mayor Jorge Vargas installed as its chairman. Japanese Prime Minister Tojo Hideki agreed to support Philippine nationalism as an expression of the Greater East Asia Co-Prosperity Sphere. His May 1943 visit to Manila was the most visible sign of his support for independence.[47]

By the next month, a Philippine Committee had been appointed—all of its members nominated by Tojo—to prepare for independence by drafting a constitution. The Japanese expected José Laurel, an associate justice of the Supreme Court, to serve as president of the new Republic of the Philippines. Laurel later claimed this was a "forced collaboration," that he had not wanted the position and agreed to take it only to help protect the Philippine people.[48]

In early September 1943, the new constitution was announced, as well as the Japanese Military Administration's intention to hand over its power, which never happened. Independence was declared on October 14th, and the next day the new republic signed a Pact of Alliance with Japan that did not include a declaration of war against the United States. When Laurel asked the United States to recognize the Philippines as a sovereign country, President Roosevelt affirmed the Commonwealth as the only legitimate government of the Philippines and pronounced Laurel's a "puppet government."[49]

The war ground on despite this political change, the Japanese maintained their occupation, and day-to-day life in Manila became more of a challenge, especially for business owners. Rationing, the official explanation for the growing food shortage, caused a variety of problems. Although Claire did not offer full meals at the Club Tsubaki, the snack items she served to complement the alcohol became more difficult to obtain. Her employees did not eat well and therefore could not always perform their best, and the club started to look shabby. A shortage of cloth meant Claire could not replace the napkins, tablecloths, and drapes she sacrificed to make shirts for the Park Avenue POWs, and the entertainers and hostesses struggled to replenish their costume wardrobes.

If customers stayed away from the Club Tsubaki, Claire knew she would not be able to contribute much to the guerrillas or the prisoners. Moreover, her medical treatment cost about 10,000 pesos, money that could have gone into the hills and the camps. Desperate to make up for lost time and to keep the club well supplied, she began dealing on the black market. Claire and Fely Corcuera cultivated a friendship with a Japanese patron who ran the navy warehouse that stored rice. They explained to him they needed rice to feed the club employees; any extra would be sent to Filipinos at a local hospital. The women offered to pay the businessman one hundred pesos for each sack of rice, most of which he turned around and spent in the Club Tsubaki. Claire bought thirty sacks of rice before the man was caught by his superiors.

In early December 1943 Claire sent notes to John Boone and to her prison contacts, confirming that she had recovered and had fully resumed her underground work. She learned about a group of POWs working in Manila's Port Area, loading crates on Japanese ships. Claire sent them supplies every week, receiving in turn information on the amount of weapons and ammunition stored in the vessels' hold. Moreover, she learned that the ships bearing the Red Cross insignia did not contain wounded soldiers, but fresh troops. Claire passed along this intelligence to Boone.

A holiday party in the ballroom at the Bay View Hotel provided another opportunity to gather nuggets of information. A Japanese conductor and composer named Ichikawa, drawn to the Club Tsubaki by Fely Corcuera's singing, invited her to perform there. Fely asked Claire to come along, certain some important military officers, the kind of people Claire liked to cultivate, would also attend the party. After meeting garden-variety colonels and majors, Claire wrangled an introduction to a Captain Kobayashi, head of investigations at Fort Santiago. "A contact worthy of exploitation," Claire decided.[50]

They made pleasant conversation, and Kobayashi expressed mild interest in Claire's nationality. She delivered the well-rehearsed lie about her Italian mother giving birth to her in the Philippines and admitted she had never been to Italy. The captain replied it was a nice country but he preferred the United States. He asked Claire if she would like to visit there once the Japanese conquered it. Yes, she allowed, it would be a nice place to visit, though she believed it was too crude to actually live there.

This assessment impressed Kobayashi, and he confided that once the Japanese occupied the United States, he would be heading its northwest government. He would give her any city she desired. While that gift obviously never materialized—Claire told the captain she would like to have Portland, Oregon, because she heard it was called the city of roses, her favorite flower—Kobayashi provided some information useful enough to pass along to Boone.

As the newness of the Club Tsubaki wore off, Claire realized she had to keep changing the establishment's entertainment to continue attracting customers. It was perhaps because of one such daring new act, however, that rumors began circulating about what went on in the club. The performance piece was prompted by the arrival of a closed-mouthed Japanese submarine commander, who, Claire knew, had information valuable to the guerrillas. "I brought up a number of subjects, but they met with no response. When I was about to give up all hope, the unexpected break came as we were about to close for the night," Claire remembered.⁵¹

The commander said he regretted he would not be staying in Manila for long. He found Claire's singing pleasant and would like to get to know her better. This would be impossible if his submarines were repaired on schedule because he would leave the next afternoon. One thing would induce him to delay his departure: if Claire agreed to perform his favorite dance. He had seen Sally Rand's famous fan dance in San Francisco and would like to see Claire's version of it. If she promised to do so, he would bring in his entire staff that evening. The opportunity to gather information about a submarine fleet was too good to pass up, so Claire agreed. She asked the commander how many officers would accompany him—she wanted to make sure the Club Tsubaki was prepared—and he told her forty. Claire knew she had her first piece of good intelligence: "Forty officers means a nice mess of subs." She sent a courier off to John Boone.⁵²

Pulling together the fan dance required some ingenuity since Claire had never seen it done. She relied on Fely Corcuera's expertise in costume design to create the right outfit, something that would cover Claire while creating the illusion of nudity. Mamerto Geronimo crafted fans from bamboo and a roll of American toilet paper. To masquerade any imperfections on stage, a small spotlight was draped with pink paper.

Despite the hasty preparations, the act was a hit. "That night, the commander and his forty guests almost lost their eyesight straining their orbs to determine whether I was really nude behind the fans . . . as they hoped, or wearing tights . . . as they feared," Claire recalled. While she was in the back room, switching the barely-there outfit for her evening gown, Fely announced that the Japanese were preparing to quit the club. She heard them comment they had to be up early for a morning departure. Though this told Claire when the submarine fleet was departing, she refused to let the officers go until she figured out where the vessels were headed.⁵³

This required delaying tactics. Claire instructed Mamerto Geronimo to spike the drinks, then joined the submarine commander at his table and said to him, "I'm going to miss you very much. Perhaps you, too, will be lonely. Would you like me to write you? I might send you my picture with the fans." It worked. The commander stayed; so did his men. Claire donned her costume again for a photography session, with the Japanese unaware the camera contained no film.[54]

When the camera finished snapping, Claire asked where she should send the pictures, and the commander offered up the information she hoped for. Claire would have to hold the photos for a couple of months until he returned, the officer explained, because he was headed to the Solomon Islands. In an active war zone, mail service was not reliable and he did not want the evening's mementos to go missing. Japanese and Allied forces had been squared off in the Solomon Islands since the spring of 1942; by late 1943 the battles intensified at Bougainville. Any information on Japanese plans, Claire knew, was invaluable to the Allies.

The delaying tactics continued after Claire dispatched a courier to John Boone with this intelligence. She needed to allow the runner time to get to Boone, who needed time to transmit the information to MacArthur's headquarters. The longer Claire kept the Japanese officers in the Club Tsubaki, the more chance the Allies had of targeting and destroying the submarines before they reached the Solomons. Claire diverted the commander, and his party remained, drinking and dancing at the Club Tsubaki, until after six o'clock in the morning. About a month later she learned all the submarines had been sunk.

The underground work of the Club Tsubaki carried on into the new year of 1944, what would be, finally, the last full year of the war. "Runners from the guerrillas continued to bring me new assignments, sometimes arriving at very inconvenient moments," Claire remembered. "I was asked to locate and describe various Jap ammunition factories and storehouses. It was up to me to note every new Nip face, ascertain the mission that had brought its owner to Manila, the length of his stay, his date of departure and destination. Much of the information that I forwarded was proverbial Greek to me." Boone and his men thrived on these bits of intelligence, so Claire stayed at it for as long as she could.[55]

———

GLADYS SAVARY WAS HAUNTED BY all the need she saw throughout Manila. She felt pleased when permission arrived from Tokyo in November 1943 for the official creation of the Neutral Welfare

Committee (NWC). Swedish Consul Helge Janson was part of a small group of Manilans who made the request for the organization, and he was designated as its head. Initially the NWC was allowed to operate as a "Special Committee" of the War Prisoners' Aid division of the YMCA, which meant its contributions to the POWs were restricted to recreation and educational items. Janson pushed the Japanese to stretch the purview of the NWC. Gladys agreed: "This is a worthy aim, but to appease hunger is more important. The boys were starving . . . they needed food and clothing."[56]

Helge Janson wanted to add food, clothing, and medicine to the approved shipments, and insisted on obtaining permission to purchase food locally. Based on the Park Avenue School scheme, he knew this latter point would enable the POWs to receive extras from local suppliers. The Swiss minister in Tokyo protested that the Red Cross already handled such matters. A brief kerfuffle followed, a kind of turf war between relief organizations, while Gladys, an official if impatient member of the NWC board, steamed ahead with a new relief project.

It centered on bean bags. Gladys decided a radical new twist on these recreational tossing toys were just what the prisoners needed. She and a group of NWC volunteers made up thousands of the bags that were duly delivered to the POWs. Though the official NWC books, open to occupation authorities for inspection, documented the distribution of "bean bags," these were not, in fact, playthings. Weighing up to a hundred pounds each, the bags were crammed with red kidney and mongo beans for eating.[57]

While Gladys considered this project a way of stretching rather than breaking the rules, Helge Janson preferred the rules reflect actual practice: "His dealings with the Japanese were conducted most correctly, efficiently, and without bootlicking." Helge received permission to send supply packages—including food, medicine, and clothing—every two weeks to POW camps and every week to civilian internment camps. The YMCA contributed a set monthly sum to the NWC that fell well below the 30,000–40,000 pesos Helge knew was needed each month.[58]

Although the NWC was not supposed to directly solicit, its members did so anyway to make up the difference. Manilans continued to show their generosity. "Contributions of food and clothing came in from all sources and we committee people were kept busy sorting and arranging all this material and getting it ready to send in," Gladys remembered. There were eight members of the committee, including Gladys, citizens of other "neutral" countries including Switzerland, Belgium, Norway, Denmark, and Ireland. Camilla Westly, one of Gladys's compatriots in the Park Avenue School relief project, served as one of the Norwegian representatives.[59]

Besides putting together the bean bags, Gladys purchased most of the food for the NWC care packages. Because of her years with the Restaurant de Paris, she knew food dealers in Manila and she knew how to bargain. She also had transportation, a bicycle she dubbed the Green Dragon. As Gladys summed up her contributions to the NWC: "I was the errand boy, the lowliest member of the committee, and I loved it."[60]

A bit of false modesty, perhaps, given how scarce and dear food became in Manila. Moreover, Gladys volunteered to serve as the courier between the NWC and the civilian internees in Santo Tomas. Despite their own dire straits, despite the stinginess Lorenza Amusategui accused them of, Gladys found the internees willing to scrounge up and donate some extra money for the NWC to use to help the military prisoners. She hopped on the Green Dragon and became a regular caller to Santo Tomas, always temporarily wealthier when she left than when she arrived. Fortunately, the camp guards rarely searched female visitors, so the money made its way into POW relief instead of the guards' pockets.

In mid-November 1943, the everyday difficulties of life under enemy occupation intensified when a typhoon unleashed more than twenty-five inches of rain, causing massive flooding. "Manila was practically a lake," Gladys recalled. "It is below sea level in parts, anyhow, and it surely was a mess in our part of town, Pasay. . . . Water came halfway up the staircase, trunks and furniture careened gaily about the drawing room. The gardens were great lakes and the streets roaring rivers with a busy *banca* (small boat) traffic." She and her neighbors were cut off for three days, but they had plenty of gin and rum to see them through.[61]

The flood caused prices to rise, the money supply tightened, and the Japanese set an early curfew and increased their harassment of people on the streets. Gladys, drawing off of her light-minded philosophy, tried to keep her sense of humor—finding her own appearance amusing as she set off on her bicycle wearing shorts and knee-high rubber boots. She got a good laugh as she rode her Green Dragon past the Japanese garrison at Rizal Stadium, where she saw thousands of wet shirts, pants, and cartridge belts hanging out to dry. The enemy soldiers waited around for their clothes, "wet and miserable, for all the world like chickens caught in a cloudburst and ailing with the pip."[62]

Despite the early curfew, despite the increased risk of being out on the street, Gladys did not give up her work for the Neutral Welfare Committee. Though the typhoon may have slowed down some of the relief efforts, there was too still much need for food and for information to give up now. Navy Commander Dr. Thomas Hayes worried about the amount of news streaming into Bilibid Prison during December 1943: " . . . the boys have gotten too gay with it. Began this morning to put the quietes on it and get it under control." He was more appreciative—"Hell of a nice contribution"—of the truckload of supplies delivered by the YMCA from "neutral sympathizers" in time for Christmas.[63]

NWC aid did not stretch outside of Manila. When Red Cross parcels arrived in Cabanatuan at the beginning of December 1943, the Japanese used this as an excuse to cut down on the rations they provided to the POWs there. As a kind of Christmas present, the Japanese allowed the prisoners to cultivate their own private gardens. Jack Wright started his on Christmas Day, putting okra, eggplant, and beans in the ground. Within two months it had such a successful yield that he expanded his plantings.[64]

This was one of the last benign gestures from the Japanese toward their prisoners, civilian and military. In early 1944, Japanese military authorities took over the administration of Santo Tomas from their civilian counterparts. The package line—the lifeline for the internees that provided food, medicine, and clothing from the outside—was shut down. "It was as though a grave had opened, a *sawali* grave, and swallowed up the internees," Gladys observed.[65]

In those first few months of 1944, a good portion of Gladys's daily work came to an end—no more meals to prepare for dozens of people, no more laundry to wash and press. She spent extra time in her garden, coaxing tomatoes, corn, lima beans, and papaya to grow, nourished with fertilizer she gathered from the street after *carromata* ponies passed by. In June 1944, the Japanese ordered the Neutral Welfare Committee to cease operations. Though they provided no explanation, Gladys believed it came from the sheer spite of the Japanese knowing they were losing the war. Now they wanted everyone to suffer.

"My conscience hurt me, being free in a comfortable house, able to move about and to eat not too badly," Gladys later wrote. She began visiting hospitals to try and cheer up the patients there, many of them recovering from interrogations in Fort Santiago. They told Gladys about torture, showed her their wounds, and she wondered how any human being could survive such horrors. Peggy Utinsky already had. Now came Claire Phillips's turn.[66]

CHAPTER 14

THE UNRAVELING (OR "THE FAT IS IN THE FIRE")

O N AN EARLY MARCH MORNING IN 1944, Claire Phillips answered her telephone. Lorenza Amusategui was on the line, letting her know in their cookie-baking code that Evangeline Neibert was ready to take the most recent batch of mail to Cabanatuan. In the middle of the call, Claire heard a distinct throat-clearing. She asked Lorenza if she was ill. When Lorenza replied no, she was not, the two women realized someone was listening in. They talked for a few minutes more, resisting hasty good-byes that would alert the eavesdropper that he had been detected.

"I knew that my good luck had been stretched like a rubber band and did not know at what moment it would snap," Claire later wrote. She took special care preparing the outgoing Cabanatuan mail. "Special care," perhaps, but in hindsight, putting anything at all in writing was a risky, if not downright naïve move. Claire censored some of the letters, since, "in their eagerness to cheer the prisoners, people would frequently mention names or express sentiments which, falling into the wrong hands, could be highly incriminating and dangerous."[1]

It made sense to cut out any identifying references from the messages, yet Claire's second step undercut that caution. On separate paper, she documented each letter as well as the amount of money enclosed. She kept one list; the other was delivered to a contact inside Cabanatuan. As Claire explained, "He checked the incoming mail against his list, so, if anything failed to arrive, we could put a tracer on it." If the Japanese found either list, they would know exactly who was involved with smuggling. Despite the revelation of her tapped telephone, Claire did not think to re-evaluate this system.[2]

Perhaps she was too busy to think such things through. That same evening, Claire prepared for the arrival of a Japanese general at the Club Tsubaki. The free-flowing alcohol—some of it spiked—resulted in the disclosure of a bit of information about a Red Cross ship masquerading as a troop transport. The general and his party spent so much money that Claire had more than enough funds for purchasing supplies for the guerrillas and POWs. The evening seemed a great success.

Not an unqualified success, though, because Claire caught the eye of a difficult customer. Mr. Kamuri—the staff referred to him as "Tarzan" because he constantly bragged about his athletic prowess—had been in Manila for about a year, relocating from Manchukuo in Japanese-occupied China to open a battery factory. He was muscular and of medium height, well-dressed and well-educated, and by Claire's estimation, "not unattractive for a Jap." She knew Kamuri was an important businessman and therefore could not be ignored; still, she did not care for him.[3]

When Claire noticed Kamuri watching her this night, she remembered what one of John Boone's couriers told her a few days earlier. The guerrillas suspected Kamuri's factory served as a front for something else. Claire realized she could make this evening more successful by charming that information out of Kamuri. She sat at his table, smiled, and said, "My duty is done now toward the honorable general. Now I can enjoy myself a little, perhaps." Kamuri accepted the flattery as his proper due, and Claire emphasized her interest by singing for him a popular 1930s jazz tune, "I Cried for You."[4]

Pleased with this personal attention, Kamuri asked Claire for a dance. As they waltzed to "The Blue Danube," she talked to him about his factory, trying to wrangle an invitation for a tour. He deflected. She brought it up again, clumsily, raising his suspicions. If he did not know her better, he said, he would think she was a spy. Claire accused Kamuri of jealousy, that he did not want any of the men at his factory to see her and desire her. "Well, I promise not to flirt with any of them if you let me come. I only want to see if you are really the big business man you always tell me you are."[5]

Kamuri did not fall for it. Instead, he asked Claire to join him for dinner at his hotel and be his "sweetheart." Claire countered with her original request. She wanted to see his factory, then she would join him at his hotel. Their banter continued as they danced, only ending when it was time for another floor show. Claire sang the evening's finale, the Fanny Brice number, "My Man," which she directed at Kamuri. As he left that night, he slipped her fifty pesos and said he would see her tomorrow. She knew she had won; she would see the factory. It would cost her, Claire understood, one way or another. This may not have been the first time Claire was faced with having to pay a steep price for information she needed. By the time she had performed the fan dance for the submarine commander, rumors had been circulating that the Club Tsubaki was nothing more than a fancy brothel. As Lorenza Amusategui later claimed, "I have people (the rest of the group) . . . who could and are willing to show Claire's true colors (one is a witness to her sleeping with Japs, in that club of hers). . . ."[6]

The morning of the anticipated tour at the battery factory, John Boone sent Claire an unusual request. He wanted her to arrange the christening of his firstborn son Phillip—named for John Phillips—who had arrived on March 13, 1944. As good practicing Catholics, John and Mellie Boone did not want to delay the baptism. Mellie was already on her way in to the city with the baby, but John, for obvious reasons, could not join them.

Claire's first stop after reading Boone's request was the Malate Convent, where Father Lalor was thrilled to hear the news about the baby. He would baptize little Phillip, he told Claire, and assumed she would stand as godmother. Claire reminded him she was not Catholic. The priest responded, "My child, in war time there's no need to be quibbling over a good woman to stand sponsor for a brave man's son." With that settled, Claire hurried over to Lorenza Amusategui's home to ask for the loan of the family's christening gown. Lorenza was happy enough to oblige. She told Claire she was worried, though, that her husband Ramon would be arrested any time now. "Don't worry, honey. Your husband is a brave man but he has excellent judgment. He will not take needless risks," Claire said.[7]

Baby Phillip looked plump and happy in Mellie Boone's arms when they arrived at the Malate Convent. Claire must have been surprised to see who walked in with Mellie: Peggy Utinsky. Sometime after her release from Fort Santiago, Peggy made contact with John Boone, and added his guerrillas to her list of aid recipients. When she learned Mellie was coming into Manila to have her baby baptized, Peggy met and accompanied them to Malate. As Peggy explained after the war, "I managed to send supplies to Boone and in return I got a receipt for them, met his wife who was in Manila and went with her when the baby was baptized."[8]

Claire and Peggy had last seen each other the morning of Peggy's arrest in September 1943. Up until that time, they had had prisoner-relief projects in common. Now they shared an association with John Boone. It is unknown what the two women talked about that day; neither one provided details of the meeting. However, within a few short months, Claire would have to rely on Peggy for a huge personal favor.

With all the blessings of the Boone baptism complete, Claire headed back to the Club Tsubaki. Mr. Kamuri had telephoned in her absence, and when she returned the call, he invited her to his office at the battery factory. Claire arrived as scheduled at two o'clock, and Kamuri tried to confine the tour to the business's showroom and his office. She got angry, yelling at him, "So! You were only fooling me. Never mind! We'll call it all off. You agreed to show me the whole place." As Claire started to walk out, Kamuri called her back, relenting. He would show her the whole factory if she promised never to tell anyone she had been here. If word got out, he would be in a lot of trouble, and he would take it out on her. Kamuri escorted her onto the factory floor where bullets, not batteries, were being manufactured. "You satisfied now?" he asked her. "Tonight I win." He told her he would see her later at the club, and Claire knew he expected that she would honor her end of the bargain.[9]

That evening, Claire avoided Kamuri until the Club Tsubaki closed. As her employees shut the lights, she tried to beg off with Kamuri, first telling him Dian was sick, then employing the age-old headache line. Kamuri, silent through most of the excuses, finally grabbed Claire's wrist and dragged her toward the private rooms, slapping her face as they moved down the corridor. The bartender, Mamerto Geronimo, followed, trying to help: "Señora, what will I tell your husband when he gets here and does not find you?" Claire shouted at him to call the military police. When Kamuri saw Mamerto reach for the telephone, he swore at Claire, kicked her, and walked out of the club. She stumbled into her bedroom and collapsed.[10]

The maneuver only delayed and intensified Kamuri's rage. He returned to the Club Tsubaki the next night and destroyed everything in the club he could get his hands on: mirrors, lights, barware, chairs, and stools. None of the customers lifted a finger to stop him, and only the arrival of the military police ended the rampage. As Claire later wrote, "I don't know who called them. There was no desire on my part to become involved with the kenpei [sic], although technically under their protection. Even when the going was extremely rough, I always felt the less they knew about me, the better off I would be."[11]

Tucked at the end of her remembrance of this episode, almost as a throwaway line, Claire divulged an intriguing bit of information. At the Club Tsubaki, she had been under the protection of the Kempeitai. She did not explain the nature of that protection. Given Lorenza Amusategui's postwar allegation about the goings on at the club, it is possible that Claire's protection was somehow linked to her willingness to provide sexual favors or sex for hire to prominent occupation officials. Perhaps, though, the protection was extended as a security measure for the important officials who patronized the club.

Considering Claire's underground work, she preferred the Kempeitai know as little about her as possible. They were already keeping tabs on her, probably had been since the opening of the Club Tsubaki. They tried to trip her up with a fake courier and now, in the spring of 1944, they tapped her telephone. The incident with Kamuri drew more attention to Claire and her club.

Not long after the military police took Kamuri away for smashing up the club, the prisoner relief project at the Park Avenue School shut down. "I overplayed my hand," Claire later admitted. "I arranged with a sympathetic Chinese confectioner to have a thousand peanut candy bars made up, and placed the whole lot of them along the road before daylight." Someone told the Japanese guards about the candy bars, and the prisoners' daily march to and from Nichols Field was rerouted, cutting off their opportunity to retrieve the nutritious snacks. Japanese soldiers arrested Claring Yuma and took her to Fort Santiago for questioning. Her smattering of Japanese impressed her captors into believing, at her insistence, she would make a valuable spy for them. As soon as they released Claring, she slipped away into the hills.[12]

The most disheartening news reached Claire on May 18, 1944. The entire Cabanatuan project had been exposed.

IN THE SPRING OF 1944, the war took a decisive turn in favor of the Allies. In mid-February, the Allies had launched a successful attack against Truk, part of the Caroline Islands, during Operation Hailstone. This was followed by similar successes in the Mariana Islands during the spring and summer. The Japanese no longer had uncontested control of the Pacific. Gladys Savary, nestled in with a congenial group of "neutral" Allied sympathizers in Manila's Pasay neighborhood, detected the change in the war. The Japanese were on the run, and it made them vindictive. Before things came to an end they would make everyone pay for their defeat, civilians and military personnel alike.

Gladys's outings on the Green Dragon dwindled during the spring and summer months. Her regular trips to Santo Tomas University, to bring food and clean laundry to civilian internees there, had ended at the beginning of 1944 with the shutdown of the package line. The medical facility at nearby Sulphur Springs, which Gladys also helped supply, closed in March when all but the most seriously ill were sent to Santo Tomas. By the end of June, Japanese authorities had shut down the Neutral Welfare Committee. At Bilibid, Thomas Hayes asked the prison's hospital director, Lieutenant Nogi Naraji, for permission to contact the committee about bringing in food for the POWs. Nogi refused, claiming the Japanese Army Headquarters did not recognize any neutral agency in Manila. That was the end of sanctioned prisoner relief in Manila. Gladys no longer had to run errands for that organization, and all the prisoners were left to rely on what the Japanese were willing to provide.[13]

Gladys occupied herself with other projects as she prepared for the end of the war. Though she optimistically believed it would happen soon, she anticipated a rough finish. In July, betting on the imminent arrival of American bombers, she dug an air raid shelter under a mango tree. It triggered her claustrophobia, so she abandoned it in favor of fortifying a cubbyhole under the stairs in her house. Gladys stockpiled enough food to outlast a siege of several months, much of which came from the vegetable garden she cultivated in the backyard. She figured that if the situation turned dire, the people living in the seven houses of the complex would pool their resources to ensure survival. Each house had its own walled garden plus another large wall enclosed all seven homes—which to Gladys seemed very secure.

Still, staying alive until liberation required vigilance and luck. Gladys noticed Japanese authorities clamping down on anything that smacked of resistance, sending more people to Fort Santiago. Two of her friends were picked up for illegally disseminating news, and under torture, one of them revealed who supplied the information. Gladys remembered, "They were all taken in for questioning; some of them were released, others never heard from again."[14]

Things were worse in the prison camps. At the beginning of 1944, Cabanatuan was a hellhole spiraling into even darker depths. The POWs, deprived of nearly everything a human body needs, most keenly felt the lack of protein. There was no meat to be had—none to purchase in town, none brought in by the Japanese—though every now and then the camp messes received some tiny dried fish whose nutritional value was next to nothing. Irvin Alexander recalled, "A small amount of granulated fish was issued in place of meat. It was very dry and salty and smelled so rotten that I had to hold my nose when I ate it." The protein deficiency sparked a rise in beriberi and edema as the men became more emaciated by the day. In their desperation, the prisoners set out to trap and cook anything they could: dogs, cats, even lizards, grasshoppers, and worms.[15]

The sole bright spot that spring was the arrival of packages from home. In March 1944, Irvin Alexander, Jack Wright, and the other prisoners each received a single bundle, via the International Red Cross, from their families. Alexander remembered, "The packages were practically all of the same size, but [that's where] their similarity ceased. My box . . . contained a thousand multi-vitamin tablets and some powdered soup for my unhappy stomach." He regretted his wife had not thought to send more food, though the vitamins proved efficient in arresting his symptoms of pellagra and beriberi. Wright also received vitamins, and treasured the chocolate bars just as much. Like most of the prisoners, he traded many of the clothing items and toiletries in his parcel for food any of the other men were willing to part with.[16]

Then, one incident erased any remaining hope of securing additional food sources: the arrest of the carabao cart drivers. At the beginning of 1944, fuel shortages forced the Japanese to exclusively use animal-driven wagons to bring the meager supplies into the Cabanatuan prison camp. Between six and ten carts, each hitched to one carabao, left the camp in the morning and returned in the afternoon. An American prisoner served as the wagon train master with about another twenty as cart drivers; three Japanese accompanied them on each trip. The drivers and the underground workers in Cabanatuan town had figured out how to utilize the carts to get mail, money, and extra food into the camp. Sometimes items were slipped onto the carts while the guards were not looking. Or packages were tucked into the bushes under the Bangod Bridge at the two watering holes for the carabao. Occasionally a cart driver and a sympathetic local sang songs to each other as coded messages. Overall, it was an effective system.[17]

"We did not know the details of the underground system from Cabanatuan to Manila, but we knew the names of a number of people working in the underground, most of whom were women," Irvin Alexander later explained. "We knew that a woman messenger traveled between Cabanatuan and Manila and that she dealt mostly with women in Manila." The woman making these trips was, of course, Evangeline Neibert—Sassy Susie. Alexander was also aware that other women of a variety of nationalities, "utterly fearless, extremely efficient and devoted to Americans and the American cause," helped her.[18]

This system would not last much longer, however. The arrests happening in Manila during the summer of 1944, some of which Gladys Savary had witnessed, represented the ripple effects of the crackdown at Cabanatuan. On May 3, 1944, the Japanese arrested six carabao drivers, including Fred Griffith Threatt. A native Louisianan, Threatt served in the military in World War I and settled on Luzon sometime after the end of that war. Though he joined up with the US Navy after the Japanese attack in December 1941 and ended up in Cabanatuan, the prisoners there regarded him as a civilian. Because of Threatt's skill with Philippine dialects, the Japanese selected him to run one of the carabao carts and deal with the market stall owners in Cabanatuan town.[19]

The drivers were taken to the guard house, and their carts and the bags of rice they hauled were searched. The Cabanatuan prisoners exchanged as much information about these events as they dared. Arthur Shreve, an artillery officer with the Quartermaster Corps, first learned of the arrests when Harold Johnson, the commissary officer and Miss U contact, asked him to hide some papers. "The fat is in the fire," Johnson said as he related the news of the cart drivers' detention.[20]

According to Shreve, the drivers had been colluding with the guards in smuggling messages into Cabanatuan, usually with the aid of a canteen with a false bottom. Fred Threatt's wife, Consuela, worked as a waitress in one of Cabanatuan's small shops. She made a show of filling his canteen with water and he made a similar show of drinking from it when he took it from her and again when he was searched at the prison gate. Fred hoped this would deflect the guards' interest in looking too closely at the canteen.

Another cart driver, Sergeant Robert Ross of the 4th Marines, had been connected with the Miss U network since the summer of 1943. Though not clear how Ross made initial contact, in July he was able to arrange for Naomi Flores to pass along medicine to treat his amoebic dysentery. Ross, known to the underground as Scrappy, worked so closely with Naomi to bring in extra items that his barracks mates referred to her as his girlfriend.[21]

Fred Threatt and the other drivers knew something serious happened when the Japanese detained them that day. Threatt whispered a warning to Colonel Johnson, prompting him to hide the documents that may have included Claire Phillips's carefully detailed lists of money donations. The men casually dropped their canteen belts and shoulder bags as the carts were inspected. Other prisoners, equally nonchalant, walked off with the incriminating items, disappearing into the barracks before the Japanese knew what had happened. By the time the men were searched, they had no contraband on them, yet the guards kept the drivers separated from the general population. "We are all very anxious," Arthur Shreve wrote in his journal, because "some money had been secured by notes signed by U.S." That would not go over well with the Japanese.[22]

The tense situation deepened over the next couple of days. Threatt and the others remained in the guard house while the Japanese raided some of the shops and market stalls in Cabanatuan town. In at least one place they found some money and notes addressed to camp prisoners, but no evidence to connect the items to the carabao cart drivers. Shreve recorded on May 11th, "Evil days are upon us," as the Japanese arrested eleven more men, including Captain Jack Le Mire, Lieutenant Colonel Edward Mack, and the two chaplains, Colonel Oliver and Captain Robert Taylor.[23]

Especially unfortunate, according to Arthur Shreve, was the fact that one of these men, "when put under pressure, squealed," resulting in another two dozen people taken away. Mack, Le Mire, Oliver, and Taylor all knew about Miss U, and the other detained men undoubtedly did as well. How many of them talked under torture and what they revealed was unknown, but none of it could be good for Peggy Utinsky and her network.[24]

Days, then weeks, passed, and the men were not released. Ralph Hibbs expressed particular concern over the detention of Lieutenant Colonel Jack Schwartz, commanding officer of the prison camp hospital. The native Texan had joined the US Army in 1928 and was the Chief of Surgical Service at Hospital No. 2 on Bataan before the surrender. In June 1942, Schwartz, code named Avocado, was already in contact with "loyal civilian agencies"—the underground—in the town of Cabanatuan. "Since detection by the Japanese would have resulted in serious punishment for the participants," he later recalled, "great care was taken." Hibbs witnessed Schwartz's arrest: "the Jap squad appeared and grabbed Jack. Surrounding him with their bayonets, they marched him down the road. He looked so small and helpless." The rest of the officers in the hospital area denied all knowledge of or involvement with any smuggling schemes. They saw no point to adding to the number of detainees.[25]

Jack Schwartz and twenty-two others were taken to Kempeitai headquarters in the town of Cabanatuan, where they remained for a week's worth of interrogation and torture as the Japanese tried to find out the identities of their civilian contacts. Lieutenant Colonel Francis S. Conaty of the Quartermaster Corps watched as the men returned to the Cabanatuan camp, and thirteen were released into the general population. Unlike Hibbs, Conaty knew right away why these men had been detained. "Our carabao drivers were confined by the Japanese the other day accused of bringing in notes and money to prisoners in the camp from Filipinos and civilian internees," he wrote in his journal, admitting "I don't know how serious it might be."[26]

Conaty was not the only prisoner trying to stay optimistic about the fate of the carabao cart drivers. Arthur Shreve was visiting at the camp hospital when a Japanese M.P. truck returned the rest of the men to the segregated area. Shreve wrote in his journal, "We are no end pleased to see them come in for we believe it will be only a matter of time before they will be returned to our side. . . . Everyone in camp feels much better as to the eventual outcome."[27]

Ten of the returned men, including Jack Schwartz, were segregated at the edge of the camp and put under guard. The Japanese considered them guilty of trafficking in unauthorized correspondence and smuggling large amounts of money. The prisoners were not given a specific sentence, though the guards led them to believe they would be executed. Instead, for a month, they were forced to sit motionless on a bench during the day and sleep on the ground at night. Then they were relocated to the guard house where they remained for two more months, once again alternating between spending time on a bench and on the floor.[28]

Although the Cabanatuan POWs might not have known exactly what the ten detainees were experiencing, they had a good idea. Francis Conaty noted that it was "too bad as they have done much to keep up morale and to enable patients in the hospital to buy some extra food. Of course," he added, "they realized they were taking chances. Hope they come out of it all right." The Japanese released Jack Schwartz to the camp hospital in early September. Ralph Hibbs saw him leave his segregated hut, "a walking skeleton certainly not more than 100 pounds, staggering slowly down the road shading his eyes from the unaccustomed sunlight." After months of "suffering unbearable dignities," Schwartz required an appendectomy and plenty of recuperation time. The Japanese pursued no more charges against him. In October he was moved from Cabanatuan to begin his journey to a labor camp in Japan.[29]

While the carabao cart drivers and their compatriots suffered their punishment that summer, the Cabanatuan prisoners faced continuing hardships. Larger and larger details of men were chosen for transfer to Japan and other locations in Asia to perform slave labor. The prisoners left behind were shuffled around to keep the barracks full. With the smuggling operation shut down, hunger among the men became unbearable. Jack Wright noticed a breakdown in morale and disciple. More men risked beatings and broken limbs to pilfer food from the garden work detail: "Canteens were ingeniously converted for smuggling by putting on sliding bottoms and sides in order to accommodate eggplant or okra which could not be put into the canteen through the small opening in the top. Pockets were sewn in G-strings to carry rice or beans in the crotch. Wooden shoes were hollowed out to provide a hiding place."[30]

The prisoners suffered more than ever because food was no longer being brought in via Manila. Too many people had been arrested in the capital, and with the breakdown of the supply line from the carabao carts, the best method of obtaining food ended. Irvin Alexander remembered, "Many of the civilians arrested in Manila were released after suffering considerable torture, but a number of them were executed. There were isolated cases of correspondence afterwards and considerable money continued to come into camp, but it was introduced by Nip soldiers who were well subsidized for their trouble." The underground at Cabanatuan had all but ceased to exist.[31]

That spring of 1944, prior to the arrest of the carabao cart drivers, the Kempeitai moved on the Manila end of the smuggling operation. On March 15th, they picked up Father Theodore Buttenbruch. By this time, Buttenbruch had already been banned from the camps because the Japanese realized he brought in a variety of contraband items during his visits. The ban had not prevented Buttenbruch from soliciting goods and assistance in Manila, so he remained under close watch until his arrest.[32]

The Kempeitai detained the German priest in Fort Santiago until May 25, 1944, as they continued to root out members of the underground. A mail courier was caught at Bilibid Prison on March 21st, his fate unknown. Father Buttenbruch's late May release coincided with the return of the carabao cart drivers to the Cabanatuan camp. It was clear the Japanese believed they learned everything they could about the smuggling operation, at least for now.[33]

In mid-June, after Buttenbruch had been free for less than three weeks, he ran into Pauline Corazon Ramirez on Calle España, near the Philippine General Hospital. Before the war, Pauline dated Army Air Corps Sergeant George P. Nord, then stationed at Nichols Field. Nord had survived the Bataan Death March only to endure imprisonment at O'Donnell, Bilibid, and Cabanatuan. Pauline's family worked with the Manila underground, so the young woman knew about Buttenbruch's involvement.[34]

The two chatted for a few minutes. Since it was a public place they did not want to draw attention to themselves by loitering for too long. Father Buttenbruch told Pauline he considered his release from Fort Santiago temporary. He knew the Japanese were watching him, and he wanted to lead them on a merry chase; he considered himself a decoy. Buttenbruch understood he was sacrificing himself, that his time was running out and the Japanese would pick him up again. He said to Pauline, "Pray for me, for I do not expect to come back the next time I am arrested."[35]

Lorenza Amusategui also had the feeling the Japanese were much too close to breaking the entire underground network. She and her husband Ramon knew since late 1943 that the Japanese stepped up surveillance of the traffic between Manila and Cabanatuan. By early 1944, the carabao carts traveling between the town of Cabanatuan and the prison camp were under additional scrutiny. American POW Ted Lewin, the infamous gambler and relentless briber, used what remaining influence he had to facilitate the delivery of extra supplies to the camp. Even that amounted to little. In April, occupation authorities moved some civilians out of Cabanatuan town to further reduce incidents of smuggling.[36]

Ramon Amusategui decided to use Horacio Manaloto as his sole contact for the prison camp, relegating Naomi Flores to an emergency substitute. While this new system might have safeguarded some of the underground workers, it slowed the flow of goods into Cabanatuan, causing additional suffering for the prisoners. Like Father Buttenbruch, Ramon set himself up as a sacrifice. He instructed everyone working with him to say the same thing if the Kempeitai picked them up for questioning: "I don't know anything outside of the fact that I have been working for Ramon de Amusategui."[37]

Manaloto made his final trip from Manila to Cabanatuan on May 1, 1944. His routine required that he return within a week, and Lorenza Amusategui remembered how Manaloto's "failure to appear at the appointed time filled our hearts with misgivings." However, those doubts were not severe enough to halt the prisoner relief network. On May 18th, the Kempeitai arrested Helen Petroff, who sent letters and money through the Amusateguis to her husband in Cabanatuan. Her arrest was "a product of her own folly," according to Lorenza, because she failed to use code names. Nevertheless, Helen worked with German Eroles at the Marfusa Restaurant in Manila's Ermita district. If she divulged his name, it would not be long before the whole network unraveled.[38]

The Kempeitai drew German's name from Helen Petroff in about a day. As soon as Ramon Amusategui heard about Helen's arrest, he realized his own would come soon. He gathered all the documents and letters he had pertaining to the Cabanatuan project and gave them to Angustias Mencarini, the woman who hosted the lunch where Claire met the other underground members. Though this would deprive the Japanese of written proof of Ramon's activities, it shifted the risk to Angustias, who was equally involved with Miss U and Claire Phillips. For some reason, no one destroyed the documents.

Next, the Amusateguis learned about German Eroles's arrest at the restaurant, and they received confirmation of their fear about Horacio Manaloto. The Japanese nabbed him in Cabanatuan, not long after the carabao cart drivers. Naomi Flores narrowly escaped capture—she climbed out a kitchen window when she saw Japanese soldiers approaching her house—and was rumored to be in the hills with the guerrillas. "This news brought into us the sharp realization we were being confronted with a huge problem in which the whole group was involved," Lorenza Amusategui later wrote.[39]

Despite the enormity of their predicament, most of the members of the Manila underground did not attempt to flee the city. The Kempeitai showed up at Ramon Amusategui's office on the morning of May 23, 1944, and took him to his home to search it and to arrest his wife as well. There were no incriminating documents; Ramon had already seen to that. He also managed to convince the officers that Lorenza had done nothing more than write a few friendly letters to some of the military prisoners. After an hour's worth of searching and interrogating, the Kempeitai took Ramon away. They left his wife behind, warning her of the severity of the situation. The couple had not been allowed to speak directly to each other while the Kempeitai were in their home. Lorenza recalled, "All we could do was to look at each other, my eyes I imagine devouring his features, as his eyes were mine, looking at me with a mixture of devotion and inexpressible sadness." Ramon could not even say good-bye to his children.[40]

Lorenza was relieved when she realized that, within their immediate circle of underground workers, no one else was scooped up by the Kempeitai. This she credited to her husband's insistence on taking full responsibility for the entire network. Lorenza noted that one other person from the larger network was picked up: "Dorothy Fuentes was arrested because the Japs had proof of her contact with a guerrilla unit." Dorothy Fuentes, High Pockets, Claire Phillips.[41]

WHEN SHE HEARD THAT GERMAN EROLES and Ramon Amusategui had been picked up, Claire Phillips called a meeting of the remaining members of the group to talk over possible scenarios. Dr. Romeo Atienza advised Claire to pack up her things and take Dian to John Boone in the hills. "The temptation was great," Claire later wrote. "Somehow or other, I could not bring myself to do it. I felt that I owed it to the memory of my departed to remain and help his former comrades, regardless of any serious consequences to myself."[42]

Claire convinced herself—and the others—that if the Japanese picked her up they would only keep her for a few weeks at most. They could not have any proof of her involvement with the underground. To make sure of that, Claire enlisted Mamerto Geronimo's help in removing all incriminating documents from their various hiding places in the Club Tsubaki. These, along with her passport, John Phillips's army papers, and receipts from the prisoners were passed along to Fely and Flora Corcuera, who buried them in glass bottles and tin cans in their family's backyard.

Then Claire waited for whatever was coming. The Japanese did not keep her in suspense long. At nine o'clock the next morning, four Kempeitai burst into Claire's living quarters at the Club Tsubaki. She sat at the kitchen table in her housecoat eating breakfast with Dian. The little girl's amah, Pressa, had gone out for bread, and Fely Corcuera, Claire's most trusted confidante, had already left for the morning. Two soldiers kept guard at the door, and the other two ordered Claire to put her hands up while they conducted a body search for weapons. They referred to her alternately as Madame Tsubaki and High Pockets, a sign the Kempeitai already knew exactly who she was.

As they nudged her toward her office, Claire told them she needed to find someone to look after Dian. She woke up Flora Corcuera, still asleep in the back despite the noisy intrusion, and whispered she had to get Dian to Boone's guerrillas. The Japanese confiscated all the items from Claire's desk and storage trunks, assuring her this evidence would be returned when she was cleared after questioning. It was an odd reassurance, given that they had already called her High Pockets. The Kempeitai allowed her to change from her housecoat into daytime clothing, and she chose practical over glamorous: a pantsuit and a pair of socks with her shoes. They walked her past the kitchen table where Flora sat with Dian, and the little girl looked at her mother but did not say a word. Claire worried a kiss good-bye might seem too final, so she told her daughter, "Be a good girl and Mummy will be home soon."[43]

Claire expected to be taken to Fort Santiago, but the Kempeitai delivered her to the Japanese Administration Building on San Luis Boulevard, just two blocks from the Club Tsubaki. The tiny guard house at the gate contained four cells, and Claire was pushed into an empty one. The cell had a barred window placed too high for her to look out of and a hole in the floor for her bathroom needs. After several hours a guard came in and blindfolded her. Claire heard other people enter, bringing objects that clanked on the rough floor. Her mouth went dry. Were these perhaps the torture devices she heard about? One voice instructed her to sit down on the chair placed behind her. Another addressed her as High Pockets and told her if she answered their questions truthfully she would soon be released. Both men spoke English, and Claire thought perhaps they had been customers at the Club Tsubaki.

The first question began with a statement. The Kempeitai knew she was not Italian—they called the Italian Consulate and checked—and she was not using her real name. What was her name? Without corroboration from the consulate, Claire realized she could no longer bluff the Italian story. "It is true that I am not an Italian," she admitted. "I am an American by birth. If you look in the files of the Bureau of Vital Statistics, you will discover that about a year ago I renounced all former loyalties and embraced Philippine citizenship. My status is that of a Philippine national. I am using my right name . . . Dorothy Fuentes."[44]

They pushed the point by asking why some people called her Claire. She was surprised they knew this because she had not used that name since shortly after her return from Bataan in July of 1942. Only a few friends from before the war knew her as Claire, and even they learned to call her Dorothy. She told the Japanese Claire was her middle name; sometimes people used it instead of her first name. These answers seemed satisfactory. If Claire's arrest had only been about her Dorothy Fuentes persona, and if the Japanese determined her birth in the United States outweighed her renunciation of former loyalties, she likely would have been released into the confines of Santo Tomas with the other civilian internees. The arrest was not only about Dorothy Fuentes, though. There was still the matter of High Pockets.

The next set of questions centered on whether or not Claire had sent and received letters from prisoners in Cabanatuan. Claire figured if she admitted to corresponding with the prisoners—and she was sure the Kempeitai had letters with her name on them—she could keep her interrogators diverted from the topic of guerrillas. She confessed to involvement with the Cabanatuan POWs. This was not enough for the Japanese. They wanted details. One of her letters was addressed to Everlasting. Who was Everlasting?

Claire's "I don't know" response earned her a punch to the temple. The men warned her to tell the truth. She pointed out she answered truthfully about her identity so they should believe her when she said she did not know Everlasting's real name. They seemed to accept this, then wanted to know how the letters traveled back and forth from Cabanatuan. Claire said, "There's a Filipino boy who came to my house every few months. I don't know his name." This provoked another punch to her head followed by kicks to her shins. The pain brought tears to her eyes that she tried to blot with the blindfold. "Tears will not help you," one of the Japanese said. "You have taken on the job of a man, so you must face the same punishment. This is no fight between man and woman . . . it is Nippon and America."

The questions and the beatings continued. The interrogators had many code names—Mutt, Papaya, Chap Bob, Sparkplug, Fancy Pants—and ordered Claire to identify them. Since she knew Ramon Amusategui and German Eroles had already been arrested, she admitted having met them when she volunteered at Remedios Hospital.[45]

Claire stuck to the story that her only contact with them concerned prisoner aid. The Japanese claimed the two men confessed Claire did much more: "They say you are also doing guerrilla work. We know you were doing guerrilla work and so were they. Speak now and we will let you off easy." Claire knew this was a lie so she did not change her story, not even when the Japanese threatened to bring Dian in and hurt her, too. When it was clear Claire would not tell them what they wanted to hear, the Japanese concluded the interrogation.[46]

A guard came in, took off Claire's blindfold, and removed the chairs and table brought in for the session, leaving her alone with no food or water. Not until the next day did she receive a cup of water, and not until the day after that a ball of rice and a cup of weak tea. This continued for two weeks—long days with little food and water and no modern sanitation facilities. The Japanese suspended Claire's interrogation, and she passed the hours by scraping a hole in a wooden board at the back of her cell so she could escape.

She never had the chance. After the first week of June 1944, two Kempeitai officers removed Claire to Fort Santiago, the place she most dreaded. Captain Kobayashi, the Club Tsubaki customer who promised her the pick of any American city once the Japanese conquered the United States, took her fingerprints. He did not acknowledge their former acquaintance. Perhaps he did not recognize the beaten, terrified woman standing before him, or maybe he did not want to admit that he had been fooled by her.

Claire's cell measured seven feet by twelve feet. The toilet consisted of a hole in the floor with a removable pan underneath it, a high-wattage lightbulb burned day and night, and the single luxury was a working faucet that provided plenty of water for drinking and washing. Claire shared the space with six other women who had been in Fort Santiago for a few months and were already thin and weak: a young Chinese woman, two American nuns, and three German Jews.[47]

Regulations forbade talking, though the women managed anyway, taking quick advantage of the times the guards moved past their door on their rounds. Claire found her cellmates' stories fascinating. As she related the Chinese woman's story: "Carmen's husband had been picked up on an unfounded charge of spreading propaganda. When she arrived with a parcel of food and clothing for him, a Japanese officer propositioned her. When she rejected the Nip's advances, they arrested her, also." The woman Claire called Carmen was Mrs. Tiu Chiao Beng, arrested on February 11, 1944, and imprisoned in Fort Santiago until the following December. She was in fact detained because the Japanese suspected both she and her husband, a Chinese school principal, had been writing and distributing anti-Japanese propaganda. Carmen endured interrogation and torture sessions as the Japanese attempted to force her confession.[48]

While there, Mrs. Beng met or heard about three American Methodist missionaries also imprisoned in the Fort, women well known in Manila for their selfless good works. Mary Boyd Stagg, Helen Wilk, and Dr. Hawthorne Darby were all associated with the Emmanuel Cooperative Hospital in the Tondo section of Manila. They had been arrested in late January and early February 1944, along with several others involved with the hospital, on suspicion of aiding and abetting the guerrillas. The women merely considered themselves humanitarians. Darby, along with nurse Helen Wilk, became involved with the underground early on, moving supplies in and out of the hospital. Mary Stagg, pastor at the Cosmopolitan Student Church, assisted their endeavors.[49]

Mary and her husband, Samuel Wells Stagg, had arrived in the Philippines in 1925, and they had a son, Samuel Boyd Stagg, known as Samboyd. When the Japanese attacked in December 1941, Samuel slipped out of Manila, eventually taking up intelligence work on the island of Palawan. Mary remained with the teenaged Samboyd; both were exempted from internment in Santo Tomas because of Mary's position as an ordained minister.[50]

Using her church as a base of operations, Mary worked with the guerrillas, passing along their requests for supplies to those who could secure the needed items. Samboyd sometimes carried verbal messages for his mother, and he knew about Claire Phillips and the Club Tsubaki, but, as he later recalled, "I stayed away from there." Though he did not specify why, it may have been that, given his age and the establishment's reputation, his mother did not want him inside a nightclub.[51]

Mother and son continued their underground work until the Japanese arrested them on January 28, 1944, and deposited them in Fort Santiago. For over three months the Staggs endured interrogation, as did Helen Wilk and Hawthorne Darby. On May 25th, Samboyd Stagg was released into internment in Santo Tomas where he declined further involvement with the guerrillas. Mary Stagg, Helen Wilk, and Hawthorne Darby were transferred to Bilibid Prison, given a court-martial, and pronounced guilty. At the end of August these three women, along with several other convicted resistance members, were executed in the Chinese cemetery. After the war, Mrs. Beng remembered the martyred missionaries from Fort Santiago. She did not, however, recall Dorothy Fuentes or Claire Phillips as one of her cellmates.[52]

The three German women in Claire's cell had been arrested for carrying what seemed to be a suspicious coded letter for Sister Mary Trinita Logue, an American Maryknoll nun confined with others at Assumption College. In fact, Sister Trinita was up to her wimple in guerrilla and prisoner relief projects. Along with the other Maryknoll sisters, the forty-nine-year-old nun began working with USAFFE in the Philippine Women's College on Taft Avenue, which had been turned into a base hospital in December 1941. When the army pulled out of the city, the nuns remained at the hospital, where they were captured by the Japanese in early January 1942 and interned at Assumption College.[53]

From those confines, Sister Trinita and the other nuns did whatever they could to help the guerrillas and the POWs. Finding the incriminating letter on the German woman gave the Japanese grounds to arrest Sister Trinita, which they did on April 11, 1944. The charges were spying, aiding the guerrillas, and—incredibly—bolstering the spirits of the Filipinos.

The Japanese interrogated and tortured Sister Trinita beginning on her first day of imprisonment. She endured at least three sessions of the water cure, and the captain in charge of her investigation deprived her of her habit. Still, the nun refused to identify other alleged participants in the underground network, and like Mrs. Beng, nowhere in her postwar narrative did the nun mention sharing a cell with Dorothy Fuentes.[54]

During the long summer of imprisonment, in addition to getting to know her cellmates, Claire Phillips benefited from some soft-hearted guards. One slipped Claire and the rest of the women extra food: a teaspoon of sugar in a twist of newspaper, twenty-one precious peanuts. Another, Sergeant Yamashita, a former patron of the Club Tsubaki, agreed to contact Fely Corcuera and ask her to send in some supplies. He returned with a package of personal care items so Claire and the others could wash with soap and brush their teeth.

These small kindnesses alleviated only a sliver of the horrors detention in Fort Santiago brought. Near the end of June 1944, Claire saw Ramon Amusategui brought in. She waited for an opportune time to talk to him, which presented itself when the prisoners were lined up and counted in front of their cells. Ramon filled her in on the other members of their group. German Eroles had been tortured to the point of near death. The Japanese then sent him out to a hospital for treatment, to make him well enough to undergo additional interrogation. Ramon was sure Horacio Manaloto had not been caught, that he reached safety somewhere in the hills, as had Maria Martinez. He told Claire it would be safe to use their names if she had to.[55]

Claire found this information reassuring and also took comfort knowing Ramon was in the cell next to hers. Two Filipino employees at the Fort helped her pass soap and a piece of towel to Ramon and, from the outside, brought notes back and forth to Fely Corcuera. Claire asked Fely to let Lorenza Amusategui know that her husband was alive and in Fort Santiago. In a return message, Fely reassured Claire that Dian was safe with John Boone, a well-intentioned lie, and, more truthfully, that Boone asked the underground to do what it could to safeguard Claire's welfare while she was in Japanese custody.

More female prisoners crowded into the cell over the summer. When the number exceeded twenty, they all moved into a slightly larger cell. More prisoners meant less food, and Claire and the other women continued losing weight and strength. In mid-August, when it seemed she had been left there to rot, Captain Kobayashi arrived for a special inspection of the cells. Claire called out to him, "You know me . . . Madame Tsubaki. Please will you find out why my investigation has not been finished? I want to have it over with and get out, so I can be with my child."[56]

It was a desperate gamble. Kempeitai investigations—or interrogations—included torture, but Claire decided she would prefer this over endless uncertainty in Fort Santiago. Kobayashi offered no pleasantries to Claire now, yet he agreed to resume her investigation. Before walking away, he informed her Dian was no longer in the apartment at the Club Tsubaki. This piece of news did not alarm Claire, if that had been Kobayashi's intent. She took it as welcome confirmation that Dian was out of reach of the Japanese, safe in the hills with the guerrillas.

The captain sent for Claire the following morning at nine o'clock and told her if she answered all of his questions truthfully, she would be released. Kobayashi then turned the investigation over to another officer and left the room, though Claire understood he would be listening. The officer spoke excellent English, and he came right to the point. He knew about Ramon Amusategui and German Eroles, and he wanted her to identify Papaya. Since Ramon told Claire she could name Maria Martinez, Claire did just that. The answer proved satisfactory.

The next question was about Mutt—Horacio Manaloto. Claire admitted Ramon Amusategui sent Mutt to her as a courier for Cabanatuan; since she never knew his real name she could not provide that information. The Japanese officer asked her about Looter and Everlasting, and Claire produced similar lies. The officer, now out of patience, called in a guard who beat Claire with a bamboo pole. After additional unsatisfactory answers, two guards shoved a hose down her throat, turned on the tap, and flooded her stomach until she passed out: the water cure.

While she was unconscious, the guards stripped Claire down to her underwear, then brought her around by burning her legs with cigars.

At six o'clock, after one more round of water torture and an additional beating, Claire was returned to her cell with a warning not to talk about how she had been treated. A week passed before the interrogation resumed, complete with a new method of torture. Guards placed bullets between Claire's fingers and squeezed.

While Claire recovered from the brutality of her interrogation, she learned General Vicente Lim was in Fort Santiago undergoing daily torture. Born in the Philippines in 1888 to Chinese mestizo parents, Lim was one of the highest ranking military officers in the country. In 1914, he became the first Filipino graduate of West Point, quickly rising through the ranks of the US Army with the elite Philippine Scouts, retiring in 1936 as a lieutenant colonel. He then joined the new Philippine Army at the rank of brigadier general and in 1940 became chief of staff. Commanding the 41st Philippine Division, Lim led his men through some of the toughest fighting at Abucay on Bataan in January 1942. After the surrender, Japanese authorities allowed the general, taken ill during the Bataan Death March, to recuperate in the Philippine General Hospital in Manila.[57]

The hospital stay was a ruse. Occupation authorities tried to recruit General Lim for a new collaborationist government. He demurred. His brother-in-law, Dr. José Rodriguez, exaggerated the severity of his illness, allowing Lim to organize and lead resistance work from his hospital bed. The general worked closely with Tony Escoda, the Manila newspaperman who headed up his own underground group. In June 1944, General MacArthur's headquarters sent orders for Lim and Escoda to make their way to Australia to help plan the Allied invasion of the Philippines. Someone betrayed them, though, and they were arrested and brought to Fort Santiago.

Although she was not tortured as often as General Lim, Claire Phillips understood what he was going through. As soon as her hands started healing, she underwent another interrogation. This time Ramon Amusategui was in the same room; the Kempeitai officer claimed he wanted them to get their stories straight. The first question they were asked concerned the small matter of when Mutt started participating in the network. Claire admitted she never noted the exact date, though she guessed it could have been July or August 1943.

An officer read aloud one of the Cabanatuan letters that had been confiscated. Now Claire understood the danger of keeping written documents: "As he read the missive, I felt like kicking my bruised and battered carcass, for it was an excellent example of how a person continually exposed to the bright face of danger, becomes careless." In the letter Claire described herself as "an American gal, running a Jap night club," pointing out, "all the money I send you comes from the Nips." Before she could offer an explanation, another beating began. When it stopped, the questions started, then the beating resumed. Ramon did not say a word. He was taken back to his cell for his interrogation. Later, as Claire once again recuperated in her cell, the prison grapevine delivered the news that Ramon's torture left one of his legs paralyzed. Sister Trinita began a prayer vigil.[58]

NEWS OF THE ARRESTS AND interrogations in Manila spread through Luzon. Soon, it reached the countryside where Yay Panlilio and Marking's men were hiding out on the Kanan River in Rizal province. Ruperto "Nik-Nik" Batara arrived at the guerrilla headquarters, with "a tale of courage so immense as to be almost incredible." Following the zoning of known guerrilla strongholds on Luzon, occupation authorities began arresting Manilans suspected of underground activities. One of those detained was Roger Moskaira, the husband of Yay's good friend Ding, who had taken Yay in when she fled the Japanese in 1942 after her final broadcast at KZRH radio.[59]

Moskaira was in Fort Santiago and Marking's immediate response was to mount a rescue. Through notes smuggled out of the Fort, Moskaira pleaded for this, afraid he would break under torture. If he talked, the remainder of the Manila network—especially those connected with Antonio Bautista's Civil Liberties Union—would be condemned. Yay's own children, in hiding in the city, would also be at risk, and then the Japanese would head straight for the guerrillas.

Yet Yay remained adamant. There would be no rescue and Roger Moskaira would not be broken by torture. Yay chose Roger to help organize and lead resistance in Manila, and Marking had concurred. Moskaira, she knew, would not talk; he would die first. And he knew, when he signed on for resistance work, that someday he might have to choose death. "Roger came through his crisis," Yay reported after the war. He was beaten for six days in a row, and still refused to talk. "None were betrayed. Punishment became milder. Soon the Japs changed tactics to bribing, offering of reward. This saved his life."[60]

The arrests and tortures of those connected with the underground continued.

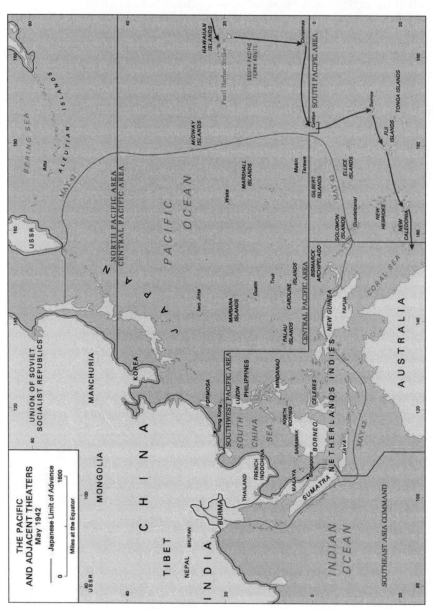

Courtesy of the U.S. Army Center of Military History.

CHAPTER 15

THE WAR RETURNS

B Y SEPTEMBER 1944, Claire Phillips had been a prisoner of the Japanese for more than three months. She tried to win her freedom by pushing forward with her interrogation, but that backfired. As long as she did not tell the Japanese what they wanted to hear, they refused to release her. The interrogation sessions—along with torture—continued.

The prison's dank environment and daily handfuls of food slop added to Claire's deteriorating health. Most debilitating was the persistent diarrhea, and when it became unbearable, she begged to see a doctor. The unsympathetic physician recommended that Claire not eat anything until her system corrected itself. After four days of the enforced fast, her remaining strength failed. She asked the guard for permission to lie down on the cell floor. Sister Trinita slapped her to her senses. "Do you want to die?" the nun asked. "Every time a man lies down in the day time, that's his finish. You know that. Now sit up and take your turn at prayer." Claire complied.[1]

The next time she was taken for interrogation, a guard woke her out of a sound sleep at 2:00 a.m. with a sharp kick in the ribs. Now the questions focused on Claire's alleged connection with the guerrillas. Despite accusations that she had passed "news" from the guerrillas to the prisoners, Claire was fairly certain that the Kempeitai had no concrete proof of her work with John Boone. After another beating failed to force Claire's confession, one of the investigating officers said, "Well, there is nothing else left to do but go ahead with your execution."[2]

A guard blindfolded Claire with an old tea towel and led her out of the room, through a long corridor, down a set of stone steps. From the fetid smell around her, she knew she was headed for Fort Santiago's underground dungeons. When the guard halted Claire, he forced her to her knees and commanded, "Bow your head." She felt the sharp edge of a sword resting against her neck. As it raised up, Claire took what she believed was her last breath, and passed out.[3]

It was a mock execution. Claire came to while a guard dragged her by her heels back to her cell. She settled on the floor to try and get some sleep, and noticed a seventeen-year-old Filipina had been added to the miserable crowd there. Claire smelled the young woman's burned flesh and attempted to alleviate her pain. The Filipina told her story as Claire tended her wounds.

She had been working as a courier for General Vicente Lim, and the Japanese caught her with money and letters destined for his hideout. Though Lim had already been arrested, the Filipina refused to provide additional details about his work. She endured horrific torture. Stripped until almost naked, she was forced to lie on wet sacks that had been spread on the floor. A guard forced an electric rod into her vagina. Every time she would not answer a question about the general, the current was switched on. Claire marveled that the young woman never gave up any information.[4]

During her own interrogation sessions, Claire also refused to talk, or at least refused to talk about anything important. She repeated information the Japanese apparently already had, offering up the names of people she assumed were safe from the Kempeitai. Claire did not know if her interrogators believed her, and after hearing her new cellmate's story, she dreaded being subjected to similar torture.

At noon on September 22, 1944, while returning from the shower, Claire and the other female prisoners heard a deep hum in the air that intensified by the minute. "American planes?" Claire wondered. The guards hustled the women back to their cells and took extra precautions to lock the doors. One woman managed a glimpse out the window and saw, high up in the sky, hundreds of planes darkening the horizon. Confirmation they were American came when the bombs start falling. Claire described the "excited guards" running through the corridors, "shouting for us to lie flat on our stomachs. I cautioned the other women to hold their mouths open and keep their fingers in their ears."[5]

For the American military prisoners, these bombings were like manna from heaven. Jack Wright was on a work detail, digging a latrine for the Japanese guards in Cabanatuan. Around 10:00 a.m. he heard airplane engines and asked one of the guards, "*Beikoku no hikooki ka?*" Are these American planes? The guard said no, then they both watched about three hundred bombers and fighters fly past. Wright knew they were American. "Men cried and laughed and embraced each other," he later remembered.[6]

Irvin Alexander hoed in the camp garden that September morning, looking for any excuse to take a rest. When he heard a strange humming sound he stopped to look around. Seeing nothing, he thought to look up. Alexander blinked "in unbelieving amazement. Directly overhead at an altitude of six to eight thousand feet was the beginning of a wave of airplanes which extended to the east in an irregular line as far as my eyes could see."[7]

Ralph Hibbs, on duty as usual that morning in the tuberculosis ward, heard the planes and felt the *bahay* shaking from the reverberations. "Wave after wave of the little black specks scurried to the west towards Clark Field. Everybody cheered and hugged each other, except me. I stared upward entranced by the formations. Too many disappointments over the years had hardened me to rumors and even the apparent."[8]

The Allies' painstaking island-hopping campaigns—with Japan as their final goal—finally put the Philippine Islands in bombing range.

Claire Phillips probably kept tabs on these events through the information she extracted from her Club Tsubaki customers. By the summer of 1942, after failing to hold Coral Sea and Midway, the war in the Pacific turned into a defensive one for the Japanese. Admiral Chester Nimitz, based in Hawaii, moved his men across the central Pacific, heading for Japan, while General MacArthur came at it from the southwest Pacific, wresting the enemy from each island they occupied.[9]

The wider war that had continued elsewhere in the Pacific theater after the surrender of Corregidor returned to the Philippines in September 1944. Part of Admiral Nimitz's Third Fleet, the Fast Carrier Task Force (TF 38), made up of seventeen fleet and light carriers and commanded by Admiral Marc Mitscher, bombed Japanese air bases, first on Mindanao, then in the Visayas, and finally, as Claire and the others experienced, Luzon. The strikes, which destroyed about five hundred enemy aircraft, were intended to pave the way for MacArthur's return to the Philippines the following month.[10]

José P. Laurel, president of the puppet-regime Republic of the Philippines, had to take care in crafting an official response to the bombing. Despite receiving independence in October 1943, Japan nevertheless retained its occupation forces in the Philippines and continued to pressure Laurel to join the Axis cause. Laurel demurred, claiming his people would not support such a move. Most Filipinos in fact preferred ties with the Americans. Still, until September 1944, the people of the Philippines had had to fend for themselves. The United States seemed very far away.[11]

Now Laurel had to confront the consequences of the return of the war to the Philippines. He had to figure out how to best protect his people, now caught in the middle of this battle. On September 22, Laurel's Proclamation No. 29 went into effect, instituting martial law and setting up nine military districts, with one governor for each, endeavoring to "suppress treason, sedition, disorder and violence." The following day came Proclamation No. 30, in which Laurel declared a state of war between the Philippines and the United States as of September 23, 1944. The Philippines acknowledged a "Pact of Alliance" with Japan to protect the "territorial integrity and independence" of the islands. The president stopped short of committing Filipino troops to actively fight against the Americans. Instead, Laurel issued an Executive Order calling for compulsory labor to shore up the Japanese military machine, and he continued the hunt for guerrillas.[12]

Claire Phillips may not have known any of these political details, yet she saw for herself that the Americans had returned, if only aerially. The temporary morale boost caused by the bombers, however, was tempered by the retaliatory punishment handed out by prison officials. Meals were reduced to one per day. For Claire, this setback was compounded by more dread and uncertainty involving her own case.

A couple of days after the first sighting of American planes, Captain Kobayashi retrieved Claire from her cell. He told her to write down everything she said during the interrogations, and had her sign and fingerprint the document. This concluded her case, and she would not be questioned again until she appeared for a court-martial. Then Kobayashi caught Claire by surprise by informing her of Maria Martinez's capture. All along Claire believed that Maria was safely away from the Kempeitai's reach. Ramon Amusategui had told her so, indicating that it would be all right to name Maria if the torture became too much. Under severe questioning, Claire *had* named her. Now Maria had been arrested and would be brought to Claire's cell that evening.

The Kempeitai picked up Maria on September 13th, about a week before that first air raid. "From the questioning I understood that letters, with money enclosures, sent by me and signed 'Papaya' . . . had been seized as they were being smuggled into Cabanatuan Camp," she recalled. Maria may have been another victim of the carabao cart incident, or perhaps the Japanese learned her whereabouts from someone else. If so, Claire only confirmed information they already had—but she could not be sure.[13]

Upon her arrival in the crowded Fort Santiago cell, Maria updated the women on war news. "The Americans have landed in Leyte," Claire remembered her saying. "A large American task force is headed for northern Luzon." If this was indeed the news Maria passed along, she was premature. General MacArthur would not make his famous landing for another month, and by that time, the circumstances of Claire and Maria would have again changed.[14]

None of the women in that cell knew exactly what the bombings meant for them, or if any American troops who had reportedly invaded the islands would reach them in time to save their lives. Rescue, in fact, would be a close call. In the meantime, like the others, Maria endured interrogations and torture during her time in the Fort. The Japanese believed she was connected to the guerrillas; she refused to admit it.[15]

Sometime around the end of September or beginning of October, a guard removed Claire and Maria from their cell, one at a time. Claire was surprised to find herself reunited with Maria and Ramon Amusategui in the Fort's main office. For a moment they all hoped this meant freedom. Then the trio was handcuffed and hustled in the back of a waiting car. The car traveled along Dewey Boulevard, headed to an unknown destination. Claire had a good view out the window, and what she saw both depressed and exhilarated her. The double lane thoroughfare that ran along the shore of Manila Bay was now denuded of its lush coconut and mango trees, and Claire mourned the loss of their beauty. As the car closed in on the harbor area, she noted the bomb destruction with satisfaction. "Most of the piers were smashed and the Bay was filled with the broken hulks of Jap vessels," she later wrote. All of this had been done by *American* planes.[16]

At last they stopped at Fort McKinley, pulling up to the old Post Exchange, now converted into a courtroom. A panel of three judges presided as charges were read against each of the prisoners. After Ramon, Maria, and Claire individually admitted their guilt, a guard shoved them out into the hallway where, for two hours, they awaited the verdicts. Claire noticed Ramon, his face flushed with fever, could not stop shaking. She thought he could not survive much longer. Eventually a guard emerged from the court room and ordered them into the car. Claire asked about the verdict, and he made a slashing motion across his throat and said, "You *patay*!" It was the Tagalog word for die. Bilibid Prison, the guard informed them, would be their place of execution. Maria started to cry. Ramon did not blink. Claire, however, felt an odd sense of relief. As she later remembered, "I figured that death would bring a speedy end to my seemingly endless ordeal of starvation, torture and illness."[17]

At Bilibid, Claire received her prisoner number: 920. She and Maria (number 921) stopped in the shower room on their way to the women's cell. In full view of the guards, the two women stripped, washed, and changed into uniforms made from men's hospital pajamas. Maria wept through the humiliation, but Claire was too angry to cry. Their cell, similar in size to the one at Fort Santiago, had a large screened window and mercifully few bugs. Ramon occupied the next cell, and Claire noticed the move had not done him any good. On her fourth day in Bilibid, she did not hear him answer roll call. When the guards ordered the prisoners to stand facing the back of their cells, Claire knew what had happened. She risked a quick look to the side and caught sight of an inert body being carried out on a stretcher. She recognized the telltale red beard. Ramon Amusategui was dead.[18]

For the next two weeks, Claire and Maria remained in their cell, forced to kneel in silence on the floor from 5:00 a.m. until 9:00 p.m. These excruciating days were punctuated with two roll calls and one fifteen-minute exercise period. Then three Filipinas, caught bringing money and supplies to the guerrillas, joined them. "The third week," Claire later wrote, "Florence Smith, an attractive young American mestiza was placed in our cell. Florence and I became good friends immediately. While the others cried and complained, Florence and I exchanged recipes, and we let our imagination flow freely."[19]

Like the other women, Florence Ebersole Smith had been arrested for helping the guerrillas. Born in northern Luzon in 1915, Florence's mother was a Filipina and her father, Charles Ebersole, was a US Army veteran of the Spanish-American War. Before the war started, Florence worked for Major E. Carl Englehart at US Army Intelligence (G-2) Headquarters at Fort Santiago, where she may have run into Yay Panlilio. In August 1941 Florence married Charles Edward Smith, a chief electrician's mate in the US Navy, who was killed in action the following February.

Florence remained in Manila after USAFFE retreated to Bataan, and because of her racial heritage she managed to avoid internment when the Japanese occupied the city in January 1942. She took a job with the

Japanese-controlled Philippine Liquid Fuel Distributing Union, where one of her duties was to write names on coupon books for those who had been approved to receive fuel. "I was told that one reason I was hired was because my handwriting was neat and legible," she later recalled. Florence worked with the guerrillas by falsifying documents that allowed them to receive coupons, ensuring they had enough fuel to operate their vehicles.[20]

Like other Allied sympathizers in Manila, Florence did as much as possible to help the Americans. In addition to forging fuel documents for the guerrillas, she collected donations for the prisoners of war, but relied on a courier to pick them up and deliver them to the camps. She never knew the man's name, never asked him if he worked with anyone else. Florence also brought food and did laundry for the Santo Tomas internees. After the Japanese arrested Florence, they confined her to a military substation for about a week, where she was interrogated and tortured with electrical devices. She was transferred to Bilibid, where she met Claire Phillips, and where the questioning sessions stretched into November.

DURING THE LATE SUMMER OF 1944, as the Japanese continued their search for American supporters in Manila, they zeroed in on the Malate Convent. A young Filipino working at Fort Santiago regularly passed along information to the Apostolic Delegate of Manila, the Pope's diplomatic representative in the Philippines. The spy discovered the Japanese had drawn up an arrest list that included the names of the Malate priests and Miss U. Father Lalor alerted Peggy Utinsky that the Japanese were after her again. He told her that he would send someone to pick her up and take her to John Boone's guerrillas in the hills.

Peggy had prepared for this eventuality, crafting an escape plan after she was released from the hospital the previous November. Around that time, an American woman approached her on the street, identifying herself as the wife of a Filipino named Soriano, a member of Boone's guerrillas. Soriano knew about Peggy and her work, and he wanted to come and see her the next time he managed to get to Manila. Peggy agreed, and Soriano came to her apartment on his next trip. While there, he said, "When you know you are going to be taken, come to us." He gave her specific instructions on where to go on the Pasig River, how to engage an interpreter, and how to arrange the passage to Orion.

Now, in September 1944, Peggy set the plan in motion. She encountered Lorenza Amusategui on a Manila street and told her she would be leaving the city soon to join the guerrillas. Lorenza was relieved by the news. She had long considered Peggy's combative personality and erratic behavior a threat to the safety of the Manila underground workers. As far as Lorenza was concerned, they would all be safer with Peggy out of the way.[21]

Peggy's departure from Manila was complicated by the fact she would not be traveling alone. When she had learned of Claire Phillips's arrest back in May, she became concerned about Dian's welfare. It is not clear why. Despite the fact that they were both members of the underground, the two women were not close. They had limited personal contact. The most time they spent together was probably when Claire was in the hospital in 1943, though neither woman ever discussed it in any detail. This may have been where Peggy first met Dian, if someone brought the little girl to visit her mother. Or perhaps Claire talked about her daughter while she was in the hospital and that was how Peggy came to know her. In any case, "Because there was no place for her to go," was the reason Peggy gave for taking custody of Dian. Even this was not quite true.[22]

After the Japanese closed the Club Tsubaki following Claire's arrest, Fely Corcuera opened a new bar. Peggy tracked her down there to find out what happened to Dian. Fely told her that the little girl was staying with Corcuera relatives in Kamuning, Quezon City, about eight miles north of Manila. Peggy and Fely both knew, though, that Claire believed Dian would be safest in the hills with John Boone's guerrillas. The arrangement in Kamuning was not working out as well as Fely thought it would. While Dian easily blended in with Fely's family, they began experiencing hostility from neighbors, who considered Fely and Flora Corcuera a bit too cozy with the Japanese, presumably because of their nightclub work. When Peggy offered to take Dian to Boone, Fely acquiesced.[23]

Anxious to remain one life-saving step ahead of the Japanese, Peggy moved quickly that September morning after Father Lalor's message arrived. "I scurried around getting ready, trying to keep the baby from being scared," she later wrote, with her habit of referring to five-year-old Dian as a baby. "But she balked at leaving behind a small yellow kitten which I had taken in because it was lost and hungry. The only way to keep her quiet was to take along that damned cat." It was fortunate that Peggy relented so quickly because two hours after she and Dian left the apartment, the Japanese arrived to arrest her. By then, Peggy, Dian, and the kitten had already been to the Malate Convent to pick up the supplies the priests packed for the guerrillas. As Peggy later explained, "I did not intend to go to them empty-handed when their need was so great."[24]

Peggy's good friend Cam Lee had waited for her at the convent, determined to help her get across Manila Bay to Orion, as per Captain Soriano's instructions. Lee fussed at Peggy for bringing along not only a little girl, but a kitten as well, because the three of them traveling together would attract too much attention. To throw off any Japanese who might have seen Peggy and her entourage leave the apartment, Lee took charge of Dian and the kitten. The Japanese, he believed, would not look twice at a Chinese man with a child.

Taking different routes, they all met up at the Pasig River, where Peggy arrived with the Filipino interpreter the good priests at Malate had provided, plus the *carretela* of supplies for the guerrillas. This was only one small part of the trip. They still had to get from the river across Manila Bay to Orion, and Lee could not locate a *banca*—a small rowboat—to take them. The best he could negotiate was a trip to nearby Abucay in a long sailboat called a *batel*. This made Peggy nervous because there were too many other passengers in the vessel, and she worried one of them might recognize her. Lee insisted it was more dangerous for her to wait for a *banca* to Orion, so he settled Peggy, Dian, and the kitten in the *batel* and bade them good-bye.

None of this set well with Peggy. The *batel* would not reach Abucay until after dark, making it more difficult for her to spot any danger before it hit. The other passengers stared at Peggy, particularly one man who kept his eyes on her until he went over to talk to the boatman. This raised Peggy's suspicions—the two men glancing at her and talking with lowered voices in Tagalog. As darkness fell, so too did rain, which Peggy knew would make the next part of her journey all the more difficult.

Then a new danger appeared, one Peggy had not anticipated: that same humming sound Claire Phillips had heard from inside Fort Santiago. "Airplanes! At first I was tremendously thrilled. At last! At last! The Yanks had come back to bomb Manila," Peggy later wrote. She wanted to scream her happiness that the Americans had finally returned, but she realized the bobbing *batel* was an easy target for the bombers. "The Yanks were on the march again and that was swell, but I did not want to be killed by a Yank bomb. That would really be too much."[25]

After the planes flew off, Peggy managed to catch some sleep until the *batel* halted to deposit its passengers on shore. As she prepared to leave the vessel, however, the boatman stopped her, saying she and Dian had to stay put. Before Peggy mustered up an argument, a *banca* slipped alongside the larger boat. Sitting inside, along with a few other men, was the Filipino who had watched her so closely earlier in the day. He ordered Peggy to bring Dian and get in; everything else she brought could be left on the *batel*. "I didn't know where I was going. I didn't know why. And I was scared to death. I was the only white woman for miles around." There was nothing else she could do except comply.[26]

Soon the *banca* maneuvered into a spot along the shore, and its passengers disembarked and began an hour-long march through a bamboo forest. The trails were slippery with the recent rain, and as she slogged on, Peggy started to feel sorry for herself: "My escorts were the most villainous specimens I ever saw and I thought my time had come. Nobody who looked like that could possibly be a friend." She had done everything she could to avoid execution in Fort Santiago and now, she believed, she would end up dead and forgotten in a remote jungle.[27]

More armed men joined the procession, each looking as vicious as the next. The group stopped at a bamboo hut that contained a homemade candle, a table, and one chair, which Peggy was given to sit on while she was questioned. Since she did not know the loyalties of the person interrogating her, she did not know the kinds of answers she should provide. First she handed over her papers. When asked what business she had in the hills, Peggy said, "I've come to look after the sick Filipinos in the mountains. I was afraid the Americans would come to Manila. It is safer for me here."[28]

When the interrogator threatened to shoot her because she was Lithuanian, Peggy realized to her great relief that she had fallen in with the guerrillas. She showed a note from John Boone that she had hidden in the hem of her skirt. That, along with the fact she knew the names of Boone's wife and child, convinced the man she was one of them. The guerrillas marched Peggy and Dian back to the shore where all the supplies Peggy brought from Manila awaited reloading on a *banca* that would take them to Orion.

By then the American bombers had returned, and the little boat docked in Orion next to a cargo ship the Japanese had outfitted with machine guns to shoot at the planes. As Peggy scrambled out of the banca, she fell and broke a bone in her foot. She started to cry and noticed a young Filipino staring at her, so she said the code phrase, "American Boy." Minutes later, Captain Soriano came running toward her. "And there I lay in a heap, practically in touching distance of the Jap cargo ship, clutching the brown baby and the yellow kitten. And no camera nearer than Manila! They do these things a lot better in the movies. I stopped crying and began to laugh."[29]

Several of Soriano's men moved Peggy and Dian to the safety of one of Orion's churches, run by a Filipino priest working with the guerrillas. The second night of their stay, two guerrillas joined them, one of whom was Warren Hendry, a Louisianan who had come to the Philippines with the US Army Air Corps. Over plates full of beans, they swapped information. Peggy filled them in on what had been happening in Manila and what she knew about the progress of the war outside of the Philippines.

The young men described life with the guerrilla forces: ragtag organizations consisting of Americans who ducked out of the Death March or escaped one of the prison camps, Filipinos who wanted the Japanese out of their country, and even Negritos, local tribesmen who disliked all outsiders. They all had little in the way of supplies, even weapons. "Yet the guerrillas were killing ten Japanese for every one of their own men who died," Peggy claimed after the war. "They had learned to fight like animals or like devils. And when they were captured, they died without revealing anything they knew."[30]

The two young men departed, carrying a message from Peggy for John Boone, letting him know she arrived well-equipped with supplies. Three nights later a guerrilla contingent of twenty-eight men showed up to take Peggy, Dian, and the provisions to a safer place in the hills. They were led by Valencia, the interrogator who threatened, just a few days earlier, to shoot Peggy. The men sat her in a bamboo chair lashed to some poles so she would not have to walk on her broken foot, and slogged through the forest in a heavy downpour. For two days they climbed up Tala Ridge to reach the headquarters of the 2nd Guerrilla Infantry Regiment, part of the Bataan Military District headed by John Boone and commanded by Lieutenant Colonel Victor Abad. A barrio situated at the northern edge of the Bataan peninsula, Tala is about halfway between Abucay and Mount Natib, on the lower edge of a small mountain.

The lieutenant colonel welcomed Peggy with a warm handshake, and said, "We need you. We need you badly. Many of my regiment are sick or wounded." Despite her broken foot, Peggy spent a full day treating everything from typhoid to jungle ulcers to gunshot wounds. When sounds of weapons fire interrupted her ministrations, Valencia ordered Peggy carried out to the cane field to hide. The Japanese, however, were not attacking. It was only some guerrillas holding an impromptu, unsanctioned target practice. This was Peggy's first taste of life in the hills.[31]

The next day, after doing all she could to treat Abad's men, Peggy headed off for a visit to John Boone's headquarters. It was quite a production. A retinue of guerrillas carried her aloft in her bamboo chair, with Dian and the kitten in her lap. A typhoon prevented her from reaching the place, so Boone came to Peggy's shelter in the storm. As Peggy later remembered, "He was a young man, about thirty-four, with reddish brown hair, blue eyes, a pleasant personality."[32]

"Thank God for you, Miss U," Boone said to her by way of a greeting. "You are needed here." Despite the late hour, they talked for a while, but about what Peggy never disclosed. Some of the conversation likely concerned their mutual acquaintance, Claire Phillips, and the Manila underground. Whatever the topic of conversation, Peggy was favorably impressed with Boone. She regarded him as an educated man, a born leader. Boone recognized Peggy's worth by commissioning her as a brevet second lieutenant and sending her back to work with Lieutenant Colonel Abad at Tala. There was more fighting in the vicinity, he told her, so that was where Peggy's nursing skills were required.

"Being a guerrilla nurse is like nothing else on earth. I was needed all right. In fact, I was the entire medical staff for the whole outfit," Peggy later asserted. There was no hospital, only hastily constructed bamboo huts to shelter the patients. "As for guerrilla nursing, all you can do is give the indicated medicine—if you have it—and trust in God. Sometimes you can't even do that much." She cared for the two hundred men of Abad's regiment while on the move, twenty new locations in a thirty-day period, despite a broken foot and a variety of illnesses. Through each of the relocations, most of them hastily executed, Peggy also looked out for Dian. The little girl learned how to conduct herself in these new surroundings. Every time Peggy said to her, "Come on, Honey, we've got to go," Dian picked up her cat and followed without a fuss. Because of her sober obedience, she became the darling of the men, who took turns carrying her on their shoulders when they could not find a horse for her to ride.[33]

Peggy made do like the men, eating vines and leaves, supplemented from time to time with monkey and boar meat. She did not thrive: "Though I had not seen a mirror, I could tell that I was skin and bone. In fact, I got so thin that I had to give up carrying a .45 and pack a .38 instead." She could not get rid of the lice in her hair, and her clothes rotted with mildew. Just when it seemed that Peggy had fallen into a routine, however hectic, Dian contracted pneumonia. The child was already in a weakened physical condition from malnutrition and the dark, humid environment. Peggy decided that to save Dian's life, she had to move her to a healthier location. An American guerrilla, Lieutenant Colonel Frank Loyd, had a camp 2,500 feet up higher in the hills. Peggy thought this would be the ideal spot. Abad ordered a dozen of his men to accompany Peggy and Dian there.[34]

Loyd, a career army officer nicknamed The Professor, had arrived in the Philippines in June 1940, assigned as Provost Marshal at Fort McKinley. After the Japanese attack in December 1941, Loyd was named Chief Instructor of the Philippine Constabulary, which had just been folded into USAFFE. On January 2, 1942, along with others from Fort McKinley, Loyd evacuated to Bataan. During the final desperate battles in early April, Loyd found himself behind enemy lines, separated from his men, and he caught up with some Americans in time to hear about Bataan's surrender. Rather than give himself up at Mariveles, Loyd decided to head for Corregidor. After he saw how the Japanese were bombarding the Rock, he concluded he would be better off if he made his way to Manila. From there he would find some way to sail to Australia.[35]

On his way to the city, Loyd met up with a few other Americans. They were all trying to reach Colonel Claude Thorp's fledgling guerrilla organization, assuming he could get them to Australia. To avoid attracting the enemy's attention, Loyd sheltered with a family in the barrio of Tala, alongside a trail up in the mountain, while the rest of the soldiers scattered into different homes in town. Loyd, convinced General MacArthur would return any day with reinforcements, decided to stay put until that happened.

When he heard about Corregidor's surrender in May, Loyd's optimism collapsed. He worried that his continued presence in Tala would endanger the Filipinos, so he built himself a hut in the jungle about a two-hour walk from the barrio, across the Orani River. Peggy, in her Lithuanian guise, had been close by then, working with the Philippine Red Cross at the Kalaguiman Hospital in Samal, near the town of Orani. Her request for medicine was a constant source of irritation to the Japanese Major Nakai, commander of the Orani garrison.[36]

In September 1942, Nakai knew Frank Loyd was at large in the vicinity and stepped up efforts to find him. The Americans in the area left Tala to form a guerrilla organization, ending up with a group of Negritos in the Zambales Mountains. Loyd, incapacitated by illness, made a narrow escape from Japanese patrols on October 19th, and decided to make his way to Colonels James Collier and Gyles Merrill in the Zambales Mountains.[37]

During his journey in early February 1943, Loyd crossed paths with John Boone, who filled him in about the guerrilla operations. Boone already had a jungle headquarters on the side of Mount Malasimbo, north of Dinalupihan. He reported to Lieutenant Edwin Ramsey, who had been under Colonel Thorp's command until Thorp's capture in 1942, in the same series of raids Loyd managed to evade.

Loyd considered joining Boone, but nagging concerns about Boone's lax security and impulsive actions convinced him to push on, even as increased Japanese raids during the early spring of 1943 made traveling difficult. In April, Loyd found an isolated spot up in the mountains, and proceeded to build a camp with a few Americans he had collected along the way. They would stay there until they could figure out a way to get to Australia. They needed help getting food and other supplies while they waited to escape. Loyd re-established contact with Boone, who linked him to the Manila network run through the Club Tsubaki. Loyd and his men also worked with Dinalupihan's priest, Father Eduardo Cabanguis, to courier information and supplies between their hideout and Manila.[38]

Their stay dragged on, and the uncertainty of their situation wore on everyone's nerves. To strengthen security, Frank Loyd and Major Royal Reynolds left the encampment in December 1943, moving another 1,800 feet up into the mountains. That location proved difficult as the Japanese stepped up their efforts to flush out the guerrillas, making supply runs into Manila all the more dangerous. Loyd and Reynolds were saved from certain starvation by the return of American bombers in September 1944. The Japanese shifted their attention to defense against these aerial attacks, and Loyd and the other guerrillas prepared for General MacArthur's imminent return.[39]

It was in this state of waiting that Peggy Utinsky found Loyd when she arrived at his encampment in the hills. It was not, perhaps, the best place for a woman and sick child, but it was the only thing Peggy could think of to save Dian's life.

YAY PANLILIO, STILL IN THE hills of Rizal province, played a similar waiting game. "Up in the hills the fighters were trying not to surrender," she remembered. Things had not been easy for Marking's force. "There was hunger, sickness.... Silence. Loneliness that reached to the stars. Bickering, back-biting, quick suspicion, blind rage, hate." Yay did not sugar-coat her experiences; the years of fear, uncertainty, and inactivity had taken a toll. That changed, however, in the summer of 1944. Supplies from General MacArthur's Australia headquarters made their way via submarine into the southern Philippine Islands and up into Luzon. Medicine, clothing, magazines, and chocolate—especially chocolate—worked wonders on the guerrillas' morale. More precious, though, was the arrival of a radio, which connected Marking with other guerrilla leaders and allowed him to transmit information to Australia.

In search of good reception for the radio, Yay and Marking led the guerrillas further up into the hills. It was there, working with the radio in the third week of September, they spotted the American planes: "The roar suddenly juggernauted over the hollow, swooping down from the heights, through the low-lying mist, down to the lowlands, away. Distantly we could hear rolling detonations." More of their couriers risked the five-day trip to Manila. Information and supplies had to flow quickly between the city and the guerrillas now that US forces were getting close. Yay worried that the Filipinos' enthusiasm for the Americans' return would lead to careless talk and actions. When that happened, the Japanese would clamp down, increasing arrests, torture, and executions.[40]

As Yay realized just how dangerous Manila had become, she no longer trusted that her twelve-year-old daughter Rae was safe in the convent where she had spent the last two years. Marking ordered his men to retrieve the girl, and when she arrived in camp, she teamed up with Marking's son, Cote. Yay observed that the children "took to guerrilla life like ducks to water." Rae and Cote grew as close as brother and sister, and Yay took comfort in her belief they were safer in the hills than in the city.[41]

On October 20th, General MacArthur waded ashore on Red Beach on the island of Leyte, wedged between Samar and Cebu islands, about 575 miles southeast of Manila. Over 100,000 troops of the Sixth Army participated in the invasion, supported by air and sea assaults. The battle for Leyte raged for sixty-seven days as the 80,000 Japanese garrisoned there fought to hold the island, losing well over half of their men in the process. American losses were considerably lighter, about 3,500. Ten days before Christmas, after conquering Leyte, the Americans moved on to Mindoro, a key spot from which to launch an invasion of Luzon.

When a message arrived via radio in October about MacArthur's landing on Leyte, it contained no orders for Marking. He itched to fight through to Leyte and join up with MacArthur, but Yay told him the time was not yet right. His main responsibility was still the radio, she reminded him; transmitting information was vital. Though Marking did not agree, he stayed put.

Two of MacArthur's liaison officers, Captain George Miller and Lieutenant Brooke Stoddard, reached Marking's camp on November 17, 1944, Marking's birthday. Miller had been briefed in Australia by General Courtney Whitney, head of intelligence for the Southwest Pacific Theater, and sent to the Philippines via submarine in October. Miller intended to rendezvous with Russell Volkmann, an American guerrilla in northern Luzon. He altered his plan because of intense enemy activity in that area. Miller linked up with Bernard Anderson instead, then moved on to Marking. Stoddard, a 1937 Princeton graduate and former banker, enlisted in the army in 1941 where he received commando training. In the fall of 1944, he joined Miller's Luzon mission.[42]

The two officers brought orders. The guerrillas must continue their surveillance and intelligence work and train men to blow up bridges. "Miller and Stoddard were the turning point," Yay later observed. "Marking and the two American officers were forever in a huddle, like the football hero and a couple of fussing coaches just before the big game." Well into December, Marking's men kept busy setting up radio transmitters throughout Rizal and Laguna, preparing for the invasion.[43]

Still, Marking wanted to fight, and as always, Yay counseled patience, something she was losing: "Marking and Miller decided between them that the Net Control Station [NCS] should be farther back, out of danger of a possible raid by the Japs. I was fast losing my grip, tired, accomplishing little, nervously irritable." Marking put Yay in charge of the NCS, sparing her the endless movement of camps, keeping her away from the battles that might begin any time. With her daughter by her side, Yay commanded seventeen guerrillas and eleven radio operators. "For the first time in the history of the outfit, I was on my own to strike a new camp and hold it." Yay understood the importance of the work. MacArthur's headquarters needed as much intelligence as possible to minimize casualties during the invasion of Luzon. Still, she was relieved to be away from Marking, his restless energy and eruptions of temper.[44]

SIX WEEKS AFTER THE SIGHTING of the American bombers, Claire Phillips was still in Bilibid Prison. Every day, from 5:00 a.m. until 9:00 p.m., she and the other women were forced to kneel on the floor of their cell. She and Florence Smith joked and flirted a bit with the prison mess personnel who delivered food. Sometimes they received extra tea for their efforts. Once a day—if the Americans had not bombed—the prisoners hustled outside to a courtyard for roll call and fifteen minutes of exercise. On November 22nd, one of the guards called out Claire's prison number. "He repeated the number distinctly, but even then I hesitated a second before I made the required response," she later recalled.[45]

The guard led her out of the cell block and into another prison building for her court-martial. "I pulled myself together and tried to walk steadily, although my weak legs refused to support me." Claire bowed before the five judges seated at the table, and through an interpreter one of them asked if she had anything to say in her defense. At first she could not think of anything to say. The interpreter slapped her and ordered her to respond, so she said, "I was only sending medicine and food to men who were less fortunate than I. I would have done this regardless of their nationality." One of the judges asked if Claire would have provided assistance to the Japanese. "I have befriended many Japanese, and have made many Japanese friends during the war," she replied. The judge did not believe Claire, and concluded she only made friends with the Japanese so she could carry out her resistance work. On behalf of the judge's displeasure, the interpreter punched her in the jaw and ordered her to plead guilty or not guilty.[46]

Claire sensed the futility of any further pleading with the judges. She admitted her guilt. As she was taken back to her cell, the interpreter let her know she would find out her sentence by the following day at the latest. Maria Martinez was next, marched out of the cell and returned a short time later, also to await sentencing. Early in the morning, a guard took both women, tied them together, then shoved them into a car. They were warned to keep their heads down. When Claire tried to look out the window to see where the car was headed, a pistol butt cracked her over the head.[47]

This time the two women ended up at the final stop of their incarceration journey: the Women's Correctional Institution located in Mandaluyong, just outside Manila. The large round structure had been built on an eighteen-hectare stretch of property in 1929. Except for the guards, women held all of the staffing positions. Claire and Maria exited the car and entered the prison, where a Japanese guard read their sentence. They received twelve years at hard labor. Any attempt at escape would be punished with a doubling of the time, which would be finished in Japan. For the duration, the guard said, "You are to have no outside contacts. No mail. No visitors. No food sent in to you." With that, Claire and Maria were turned over to the jurisdiction of the prison superintendent to begin serving their sentences. Although the rules sounded harsh, both women must have felt relieved to be in a prison that did not subject its inmates to interrogation and torture.[48]

Arrests of suspected underground members continued through the late fall of 1944. As he had anticipated, Father Buttenbruch was picked up again, on Taft Avenue on November 13th, as Manila was subjected to a second day of particularly intense American bombing. Buttenbruch, still a busy man with a variety of aid projects both sanctioned and illicit, refused to allow the raids to deter him. He took a morning meeting at Manila's City Hall with Engracio Fabre, director of the Bureau of Religious Affairs, probably to discuss the necessary permits for an emergency hospital he planned to open.[49]

That done, the German priest traveled about a mile and a half down Taft Avenue to attend a noon luncheon at the Philippine Women's University. It was now functioning mostly as a hospital, and Buttenbruch wanted to discuss using some of their beds for his proposed site. In the afternoon, as an air raid siren blasted, the priest was back at City Hall for further discussion of his plans. He later disappeared somewhere along Taft Avenue after leaving the municipal building when the all-clear sounded.

The streets teemed with Japanese soldiers and members of the Makapili, any one of which may have been on the lookout for Buttenbruch. Recently established in November 1944 and known officially as the Alliance of Philippine Patriots, the Makapili served as a pro-Japanese Philippine military force, not an official army. Buttenbruch probably ended up at the Cortabitarte Garrison, the Southern Manila Branch of the Military Police. The Kempeitai had arrested too many people for Fort Santiago to hold, so the Japanese requisitioned a pair of houses in the Malate district. One was turned into Kempeitai offices while the other was used for the detention and interrogation of prisoners, most of them confined to three cells that had been partitioned in the garage.

Fermin Miyasaki, a Filipino-Japanese working at Cortabitarte as an interpreter for the Kempeitai, took particular notice of the tall and stocky bespectacled prisoner with his distinctive white hair and long white cassock. Conchita Liboro Benitez, daughter-in-law of the president of the Philippine Women's University, heard that Buttenbruch, along with her uncle José Araneta and Josefa Escoda, was executed there in early December 1944. They were all betrayed, she believed, by a Kempeitai interpreter known as Mr. Hiroshi.[50]

No one knew for certain, but if Father Buttenbruch was in a group of prisoners along with Araneta and Escoda, he likely remained alive until early January 1945. He may have been transferred to the main prison at Fort Santiago to be questioned by Captain Yanase Shoichi, who had been in charge of his previous interrogation. Others in the underground heard about these prisoners until sometime during the first week of January 1945, when they were removed from the Fort and disappeared. Removals, transfers, disappearances—all became common during the last weeks of the occupation.[51]

ONE SUCH TRANSFER INVOLVED Gladys Savary's nephew, Edgar Gable, who let her know the prisoners were being moved out of

Cabanatuan to an unknown destination. Gladys noticed more and more trucks traveling through Manila carrying American POWs, usually depositing them at Bilibid Prison while arrangements were made for their final destinations. In one of those trucks Gladys saw a young man she knew had been in Edgar's barracks. She stopped by Bilibid Prison as often as she could, hoping to catch a glimpse at the prisoners there, hoping to find her nephew. She did not.

Gladys spent the summer of 1944 hoarding food in anticipation of a drawn-out last stand by the Japanese. She and her friends devised a code to use during their telephone conversations so they could relay the latest war news. While Claire Phillips had relied on baking phrases to organize the collection and distribution of relief supplies, Gladys's circle talked about playing bridge. Gladys was not good at this kind of thing; she forgot about the coded bridge language and was often left wondering if she missed out on a tournament.

The best news, though, did not come from the radio. It arrived directly from the skies over Manila. On September 21st, Gladys went to the market first thing in the morning, as usual, even though this daily ritual had long ago become an exercise in futility—there was rarely anything worth buying. Then she headed into her garden to pick some lima beans to fix for lunch. The first airplane sounds barely registered. The Japanese had informed Manilans of two days of scheduled air and ground defense maneuvers. Gladys assumed they had commenced. A plane burst into flames and the local radio station issued an air-raid alert. This was not a practice drill; the Americans had returned.

The neighborhood children were in Gladys's house for their bi-weekly kindergarten class, and she helped the teacher gather them into the stairway cubbyhole, piled with pillows and mattresses. With the little ones safe, Gladys dashed off to watch the action. "It was a wonderful show," she wrote that night in her journal. "Who *could* have had such a wonderful sense of humor as to crash the Jap party? They bombed all morning, intermittently. In our part of town it was Nichols Airfield, and it was very close. So close that the swoosh of bombs blew our skirts sky-high if we were moving about—as I was, constantly."[52]

The parents came for their kindergarteners at noontime, after the American planes finished dropping their payloads. Although the interior of Gladys's house sustained some damage, all of the children were fine. Everyone was in such high spirits that Gladys organized an impromptu picnic. So far, the worst to happen was the cutting of utilities, which did not bother Gladys. She could not wait for the bombers to return.

Over the next couple of days, the Manila radio station blared the news that a state of war existed between the Philippine Republic and the United States. Following the morning raid on September 21st, the American bombers returned again in the afternoon, targeting Japanese ships docked at Manila Bay and planes at various airfields. The next day they concentrated on the port area and the Japanese embassy. During the next few weeks, American planes bombed the Philippines, almost always taking out military targets but occasionally hitting civilian locations, causing damage as well as casualties. Japanese authorities tried to use this to turn public opinion against the Americans. Most Filipinos endured the bombings, cheering on the Americans as much as they dared.

Rumors about the progress of the war made their way into Bilibid's isolation ward, but nothing was confirmed until the day in September 1944 when Bill Berry saw the American planes with his own eyes. It was laundry day—which sounded a bit too grand for the few clothing items Berry owned and the crude washing facilities—and the raid took him by surprise. "When I first saw the carrier-based planes overhead," he later wrote, "I didn't realize that they were ours until they started diving and bombing. That was exciting."[53]

The thrill of seeing those American planes for the first time set up high hopes for the prisoners. In Cabanatuan, Jack Wright did not see any more of them for three weeks: "That was a period of excited anticipation. We talked constantly of the ways in which we thought we might be released. We made plans to get back with the fighting troops. We made plans for our return to the States. We planned every minute and every inch of the campaign to reconquer the Philippine Islands." This was exactly what the Japanese worried about, so they stepped up the transfer of prisoners out of Cabanatuan, with hundreds departing throughout October. All able-bodied POWs were to be shipped to Japan as slave labor. Bill Berry estimated that, every week or two, about fifteen hundred prisoners were sent to Manila, where they temporarily stayed in Bilibid before embarking to Japan.[54]

Most of Jack Wright's closest friends left on October 12th, and he followed in four days. Edgar Gable probably left around the same time. Irvin Alexander had been expecting the transfer: "A few of my close friends used to discuss the advisability of remaining in the Philippines or going with the detail to Japan in view of the rapid approach of the American forces. Most of us were of the opinion that the Nips would take such steps as might be available to prevent us from falling into the hands of our own troops." The Japanese only allowed the sickest prisoners, along with some medical personnel and support staff, to remain in Cabanatuan. Alexander did not like his odds for surviving this final move, so he wrote a farewell letter to his wife and left it with a friend who was staying behind. Still, he tried to look for a bright spot: no more exhausting farm labor, no more brutal guards, a chance for a new experience in Bilibid Prison before heading to parts unknown.[55]

About five hundred extremely ill men, along with Dr. Ralph Hibbs, watched as hundreds of their compatriots were trucked out of Cabanatuan. By December 1944 only thirty-five medical officers remained. Because Hibbs had been treating the most severe cases, he was one of the last of the medical personnel in the camp. With the final departures, James Duckworth now took charge and named Hibbs his adjutant.

As the American prisoners were moved around, Japanese military personnel also shifted, getting into position for their final confrontation with the Allied forces. In mid-October 1944, the Japanese Navy moved into Gladys Savary's compound in Pasay, forcing her to leave the house she had been renting since the summer of 1942. Although they initially agreed to give Gladys two weeks to find a new place to stay, they reneged and insisted on immediate occupancy. "The Navy of his Imperial Majesty has need of these houses," Captain Toda informed Gladys when he showed up at her home, interrupting her lunch. "There is a war on which we must win, and you must give up your houses."[56]

Fortified with the cocktails she drank with her meal, Gladys said, "What kind of Navy have you? In my country the Navy does not need houses to sleep in, they sleep on their ships. Perhaps it is true you have no more ships?" The captain was so enraged by Gladys's impertinence that she made him coffee to try and calm him. He became angry all over again when she refused to take a cup out to his driver, saying she did not serve servants. Toda warned her that her attitude would get her in trouble and told her he would be back in the morning to move into her house. It did not quite work out that way. One of the captain's aides ended up moving into Gladys's place after Toda's ship was sunk in Manila Harbor.[57]

Gladys moved in with Helge and Dorothy Janson on October 22nd, two days after General MacArthur brought American troops back to the Philippines via the Leyte invasion. Heartened by the US bombings and the Leyte invasion, Gladys anticipated the end of the war. It came slowly. Throughout November and December 1944, she kept looking for the Americans; instead she watched conditions in Manila further deteriorate. The Japanese picked up anyone for any reason at all. Helge Janson received a warning that his blatant pro-American sympathies were about to get him in big trouble. Some Japanese soldiers pulled Gladys from her bicycle and questioned her for hours before letting her go. They never told her exactly what she had been suspected of.

CHAPTER 16

BLOODLETTING
AND LIBERATION

A T THE WOMEN'S CORRECTIONAL INSTITUTION WITH MARIA
Martinez, Claire Phillips filled out her prison registration forms
in the name of Dorothy Claire Fuentes. During her admittance search,
a prison trustee found the wristwatch Claire managed to keep hidden
throughout her prison ordeal, the last nice thing she owned. When the
woman insisted Claire surrender it to the prison safe, Claire demanded to
speak with the superintendent, Mrs. Garcia. Nothing Claire said about how
she and Maria had been helping military prisoners roused any sympathy in
the woman, who reminded Claire and Maria they were prisoners just like
the other women and would be treated as such: "You will receive no special
privileges, so don't ask for any." Mrs. Garcia kept Claire's watch, telling her
she would get it back upon release, then dismissed both prisoners.[1]

After relinquishing their clothing, Claire and Maria donned the required
prison garb of faded denim blue sacks marked with "M.P." They were taken

to a dormitory of designated military prisoners—though neither woman apparently caught the irony—and put in a room with several other women where they all swapped stories. One cellmate Claire described as a "pretty American girl named Margie," was probably Margaret Folsom, serving the last month of a two-year sentence for escaping from Santo Tomas. Another may have been Pauline Costigan, a Filipina married to an American reservist who had been recalled to active duty in Manila in December 1941. The couple ended up in Batangas, in southwestern Luzon, working with a guerrilla unit. For over two years, Pauline served as a runner, until her capture at the end of March 1944. She endured the water cure three times as the Japanese attempted to force her to talk about American submarines that had made contact with the guerrillas. Like Claire, she never talked, and was court-martialed and sentenced to three years at hard labor in the Women's Correctional Institution.[2]

Although the inmates here were all underfed, conditions in the prison proved much better than anything Claire previously experienced. In addition to being able to talk while in their cells, the women could move about, both inside the single-story building and the inner courtyard. Each woman had a bed made of wooden planks and sawhorses, complete with bedspread, pillow, and mosquito netting. Each had her own spoon to carry to the mess hall three times a day for meager, dwindling rations. To contribute to their own upkeep, the women worked six hours a day in the prison's vegetable garden.

Florence Smith received a five-year sentence for spreading anti-Japanese propaganda and soon joined these prisoners. She and Claire picked up where they left off in Bilibid and teamed up for garden work, sharing a shovel between them. As this friendship strengthened, Claire's relationship with Maria Martinez deteriorated. Maria may have blamed Claire for her capture, or maybe they were simply worn out by their ordeal. It rankled Claire to see Maria shirk her share of the garden work: "All of us labored thus [in pairs], except Marie [sic] who had a system. Selecting the huskiest Filipino girl for her partner, she acted as supervisor while the girl dug." Long hours working in the garden yielded meager results, especially when divided among all of the prisoners. Claire grew alarmed about her weight loss—she dropped down to one hundred pounds from her normal 145—so she and Maria talked about how to supplement their diets.[3]

Maria convinced one of the guards to take a message to her family in Manila, who managed to bribe the appropriate people to gain access to the prison. Maria's mother and sister, accompanied by a guard from Fort Santiago and Señorita Del Rosario, the manager at Claire's old apartment house, showed up with bags of food and toiletries. Del Rosario recognized Claire at once and addressed her as Mrs. Phillips—thankfully, the guards did not raise any questions. She expressed sympathy for Claire's plight and boasted that because of her work at Fort Santiago, she had enough connections to arrange for Claire's release. This would require bribery, of course, and since Claire had no money, she never saw the benevolent señorita again.

Despite Maria's bounty, she was, by Claire's estimation, much too stingy with sharing: "She now grudgingly offered me a few spoonfuls of the food brought in to her." Claire decided to secure her own supply of care packages, and figured Fely Corcuera would be just the person to arrange for them. Claire's friendship with Maria stretched far enough that Maria offered the use of her contact to send a note out. The first time Fely appeared at the prison with food, the superintendent Mrs. Garcia turned her away because she did not have the necessary permit. The next day Pressa, another of Claire's former servants, showed up and was also denied entrance. The assistant superintendent passed along her message that Dian was safe in the hills. That night, one of the prison trustees, a woman named Pilar, gave Claire a small package of food that Pressa brought.[4]

Claire began working with Pilar, promising her a cut of everything that came in from her Manila contacts. Fely, Pressa, and even the Roxas family managed to send in some food, but everything was scarce by now. Claire convinced Mrs. Garcia to arrange for the sale of her confiscated wristwatch, which brought in enough pesos to buy ten pounds of rice, three pounds of sugar, a pound of beans, some vinegar and coconuts, and six eggs. Claire shared all of it with Florence Smith and two other military prisoners in her cellblock. The supplies did not last long, and starvation set in.

BY CHRISTMAS OF 1944, MANILA was on lockdown in anticipation of an American invasion. With the airfields wiped out by American bombs, the Japanese turned Dewey Boulevard into an airstrip. Civilians were not allowed near it or Manila Bay. Santo Tomas was shut up tight, now run by the Japanese military, which refused to allow even holiday packages brought in. Based on nothing more than caprice, they permitted the delivery of a small amount of parcels for a newer camp that had been opened in 1943 at Los Baños. Gladys Savary put together a few bundles of mostly tobacco products, which the internees seemed to crave as much as food. Using the dwindled funds from the Neutral Welfare Committee, she also purchased fruit and eggs for the internees on temporary release from Santo Tomas for treatment at the Philippine General Hospital.

The remaining civilians in Gladys's Pasay neighborhood visited each other on Christmas Day, handing out modest presents to the children, admiring the small tree Gladys managed to decorate. The conversations centered more on war news than on holiday cheer. Even the children, Gladys realized, were interested in every little detail about the war. The adults tried to divert their attention, yet all they were interested in was mimicking the sounds made by machine guns and bombers. Gladys and her friends discussed the big, worrisome questions: "Would the Japanese leave the city intact? Or would they destroy it, using scorched earth policy? Or would they fight it out there?"[5]

A few of Gladys's friends, fearing the Japanese intended to make a big last stand in Manila, had already left the city. Some headed about sixty miles south along the Manila Bay coastline to Nasugbu in Batangas, others north to Baguio. Though Gladys feared the scorched-earth policy, she saw no point in leaving Manila—she felt safest in familiar territory. The military prisoners, of course, had no choice in where they stayed. After being moved from Cabanatuan to Bilibid, they waited to be shuffled out to their final destinations. On December 13, 1944, Bill Berry, confined to a medical isolation ward in Bilibid, heard the Japanese round up every remaining able-bodied POW for transfer to Japan: "By this time, they were scraping pretty hard at the bottom of the barrel. They went through each cell block, one by one, man by man, and picked out the ones they were going to ship out—including those who could barely hobble."[6]

Jack Wright was part of the December 13th roundup of about 1,600 men, as was Edgar Gable. Before departing Bilibid, Wright wrote to his wife: "Thought sure we would be home within a month or so, but fate stepped in again. I pray for our reunion soon, and when it comes I know we will more than make up for this awful nightmare." He gave the letter to Lieutenant Robert F. Augur, who was too disabled to be moved. Irvin Alexander, also waiting in Bilibid for his final transfer, had already left a letter for his wife, buried in a safe spot in Cabanatuan. Around December 10th the Japanese distributed woolen clothing and blank postcards for the POWs to write brief messages home. Alexander understood their departure was imminent. Two days later the prisoners underwent a cursory medical examination to make sure they were healthy enough for the journey. As for Alexander, "I was fit to travel because I could walk."[7]

The POWs made a final march through the streets of Manila to the port area. It was the fifth time Jack Wright had done so, and once again he looked at the Filipino civilians who watched the prisoners: "In their eyes we could read what they had been through during the Japanese occupation—eyes that had seen brothers and sisters, fathers and mothers, tortured and slaughtered by cruel oppression. In their bodies we could see the stories of starvation, exposure, and beatings. Yet there was a frequent furtive sign made, the V for Victory." Irvin Alexander, who had not been in Manila for three years, was struck by the changes in the city, especially the lack of streetcars and private automobiles. He smelled the buses on the streets, which now used alcohol as fuel.[8]

Jack Wright, Irvin Alexander, Edgar Gable, and about 1,600 other prisoners boarded the *Oryoku Maru*, a converted 1930s passenger liner, packed into three holds with little food, water, or air, one reason such vessels were referred to as "hellships." The *Oryoku Maru* was bombed by American planes several times on its voyage; the Japanese had not marked it as a POW vessel. On December 15th, the prisoners were ordered to abandon ship and swim to the nearest shore, a half mile to a former US Naval Station at Olangapo on Subic Bay. It was tantamount to a death sentence. The men were too debilitated to walk, much less swim, and American planes continued their attack.

Five days later, the prisoners boarded trucks to a provincial jail in San Fernando, Pampanga. The town, a key railroad hub, had been nearly flattened by American bombers, and the sight made the POWs smile. After four days they piled into train cars for a journey north to the Lingayen Gulf, boarding the *Enoura Maru* on December 27th. It was the same thing all over again: appalling conditions and bombing raids. On New Year's Eve, the men rioted because of hunger. On January 1, 1945, the ship docked at Takao on the southwest end of Formosa (today Taiwan), but the men remained confined in the hold.[9]

In Manila, the Japanese continued to arrest anyone they suspected of involvement in the underground. On December 23, 1944, the Kempeitai picked up Benigno Del Rio, a Manila journalist in his late thirties. Next they brought in Fathers Kelly and Lalor from the Malate Convent, along with their Irish helper, Sullivan. They all ended up in the Cortabitarte Garrison, shoved into one of the garage cells that already contained several other prisoners. Del Rio was tortured for three days out of his week-long captivity. He was not sure how the Japanese treated the religious men from Malate, but they were all released at about the same time.[10]

During roll calls at Cortabitarte, Del Rio heard the names of some of the other prisoners, including Joaquin and Angustias Mencarini—the Spanish couple who worked with Miss U and Claire Phillips. Del Rio knew Angustias had been arrested because of her underground association with the Americans. Two days after Christmas, Del Rio heard the Mencarinis being tortured. Through a hole in the wall he saw Angustias's newly blackened eye.[11]

Angustias Mencarini's arrest raised concern among the Santo Tomas internees, many of whom had been involved with a variety of underground activities. Now that the Japanese had her, they worried it would not be long before some of the people in camp were picked up, too. Earl Carroll, a member of the camp's internee Executive Committee, learned of Angustias's arrest on December 21, 1944: "She had secured money for the camp and for individuals, had assisted in the operation of two hospitals on the outside for the sick and aged internees. She also had assisted them in contacting prisoners of war at Cabanatuan and the guerillas [*sic*]." When Earl Carroll informed Carroll Grinnell, another Executive Committee member, of the arrest, Grinnell became agitated. "This is it," he said.[12]

———

A FEW WEEKS BEFORE CHRISTMAS, as MacArthur's forces secured Leyte and turned their attention to Mindoro, Peggy Utinsky and Dian joined Frank Loyd's Tala hideaway in the mountains. "I came up the hill to see the funniest sight of my life," Peggy later wrote about their first meeting. Two men stood outside a nipa hut, waiting to greet her, and she was incredulous that they were American officers. Everything about Loyd and Royal Reynolds was shaggy, from their long hair and beards to their patched clothing. Loyd, plagued with rheumatism, could not stand up straight. They stared at each other for a moment, then Peggy asked, "Well, have I got into the House of David?"[13]

Loyd and Reynolds invited the newcomers into their sparsely furnished hut, where Peggy sat in the lone chair while the men brewed some mango tea. Loyd noted in his journal, "Have had a guest since December 13th. A Mrs. Utinsky, wife of an American officer." He summarized Peggy's activities since the beginning of the war: the fake Lithuanian citizenship, her Red Cross work, the smuggling operation. "What she got away with is unbelievable." He acknowledged Dian's presence, but not her name or her mother's. "Brought with her a five year old daughter of an American woman (by a Filipino husband) who had helped her in her prisoner relief work. That woman has been in Jap prison seven months—probably now dead."[14]

Loyd's journal entry repeated Peggy's story that Claire Phillips functioned as a subordinate operative in the Miss U network. At this stage of the war, for the practical purposes of prisoner relief, the point was moot since both Miss U and High Pockets were out of that particular game. However, Loyd's assumption that Claire had died sheds interesting light on Peggy's relationship with Dian. The longer Peggy took care of the little girl, the closer the two became. "Dian was the best baby I ever saw. No authority on child care would ever recommend the kind of life Dian had to live . . . constantly in danger of her life. Yet she never cried and never complained," Peggy remembered. She admitted an initial prejudice against mixed marriages, "But after knowing Dian, and having her with me for so long a time, I understood it a lot better."[15]

Peggy and Dian spent the worst of times together, and Peggy doted on the child as if she were her own. If Peggy believed, as Loyd wrote in his journal, that Claire had not survived her imprisonment in Fort Santiago, she might have also assumed the temporary custody situation would become permanent—she would become Dian's mother. To a woman who lost everything to this war, she might have viewed gaining a daughter as just compensation.

Her conversation with the American officers, as recorded by Loyd, also revealed a different experience with the guerrillas than what Peggy would later recount. Loyd described how the Japanese raided Victor Abad's camp, "and of course the Filipino and all his cohorts with his headquarters fled and left her and the little sick girl to look out after themselves." Abad regarded Peggy not as a valued member of his unit but as a nuisance and a burden, therefore expendable. "Under the guise of being afraid of eight days of Jap raiding . . . he slipped her out to my place," Loyd recounted.[16]

There were two more events involving the guerrillas that Peggy never disclosed after the war, probably because they cast the guerrillas in a bad light and demonstrated what little regard Abad had for her. Writing in his journal on New Year's Day 1945, Loyd documented his latest meeting with John Boone, which happened just after Christmas 1944. Loyd had a high opinion of Boone: "He is a capable guerrilla leader and a remarkable development from an enlisted man of two years service at the time the war began." After this meeting with Boone, Loyd wrote nothing good about Abad, and all the negatives centered on Abad's treatment of Peggy. It is not clear if Peggy told Loyd about the following episodes. Since he did not write about them until after his meeting with Boone, it is more likely the stories came to Loyd from that source.[17]

Sometime after Peggy arrived on Bataan in September 1944, Abad sent her back to Manila to retrieve an American flag and pick up some paint. Perhaps he told her the guerrillas needed these items to signal the US troops when they arrived. No matter the rationale, Loyd found this outrageous: "When they knew she had left Manila because she was sus-pected by the Japs and had been imprisoned previously . . . and had she been seen by the Japs the very fact that she was a white woman would have caused them to search her baggage, and they certainly would have killed her for possessing the American flag."[18]

A Filipino could have been sent on this errand, Loyd reasoned, with much less risk, without attracting any attention at all. The fact that Abad sent Peggy showed that she was the most expendable of the group and he did not care about her safety. Peggy may have told herself that Abad chose her for this mission because she had successfully skirted around the Japanese for so long. Still, on some level it caused her discomfort. Years later she could not acknowledge it, probably because she could offer no reasonable explanation for it—or for the incident that finally drove her from Abad's camp.

Sometime after Peggy's errand to Manila, the Bay Side Brigade, Victor Abad's men, captured a Filipina whom they accused of spying for the Japanese. They brought her and her three-year-old son to Abad's head-quarters. Abad presumed the woman's guilt and decided she should die. He proposed a mercy killing, and directed Peggy to inject mother and child with a fatal dose of strychnine. When Peggy refused, Abad ordered a grave dug and told the Filipina to lie down in it with her son on top of her. He made Peggy watch as he dispatched both with a single shot. Peggy's horror at such casual brutality drove her to seek shelter with Loyd and Reynolds.[19]

This guerrilla hut turned out to be one of the safest places Peggy had stayed in a very long time. Dian recuperated in the clear mountain air, and Loyd fashioned a doll for her out of some of Peggy's medical sup-plies. They delayed their Christmas celebration until Loyd and Reynolds returned from their meeting with Boone and the other guerrillas, but nobody minded. Dian played for hours on end with her new toy, and Peggy delighted in reading the leaflets and Christmas cards dropped by the American planes.

When the men returned, Peggy cooked a couple of chickens and served them with fresh vegetables and some bananas—a true feast, something to sustain them over the turbulent weeks to come. Loyd delivered a letter for Peggy from Boone, laying out the current medical needs in the Bataan Military District. Boone's letter also carried a surprising piece of intelligence from Father Lalor in Manila: Claire Phillips was in fact alive. Any plans Peggy may have been making about Dian would now have to be revised.[20]

In early January 1945, the Americans sailed battleships, cruisers, and destroyers from their secured positions on Leyte, followed by transports and amphibious vessels. Their destination was the Lingayen Gulf on the western side of Luzon, about two hundred miles north of Manila—the same place the Japanese chose for their main invasion in 1941. The Japanese responded with kamikazes, sinking twenty-four ships and crippling sixty-seven more. It was not enough to stop General Walter Krueger's Sixth Army, which began landing at Lingayen on January 9th.

The initial landing force of 60,000 American troops caught the Japanese by surprise. After US forces captured the island of Mindoro, just to the southwest of Luzon, in the second half of December 1944, the Japanese expected an invasion of Luzon to come from that direction. General MacArthur encouraged this expectation by ordering Filipino guerrillas to begin sabotage operations in southern Luzon and focusing reconnaissance missions and bombing raids there. General Yamashita was fooled enough that he kept his headquarters in Manila, yet he hedged his northern bets, too. There Japanese troops built a series of caves and tunnels inland from the beaches, planning to draw US troops away from the shoreline before beginning defensive attacks.

The Japanese activity in the north gave the Sixth Army time to raise its troop strength to 280,000. Every man was needed to face Yamashita's 260,000, which were divided into three locations: the Shobu Group of 152,000 in northern Luzon, the Kembu Group of 30,000 near Clark Air Field and Bataan, and the Shimbu Group of 80,000 in southern Luzon. With the invasion, Yamashita deployed the bulk of his forces into three key mountain areas and 20,000 to Manila, and he utilized delaying tactics, fighting a bitter battle of attrition to impede American progress toward Manila.[21]

Frank Loyd and his men were now gone more often than not from the guerrilla encampment, doing what they could to assist the returning Americans. Peggy wanted to accompany him and provide medical treatment for the guerrillas while they were in the field. "You have done enough. Suppose you get killed—I could not take care of Dian," he said to her. With the "big show" underway, Loyd relocated his camp closer to John Boone to better coordinate their activities.[22]

Other American guerrillas in the area did not share Loyd's willingness to work with Boone. Five days after the Sixth Army landed, Leon Beck was on the move. Beck, who fought with the 31st Infantry on Bataan and considered Boone a deserter, had slipped out of the Death March at the small town of San Juan. He found and joined Claude Thorp's Luzon Guerrilla Force. Shortly before the Americans returned, Beck married a local woman, Veneranda Luna. His January 1945 mission required him to leave the guerrilla camp in Zambales, on the west coast of central Luzon, and deliver a radio set to Boone on Bataan. "He knew it was coming, he already had had one set and lost it some way. . . . He had a little shack built ready to receive this. It was right on the edge of the trees around the base of a hill," Beck recalled.[23]

On Boone's order, specially trained Filipino radio operators, brought to Luzon by submarine, started transmitting a coded message from the new device. Alarmed by the sound of Zeros flying overhead, Beck advised Boone to shut off the radio. "Aw, hell no! We're on different frequencies; you can't pick up this American radio set," Boone said. As if on cue, the enemy planes blasted Boone's shelter, setting it on fire, destroying the radio. Beck, startled by Boone's hubris, was appalled at the guerrilla leader's next action. Boone fled the shack, apparently unconcerned about anyone else's welfare, even leaving his wife Mellie and their children behind. For Beck, also married to a local woman, such behavior was unconscionable, the mark of a coward. "John P. Boone ripped his ass with me" that day, Beck later concluded.[24]

For Loyd, Victor Abad proved more of a problem. When Boone detailed some of the guerrillas to help Loyd move Peggy and the rest of the camp, Abad pulled them away, leaving Loyd's fledgling camp without food and shelter. This episode reinforced Loyd's belief that Peggy's presence among the guerrillas was unwanted. "To add to the difficulties," Loyd wrote in his journal mid-month, "Mrs. Utinsky and the little girl are still here with us. No satisfactory arrangement has yet been made for her elsewhere, and I cannot let her go until I can be sure she will be kept safely."[25]

To keep Peggy occupied on a project with "propaganda value in stimulating the war effort," Loyd assigned her the task of drawing up a list of collaborators. Peggy threw herself into the task because she believed the Counter Intelligence Corps would use the information to round up and punish the guilty. After all she had endured, she longed for retribution. She covered nearly thirty pages with names of collaborators and spies, conversely, also identifying those who assisted Miss U and other relief efforts. If the guilty were to be punished, the heroes should be rewarded.[26]

Victor Abad, meanwhile, continued to frustrate Loyd's attempts to settle Peggy and Dian in a safe location in Tala. During the third week of January, Loyd thought he had finally convinced Abad how important it was to look after them. Loyd "almost burst" when he learned Abad had done nothing to prepare a new hut for them: "My first reaction was to have Boone relieve him of his command, but that would only upset Bay Side guerrillas who actually are *not* commanded but do pretty well as they please." A local family took in Peggy and Dian, a compromise Loyd accepted when he realized better arrangements would never be made. He confessed in his journal, "It's a great relief to be free from Mrs. Utinsky's incessant chatter. Just like a phonograph with an endless talking record." Loyd preferred to focus on the rapidly changing circumstances of the war on Luzon, one of which involved the liberation of the military prisoners Peggy's Miss U organization had been helping.[27]

After the Sixth Army's landing at the Lingayen Gulf on January 9, 1945, General MacArthur pressed General Krueger to get his troops to Manila as quickly as possible. The Japanese, who had offered little resistance at Lingayen, would stand and fight in the capital city, MacArthur knew, and he saw no sense in delaying the inevitable confrontation. Krueger had received G-2 intelligence reports about the POW camp at Cabanatuan, detailing the desperate conditions of the five hundred or so remaining prisoners. Much of this information came from the local guerrilla leader, Major Robert Lapham, who had originally been part of Claude Thorp's team. Lapham now commanded the Luzon Guerrilla Army Forces, known as Lapham's Raiders, centered in Nueva Ecija, near the prison camp. He believed the Japanese intended to kill all the remaining Cabanatuan prisoners before pulling out, and he wanted something done to save them.[28]

Krueger decided to launch an attack on the camp, and about 120 men of the 6th Ranger Battalion, supported by the Sixth Army's Special Reconnaissance Unit—called the Alamo Scouts—and two hundred Filipino guerrillas commanded by Captain Juan Pajota, led the raid on January 30, 1945. Ralph Hibbs was still there in Cabanatuan, one of the last remaining doctors, and he had been anticipating something like this.

Earlier in the month the Japanese guards had abandoned the prisoners, warning them not to leave. They returned just when the POWs started to believe they were free. Hibbs and the others understood the end was near, but they did not know how or when. Still, the doctor had a plan in place for when the shooting started, which he dubbed "War plan pink—#57." He would crawl into the ditch leading to the duck pond, swim to the opposite shore, and board a ferry to freedom, a fantasy supported by the notion that someone in the mess would loan him a butcher knife for protection.[29]

When the Rangers came blasting into the camp on the night of January 30th, to Hibbs all of the noises sounded like "someone's Fourth of July." In a variation on his war plan, he hid in a drainage ditch because he did not recognize the Ranger uniforms and could not quite figure out what was going on. When one of the Rangers identified himself and told Hibbs the POWs had to get out of the camp fast, he still hesitated. The Ranger physically hustled him toward the front gate. Colonel James Duckworth, the senior American officer in Cabanatuan, showed similar reluctance, challenging the Rangers on chain of command issues. He, too, had to be prodded and coerced to the gate.[30]

After years of wishing and waiting for liberation, the prisoners had a hard time believing it had arrived. There was no time to ponder the situation. The debilitated men had to hurry—some on their own steam, some with considerable assistance—through the rice fields to the Pampanga

River while the Rangers held off the Japanese. There, Filipinos with cara-bao carts helped the prisoners cross the river's sandbar to freedom. The raid on Cabanatuan had taken thirty minutes. That night, Ralph Hibbs ate his first full meal in nearly three years.[31]

The operation was such an unqualified success that General MacArthur visited the 1st Cavalry headquarters in Guimba, twenty-three miles north of Cabanatuan. He instructed General Verne D. Mudge to use a similar method to free American prisoners in Manila. Mudge created "flying col-umns," special motorized squads equipped for rapid movement, and put them under the command of Brigadier General William C. Chase. On February 1, 1945, the flying columns began their one-hundred-mile push south to Manila. Two days later they liberated Santo Tomas and the day after that, Bilibid Prison. It took a few more days to locate smaller, scat-tered concentrations of American prisoners.

AT THE BEGINNING OF JANUARY 1945, the guerrillas made con-tact with Claire Phillips through the prison trustee, Pilar. "The guard at the outside gate was contacted by a guerrilla officer. This man has a mes-sage for you. It is fixed so that you can speak to him about midnight," she said to Claire, and left the cell unlocked. While the other women slept, Claire walked to the appointed place and whistled for her contact. "The bushes outside swayed slightly, a man stepped out, and came to the win-dow." The man addressed her as High Pockets and gave her the welcome news that the guerrillas planned a rescue: "The guard at the outside gate is one of our men. His name is Fred. I placed him here as soon as we heard where you were. Fred will get pencil and paper to you. Draw a diagram of the inside of your building, the walls, and the courtyard."[32]

Before he left, Claire asked if he knew anything about her daughter. He reassured her Dian was safe with John Boone. Pilar delivered the prom-ised pencil and paper the next day, and Claire devoted two days' worth of her free time to making as accurate a sketch as possible. On the evening of January 9th, Claire heard a familiar whistle at the window down the hall. She picked the feeble lock on the cell door, took her diagram, and went to meet her contact. After he pulled the document through the bars, he told

Claire about the landing at the Lingayen Gulf. She decided, "Then I'll wait for them to liberate me. Since I've waited this long, I can wait a little longer." The guerrilla promised Claire he would try to get to the prison twice a week to give her updates on the location of the American troops so she would be prepared for her rescue.[33]

The days leading up to liberation were far from dull. Every day Claire saw American planes fly overhead, so low that the stars painted on their wings were clearly visible. Bombs fell every day; Japanese anti-aircraft guns could do little about them. Still, on February 1st, Claire received a chilly reminder of what the Japanese were still capable of. At the nearby psychiatric hospital, soldiers rounded up all the Caucasian patients, herded them out on the lawn, and shot them. One of the guards warned Claire the same thing could happen in the women's prison.

By this point, however, the superintendent, Mrs. Garcia, seemed to have embraced the inevitability of an Allied victory and began taking steps to help the prisoners. She instructed the guard at the gate to use a buzzer to warn when any Japanese soldiers approached so the white women had time to hide. After word arrived that the Americans liberated Santo Tomas, Mrs. Garcia returned the prisoners' personal clothing to them.

Then, on Saturday morning, February 10, 1945, the prison priest brought the news that American soldiers were on the way. Claire later remembered, "I had been a prisoner for eight months and eighteen days, but the last few hours of tense waiting seemed to be the longest." Finally, she heard the shout heralding their arrival, and Claire saw ten tall uniformed men of the 1st Cavalry standing in the prison courtyard. She touched the arm of the nearest soldier to make sure he was real and asked if she could kiss him. "Well, if you don't, I'm going to kiss you, sister. You're the first white woman from God's country I've seen in over two years," he said.[34]

Colonel Charles C. Young, a civil affairs officer with the 1st Cavalry, gathered up some prison records, and asked the women to pose for a photo on the front steps. Reporters were on the scene, too, taking the names of the liberated prisoners. Subsequent newspaper articles offered sketchy information about the resistance activities of "Claire Fuentes." Young then piled the women into a truck bound for the relative safety of Santo Tomas

University. "It was not a tranquil ride for the ping of sniper's bullets, the staccato chatter of machine guns, and the burping of mortars came from all directions," Claire later wrote. "We frequently saw G.I.'s tossing hand grenades into shallow, hastily-built air raid shelters where many Japs had sought refuge and were fighting to the death rather than surrender."[35]

SEVENTH HEAVEN CAMP, AS MARKING referred to Yay Panlilio's Net Control Station (NCS) in the mountains of Rizal province, provided her a brief respite from the war—and from Marking. The January 1945 landing of US troops at the Lingayen Gulf increased enemy activity throughout the island, putting Marking's entire guerrilla contingent on the move, including the NCS. They settled at Karakatmon, northeast of Laguna de Bay. They built a trio of camps at varying hillside levels for different functions; the long-awaited supplies—food, medicine, weapons, and ammunition—were air-dropped into the lower camp.[36]

During early February 1945, word filtered through that the 1st Cavalry was making its way through Manila and would soon enter Rizal province. George Miller suggested the time had come for Marking to make contact with the Americans. Rather than marshal a small greeting party, the guerrilla leader decided to bring out his whole fighting force. "And so, for the last time, we rolled from the highlands down into the lowlands," Yay remembered. She left the Net Control Station in the capable hands of a few guards who also watched over a cache of remaining supplies. Her daughter Rae traveled on horseback with Leon Cabalhin. "I knew that as a normal mother, I should worry," Yay later admitted. As a guerrilla mother, she believed in the chivalry and goodness of Marking's men, trusting them to keep her daughter safe. "Rae would roll in when the fighters rolled in."[37]

They made it as far west as Cardona before Marking decided, for the safety of the guerrilla force, they should wait for the 1st Cavalry to reach them. A reconnaissance team soon arrived, and Yay learned that Carlos Romulo, her old boss at the *Herald*, was in Manila and wanted to see her. Marking raged with jealousy, accusing Yay of preferring Romulo, telling her that once she went to him in Manila, she would never return.

Eventually his temper subsided, and he apologized and asked Yay to forgive him. For Yay, it was no longer a matter of forgiveness. She decided the only way to cure Marking of his jealousy was not to placate him, but to leave him—to go to Manila—to prove she would come back. When Marking saw her with her packed bags, he pulled a gun on her.

Men from the 1st Cavalry were in the next room and Yay requested their help to reach Captain Stoddard. "I can't take it any more. I'm leaving," she said to Stoddard, who did not ask for details. He found room for her in an armored car leaving for Manila. Marking had exploded in another rage, and Yay admitted to herself, "I was leaving to keep us from killing each other." They would not kill each other; instead, they would each head into a different danger zone. Yay ended up in Manila, which the Japanese intended to hold at all cost.[38]

FOR GLADYS SAVARY, JANUARY 9, 1945—the day of the American landing at Lingayen—was "The Great Day, *our* Great Day!" Like other Manila residents, Gladys understood the important and dangerous role the city would play in the final showdown between the Americans and the Japanese. General Yamashita's men fortified Manila, neighborhood by neighborhood, street by street, and Gladys watched as they mined the main north-south streets. On her own two-block-long street, where she now lived with Helge Janson's family, enemy soldiers built a log barricade studded with dynamite, sharpened sticks, and wrapped with barbed wire. Gladys referred to this as "Janson's Last Stand," convinced that "if the Americans ever encountered anything so formidable as this tank trap, they'd turn right around (and that's a joke)."[39]

As Manilans braced for the siege, Gladys tried one last time to provide assistance to the Santo Tomas internees, whom she viewed as sitting ducks. In mid-January, an English-speaking Japanese civilian showed up at the Janson house in Pasay because, he said, he knew Helge Janson had headed up the Neutral Welfare Committee. He explained to Gladys and Helge that he had been in charge of transferring the Baguio internees to Bilibid Prison. He was very worried about the welfare of the civilians in Santo Tomas and Bilibid, and he hoped Helge could help him help them.[40]

Gladys had her doubts about this man. She worried that he was really Kempeitai, trying to round up the last American sympathizers in the city or that he was trying to cheat them out of money and supplies. Yet Gladys and Helge could not pass up an opportunity to try to help. Helge gave the man the remaining pesos from the Neutral Welfare Committee's treasury and told him to distribute it however he saw fit. The man also agreed to take a letter from Helge to the Executive Committee of Santo Tomas informing them of the current situation with the invasion. Gladys carefully worked out a budget and purchasing plan, and located enough merchants around Manila willing to dedicate their remaining stocks to the prisoners, even on credit.[41]

The scheme collapsed. The man, after claiming he delivered the letter to Santo Tomas, visited Helge and Gladys one more time, and then disappeared. Japanese authorities in Santo Tomas continued to refuse any outside assistance for the internees. Gladys heard about the rapid advance of the Sixth Army toward Manila and hoped the Japanese would leave the city. "The idea that Manila would be ruined occurred to all of us as abstract theory," she later wrote. "We told ourselves we must be prepared, the town would undoubtedly be blown up; but actually we couldn't believe it, in our hearts."[42]

By late January, though, Gladys had accepted the reality that the Japanese had no intention of leaving Manila any time soon. Enemy soldiers repeatedly climbed over the Jansons' garden wall, ordering the inhabitants of the house to evacuate. Helge obtained a document from the Japanese ambassador identifying him as a consul representing several neutral countries. This convinced the soldiers to leave them alone.

At the beginning of February, Gladys visited friends in the Ermita district, taking a two-and-a-half-mile walk that showed her how badly the American bombings had damaged the city. She stopped at the Philippine General Hospital to talk with the patients, most of them from the Santo Tomas internment camp, who told her the internees were starving to death there. Gladys walked past the Restaurant de Paris, now empty and guarded by a lone sentry. She caught a glimpse of the inside, bare but in good condition, and wondered how long it would be before she could resume her business.

On February 2nd, with American troops about twenty miles outside of Manila, Gladys and the Jansons huddled over their illegal radio listening to news of the liberation of Cabanatuan. A "real swashbuckling, D-Artagnan job. It must have been a real thriller-diller," Gladys wrote in her diary. While she tried to believe Edgar Gable was among the rescued, in her heart she knew he was not. Those final days held more fear than thrills, though. Gladys noted, "It is this waiting that kills me. For us who have been seemingly free in a captive city, it is almost harder. We are filled with fear and anxiety for those inside the prisons, we agonize over the starving natives, and, mingled with all that, we have a worrying tinge or two about our own fate."[43]

It was a common concern throughout the city. Bill Berry, confined to one of Bilibid's hospital wards, was one of a few hundred prisoners exempted from transport to Japan. The news of the Lingayen landing, he remembered, "was certainly the occasion for a great deal of joyfulness" for the prisoners. However, it put the guards on edge. The POWs' optimism dimmed as they fretted over how these guards might respond to an American assault on Bilibid, especially after word spread of last month's massacre of prisoners on Palawan Island, some 670 miles south of Luzon.[44]

Within three weeks, the American Sixth Army was close enough to Manila that Berry could hear the repeated artillery fire. During the first days of February, he caught the sounds of machine guns, rifles, and pistols. The ground shook with what he assumed were armored vehicles, and on February 3, 1945 he was convinced—and rightly so—that American forces were outside the prison walls. The next morning, the Japanese guards changed into civilian clothing and walked out of Bilibid, leaving a note advising the prisoners of their freedom. By mid-afternoon of February 4th, Berry found himself chatting with the newly arrived Yanks of one of the 1st Cavalry's flying columns.[45]

Between the liberations of Santo Tomas and Bilibid, thousands of Americans and other Allied national were freed, but the war was hardly over. As Bill Berry acknowledged, "The battle for Manila was still raging around us. We could hear the artillery blasts in the distance. We could hear the shells whistling over our heads as they traveled toward their targets. And we could hear them hit. A tremendous amount of artillery fire was going on right over our heads. But to us it all sounded like music. It was like the Fourth of July." Berry's freedom was assured now.

Outside those prison walls in early 1945, however, freedom was by no means a guarantee. Throughout February 1945, the Japanese did their best to obliterate Manila, without any pretense whatsoever of focusing on military objectives. For example, over 90 percent of all property in Spanish neighborhoods, including historic and irreplaceable convents and churches, was destroyed. The Kempeitai rounded up the Spanish religious men, herded them into shelters, and tossed in hand grenades. An attack on the Spanish Consulate on Colorado Street resulted in the deaths of at least fifty people who were either burned alive or bayoneted by enemy soldiers.[46]

A squad of Japanese soldiers walked into the headquarters of the Philippine Red Cross, at the corner of General Luna and Isaac Peral Streets in the Ermita district, on Saturday, February 10, 1945. They shot and bayoneted all occupants. When they finished, they helped themselves to the lunch their victims had been getting ready to eat. Two days later, a Japanese officer accompanied by twenty soldiers entered De La Salle College on Taft Avenue, where seventy people, including about thirty women and children, fifteen brothers, and a priest, had taken refuge. They bayoneted everyone and piled the bodies, both dead and dying, at the foot of the stairs. Once the Japanese departed, Father Superior Francis Cosgrave, despite his severe injuries, began administering last rites. He was one of only a handful of survivors rescued three days later by American soldiers.[47]

In the house-to-house fighting along Taft Avenue, some Japanese Marines reached Pilar Campos's home at number 1462 on February 13th. They had a particular interest in this locale. Japanese intelligence officers had been keeping an eye on Pilar's activities since 1942, when her efforts to aid American prisoners landed her in Fort Santiago for a time. Most recently, on Wednesday, February 7th, four Navy intelligence officers searched her home and not only found a shortwave radio, but also the footlocker Pilar had packed with Ralph Hibbs's belongings at the start of the war. When they confiscated these items, they stole money, jewelry, and food as well.[48]

On February 13th, the Marines knocked on Pilar's front door demanding admission. She opened the door as far as its safety chain would allow and told them to get their commanding officer. The Marines shot through the door instead, and a bullet caught her in the stomach. After breaking their way inside, they dragged Pilar out to the front lawn where she was bayoneted and left for dead. A refugee who had been staying in the house tried to help Pilar by shifting her into a more comfortable position and giving her some water. Before he could do anything else, the Japanese started shooting at him. He ran for his life. It took twenty-eight-year-old Pilar Campos three days to die, alone, and cut off from help.[49]

While recuperating at an R & R camp near the Lingayen Gulf, Ralph Hibbs received the news about Pilar from two middle-aged Filipinos, friends of the Campos family. Hibbs never stopped worrying about her, especially when he heard about the horrific fighting in Manila. Knowing Pilar, he did not envision her hiding away from it. As he later wrote, "My suffering and sacrifice paled in the reality of this patriot's devotion. She volunteered, stepped forward, stood tall, and died helping others. . . . She died a soldier's death with bravery as her only weapon."[50]

At the beginning of February 1945, the Pasay neighborhood where Gladys and the Jansons lived was relatively quiet, most of the noise generated by Japanese troops moving out. On February 3rd, they listened to the Voice of Freedom on the radio, and a friend telephoned with the news that Santo Tomas had been liberated and Malacañan Palace, the official residence of the president and the headquarters of the Philippine government, was once again flying the American flag. Electricity and phone lines went down soon after, and the sounds and stench of battle crept closer to Pasay. After a few days without news and unable to contain her curiosity any longer, Gladys climbed over her back wall and ventured into the neighborhood. The streets were mostly empty, the buildings destroyed. She had a close call with some Japanese soldiers shooting at Filipino looters and got caught in a bombing raid, which more than satisfied her curiosity.

On February 10th, the day of Claire Phillips's liberation, bombs fell on Pasay, and for the first time Gladys seriously worried about her survival: "We have all made our wills (several times over, mentally). We don't dare say what we are all thinking. It's the end." All changed the next day, which Gladys described as "Wottaday, wottaday." It started in the early morning hours, with Gladys and Dorothy Janson hauling water up to the roof to Helge who, working while being shot at from beyond the garden wall, used it to keep fire from latching on to their home. Only the wind changing direction saved the structure. Before breakfast, everyone was exhausted and jumpy from the sounds of guns and bombs. Gladys heard Filipinos running and shouting on the street and assumed they were looters. Then a neighbor at their front gate called out, "The Americans are here, just in the next street."[51]

Nothing could restrain Gladys and Dorothy once that news was broadcasted. They dashed out of the house and down Park Avenue, intent on greeting their liberators. At their first sighting of a yellow-complexioned soldier clad in an unfamiliar uniform, Dorothy called out to Gladys, "It's the Japs back again." She turned to run back to the house. They heard the soldier call out, "Hey you, are youse Americans?" The women stopped dead in their tracks. "It isn't Japs. It's Brooklyn!" Gladys said. The soldier was one of a dozen American paratroopers, wearing a uniform the women had never seen before, their skin yellowed by the anti-malaria drug atabrine. The men were delighted to find American women alive in Pasay; they had been told that all the white people in the area had been murdered. The soldiers had orders to patrol the neighborhood, to make sure all enemy troops had gone. Gladys took them to the Park Avenue school, just in case any prisoners remained. Nothing was left except graves.[52]

Twenty paratroopers moved into the compound behind the Jansons, and they all celebrated together. Gladys and Dorothy offered up coffee and the only other thing they had plenty of: red beans. When the Americans contributed their K-rations to the feast, complete with crackers and cheese, Gladys broke out her last bottle of Scotch. She had been saving it for an important occasion, and this qualified. The impromptu party became so merry with loud conversation and laughter that Japanese snipers took aim at the compound, luckily missing everyone inside.

This was a bit of isolated revelry. Throughout the city, Japanese atrocities continued over the next couple of days. Gladys recounted some of them in her diary: "The Japanese have been firing whole sections with gasoline, then shooting people as they try to escape. Their favorite sport is to toss hand grenades into houses, and then shoot people as they try to run. Thank heaven, we never left our gates." As Japanese troops had withdrawn from Pasay in the first days of February, they had not engaged in the house-to-house destruction now occurring in other parts of the city. Still, about halfway through the battle of Manila, Gladys noted, "The Japanese are fighting like animals, desperate animals."[53]

★ ★ ★

CHAPTER 17

FREEDOM

B UREAUCRACY REIGNED ON THE SANTO TOMAS INTERNMENT campus in February 1945. Members of the US Counter Intelligence Corps (CIC) registered Claire Phillips and the other women from the Women's Correctional Institution, giving out room assignments and meal tickets. Claire stood in line for an hour to receive her first full meal in freedom, and though she knew she should be careful, she could not resist wolfing down the tinned meat, reconstituted potatoes, bread, fruit, and coffee. She walked around the university grounds, hoping the exercise would get her digestive system working as it should. Yet Claire could not keep the food down, and she found herself in the camp hospital, diagnosed with anemia, scurvy, and a variety of skin infections. A doctor restricted Claire's diet to soup and eggnog. By this time, her weight had dipped to ninety-five pounds, her hair came out in handfuls, and all of her teeth were loose.

Claire received her first visitor while she was hospitalized, her former servant, the "faithful little Pressa." While they caught up, a Red Cross worker offered pen and paper to Claire to write home to her mother. She also wrote to John Phillips's mother. When army officials informed Claire she was scheduled to be flown stateside as soon as possible, she told them about Dian. She could not possibly leave without her daughter. A radio message was dispatched to John Boone, and he answered, "Dian will be sent down without delay in the custody of two army officers."[1]

———

ON FEBRUARY 5, 1945, Peggy Utinsky received word from Frank Loyd that the time had come for her to take Dian and head for Manila and the protection of the American Army. They left at once. The first leg of the trip took them down to Victor Abad's 2nd Regiment headquarters near Tala. The Negrito guides hacked a path through the bamboo forest up and down a mountain route so steep that at one point they dragged Peggy up a mountain face down on her stomach. She did not care, though, because in her head she sang, "The Yanks have come! The Yanks are here!"[2]

Abad welcomed Peggy and tried to convince her to stop long enough for dinner. She was in too much of a hurry to get to Manila to waste time eating with a man who had caused her so much grief. At her insistence, they moved out immediately, and she traveled east with Abad and the 2nd Regiment as far as Orani. Although they arrived after dark, they observed the remnants of a battle that had taken place earlier that day. Abad decided they should stay put for the night to avoid a countryside crawling with retreating Japanese. Peggy conceded his point; still, she woke at dawn the next morning, eager to get moving. Abad again hesitated, arguing that there were too many snipers in the area for a safe journey. He did not want to risk losing any of his men. Peggy disagreed—probably vehemently—and Abad said to her, "Lieutenant, you are on your own."[3]

That was fine with Peggy. She bought an old horse from a Filipino willing to travel with her and Dian until they met up with American troops, an agreement facilitated by Peggy's promise to hand over ten US dollars at the end of the trip. She got up on the horse but could not fit her feet into the stirrups because of the oversized men's shoes she wore. The rest of her outfit was also cobbled together from hand-me-downs: a red dress made from a curtain, a battered wide-brimmed straw hat, socks knitted from string, and a handmade gun belt to hold her .38.

After several hours the trio spotted a group of green-uniformed soldiers crouched in a roadside ditch. "I stopped the horse, feeling cold and sick all over. Green meant Japs! I had to think fast, to concoct a story that would sound convincing. It had to be the very best story of my life, or it would be my last one," Peggy later wrote. One of the soldiers stood up, and Peggy noted his height and his bright red hair. Her voice came out in a sob as she said to Dian, "Oh, Honey, only a Yank grows like that!" The Americans stared at Peggy before breaking into a song she never heard before, "Pistol-packing mama, lay that pistol down!"[4]

The men belonged to the Sixth Army, and they had as many questions for her as she had for them. Colonel Evan M. Houseman, after reading the letter of introduction Peggy carried from Frank Loyd, remarked, "Woman guerrilla! Goddam, what is this war coming to?" He offered to arrange transportation for her to Dinalupihan, but she refused the first conveyance—a stretcher that reminded her too much of weakness. Peggy consented to ride in a *carretela*, and carried on a rolling conversation with the soldiers until they all reached Dinalupihan.[5]

The transformation of the barrio rendered Peggy speechless. The last time she had seen it, the place was in ruins, but now she looked on at a vast array of tanks and guns, weapons as unfamiliar as the army uniforms. As she later wrote, "You can dream and imagine what victory will be like—and I had done that for months and months—but never had I conceived of anything like the sight before me."[6]

Her escorts delivered her to Colonel Winfred Skelton, who was not at all surprised to see her. Frank Loyd and John Boone had come through Dinalupihan that morning and said to keep an eye out for Peggy. Skelton told her she had time for a cup of coffee before a plane would take her to General MacArthur's headquarters on Luzon. In fact, she had just enough time to arrange for the colonel to pay her Filipino guide the ten dollars she had promised. Peggy dodged an overeager reporter before she and Dian flew north to Hacienda Luisita, the sugar plantation turned army headquarters.

Lieutenant General Charles P. Hall, commander of XI Corps, greeted Peggy and Dian and arranged for food—Peggy marveled at such casual

offers of food and drink wherever she went. She handed over the list of collaborators and underground members she had drawn up, then asked permission to visit the men who had been rescued from Cabanatuan. First,
though, she took a bath and had a good night's sleep. For the first time
in a very long time, she looked at herself in the mirror, where a five feet
tall, eighty-five-pound woman with gray hair stared back at her. *This* was
Brevet Second Lieutenant Utinsky. "I couldn't find Peggy Doolin at all."[7]

The next day, Major Ike Kampmann accompanied Peggy on a flight
to the evacuation camp at Calasiao, where she met James Duckworth
in person for the first time. He filled her in on the final weeks of life in
Cabanatuan and the camp's rescue on January 30th. At another evacuation camp, Peggy met Alfred Oliver, the army chaplain at O'Donnell and
Cabanatuan, who related his tale of the Rangers' raid. He wrote a note
for Peggy attesting to her prisoner relief work: "It is the opinion of the
undersigned that Brevet Lieutenant Utinsky did more than any other one
person for the morale and physical well being of the Allied Prisoners of
War held at Camp O'Donnell and Prison Camp No. 1, Cabanatuan." It
is not clear what prompted him to do so, though Peggy may have already
been thinking about collecting proof of what she had accomplished during the occupation.[8]

While they talked, a man identifying himself as Colonel Hill made an
introduction to Peggy. If he had been recently promoted, this may have
been Major Robert Hill of Manila. Hill told Peggy he knew Jack Utinsky
well. They had served in the First World War, were together in Siberia,
and resigned from the army at the same time. After the Japanese invasion
in 1941, the two men ended up on Bataan and surrendered together on
Corregidor. Hill had been with Jack when he died at Cabanatuan. Now
there was no longer any reason for Peggy to hold out hope that her husband
had survived. If Peggy broke down at this news, she never admitted it.[9]

After meeting with the liberated prisoners, Peggy returned to
MacArthur's headquarters. General Courtney Whitney, head of intelligence operations, told Peggy she should go back to work for the Red Cross
at nearby Gerona. She was not interested. Her unpleasant encounter with
the Red Cross doctor Joaquin Canuto during her second trip to Bataan

in the spring of 1942 still stuck in her mind, and she preferred not to get involved with the organization again. Peggy wanted to return to Manila. She wanted to find out what happened to the other members of her network and make sure the collaborators received their comeuppance.

Peggy's chance came with an offer from the CIC to work with them, so off she headed to Manila, tagging along with whichever military group moved the quickest. When she realized at one point how close she was to Cabanatuan, though, she could not resist stopping to see where Jack was buried. Lieutenant James McElhinney accompanied Peggy and Dian into the deserted camp and pointed to a huge mound of dirt that marked a mass grave. "In a way that was as bitter a shock as I had had since the moment when I knew Jack was dead." It was a final good-bye.[10]

A good-bye that turned out not to be so final occurred shortly after Peggy reached Manila. Though an M.P. tried to turn her away because the city was still a battle zone, she talked her way in, emphasizing her work with the CIC. How Peggy learned about Claire Phillips's rescue from the Women's Correctional Institution is not known. She understood, though, that she had to return Dian to her mother in Santo Tomas, which turned out to be more difficult than she expected: "You cannot take care of a child for so long a time without coming to love it, and I hated to let Dian go. So far as she was concerned, she no longer knew her mother, and she cried at having to leave me. It was hard on her mother, too, when she discovered that her own child no longer recognized her or felt at ease with her."[11]

Still recuperating from her prison ordeal, Claire waited in the liberated internment camp for Dian to be returned to her. John Boone had sent word that two officers would deliver the little girl to Manila, so Claire must have been surprised to see Peggy walk in with Dian. Yet she mentioned nothing about Peggy when she wrote about the incident after the war, just as Peggy did not identify Claire by name in her memoir. This, perhaps, was one source of tension between the two women—love for a child that only one of them could have.

At that point, Claire worried about Dian's reaction to her after their separation of nine months, a period of time which, to a child, can seem like forever. Given what Dian had recently experienced—strange people and strange places, constant flight from the Japanese, malnutrition and illness—she must have suffered from some kind of psychological trauma. Claire chose not to focus on the negatives. The day after she and Dian were reunited, they ventured out into the camp to look through a pile of clothing collected by the Red Cross from departing internees. As they picked out dresses and shoes, Dian asked, "Are you my Mummy?" When Claire said yes, Dian placed her hand in her mother's, and Claire believed everything was all right.[12]

Despite the difficulty of letting Dian go, Peggy walked out of Santo Tomas and turned to her CIC work. Courtney Whitney, who had also just arrived in Manila, tracked her down and assigned her an aide, Eugene Smith, to accompany her around the city. Word of Peggy's whereabouts traveled quickly, and that afternoon she received the best news she had had in a long time: a cable from her son, Charley. He wanted to know how she had come through the war. This may have raised Peggy's hopes for a renewed family life.

Now, though, there were things Peggy wanted to do. One of her first stops was the Malate Convent: "Nothing was standing but the walls of the church. There were parts of bodies all over the place, and blood was spattered everywhere. Everyone was dead," Peggy recalled later. Around February 9, 1945, members of the Japanese Navy turned up at the convent and killed everyone, including Fathers John Heneghan and Patrick Kelly. John Lalor happened to be away from Malate that day and so was spared. He was there on February 13th when the convent grounds were repeatedly shelled. A bomb hit the wall where he stood, killing him by concussion.[13]

The sight of the Malate ruins spurred Peggy to find collaborators. She was particularly determined to find proof that a certain American newspaperwoman had been responsible for the arrest of many Miss U operatives and their contacts in Santo Tomas. Peggy believed that this woman, whom she did not identify by name in her memoir, had herself been interned in Santo Tomas when Ernest Johnson, one of the camp leaders, was transferred there from the Philippine General Hospital. According to Peggy, this woman struck up a friendship with Johnson. When he told her about his involvement with the guerrillas and the Cabanatuan prisoners, she reported him to the camp authorities.

No one took Peggy's accusation seriously until Navy Lieutenant Thor Johnson, Ernest Johnson's son, arrived in Manila to investigate his father's disappearance. After talking with Dr. Antonio Sison, he discovered that Ernest Johnson's body was found near the Cortabitarte Garrison in a mass grave along with other men from Santo Tomas's Executive Committee who had been executed. Something led Thor Johnson to the very same woman Peggy accused. The suspect was finally arrested, and a search of her clothing revealed incriminating documents hidden inside a double brassiere. On February 22nd, Ernest Johnson and the others were reburied in a special plot on the grounds of Santo Tomas.[14]

By the third week of February 1945, Peggy turned over to the CIC a list of American POWs that she had compiled from informants and hearsay, some from records she had buried for safekeeping. On March 7th, Colonel Emil Krause, investigating Japanese atrocities for the Inspector General's Division, interviewed Peggy at Santo Tomas. She identified herself as a nurse, specifying she had worked at Remedios Hospital and that she had been given the rank of brevet lieutenant while she was nursing with the guerrillas.

Peggy explained about Jack Utinsky and then described her wartime work: "I built an organization in Manila known as the Miss U by which method I managed to get food and medicines into prison camps. My experiences have been so numerous with the Japanese, that I could not begin to cover them or know where to start talking about them in logical order. The best thing I can do is to give to you copies of affidavits and letters which tell in detail of Japanese atrocities and of the suffering of American soldiers." She handed over a variety of documents, including letters from Alfred Oliver and Frank Loyd plus notes of her observations of conditions in O'Donnell, Cabanatuan, and Park Avenue.[15]

Now, finally, Peggy believed her war work had ended. It was time to go back to the States. Before leaving the Philippines, she visited her friend Cam Lee, to make sure he was all right. She took twenty dollars with her, not a huge sum of money, certainly not enough to even begin to repay him for all he had done for her, but enough to keep him going. Lee seemed touched by the gesture and showed Peggy that he had collected the same amount for her, assuming all her aid work had left her broke. "You keep it. I'll be all right. I am going home and something will happen," she said. Lee nodded in agreement; he knew her well. "Yes, Miss Peggy, for you something always happens."[16]

AFTER LEAVING MARKING'S CAMP WITH members of the Signal Corps, Yay Panlilio's first stop in Manila was Malacañan Palace, to see Carlos Romulo. Then she visited her friends who had been interned at Santo Tomas and were still there, waiting for the city to be secured. "In the shattered turmoil of retaken Manila, there was little that I found at all, except old friends. That was all I wanted," she recalled. For the first time since 1941, she did not head into war. Yay located Herbert and Janet Walker, who had kept an eye on her children, as well as many of the journalists she knew before the war: David Sternberg, radio station manager for the Far East Broadcasting Company, and Bessie Hackett, society editor of the Manila *Bulletin* who wrote for the Santo Tomas newspaper, the *Internews*. [17]

It was enough for Yay to spend her time socializing; it was the kind of relaxation she had not known for more than three years. Too soon, Marking appeared in Santo Tomas looking for her, and she did not want to be found. Bessie Hackett stashed Yay and her children—including Rae, who had been safely delivered by her guerrilla escort—in one of the camp's shanties. All the friends pitched in to keep them supplied with food and information. They pretended to help Marking look for Yay, leading him around to all of the places she was not.

While hiding from Marking, Yay had a welcome reunion with her half-brother, Raymond Corpus, her daughter Rae's namesake, now a corporal with the 640th Tank Destroyer Battalion, Company B. He had fought his way through the Pacific theater, starting at Guadalcanal, ending on the beach at the Lingayen Gulf. Yay had not seen him since they were children, and her children did not even know they had an uncle. Ray brought a message from their mother, who wanted Yay and the children to come home to California. When Ray gave her five hundred pesos to get the trip started, Yay realized this was the best solution for her family.

Courtney Whitney stopped by to thank her for what she had done during the war, "You've done splendid work, young woman. Good luck to you." With a great sense of relief, Yay and the children packed their belongings, climbed into an army truck, and headed to the Manila docks to board a ship to take them to the States.[18]

ON FEBRUARY 16, 1945, GLADYS Savary considered Pasay safe enough to venture out of the house to search for supplies. New market stalls offered some fruit and vegetables, and Gladys was particularly pleased to purchase some pork. She had a spring in her step as she made her way back to the compound when she saw an army jeep parked on her street. She asked the worried-looking officer in the driver's seat if she could help. He said, "Can you tell me where—damn it to h—Is that you, Gladys? Everybody in Santo Tomas claims you're dead! And they made me come out to look for yours and the Jansons' bodies!"[19]

Gladys recognized Edward Miller "Pete" Grimm, now a colonel on General MacArthur's staff. Pete and Gladys had known each other in Manila before the war, when Grimm had worked organizing the city's piers for the Luzon Stevedoring Company. Pete joined the army in 1941, and MacArthur put him in charge of cargo and transportation for the Southwest Pacific. Pete came along when the Sixth Army began its Philippine campaign in 1944, and he was now working at the newly liberated Santo Tomas internment camp.

Gladys brought Grimm into the house she shared with the Jansons. He told them about the liberation of Santo Tomas, that at least eighteen people had been killed by wayward bombs and gunfire, with another hundred injured. Most of the city neighborhoods, he reported, had been reduced to burning rubble. The Japanese killed as many Caucasians and Filipinos as possible while they retreated, and that was why Pete had given up Gladys for dead.

In fact, while Gladys and the Jansons socialized with Pete Grimm, the battle of Manila, which would not end for another two weeks and would cost about 100,000 lives, was only at its halfway point. The 1st Cavalry Division had reached the city of over 800,000 people on February 3rd and liberated prisoners at Bilibid and Santo Tomas in rapid succession. Despite

General Yamashita's orders for all Japanese troops to evacuate—he did not believe the city could be defended—Rear Admiral Iwabachi Sanji decided to stay and fight. The 1st Cavalry was soon joined by the 37th Division and the 11th Airborne, engaging the Japanese in street-by-street, house-by-house combat. The last remnants of enemy resistance in Manila were finally pacified on March 3, 1945.[20]

After a brief visit, Pete Grimm took his leave of Gladys and the Jansons. Though he brought mostly painful news, Gladys hated to see him go: "He was our first visitor from the other side, and we parted with him reluctantly." Though the battle of Manila continued, most of it was concentrated well north of Pasay by now, and Gladys felt more confident that the war would end soon. After hearing rumors and stories about what various people had done during the fighting, Gladys wondered who the heroes were. "At the risk of sounding unfair, it seems to me from all I hear, that the guerrillas haven't been the little heroes they should have been, around here, anyway."[21]

More of Gladys's friends and acquaintances started showing up in Pasay, many now commissioned with the Army, and she celebrated their returns with food and drink, just like the restaurateur of the old days. They reciprocated when possible, whisking Gladys away in a jeep for a party hosted by some major or colonel. At one such event, the colonel host produced a bottle of Cointreau, and Gladys helped concoct sidecars for the guests. The dinner that followed was, according to Gladys, "out of this world!": steak, potatoes, corn, bread and butter, and apple pie topped with cheese. Life in Manila, in certain areas and for some Americans at least, was starting to return to normal.[22]

By early March 1945, Gladys began to forget the worst of the battle. The bulk of Japanese forces had withdrawn by February 27th, leaving US troops to mop up the stragglers. Now Manila could be used as a base from which the Americans would launch their final push for victory in the Pacific. Gladys observed, "It's an unreal world. The long wait is over and Manila is free. And what a Manila!" She realized the war left her with very little. Her money and most of her possessions were gone, as was her ex-husband and her nephew Edgar Gable. Many of the Manilans she knew before the war prepared to leave the Philippines. Gladys was determined to remain—"for my home is here, my life is here"—so she did what she always had done: invite others to stay with her, pool their resources, drink, and try to laugh. She rented another house and opened a new restaurant.[23]

REUNITED WITH HER DAUGHTER DIAN in Santo Tomas, Claire Phillips experienced a contentment that had eluded her since before the war. This positive feeling was bolstered when Claire met forty-nine-year-old Frederick C. Painton, war correspondent for *Reader's Digest*. After wrapping up his coverage of the war in Europe in the spring of 1944, Painton had moved on to the Pacific theater and arrived in the Philippines in time for the battle of Manila. He now lived and worked with a B-29 crew, but like many members of the US military, he found time to visit with the liberated internees on the grounds of Santo Tomas. Painton probably assumed that among the few thousand American civilians, there were at least a few thousand good stories on that campus.

One of them was Claire's, which had already received brief news coverage. Painton was determined to bring her story to a wider audience. He helped shape the image Claire insisted on presenting for the rest of her life, that of a generous, loving, grieving widow with enough grit and determination to risk her life to help her country in its time of need. By the time Claire left the Philippines, "I Was an American Spy," a feature-length as-told-to story, had already appeared in *The American Mercury*.

Still, Claire remained in Santo Tomas for several weeks to receive the medical attention she needed. Every day, to help regain her health, she took Dian on a short stroll around the campus. It may have been during one of those walks that Claire met a soldier named Dale Risdon, who snapped some photographs of her with Dian. During another, Claire caught sight of her old friend Mona passing by the main gate. Mona seemed a bit embarrassed to have run into Claire again, and she provided a vague explanation of how she had survived. Her Japanese boyfriend had gone off with the Japanese Army. When American planes began bombing Manila in September 1944, Mona took refuge outside of the city and did not return until it was safely in the hands of the Americans. Claire pointed out her change of allegiance—once again—and Mona said, "I don't know what you mean. Had to look out for myself during this horrible war, didn't I?" Claire had to admit, "Yes. We all did."[24]

Now that she was feeling stronger, Claire wanted to find out what happened to her friend Louise De Martini, one of the 2,100 Santo Tomas internees moved to a new camp southeast of Manila at Los Baños in the spring of 1943. The 11th Airborne, supported by Filipino guerrilla forces, had liberated the camp on February 23, 1945, a dramatic rescue that rivaled the one at Cabanatuan. Claire secured a travel pass for Muntinlupa, where the liberated prisoners were recuperating, and there she found her friend happy and well and deeply in love with a fellow internee named Bob Humphreys. As Claire later wrote, "Louise told me that they had heard about my arrest and never expected to see me again. They too, had suffered, but that seemed forgotten in their current happiness."[25]

During her final days at Santo Tomas, as she and Dian awaited repatriation to the United States, Claire received visitors and learned the fate of the others she had worked with in the underground. Claring Yuma, her partner in the Park Avenue School scheme, returned from her hiding place in the hills, and showed up at Santo Tomas to tell Claire that their "Park Avenue boys" had all been taken away to Japan. Naomi Flores, Evangeline Neibert, German Eroles, Dr. and Maria Fe Atienza all stopped by as well. To Claire, they all looked "much older and very emaciated. We sat inside a large army pyramidal tent, and talked for two hours . . . sometimes all at once."[26]

They told her how Father Lalor died and that the Mencarinis had been imprisoned in Fort Santiago and simply disappeared. Claire related what she knew of Ramon Amusategui's imprisonment and death, and German Eroles filled her in about Ramon's wife Lorenza. The Japanese arrested her in January but released her when she suffered a nervous breakdown from which she was still recovering. One of Lorenza's sisters took in the couple's two little boys. However traumatized Lorenza Amusategui might have been by Ramon's arrest and then her own, she had put on a show for her captors, acting insane so they would let her out of prison.

Finally, Claire and Dian hitched a ride in an army jeep to suburban Quezon City to reclaim the papers Claire left with Fely Corcuera for safekeeping. "We received a very enthusiastic welcome at Fely's home, and we dug up my records," Claire later wrote. "The papers were yellow and crumpled, but well preserved in the large demijohns which contained them. . . . All of my boys' notes were intact as well as the hard-won lists of men in the various prison camps. When I exhibited the latter to military intelligence officers, they made careful copies. I would not relinquish the originals . . . they meant so much to me." Claire was now ready to leave the Philippines.[27]

———

JOY OVER MANILA'S LIBERATION MIXED with sadness about what had been lost. "We drove past my old restaurant, where we have been so gay and happy, and have worked so hard. It was a small heap of ashes, not even one small memento remained," Gladys Savary wrote in her diary on March 10, 1945. It was impossible to go back to the good old days, she knew. "That part of my life is over, perhaps our whole way of living is over." Gladys now felt out of place. Compared to what the Americans in Santo Tomas suffered and what happened to civilians in other parts of Manila, she admitted, "I was somewhat embarrassed that I had no wounds to show, no shrapnel nor bullets in my bones—only a few scars on my knees and shins where I had fallen from the bicycle, or climbed a wall too vigorously."[28]

Manila buzzed with activity. Though the war was not finished, people poured into the city hoping for a ringside seat for the much-anticipated ending. Parties went on almost around the clock, and Gladys realized she would have a steady clientele if she opened another restaurant. Her former restaurant staff began showing up at the new house she rented in Pasay (later called Rizal City) on Dewey Boulevard. They encouraged her to go back into business, promising to work for meals until she was on her feet financially. With all these people willing to pitch in, Gladys converted the main floor of the house into a restaurant and bar, moving her living quarters to the second story.

By the middle of the summer of 1945, Gladys's simply-named French Restaurant, which she referred to as the café, opened for business. Enlisted men flocked to the place for lunch, with the evening clientele made up mostly of civilians and officers. The only entertainment available, besides convivial conversation, was a litter of puppies delivered by Gladys's dog,

Spec. "It was a mark of distinction to get invited up to my private apartment to see the pups! Many a dignified general and colonel sat upon my floor, playing with them. It was a good way to make the patrons forget the shortcomings of our little venture," she later wrote. Food prices were sky high—though Gladys managed to provide shrimp, steak, ham, and eggs—and alcohol was in short supply, yet customers packed the place.[29]

The lack of electricity, gas, and running water made the work difficult; still, Gladys enjoyed the socializing her restaurant provided. She remembered the US Consulate reopening sometime in the late spring or summer, reliable mail service resumed, and gradually supplies of all kinds were easier to come by. Gladys once again augmented her restaurant income with rent. She took over the homes of three neighbors who had been repatriated and rented them out as guest houses. Even without reliable utilities, the places were snapped up by those eager to get in on the profits of rebuilding the war-ravaged country.

Gladys thought a lot about what had happened and what was yet to come: "The city was a horrid mess. There was no time to clean it up, and ruins and devastation were everywhere." Military officers who arrived from Europe, where the war ended with Germany's surrender in May 1945, remarked that only Warsaw in Poland had been subjected to more destruction than Manila. Even now, with the fighting pushed into northern Luzon, the city streets were not completely safe; robberies and assaults were commonplace.[30]

"I was uneasy all this time, no news of the prisoners who had been sent to Japan," Gladys also remembered of that summer. The last information she had received about Edgar Gable indicated he had been taken to Japan. It was months now since the liberation of Cabanatuan and Bilibid, and Edgar's name had not turned up on any list of the rescued nor had he shown up in person. Gladys began to accept he was among the large number of POWs "swallowed up in mystery."[31]

What was mystery to Gladys, however, was a new hell for the American prisoners transferred to slave labor camps in Japan and other locations in Asia. On January 9, 1945, Edgar Gable had been one of five hundred POWs on board the *Enoura Maru*, anchored at Takao Harbor in Formosa, when a US Navy bomber hit the vessel. Two hundred and fifty prisoners, including Edgar, were killed. Irvin Alexander survived the raid. As he ate breakfast that morning he heard anti-aircraft fire and the screech of a bomber: "Several planes honored us with attacks, a bomb from one of them exploding on the deck just outside the far corner of the hold. The heavy steel crosspieces were blown down on top of the men who were lying in the middle of the hold, and fragments of steel were generously sprinkled over most of the hold."[32]

Jack Wright, one of the fittest Formosa POWs, was fortunate enough to be out on a work detail, earning extra rations, when the ship was bombed. "The carnage was beyond description," he later remembered. "Those were the men who had held Bataan and Corregidor until they were starved into surrender. They could take punishment. They were brave, hard. They were men who made a man proud to be an American. Now they were a conglomeration of butchered bodies; broken, twisted, hardly recognizable as human beings."[33]

After clearing away the dead bodies, Wright, Alexander, and the other survivors transferred to the *Brazil Maru*, leaving Formosa in a convoy on January 14, 1945, arriving on the Japanese island of Kyushu at the end of the month. There, the men underwent a medical inspection. Those who did not pass were taken to a hospital in Moji, others were trucked to a nearby camp, and the remainder marched to the railroad station. Wright and Alexander ended up at Fukuoka Camp Number 1, which contained just over nine hundred Allied prisoners.[34]

The prisoners received food, were allowed to trade for cigarettes, and spent time working in the camp garden. On April 26, 1945, they again transferred, this time to Fusan, Korea. Part of the group was sent on to Mukden, Manchuria, while the others, including Wright and Alexander, ended up in Jinsen, west of Seoul. Prisoners there received three meals a day, plus tea (or hot water) twice a day; those on work details got extra rations and in May, Red Cross parcels arrived. So the POWs existed, until August 16th, when the Japanese camp commander announced the end of the war. Wright and the others laughed when they heard Japan had been forced to surrender because of a new bomb used by the United

States—they believed it was just another Japanese face-saving explanation. For the first three weeks of their freedom, the men remained in the camp while the Americans dropped in food supplies. On September 8, 1945, they began their journey home.[35]

While Gladys waited to hear final news about her nephew, information trickled in about Manilans who had been involved with smuggling supplies into the POW camps. She described Tony and Josefina Escoda as the "great heroes of the whole prisoner-aid movement," identifying them as the first to get food and medicine into Camp O'Donnell. She lamented the long list of people arrested, tortured, and killed for helping others in need: "My small bit was nothing, yet many people were killed for less than my activities. I was indeed fortunate."[36]

The meaning of collaboration preyed on her mind. Though identifying collaborators consumed much of Peggy Utinsky's last weeks in the Philippines, Gladys viewed such efforts as futile. The CIC and the FBI provided her endless amusement as they tried to "sort out the collaborators from the non-collaborators—a hopeless job," Gladys believed. "There was such a fine line, so far as the Filipinos were concerned, it was well-nigh impossible. What was hard for them to realize was that the Philippines had been occupied for more than three years by the Japanese, that the puppet government was in reality the Japanese government and the Filipinos had to abide by the rulings of the Japanese. There was no choice for them, actually."[37]

Then in August, the war ended. It was a typical summer evening at Gladys's café, with the first of the dinner patrons sipping cocktails as they awaited their meals. An acquaintance of Gladys's arrived, driving erratically, clearly excited. "All gone, Japan's all finished, blown up, no more," he said, and continued on about a terrible new weapon. None of it made sense to Gladys; she assumed he was drunk. A Navy officer arrived a few hours later and filled in the details about Hiroshima and the atomic bomb. Though Gladys felt some fleeting concern for the civilians there, she decided that since this weapon brought about a speedy end to the war, "let there be more of them." It took one more, at Nagasaki on August 9th, to finish the war.[38]

The Japanese surrender on August 15, 1945, triggered the release of the remaining American POWs. When Gladys learned many of them would come through Manila on their way to the United States, she tried to convince the Red Cross to let her work with them at the airport's welcoming station. She knew so many who had been taken prisoner at Bataan and Corregidor and she wanted to be on hand when they finally came home. She also wanted to find Edgar, or at least hear news of him. The Red Cross—which had tried repeatedly in recent months to repatriate Gladys—turned her down. She had to wait for the men to come to her: "More old Manila boys came along, and for many days the little makeshift restaurant was a rendez-vous for those who had returned, literally, from the dead."[39]

"Zombies," Associated Press war correspondent Kenneth L. Dixon called them, a term he picked up from Gladys. Dixon, who had been trav-eling with American troops since 1942, including frontline reporting from the Battle of the Bulge, was now on the Pacific beat, stationed in Manila. He knew if he wanted to meet important and interesting people, he had to go to Gladys's café, which he described as "a section of cobblestones under a porch roof." Every night, at least three or four liberated prisoners turned up there, grateful that at least one thing remained unchanged in Manila: Gladys Savary still ran a restaurant. After complimenting their hostess ("Good old Gladys. You're about all that's left of Manila that hasn't changed. You don't even look any older—at least not much."), they asked about the other men they had been imprisoned with. "Here we go again," Gladys interrupted, "roll call of the zombies."[40]

The Gladys Savary that Ken Dixon met was "tall, serene, whitehaired, and ageless." Gladys agreed with three of those adjectives. When she later copied Dixon's article into her memoir, she omitted the reference to her hair color. The article was a sentimental piece, with strong overtones of you-can't-go-home-again. After the former POWs concluded their roll call, the evening was at an end: "Finally the lamps burning low and one by one the living dead got up to go—back to their billets, and soon on to the United States—and each told Gladys he'd never be back, that there was nothing left."[41]

YAY PANLILIO'S LAST FEW DAYS in Manila consisted of successfully hiding from Marking in a shanty in the liberated Santo Tomas internment camp. She and her three children sailed for the United States on April 2, 1945, on a troop transport ship, the SS *John Lykes*. Here the story comes full circle. On board, Yay met Claire Phillips, who chatted away about her espionage activities at the Club Tsubaki and her doomed marriage to John Phillips. Claire tried to make friends; Yay resisted. Though they had underground work in common, Claire had supplied the guerrillas while Yay had *been* a guerrilla. Claire's stories were greeted with growing skepticism by many of the other passengers, and she tried to enlist Yay's support, Yay kept herself at a distance.[42]

Peggy Utinsky, however, could not avoid getting drawn in. Two pictures, snapped by a Signal Corps photographer in late March 1945, document that Peggy ran into Claire and Dian while they waited to board the *Lykes*. The one Peggy would later include in her memoir shows her standing outdoors with Dian. Peggy, wearing a skirt and blouse, a holster and gun on her hip, appears to be explaining something as the little girl touches a tree. Neither of them is smiling, yet they look at ease with each other. The caption taped to the back of the photo describes Peggy as an "Angel of the underground." It identifies Dian as her daughter.[43]

Claire is not in this picture. She appears in the other one, which neither she nor Peggy included in her book. In it, the two women sit unsmiling on a bench, in what looks like a waiting room. They seem ill at ease, a bit wary, as if they are total strangers thrown together unwillingly. Once on board they appeared to have made no effort at friendship. In fact, as reflected in the opening of this story, they argued during the voyage about money and about receipts that had been collected from the prisoners they had aided.

The fight stemmed from Claire's claims about her underground work during the war. She bragged about the Club Tsubaki, her work on behalf of the prisoners of war, especially those at the Park Avenue School, and her connections with the guerrillas. Claire continued to lie about being the wife of John Phillips. She hinted that she intended to file a claim for his soldier's insurance policy and for reimbursement from the US government for her prisoner relief programs.[44]

Then came the whole flap about the alleged robbery, which revealed Peggy's connection with Claire. Yet Peggy refused to corroborate Claire's version of her underground work. Instead, she verified that Claire planned to file a claim for John Phillip's insurance policy, which she was not entitled to. Peggy also told the FBI agent that *she* had buried Claire's papers along with her own and examined the documents before returning them to Claire. Peggy was positive there were no promissory notes from POWs or from John Boone, and she was certain Claire destroyed some documents to gain sympathy.[45]

It is impossible to know if Peggy was telling the truth. Out of all the passengers on board, she was the one who stood to gain the most by stealing the IOUs and promissory notes. Peggy could add them to her own documents, boosting her claim for monetary compensation from the US government. However, if a real theft had occurred, Claire would have known Peggy was the most likely suspect. Yet she never suggested the FBI agents search Peggy's cabin to recover the documents.

While making her statement to the FBI, Claire admitted to at least a couple of deceptions. One concerned her 1944 arrest in Manila by the Kempeitai. Sometime in 1943, Maria Martinez, working for the guerrilla leader Hugh Straughn, recruited a young woman named Emma Link Infante. Emma and her husband Ramon owned a bar just down the street from the Club Tsubaki, and the two establishments carried on a business rivalry complicated by personal relationships. Emma was sleeping with a Japanese officer, while Claire allegedly had an affair with Ramon. In the spring of 1944, Emma intercepted a message Claire had written, assuming it was a coded love note to her husband. Hoping to get Claire into trouble with occupation authorities over morality issues, Emma turned the note over to her Japanese lover.

Claire's letter contained a message for the guerrillas about supplies she was preparing to send. The receipt of this intercepted message coincided with other Japanese investigations underway during the spring of 1944 stemming from the carabao cart incident in Cabanatuan, ensuring Claire's arrest. However, Claire asserted to the FBI agent, she would have been released immediately if not for Emma Infante's jealousy and her Japanese connections. Claire may have been right about those connections. In early April 1945, when Claire was on her way home, the US Army arrested Emma on a charge of "active collaboration with the Japanese," detaining her, ironically, at the Women's Correctional Institution at Mandaluyong. It was because of a morals charge, Claire admitted, that she was kept in prison. Moreover, she had not been subjected to the torture there that she had earlier claimed.[46]

The other confession Claire made to the FBI was that she had never married John Phillips. She did not provide a clear explanation as to why she lied about that in *The American Mercury* article or in subsequent testimony to immigration officials. Claire told the agent that her first husband, Manuel Fuentes, had secured a divorce in Reno, Nevada, in September or October 1941, and that he had sent her a letter informing her of that action. In subsequent FBI interviews, Claire stated of her relationship with Phil that she had "merely known of such a person and understood that he was killed." That last statement was also false. Phil had written at least one letter home to his family telling them about Claire, a relationship that was more than passing.[47]

Based on the *Lykes* interviews, the FBI concluded: "The investigation conducted reflected strongly not only that her story was false but that she possibly collaborated with the Japanese during the occupation of the Philippines." The Bureau opened a file on Claire Phillips and launched an investigation into whether or not she had violated the National Stolen Property Act, committed mail fraud, and perjured herself to the Immigration and Naturalization authorities.[48]

On May 2, 1945, the SS *John Lykes* docked in Los Angeles, and Peggy Utinsky and Claire Phillips disembarked into their new lives carrying the weight of their wartime baggage. Their hostility onboard ship, which at one point turned into an argument, reveals that, despite the "angel" designation bestowed on them by grateful recipients of their aid, the two women were, of course, flawed human beings. Their passionate natures led them to do good works, but also drew them into more troublesome activities.

In her determination to help the prisoners and the guerrillas, and at the same time save Dian's life and her own, Claire may have been unwilling to draw a firm line between flirting with the enemy to secure information and sleeping with the enemy to guarantee personal safety. In her grief over being unable to prevent Jack Utinsky's death, Peggy turned to anger—and perhaps alcohol—that alienated many of the people she relied on for the success of Miss U and sometimes caused her to take unnecessary risks.

At the end of the war, Peggy and Claire each had little left, except the fact they had made contributions to the US victory in the Philippines. As they struggled to make sense of what happened during the war and what they wanted to do with the rest of their lives, documenting their efforts and successes took on increasing importance.

CHAPTER 18

PEEKING THROUGH THE FENCE
AT A WAR

W HEN THE SS *JOHN LYKES* DOCKED IN LOS ANGELES IN MAY 1945, Yay Panlilio and her family surrendered themselves into the capable hands of the Red Cross: "America, through its organized channels, gave us food, shelter, and clothing." Mere weeks after living in a war-ravaged city dependent on US military supplies for its survival, Yay and her children entered a May Company department store that looked to them like a "fairyland." They hopped on an escalator for the first time, stocked up on new clothing, and ate lunch in the store's restaurant before beginning their trip to Auburn, California.[1]

The Panlilios rode the train north, traveling over four hundred miles to the western foothills of the Sierra Nevada Mountains. Yay's stepfather, Ildefonso Corpus, met them at the station and drove them to the family's small chicken farm. He and his wife Valentina were delighted to be reunited with their daughter and to meet their grandchildren. Valentina was obviously ailing from the bad heart that would take her life the next year, yet her grandmotherly instincts kicked in. She gave each child a set of chores and began instructing them in manners. With her children well in hand, Yay set up her typewriter and went back to work. Her guerrilla-fighting days were over; she was a journalist again.

The first weeks were peaceful, devoted to healing and to family. Marking intruded soon enough, inundating Yay with personal letters and copies of military documents. One, dated March 10, 1945, acknowledged that "Marking's Guerrillas" had been inducted into the U.S. Army, and carried the letterhead of the Philippine Island Forces. Its single organized regiment was officially named the Yay Regiment, "in honor of our beloved guerrilla mother." Marking used this honest demonstration of affection for Yay for his own purposes. The thirty-three letters he sent her contained his declarations of love: "True love is sometimes dangerous. I guess I have told you before that Filipinos are very serious about love, they can kill or be killed or go to jail or go crazy. You will be sorry if I go crazy."[2]

In the last letter of that batch, Marking informed Yay that he had received orders for an important mission. This was no empty boast. Marking had been instructed to deploy his Yay Regiment twenty-five miles northeast of Manila to the Angat River, where the Japanese were dug in around the Ipo Dam. The Americans wanted to guarantee the capital city a consistent water supply and prevent the Japanese from poisoning it. Also dispatched on the mission, which commenced May 10, 1945, was the US 43rd Infantry Division, commanded by Major General Leonard "Red" Wing. Yay followed the news of the pivotal battle on the radio. On May 17th, the American and Filipino forces captured the dam intact, with Marking's men securing its northern edge. Two days later, the mopping-up operations completed, enemy resistance in the area ended. "Marking had gotten his fight," Yay observed.[3]

Battles continued elsewhere in the Philippines, many now concentrated in northern Luzon. Political changes followed the military developments. José Laurel, president of the puppet government, abandoned the islands in mid-April 1945, decamping to Japan along with his family and a few other high-ranking Philippine government officials. With the return of the American troops at the beginning of that year, and the subsequent liberation of Manila, MacArthur had reaffirmed the Commonwealth government and the presidency of Sergio Osmeña. Osmeña had served as the first vice president of the Commonwealth when it launched in 1935, and evacuated from Corregidor with President Manuel Quezon in 1942. The two politicians were the leaders of the government-in-exile in Washington, D.C. When Quezon died in 1944, Osmeña assumed the office. Later that year, to ensure continuity in government despite the disruptions of war, he had accompanied MacArthur on the Leyte landing. Now he was back in Manila.[4]

During the summer of 1945, Marking sent more letters and news clippings to Yay, detailing the projected birth of new Yay regiments, which would culminate in a Yay brigade. He anticipated more than enough fighting in the weeks ahead to make up for the years of inaction. Most of all, Marking wanted Yay back; he offered to marry her, to buy a printing press so she could start her own newspaper or magazine, anything just so that she would consent to be with him. Some of his letters came by mail. Others were hand delivered by soldiers returning stateside from Philippine duty, who added their verbal pleas to Marking's written ones. A registered envelope arrived with $1,250 in checks and money orders, some of it from a "Yay Trust Love Fund" started by the guerrillas. They wanted Yay to live comfortably—and perhaps purchase a passage back to the Philippines.[5]

"It was water on stone, drip-dripping away, wearing me down," Yay later admitted. Marking's relentlessness paid off; she sent replies, which he took as a sign that all was forgiven. In early August 1945, the United States dropped atomic bombs on the Japanese cities of Hiroshima and Nagasaki. Japan finally accepted defeat. As the war in the Pacific drew to a close, Marking secured leave, notified Yay of his anticipated arrival date at her parents' farm, and begged her to be there. Yay waited for him: "If that man ever gets near me again, I'll teach him another bitter lesson. I'll teach him a lesson he'll never forget. I'll marry him."[6]

Yay Panlilio and Marcos Agustin were reunited. "Then, all wars ended, we started home, to build the peace." They had both been married before and needed lawyers to work out the tangled legal issues. Their marriage was recorded on September 11, 1945, shortly before they headed to the Philippines. The country was in its final months of the Commonwealth government, still a colony of the United States, though with a specific date for independence. As a journalist, Yay would find many stories to cover; Marking would have more difficulty easing into the peace.[7]

Most of the couple's time was spent trying to obtain official recognition for their guerrilla organization. With recognition came back pay, money sorely needed by almost everyone in the Philippines. In late September 1945, President Osmeña issued Executive Order No. 68, calling for the demobilization of all guerrilla organizations, making plain that dissolution carried no stigma against those still applying for recognition. It was anticipated that all applications would be received and processed sometime in 1946, though the date was extended several times because of the volume of requests and the tangled process of verification.

The 1945 executive order also contained a provision for paying unrecognized guerrillas as laborers. Marking, who by 1946 was a colonel with the special staff of the general headquarters of the Philippine Army, reacted so badly to the order that he received an administrative reprimand. As he told a local newspaper in the spring, he viewed this as an attempt by the US Army to withhold recognition from many of his men, whose applications were still pending, and to downplay their war efforts by demoting them to "mere" laborers.[8]

It was this comment that prompted the reprimand. Basically, Marking had accused the United States of being cheap. Still more troublesome to the higher-ups were Marking's insinuations about what had always been portrayed as a cozy colonial relationship. That was as much a myth as any alleged "Bataan brotherhood" between American and Filipino soldiers. Americans always saw themselves as the masters, and their handling of the guerrilla recognition issue was yet another example.[9]

Marking expanded his public criticism of the guerrilla-recognition program on June 28, 1946, just days before the Philippines became an independent country. The Commonwealth had been established in 1935 as part of a specific timetable for full independence, public recognition that the United States did not intend to hold the Philippines as a colony indefinitely. Had World War II not intervened, that independence would have been granted in 1945, following a decade of Filipino experience with self-government. War had disrupted the timeline. Once the Japanese were defeated, however, a new date was set, one that reinforced the symbolic ties between the United States and the Philippines—July 4, 1946.

Marking took advantage of this much-anticipated event to gain attention for his cause. On June 28th, he rallied thousands—estimates run between 10,000 and 25,000—of his unrecognized guerrilla fighters for a demonstration in Manila, where the independence festivities were to be held. After a mass meeting, the men marched to Malacañan Palace, the president's official residence. They delivered petitions to Manuel Roxas, the man who defeated Sergio Osmeña in the recent presidential election, and Paul McNutt, the soon-to-be ex-American High Commissioner. Both men promised to look into the matter. Roxas reminded the protesters, who were orderly, that it was a matter for the US military. Lieutenant General Wilhelm D. Styer, Commander in Chief of US Army Forces in the Western Pacific, had the final say. However, in July, President Roxas, perhaps concerned about the possibility of a violent confrontation, recommended recognition for every guerrilla who surrendered his weapon. The US Army vetoed the request.[10]

Because of her position in Marking's Guerrillas and her status as his wife, Yay Panlilio routinely attended the recognition meetings, often speaking on the guerrilla leader's behalf. After her years with the resistance fighters, Yay was comfortable in this role and at ease around the men. And she felt strongly about the issue of recognition, which was an expression of the bond between her two countries. Yay considered herself a citizen of the United States and the Philippines; she fought for both countries when she joined Marking's group. Now she wanted the United States to recognize the Philippines as an equal. She wanted public acknowledgment of the crucial role the Filipino guerrillas played in the war.

The sticking point was the actual number of people who served with the guerrillas. The US Army estimated that about one in every eight people on the island of Luzon—men, women, and children—had submitted a recognition claim. Fewer than 200,000 of the one million would be approved; the rest, according to the army, were clearly part-time guerrillas or "pure, unadulterated frauds." Distinctions between part-time and full-time guerrillas made little sense to the Filipinos who endured the Japanese occupation.[11]

Yet by early 1947, Marking conceded that many guerrilla units throughout the Philippines had inflated their rosters in anticipation of later recognition and compensation. This was the closest he came to admitting he had done the same. Accompanied by a few former guerrilla officers, Yay and Marking headed out to Rizal province to conduct their own investigations of their units' rosters. With his typical bluster, Marking berated former unit commanders for trying to get recognition for "undeserving" people, while Yay smoothed ruffled feathers. Nonetheless, as she knew, Marking believed that he could get the US Army to accept 12,725, in his mind an accurate figure. Yay had not broken the news to him that the army estimated that only 3,738 claims were likely valid.[12]

With the issue far from resolved, the former guerrillas continued to get together and plan strategy. Tempers flared at those meetings, weapons were drawn, and on at least one occasion a gunfight had been narrowly averted. By July 1947, Yay was so worried about all the hard feelings, she thought it likely the ex-guerrillas might attempt to assault or assassinate American army personnel. She reported her concerns to the army. Several officers misconstrued this as a threat, as they did her subsequent comments that her "boys" were still ready to fight and when they did, "things would pop."[13]

In the end, the US Army concluded that the threats from Marking and Yay Panlilio amounted to empty posturing. Officials noted that Marking, now working for the Philippine government—first as Chief of the Secret Service, then as head of the National Bureau of Investigation—had political ambitions. They assumed he would keep a tight rein on his former comrades because he wanted respectability and power for himself and for his wife. Sanctioning violence would not accomplish that. Besides, by 1949 the couple managed to secure recognition for over 12,000 former Marking's guerrillas, very close to the number he had in mind all along.[14]

With this highly politicized matter finally settled, Yay turned her full attention to her writing career. She worked on her wartime memoir, published by the Macmillan Company in 1950 under the title *The Crucible*. The book received favorable reviews in the few publications that acknowledged it. Additional sales may have been spurred when that fall, Yay received the Medal of Freedom, which President Harry Truman had created by Executive Order 9586 in July 1945 to honor civilians living outside the continental United States who had aided the war effort against the Axis powers. Considering Yay's heritage and her determination to save both of her countries during the war, receiving this medal meant everything.[15]

In 1955 Yay began writing a weekly column, "Where a Country Begins," for the *Weekly Women's Magazine* in Manila. For six years, she used the column to explore the cultural and political complexities of the Philippine Islands. Perhaps not surprisingly, her marriage to Marking lasted only a few years. Yay returned to the United States in the 1970s, when President Ferdinand Marcos imposed martial law, which lasted until 1981. Yay was living in New York City when she died in 1978, her role as a guerrilla leader and an avenging angel for her two countries, forgotten.[16]

GLADYS SAVARY DID NOT LEAVE Manila at the end of the war, or at least not permanently. After she opened the French Restaurant in the summer of 1945, Gladys earned a reliable income, and after all these years, despite the war and its devastation, Manila was home. In the spring of 1946 she returned to the United States for a visit, so she was not present for the celebrations of Philippine independence on July 4th. When she returned to Manila, Edgar Gable's widow, Marian, accompanied her to help run the restaurant. Life was almost as it had been before the war. Gladys had a business to tend, a steady stream of customers and friends to drink and chat with, and a trusted relative to rely on.[17]

Two years later, Gladys applied for compensation under the US War Claims Act of 1948, which was passed to assist those who had been in enemy detention. Her success depended on a broad interpretation of "custody," and in 1951 the General Counsel of the War Claims Commission, Abraham S. Hyman, ruled in her favor, finding that although Gladys had not been interned or imprisoned, "The evidence supports a finding that claimant as by force of the Japanese Army restrained in her movements and activities, was subjected to arrest, and surveillance, and her premises searched and property seized to such an extent that she was captured and held by the Japanese Imperial Government." She received $60 for each month of the occupation.[18]

The French Restaurant operated until 1949, when Gladys and Marian Gable closed it and departed Manila amid public controversy over city-wide payoffs and graft. In a letter to the *Manila Daily Bulletin*, reminiscent of the one she had sent to *Time* magazine from Venezuela twenty years earlier, Gladys identified unfair taxation and "palm-crossing" as her reasons for giving up the restaurant and returning to the United States. (Marian Gable had her own reason: she was to remarry.) City officials vowed to investigate Gladys's allegations, though some claimed she "twisted her facts" to justify a hasty, unprofitable departure. One voice raised in her defense came from none other than Colonel Marking, now identified as the Chief Confidential Agent for the Philippine government: "The most we can do now is to find ways and means to prevent such a misfortune to be repeated, especially to persons like Madame Savary and others who came to our shores and became real friends and who have the liking and sympathy of the Filipino people."[19]

Not quite ready for retirement, in 1950, Gladys opened her third and final establishment, a restaurant called Ramor Oaks, in Atherton, California. The restaurant became a gathering place for a number of friends from the old Manila crowd, many of whom now resided along the West Coast. Gladys modeled the place after the prewar Restaurant de Paris and her friends felt very much at home. Her ongoing contact with them may have sparked her decision to write a memoir of her Manila years.

Gladys self-published *Outside the Walls* in 1954. She made clear she wanted her friends to understand her perspective on wartime Manila: "What happened to me, my little trials and tribulations under the Japanese rule, how I reacted—for I am typical of the human race: each of us finds his or her own case of supreme interest. People's different points of view are like little boys peeking through a fence at a ball game—it depends on where the knothole is, what they see of the game. So we all peeked through the fence at a war, and all saw it differently." [20]

Gladys was particularly anxious that readers know she did not sit out the war in luxury, that she had suffered as all Manilans had, even that everyone's suffering was a bit different. She reflected on her experiences rather than merely recounting them. In the end, Gladys seemed to accept that she had done what she could during the war to help others. If she had survived it was because of a light-minded attitude, a bit of luck, and some alcohol.

Gladys sold Ramor Oaks the year after her book came out, and set sail for England. Why she chose England is not clear. London was the last place she had received word from André Savary, so it is possible they arranged to meet up—for old time's sake. Having not heard from him after all these years, it was not even clear to her that he had survived the war. Maybe she wanted to find out. Whether or not a reunion took place, she was back in the States by 1956. Around 1970, Gladys moved to North Hollywood. She submitted an article to the local paper, a reminiscence of a wartime Fourth of July celebration during an enemy occupation. It was the last time she commented publicly on the war. Gladys Savary died in 1985 in Palo Alto, California, at the age of 92, the longest-lived, least-recognized, but perhaps most perceptive and contented of the four women. [21]

─────

THE WAR HAD PROVIDED CLAIRE PHILLIPS with the opportunity to become famous, and after it was over she had no intention of spending the rest of her life away from the limelight. In response to the trouble on board the SS *John Lykes* during April 1945 and in "view of the fact that this individual gave a fantastic story of her activities while in the Philippines which had many discrepancies," the FBI launched an investigation of Claire when she returned to the States. By this time, however, Claire was already becoming a public heroine. She was determined to capitalize on her "fantastic story."

An Army officer from the Public Relations Office met Claire in Los Angeles when the ship docked on May 2nd. *The American Mercury* published her as-told-to story with Frederick Painton, and throughout the summer she gave interviews to the press. All of these stories repeated the same sequence of events Claire had outlined for Painton back in Manila, complete with her Christmas Eve wedding to John Phillips. The CBS Sunday radio program, *I Was There* featured Claire on June 17, 1945. The renowned gossip columnist Louella Parsons wrote about Claire in July and August, when she was in Los Angeles, making the rounds of the movie studios. This must have been a dream come true—after all those years as a struggling entertainer, Claire had the spotlight. It was clear, according to the FBI, that she intended to broker a Hollywood deal "for the filming of her false story and the possibility of her receiving a leading role in such picture."[22]

The American Mercury story also attracted the attention of family members still awaiting news about the fate of their loved ones in the Philippines. Celia Thorp, wife of the guerrilla leader Claude Thorp, sent a letter to Claire, asking if Claire could confirm the information she received: that Claude had been captured and executed by the Japanese. Claire responded in a letter dated May 14, 1945, addressing the woman as "My Dear Mrs. Thorp": "I can't tell you how happy I was to get your letter, altho I am afraid I cannot do much to help you."[23]

Claire explained that she had worked with Captain John Boone's guerrillas, under Colonel Edwin Ramsey's command, and therefore had heard about Claude Thorp, but never knew him personally. Her letter to Celia was riddled with misspelled words and poor grammar: "I am quite sure your husband was shot in the Chinese cemetary [*sic*] by the Jap's [*sic*] . . . I don't remember the date, but I think it was the fall of 1943. But as soon as I write to Capt. Boone again I will ask him to give me all the data he can. Maybe he can help you more than I can. That's where the Jap's [*sic*] held most of their exicutions [*sic*] and after mid_night [*sic*] and before dawn."[24]

Claire referred to Boone as a captain, but by this point he had been promoted to major. At the end of the war he returned stateside for medical treatment at Brooke General Hospital, Fort Sam Houston, in San Antonio. Once he recovered, in November 1945, Boone was transferred to Fort Ord, California, to await return to duty in the Philippines. Claire stayed in touch, but the FBI, anxious to interview him about Claire's wartime activities, had a hard time tracking him down.[25]

Claire commiserated with Celia Thorp: "I know how you feel, that you will not give up hope until there is not a doudt [sic] or stone unturned. That is how I was about my husband. Even after several men and two chaplains had written that they were sure it was no mistake, I still could not believe it was true that I would never see my husband again."[26]

There was one more letter from Claire to Celia Thorp, dated about a month later. It revealed what Claire kept out of the public eye. Celia had asked about Claire's health, and she responded, "It is not bad concidering all I went thru. Altho I am terribly nervous now and I used not to have a nerve in my body. At least I never, ever felt nervous before.... Of course I am anemic and malnutrition is common with every one that came back. But I am picking up very well. Just this nervous tention [sic] which seems to stay with me."[27]

Today, Claire would be diagnosed with post-traumatic stress disorder, an unidentified condition in 1945. Most Americans could not have understood what had happened to her in the Philippines and would not have comprehended her distress. Although World War II brought hundreds of thousands of American women into military service, especially through the WACs and the WAVES, regulations kept them away from active battle zones. These women had volunteered for service, received training, orders, supplies, and pay. Claire, a civilian, lived through an invasion, occupation, and liberation. She had been caught in an isolated, bloody corner of the war, and had had to live by her wits. Few Americans would have recognized or understood the cost to a woman like Claire.[28]

Despite her nerves, Claire kept busy cultivating her heroine persona. She traveled between Portland, where she and Dian stayed with Claire's mother, and California over the next several months to explore movie possibilities, but made little progress. Her postwar public identity heavily relied on her sham marriage to John Phillips, and she did not want anyone questioning it. Claire continued corresponding with Vada Phillips, Phil's mother, who lived in Wasco, California, about two hours north of Los Angeles. At the same time, however, Claire resumed her relationship with Manuel Fuentes, her legal husband. Manuel had also returned to the United States and was now working at Fort Mason and living on Powell

Street in San Francisco. Claire and Dian stayed there with him for a time, though Claire no longer used his name and spent limited time out in public with him.[29]

In mid-September 1945, Claire thought it was time for a face-to-face meeting with Vada Phillips, so she visited Phil's mother in Wasco. The more Vada talked to Claire, the more she was convinced that her son would never have married this woman. Vada later told an FBI agent that certain things had convinced her that Claire "had not been married to her deceased son, nor at any time did she appear interested in some of his past as a boy or in knowing any of the intimate things concerning John." The two women never met again.[30]

The NBC radio program *Cited for Valor* featured an interview with Claire on October 9, 1945, and included a dramatization of her story. She was presented on air as a "charming woman who became the center of a web of patriotic intrigue." About two weeks later, Claire spoke to the San Francisco chapter of the American Legion, and her photo appeared on the front page of the *California Legionnaire*. Claire had hoped that all of these appearances would raise her public profile, improving her chances for a movie contract, yet by early 1946, nothing had materialized. It is possible that she was unaware of the FBI's ongoing investigation, or that its agents also talked to Hollywood people, which may have caused the studios to back off. "War pictures have run their cycle," one report asserted. In any case, the film companies considered Claire's story "of no particular value at this time although five years from now it may become valuable."[31]

By the end of the summer of 1945, the FBI concluded—after consulting with the Counter Intelligence Corps—that Claire had not engaged in any "pro-Japanese activities" during the war. Agents in Portland also determined that Claire held no subversive political views. By the end of that year, Claire filed a claim for $15,000 (worth about $193,000 in 2015) with the General Accounting Office for payment of the services she rendered to the American guerrilla forces in the Philippines. This prompted an investigation by the Claims Division of the War Department.[32]

In her sworn deposition, she used the name Claire M. Phillips and testified she had lost almost all of her personal records, including IOUs and receipts, because of her arrest and imprisonment by the Japanese. She did not mention the alleged theft on board the SS *John Lykes*. Claire broke down the requested $15,000 as follows: $6,000 distributed in cash, $1,000 worth of clothing, $3,000 in medicine and toiletries, and $5,000 worth of food. The claim was supported by an affidavit from Major John Boone, dated October 12, 1945, while he was stationed at the Santa Barbara Redistribution Detachment. He confirmed the value of her donations and testified that "receipts which were issued by affiant, Major John P. Boone to Mrs. Claire Phillips were issued some in her name and the balance in the name of 'Highpockets,' her code name, and that affiant is informed that all of said receipts have been lost or stolen."[33]

As this investigation proceeded, Claire realized she might never see a settlement. She turned to Manuel Fuentes for financial support. Although they were not yet divorced, they considered the marriage over, and Manuel had returned to his job in the Philippines. Still, he agreed to pay Claire $200 a month, which was not enough to support her and Dian. In February 1946 Claire tried for some quick cash by applying for John Phillips's Army death benefits. A captain in the First Gratuity Pay Branch of the Office of Special Settlements turned down the request since it had not been accompanied by documentation of a legal marriage. If Claire could not provide this proof by the end of March, she was told, the benefit sum of $500 would be paid to Vada Phillips. In mid-March, Claire sent another letter to Vada, offering up a unique perspective on the dispersal of the money. Claire informed Vada that the War Department gave Claire permission to *allow* John Phillips's insurance to be paid out to his mother. "I feel that you are more entitled to it that I am, and really do want you to have it," she wrote.[34]

If Claire had been hoping Vada would turn the money over to her, she must have been disappointed. Claire's clumsy attempt to obtain the death payment had attracted the attention of the Army's Field Investigation Branch of the Office of Dependency Benefits in New York City. The FBI tracked that investigation while continuing its own. In early October 1946, a memo from FBI director J. Edgar Hoover concluded that Claire had not violated the National Stolen Property Act but might still be prosecuted for fraud in connection with her $15,000 reimbursement claim. At the end of that investigation, the Bureau intended to interview Claire again. Hoover advised, "If prosecution has not been authorized, the subject should be specifically admonished to stop making unwarranted claims in connection with her alleged espionage activities. She should also be admonished to cease intimating that she has had any connection with the Federal Bureau of Investigation."[35]

Claire enlisted the help of Ed Riley, mayor of Portland, Oregon. He turned to Senator Wayne Morse for assistance in collecting this claim through congressional action for a "respected citizen" of Portland. At the end of October 1946 Assistant US Attorney William Ritzi declined to prosecute Claire on a charge of making false claims in connection with the reimbursement request. Ritzi based his decision on the War Department's inability to determine whether or not Claire's claim was unfounded. Moreover, the army determined there was no precedent for it to pay out such a claim; this could only be accomplished through a special act of Congress. The Army's Contract Claims Commission officially denied Claire's request in early December 1946.[36]

This did not put an end to her quest for recognition. Throughout that year, Claire spent considerable time in Los Angeles, trying to secure a movie deal and getting started on a companion project, the book-length account of her wartime experiences. While Claire knew she had a great story to tell, she did not, as evidenced in samples of her personal letters, possess the writing skills to produce a book on her own. She chose Myron B. Goldsmith, a World War I veteran and professional writer, as her partner. John Boone provided the foreword.[37]

Manila Espionage was published in the late spring of 1947 by Binfords & Mort, a small but well-regarded Oregon house catering to Pacific Northwest authors and subjects. Sales were likely modest, and while some local articles mentioned the book, it did not receive reviews in any major periodicals. Claire kept her job in the manufacturing branch office of the National Laundry Company in Portland, at least for a while longer. She may have been receiving some money, especially child support, from Manuel Fuentes, though the couple divorced in 1947.[38]

Claire was not one to remain single for long. When she visited a hospital in Vancouver, Washington, on Christmas Day of 1947, she met Robert Clavier, a thirty-one-year-old Cabanatuan survivor. He was still recuperating from his ordeal and suffered from tuberculosis. They decided to get married anyway, tying the knot at a Vancouver Presbyterian church on January 16, 1948. In light of what Claire had been planning for her future, Clavier seemed the perfect, romantic choice for a new spouse. He had survived the prison camp that had killed her wartime husband, and his survival could be linked to Claire's High Pockets activities. The marriage only lasted a few years, though, and Claire continued to use the name Phillips in public. [39]

Manila Espionage kept Claire in the public eye. It did not, however, attract the kind of attention she hoped for. The FBI reopened the investigation it had shuttered at the end of 1946. Now the Bureau anticipated some further developments, especially since Claire pursued her reimbursement claim in Congress, this time for $6,000 (worth over $58,000 in 2015) in compensation, an amount she believed was much too low. Despite Senator Wayne Morse's unwavering support, in 1947 and 1948, bills in both houses did not pass. The repeated failures had more to do with questions over jurisdiction and liability than anything else, yet Claire felt she had been treated unfairly. [40]

In his ongoing quest to help Claire Phillips, Senator Morse asked one of his aides to contact the FBI for any information it might have on her. The FBI tried to pass the aide off to the War Department, but she insisted the senator needed the Bureau's input. An agent provided the senator with an oral report on Claire's background, stressing that the FBI "has no first-hand information concerning any activities on the part of the subject in connection with aiding the guerrilla forces." General Courtney Whitney, who ran intelligence for General MacArthur in the Southwest Pacific theater, confirmed this for Morse's office: "I have no record or recollection concerning the activities of Mrs. Phillips in connection with the resistance movement." [41]

In terms of "background," the FBI focused on the inconsistencies in Claire's various statements over the last couple of years. One of the agents wrote on a document in Claire's file, "She's a prostitute. Got a lot of publicity and is a phony." Two additional agents jotted below that, "I concur." It is uncertain if this particular assessment was passed along to Senator Morse; still, he did not abandon Claire's claim.[42]

Claire's hopes for a satisfactory settlement were buoyed in 1948 when she received the Medal of Freedom. Despite all the questions raised by the FBI and the difficulties involved with Senator Morse's investigation, Claire's name was put forward for this honor by General MacArthur's office, and the award was conferred by General Mark Clark on August 19, 1948, at Fort Lewis, Washington.

Congress's lack of action over the reimbursement bill did not prevent Claire from pursuing a movie deal. She met with an independent producer, David Diamond, in Hollywood in March 1950. During the trip, Claire was brought to a radio studio for a surprise taping of the popular NBC program *This Is Your Life*. The show aired on Wednesday night, March 15th, and proud Oregonians chipped in with gifts to honor Claire's wartime achievements. A local realtor and housing developer presented Claire with a brand-new three-bedroom home, complete with furniture and appliances provided by the Ramblers Club of the Jewish Community Center. Lewis and Clark College pledged a four-year music scholarship to young Dian Clavier.[43]

That Hollywood meeting proved fruitful. It had taken five years, but it finally happened. David Diamond signed with Allied Artists to make the picture, called *I Was an American Spy*, which began filming in early 1951. Paid $1,500 (about $13,500 in 2015) for the rights to her story, Claire was also hired as a technical adviser. Ann Dvorak, perhaps best known for her role in 1932's *Scarface*, was cast as Claire Phillips, with Gene Evans as John Boone. General Mark W. Clark, chief of Army Field Forces and the man who had presented Claire with her Medal of Freedom in 1948, provided a prologue to the film, focusing on values of loyalty and patriotism. Print ads featured glowing testimonials of Claire's wartime activities from Oregon Senator Wayne Morse.[44]

At the beginning of May 1951, Claire traveled to Washington, D.C. for the movie's world premiere, scheduled for May 16th at the RKO Keith

Theater on 15th Street NW, near the White House and the Statler Hotel where she was staying. During the first week of her promotional visit to the capital city, Claire marshalled some moxie and sent a telegram to J. Edgar Hoover, inviting him and a guest to the event. The FBI director replied, disingenuously, that it was a thoughtful gesture, and "I would be happy to be with you on this occasion; however, a previous engagement will preclude my having that pleasure."[45]

For all the carefully orchestrated photo opportunities and luncheon talks, and despite Claire's considerable charisma, *I Was an American Spy* failed to take off. The review in *The New York Times* described the movie as a "seemingly earnest account" of Claire's wartime espionage, but found it not "especially stimulating, either as a narrative or as a tribute to personal courage." More successful was the movie's theme song, the 1940 tune "Because of You," performed by Tony Bennett, giving the popular singer his first major hit and keeping him at the top of the Billboard chart for ten weeks in 1951–1952.[46]

Just after filming of the movie commenced, the US Senate introduced another bill concerning reimbursement to Claire Phillips, this time recommending the issue be settled by the US District Court in Oregon. In 1952 the case was taken up by the Court of Claims, with Claire petitioning for relief in the whopping amount of $146,850 (worth over $1.3 million in 2015). The subsequent investigation took nearly five years as the government tracked down others who worked on behalf of the prisoners and guerrillas on Luzon during the war. Among those giving testimony were Fely Corcuera Santos, Naomi Flores Jackson, Maria Martinez, Lorenza Amusategui O'Malley, and Peggy Utinsky.[47]

Of those, only Fely Corcuera, considered Claire Phillips's principal witness, was sympathetic. Fely arrived in the United States in October 1947 to enroll in postgraduate studies at the university in Portland, Oregon. She resumed her friendship with Claire, who probably helped facilitate her visit. Fely also met and married Dr. Ernesto Santos, with whom she moved to Hawaii in the 1950s. However supportive Fely's testimony, it did not strengthen Claire's case. Beyond acknowledging that she worked at the Club Tsubaki and had tried to keep it going after Claire's arrest, she stated that she "could not estimate the extent of plaintiff's [Claire Phillips] contributions to the guerrillas or to the prisoners of war."[48]

Warren E. Burger, then the Assistant Attorney General in the Justice Department, sent a letter to Peggy Utinsky in October 1954, advising her of Claire's upcoming trial and requesting she make herself available to give testimony. At the time, Peggy was on a speaking tour in southern California, promoting her own book. She contacted the FBI office in Los Angeles, requesting help from the Bureau in making these arrangements. She gave her statement the following October in San Francisco, confirming what the other witnesses said: that Claire Phillips was a minor member of the Miss U organization. According to Peggy, Claire "never donated anything other than money; that plaintiff sent pesos in small amounts to several members of the 31st Infantry whom she knew and who had been imprisoned in Cabanatuan," totaling perhaps 2,000 pesos.[49]

Particularly damaging to Claire's case was the recovery of a diary she kept during the war. Only three entries out of eighty-four documented money sent to the prison camps, each one noting modest amounts of one hundred to five hundred pesos. One entry on June 7, 1943, mentioned that in response to a letter received from John Boone, Claire dispatched one hundred pesos and some medicine to the guerrillas. Though she claimed to have sold the house she lived in with Manuel Fuentes before the war and sent the 30,000 pesos in proceeds to Boone in 1943, Boone denied ever receiving such a sum. Claire could not recall any of the details about the house sale.[50]

Her credibility was further damaged by her contradictory testimony about her alleged marriage to John Phillips. Letters turned over to the court by Evangeline Neibert documented how Claire planned to get $50,000 from the US government, which she promised to share with Evangeline and Naomi Flores. Claire began writing to Evangeline in June 1947, explaining she had retained a lawyer who needed Evangeline to corroborate Claire's story. "I waited and waited for Mrs. U. to do something for us," she told Evangeline, referring to Peggy Utinsky, "but she has really forgotten us. I think she started forgetting when we arrived in the US or maybe before we left Manila. She sure was a different person on the ship, than when we were all working together." After two years, that shipboard incident loomed large in Claire's mind. During the war, Claire had thrived when she surrounded herself with a small coterie of supporters—Fely, Evangeline, Naomi, Maria Martinez, Florence Smith. Now she felt abandoned.[51]

These statements suggest that Claire believed she had an agreement about reimbursement with Peggy that was no longer being honored. Claire's letter emphasized that she was willing to split the money with Evangeline and Naomi, "*But NOT Mrs. U. Let her get her own. I am not just making a promise like Mrs. U. did.*" Subsequent letters encouraged Evangeline to use large numbers when discussing the amount of aid the underground workers dispensed. "I know you cant [sic] remember the exact amounts and dates of trips, but no one can check and find out the difference," Claire assured her. "We are not trying to cheat any one, we are only trying to get paid for the good work we did. Am I right?" She even included a sample letter for Evangeline to copy, sign, and send to her attorney.[52]

Despite Claire's promises of large amounts of money and assistance in getting to the United States, neither Evangeline nor Naomi could bring herself to do as Claire asked. Naomi's testimony referred to small amounts of money passing into the POW camps. She remembered Claire "used to write to about five prisoners, including with her letters sometimes five and sometimes ten pesos; that on one occasion she sent 20 pesos; and, on another, 200." A week before Lorenza Amusategui was scheduled to testify in September 1955, Claire tried a similar tactic. She addressed Lorenza by her nickname, "Larry," reminding her, "We were good friends in Manila, so why cant [sic] we be now. You and I both know, there never was any hard feeling among the group, we all worked together for one cause and each did what he or she could do."[53]

Claire wanted to know why Larry, her "old pal," failed to reply to an earlier letter and was also curious: "Why are you to be a witness *for* the Gov.? Does this have some thing to do in regards to your claim in now? I am sure you would not *hurt me*, but wonder how much you will *help me*." Lorenza had indeed recently settled her claim with the US government in the amount of $30,000 for the money and supplies she and her husband Ramon provided to the POWs. This, despite the fact that, like Claire, Lorenza had lost or destroyed receipts, notes, and IOUs. Unlike Claire, Lorenza had not lied about her personal circumstances, and she had at least one friend well placed to help her.[54]

Lorenza survived the war as a widow, and as she pulled her life back together in Manila, she met a lieutenant colonel with the US Air Transport Command, Oliver La Farge. A Pulitzer Prize–winning novelist (for a 1929 book called *Laughing Boy*), La Farge became fascinated with Lorenza's stories about her anti-Japanese work and the consequences she suffered because of it, especially the loss of her husband, Ramon. The two became correspondents once La Farge returned home to New Mexico. He assisted Lorenza with securing recognition for Ramon's status as a guerrilla officer and his involvement with smuggling supplies to the military prisoners. [55]

It had been Ramon Amusategui's dream that his children grow up in America, and his widow was as anxious to achieve this as she was to receive recognition and compensation. Lorenza insisted she did not want any monetary compensation "in exchange of past deeds, because I do not believe in mixing charity with credit." She seemed particularly concerned with that last point, mixing charity with credit. "I suppose I should have followed the attitude taken by some individuals such as Claire Phillips, and made a big publicity of past deeds . . . then maybe US authorities would know of my existence," she wrote to Oliver La Farge. "Never have I read so many lies as C.P.'s article, 'I Was an American Spy.'" Lorenza could not find one good thing to say about Claire.[56]

In summation, lawyers for the US government submitted that Claire Phillips was "guilty of false testimony and of fraud upon this Court. Congress should be advised that, had her claim been presented under the Court's general jurisdiction, it would have been forfeited for such fraud." In July 1957, Chief Judge of the Court of Claims, John Marvin Jones, handed down an opinion that was not quite as harsh in tone as the government's brief. Jones agreed that Claire had "greatly exaggerated" much of her story and that witness testimony clearly proved that. "Yet when all the rubbish is cleared away it is rather well established by outside testimony that she furnished to prisoners of war and to organized guerrillas funds and supplies of the value of 8,500 pesos." Therefore, the Court of Claims recommended Congress reimburse Claire in the amount of $1,349.21 (worth about $11,000 in 2015) because "her sympathies and efforts were on our side in a time of great emergency."[57]

Despite the Court of Claims's more conciliatory tone, the monetary award must have seemed a slap in the face to Claire. After the heady early years of the 1950s—appearing on a popular national radio program, seeing a movie based on her own experiences—the decade ended with a decided reversal of fortune. Claire became a divorcée for the second time and, for some unknown reason, was estranged from her only daughter. Plus she had money woes again, which sent her back to working in a bar.

Claire died in Portland, Oregon, on May 22, 1960, from meningitis. A four-paragraph obituary, identifying her simply as Claire Phillips, appeared in *The Oregonian* about a month later. It focused on her wartime activities, her book, and her appearance on *This Is Your Life*. In the end, as in the beginning, it was fame that mattered.[58]

AFTER DISEMBARKING FROM THE SS *John Lykes* in California in early May 1945, Peggy Utinsky headed east to Washington, D.C. She lived for a time with the family of Alfred Oliver, the former army chaplain at O'Donnell and Cabanatuan who had been a "Miss U" contact. When he had met Peggy in person in the Philippines in February 1945, Oliver was so impressed that he wrote to General MacArthur's headquarters, recommending she be sent out "to address Women's Clubs on the subject of her experiences in order to arouse America." The war in the Pacific had not yet ended; no one knew how long the Japanese would hold out. Nonetheless, it is unlikely Peggy objected to Oliver's plan. She was a middle-aged widow, had limited contact with her adult son, and lost all her possessions in the war. She was also still recuperating from a physically and emotionally taxing ordeal. Somehow, Peggy had to earn a living.[59]

The Red Cross may have offered another option. Major John L. Lucas, a member of the Army Corps of Engineers who had been freed by the raid on Cabanatuan, was a patient at Walter Reed Hospital in Washington when he met Peggy in the summer of 1945. Lucas had known about and benefited from the aid smuggled in to the prisoners at Cabanatuan. He was particularly anxious for news of Maria Martinez, one of Miss U's operatives. Peggy told him she saw Maria in Manila after the liberation and that she had looked fine. The major sent Maria a long letter of appreciation, enclosing a $25 money order: "I was afraid if and when the Japanese found out about your activities for the benefit of the American Prisoners as to what they might do to you, there are so many of us who owe our being alive to you for the food, money, medicines and the cheery letters you sent us." Lucas informed Maria that the American Red Cross had offered Peggy a job, though he did not know if she would take it.[60]

Peggy remained in Washington through the end of 1946. There is no evidence she took the Red Cross offer. She had recently declined to work with the organization on Luzon while she awaited repatriation, and there is no indication that she now held it in any greater esteem. Peggy's money problems were alleviated in an unexpected way. Though the US Army declined to recognize her rank of brevet lieutenant with the guerrillas—John Boone lacked the authority to issue such an appointment—making Peggy ineligible for back military pay, Congress came through. In July 1946, the US House of Representatives passed H.R. 6213, a bill introduced by the chair of the Committee on Claims, Daniel McGehee of Mississippi. The bill approved reimbursement to Peggy Utinsky in the amount of $9,820 (worth about $118,000 in 2015) for the personal possessions she sold to benefit the POWs. The Senate concurred, and Private Law 781 passed on July 25, 1946. The government considered this full settlement on all war claims Peggy might have.[61]

Three months later, Peggy received the Medal of Freedom, one of many women from the Philippines, including Yay Panlilio and Claire Phillips, upon whom this honor was conferred. Nancy Belle Norton, the elderly retired schoolteacher, had received the award in 1945, its inaugural year. Repatriated to the United States after the war, Nancy Belle made the rounds of veterans' hospitals and various reunions, keeping in touch with the men who survived the Philippine prison camps. These grateful men referred to her affectionately as "Ma Norton" or the "White Angel," terms she deflected modestly: "Why landsakes, I wanted to do so much more than I could. Please don't say I was a heroine. I just did what I could. Anybody would have done the same."[62]

Peggy's award originated with the War Department, and Major General Edward F. Witsell of the Adjutant General's Office sent her a letter informing her she had been selected. The citation acknowledged her "extremely hazardous and valuable services" concerning aid to the POWs and guerrillas in the Philippines. Three generals—Claude B. Ferenbough, Charles P. Hall, and Peggy's old friend Walter K. Wilson—presented the medal in a small ceremony in Washington, D.C. There is no evidence that her son Charley or any other family member attended.[63]

The War Department conferred this honor despite a curious notation in Peggy's case file. The Supreme Commander for the Allied Powers (SCAP) created a Legal Section in early 1945 to investigate war crimes. Peggy's file contained statements she made about her activities with Miss U, the beatings she endured by Japanese soldiers, and her imprisonment in Fort Santiago. At the end of the year, First Lieutenant Sheldon A. Key of the Judge Advocate General Department recommended Peggy's file be closed, noting she was now in the United States and would presumably not prove very valuable in tracking down war criminals. Key also passed along some information from a Lieutenant Nelson who described Peggy as "unreliable," and who claimed to have interviewed other witnesses who said Peggy "pointed them out" to the Japanese. Yet none of these witness statements appeared in Peggy's file, nor was she investigated for or charged with collaboration.[64]

In 1947, Peggy moved to San Antonio, Texas, for reasons that are not entirely clear. It is possible her son was living in the area and she wanted to be close to him. If so, the proximity probably ended up causing her grief. There is no evidence that mother and son spoke to each other after the war, nor any hint as to the source of estrangement. To support herself, Peggy may have taken a job at Brooke General Hospital in San Antonio, an army medical facility. That may have been where she met the writer and composer Ora Pate Stewart. The wife of an Air Force officer, Ora had recently given birth, and she hired Peggy to provide at-home nursing services.

The two become fast, lifelong friends, with Peggy sometimes living for months at a time in the Stewart home, the children calling her Aunt Margaret. Ora noticed the toll that Peggy's wartime experiences had taken on her, physically and psychologically. Like Claire Phillips, Peggy probably suffered from post-traumatic stress disorder. Peggy, however, was lucky to have someone in her life who recognized the pain she was in and offered help.

Ora encouraged Peggy to write down her story—it would be therapeutic, she insisted—and Peggy devoted most of that year to the project. Confronting the war years, if only on the page, kept Peggy tied to the other survivors of the Japanese occupation. G.G. Estill, a San Antonio illustrator, inked the black-and-white drawings for the book, similar to the ones he produced for Calvin Ellsworth Chunn's collection of Cabanatuan writings, *Of Rice and Men*. Peggy was well-connected and highly-regarded enough that retired General Jonathan Wainwright contributed the foreword to her book. He hailed Peggy's "gallantry and intrepidity" as "worthy of the best traditions of our country." An accomplished author, Ora Stewart may have had a hand in the actual writing of the memoir, advising Peggy on both style and content. Ora also placed it with her publisher, The Naylor Company.[65]

As the book's publication date approached in the spring of 1948, Peggy's health collapsed. She landed in the hospital, listed in critical condition due to long-term complications from the injuries she sustained in Fort Santiago. Peggy recuperated enough to serve as a panelist, along with Ora Pate Stewart and publisher Joe Naylor, at the Southwest Writers Conference in Corpus Christi that June. [66]

Still, Peggy seemed haunted by her wartime experiences. She spent the next few years supporting herself by working in day care centers, lecturing about her underground activities, and selling copies of her book. She enjoyed the traveling and socializing associated with public lectures, however, she did not seek fame like Claire Phillips. Her life intersected just one more time with Claire's, when she gave testimony in 1955 for the Court of Claims case.

Peggy Utinsky outlived Claire Phillips by a decade. In the 1950s, Peggy moved around a bit, living for a time in Indiana, before finally settling in

Long Beach, California. She never remarried, and she drifted out of contact with Jack Utinsky's family. There is no evidence she ever saw Dian again or re-established contact with her son. Peggy never fully regained her health after those days of torture in Fort Santiago. She spent her last years in a nursing home, suffering from a form of Alzheimer's disease. She died there in 1970.

THE STORIES OF THESE FOUR women have provided a peek behind the fence of occupied Manila to show the multiple viewpoints of those who experienced the same war. Yay Panlilio, Gladys Savary, Claire Phillips, and Peggy Utinsky each made their own choices about how they would confront the enemy, and they came to their own conclusions about the meaning of their actions.

Yay capitalized on the fact that she was American and Filipino. She had to fight for both of her countries to help save them from the enemy. After the war, she worked to ease the shift into a postcolonial relationship as the Philippines finally became an independent country. Gladys relied on her entrepreneurial skills and a touch of light-mindedness to help her survive living in an occupied city with sketchy identity papers. Those same skills and attitude eased her transition into the postwar period, allowing her to carry on much the same as she always had.

Claire drew inspiration from her skill as a performer, which provided the strength she needed to risk her life to help the POWs and the guerrillas. After the war, she portrayed her underground activities as a romantic adventure and felt entitled to profit from it. Because of her background in nursing, Peggy took the same risks, yet she experienced a deep sense of loss that she could never shake. She may have considered the congressional compensation and the Medal of Freedom her just due, but she could not understand Claire's constant need for public acclaim. The war had brought them together, briefly and fretfully, only to serve in the end as a wedge between them. There were no angels here, simply women who experienced war, one by one.

Introduction
 1. Descriptions of the *Lykes* are found in Angus Lorenzen, "Going Home," accessed January 25, 2015, http://historypublishingco.com/articles/articles_224.php.
 2. Claire Maybelle Phillips, FBI File, 9 June 1945, 8.
 3. Claire Maybelle Phillips, FBI File, 9 June 1945, 6, 8–9.
 4. Claire Maybelle Phillips, FBI File, 9 June 1945, 6.
 5. Claire Maybelle Phillips, FBI File, 9 June 1945, 8.
 6. Martha Gellhorn, *The Face of War* (New York: Simon and Schuster, 1959).

Chapter 1
 1. For a particularly insightful discussion of these imperialist issues, see Michael H. Hunt and Steven I. Levine, *Arc of Empire: America's Wars in Asia from the Philippines to Vietnam* (Chapel Hill: University of North Carolina Press, 2012), ch. 1.
 2. Hunt and Levine, *Arc of Empire*, 12–13.
 3. Hunt and Levine, *Arc of Empire*, 20.
 4. For a more comprehensive overview of these events, see, for instance, Paul A. Kramer, *Blood of Government: Race, Empire, the United States, and the Philippines* (Chapel Hill: University of North Carolina Press, 2006), ch. 1.
 5. Hunt and Levine, *Arc of Empire*, 20; Daniel B. Schirmer, *Republic or Empire: American Resistance to the Philippine War* (Cambridge, MA: Schenkman Publishing Company, Inc., 1972), 7–8, 171–186.
 6. Kramer, *Blood of Government*, 109; Hunt and Levine, *Arc of Empire*, 17–19. See also Edward M. Coffman, *The Regulars: The American Army, 1898–1941* (Cambridge, MA: Harvard University Press, 2004), chs. 1 and 2.
 7. H. W. Brands, *Bound to Empire: The United States and the Philippines* (New York: Oxford University Press, 1992), 29–34; Kristin L. Hoganson, *Fighting for American Manhood: How Gender Politics Provoked the Spanish-American and Philippine-American Wars* (New Haven: Yale University Press, 1998), 6–7; Hunt and Levine, *Arc of Empire*, 51–54; Kramer, *Blood of*

Government, ch. 2. Additional details can be found in Stanley Karnow, *In Our Image: America's Empire in the Philippines* (New York: Random House, 1989), chs. 6 and 7; Coffman, *The Regulars*, chs. 1 and 2; and Gregg Jones, *Honor in the Dust: Theodore Roosevelt, War in the Philippines, and the Rise and Fall of America's Imperial Dream* (New York: New American Library, 2012).

8. Hunt and Levine, *Arc of Empire*, 44.
9. Kramer, *Blood of Government*, 112; Karnow, *In Our Image*, 174, 201.
10. Coffman, *The Regulars*, 34.
11. Hunt and Levine, *Arc of Empire*, 49–50; Brands, *Bound to Empire*, 65–68.
12. Joan M. Jensen, *Army Surveillance in America, 1775–1980* (New Haven, CT: Yale University Press, 1991), 100, 103; Alfred W. McCoy, *Policing America's Empire: The United States, the Philippines, and the Rise of the Surveillance State* (Madison: University of Wisconsin Press, 2009), 297. This Military Information Division operated separately from the one that had been headquartered in Washington, D.C. since the 1890s, but the Philippine MID merged with the D.C. operation in 1902.
13. Hunt and Levine, *Arc of Empire*, 56.
14. Brands, *Bound to Empire*, 90–95; Hunt and Levine, *Arc of Empire*, 56. For additional information about the many governor-generals, see Lewis E. Gleeck, Jr., *The American Governors-General and High Commissioners in the Philippines: Proconsuls, Nation-Builders and Politicians* (Quezon City, Philippines: New Day Publishers, 1986).
15. Quoted in Brands, *Bound to Empire*, 108, and Karnow, *In Our Image*, 245.
16. Brands, *Bound to Empire*, 114–116.
17. Brands, *Bound to Empire*, 115.
18. Brands, *Bound to Empire*, 116–118.
19. McCoy, *Policing America's Empire*, 298.
20. Theodore Friend, *Between Two Empires: The Ordeal of the Philippines, 1929–1946* (New Haven, CT: Yale University Press, 1965), 17–18.
21. Brands, *Bound to Empire*, 114–116, 119–120.
22. Brands, *Bound to Empire*, 125; Karnow, *In Our Image*, 250.
23. Brands, *Bound to Empire*, 140–142.
24. Brands, *Bound to Empire*, 148–149.

Chapter 2
1. Margaret Utinsky, *"Miss U"* (San Antonio, TX: The Naylor Company, 1948), 1, 14. This birth and childhood information is consistent with what Peggy listed on the SS *John Lykes* passenger roster in 1945. In her memoir she mentioned growing up in Canada, and years later she clarified that she grew up in orphanages there. Her name does not appear on any US census records in the early twentieth century, and one of the California state death certificates lists Canada as her birthplace. No documentation of Peggy's birth, first marriage, or the birth of her son has been located.
2. Sherrilyn Coffman, "Margaret Utinsky," *American Journal of Nursing* 109:5 (May 2009), 72–76.

3. Utinsky, *"Miss U,"* 65. Peggy's name does not appear on any extant ships' rosters nor is there an extant passport application.
4. Utinsky, *"Miss U,"* 65.
5. US Military Registers, 1862–1970, 1127, Ancestry.com. First Lieutenant John P. Utinsky is listed in the "Casualties: Appointments Terminated" section of the 1918 register. West Virginia birth records list the year as 1897 but a subsequent census record puts his birth year in 1898. Peggy wrote that Jack had come to the Philippines in 1913. See Utinsky, *"Miss U,"* 65. Jack Utinsky's relatives, however, remember him joining up at age seventeen and leaving for the Philippines, never to return. This means he would not have arrived in the islands until 1914. And the 1929 Springfield, Illinois, City Directory on Ancestry.com listed Jack Utinsky as living at home with his parents on Logan Avenue, working as a clerk.
6. John A. Glusman, *Conduct Under Fire: Four American Doctors and Their Fight for Life as Prisoners of the Japanese 1941–1945* (New York: Viking, 2005), 88.
7. Utinsky, *"Miss U,"* 65.
8. Utinsky, *"Miss U,"* 65.
9. Brands, *Bound to Empire*, 153–154. Details of this debate among Filipino politicians can also be found in Friend, *Between Two Empires*, chs. 5, 8, and 9.
10. Brands, *Bound to Empire*, 156–157.
11. Brands, *Bound to Empire*, 163.
12. The description of the Sakdal uprising comes from Frederic S. Marquardt, *Before Bataan and After: A Personalized History of Our Philippine Experiment* (Indianapolis: The Bobbs-Merrill Company, 1943), 192–193. Reports on Aguinaldo's activities can be found in "Memorandum for the Superintendent," October 1 and 5 1935, Frank Murphy papers, microfilm reel 24, Bentley Historical Library, University of Michigan.
13. Letter from Secretary of War George Dern to Frank Murphy, November 13, 1935, Frank Murphy papers, microfilm reel 24, Bentley Historical Library, University of Michigan; Telegram from McDonald to Frank Murphy, November 25, 1935, Frank Murphy papers, microfilm reel 25, Bentley Historical Library, University of Michigan; Gleeck, Jr., *The American Governors-General and High Commissioners in the Philippines*, 309–310.
14. McCoy, *Policing America's Empire*, 363; Coffman, *The Regulars*, 35.
15. Quoted in Richard Connaughton, *MacArthur and Defeat in the Philippines* (New York: The Overlook Press, 2001), 43. A variation of this quote can be found in Karnow, *In Our Image*, 270.
16. Bill Sloan, *Undefeated: America's Heroic Fight for Bataan and Corregidor* (New York: Simon and Schuster, 2012), 9; Carol Morris Petillo, *Douglas MacArthur: The Philippine Years* (Bloomington: Indiana University Press, 1981), 170–173; Connaughton, *MacArthur and Defeat in the Philippines*, 45; Karnow, *In Our Image*, 270; Glusman, *Conduct Under Fire*, 37.
17. For an overview, see Edward S. Miller, *War Plan Orange: The US Strategy to Defeat Japan, 1897–1945* (Annapolis, MD: Naval Institute Press, 1991).
18. Glusman, *Conduct Under Fire*, 51; Ronald Spector, *Eagle Against the Sun: The American War with Japan* (New York: The Free Press, 1985), 56.

19. Gladys Savary, *Outside the Walls* (New York: Vantage Press, 1954), 2.

20. An article in the *Oakland Tribune* from January 22, 1912, suggests that Gladys Slaughter may have attended UC Berkeley, and an article in an Oshkosh, Wisconsin paper from 1919 mentioned she was visiting from Chicago.

21. Gladys's physical description is taken from her passport application, accessed from Ancestry.com; Savary, *Outside the Walls*, 2–4.

22. Savary, *Outside the Walls*, 4, 63.

23. Savary, *Outside the Walls*, 5.

24. Savary, *Outside the Walls*, 5.

25. Savary, *Outside the Walls*, 5.

26. Savary, *Outside the Walls*, 8. On Culion, Gladys became acquainted with the man known as Ned Langford, an American veteran of the Spanish-American War, who contracted leprosy while stationed in the Philippines. A fictionalized version of Langford's story, *Who Walk Alone*, would become a bestseller for the Henry Holt publishing company in 1940, winning the National Book Award, and remaining in print for decades. Gladys "had the greatest sympathy for him, but he had a not too difficult life, a pension, a salary and the treatment of the best leprologists available."

27. Savary, *Outside the Walls*, 10.

28. Savary, *Outside the Walls*, 13; *American Chamber of Commerce Journal*, December 1936, 43, University of Michigan Digital Library, http://quod.lib. umich.edu/cgi/t/text/textidx?c=philamer;idno=AAJ0523.1936.007.

29. Savary, *Outside the Walls*, 11. Sascha Jensen, an American who grew up in Manila and was interned during the war, knew Gladys Savary almost her entire life. Jensen has firsthand knowledge about the restaurant's popularity and knew who ate there.

30. Yay Panlilio, *The Crucible: An Autobiography* (New York: The MacMillan Company, 1950), 335, 331; 1920 Census, Ancestry.com. This census puts the Corpuz [*sic*] family in Denver that year and identifies Yay's given name as Valeria. The 1930 Census lists Valeria Panlilio (16) and Edward Panlilio (25) as residents of Roseville, California, about sixteen miles southwest of where the Corpus family settled in Auburn. According to the register of the *Lykes*, accessed on Ancestry.com, Randall Ray [Rae] Panlilio was born in Manila in 1933, with brothers Edward Jr. following in 1936 and Curtis in 1938.

31. Florence Horn, *Orphans of the Pacific: The Philippines* (New York: Reynal & Hitchcock, 1941), 58–59.

32. Dominador D. Buhain, *A History of Publishing in the Philippines* (Quezon City, P.I.: Rex Printing Company, 1998), 31.

33. Claire Phillips and Myron B. Goldsmith, *Manila Espionage* (Portland, OR: Binfords & Mort, Publishers, 1947), The 1910 Federal Census, Ancestry.com, seems the most accurate.

34. Claire M. Phillips, Federal Bureau of Investigation, File No. 105–377, June 9, 1945, 2; August 29, 1945, 1; March 15, 1948, 2. The arrest was verified after Claire was fingerprinted in 1945.

35. Louise De Martini's biographical information is from documents located on Ancestry.com. In July of 1941 the US Army appropriated the *Pierce*, along with

the others in the line, converted it to military use, and renamed it the *Hugh L. Scott*. After it was transferred to the Navy in 1942, the ship was torpedoed by a German submarine off the coast of North Africa. Fifty-nine men died. For a description of prewar Manila, see for instance, Bob Stahl, *Fugitives: Evading and Escaping the Japanese* (Lexington: University of Kentucky Press, 2001), 8–9.

36. While it is clear that Claire headed for Manila because of her career, she told different stories about that time in her life. This information about her 1938 employment and about her marriage to Fuentes is from her FBI file.

37. Claire Phillips, FBI File 105–377, 2.

38. Claire Phillips, FBI File 105–377, 2; Dian's birthdate is listed as February 7, 1939, on the passenger list for the *S.S. John Lykes*.

Chapter 3

1. Horn, *Orphans of the Pacific*, 60.
2. Panlilio, *The Crucible*, 4.
3. Federico V. Magdalena, "*Dabao-Kuo* and the Construction of the Philippine State," Paper presented at the 41st Annual Conference of Asian Studies on the Pacific Coast, June 15–17, 2007, Honolulu, Hawaii, accessed May 24, 2013, www2.hawaii.edu/~fm/Dabao-kuo.doc; Catherine Porter, *Crisis in the Philippines* (New York: Alfred A. Knopf, 1942), 91, 98–99. On Japanese immigration to the Philippines, see also Furiya, Reiko, "The Japanese Community Abroad: The Case of Prewar Davao in the Philippines," 155–172, and Hashiya, Hiroshi, "The Pattern of Japanese Economic Penetration of the Prewar Philippines," 113–138, both in Shiraishi, Saya S. and Takashi Shiraishi, eds., *The Japanese in Colonial Southeast Asia* (Ithaca, NY: Cornell University Press, 1993); Lydia N. Yu-Jose, *Japan Views the Philippines, 1900–1944* (Manila: Ateneo de Manila University Press, 1992), 123–127.
4. Horn, *Orphans of the Pacific*, 94, 96; *American Chamber of Commerce of the Philippines*, vols. 1–2, 1921, 61, accessed June 13, 2015, https://books.google.com/books?id=fM1BAQAAMAAJ&pg=RA1-PA15&dq=american+chamber+of+commerce+of+the+philippines+1921&hl=en&sa=X&ved=0CCIQ6AEwAWoVChMIiuP4w6qNxgIVjAySCh1hXQDz#v=onepage&q=american%20chamber%20of%20commerce%20of%20the%20philippines%201921&f=false. Gaches arrived in Manila in 1900, shortly after graduating from Stanford University, to take a position with the Bureau of Posts. He remained with the government until 1910 when he went to work as treasurer of Heacock's, then a jewelry store. During the 1920s, Gaches became its president and general manager, overseeing its transition to a full-scale department store, a modern, elegant establishment that rivaled any of those found in the United States once it moved into a new building in 1938. In 1939, Gaches hired fellow Stanford alum, Bertrand Silen, as KZRH's station manager. Beliel was very active in the Manila business community and in its political circles. His work on the Free French Committee meant that he probably knew Gladys Savary, if he didn't already know her from the restaurant. Gaches, Silen, and Beliel all ended up interned in Santo Tomas.

5. Panlilio, *The Crucible*, 2; Richard Gardner, "Golden's Missing Heroes," February 2, 2007, accessed May 21, 2013, denverpost.com.

6. Sloan, *Undefeated*, 3–4; Glusman, *Conduct Under Fire*, 45. See also Coffman, *The Regulars*, chs. 9 and 10.

7. Ralph Emerson Hibbs, *Tell MacArthur to Wait* (New York: Carlton Press, 1988), 16–18.

8. Glusman, *Conduct Under Fire*, 53.

9. Utinsky, "Miss U," 65; "Tales of Sacrifice for American Captives Told Lions by Authoress," *Kokomo* (IN) *Tribune* May 15, 1952, 14, accessed June 13, 2015, http://access.newspaperarchive.com.ezproxy.uwsp.edu/us/indiana/kokomo/kokomo-tribune/1952/05-15/page-14?tag=margaret+utinsky&rtserp=tags/margaret-utinsky?page=2&ndt=by&py=1950&pey=1959. Peggy Utinsky was never any more specific about the circumstances surrounding her son's departure from the Philippines. It is also possible she had returned to the States earlier in the 1930s as well. The 1932 St. Louis, Missouri City Directory available on Ancestry.com (US City Directories, 1821–1989) lists a Margaret E. Doolin, nurse at the Christian Hospital, renting a room on Cleveland Ave. Why she would have resumed using her maiden name, though, is a mystery, and there was no Charles Rowley listed at the same address. Hospital employment records for that time period are not extant.

10. Brands, *Bound to Empire*, 179–181; Ricardo T. Jose, "Labor Usage and Mobilization During the Japanese Occupation of the Philippines, 1942–1945," in Paul H. Kratoska, ed., *Asian Labor in the Wartime Japanese Empire: Unknown Histories* (Armonk, NY: M. E. Sharpe, Inc., 2005), 269; "Quezon Suggests Semi-Independence," *The New York Times*, March 27, 1940, accessed April 13, 2015, http://archive.atlantic-archive.org/869 /.

11. Utinsky, "Miss U," 65, 94–97; "Tales of Sacrifice," 14.

12. Bernice Archer, *Internment of Western Civilians Under the Japanese, 1941–1945* (New York: Routledge, 2005), n.p.; Google Books; Frances B. Cogan, *Captured: The Japanese Internment of American Civilians in the Philippines* (Athens: University of Georgia Press, 2000), 26.

13. Utinsky, "Miss U," 65; "Walter King Wilson, Sr.," accessed June 26, 2013, arlingtoncemetery.net/wkwilson.htm.

14. McCoy, *Policing America's Empire*, 300.

15. Utinsky, "Miss U," 5. It's unclear that this regulation would have applied to Peggy because it is unclear that Jack Utinsky was in active military service prior to December 8, 1941. His POW record lists him as a civilian.

16. Utinsky, "Miss U," 5.

17. Utinsky, "Miss U," 5.

18. Brands, *Bound to Empire*, 185–187; Connaughton, *MacArthur and Defeat in the Philippines*, 113, 117; Glusman, *Conduct Under Fire*, 38–39.

19. Utinsky, "Miss U," 103.

20. Phillips, *Manila Espionage*, 1; Claire Phillips, FBI File.

21. Phillips, *Manila Espionage*, 1; Edna Binkowski, *Code Name: High Pockets* (Limay, P.I.: Valour Press, 2006), 11–12; Claire Phillips FBI File 105-377, 3.

For information on the ship, see Stahl, *Fugitives*, 5; Otto Friedrich, *City of Nets: A Portrait of Hollywood in the 1940s* (Berkeley: University of California Press, 1986), 95; Robert A. Schanke, *"That Furious Lesbian": The Story of Mercedes de Acosta* (Carbondale: Southern Illinois University Press, 2003), 117.

22. Phillips, *Manila Espionage*, 2. The weather information was listed in the *Manila Daily Bulletin*, September 20, 1941, 1.
23. Stahl, *Fugitives*, 2.
24. Phillips, *Manila Espionage*, 2.
25. McCoy, *Policing America's Empire*, 236, 244, 367; Neile Adams McQueen, *My Husband, My Friend: A Memoir* (Bloomington, IN: AuthorHouse, 2012), 17. Fanny Lewin, Ted's wife, was godmother to a mestiza named Ruby Neilam "Neile" Adams, who would later marry the American actor Steve McQueen. Neile's mother was the dancer who used the stage name Miami and who reportedly was a favorite of General Douglas MacArthur. Ted Lewin ended up as a POW in Cabanatuan, and James Clavell's 1962 novel *King Rat* is based on Lewin's alleged activities there.
26. McCoy, *Policing America's Empire*, 351, 356, 367.
27. McCoy, *Policing America's Empire*, 368–369.
28. Phillips, *Manila Espionage*, 5–6.
29. "U.S., P.I. Troops Pass War Test 'With Honors,'" *Manila Daily Bulletin* October 15, 1941, 1; "At the Night Clubs," *Manila Daily Bulletin*, October 15, 1941, 4.
30. World War II Prisoners of War Roster; Prisoners of the Japanese Roster; both on Ancestry.com; Glusman, *Conduct Under Fire*, 52.
31. Claire M. Phillips, FBI File, 105–377, January 14, 1946, 8. Most names have been redacted from the file so it is not entirely clear if Phillips wrote to his mother or to another female relative, but he only mentioned Claire in one letter.
32. Phillips, *Manila Espionage*, 6.
33. Phillips, *Manila Espionage*, 6.
34. Glusman, *Conduct Under Fire*, 38.
35. William A. Berry (with James Edwin Alexander), *Prisoner of the Rising Sun* (Norman: University of Oklahoma Press, 1993), 3.
36. Berry, *Prisoner of the Rising Sun*, 6.
37. Berry, *Prisoner of the Rising Sun*, 9.
38. Berry, *Prisoner of the Rising Sun*, 9, 12.
39. Phillips, *Manila Espionage*, 7; "Hull Resumes Talks with Japanese Envoys," and "Quezon Reaffirms His Loyalty to U.S.," *Daily Tribune*, December 2, 1941, 1. This was also the day the Japanese military received word that war would commence in six days. See Eri Hotta, *Japan 1941: Countdown to Infamy* (New York: Alfred A. Knopf, 2013), 278.
40. Phillips, *Manila Espionage*, 7–8.
41. Savary, *Outside the Walls*, 14. In the memoir, Gladys describes one trip away from the Philippines, but passenger liner documents show she arrived in New York from Marseille, France, on June 24, 1937, and arrived in Los Angeles from Manila on January 29, 1938. See Ancestry.com.
42. Savary, *Outside the Walls*, 12–13.

43. Savary, *Outside the Walls*, 13. Gladys's close friend Dorothy Janson revealed the Savarys' divorce in "General Homma Gave a Party," 6, unpublished mss., copy in possession of the author. Gladys never acknowledged it in her book.
44. Savary, *Outside the Walls*, 13.
45. Savary, *Outside the Walls*, 13. New Zealander Laurie Reuben (L.R.) Nielson moved to Manila with his American wife Annette (known as Bumpy) during the first half of the 1930s. He organized a group of investors to build Nielson Airport in 1937, the first commercial airfield in the Philippines. After the occupation, Annette and their two sons were interned in Santo Tomas, but L.R. was taken to Hong Kong and never returned. At the end of the war the only part of his business empire that remained was the airport tower.
46. Savary, *Outside the Walls*, 15; Glusman, *Conduct Under Fire*, 52.
47. Spector, *Eagle Against the Sun*, 106; Connaughton, *MacArthur and Defeat in the Philippines*, 137–138; Douglas MacArthur, *Reminiscences* (New York: McGraw-Hill Book Company, 1964), 110.
48. Hotta, *Japan 1941*, 242–246.
49. Hotta, *Japan 1941*, 250–252; Glusman, *Conduct Under Fire*, 46.
50. Karnow, *In Our Image*, 282–284; Friend, *Between Two Empires*, 203.
51. Savary, *Outside the Walls*, 15; Ancestry.com. Savary's second marriage took place on March 22, 1941.
52. Information on these holiday weekend events can be found in the *Daily Tribune*, December 5–7, 1941.

Chapter 4
1. Connaughton, *MacArthur and Defeat in the Philippines*, 162; Spector, *Eagle Against the Sun*, 1, 4–6; Karnow, *In Our Image*, 287.
2. Karnow, *In Our Image*, 285–286, 288; Brands, *Bound to Empire*, 188–189; Connaughton, *MacArthur and Defeat in the Philippines*, 160; MacArthur, *Reminiscences*, 117. There is conflicting information about what happened that morning. According to Karnow, MacArthur was informed at about 3:40 a.m.; Brands puts it at just a few minutes after 3:00. Spector says that word of the Pearl Harbor attack reached Manila at 2:30 a.m. and that within an hour MacArthur knew that the war had started. See Spector, *Eagle Against the Sun*, 107. The conflicting accounts are due to erratic record-keeping during those hectic hours and some willful rearranging of surviving accounts.
3. Spector, *Eagle Against the Sun*, 107; Brands, *Bound to Empire*, 189; Karnow, *In Our Image*, 288; Connaughton, *MacArthur and Defeat in the Philippines*, 164.
4. Spector, *Eagle Against the Sun*, 107; MacArthur, *Reminiscences*, 120.
5. Connaughton, *MacArthur and Defeat in the Philippines*, 163.
6. Connaughton, *MacArthur and Defeat in the Philippines*, 163.
7. Phillips, *Manila Espionage*, 8.
8. Phillips, *Manila Espionage*, 9.
9. Berry, *Prisoner of the Rising Sun*, 14.
10. Karnow, *In Our Image*, 289; Connaughton, *MacArthur and Defeat in the Philippines*, 167–170; "Nichols Field Raided!" *Manila Tribune*, December 9, 1941, 1.

11. Phillips, *Manila Espionage*, 12.
12. Phillips, *Manila Espionage*, 12.
13. Phillips, *Manila Espionage*, 12.
14. Phillips, *Manila Espionage*, 13.
15. Phillips, *Manila Espionage*, 14.
16. Phillips, *Manila Espionage*, 14.
17. Phillips, *Manila Espionage*, 15.
18. Phillips, *Manila Espionage*, 15.
19. Phillips, *Manila Espionage*, 15.
20. See the *Daily Tribune*, December 16–20, 1941. By this point, the newspaper had shrunk to four pages per issue.
21. Phillips, *Manila Espionage*, 16.
22. Brands, *Bound to Empire*, 190; Connaughton, *MacArthur and Defeat in the Philippines*, 180–181; MacArthur, *Reminiscences*, 123.
23. David Joel Steinberg, *Philippine Collaboration in World War II* (Ann Arbor: University of Michigan Press, 1967), 29. Jeannette Rankin (R-MT) was the lone dissenting vote against war with Japan. The other Axis powers, Germany and Italy, declared war on the United States on December 11, 1941.
24. Steinberg, *Philippine Collaboration in World War II*, 30–31.
25. Phillips, *Manila Espionage*, 17; Cecil B. Currey, "Chaplain on the Bataan Death March," *The Army Chaplaincy*, Winter–Spring 2006, 1, np.
26. Phillips, *Manila Espionage*, 17. Claire referred to Packer as Packard in her memoir. But Earl C. Packer was a captain with the 31st Infantry's Headquarters Company. See "World War II Prisoners of the Japanese," Ancestry.com.
27. Phillips, *Manila Espionage*, 19.
28. Phillips, *Manila Espionage*, 19.
29. Phillips, *Manila Espionage*, 20.
30. Spector, *Eagle Against the Sun*, 108–110; Karnow, *In Our Image*, 291–292; Glusman, *Conduct Under Fire*, 74–75.
31. Glusman, *Conduct Under Fire*, 75.
32. Glusman, *Conduct Under Fire*, 66–67; Petillo, *MacArthur*, 202–203.
33. Glusman, *Conduct Under Fire*, 75. See also Louis Morton, "Decision to Withdraw to Bataan," http://www.history.army.mil/books/70-7_06.htm.
34. Steinberg, *Philippine Collaboration in World War II*, 32; Karnow, *In Our Image*, 295; Connaughton, *MacArthur and Defeat in the Philippines*, 192.
35. Connaughton, *MacArthur and Defeat in the Philippines*, 192–193.
36. Phillips, *Manila Espionage*, 22.
37. Phillips, *Manila Espionage*, 22–23.
38. Phillips, *Manila Espionage*, 24–25.
39. Glusman, *Conduct Under Fire*, 83; Spector, *Eagle Against the Sun*, 110.
40. Phillips, *Manila Espionage*, 25.
41. Phillips, *Manila Espionage*, 27.
42. Phillips, *Manila Espionage*, 27.
43. Binkowski, *Code Name: High Pockets*, 21; Phillips, *Manila Espionage*, 28.

44. Phillips, *Manila Espionage*, 28–29.
45. Savary, *Outside the Walls*, 16.
46. Savary, *Outside the Walls*, 17.
47. These various events were reported in the *Daily Tribune* on December 9–10, 1941.
48. Savary, 18.
49. "USAFFE Mop Up After Stopping Foe at Lingayen," *Daily Tribune*, December 12, 1941, 1.
50. Savary, *Outside the Walls*, 19.
51. "Notes on Fred Stevens," *American Chamber of Commerce of the Philippines*, March 1941, 11, accessed June 13, 2014, http://quod.lib.umich.edu/p/phil-amer/AAJ0523.1941.001?view=toc. More information on the formation of the ACC can be found in Lewis E. Gleeck, Jr., *The Manila Americans, 1901–1964* (Manila: Carmelo and Bauermann, 1977), 243 and Frederic H. Stevens, *Santo Tomas Internment Camp, 1942–1945* (Limited private edition: Frederic H. Stevens, 1946), 2–3.
52. Savary, *Outside the Walls*, 20.
53. Savary, *Outside the Walls*, 21.
54. Savary, *Outside the Walls*, 21; "'Open City' Plan Studied," *Manila Tribune*, December 25, 1941, 1.
55. Robert Ryal Miller, "Edgar Gable's Prison Camp Diary," *South Dakota Department of History Report and Historical Collections, Vol. XXX.* (Pierre, SD: South Dakota Historical Society, 1960), 318; Savary, *Outside the Walls*, 22–23. Gladys did not specify the date, but given the Open City declaration, December 26th is the most likely.
56. Savary, *Outside the Walls*, 21–22.
57. Savary, *Outside the Walls*, 22.
58. Savary, *Outside the Walls*, 22. The original diary has not surfaced, though Gladys transcribed portions of it into her memoir.
59. Savary, *Outside the Walls*, 23.
60. Savary, *Outside the Walls*, 23.
61. "The Day After Pearl Harbor," philippinecommentary.blogspot.com/2005/12/day-after-pearl/harbor.html, accessed online July 1, 2013. Halsema also noted that Quezon's story of the meeting differs from his. According to Quezon, he received a written request from a female reporter for a comment about Pearl Harbor. Halsema told me this story during a series of conversations in the 1990s. See also Cogan, *Captured*, 36, and James Halsema, *The Internment Camp at Baguio*, Interview by Michael P. Onorato, Oral History Program (Fullerton: California State University, Fullerton, 1987), 2–3. Yay did not provide a firsthand account of this in her memoir.
62. Panlilio, *The Crucible*, 2.
63. Panlilio, *The Crucible*, 2; Hiroshi Masuda, *MacArthur in Asia: The General and His Staff in the Philippines, Japan, and Korea* (Ithaca: Cornell University Press, 2012), 20; Paul P. Rogers, *The Good Years: MacArthur and Sutherland* (New York: Praeger Publishers, 1990), 53.

64. Panlilio, *The Crucible*, 1–2.
65. Panlilio, *The Crucible*, 3.
66. Glusman, *Conduct Under Fire*, 53; "30 Emergency Stations Over All City Ready," *Manila Tribune*, December 9, 1941, 5.
67. Utinsky, "Miss U," 11.
68. Pedro M. Picornell, *The Remedios Hospital, 1942–1945: A Saga of Malate* (Manila: DeLaSalle University Press, 1995).
69. This information can be found at http://www.columbans.eu/index.php/ about-us/history/587-columban-martyrs .
70. Glusman, *Conduct Under Fire*, 77.
71. Utinsky, "Miss U," 66.
72. Utinsky, "Miss U," 66. In its December 30, 1941 issue, the *Daily Tribune* acknowledged that the Japanese refused to recognize Manila as an open city.
73. "Army Goods are Given Away Free," *Daily Tribune*, January 2, 1942, 1; Utinsky, "Miss U," 6.

Chapter 5
1. Savary, *Outside the Walls*, 24.
2. Savary, *Outside the Walls*, 24.
3. Savary, *Outside the Walls*, 25–26.
4. Juan Labrador, *A Diary of the Japanese Occupation: December 7, 1941–May 7, 1945* (Manila, P.I.: Santo Tomas University Press, 1989), 41.
5. Convention (IV) respecting the Laws and Customs of War on Land and its annex: Regulations concerning the Laws and Customs of War on Land, The Hague, October 18, 1907, accessed June 13, 2015, https://www.icrc. org/applic/ihl/ihl.nsf/0/1d1726425f6955aec125641e0038bfd6. See also Ronald C. Rosbottom, *When Paris Went Dark: The City of Light Under German Occupation, 1940-1944* (New York: Little, Brown and Company, 2014), 97–98, and Eyal Benvenisti, *The International Law of Occupation*, 2nd ed. (New York: Oxford University Press, 2012).
6. Theodore Friend, *The Blue-Eyed Enemy: Japan Against the West in Java and Luzon, 1942–1945* (Princeton: Princeton University Press, 1988), 60–67; Propaganda Corps of the Imperial Japanese Forces, ed., *Ideals of the New Philippines*, n.p., n.d.; and Marcelino A. Foronda, Jr., *Cultural Life in the Philippines During the Japanese Occupation, 1942–1945* (Manila, P.I.: De La Salle University, 1978).
7. Glusman, *Conduct Under Fire*, 94; Savary, *Outside the Walls*, 27.
8. "Japanese Army Forms Civil Administration," *Daily Tribune*, January 24, 1942, 1.
9. Savary, *Outside the Walls*, 27.
10. Savary, *Outside the Walls*, 28.
11. Savary, *Outside the Walls*, 28.
12. Savary, *Outside the Walls*, 29–28.
13. Karnow, *In Our Image*, 291; Savary, *Outside the Walls*, 29.
14. "Quezon Told of Japan's Real Aim," *Daily Tribune*, January 4, 1942, 1. See also Layton Horner, *Japanese Military Administration in Malaya and the Philippines*, Ph.D. dissertation, University of Arizona, 1973, UMI microfilm.

15. Warning notice from the Commander of the Japanese Landing Forces published in the *Daily Tribune*, January 6, 1942, 3.
16. Cogan, *Captured*, 53.
17. Savary, *Outside the Walls*, 31.
18. Savary, *Outside the Walls*, 33.
19. Cogan, *Captured*, 45–46; Theresa Kaminski, *Prisoners in Paradise: American Women in the Wartime South Pacific* (Lawrence: University Press of Kansas, 2000), 55; Stevens, *Santo Tomas Internment Camp*, 6.
20. Labrador, *A Diary of the Japanese Occupation*, 41–42; Cogan, *Captured*, 61; Kaminski, *Prisoners in Paradise*, 55. Labrador estimated the numbers at three hundred Americans, one hundred Brits that first day.
21. Savary, *Outside the Walls*, 35; Proclamation by the Commander-in-Chief of the Japanese Expeditionary Forces published in the *Daily Tribune*, January 10, 1942, 1.
22. Savary, *Outside the Walls*, 35.
23. Savary, *Outside the Walls*, 39–40.
24. Cogan, *Captured*, 115–116.
25. Cogan, *Captured*, 111; Kaminski, *Prisoners in Paradise*, 3; P. Scott Corbett, *Quiet Passages: The Exchange of Civilians Between the United States and Japan During the Second World War* (Kent, OH: Kent State University Press, 1987), 50.
26. Utinsky, "Miss U," 2.
27. Utinsky, "Miss U," 2; quoted in Glusman, *Conduct Under Fire*, 94.
28. Utinsky, "Miss U," 2.
29. Utinsky, "Miss U," 5.
30. Utinsky, "Miss U," 1.
31. Utinsky, "Miss U," 1.
32. Utinsky, "Miss U," 1.
33. Utinsky, "Miss U," 1.
34. Utinsky, "Miss U," 8.
35. Utinsky, "Miss U," 8.
36. Utinsky, "Miss U," 8.
37. Panlilio, *The Crucible*, 3.
38. Panlilio, *The Crucible*, 4.
39. Panlilio, *The Crucible*, 5.
40. "Radio Station Is ReOpened," *Daily Tribune*, January 18, 1942, 4; Panlilio, *The Crucible*, 5.
41. Panlilio, *The Crucible*, 6.
42. Panlilio, *The Crucible*, 6.
43. Information about Antonio Bautista, the Civil Liberties Union, and the Free Philippines can be found in Buhain, *A History of Publishing in the Philippines*; Alfredo Roces, *Looking for Liling* (Anvil Publishing Company, 2000); Adalia Marquez, *Blood on the Rising Sun* (New York: DeTanko Publishers, Inc., 1957).
44. Panlilio, *The Crucible*, 6.
45. "Acts Punishable by Death Listed by Army," *Daily Tribune*, January 14, 1942, 1.
46. Panlilio, *The Crucible*, 7.

47. Panlilio, *The Crucible*, 7–8.
48. Panlilio, *The Crucible*, 9.

Chapter 6

1. Phillips, *Manila Espionage*, 30.
2. Gavan Daws, *Prisoners of the Japanese: POWs of World War II in the Pacific* (New York: William Morrow and Company, Inc., 1994), 69.
3. Phillips, *Manila Espionage*, 33. Claire misspelled the family's name as Dymson. Many of the names in her memoir are misspelled, likely because of her unfamiliarity with Philippine culture and her limited formal education.
4. Phillips, *Manila Espionage*, 32; Michael Norman and Elizabeth M. Norman, *Tears in the Darkness: The Story of the Bataan Death March and Its Aftermath* (New York: Farrar, Straus and Giroux, 2009), 111.
5. Phillips, *Manila Espionage*, 33–34.
6. Interview with Leon O. Beck by Doug Clanin, 61, M0863, "Philippine Guerrillas," Sanford/Clanin Philippine Resistance Records, Indiana Historical Society Collection. Copy in author's possession.
7. Glusman, *Conduct Under Fire*, 95.
8. Hibbs, *Tell MacArthur to Wait*, 49.
9. Glusman, *Conduct Under Fire*, 95–96; Norman and Norman, *Tears in the Darkness*, 111.
10. Hibbs, *Tell MacArthur to Wait*, 50.
11. Spector, *Eagle Against the Sun*, 116; Hibbs, *Tell MacArthur to Wait*, 53.
12. Dominic J. Caraccilo, ed. *Surviving Bataan and Beyond: Colonel Irvin Alexander's Odyssey as a Japanese Prisoner of War* (Mechanicsburg, PA: Stackpole Books, 1999), 61–62.
13. Caraccilo, *Surviving Bataan and Beyond*, 62.
14. Diary of Mrs. R. W. [Maude Denson "Denny"] Williams, 6, RG 407, NARA, Box 143B, Folder 6. For additional information on Carroll, see Oral History of Brigadier General (Ret.) Percy J. Carroll, 1981, Washington University School of Medicine, Oral History Project, beckerexhibits.wustl.edu/oral/transcripts/carroll.html.
15. Diary of Denny Williams, 6, RG 407, NARA, Box 143B, Folder 6.
16. Diary of Denny Williams, 7. See also Denny Williams, *To the Angels* (San Antonio, TX: Denson Press, 1985).
17. Phillips, *Manila Espionage*, 37.
18. Phillips, *Manila Espionage*, 38.
19. Phillips, *Manila Espionage*, 40. Again, Claire likely got the spelling of Damian's name wrong, perhaps because of the way she heard it pronounced. In her book, she refers to the young man as Demyon, but it was probably Damian. See Binkowski, *Code Name: High Pockets*, 28.
20. Phillips, *Manila Espionage*, 49. Claire misspelled Sobrevinas as Sobervenas. For the correct spelling, see Affidavit of Carlos C. Sobrevinas, 18 July 1949, Wayne Morse Collection, University of Oregon Libraries, Division of Special Collections and University Archives, Box 8.

21. Phillips, *Manila Espionage*, 52.

22. In one place Claire pinpoints these events as occurring in early March, in another she recalled listening to a newscast about the fall of Singapore, which happened in mid-February. See *Manila Espionage*, 50, 58. Claire misspelled Cabanguis as Cabaginis. The correct spelling can be found in Binkowski, *Code Name: High Pockets*, 29, and the Diary of Lieutenant Colonel Frank Loyd, 104, typescript photocopy provided by Chris Schaefer in author's possession.

23. Phillips, *Manila Espionage*, 53.

24. Phillips, *Manila Espionage*, 53.

25. Malcolm Decker, *From Bataan to Safety: The Rescue of 104 American Soldiers in the Philippines* (Jefferson, NC: McFarland & Company, Inc., Publishers, 2008), 9. This information came from Boone's son, Phil.

26. Norman and Norman, *Tears in the Darkness*, 90.

27. Phillips, *Manila Espionage*, 58.

28. Phillips, *Manila Espionage*, 59.

29. Phillips, *Manila Espionage*, 58. Because of this chaos, Rudolph Mramor, John Boone, and Marion Henderson were all listed as missing in action. Another private from D Company, Earl Baxter, was also with Boone during that hectic day of January 6th and hid out with the others in the hills of Bataan. The stress of trying to avoid contact with the enemy provoked him to commit suicide right after telling Boone and the others, "I can't take it any more." Leon Beck interview by Doug Clanin, 62, M0863, "Philippine Guerrillas," Sanford/Clanin Philippine Resistance Records, Indiana Historical Society Collection.

30. Phillips, *Manila Espionage*, 60.

31. Phillips, *Manila Espionage*, 61.

32. Hibbs, *Tell MacArthur to Wait*, 67.

33. Caraccilo, *Surviving Bataan and Beyond*, 99.

34. Hibbs, *Tell MacArthur to Wait*, 85–86; Norman and Norman, *Tears in the Darkness*, 116–117.

35. Spector, *Eagle Against the Sun*, 117; Norman and Norman, *Tears in the Darkness*, 113.

36. Louis Morton, *The Fall of the Philippines* (Washington, D.C.: Center of Military History, United States Army, 1953), 354–355.

37. Quoted in Norman and Norman, *Tears in the Darkness*, 128, and in many other sources, sometimes with slight variations. The Normans interviewed Frank Hewlett's daughter, who was quite clear that her father did not create the poem, only reproduced (and possibly improved on) it. See n. 40, 408.

38. Spector, *Eagle Against the Sun*, 132; Karnow, *In Our Image*, 298–299; Berry, *Prisoner of the Rising Sun*, 50; quoted in Glusman, *Conduct Under Fire*, 131. Berry put the date at March 11th, which was the day preparations were underway, but the group actually slipped out in the early morning hours of March 12th. See Morton, *The Fall of the Philippines*, 359. Lee was imprisoned in Cabanatuan and died on the *Enoura Maru* in January 1945.

39. Hibbs, *Tell MacArthur to Wait*, 85; Glusman, 134–135.

40. Glusman, *Conduct Under Fire*, 136; Hibbs, *Tell MacArthur to Wait*, 83.

41. Claire only used the name Pacio in her book. Edna Binkowski has identified him as Bonifacio Reyes. See *Code Name: High Pockets*, 82.
42. Phillips, *Manila Espionage*, 64.
43. Phillips, *Manila Espionage*, 66.
44. Phillips, *Manila Espionage*, 67.
45. Glusman, *Conduct Under Fire*, 155, 157; Spector, *Eagle Against the Sun*, 135.
46. Norman and Norman, *Tears in the Darkness*, 143–144.
47. Diary of Denny Williams, 10.
48. Diary of Denny Williams, 11–12, 14–15.
49. Norman and Norman, *Tears in the Darkness*, 144–146, 151.
50. Quoted in Glusman, *Conduct Under Fire*, 161, and in Norman and Norman, *Tears in the Darkness*, 153.

Chapter 7
1. Phillips, *Manila Espionage*, 68.
2. Glusman, *Conduct Under Fire*, 117; Shunsuke Tsuimi, *An Intellectual History of Wartime Japan: 1931–1945* (New York: Routledge, 2011), 73.
3. Norman and Norman, *Tears in the Darkness*, 163. According to Edwin Hoyt, the Japanese had anticipated around 25,000. See *Japan's War: The Great Pacific Conflict* (New York: Cooper Square Press, 2001), 270.
4. Glusman, *Conduct Under Fire*, 161–163; Hoyt, *Japan's War*, 269.
5. Hibbs, *Tell MacArthur to Wait*, 109.
6. Caraccilo, *Surviving Bataan and Beyond*, 26–27.
7. Caraccilo, *Surviving Bataan and Beyond*, 33.
8. Caraccilo, *Surviving Bataan and Beyond*, 42–43; Glusman, *Conduct Under Fire*, 164. The number of men packed into each boxcar varied, as did the length of the trip. Alexander put the distance at thirty miles; it may have been closer to twenty-five. The number of deaths also varies from source to source.
9. Berry, *Prisoner of the Rising Sun*, 54.
10. Berry, *Prisoner of the Rising Sun*, 46.
11. Hibbs, *Tell MacArthur to Wait*, 118.
12. Berry, *Prisoner of the Rising Sun*, 40.
13. Glusman, *Conduct Under Fire*, 147, 166.
14. Glusman, *Conduct Under Fire*, 171, 173; Diary of Denny Williams, 1–3, RG 407, NARA, Box 143B, Folder 6.
15. Glusman, *Conduct Under Fire*, 172, 174, 179; Berry, *Prisoner of the Rising Sun*, 57, 60.
16. Berry, *Prisoner of the Rising Sun*, 63–65; Glusman, *Conduct Under Fire*, 188, 190.
17. Berry, *Prisoner of the Rising Sun*, 65; Glusman, *Conduct Under Fire*, 194.
18. Berry, *Prisoner of the Rising Sun*, 66; Glusman, *Conduct Under Fire*, 196.
19. Utinsky, "Miss U," 10.
20. Utinsky, "Miss U," 10.
21. Savary, *Outside the Walls*, 63.
22. Savary, *Outside the Walls*, 65.
23. Savary, *Outside the Walls*, 66.

24. Berry, *Prisoner of the Rising Sun*, 72.
25. John M. Wright, Jr., *Captured on Corregidor: Diary of an American P.O.W. in World War II* (Jefferson, NC: McFarland & Company, Inc., 1988), 4, 6, 43; 2007 Distinguished Graduate Award, West Point Association of Graduates, www. westpointaog.org. Wright's biographical information comes from the US censuses of 1920, 1903, and 1940, all on Ancestry.com.
26. Wright, *Captured on Corregidor*, 6; E. Bartlett Kerr, *Surrender and Survival: The Experience of American POWs in the Pacific 1941–1945* (New York: William Morrow and Company, Inc., 1985), 70–71; Glusman, *Conduct Under Fire*, 203.
27. Wright, *Captured on Corregidor*, 7; Glusman, *Conduct Under Fire*, 203–204.
28. Glusman, *Conduct Under Fire*, 204; Wright, *Captured on Corregidor*, 9.
29. Savary, *Outside the Walls*, 54.
30. Letter from Edgar Gable to Gladys Savary, 4-11-42 [*sic*].
31. Phillips, *Manila Espionage*, 69.
32. Phillips, *Manila Espionage*, 70. The timing of this means that Claire did not witness the Bataan Death March.
33. Phillips, *Manila Espionage*, 71.
34. Phillips, *Manila Espionage*, 73.
35. Doyle Decker, "Reminiscences," 6, Indiana Historical Society. Decker never provided a first name for Sergeant Phillips, but given the location and timing, it is very possible this was John Phillips.
36. Decker, "Reminiscences," 6.
37. Malcolm Decker, *From Bataan to Safety*, 16.
38. Doyle Decker, "Reminiscences," 7–8; Malcolm Decker, *From Bataan to Safety*, 22.
39. Phillips, *Manila Espionage*, 73.
40. Phillips, *Manila Espionage*, 74.
41. Utinsky, "Miss U," 11.
42. Utinsky, "Miss U," 12.
43. Utinsky, "Miss U," 14.
44. Alfonso J. Aluit, *The Conscience of a Nation: A History of the Red Cross in the Philippines, 1896–1972* (Manila: Printorama, Inc., 1972), 323–324; "P.I. Red Cross Board Organized," *Daily Tribune*, May 5, 1942, 1; "Red Cross to Campaign for Funds," *Daily Tribune*, May 9, 1942, 1.
45. Utinsky, "Miss U," 15.
46. This information on the Kummers is from passenger liner lists, naturalization applications, and draft registrations from Ancestry.com; Utinsky, "Miss U," 16. Elizabeth's name was sometimes spelled Elisabeth.
47. Confidential Extract, Memorandum for the Officer in Charge, Subject: Dr. Leung Kwong Luk, from Walker S. Harrison, Sp. Agent, SIC, 6 July 1945, RG 331, NARA, Box 1993, File No. 40–905. See also Perpetuation of Testimony of Mrs. Trinidad Jaucin Demas, War Crimes Office, Judge Advocate Generals' Department, 9 November 1945, 2, RG 331, NARA, Box 2008, Folder 7.
48. Aluit, *The Conscience of a Nation*, 324, 518; Utinsky, "Miss U," 17. Aluit spells the name as "Gan."

49. Utinsky, *"Miss U,"* 18.
50. Utinsky, *"Miss U,"* 20.
51. "Report of Investigations of Alleged Atrocities by Members of the Japanese Imperial Forces in Manila," 31, Headquarters XIV Corps, 9 April 1945, RG 331, NARA, Box 1993, Folder 1.
52. Utinsky, *"Miss U,"* 21.
53. Takefumi Terada, "The Japanese Catholic Women's Religious Corps and Its Activities in the Philippines During World War II," *Anthropological Studies of Gospel and Civilization* 31 (October 2002): 294, accessed May 31, 2014, http://hdl.handle.net/10502/1459.
54. Utinsky, *"Miss U,"* 21.
55. Utinsky, *"Miss U,"* 22.
56. Utinsky, *"Miss U,"* 22.
57. Glusman, *Conduct Under Fire*, 209.
58. Wright, *Captured on Corregidor*, 10.
59. Berry, *Prisoner of the Rising Sun*, 82–83. See also Wright, *Captured on Corregidor*, 10.
60. Kerr, *Surrender and Survival*, 75; Utinsky, *"Miss U,"* 24.
61. Savary, *Outside the Walls*, 78.
62. For a description of the prison, see for instance Glusman, *Conduct Under Fire*, 214–216.
63. Letter from Johnny P. Turner to Captain Smith, March 15, 1946, 2, RG 389, NARA, Box 2135, Cabanatuan Camp Folder.
64. Savary, *Outside the Walls*, 78; Wright, *Captured on Corregidor*, 12.
65. Utinsky, *"Miss U,"* 24–25.
66. Utinsky, *"Miss U,"* 29. It is not exactly clear when Peggy went back to Bataan, but given the fact that Hospital No. 1 was dismantled and its remaining prisoners transferred to O'Donnell during the last week of June 1942, she must have been on the peninsula sometime earlier that month. See Ralph Hibbs, *Tell MacArthur to Wait*, 125.
67. Utinsky, *"Miss U,"* 30.
68. Utinsky, *"Miss U,"* 31. The town is misspelled as Caligaman in the book.
69. Utinsky, *"Miss U,"* 32.
70. This biographical information comes from Ancestry.com documents.
71. Utinsky, *"Miss U,"* 34.
72. Aluit, *The Conscience of a Nation*, 325; Utinsky, *"Miss U,"* 35.
73. Utinsky, *"Miss U,"* 36. Le Mire had made the army a career, and after a final posting at Fort William McKinley had been honorably discharged in 1941. But as a reservist, he was soon called back to active duty, ending up at Hospital No. 1 as part of the Medical Administration Corps. Burr, like Andrew Rader, was a doctor with the 12th Medical Battalion, and Osborne a doctor with the Medical Corps. This basic biographical information is from documents located on Ancestry.com.
74. Utinsky, *"Miss U,"* 36.
75. Utinsky, *"Miss U,"* 37.

Chapter 8

1. Utinsky, *"Miss U,"* 26; "Forgotten Heroine Lives on Relief in Dank Shack," *Pasadena* (CA) *Independent*, October 24, 1948, accessed August 16, 2013, www.cnac.org/emilscott/milliesanders01.html. Peggy described Millie as "a Negro woman named Minnie Sanders."
2. Utinsky, *"Miss U,"* 26.
3. Utinsky, *"Miss U,"* 28.
4. Utinsky, *"Miss U,"* 28.
5. Utinsky, *"Miss U,"* 29; "Report of Investigation of Alleged Atrocities by Members of the Japanese Imperial Forces in Manila," Headquarters XIV Corps, April 9, 1945, 31, RG 331, NARA, Box 1993, Folder 1.
6. "Report of Investigation of Alleged Atrocities," 31.
7. Utinsky, *"Miss U,"* 37; "St. Luke the Physician," *The American Chamber of Commerce Journal*, February 1940, 13, 30. The hospital was founded in 1903 by American Episcopal missionaries.
8. Utinsky, *"Miss U,"* 38; Hibbs, *Tell MacArthur to Wait*, 125; census and POW records from Ancestry.com.
9. Passenger liner manifest, passport application, World War I draft registration of Edwin M. Van Vorhees all from Ancestry.com; Utinsky, *"Miss U,"* 39. Peggy misspelled his name in her book.
10. Utinsky, *"Miss U,"* 39. Peggy did not specify when she received the letter, but given the duration of her illness and recovery and the arrival of certain officers at Camp O'Donnell, July seems the most logical.
11. Savary, *Outside the Walls*, 50–51.
12. Savary, *Outside the Walls*, 67.
13. Savary, *Outside the Walls*, 67.
14. Savary, *Outside the Walls*, 67–68.
15. Savary, *Outside the Walls*, 52.
16. Savary, *Outside the Walls*, 69–70, 72.
17. Savary, *Outside the Walls*, 72.
18. Savary, *Outside the Walls*, 72.
19. Savary, *Outside the Walls*, 74.
20. Savary, *Outside the Walls*, 75.
21. Utinsky, *"Miss U,"* 40.
22. Utinsky, *"Miss U,"* 40; Kerr, *Surrender and Survival*, 63.
23. Utinsky, *"Miss U,"* 42.
24. Descriptions of Tsuneyoshi are found in Kerr, *Surrender and Survival*, 60, and Daws, *Prisoners of the Japanese*, 84.
25. Caraccilo, *Surviving Bataan and Beyond*, 43–44.
26. Caraccilo, *Surviving Bataan and Beyond*, 125–126.
27. Kerr, *Surrender and Survival*, 63.
28. Bill for the Relief of Mering Bichara, 82nd Congress, 1st Session, September 25, 1951.
29. Alvin C. Poweleit, M.D. *USAFFE: The Loyal Americans and Faithful Filipinos, A Saga of Atrocities Perpetrated During the Fall of the Philippines, the Bataan*

Death March, and Japanese Imprisonment and Survival. [np] (1975), 62–63; Kerr, *Surrender and Survival*, 63. Poweleit remained in O'Donnell until his transfer to Cabanatuan in January 1943.

30. Utinsky, *"Miss U,"* 42–43.
31. Caraccilo, *Surviving Bataan and Beyond*, 127.
32. Ernest B. Miller, *Bataan Uncensored* (Little Falls: Military Historical Society of Minnesota, 1991), 242.
33. Miller, *Bataan Uncensored*, 236–237; Caraccilo, *Surviving Bataan and Beyond*, 132.
34. Miller, *Bataan Uncensored*, 242; Caraccilo, *Surviving Bataan and Beyond*, 132.
35. Caraccilo, *Surviving Bataan and Beyond*, 131; Kerr, *Surrender and Survival*, 62–63.
36. Daws, *Prisoners of the Japanese*, 88–89. Lewin survived the war.
37. Utinsky, *"Miss U,"* 44.
38. Utinsky, *"Miss U,"* 44.
39. Utinsky, *"Miss U,"* 45.
40. Utinsky, *"Miss U,"* 44, 46.
41. Utinsky, *"Miss U,"* 52.
42. Utinsky, *"Miss U,"* 52–53.
43. Naomi Flores, statement given July 2, 1947, 1, in the Oliver LaFarge Collection, Harry Ransom Center, University of Texas, Austin. The exact date of this encounter is unknown. Peggy never specifies, but implies that it happened after her first visit to Capas. Flores specifies July, yet indicates Peggy had recently received Atienza's letter but had not yet gone to Capas. Bautista and his organization are discussed here in Chapter 7.
44. Affidavit of Maria Martinez, January 30, 1946, 1, RG 407, NARA, Box 136, Folder 10.
45. Affidavit of Maria Martinez, 4.
46. Utinsky, *"Miss U,"* 53.
47. Utinsky, *"Miss U,"* 57. The biographical information on Evangeline Neibert is from documents available on Ancestry.com.
48. Utinsky, *"Miss U,"* 46.
49. Utinsky, *"Miss U,"* 47.
50. Utinsky, *"Miss U,"* 47.
51. Utinsky, *"Miss U,"* 48.
52. Utinsky, *"Miss U,"* 48.
53. Utinsky, *"Miss U,"* 50.
54. Utinsky, *"Miss U,"* 51.
55. Utinsky, *"Miss U,"* 51. Kelly died in February 1943 and Meir in October 1944. Booth survived the war.
56. Utinsky, *"Miss U,"* 51.
57. Utinsky, *"Miss U,"* 52.
58. Utinsky, *"Miss U,"* 46–47.
59. Utinsky, *"Miss U,"* 52.
60. Utinsky, *"Miss U,"* 57.

61. Utinsky, *"Miss U,"* 57.
62. Utinsky, *"Miss U,"* 59.
63. For additional details on Horan's activities, see Bernard Norling, *The Intrepid Guerrillas of North Luzon* (Lexington: University Press of Kentucky, 1999).
64. Utinsky, *"Miss U,"* 62. Information on Albert Holland can be found in Earl Carroll, "The Secret Story of Santo Tomas," ch. 2, August 19, 1945, WORLDWAR2-L Archives online. http://archiver.rootsweb.ancestry.com/th/read/PHILIPPINES/200312/1070504833.
65. Affidavit of Maria Martinez, 5.

Chapter 9
1. Affidavit of Carlos C. Sobrevinas, July 18, 1949, Wayne Morse Collection, University of Oregon Libraries. Sobrevinas did not provide any details of the journey.
2. Phillips, *Manila Espionage*, 76, 78.
3. Phillips, *Manila Espionage*, 79.
4. The address is from Binkowski, *Code Name: High Pockets*, 67.
5. According to Carling Sobrevinas's postwar statement, however, Claire had left her documents with his family. See n. 1 above.
6. Lorenza Vazquez de Amusategui, "Contraband for Cabanatuan," 5–7, Lorenza de Amusategui file, Oscar La Farge Collection, Harry Ransom Center.
7. On Ana Fey and her nightclub, see Binkowski, *Code Name: High Pockets*, 69; Phillips, *Manila Espionage*, 86. Isaac Peral has been renamed United Nations Avenue.
8. Phillips, *Manila Espionage*, 86.
9. Phillips, *Manila Espionage*, 86–87.
10. Phillips, *Manila Espionage*, 88.
11. Phillips, *Manila Espionage*, 91.
12. Phillips, *Manila Espionage*, 91.
13. Phillips, *Manila Espionage*, 93.
14. Phillips, *Manila Espionage*, 93.
15. Phillips, *Manila Espionage*, 94.
16. The address is found in Binkowski, *Code Name: High Pockets*, 79; the ad for the opening of the club was in *The Daily Tribune*, October 15, 1942, 3; Phillips, *Manila Espionage*, 96.
17. Phillips, *Manila Espionage*, 96.
18. Binkowski, *Code Name: High Pockets*, 79.

Chapter 10
1. Kerr, *Surrender and Survival*, 79.
2. Wright, Jr., *Captured on Corregidor*, 12–13; Berry, *Prisoner of the Rising Sun*, 89.
3. Wright, *Captured on Corregidor*, 13.
4. Wright, *Captured on Corregidor*, 14–15.
5. Berry, *Prisoner of the Rising Sun*, 95–96.
6. Berry, *Prisoner of the Rising Sun*, 104.

7. Diary of Albert Fields, 4–5, RG 407, NARA, Box 130, Folder 1.
8. Descriptions of the prison camp diet are pretty consistent across the sources. This one comes from Diary of P. R. Cornwall, 25–26, RG 407, NARA, Box 129, Folder 5.
9. Caraccilo, *Surviving Bataan and Beyond*, 138.
10. Caraccilo, *Surviving Bataan and Beyond*, 139.
11. Caraccilo, *Surviving Bataan and Beyond*, 146.
12. Kerr, *Surrender and Survival*, 104.
13. Daws, *Prisoners of the Japanese*, 110–111.
14. Diary of E. R. Fendall, 104, RG 407, NARA, Box 129, Folder 13.
15. Diary of Albert Fields, 8, RG 407, NARA, Box 130, Folder 1.
16. Diary of Albert Fields, 9; Eugene C. Jacobs, "Sick Call," in Calvin Ellsworth Chunn, ed., *Of Rice and Men: The Story of Americans Under the Rising Sun* (Los Angeles: Veterans' Publishing Company, 1947), 43.
17. [Naomi Flores] "The So-Called Miss 'U' Group and its Activities," 9, Miss "U" Group file, RG 407, NARA, Records of the Adjutant General's Office, Guerrilla Unit Recognition Files, Philippine Archives Collection, Box 371, File 126; *International Review of the Red Cross*, May 1966, 246, accessed August 3, 2013, http://www.loc.gov/rr/frd/Military_Law/pdf/RC_May-1966.pdf. Seraspi received the Florence Nightingale Medal from the Red Cross for her prisoner relief work.
18. [Flores] "The So-Called Miss 'U' Group and its Activities," 10, Miss "U" Group file, RG 407, NARA, Box 371, File 126.
19. Clark Lee, "Japan's 'Con' Man," August 19, 1943, accessed June 17, 2015, http://fultonhistory.com/Newspapers%2021/Belmont%20NY%20 Dispatch/Belmont%20NY%20Dispatch%201943-1945/Belmont%20NY%20 Dispatch%201943-1945%20-%200267.pdf.
20. Phillips, *Manila Espionage*, 100.
21. Phillips, *Manila Espionage*, 100.
22. Caraccilo, *Surviving Bataan and Beyond*, 149–150.
23. Diary of Albert Fields, 21, RG 407, NARA, Box 130, Folder 1; Caraccilo, *Surviving Bataan and Beyond*, 149.
24. Phillips, *Manila Espionage*, 100.
25. Phillips, *Manila Espionage*, 101.
26. While Peggy is clear that she made her last trip to Capas in December 1942, she is vague on when she first sent Naomi Flores to Cabanatuan. See *"Miss U,"* 62–63. Flores put that first trip in October. See [Flores] "The So-Called Miss 'U' Group and its Activities," 9–10, Miss "U" Group file, RG 407, NARA, Box 371, File 126.
27. Lorenza de Amusategui, "Contraband for Cabanatuan," 17, Lorenza de Amusategui File, Oliver La Farge Collection, Harry Ransom Center. Amusategui was clear that Naomi Flores had been very specific about the date of that first meeting with Mack.
28. Utinsky, *"Miss U,"* 64.
29. Utinsky, *"Miss U,"* 64. Mack died in Japan in 1945 in Fukuoka #3.

30. Utinsky, *"Miss U,"* 66.
31. Utinsky, *"Miss U,"* 66.
32. The financial transactions are described in the Diary of P. R. Cornwall, n.p., RG 407, NARA, Box 129, Folder 5, 29–30.
33. Utinsky, *"Miss U,"* 56.
34. Utinsky, *"Miss U,"* 68–69.
35. Glusman, *Conduct Under Fire,* 273.
36. Glusman, *Conduct Under Fire,* 273–274. Dr. John Bumgarner, who had shared an apartment with Ralph Hibbs in Manila and was later imprisoned at Cabanatuan, confirms Campos's activities in *Parade of the Dead: A U.S. Army Physician's Memoir of Imprisonment by the Japanese, 1942–1945* (Jefferson, NC: McFarland & Company, Inc., 1995), 109, 121.
37. Hibbs, *Tell MacArthur to Wait,* 169; Caraccilo, *Surviving Bataan and Beyond,* 290.
38. Chunn, *Of Rice and Men,* 22. See also Glusman, *Conduct Under Fire,* 228.
39. Savary, *Outside the Walls,* 76.
40. Savary, *Outside the Walls,* 81.
41. Savary, *Outside the Walls,* 82.
42. Utinsky, *"Miss U,"* 69–70.
43. Utinsky, *"Miss U,"* 70.
44. Utinsky, *"Miss U,"* 71.
45. Phillips, *Manila Espionage,* 103; Glusman, *Conduct Under Fire,* 226; List of Allied personnel who died before the formal establishment of POW, 22, RG 407, NARA, Box 23 (Invasion and Surrender Death Reports), no folder number; Diary of Edward R. Wernitznig, np, RG 407, NARA, Box 143B, Folder 4.
46. Phillips, *Manila Espionage,* 103–104.
47. Phillips, *Manila Espionage,* 104.
48. Utinsky, *"Miss U,"* 118.
49. Phillips, *Manila Espionage,* 107.
50. Currey, "Chaplain on the Bataan Death March." Taylor referred to her as "Clara Phillips," and remembered that she was later arrested by the Japanese.

Chapter 11
1. Phillips, *Manila Espionage,* 104–105.
2. Phillips, *Manila Espionage,* 105.
3. Glusman, *Conduct Under Fire,* 345–346.
4. Glusman, *Conduct Under Fire,* 346–347.
5. "21 Are Executed," *The Tribune* [Manila, P.I.], November 9, 1942, 1.
6. Phillips, *Manila Espionage,* 107.
7. Phillips, 106; Chris Schaefer, *Bataan Diary, An American Family in World War II, 1941–1945* (Houston: Riverview Publishing, 2004), 377.
8. Phillips, *Manila Espionage,* 107. At the time, Boone had about fifty Americans and a thousand Filipinos in his outfit.
9. Doyle Decker, "Reminiscences," 11, Indiana Historical Society. See also Malcolm Decker, *On a Mountainside: The 155th Provisional Guerrilla Battalion*

Against the Japanese on Luzon (Las Cruces, NM: Yucca Tree Press, 2004), 135–136.

10. Doyle Decker, "Reminiscences," 8–9.
11. Robert Lapham and Bernard Norling, *Lapham's Raiders* (Lexington: University of Kentucky Press, 1996), 14–15; 1st Lieutenant Herminia S. Dizon, "The Complete Data Covering the Guerrilla Activities of the Late Col. Claude A. Thorp," www.battlingbastardsbataan.com/dizon.htm.
12. Malcolm Decker, *From Bataan to Safety*, 24; Schaefer, *Bataan Diary*, 60, 111–112; Dizon, "The Complete Data Covering the Guerrilla Activities of the Late Col. Claude A. Thorp"; Lt. Col. Claude A. Thorp, Memo No. 2, June 15, 1942, RG 407, NARA, Box 250, File 500-3-10; General Headquarters Southwest Pacific Area, "Guerrilla Resistance Movements in the Philippines," 1945, 11, RG 407, NARA.
13. Thorp, "Philippine Guerrillas," M0863, Indiana Historical Society Collection, Box 10, Folder 4; General Headquarters Southwest Pacific Area, "Guerrilla Resistance Movements in the Philippines," 1945, 9, RG 407, NARA.
14. Doyle Decker, "Reminiscences," 10.
15. Malcolm Decker, *From Bataan to Safety*, 8.
16. "Special Operations in the Pacific," 65–66, www.history.army.mil/books/wwii/70-42/70-424.html; General Headquarters Southwest Pacific Area, "Guerrilla Resistance Movements in the Philippines," 1945, n.p., RG 407, NARA, Box 255; Glusman, *Conduct Under Fire*, 345. De Jesus was captured by the Japanese in 1944 and executed in Fort Santiago.
17. Glusman, *Conduct Under Fire*, 345.
18. Utinsky, *"Miss U,"* 82–83.
19. Lapham and Norling, *Lapham's Raiders*, 49; Dizon, "The Complete Data Covering the Guerrilla Activities of the Late Col. Claude A. Thorp"; Lapham and Norling, *Lapham's Raiders*, 54–55; Schaefer, *Bataan Diary* Research, www.BataanDiary.com.
20. General Headquarters Southwest Pacific Area, "Guerrilla Resistance Movements in the Philippines," 1945, 10, RG 407, NARA, Box 255; Lapham and Norling, *Lapham's Raiders*, 36, 54; Schaefer, Bataan Diary Research, www.BataanDiary.com.
21. Memo from Edwin P. Ramsey to All District Commanders, October 12, 1943, RG 407, NARA, Box 246, ECLGA Folder.
22. General Headquarters Southwest Pacific Area, "Guerrilla Resistance Movements in the Philippines," 1945, 11, RG 407, NARA, Box 255; Lapham and Norling, *Lapham's Raiders*, 63.
23. General Headquarters Southwest Pacific Area, "Guerrilla Resistance Movements in the Philippines," 1945, 12, RG 407, NARA, Box 255; Utinsky, *"Miss U,"* 83; Schaefer, Bataan Diary Research, www.BataanDiary.com.
24. Utinsky, *"Miss U,"* 83.
25. Statement of Naomi Flores, 4–5, 1947, Lorenza de Amusategui file, Oliver La Farge Collection, Harry Ransom Center; Lorenza de Amusategui, "Personal

Narrative *in Re* 'The Miss U' Undercover Group," 9, Lorenza de Amusategui file, Oliver La Farge Collection, Harry Ransom Center.

26. Republic of the Philippines Supreme Court, Lily Raquiza, et. al vs. Lt. Col. L. J. Bradford, et. al, G.R. No. L-44, September 13, 1945, http://www.lawphil.net/judjuris/juri1945/sep1945/gr_l-44_1945.html; Affidavit of Maria Martinez, 7, RG 407, NARA, Box 136, Folder 10. The Infante marriage information can be found on Ancestry.com.

27. Affidavit of Maria Martinez, 7–8, RG 407, NARA, Box 136, Folder 10. After the war, the US Army declined to officially recognize Straughn's guerrilla unit. See Explanation of Non-Recognition of Col. Straughn's Unit, RG 407, NARA, Box 246, Bataan Military District Folder.

28. Letter from John Boone to Maria Martinez, January 6, 1944, RG 407, NARA, Box 136, Folder 10.

29. Utinsky, *"Miss U,"* 83–84.

30. Utinsky, *"Miss U,"* 84. Peggy may have misremembered George Arnevic's name or may have opted to use a pseudonym. The name, like Captain Burson's, does not appear on any POW or guerrilla rosters.

31. Utinsky, *"Miss U,"* 85, 87.

32. Utinsky, *"Miss U,"* 88.

33. Statement of Naomi Flores, 6, Lorenza de Amusategui File, Oliver La Farge Collection, Harry Ransom Center.

34. Statement of Naomi Flores, 6–7, Lorenza de Amusategui File, Oliver La Farge Collection, Harry Ransom Center.

35. Statement of Naomi Flores, 6–7; Binkowski, *Code Name: High Pockets,* 133.

36. Statement of Naomi Flores, 7.

37. Utinsky, *"Miss U,"* 89.

38. Utinsky, *"Miss U,"* 90.

39. Utinsky, *"Miss U,"* 90. Peggy identified the day of the week as Friday, but if she had the date correct, she had the wrong day. Walter Jasten spent time in both Cabanatuan and Bilibid until he was chosen for a work detail headed for Japan. He left the Philippines in October 1944 but did not make it to Japan alive. Zena Jasten was later rounded up for internment at Santo Tomas and she died of breast cancer several months after liberation.

40. Panlilio, *The Crucible,* 12–13.

41. Panlilio, *The Crucible,* 13.

42. Panlilio, *The Crucible,* 14.

43. Panlilio, *The Crucible,* 91–96.

44. Panlilio, *The Crucible,* 107.

45. "Have Bolo Will Travel: World War II Weaves Stories of Survival," *Asian Journal* [San Diego, CA], May 31–June 6, 2013, accessed May 31, 2013, http://asianjournalusa.com/have-bolo-will-travel-p7026-95.htm.; Panlilio, *The Crucible,* 15.

46. "Have Bolo Will Travel"; Panlilio, *The Crucible,* 16.

47. Panlilio, *The Crucible,* 14.

48. Panlilio, *The Crucible,* 18.

49. Panlilio, *The Crucible*, 20.
50. Panlilio, *The Crucible*, 22.
51. Panlilio, *The Crucible*, 25.
52. Panlilio, *The Crucible*, 26–27.
53. Chuck Thompson, *Twenty-Five Best World War II Sites: Pacific Theater* (San Francisco: Greenline Publications, 2002), 173; Panlilio, *The Crucible*, 28–29.
54. Panlilio, *The Crucible*, 34.
55. Panlilio, *The Crucible*, 42.
56. Panlilio, *The Crucible*, 50.
57. Panlilio, *The Crucible*, 58.
58. Panlilio, *The Crucible*, 58–59.
59. Panlilio, *The Crucible*, 62–63.
60. Panlilio, *The Crucible*, 81, 78.
61. Panlilio, *The Crucible*, 86.
62. Panlilio, *The Crucible*, 110.
63. Panlilio, *The Crucible*, 115.
64. Panlilio, *The Crucible*, 119, 127–128.
65. Panlilio, *The Crucible*, 125.
66. Phillips, *Manila Espionage*, 117.
67. Phillips, *Manila Espionage*, 117.
68. Phillips, *Manila Espionage*, 117.
69. Phillips, *Manila Espionage*, 118.
70. Phillips, *Manila Espionage*, 120. There are no extant documents that confirm any of these messages were addressed directly to Claire Phillips. The orders would have gone to the guerrilla leaders, who in turn delegated specific tasks.
71. Phillips, *Manila Espionage*, 132. After the war, however, none of those "bona-fide" leaders remembered this message clearinghouse function of the Club Tsubaki. For more on this, see chapter 18.
72. Phillips, *Manila Espionage*, 118.
73. Phillips, *Manila Espionage*, 120. It is possible this may have been Captain Arita Yuzou, who was assigned to a carrier force around this time.
74. Phillips, *Manila Espionage*, 121. Allied planes led a successful bombing raid over Rabaul in November 1943.
75. Phillips, *Manila Espionage*, 137. Claire may have misremembered what Nagahama told her, or perhaps he lied to her in addition to bragging. Straughn and the others who were executed in the Chinese Cemetery were probably beheaded.
76. Panlilio, *The Crucible*, 129.
77. Panlilio, *The Crucible*, 132.
78. Panlilio, *The Crucible*, 134, 139, 141.
79. Panlilio, *The Crucible*, 144.
80. Panlilio, *The Crucible*, 165.
81. Panlilio, *The Crucible*, 167–168.
82. Panlilio, *The Crucible*, 172.

Chapter 12

1. Phillips, *Manila Espionage*, 110. The date of the Boones' wedding is from Schaefer, *Bataan Diary*, 377. Filomena (Mellie) G. Boone was born October 22, 1922, in the Philippines. She married John Boone on February 19, 1943, in a ceremony performed by Lt. Edwin Ramsey. The couple had four children. Phillip G. Boone was born March 13, 1944, and both Peggy Utinsky and Claire Phillips attended his christening. Mellie and the children came to the United States in 1952. She was listed as working for or being affiliated with Headquarters Battery, 1st Field Artillery, Fort Ord, California. She died in 1965 and was interred in Arlington National Cemetery in 1980.

2. Phillips, *Manila Espionage*, 110.

3. Phillips, *Manila Espionage*, 111. Chris Schaefer put the meeting in early March 1943. See *Bataan Diary*, 187.

4. Phillips, *Manila Espionage*, 111.

5. Phillips, *Manila Espionage*, 112–113. Lorenza Amusategui also identified a "Captain Torres," a member of USAFFE, as a frequent visitor of her husband's. Given the nature of their work, she assumed it was not his real name. See Lorenza de Amusategui, "Contraband for Cabanatuan," 28, Lorenza de Amusategui File, Oliver La Farge Collection, Harry Ransom Center.

6. Phillips, *Manila Espionage*, 113.

7. Utinsky, *"Miss U,"* 73.

8. Utinsky, *"Miss U,"* 73–74; Lorenza de Amusategui, "Personal Narrative," 14–15, Lorenza de Amusategui File, Oliver LaFarge Collection, Harry Ransom Center.

9. Phillips, *Manila Espionage*, 114.

10. Phillips, *Manila Espionage*, 114.

11. Phillips, *Manila Espionage*, 115.

12. Savary, *Outside the Walls*, 81.

13. U.S. Census reports, 1900, 1910, and 1920; 1923 Passport Application for Mamie Belle Norton, Ancestry.com; 1916 Passport Application for Roscoe Lautzenhiser, Ancestry.com. Norton's activities are also discussed in Glusman, *Conduct Under Fire*, 227.

14. Hill Williams, "Prison Camp 'Angel Visits in Richland," *Tri-City Herald* (Pasco, KY), October 7, 1951, 1, 3.

15. Glusman, *Conduct Under Fire*, 236; Myrtle Gaylord, "American Spy 'Meanest Guard' at Prison Camp," *Spokane Daily Chronicle*, December 13, 1946, 1; Williams, "Prison Camp 'Angel,'" 3.

16. Glusman, *Conduct Under Fire*, 227.

17. Hibbs, *Tell MacArthur to Wait*, 132.

18. Glusman, *Conduct Under Fire*, 227.

19. Hibbs, *Tell MacArthur to Wait*, 135.

20. Hibbs, *Tell MacArthur to Wait*, 140.

21. Wright, *Captured on Corregidor*, 47.

22. Wright, *Captured on Corregidor*, 48.

23. Wright, *Captured on Corregidor*, 50.

24. Savary, *Outside the Walls*, 103.

25. Savary, *Outside the Walls*, 104.

26. Savary, *Outside the Walls*, 89.

27. "Report of Investigation of Alleged Atrocities by Members of the Japanese Imperial Forces in Manila and other parts of Luzon, Philippine Islands," Headquarters XIV Corps, 1945, 8, RG 331, NARA, Box 1993, Folder 1.

28. "Report of Investigation of Alleged Atrocities by Members of the Japanese Imperial Forces in Manila," 9 April 1945, 32; Santo Tomas Internment Camp, January 4, 1942, to September 27, 1943, 9, RG 389: Records of the Office of the Provost Marshal General, NARA, Box 2154, Santo Tomas Camp, Philippines Folder. Captain Lee Stevens died on a hellship in 1944.

29. Diary of Denny Williams, 20, RG 407, NARA, Box 143B, Folder 6.

30. Bill Williams left Cabanatuan on a work detail in October 1944, and died on a hellship. Denny Williams's diary ended in December 1944. She went on to serve as a nurse during the Korean War and never remarried.

31. Santo Tomas Internment Camp, January 4, 1942 to September 27, 1943, p. 9, RG 389, NARA, Box 2154, Santo Tomas Camp, Philippines Folder.

32. Statement of Naomi Flores, July 2, 1947, 4, Oliver La Farge Collection, Harry Ransom Center. Bell the prisoner has been described as a private and a sergeant, though all sources agree he was African American and elderly, probably in his mid-sixties. Bell died in Cabanatuan in March 1944. See Alan J. Levine, *Captivity, Flight, and Survival in World War II* (Westport, CT: Praeger Publishers, 2000), 142; Diary of F.S. Conaty, 1, RG 407, NARA, Box 129, Folder 3; Diary of Ralph Crandall, 42, RG 407, NARA, Box 129, Folder 7.

33. Affidavit of Maria Martinez, 5, 9.

34. Statement of Naomi Flores, 2 July 1947, 4, Oliver La Farge Collection, Harry Ransom Center; Letter from Frank L. Tiffany to Maria Martinez, [March 1943], RG 407, NARA, Box 136, Folder 10. See also Letter from Maxwell M. Andler to Maria Martinez, [n.d.], RG 407, NARA, Box 136, Folder 10. Andler survived the war and went on to practice neurosurgery in California.

35. Letter from Dick to Maria Martinez, July 11, 1943, RG 407, NARA, Box 136, Folder 10.

36. Diary of Philip H. Meier, 3, RG 407, NARA, Box 136, Folder 13. Morgan related these events to Meier and showed him the note from Martinez.

37. Utinsky, *"Miss U,"* 79.

38. Wright, *Captured on Corregidor*, 50–51, 53. The description of the farm work comes from Chaney, 96, RG 407, NARA. This food system is also explained in Cornwall, "Chow Now," in Chunn, ed., *Of Rice and Men*, 33.

39. Wright, *Captured on Corregidor*, 57. On the Japanese guards and their nicknames, see also Chunn, ed., *Of Rice and Men*, 54–55.

40. Wright, *Captured on Corregidor*, 54.

41. Hibbs, *Tell MacArthur to Wait*, 174.

42. Wright, *Captured on Corregidor*, 56–57.

43. War Diary of Calvin F. Chunn, 31, RG 407, NARA, Box 128, Folder 9; Caraccilo, *Surviving Bataan and Beyond*, 150. See also Diary of Albert Fields, 41, RG 407, NARA.

44. Utinsky, "Miss U," 77.
45. Lorenza Vazquez de Amusategui, "Personal Narrative in Re 'The Miss "U' Undercover Group," 1947, 11–12, Lorenza de Amusategui File, Oliver La Farge Collection, Harry Ransom Center. Harold Johnson survived transport on the hellship *Oryoku Maru* to Japan in December 1944, and was moved again to Korea before his liberation in September 1945. He went on to serve in the Korean War, was promoted to General, and served as the Army Chief of Staff in the 1960s.
46. Utinsky, "Miss U," 77.
47. Utinsky, "Miss U," 78.
48. Phillips, *Manila Espionage*, 117.
49. Labrador, *A Diary of the Japanese Occupation*, 195–197.
50. Phillips, *Manila Espionage*, 122.
51. Phillips, *Manila Espionage*, 122–123.
52. Savary, *Outside the Walls*, 90.
53. Savary, *Outside the Walls*, 90.
54. Kaminski, *Prisoners in Paradise*, 199–200; Savary, *Outside the Walls*, 90–93; Dorothy Janson, "Prisoners of War and the YMCA," *American Historical Collection* [n.d.]: 18.
55. "Perpetuation of the testimony of Ralph Burdell Scheibley," April 20, 1945, 1, War Crimes Office, Judge Advocate General's Department, War Department," RG 331, NARA, Box 1996, Folder 10. See also Kerr, *Surrender and Survival*, 155–156.
56. Scheibley, 2. For other prisoners' comments about food at Pasay, see P.I. Camp #1 Cabanatuan, CINCPOA E & E Report No. 33, March 19, 1945, n.p., RG 389, NARA, Box 2135, Capt. Walter G. Hoberg, Camp Conditions Section, Japanese Camps File.
57. Utinsky, "Miss U," 48.
58. Utinsky, "Miss U," 49.
59. Phillips, *Manila Espionage*, 124; Binkowski, *Code Name: High Pockets*, 109.
60. Phillips, *Manila Espionage*, 125.
61. Phillips, *Manila Espionage*, 126.
62. Phillips, *Manila Espionage*, 127.
63. Phillips, *Manila Espionage*, 129.
64. Phillips, *Manila Espionage*, 130; Savary, *Outside the Walls*, 91.
65. Savary, *Outside the Walls*, 90–91; Lorenza de Amusategui, "Personal Narrative in Re 'The Miss U' Undercover Group," Lorenza de Amusategui file, Oscar La Farge Collection, Harry Ransom Center. According to documents on Ancestry.com, one of the Westly sons, Einar Camillo Westly, was born in Hawaii in 1915, lived in California for a time, and graduated Stanford in 1938. His future wife, Nell Joyce, was born in Manila in 1914; their son Einar Michael was born in Manila in September 1941. By 1943 Einar and perhaps the whole family was in Santo Tomas. They were repatriated together on the *John Lykes* in May 1945.

Chapter 13

1. Phillips, *Manila Espionage*, 133. Claire referred to the bartender as Memerto. He was in fact, Mamerto Geronimo, brother of one of the Club Tsubaki's hostesses, Judith Geronimo, who had worked with Claire at Ana Fey's. See Binkowski, *Code Name: High Pockets*, 78–79.

2. Phillips, *Manila Espionage*, 134.

3. Glusman, *Conduct Under Fire*, 273.

4. Wright, *Captured on Corregidor*, 61.

5. Abe Mark Nornes interviewed some American veterans who participated in the filming, though they were uncertain when it occurred. See "Nippon . . . Philippines . . . Peace," http://deepblue.lib.umich.edu/bitstream/handle/2027.42/90891/Dawn_of_Freedom.pdf?sequence=1.

6. Phillips, *Manila Espionage*, 161; Nornes, "Nippon . . . Philippines . . . Peace," 67, 63.

7. Diary of P. R. Cornwall, n.p., RG 407, NARA, Box 129, Folder 5, 33–34; Diary of Arthur L. Shreve, 28, RG 407, NARA, Box 143, Folder 10.

8. Hibbs, *Tell MacArthur to Wait*, 188–189.

9. Phillips, *Manila Espionage*, 137.

10. Phillips, *Manila Espionage*, 139. There is no extant corroboration of this story.

11. Phillips, *Manila Espionage*, 140.

12. Phillips, *Manila Espionage*, 151.

13. Utinsky, "Miss U," 74–75.

14. Utinsky, "Miss U," 112. Passenger liner information available from documents on Ancestry.com also indicates that Pearl Yearsley knew Elizabeth Kummer. Robin Yearsley died in 1945 in a Tokyo POW camp.

15. Utinsky, "Miss U," 111–112.

16. Statement of Naomi Flores, 8, Oliver La Farge Collection, Harry Ransom Center.

17. Affidavit of Maria Martinez, 5–6, RG 407, NARA, Box 136, Folder 10. Martinez put the arrest in September, but stated Peggy Utinsky was held for fifteen days at Fort Santiago.

18. Statement of Naomi Flores, 8, Oliver La Farge Collection, Harry Ransom Center.

19. Statement of Naomi Flores, 8.

20. Utinsky, "Miss U," 91.

21. Utinsky, "Miss U," 91.

22. Phillips, *Manila Espionage*, 151.

23. Phillips, *Manila Espionage*, 151–152.

24. Phillips, *Manila Espionage*, 152.

25. Utinsky, "Miss U," 92.

26. Utinsky, "Miss U," 92.

27. Utinsky, "Miss U," 93.

28. Utinsky, "Miss U," 98.

29. Utinsky, "Miss U," 103. Additional testimony concerning Peggy's arrest and interrogation can be found in "Report of Investigation of Alleged Atrocities,"

29–30, RG 331, NARA, Box 1993, Folder 1. Though it is narrated in the third person, it is clear the information came from Peggy.

30. Utinsky, "*Miss U,*" 105.
31. Utinsky, "*Miss U,*" 107.
32. Utinsky, "*Miss U,*" 115.
33. Utinsky, "*Miss U,*" 116–117.
34. Utinsky, "*Miss U,*" 117.
35. Phillips, *Manila Espionage,* 159.
36. Lorenza de Amusategui, "Personal Narrative," 12–13, Lorenza de Amusategui File, Oliver La Farge Collection, Harry Ransom Center.
37. Lorenza de Amusategui, "Personal Narrative," 13.
38. Lorenza de Amusategui, "Personal Narrative," 15.
39. Lorenza de Amusategui, "Personal Narrative," 14.
40. Lorenza de Amusategui, "Personal Narrative," 15–16.
41. Lorenza de Amusategui, "Personal Narrative," 17. Lorenza wrote up a slightly different version of her story "Contraband for Cabanatuan," Lorenza de Amusategui File, Oliver La Farge Collection, Harry Ransom Center, and discussed the bribery on p. 13.
42. Naomi Flores, "The So-Called Miss 'U' Group and its Activities," 11, Oliver La Farge Collection, Harry Ransom Center.
43. Lorenza de Amusategui, "Personal Narrative," 17, Lorenza de Amusategui File, Oliver La Farge Collection, Harry Ransom Center.
44. Lorenza Amusategui, "Personal Narrative," 17.
45. Lorenza Amusategui, "Personal Narrative," 18.
46. Phillips, *Manila Espionage,* 159.
47. Steinberg, *Philippine Collaboration in World War II,* 72.
48. Brands, *Bound to Empire,* 201, Steinberg, *Philippine Collaboration in World War II,* 73–76, 80.
49. Steinberg, *Philippine Collaboration in World War II,* 85.
50. Phillips, *Manila Espionage,* 155.
51. Phillips, *Manila Espionage,* 155.
52. Phillips, *Manila Espionage,* 156.
53. Phillips, *Manila Espionage,* 156.
54. Phillips, *Manila Espionage,* 157.
55. Phillips, *Manila Espionage,* 159.
56. Summary of Letters Written in Swedish, 2, RG 389, NARA, Box 254, Civilian Internees Philippines Folder; Savary, *Outside the Walls,* 92.
57. Savary, *Outside the Walls,* 92.
58. Savary, *Outside the Walls,* 93; Summary of Letters Written in Swedish to Hugo Cedergren from the Swedish Foreign Office Regarding WPA Work in the Far East, June 30, 1944, 1–2, RG 389, NARA, Box 2154, Civilian Internees Philippines Folder. The exact amount of the YMCA donation was not specified.
59. Savary, *Outside the Walls,* 92; Summary of Letters Written in Swedish, 2–3, RG 389, NARA, Box 254, Civilian Internees Philippines Folder.

60. Savary, *Outside the Walls*, 93.
61. "Typhoon Wrecks Manila," *The Canberra* (Australia) *Times*, November 19, 1943, http://trove.nla.gov.au/ndp/del/article/2657930; Savary, *Outside the Walls*, 106.
62. Savary, *Outside the Walls*, 107.
63. Diary of Commander Hayes, 46, 48, RG 407, NARA, Box 130, Folder 15.
64. Wright, *Captured on Corregidor*, 62. See also Caraccilo, *Surviving Bataan and Beyond*, 169. Irvin Alexander remembered the parcels much more than the Christmas celebration.
65. Savary, *Outside the Walls*, 118.
66. Savary, *Outside the Walls*, 120.

Chapter 14
1. Phillips, *Manila Espionage*, 162.
2. Phillips, *Manila Espionage*, 163.
3. Phillips, *Manila Espionage*, 165. With the limited information Claire provided in her memoir about this man, it has not been possible to verify anything more about him or his company. She frequently misspelled names in her book, making corroboration that much more difficult. It is possible this man was connected with the Komori Battery Factory that operated in Japan in the 1920s and 1930s. See Ko Unoki, *Mergers, Acquisitions and Global Empires: Tolerance, Diversity and the Success of M&A* (New York: Routledge, 2013), 104–107.
4. Phillips, *Manila Espionage*, 165.
5. Phillips, *Manila Espionage*, 165.
6. Letter from Lorenza Amusategui to Oliver La Farge, November 7, 1945, 3, Lorenza de Amusategui File, Oliver La Farge Collection, Harry Ransom Center.
7. Phillips, *Manila Espionage*, 166–167. Lorenza Amusategui did not recount this episode in her postwar testimony.
8. Utinsky, *"Miss U,"* 118.
9. Phillips, *Manila Espionage*, 167–168.
10. Phillips, *Manila Espionage*, 168.
11. Phillips, *Manila Espionage*, 169.
12. Phillips, *Manila Espionage*, 169.
13. Diary of Commander Hayes, 111, RG 407, NARA, Box 130, Folder 15.
14. Savary, *Outside the Walls*, 127.
15. Cornwall, "Chow Now," in Chunn, ed., *Of Rice and Men* 34; Caraccilo, *Surviving Bataan and Beyond*, 169.
16. Caraccilo, *Surviving Bataan and Beyond*, 171; Wright, *Captured on Corregidor*, 66–67.
17. An Oral History of Robert A. Ross, Sr., 2002, accessed February 15, 2014, http://www.lindavdahl.com/Bio%20Pages/R.Ross/RRoss.bio.htm; Binkowski, *Code Name: High Pockets*, 153.
18. Caraccilo, *Surviving Bataan and Beyond*, 166–167.
19. This biographical information was pieced together from the obituary of one of Threatt's sons and from documents on Ancestry.com. See Obituary of Benjamin

F. Threatt, *San Jose Mercury News*, October 5, 2008, accessed February 15, 2014, http://www.legacy.com/obituaries/mercurynews/obituary.aspx?page=lifestory&pid=118400705.

20. Diary of Arthur L. Shreve, 22, RG 407, NARA, Box 143, Folder 11.

21. James W. Chaney Diary, 100–111, RG 407, NARA, Box 128, Folder 7. Ross survived the war.

22. Diary of Arthur L. Shreve, 22, RG 407, NARA, Box 143, Folder 11.

23. Diary of Arthur L. Shreve, 22. See also Kerr, *Surrender and Survival*, 197–198. Kerr connected the carabao cart arrests with those that took place in Manila later in May 1944, though he incorrectly stated that Peggy Utinsky was arrested then, too.

24. Diary of Arthur L. Shreve, 22, RG 407, NARA, Box 143, Folder 11.

25. Affidavit of Lieutenant Colonel Jack William Schwartz, 1946, accessed February 15, 2014, http://www.mansell.com/pow_resources/camplists/philippines/Cabanatuan/schwarz_jack_1_affidavit.html; Hibbs, *Tell MacArthur to Wait*, 177–178. See also Diary of James W. Chaney, 165–168, RG 407, NARA, Box 128, Folder 7. Schwartz's original affidavit is located in RG 331, NARA, Box 920, Folder 7. Even after the war, Hibbs did not admit that he knew anything about the underground's operations.

26. Diary of F. S. Conaty, 2–3, RG 407, NARA, Box 129, Folder 3. Conaty put the date as May 24, but Shreve noted it on the 21st.

27. Diary of Arthur L. Shreve, 24, RG 407, NARA, Box 143, Folder 11.

28. Affidavit of Jack Schwartz; Diary of F. S. Conaty, 2–3, RG 407, NARA, Box 129, Folder 3; Caraccilo, ed., *Surviving Bataan and Beyond*, 167.

29. Diary of F. S. Conaty, 2–3, RG 407, NARA, Box 129, Folder 3; Hibbs, *Tell MacArthur to Wait*, 178; Affidavit of Jack Schwartz. Schwartz was one of four of those detainees who survived the war, along with Threatt, Taylor, and Oliver. Conaty buried his diary before leaving Cabanatuan in mid-October 1944. He did not survive the war.

30. Wright, *Captured on Corregidor*, 71.

31. Caraccilo, *Surviving Bataan and Beyond*, 168.

32. "Eventual Fate of Fr. Theodore Buttenbruch," MPC (PA) Advisory Division, Provost Marshal Section, Headquarters AFWESCPA, Manila Office, 1946, 1–2, RG 331, NARA, Box 1993, Folder 1.

33. Diary of Commander Hayes, 80, RG 407, NARA, Box 130, Folder 15.

34. Greta Janz, "Needs Information," *The Quan*, January 2003, 4, accessed February 16, 2014, http://philippine-defenders.lib.wv.us/QuanNews/quan2000s/January2003.pdf.

35. "Supplemental Information Report of Investigation Re-Disappearance of Father Theodore Buttenbruch-Society of the Divine Word," Office of the Provost Marshal Manila, 1946, 1, RG 331, NARA, Box 1993, Folder 1. By the time Pauline Ramirez gave her statement in 1946, she was married to George Nord. He survived transport in a hellship to Japan and the subsequent slave labor, and the two ran into each other in Manila after the war ended in 1945.

36. [Naomi Flores], "The So-Called Miss 'U' Group and its Activities," 8, Miss "U" Group, Records of the Adjutant General's Office, Guerrilla Unit Recognition Files, RG 407, NARA, Box 371, File 126.

37. Lorenza de Amusategui, "Personal Narrative in re 'The Miss U' Undercover Group," 26, Lorenza de Amusategui file, Oliver La Farge Collection, Harry Ransom Center.

38. Amusategui, "Personal Narrative," 25–26; Binkowski, Code Name: High Pockets, 154; Phillips, Manila Espionage, 170. Claire Phillips remembered Petroff's arrest happening on May 20, 1944.

39. Binkowski, Code Name: High Pockets, 153–154; Amusategui, "Personal Narrative," 26.

40. Amusategui, "Personal Narrative," 27.

41. Amusategui, "Personal Narrative," 27.

42. Phillips, Manila Espionage, 171.

43. Phillips, Manila Espionage, 173.

44. Phillips, Manila Espionage, 175.

45. Phillips, Manila Espionage, 176.

46. Phillips, Manila Espionage, 178.

47. Phillips, Manila Espionage, 180–182.

48. Phillips, Manila Espionage, 181.

49. Dr. Rebecca Parrish, A Tribute to Dr. Hawthorne Darby, 9–10 (Lafayette, IN?, privately published, 1946); American Foreign Service, Presumptive Report of the Death of an American Citizen, Helen Jonaline Wilk, 1947, Reports of Deaths of American Citizens Abroad, 1835–1974, accessed from Ancestry. com; Donald P. Smith, We Survived War's Crucible: A True Story of Imprisonment and Rescue (Bloomington, IN: Authorhouse, 2007), 27, accessed from Google Books.

50. Samuel Boyd Stagg interview with Chris Schaefer, August 2, 2002, 1–2, transcription copy in possession of author.

51. Stagg interview, 2.

52. Stagg interview, 5–6; Mrs. Tiu Chiao Beng, "Atrocities Committed in Fort Santiago During Nagahama's Time," 1, RG 331, NARA, Box 2008, Folder 7. Samuel Stagg survived the war, but there are no extant documents concerning his experiences.

53. Phillips, Manila Espionage, 181–182.

54. Extract from Report No. 10, War Crimes Branch, J.A. Section, Headquarters, USAFFE, Deposition of Sister Mary Trinita Logue, RG 331, NARA, Box 1993, File 40-400. During July 1944, all but two of the forty-five nuns at Assumption Convent were transferred to the internment camp at Los Baños.

55. Phillips, Manila Espionage, 184.

56. Phillips, Manila Espionage, 187.

57. "Vicente Lim 1914," West Point Associate of Graduates, accessed February 23, 2014, http://apps.westpointaog.org/Memorials/Article/5282/.

58. Phillips, Manila Espionage, 194.

59. Panlilio, *The Crucible*, 175.
60. Panlilio, *The Crucible*, 178.

Chapter 15
1. Phillips, *Manila Espionage*, 195.
2. Phillips, *Manila Espionage*, 197.
3. Phillips, *Manila Espionage*, 197.
4. Phillips, *Manila Espionage*, 198.
5. Phillips, *Manila Espionage*, 199.
6. Wright, *Captured on Corregidor*, 74–75.
7. Caraccilo, *Surviving Bataan and Beyond*, 180–181.
8. Hibbs, *Tell MacArthur to Wait*, 199.
9. Hunt and Levine, *Arc of Empire*, 82–85.
10. Spector, *Eagle Against the Sun*, 422–424.
11. Steinberg, *Philippine Collaboration in World War II*, 83–86. See also Brands, *Bound to Empire*, 201, and Nakano Satoshi, "Appeasement and Coercion," in Ikehata Setuho and Ricardo Jose, eds., *The Philippines Under Japan: Occupation Policy and Reaction* (Manila, P.I.: Ateneo de Manila University Press, 1999), 26.
12. Brands, *Bound to Empire*, 206; José P. Laurel, Proclamation No. 29, 21 September 1944; José P. Laurel, Proclamation No. 30, 22 September 1944, accessed March 9, 2014, http://www.lawphil.net/executive/proc/proc_30_1944.html. See also Steinberg, *Philippine Collaboration in World War II*, 97–98.
13. Affidavit of Maria Martinez, January 30, 1946, 9, RG 407, NARA, Box 136, Folder 10.
14. Phillips, *Manila Espionage*, 199.
15. Affidavit of Maria Martinez, 9.
16. Phillips, *Manila Espionage*, 200.
17. Phillips, *Manila Espionage*, 201.
18. Lorenza Amusategui listed the date of her husband's death as October 14, 1944, and she bitterly resented Claire's depiction of Ramon's death. See Lorenza de Amusategui, "Personal Narrative," 28, Lorenza de Amusategui File, Oliver La Farge Collection, Harry Ransom Center.
19. Phillips, *Manila Espionage*, 203–204.
20. Florence Ebersole Smith Finch, Oral History Interview, Ithaca, NY, 2007, www.uscg.mil/history/weboralhistory/FlorenceFinchHistory.pdf. After liberation, Florence Smith moved to New York to live with her Ebersole relatives. She joined the Coast Guard Women's Reserve, serving from July 1945 until her discharge in May 1946. Smith was awarded the Asiatic-Pacific Campaign Ribbon, the first woman to receive that honor. In 1947 she also received the Medal of Freedom, largely based on the testimony of her former boss Englehart, who had been a POW and served as one of her underground contacts.
21. Lorenza de Amusategui, "Contraband for Cabanatuan," 56, Lorenza de Amusategui File, Oliver La Farge Collection, Harry Ransom Center.

22. Utinsky, *"Miss U,"* 118.
23. Binkowski, *Code Name: High Pockets,* 163, 168–169.
24. Utinsky, *"Miss U,"* 119.
25. Utinsky, *"Miss U,"* 122.
26. Utinsky, *"Miss U,"* 123.
27. Utinsky, *"Miss U,"* 124.
28. Utinsky, *"Miss U,"* 124.
29. Utinsky, *"Miss U,"* 125–126.
30. Utinsky, *"Miss U,"* 128.
31. Utinsky, *"Miss U,"* 131.
32. Utinsky, *"Miss U,"* 132.
33. Utinsky, *"Miss U,"* 133, 135.
34. Utinsky, *"Miss U,"* 136. Locals tended to use the words "hill" and "mountain" interchangeably.
35. Schaefer, *Bataan Diary,* 60, 111–112.
36. Schaefer, *Bataan Diary,* 92.
37. Schaefer, *Bataan Diary,* 115, 255.
38. Schaefer, *Bataan Diary,* 164, 192.
39. Schaefer, *Bataan Diary,* 235, 248.
40. Panlilio, *The Crucible,* 258.
41. Panlilio, *The Crucible,* 270.
42. "Special Operations in the Pacific," accessed June 5, 2013, www.history.army. mil/books/wwii/70-42/70-424.html.
43. Panlilio, *The Crucible,* 277, 279.
44. Panlilio, *The Crucible,* 288–289.
45. Phillips, *Manila Espionage,* 205.
46. Phillips, *Manila Espionage,* 205–206.
47. Affidavit of Maria Martinez, 10. Martinez put her court-martial date at November 21, 1944, during which she received a twelve-year sentence. "Two days later, I was transferred to the Women's Correctional Institution at Mandaluyong. There were eleven other women, also military prisoners among them two were Charity sisters. We were not beaten there and although the food was nearly impossible to eat." Her family smuggled food in to her. She was liberated with the others, including Claire Phillips, on January 10, 1945. Although Claire mentioned Maria by name and discussed her in detail, Maria did not specifically mention Claire in her affidavit.
48. Phillips, *Manila Espionage,* 207.
49. "Supplemental Information Report of Investigation Re-Disappearance of Father Theodore Buttenbruch-Society of the Divine Word," Office of the Provost Marshal Manila, 1946, 2, RG 331, NARA, Box 1993, Folder 1.
50. "Eventual Fate of Fr. Buttenbruch," 2–3; Father Enrique Ederle, S.V.D., "Father Theodore Buttenbruch of the Society of the Divine Word," 1945, 1–2, RG 331, NARA, Box 1993, Folder 1; "Supplemental Information Report," 2, RG 331, NARA, Box 1993, Folder 1. According to Castro Alvano y Altomera, Detective Inspector in Quezon City during the occupation,

"[H]e had brought the subject to downtown Manila in his car on many occasions [to visit Engracio Fabre]." Alvano recalled that the subject was held in Fort Santiago for several months and later released; that he did not know of the Father's disappearance until several days after it was reported to have occurred; that he knew the subject was warned about his activities but "believed the warnings useless as Father Buttenbruch was a headstrong person."

51. "Eventual Fate of Fr. Buttenbruch," 2–3, RG 331, NARA, Box 1993, Folder 1; Letter from J. Antonio Araneta to Major Glicerio Opinion, War Crimes Commission, October 19, 1945, RG 331, NARA, Box 1993, Folder 21; Statement of Elvira Llanes, 1946, RG 331, NARA, Box 2008, Folder 7; Extract from Report No. 10, War Crimes Branch, J.A. Section, Headquarters, USAFFE, Deposition of Sister Mary Trinita Logue, RG 331, NARA, Box 1993, File 40-400.

52. Savary, *Outside the Walls*, 129.

53. Berry, *Prisoner of the Rising Sun*, 209.

54. Wright, *Captured on Corregidor*, 75; Berry, *Prisoner of the Rising Sun*, 208.

55. Wright, *Captured on Corregidor*, 76; Caraccilo, *Surviving Bataan and Beyond*, 177, 182–183.

56. Savary, *Outside the Walls*, 132.

57. Savary, *Outside the Walls*, 132–133.

Chapter 16

1. Phillips, *Manila Espionage*, 209.

2. Phillips, *Manila Espionage*, 209; In the Matter of the Torture of Pauline Obra by the Japanese, Affidavit, October 22, 1945, 1, RG 331, NARA, Box 2008, Folder 7; Santo Tomas Internment Camp, January 4, 1942 to September 27, 1943, 9, RG 389: Records of the Office of the Provost Marshal General, NARA, Box 2154, Santo Tomas Camp, Philippines Folder. Mrs. Margaret Folsom is identified as one of the rescued women in "Flying Squad Rescues Twelve Women," *San Bernadino County Sun*, February 12, 1945, 2, accessed June 6, 2014, http://www.newspapers.com/newspage/49467101/.
The 1945 *Eberle* roster on Ancestry.com lists Pauline Costigan with her maiden name, as a single woman. The American reservist, Thomas Myers, may have been her common law husband. In the United States, she married a man named Obra.

3. Phillips, *Manila Espionage*, 210.

4. Phillips, *Manila Espionage*, 212.

5. Savary, *Outside the Walls*, 143.

6. Berry, *Prisoner of the Rising Sun*, 209–210.

7. Wright, *Captured on Corregidor*, 86; Caraccilo, *Surviving Bataan and Beyond*, 191. Wright's wife received the letter in early 1945, while her husband was still a prisoner in Japan.

8. Wright, *Captured on Corregidor*, 86; Caraccilo, *Surviving Bataan and Beyond*, 191–192.

9. Wright, *Captured on Corregidor*, 106; Caraccilo, *Surviving Bataan and Beyond*, 192–201.
10. Benigno Del Rio, "Seven Days in Hell (In Hands of Nippon Gestapo)," 1945, 1–3, 14," RG 331, NARA, Box 1993, Folder 15.
11. Del Rio, "Seven Days in Hell," 1–3. Del Rio also mistakenly reported hearing Ramon Amusategui's name.
12. Deposition of Lemuel Earl Carroll in the Matter of the Execution of Carroll G. Grinnell, Alfred Duggleby, Ernest E. Johnson and Clifford L. Larsen by the Japanese Military Police at Manila, P.I. in January 1945, 3, RG 331, NARA, Box 1993, Folder 13. The Japanese arrested Carroll Grinnell, Alfred Duggleby, Ernest Johnson, and Cliff Larsen two days later on charges of aiding the guerrillas.
13. Utinsky, *"Miss U,"* 141, 142.
14. Journal of Frank Loyd, 159. Copy in possession of the author, courtesy of Chris Schaefer and the Loyd family.
15. Utinsky, *"Miss U,"* 139.
16. Loyd journal, 159–160.
17. Loyd journal, 162.
18. Loyd journal, 163.
19. Loyd journal, 163.
20. Letter from John Boone to Miss U, [Margaret Utinsky], December 24, 1944, John Boone Collection, MacArthur Memorial Library.
21. Spector, *Eagle Against the Sun*, 519–520.
22. Utinsky, *"Miss U,"* 145; Loyd journal, 164.
23. Interview of Leon Beck by Doug Clanin, 71, M0863, "Philippine Guerrillas," Sanford/Clanin Philippine Resistance Records, Indiana Historical Society Collection.
24. Interview of Leon Beck, 71–72.
25. Loyd journal, 164.
26. Loyd journal, 164; Utinsky, *"Miss U,"* 146.
27. Loyd journal, 167–168.
28. Spector, *Eagle Against the Sun*, 520–521; Recapitulation of Recognized Guerrilla Units by Major Commands, 1948, 1–2, RG 407, NARA, Box 249, List of Recognized Guerrilla Units by Major Commands Folder; Hampton Sides, *Ghost Soldiers: The Forgotten Epic Story of World War II's Most Dramatic Mission* (New York: Doubleday, 2001), 20–21.
29. Hibbs, *Tell MacArthur to Wait*, 212–213.
30. Hibbs, *Tell MacArthur to Wait*, 213; Sides, *Ghost Soldiers*, 276–278.
31. Sides, *Ghost Soldiers*, 289–290, 295, 304.
32. Phillips, *Manila Espionage*, 217.
33. Phillips, *Manila Espionage*, 218.
34. Phillips, *Manila Espionage*, 220–221; "Asylum Gaol for Women," *The Courier-Mail* (Brisbane, Australia), February 13, 1945, 1, accessed June 6, 2014, http://trove.nla.gov.au/ndp/del/article/48943670. The article describes the rescue of twelve women from the Mandaluyong insane asylum by the 1st Cavalry

Division "flying squad." Claire is identified as Claire Fuentes, an American imprisoned because she had been caught smuggling items into Cabanatuan and Santo Tomas. See also "Americans Astride Main Roads North of Manila," *Advocate* (Burnie, Tasmania), February 13, 1945, 5, accessed June 6, 2014, http://trove.nla.gov.au/ndp/del/article/68914073.

35. Phillips, *Manila Espionage*, 222.
36. Panlilio, *The Crucible*, 308–310.
37. Panlilio, *The Crucible*, 318, 321.
38. Panlilio, *The Crucible*, 326–327.
39. Savary, *Outside the Walls*, 144–145.
40. Savary, *Outside the Walls*, 146.
41. Savary, *Outside the Walls*, 147–148.
42. Savary, *Outside the Walls*, 148.
43. Savary, *Outside the Walls*, 158–159, 154.
44. Berry, *Prisoner of the Rising Sun*, 214.
45. Berry, *Prisoner of the Rising Sun*, 215–216.
46. Office of the Resident Commissioner of the Philippines to the United States, *Report on the Destruction of Manila and Japanese Atrocities*, Washington, D.C., 1945, 7, 9.
47. *Report on the Destruction of Manila*, 35–36, 18.
48. Statement of Mrs. Nena Pacheco De Fexer, Eye Witness and Survivor in Mrs. Pedro J. Campos' Residence Massacre, February 13, 1945, 2, RG 331, NARA, Box 1993, Folder 3.
49. Hibbs, *Tell MacArthur to Wait*, 232–233. See also Statement of Mrs. Nena Pacheco De Fexer taken by John J. O'Connell, CWO, February 22, 1945, RG 331, NARA, Box 1993, Folder 3 and De Fexer, February 13, 1945, 5.
50. Hibbs, *Tell MacArthur to Wait*, 234.
51. Savary, *Outside the Walls*, 173–175.
52. Savary, *Outside the Walls*, 175.
53. Savary, *Outside the Walls*, 178.

Chapter 17

1. Phillips, Manila *Espionage*, 222–223.
2. Utinsky, "Miss U," 147.
3. Utinsky, "Miss U," 148.
4. Utinsky, "Miss U," 149.
5. Utinsky, "Miss U," 151.
6. Utinsky, "Miss U," 152.
7. Utinsky, "Miss U," 155. On Skelton's involvement in these military operations, see Robert Ross Smith, *Triumph in the Philippines*, 325–327, accessed June 10, 2014. http://books.google.com/books?id=BSrFX51AGPMC&pg=PA326&lpg=PA326&dq=colonel+skelton+dinalupihan+philippines+world+war+II&source=bl&ots=jezXoiTm_7&sig=b6R0XIzgR6-1SS1BPeLiCuXOaGI&hl=en&sa=X&ei=88WZU93JGoewyATcj4KgAg&ved=0CB0Q6AEwAA#v=onepage&q=colonel%20skelton%20dinalupihan%20philippines%20world%20war%20II&f=false.

8. Utinsky, *"Miss U,"* 158.
9. Utinsky, *"Miss U,"* 158.
10. Utinsky, *"Miss U,"* 159.
11. Utinsky, *"Miss U,"* 161.
12. Phillips, *Manila Espionage*, 223.
13. Picornell, *The Remedios Hospital*, 39–44. Sources vary concerning the exact date of the mass arrest, some putting it as early as February 7th and some as late as February 10, 1945. Eugene Smith, originally with the Army Air Corps, lost part of his leg at the beginning of the war and managed to avoid imprisonment in Cabanatuan. He worked with Ramon Amusategui and the Malate priests, so he knew Peggy during the war. See Letter from Eugene Smith to John Boone, 26 November 1945, John Boone Collection, MacArthur Memorial Library.
14. Utinsky, *"Miss U,"* 167. There are no other extant documents that mention this American newspaperwoman.
15. "List of American POWs, compiled by Mrs. Utinsky, an American Civilian serving with the guerrilla [*sic*] as nurse," RG 407, NARA, Box 57, File 88; "Testimony of Mrs. Margaret Utinsky, Manila, P.I., taken at Santo Tomas Internment Camp, Manila, P.I., 7 March 1945," RG 331, NARA, Box 1993, Folder 1; "Copies of Letters regarding Mrs. Margaret Utinsky, Headquarters 12th Replacement Battalion, USAFFE, APO 70" RG 331, Box 1993, Folder 1. The extant documents of the POW list amount to thirteen typed pages of an A–G alphabetical listing of names and locations. Some information was written in, and the edges of the pages are brown as if they had sat in dirt in a metal box. Krause's report reads that Peggy was "commissioned in the ASANC [*sic*] as a first lieutenant before the fall of Corregidor."
16. Utinsky, *"Miss U,"* 167–168.
17. Panlilio, *The Crucible*, 328–329.
18. Panlilio, *The Crucible*, 332.
19. Savary, *Outside the Walls*, 180.
20. Spector, *Eagle Against the Sun*, 523–524.
21. Savary, *Outside the Walls*, 181–182.
22. Savary, *Outside the Walls*, 184.
23. Savary, *Outside the Walls*, 187.
24. Phillips, *Manila Espionage*, 224–225.
25. Phillips, *Manila Espionage*, 225.
26. Phillips, *Manila Espionage*, 225.
27. Phillips, *Manila Espionage*, 226. None of those copies appeared in any of the NARA collections.
28. Savary, *Outside the Walls*, 188, 190.
29. Savary, *Outside the Walls*, 193.
30. Savary, *Outside the Walls*, 196.
31. Savary, *Outside the Walls*, 197.
32. Caraccilo, *Surviving Bataan and Beyond*, 206.
33. Wright, *Captured on Corregidor*, 123.

34. Caraccilo, *Surviving Bataan and Beyond*, 211, 305; Wright, *Captured on Corregidor*, 123, 137.

35. Wright, *Captured on Corregidor*, 159, 168.

36. Savary, *Outside the Walls*, 197–198.

37. Savary, *Outside the Walls*, 199.

38. Savary, *Outside the Walls*, 201.

39. Savary, *Outside the Walls*, 203.

40. Savary, *Outside the Walls*, 203–205.

41. Savary, *Outside the Walls*, 203, 205–206; Kenneth L. Dixon, "In the Pacific," *The Palm Beach Post*, October 5, 1945, accessed June 16, 2014, http://news.google.com/newspapers?id=YXcyAAAAIBAJ&sjid=ybYFAAAAIBAJ&pg=5805%2C280292. Gladys made at least one other alteration in the transcription, preferring "tall, thin, and tired" to Dixon's original "tall, lean, gaunt."

42. Ancestry.com, roster of the SS *John Lykes*, May 1945.

43. Utinsky, *"Miss U,"* n.p.; Signal Corps photo 45-13519, March 25, 1945, Signal Corps photo collection, National Archives, College Park, Maryland.

44. Claire Maybelle Phillips, FBI File, June 9, 1945, 8.

45. Claire Maybelle Phillips, FBI File, June 9, 1945, 8.

46. Claire Maybelle Phillips, FBI File, June 9, 1945, 5; *Lily Raquiza, et.al. vs. Lt. Col. L.J. Bradford, et. al.*, September 13, 1945, 2, Supreme Court, Republic of the Philippines, accessed June 27, 2014, http://www.lawphil.net/judjuris/juri1945/sep1945/gr_l-44_1945.html.
Claire Maybelle Phillips, FBI File, August 20, 1945, 1–2.

47. Claire Maybelle Phillips, FBI File, June 9, 1945, 3; Claire Maybelle Phillips, FBI File, August 20, 1945, 2.

48. Claire Maybelle Phillips, FBI File, August 20, 1945, 2; Claire Maybelle Phillips, FBI File, September 21, 1945.

Chapter 18

1. Panlilio, *The Crucible*, 333.

2. Panlilio, *The Crucible*, 337–339.

3. "Large Jap Force Trapped by Yanks and Guerrillas," *Joplin* (MO) *Globe*, May 19, 1945, 1, newspaperarchive.com; Panlilio, *The Crucible*, 341.

4. Karnow, *In Our Image*, 321–322.

5. Panlilio, *The Crucible*, 343.

6. Panlilio, *The Crucible*, 343, 348.

7. Panlilio, *The Crucible*, 348. According to Yay's FBI file, the couple married on September 11, 1945, but the location of the wedding was not identified. Marking re-entered the Philippines that December, and presumably Yay accompanied him. FBI file was obtained through FOIPA No. 1199013-000, June 26, 2013; copy in possession of the author.

8. Memo to Chief of Staff, Philippine Army from 1st Lt. L. J. Gutheridge, US Army Forces Western Pacific, May 15, 1946, RG 407: Records of the Adjutant General's Office, NARA, Box 249, no file number. The text of Osmeña's Executive Order can be found online at http://www.gov.ph/1945/09/26/executive-order-no-68-s-1945/.

9. Memo to Chief of Staff, Philippine Army from Col. W. P. Moore, US Army Forces Western Pacific, April 1, 1946, RG 407, NARA, Box 249, Field Examination, BMA, Anderson's Guerrillas Folder.

10. US Army Recognition Program of Philippine Guerrillas, c. 1949, 193–194, 131, accessed June 18, 2014, http://media.nara.gov/dc-metro/rg-554/629817-army-recognition-philippine-guerrillas-1182341/1182341.pdf; "World News Front," *Oakland* (CA) *Tribune*, June 28, 1946, 3, newspaperarchive.com. Newspaper reports put the number of protestors at 25,000; the US Army estimated 8,000–10,000.

11. US Army Recognition Program of Philippine Guerrillas, c.1949, 12, accessed June 18, 2014, http://media.nara.gov/dc-metro/rg-554/629817-army-r ecognition-philippine-guerrillas-1182341/1182341.pdf.

12. Account of investigation of the Marking's Fil-American Troops, [c.1947], 2, RG 407, NARA, Box 326, File #109-1, General Headquarters, Markings Fil-American.

13. Account of the investigation of Marking, 7; Conversation with Yay Panlilio Agustin, November 21, 1947, 42, RG 407, NARA, Box 325, File# 109-1, General Headquarters, Markings Fil-American.

14. Composite roster and recognition strength, MFAT, October 27, 1947, 70–71, RG 407, NARA, Box 325, File# 109-1, General Headquarters, Markings Fil-American; US Army Recognition Program of Philippine Guerrillas, 30.

15. "Executive Order 9586: The Medal of Freedom," July 6, 1945. Nominations usually came through the secretaries of state, war, and the navy, and the medals could be given posthumously.

16. Marking, Mrs. Yay Panlilio, Associated Press, Name Card Index to AP Stories, 1905–1990, accessed June 26, 2014, AncestryLibrary.com. Agustin Marking's date of death is unknown, though there is a grave bearing his name (which he changed from Marcos Agustin in the late 1940s) in Calabarson, Rizal, P.I.

17. Savary, *Outside the Walls*, 206; California Passenger and Crew Lists, 1893–1957, AncestryLibrary.com.

18. General Counsel Opinion No. 23, Claim of Gladys Slaughter Savary, 1951, RG 299: Foreign Claims Settlement Commission, NARA, Box 2.

19. Gladys Savary, "I Go Now," *Manila Daily Bulletin*, March 17, 1949; "RC Police Chief Welcomes Probe; BIR Officer Gives Side of Savary Case," *Manila Daily Bulletin*, March 21, 1949; Letters to the Editor, *Manila Daily Bulletin*, March 18, 1949; The Savary Case, RG 59: General Records of the Department of State, NARA, Box 7430.

20. Savary, *Outside the Walls*, 2. Information about Gladys's postwar life can be traced through articles in the *San Mateo Times*, 1954–1956, available on newspaperarchive.com.

21. UK Incoming Passenger Lists, 1878–1960, Ancestry.com; Letter to the Editor, "War-Time Memories Return on Fourth of July," *Van Nuys Valley News*, July 10, 1970, newspaperarchive.com.

22. Letter from Claire Phillips to Mrs. Claude [Celia] Thorp, June 12, 1945, Claude Thorp File, M0863, "Philippine Guerrillas," Indiana Historical Society Collection, Box 10, Folder 5; Claire Maybelle Phillips, FBI File, August 20, 1945, 1.

23. Letter from Claire Phillips to Mrs. Claude [Celia] Thorp, May 14, 1945, Claude Thorp File, Box 10, Folder 5.

24. Letter from Claire Phillips to Mrs. Claude [Celia] Thorp, May 14, 1945.

25. Claire Maybelle Phillips, FBI File, May 24, 1946.

26. Letter from Claire Phillips to Mrs. Claude [Celia] Thorp, May 14, 1945, Claude Thorp File, M0863, "Philippine Guerrillas," Indiana Historical Society Collection, Box 10, Folder 5.

27. Letter from Claire Phillips to Mrs. Claude [Celia] Thorp, June 12, 1945.

28. A group of US Army and Navy nurses had been taken prisoner in the Philippines and spent most of the duration of the war with the civilians in Santo Tomas. Still, they were military, not civilian, women. See, for instance, Elizabeth M. Norman, *We Band of Angels: The Untold Story of American Women Trapped on Bataan* (New York: Random House, 2013).

29. Claire Maybelle Phillips, FBI File, May 8, 1946, 3; Claire Maybelle Phillips, FBI File, April 8, 1946, 1.

30. Claire Maybelle Phillips, FBI File, July 29, 1946, 3.

31. Claire Maybelle Phillips, FBI File, November 2, 1945; Claire Maybelle Phillips, FBI File, January 20, 1946, 2, 6, 7.

32. Claire Maybelle Phillips, FBI File, August 29, 1945 and June 14, 1946, 1.

33. Claire Maybelle Phillips, FBI File, June 10, 1946, 2–5. She was represented by a San Francisco attorney, J. Thaddeus Cline.

34. Claire Maybelle Phillips, FBI File, August 16, 1946, 1; Claire Maybelle Phillips, FBI File, July 29, 1946, 4.

35. Claire Maybelle Phillips, FBI File, September 13, 1946 and October 3, 1946.

36. Claire Maybelle Phillips, FBI File, October 17, 1946, 2; November 19, 1946; 9 January 1947.

37. Claire Maybelle Phillips, FBI File, March 8, 1947; "Claire Phillips' Book," *The Oregonian*, August 3, 1947, n.p., copy in possession of author. Claire had originally hired a practical nurse from west Los Angeles to help her write the book, but the arrangement did not work out.

38. "Author Recalls Espionage, Jap Torture During War," *The Oregonian*, March 30, 1947, n.p.

39. "Ex-Spy Wed in Vancouver," *The Oregonian*, January 19, 1948, n.p. Copies of both articles are in possession of author. A Certificate of Marriage can be found in Washington Marriage Records, 1865–2004 at AncestryLibrary.com. Clavier had been born in Montana and was married and divorced before he enlisted in the Army Signal Corps in April 1941. Claire and Robert Clavier separated sometime in 1953 and were divorced the following year; he died in 1970.

40. Claire Maybelle Phillips, FBI File, October 25, 1947; *Clavier v. The United States*, U.S. Court of Claims, 2–52, 1957, 3.

41. Memo from General Courtney Whitney, April 10, 1948, Courtney Whitney Personal Correspondence, 1945–1948, RG-16, Box 10, Folder 4, MacArthur Memorial Library.

42. Claire Maybelle Phillips, FBI File, March 15, 1948, 2.

43. "Janesville Vet to Appear on Network from Hollywood," *Janesville* (WI) *Daily Gazette*, February 28, 1950, 5; "Ex-Spy Gets Lucky Break," *The Oregonian*, March 16, 1950, n.p.; "Radio Star Will Perform at Affair Honoring Spy," *The Oregonian*, April 7, 1950; "Wartime Spy in Philippines Receives Gifts of Bungalow, Appliances at Ceremonies," *The Oregonian*, April 10, 1950, n.p. Copies of these articles are in possession of the author. Dian Clavier dropped out of high school and never attended Lewis and Clark.

44. Edwin Schallert, "Heroic Actress-Spy of Philippines Helps Screen Her Own Torture Story," *The Los Angeles Times*, January 14, 1951, n.p. A copy of this article, along with copies of various pieces of publicity, are included in Claire Phillips's FBI file.

45. Telegram from J. Edgar Hoover to Claire Phillips, May 8, 1951, Claire Phillips FBI file.

46. "Spy Story Opens at the Holiday," *The New York Times*, July 4, 1951.

47. *Clavier v. The United States*, Congressional No. 2-52, Defendant's Exceptions and Brief, March 12, 1957, 3, 8–10. Only this and the published court opinion are available. The full case file, which presumably would have contained transcriptions of all proceedings, went missing somewhere between the Court of Claims and the National Archives.

48. "Spy Turns Co-Ed," *Kentucky New Era*, October 17, 1947, 1, accessed July 1, 2014, http://news.google.com/newspapers?nid=266&dat=19471017&id=V u0rAAAAIBAJ&sjid=XWcFAAAAIBAJ&pg=2149,5931826; Ann Connell, "ANNotations . . . Among the Cards," *Eugene* (OR) *Register-Guard*, January 6, 1956, accessed July 1, 2014, http://news.google.com/newspapers?nid=1310&dat =19560106&id=6BBWAAAAIBAJ&sjid=ceIDAAAAIBAJ&pg=4846,784595; *Clavier v. The United States*, 8.

49. Claire Maybelle Phillips, FBI File, October 15, 1954, October 18, 1955, October 26, 1955; *Clavier v. The United States*, 14.

50. *Clavier v. The United States*, 12–13, 23–24.

51. *Clavier v. The United States*, 18–22, 25–26.

52. *Clavier v. The United States*, 25–26, 29–31.

53. *Clavier v. The United States*, 13, 32.

54. *Clavier v. The United States*, 31–32, 14; *Clavier v. The United States*, Congressional No. 2-52, Opinion, July 12, 1957, 12. Congress enacted Private Law 478 on August 11, 1955, to pay Amusategui.

55. For her account of wartime activities, see Lorenza de Amusategui, "Personal Narrative in Re 'The Miss U Undercover Group,' (c.1947), RG 407, NARA, Box 143A, Folder 8.

56. Letter from Lorenza Amusategui to Querida primos [Oliver La Farge], November 7, 1945, 2–3, Oliver La Farge Collection, Harry Ransom Center, University of Texas.

57. *Clavier v. The United States*, 36; *Clavier v. The United States*, Congressional No. 2-52, Opinion, July 12, 1957, 14.

58. Obituary of Claire Phillips, *The Oregonian*, May 24, 1960, 17. Copy in possession of author.

59. Testimony of Colonel Alfred C. Oliver. Jr., July 17, 1945, 3, RG 331, Closed Case Files: Margaret Utinsky, NARA, Box 1063, Folder 34. When the FBI interviewed Peggy in 1945 about Claire Phillips, Peggy said she could be reached in care of Oliver or through her son, now a captain at the Water Division Marine Department, Hogg Island Terminal, Philadelphia. The passenger roster of the *S.S. John Lykes* listed an in-care-of residence as Oliver's D.C. home, indicating the arrangement had been made prior to departure. Oliver's message to HQ also stated Peggy should be sent back to the Philippines at the conclusion of her lectures, but gave no specific reason.

60. Letter from John L. Lucas to Maria Martinez, August 13, 1945, RG 407, NARA, Box 136, Folder 10.

61. Sherrilyn Coffman, "Margaret Utinsky," *American Journal of Nursing* 109 (May 2009): 72–76, accessed July 1, 2014, http://journals.lww.com/ajnonline/Fulltext/2009/05000/Margaret_Utinsky.43.aspx; and "Bill to Reimburse Nurse," *The New York Times*, July 3, 1946, accessed online. See also Bill for the Relief of Mering Bichara, House of Representatives, 82nd Congress, Committee on the Judiciary, September 25, 1951, 3; *Mrs. Claire Phillips Clavier v. The United States*, U.S. Court of Claims, 2–52, 1957.

62. Williams, "Prison Camp 'Angel,'" 3; Gaylord, "American Spy," 1. For additional accolades about Norton's wartime work, see "The 'Angel of Bataan,' WWII Heroine, is Dead," *Stars and Stripes* (Pacific edition), December 7, 1963, 40.

63. Reproductions of Witsell's letter and a photo of the award ceremony are included in Peggy's book.

64. "The Command Structure: AFPAC, FEC, and SCAP," accessed June 27, 2014, http://www.history.army.mil/books/wwii/MacArthur%20Reports/MacArthur%20V1%20Sup/ch3.htm; Closed Case Files: Margaret Utinsky, RG 331, NARA, Box 1063, Folder 34.

65. Chunn, ed., *Of Rice and Men*; telephone interview with David Grant Stewart, September 27, 2009; Utinsky, "*Miss U*," viii. Stewart believed it was possible his mother met Peggy at some kind of military function in St. Louis, MO, in 1946 and encouraged her to come to San Antonio. According to Stewart, Peggy talked about her son all the time, but mother and son never visited each other.

66. "Woman Guerrilla Fighter in Critical Condition," *El Paso* (TX) *Herald-Post*, April 22, 1948, 2.

BIBLIOGRAPHY

Archival Sources

Gable, Edgar Slaughter Papers. South Dakota Historical Society, Pierre, SD.

John Boone Collection, RG-122, MacArthur Memorial Library.

Courtney Whitney Collection, RG-16, MacArthur Memorial Library.

M0863, "Philippine Guerrillas," Sanford/Clanin Philippine Resistance Records, Indiana Historical Society Collection.

RG 59: General Records of the Department of State. National Archives & Records Administration (NARA).

RG 299: Foreign Claims Settlement Commission, 1951. National Archives & Records Administration (NARA).

RG 331: Allied Operational & Occupation Headquarters, World War II. Supreme Commander for the Allied Powers, Legal Section, Manila Branch. "Illegal Acts by Japanese in the Philippines," 1945–1947. National Archives & Records Administration (NARA).

RG 389: Records of the Office of the Provost Marshal General. National Archives & Records Administration (NARA).

RG 407: Records of the Adjutant General's Office, Philippine Archives Collection. National Archives & Records Administration (NARA).

Oliver La Farge Collection, Harry Ransom Center, University of Texas, Austin.

Wayne Morse Collection, University of Oregon Libraries, Division of Special Collections and University Archives.

Primary Source Documents

Affidavit of Lieutenant Colonel Jack William Schwartz, 1946. http://www.mansell.com/pow_resources/camplists/philippines/Cabanatuan/schwarz_ack_l_affidavit.html.

Bill for the Relief of Mering Bichara, 82nd Congress, 1st Session, September 25, 1951.

Claire Phillips Clavier v. The United States, Congressional No. 2-52, Defendant's Exceptions and Brief, March 12, 1957.

Federal Bureau of Investigation Files, Claire Maybelle Phillips, 1945–1947. Obtained through FOIA. Copy in possession of the author.

Federal Census Records, 1900–1940. Accessed from Ancestry.com.

Janson, Dorothy. "General Homma Gave a Party." Unpublished manuscript. Copy in possession of the author.

Japanese POW roster, online. http://www.west-point.org/family/japanese-pow/Rosters.htm.

Murphy, Frank, papers of. Microfilm, Bentley Historical Library, University of Michigan.

Passenger List, SS *John Lykes*, May 1945. Accessed from Ancestry.com.

Republic of the Philippines Supreme Court. *Lily Raquiza, et. al vs. Lt. Col. L.J. Bradford, et. al*, G.R. No. L-44, 13 September 13, 1945. http://www.lawphil.net/judjuris/juri1945/sep1945/gr_l-44_1945.html.

José P. Laurel, Proclamation No. 29, 21 September 1944; José P. Laurel, Proclamation No. 30, 22 September 1944, http://www.lawphil.net/executive/proc/proc_30_1944.html.

Stagg, Samuel Boyd. Stagg Interview with Chris Schaefer, August 2, 2002. Transcription copy in possession of the author.

US Army Recognition Program of Philippine Guerrillas, c.1949; http://media.nara.gov/dc metro/rg-554/629817-army-recognition-philippine-guerrillas-1182341/1182341.pdf.

US Military Registers, 1862–1970, accessed from Ancestry.com.

Published Primary Sources

American Chamber of Commerce Journal, December 1936. University of Michigan Digital Library. http://quod.lib.umich.edu/cgi/t/text/textidx?c=philamer;idno=AAJ0523.1936.007

American Chamber of Commerce of the Philippines Vols. 1–2, 1921. https://books.google.com/books?id=fM1BAQAAMAAJ&pg=RA1-PA15&dq=american+chamber+of+commerce+of+the+philippines+1921&hl=en&sa=X&ved=0CCIQ6AEwAWoVChMIiuP4w6qNxgIVjAySCh1hXQDz#v=onepage&q=american%20chamber%20of%20commerce%20of%20the%20philippines%201921&f=false.

American Chamber of Commerce of the Philippines, 1941. http://quod.lib.umich.edu/p/philamer/AAJ0523.1941.001?view=toc.

Ashton, Paul. *Bataan Diary*. [n.p.], 1984.

Berry, William A. (with James Edwin Alexander). *Prisoner of the Rising Sun*. Norman: University of Oklahoma Press, 1993.

Bumgarner, John R., M.D. *Parade of the Dead: A U.S. Army Physician's Memoir of Imprisonment by the Japanese, 1942–1945*. Jefferson, NC: McFarland & Company, Inc., Publishers, 1995.

Caraccilo, Dominic J., ed. *Surviving Bataan and Beyond: Colonel Irvin Alexander's Odyssey as a Japanese Prisoner of War*. Mechanicsburg, PA: Stackpole Books, 1999.

Carroll, Earl. "The Secret Story of Santo Tomas," Chapter 2, August 19, 1945, WORLDWAR2 Archives online. http://archiver.rootsweb.ancestry.com/th/read/PHILIPPINES/200312/1070504833.

Chunn, (Major) Calvin Ellsworth, ed. *Of Rice and Men: The Story of Americans Under the Rising Sun.* Los Angeles: Veterans' Publishing Company, 1947.

Dizon, Herminia S. "The Complete Data Covering the Guerrilla Activities of the Late Col. Claude A. Thorp," www.battlingbastardsbataan.com/dizon.htm.

Finch, Florence Ebersole Smith. Oral History Interview, Ithaca, NY, 2007. www.uscg.mil/history/weboralhistory/FlorenceFinchHistory.pdf.

Halsema, James. *The Internment Camp at Baguio.* Interview by Michael P. Onorato, Oral History Program. Fullerton: California State University, Fullerton, 1987.

Hibbs, Ralph Emerson, M.D. *Tell MacArthur to Wait.* New York: Carlton Press, Inc., 1988.

International Review of the Red Cross, May 1966. http://www.loc.gov/rr/frd/Military_Law/pdf/RC_May-1966.pdf.

Janson, Dorothy. "Prisoners of War and the YMCA," *American Historical Collection* [n.d.]

Labrador, Juan. *A Diary of the Japanese Occupation: December 7, 1941–May 7, 1945.* Manila, P.I.: Santo Tomas University Press, 1989.

Lapham, Robert, and Bernard Norling, *Lapham's Raiders.* Lexington: University of Kentucky Press, 1996.

Loyd, Frank. Journal of Frank Loyd. Copy in possession of the author, courtesy of Chris Schaefer and the Loyd family.

MacArthur, Douglas. *Reminiscences.* New York: McGraw-Hill, 1964.

McQueen, Neile Adams. *My Husband, My Friend: A Memoir.* Bloomington, IN: AuthorHouse, 2012.

Miller, Ernest B. *Bataan Uncensored.* Little Falls, MN: Military Historical Society of Minnesota, 1991.

Miller, Robert Ryal, ed. "Edgar Gable's Prison Camp Diary," 318–348, in *South Dakota Department of History Report and Historical Collections,* Vol. 30. Pierre, SD: South Dakota Historical Society, 1960.

Nornes, Abe Mark. "Nippon . . . Philippines . . . Peace." http://deepblue.lib.umich.edu/bitstream/handle/2027.42/90891/Dawn_of_Freedom.pdf?sequence=1.

Office of the Resident Commissioner of the Philippines to the United States. *Report on the Destruction of Manila and Japanese Atrocities,* Washington, D.C., 1945.

Panlilio, Yay. *The Crucible: An Autobiography.* New York: The MacMillan Company, 1950.

Phillips, Claire, and Myron B. Goldsmith. *Manila Espionage.* Portland, OR: Binfords & Mort, Publishers, 1947.

Poweleit, Alvin C., M.D. *USAFFE: The Loyal Americans and Faithful Filipinos, A Saga of Atrocities Perpetrated During the Fall of the Philippines, the Bataan Death March, and Japanese Imprisonment and Survival.* [n.p.], 1975.

Propaganda Corps of the Imperial Japanese Forces, ed., *Ideals of the New Philippines* [n.p., n.d.], Manila, P.I.: 1944(?); http://ebooks.filipinaslibrary.org.ph/ideals_of_new_philippines_new_order__short_essays_parts_i-ii/.

Ross, Robert A., Sr. Oral History, 2002. http://www.lindavdahl.com/Bio%20Pages/R.Ross/RRoss.bio.htm.

Savary, Gladys. *Outside the Walls.* New York: Vantage Press, 1954.

Stevens, Frederic H. *Santo Tomas Internment Camp, 1942–1945* (Limited private edition: Frederic H. Stevens, 1946), 2–3.
Utinsky, Margaret. *"Miss U."* San Antonio, TX: Naylor, 1948.
Williams, Denny. *To the Angels.* San Antonio, TX: Denson Press, 1985.
Wright, John M., Jr. *Captured on Corregidor: Diary of an American P.O.W. in World War II.* Jefferson, NC: McFarland & Company, Inc., Publishers, 1988.

Newspapers
Advocate (Burnie, Tasmania), 1945.
Asian Journal (San Diego, CA), 2013.
The Canberra (Australia) *Times*, 1943.
The Courier-Mail (Brisbane, Australia), 1945.
The Daily Tribune, 1941, 1942.
El Paso (TX) *Herald-Post*, 1948.
Eugene (OR) *Register-Guard*, 1956.
Janesville (WI) *Daily Gazette*, 1950.
Joplin (MO) *Globe*, 1945.
Kentucky New Era, 1947.
Manila Daily Bulletin, 1941, 1949.
The New York Times, 1940, 1946.
Oakland (CA) *Tribune*, 1946.
The Oregonian, 1947–1950.
The Palm Beach (FL) *Post*, 1945.
The Quan, 2003.
San Bernardino (CA) *County Sun*, 1945.
San Jose (CA) *Mercury News*, 2008.
San Mateo (CA) *Times*, 1954–1956.
Spokane (WA) *Daily Chronicle*, 1946.
Stars and Stripes (Pacific edition), 1963.
Tri-City Herald (Pasco, KY), 1951.
Van Nuys Valley (CA) *News*, 1970.

Books and Articles: Secondary Sources
Aluit, Alfonso J. *The Conscience of a Nation: A History of the Red Cross in the Philippines, 1896–1972.* Manila: Printorama, Inc., 1972.
Archer, Bernice. *Internment of Western Civilians Under the Japanese, 1941–1945.* New York: Routledge, 2005.
Benvenisti, Eyal. *The International Law of Occupation*, 2nd ed. New York: Oxford University Press, 2012.
Binkowski, Edna. *Code Name: High Pockets.* Limay, P.I.: Valour Press, 2006.
Brands, H. W. *Bound to Empire: The United States and the Philippines.* New York: Oxford University Press, 1992.
Buhain, Dominador H. *A History of Publishing in the Philippines.* Quezon City, P.I.: Rex Printing Company, 1998.

Coffman, Edward M. *The Regulars: The American Army, 1898–1941*. Cambridge, MA: Harvard University Press, 2004.

Coffman, Sherrilyn. "Margaret Utinsky." *American Journal of Nursing* 109, no: 5 (May 2009): 72–76: http://journals.lww.com/ajnonline/Fulltext/2009/05000/Margaret_Utinsky.43.aspx.

Cogan, Frances B. *Captured: The Japanese Internment of American Civilians in the Philippines*. Athens: University of Georgia Press, 2000.

Connaughton, Richard. *MacArthur and Defeat in the Philippines*. New York: The Overlook Press, 2001.

Corbett, P. Scott. *Quiet Passages: The Exchange of Civilians Between the United States and Japan During the Second World War*. Kent, OH: Kent State University Press, 1987.

Currey, Cecil B. "Chaplain on the Bataan Death March," *The Army Chaplaincy*, Winter–Spring 2006, 5–6.

Daws, Gavan. *Prisoners of the Japanese: POWs of World War II in the Pacific*. New York: William Morrow and Company, Inc., 1994.

Decker, Malcolm. *From Bataan to Safety: The Rescue of 104 American Soldiers in the Philippines*. Jefferson, NC: McFarland & Company, Inc., Publishers, 2008.

———. *On a Mountainside: The 155th Provisional Guerrilla Battalion Against the Japanese on Luzon*. Las Cruces, NM: Yucca Tree Press, 2004.

Foronda, Marcelino A., Jr. *Cultural Life in the Philippines During the Japanese Occupation, 1942–1945*. Manila, P.I.: De La Salle University, 1978.

Friend, Theodore. *Between Two Empires: The Ordeal of the Philippines, 1929–1946*. New Haven, CT: Yale University Press, 1965.

———. *The Blue-Eyed Enemy: Japan Against the West in Java and Luzon, 1942–1945*. Princeton, NJ: Princeton University Press, 1988.

Friedrich, Otto. *City of Nets: A Portrait of Hollywood in the 1940s*. Berkeley: University of California Press, 1986.

Furiya, Reiko. "The Japanese Community Abroad: The Case of Prewar Davao in the Philippines," in Shiraishi, Saya S. and Takashi Shiraishi, eds. *The Japanese in Colonial Southeast Asia*. Ithaca, NY: Cornell University Press, 1993, 155–172.

Gardner, Richard. "Golden's Missing Heroes." February 2, 2007, denverpost.com.

Gleeck, Lewis E. Jr. *The American Governors-General and High Commissioners in the Philippines: Proconsuls, Nation-Builders and Politicians*. Quezon City, P.I.: New Day Publishers, 1986.

———. *The Manila Americans, 1901–1964*. Manila, P.I.: Carmelo and Bauermann, 1977.

Glusman, John A. *Conduct Under Fire: Four American Doctors and Their Fight for Life as Prisoners of the Japanese 1941–1945*. New York: Viking, 2005.

Hashiya, Hiroshi. "The Pattern of Japanese Economic Penetration of the Prewar Philippines," in Shiraishi, Saya S. and Takashi Shiraishi, eds., *The Japanese in Colonial Southeast Asia*. Ithaca, NY: Cornell University Press, 1993, 113–138.

"Have Bolo Will Travel: World War II Weaves Stories of Survival," in *Asian Journal* (San Diego, CA), May 31–June 6, 2013; http://asianjournalusa.com/have-bolo-will-travel-p7026-95.htm.

Hoganson, Kristin L. *Fighting for American Manhood: How Gender Politics Provoked the Spanish-American and Philippine-American Wars.* New Haven, CT: Yale University Press, 1998.

Horn, Florence. *Orphans of the Pacific: The Philippines.* New York: Reynal and Hitchcock, 1941.

Horner, Layton. *Japanese Military Administration in Malaya and the Philippines,* Ph.D. dissertation, University of Arizona, 1973, UMI microfilm.

Hotta, Eri. *Japan 1941: Countdown to Infamy.* New York: Alfred A. Knopf, 2013.

Hoyt, Edwin. *Japan's War: The Great Pacific Conflict.* New York: Cooper Square Press, 2001.

Hunt, Michael H. and Steven I. Levine. *Arc of Empire: America's Wars in Asia from the Philippines to Vietnam.* Chapel Hill: University of North Carolina Press, 2012.

Jensen, Joan M. *Army Surveillance in America, 1775–1980.* New Haven, CT: Yale University Press, 1991.

Jones, Gregg. *Honor in the Dust: Theodore Roosevelt, War in the Philippines, and the Rise and Fall of America's Imperial Dream.* New York: New American Library, 2012.

Kaminski, Theresa. *Prisoners in Paradise: American Women in the Wartime South Pacific.* Lawrence, KS: University Press of Kansas, 2000.

Karnow, Stanley. *In Our Image: America's Empire in the Philippines.* New York: Random House, 1989.

Kerr, E. Bartlett. *Surrender and Survival: The Experience of American POWs in the Pacific 1941–1945.* New York: William Morrow and Company, Inc., 1985.

Kramer, Paul A. *The Blood of Government: Race, Empire, the United States, and the Philippines.* Chapel Hill: University of North Carolina Press, 2006.

Lee, Clark. "Japan's 'Con' Man," August 19, 1943, fultonhistory.com.

Levine, Alan J. *Captivity, Flight, and Survival in World War II.* Westport, CT: Praeger Publishers, 2000.

Magdalena, Federico V., "Dabao-Kuo and the Construction of the Philippine State," Paper presented at the 41st Annual Conference of Asian Studies on the Pacific Coast, June 15–17, 2007, Honolulu, Hawaii, www2.hawaii.edu/~fm/Dabao-kuo.doc.

Marquardt, Frederic S. *Before Bataan and After: A Personalized History of Our Philippine Experiment.* Indianapolis: The Bobbs-Merrill Company, 1943.

Marquez, Adalia. *Blood on the Rising Sun.* New York: DeTanko Publishers, Inc., 1957.

Masuda, Hiroshi. *MacArthur in Asia: The General and His Staff in the Philippines, Japan, and Korea.* Ithaca, NY: Cornell University Press, 2012.

McCoy, Alfred W. *Policing America's Empire: The United States, the Philippines, and the Rise of the Surveillance State.* Madison: University of Wisconsin Press, 2009.

Miller, Edward S. *War Plan Orange: The US Strategy to Defeat Japan, 1897–1945.* Annapolis, MD: Naval Institute Press, 1991.

Morton, Louis. *The Fall of the Philippines.* Washington, D.C.: Center of Military History, United States Army, 1953. http://www.history.army.mil/books/70-7_06.htm.

Norling, Bernard. *The Intrepid Guerrillas of North Luzon.* Lexington: University Press of Kentucky, 1999.

Norman, Elizabeth M. *We Band of Angels: The Untold Story of American Nurses Trapped on Bataan by the Japanese*. New York: Random House, 2013.

Norman, Michael, and Elizabeth M. Norman. *Tears in the Darkness: The Story of the Bataan Death March and Its Aftermath*. New York: Farrar, Straus and Giroux, 2009.

Parrish, Dr. Rebecca. *A Tribute to Dr. Hawthorne Darby*. Lafayette, IN?. Privately published, 1946.

Petillo, Carol Morris. *Douglas MacArthur: The Philippine Years*. Bloomington: Indiana University Press, 1981.

Picornell, Pedro M. *The Remedios Hospital, 1942–1945: A Saga of Malate*. Manila, P.I.: DeLaSalle University Press, 1995.

Porter, Catherine. *Crisis in the Philippines*. New York: Alfred A. Knopf, 1942.

Roces, Alfredo. *Looking for Liling*. P.I.: Anvil Publishing Company, 2000.

Rogers, Paul P. *The Good Years: MacArthur and Sutherland*. New York: Praeger Publishers, 1990.

Rosbottom, Ronald C. *When Paris Went Dark: The City of Light Under German Occupation, 1940–1944*. New York: Little, Brown and Company, 2014.

Schaefer, Chris. *Bataan Diary: An American Family in World War II, 1941–1945*. Houston, TX: Riverview Publishing, 2004.

Schanke, Robert A. *"That Furious Lesbian": The Story of Mercedes de Acosta*. Carbondale: Southern Illinois University Press, 2003.

Schirmer, Daniel B. *Republic or Empire: American Resistance to the Philippine War*. Cambridge, MA: Schenkman Publishing Company, Inc., 1972.

Setuho, Ikehata, and Ricardo Jose, eds., *The Philippines Under Japan: Occupation Policy and Reaction*. Manila, P.I.: Ateneo de Manila University Press, 1999.

Shiraishi, Saya S., and Takashi Shiraishi, eds. *The Japanese in Colonial Southeast Asia*. Ithaca, NY: Cornell University Press, 1993.

Sides, Hampton. *Ghost Soldiers: The Forgotten Epic Story of World War II's Most Dramatic Mission*. New York: Doubleday, 2001.

Sloan, Bill. *Undefeated: America's Heroic Fight for Bataan and Corregidor*. New York: Simon and Schuster, 2012.

Smith, Donald P. *We Survived War's Crucible: A True Story of Imprisonment and Rescue*. Bloomington, IN: Authorhouse, 2007.

Smith, Robert Ross. *Triumph in the Philippines*. http://books.google.com/books?id=BSrFX51AGPMC&pg=PA326&lpg=PA326&dq=colonel+skelton+dinalupihan+philippines+world+war+II&source=bl&ots=jezXoiTm_7&sig=b6R0XIzgR61SS1BPeLiCuXOaGI&hl=en&sa=X&ei=88WZU93JGoewyATcj4KgAg&ved=0CB0Q6AEwAA#v=onepage&q=colonel%20skelton%20dinalupihan%20philippines%20world%20war%20II&f=false.

"Special Operations in the Pacific," www.history.army.mil/books/wwii/70-42/70-424.html.

Spector, Ronald. *Eagle Against the Sun: The American War with Japan*. New York: The Free Press, 1985.

Stahl, Bob. *Fugitives: Evading and Escaping the Japanese*. Lexington, KY: University of Kentucky Press, 2001.

Steinberg, David Joel. *Philippine Collaboration in World War II.* Ann Arbor: University of Michigan Press, 1967.

Takefumi Terada, "The Japanese Catholic Women's Religious Corps and Its Activities in the Philippines During World War II," in *Anthropological Studies of Gospel and Civilization* 31: October 2002, 293–308.

Thompson, Chuck. *Twenty-Five Best World War II Sites: Pacific Theater.* San Francisco: Greenline Publications, 2002.

Tsuimi, Shunsuke. *An Intellectual History of Wartime Japan: 1931–1945.* New York: Routledge, 2011.

Unoki, Ko. *Mergers, Acquisitions and Global Empires: Tolerance, Diversity and the Success of M&A.* New York: Routledge, 2013.

"Vicente Lim 1914," West Point Associate of Graduates, http://apps.westpointaog.org/Memorials/Article/5282/.

Welch, Bob. *Resolve: From the Jungles of WWII Bataan, the Epic Story of a Soldier, a Flag, and a Promise Kept.* New York: Berkley Caliber, 2012.

Yu-Jose, Lydia N. *Japan Views the Philippines, 1900–1944.* Manila, P.I.: Ateneo de Manila

INDEX

Papaya. *See* Martinez, Maria
Park Avenue School (Pasay Elementary
    School), 273–79, 313, 381
Parker, George M., 68, 108
Parsons, Charles (Chick), 226
Parsons, Louella, 413
Pasay Elementary School (Park Avenue
    School), 273–79, 313, 381
Pearl Harbor attack (1941), 55–61,
    72–74, 78–79
Pedro (Filipino mechanic), 276, 278
Petroff, Helen, 321–22
Philippine Commission, 10–11
Philippine Commonwealth, 13, 300
Philippine Executive Commission, 299
Philippine Scouts, 51, 75, 156
Philippine Women's Federation, 216–17
Philippine Women's University
    (Manila), 80, 354–55
The Philippines Herald (newspaper),
    29–30, 33–34, 35, 76–77, 100
Phillips, Claire
    arrest and detention of, 323–332,
        335–37, 339–341, 353–54,
        360–62, 373–75, 401–2
    arrival in Philippines and life before
        the war, 30–32
    attack on Pearl Harbor and the
        Philippines and, 57–58, 59–61,
        64–66, 68, 69–72
    on Bataan Peninsula, 72, 105, 107–8,
        111–18, 121–24, 127–28, 139–141,
        143, 188–89
    J. Boone and: baptism and, 310–11;
        claims and, 416; D. Clavier and,
        323, 384, 387; underground
        activities and, 115–18, 122, 143,
        192, 194, 209, 222–23, 225,
        227–28, 248–251, 300–301,
        302, 413
    Buttenbruch and, 210–12, 220
    claims and, 415–17, 420–25
    D. Clavier and: attack on Pearl
        Harbor and the Philippines and,
        57–58, 59–61, 64–66, 68, 69–72;

on Bataan Peninsula, 72, 107–8,
    111–14, 121–24; J. Boone and, 323,
    384; on S.S. *John Lykes*, 3, 400;
    in Manila, 42–43, 45, 192, 212,
    220–21, 227, 281, 323; in Oregon,
    41–42, 414–15; at Santo Tomas,
    387–88, 393–95
Club Tsubaki and: apartment in,
    227; Boone's guerrillas and, 228,
    255–59, 281, 300–303; Christmas
    1942 celebrations and, 224–25;
    Kamuri and, 309–10, 311–13;
    Kempeitai and, 280–81, 323–24;
    opening of, 200–201, 209–10; Park
    Avenue School and, 276–79; POWs
    and, 222–23, 255–59, 272–73, 281,
    284–86, 300–301, 308–9
De Martini and, 30–31, 42, 45, 122,
    191, 192, 394
death of, 425
as Dorothy Fuentes, 190–200,
    284–85. *See also* Club Tsubaki
as entertainer in Manila, 43–46,
    195–200
FBI and, 3–4, 412–13, 415–17, 418–19
Fuentes and: divorce, 69–70, 402,
    417; in Manila, 31–32, 41–42; in
    the US after the war, 414–15, 416
heroine persona of, 393, 402, 412–15,
    418–420
as High Pockets, 225, 228, 273,
    276–77, 323–24, 373
on S.S. *John Lykes*, 3–5, 400–403
Martinez and, 330, 339, 360–62, 420
Miss U network and, 194, 222–23
Y. Panlilio and, 3, 400
J. Phillips and: alleged marriage
    with, 141, 143, 212, 402, 421;
    relationship with, 4, 45–46,
    48, 52–53
V. Phillips and, 414–15, 416
post-traumatic stress disorder
    and, 414
Remedios Hospital and, 193–94,
    198, 223